United States Naval Aviation, 1919–1941

Aircraft, Airships and Ships Between the Wars

E. R. JOHNSON

McFarland & Company, Inc., Publishers

Jefferson, North Carolina, and London

All three-view illustrations are by Lloyd S. Jones.
All photographs are courtesy David W. Ostrowski,
unless otherwise noted.

LIBRARY OF CONGRESS CATALOGUING-IN-PUBLICATION DATA

Johnson, E.R., 1948–
United States naval aviation, 1919–1941 :
aircraft, airships and ships between the wars /
E.R. Johnson.
p.   cm.
Includes bibliographical references and index.

ISBN 978-0-7864-4550-9
softcover : 50# alkaline paper ∞

1. United States. Navy—Aviation—History—20th century.
2. Airplanes, Military—United States—History—20th century.
3. Military airships—United States—History—20th century.
4. Aeronautics, Military—United States—History—20th century.
I. Title.
VG93.J627   2011   359.9'4097309042—dc22   2011006978

BRITISH LIBRARY CATALOGUING DATA ARE AVAILABLE

Front cover: *from top* Rigid Airship USS *Macon* ZRS-5 in 1935;
Martin T4M-1 attached to VT-2B of the Saratoga Air Group in 1931;
Vought OS2U-1 sited on a Type P-6 catapult in 1940 (Lloyd S. Jones)

Manufactured in the United States of America

*McFarland & Company, Inc., Publishers
Box 611, Jefferson, North Carolina 28640
www.mcfarlandpub.com*

Contents

Preface

By June 1942, within six months of Japan's devastating attack on Pearl Harbor, the U.S. Navy had checked the Japanese military advance in the Pacific to the extent that the United States could return to its original war plan of defeating Germany first. That the Navy was able to accomplish this with six fleet aircraft carriers—two of which were based in the Atlantic at the time—and little more than 1,000 combat aircraft was not a miracle or simply a matter of luck but the culmination of more than 20 years of determined preparation. This book explains and illustrates, in terms of individual aircraft, airship, and ship development, the process of trial and error that ultimately enabled naval aviation to succeed in those critical, early months of the war. The book is introduced by a historical summary listing the major influences that shaped the course of naval aviation during the period.

For organizational purposes, the book is divided into three main parts. Part I covers heavier-than-air development in chronological order, subdivided by attack aircraft, fighter aircraft, observation and scout aircraft, patrol aircraft, and trainer, transport, and utility aircraft. Part II covers lighter-than-air development in chronological order, subdivided by rigid airships (dirigibles) and non-rigid airships (blimps). Part III covers aviation-related ship development in chronological order, subdivided by aircraft carriers, seaplane and airship tenders, and seaplane-equipped warships. With the exception of seaplane-equipped warships, each subdivision is preceded by a procurement synopsis to summarize and interrelate the chronology of events. Supplementing the main parts are four appendices: foreign aircraft and airships in chronological order; racing and experimental aircraft in chronological order; aircraft, airship, ship and aviation unit designations, nomenclature, and abbreviations; and status of naval aviation in December 1941. A glossary of aviation terms follows.

Introduction: Influences That Shaped U.S. Naval Aviation, 1919–1941

"Naval aviation cannot take the offensive from the shore; it must go to sea on the back of the fleet.... The fleet and naval aviation are one and inseparable."
—Rear Admiral William A. Moffett, first chief of the
Naval Bureau of Aeronautics, 1921–1933.

World War I

At the time the United States entered World War I in April 1917, Naval Aviation, both within the U.S. Navy and the U.S. Marine Corps, was little more than a vestigial organization, then consisting of 54 aircraft and 48 pilots. Nineteen months later, in November 1918, it had grown to a force of 2,107 aircraft and 15 airships, with 6,716 officers and 30,693 enlisted personnel in Navy units, and 282 officers and 2,180 enlisted personnel in Marine units. Even after the inevitable postwar downsizing of the fleet, Naval Aviation managed to emerge from the process as an important force in being, which, by 1920, still maintained a strength of about 850 aircraft and 30 airships in Navy units, with another 88 aircraft allocated to the Marines. Though Naval Aviation would not regain and surpass its 1918 force levels for another 23 years, World War I had nevertheless left behind a strong foundation upon which a postwar aviation establishment could be built.

Naval Treaties of 1922, 1930, and 1936

The disarmament of Germany after World War I left Great Britain with the largest navy in the world, the United States a close second, Japan third, France fourth, and Italy fifth. In order to avoid a repeat of the unrestrained naval arms race that had taken place both before and throughout the war, these five nations met in Washington, D.C., in late 1921 to negotiate a treaty placing limits on existing and future naval armaments. The Washington Naval Treaty, signed by the five participants in February 1922 and ratified by the U.S. government in June 1923, established an allowable ratio (expressed in thousands of tons displacement) between Great Britain, the United States, Japan, France, and Italy of 5:5:3:1:1 with regard to "capital ships," which included battleships and battlecruisers.

Of great future significance to Naval Aviation, a similar ratio extended to construction of aircraft carriers: Britain and the U.S., 135,000 tons each; Japan, 81,000 tons; and France and Italy, 60,000 tons each. Although the offensive capability of carriers was largely untested at the time of the treaty, Britain already had two with a third nearing completion, and the U.S. and Japan each had one. Faced with controlling the largest ocean areas (the Atlantic and the Pacific in the case of Britain and the U.S.), these three nations originally viewed carriers as a means to broaden fleet reconnaissance and spot for the big guns of capital ships, with secondary emphasis on the strike role, and perhaps as important, all three had battleships or battlecruisers under construction, otherwise illegal under the treaty, which could be completed as carriers (i.e., Britain—*Eagle, Courageous*, and *Glorious*; U.S.—*Lexington* and *Saratoga*; and Japan—*Akagi* and *Kaga*). Although reconnaissance would remain a vital carrier function, the U.S. and Japan, to a much greater extent than Britain, afterward used their new carriers to evolve multi-mission capabilities such as anti-carrier tactics, attacks on shore bases, and support of amphibious assaults.

Of related significance, the Washington Treaty, though limiting new cruiser construction to a maximum displacement of 10,000 tons and gun armament of 8 inches, placed no restriction on tonnage, thereby triggering a cruiser construction "race" between the five participating powers. Continuing negotiations through the 1920s led to adoption of the London Naval Treaty of 1930, which made a distinction between gun armament of "heavy" cruisers (up to 8 inches) and "light" cruisers (up to 6.1 inches) and set limits on both the tonnage and number of ships allowed: Britain, 339,000 tons/15 heavy cruisers; U.S., 323,500 tons/18 heavy cruisers; and Japan, 208,850 tons/12 heavy cruisers. Between 1929 and 1939, applying this formula, the U.S. Navy placed 27 new "treaty" cruisers in commission—18 heavy, 9 light—each of which was equipped to handle two or more floatplane scouts. Added to this were the 19 remaining battleships (16 after 1930), 10 pre-treaty light cruisers, and two gun-boats, so that by 1939 the fleet possessed 55 warships operating approximately 170 floatplanes between them.

The final treaty, the Second London Treaty of 1936, made no important changes except for an "escalator clause," invoked after Japan refused to sign the treaty, that allowed the armament of two planned U.S. battleships (i.e., BB-55 and -56) to be increased to 16 inches. These were the first Navy battleships designed from the outset to accommodate floatplanes. After 1936, Navy shipbuilding programs relative to battleships, cruisers, and carriers were timed to place new vessels in service beyond the expiration of all treaty restrictions in 1942; however, the start of war in Europe in September 1939 effectively ended the treaty system altogether. Nonetheless, the treaties had irrevocably moved the U.S. and Japan onto a path in which major sea engagements fought a few years hence would be decided, not by converging lines of battleships, but by aircraft launched from fleets out of sight of one another.

Fleet Tactics

Naval Aviation, while not displacing the primacy of the battle line, still evolved into a key component of fleet battle tactics during the period between the wars. Fleet tactics as a whole, including the specific role to be played by aircraft within the Battle and Scouting Fleets, were largely formulated and practiced over a period of 17 years (1923–1940) through a series of 21 different Fleet Problems. Even from the very start, aircraft were seen as a means of extending the fleet's striking power, adding over-the-horizon reconnaissance and attack capabilities that had not previously existed. During Fleet Problem I in 1923, before *Langley* possessed an operational air group, battleships were used to simulate aircraft carriers, and their floatplanes functioned as fictitious air groups.

The potential shown by *Langley*'s still incomplete air group during Fleet Problem V in 1925 helped speed the completion of fleet carriers *Lexington* and *Saratoga*. Although "sunk" afterward, *Saratoga*, in Fleet Problem IX of 1929, convincingly demonstrated how a detached carrier could circumvent an enemy fleet to attack shore installations (i.e., the Panama Canal in this case). The next year, in Fleet Problem X, the tactical advantage abruptly shifted between opposing fleets when *Saratoga* and *Langley* were both "disabled" by a surprise attack launched from *Lexington*. In mock air attacks against the Battle Fleet at anchorage in Pearl Harbor, carried out in Fleet Problem XIII in 1932 and again in Fleet Problem XIX in 1938, the Battle Line was "eliminated" as an effective fighting force on both occasions. Ironically, virtually the same tactics would be copied by the Imperial Japanese Navy in December 1941.

One of the earliest influences on tactics was the advent of aerial gun spotting for battleships. By using aircraft to pinpoint targets, accuracy beyond 18,000 yards increased by a factor of 200 percent. Initially, from 1919 to 1922, surplus World War I landplane fighters had been launched from turret platforms on one-way flights, but catapult developments during 1922 enabled a switch to recoverable floatplanes, with 18 battleships having been fitted with one or more catapults by 1925. Battleships likewise carried the first shipboard aircraft intended primarily for fleet air defense—float-equipped single-seat fighters—from 1925 until 1928, when the concept was overtaken by carrier-based wheeled fighters once *Lexington* and *Saratoga* joined the Battle Fleet. The ability of cruisers to carry floatplanes, starting in 1924, brought about an equally dramatic change in tactics, in so far as these ships could now use aircraft to scout large areas of ocean without distancing themselves from the main body of the fleet. However, related efforts to incorporate aircraft-carrying, rigid airships (i.e., *Akron* and *Macon*) into the fleet as long-range scouts ended in disaster, with the entire program being abandoned in mid–1935.

By far, however, the biggest change in fleet tactics was wrought by the introduction of aircraft carriers, especially as *Lexington* and *Saratoga* began participating in 1929. At first, torpedo attack was seen as a carrier's primary anti-ship tactic, with the objective of hindering the enemy's battle line until our own battleships could maneuver into optimal position (i.e., crossing the "T" in line astern formation) to administer the coup de grâce. But starting in 1930, this tactic began giving way to an anti-carrier doctrine: simply stated, before the opposing battle lines were in a position to maneuver, the carrier force would use its aircraft to seize control of the air first by sinking or disabling the enemy's carrier force. Lacking air cover, the enemy fleet would be at a serious disadvantage as our battleships moved into position—crossed the T—to inflict a killing blow from maximum range. Moreover, if carriers were the primary targets, a low and slow-moving torpedo attack would be unnecessary; instead, the thin carrier decks could easily be taken out of action by dive-bombing attacks. Equally important, carriers gave the fleet the ability to launch surprise attacks on shore installations or to provide air cover and close air support during amphibious assaults, and a fleet equipped with two or more carriers could perform these missions independently and simultaneously. Central to the carrier doctrine was emphasis on "aggressive offensive action," which meant finding the enemy force first and launching an air strike just as soon as it came within range.

An essential building block in the implementation of the Navy's carrier doctrine was coordination of flight deck operations. As early as 1925 deck crews aboard *Langley* departed from a "clear-deck" landing procedure, which allowed no more than six aircraft in the air at any time, in favor of a "deck park," where recovered aircraft were immediately moved up to the bow so incoming aircraft could land right behind them. Other innovations included erecting a traverse crash barrier between the deck park and planes landing-on, plus specialized teams of flight deck personnel identified by variously colored jerseys. By 1927, despite limited deck space, *Langley* was able to keep 22 aircraft in the air at any given time, and when *Lexington* and *Saratoga* began operating, this number increased to 83. Another Navy policy that strengthened anti-carrier tactics (vis-à-vis the

Battle formation as seen in 1939. Three battleships in the van with the *Enterprise* (CV-6) Air Group overhead.

Japanese) was early emphasis on the scouting function, giving air groups a higher ratio of scouts and bombers versus fighters and torpedo planes, and this policy eventually evolved into development of one type of aircraft—the scout-bomber—to perform both roles. Still, from a tactical perspective, the torpedo remained the only aerial weapon capable of inflicting serious damage on heavily armored ships, so with the *Yorktown* class and the planned *Essex* and *Independence* classes after it, this concern led to a restoration of one torpedo squadron (VT) to future air group complements. Henceforth and until the middle of World War II, a U.S. Navy carrier air group typically consisted of four squadrons of 22 aircraft each, a VF, a VS, a VB, and a VT, plus a five or six-plane utility unit. Comparatively, a Japanese carrier air group of the same period consisted of four squadrons of 65 aircraft, one fighter, one dive-bomber, and two torpedo, with no units dedicated to scouting.

Another decisive advantage of U.S. Navy carrier doctrine (versus the Japanese) lay in the independent authority of carrier captains and air group commanders (CAGs) to make tactical decisions on the spot, as the situation demanded. When the Pacific Battle Line ceased to exist as an effective fighting force on December 7, 1941, the Navy already possessed carrier tactics of sufficient flexibility that they could be readily adapted to the naval forces remaining. Following the Pearl Harbor attack, since they were no longer tied to support of the battle line, U.S. Navy carriers were given the added capability to maneuver independently and thus respond to rapidly changing tactical conditions much faster than their Japanese counterparts. Though outnumbered and outgunned by the Japanese fleet, superior tactics employed by U.S. Navy carriers during the early months of the war made a critical and decisive difference between victory and defeat.

Figure 1: Typical Cruising Formation

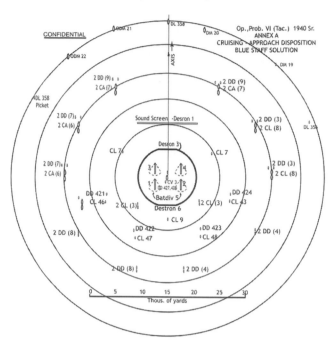

Figure 2: Typical Approach Formation

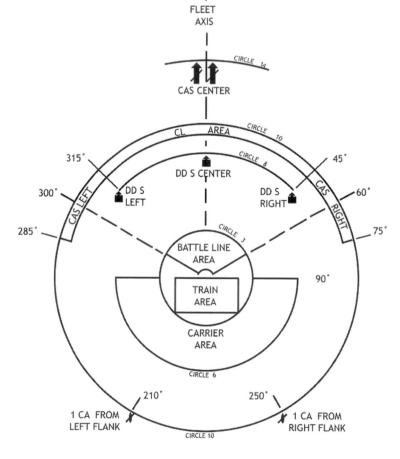

Battle fleet diagram from the late 1930s.

U.S. Government Support

Presidential and congressional support of Naval Aviation and the Navy in general can be said to have been uniformly unenthusiastic until 1932, when Franklin Delano Roosevelt became president and Democratic majorities swept both houses of the U.S. Congress. Roosevelt, a former assistant secretary of the Navy during World War I, not only championed a strong Navy but also believed Naval Aviation should play a bigger role within it. The Vinson-Trammell Expansion Act of 1934 authorized (not as yet funded) the Navy to build up its fleet to levels authorized by the Washington and London Treaties and of great importance to Naval Aviation, permitted new operational aircraft to be ordered in proportion to the number of aircraft carriers, battleships, and cruisers that would be built. In 1936, Congress funded construction of *Yorktown, Enterprise,* and *Wasp,* along with six new cruisers, followed in 1937 by two battleships, and in 1938 by *Hornet, Curtiss* (AV-4), and *Barnegat* and *Biscayne* (AVP-10 and -11), effectively tripling the size of Naval Aviation before the end of the decade.

But the most far-reaching legislation came with passage of the Two-Ocean Naval Expansion Act of 1940. Among other things, the act called for construction of 18 new *Essex* class aircraft carriers, seven battleships, plus the thousands upon thousands of aircraft needed to equip them. Some experts have characterized this act as tantamount to a declaration of war against Japan, to-wit: in order to have any practical strategic advantage, Japan would be compelled to attack American forces and possessions in the Pacific before the ships and aircraft authorized under the Act could begin entering service in 1942 and 1943.

Naval Leadership

It goes without saying that none of the foregoing factors—ships, aircraft, tactics, procedures, or government—would have shifted the advantage in the absence of effective leadership. During the period between the wars, as Naval Aviation grew in stature, a number of senior Navy officers were placed in major leadership positions. Most of these men came into their jobs with virtually no practical aviation experience, but together, with great imagination, they forged Naval Aviation into a potent fighting force.

Rear Admiral William A. Moffett. Considered by many to be the "architect of Naval Aviation," Moffett, at age 52, joined the aviation establishment after a brilliant career serving aboard cruisers and battleships. He had been awarded the Medal of Honor in 1914 for his actions in the invasion of Vera Cruz, Mexico, while commanding the cruiser *Chester.* As the first chief of the newly formed U.S. Naval Bureau of Aeronautics (BuAer) in 1921, Moffett became a leading advocate of the belief that aircraft and airships should be integral to the fleet itself, giving strong emphasis to their ability to operate directly with or from ships in an offensive role. Under his guidance, BuAer became a nucleus of aviation ideas and a focal point for development of new aircraft and airships. In this role, Moffett also oversaw pilot and aircrew training programs, construction of new air bases, and development of catapults and carrier-arresting equipment. He was one of the 60 people lost when the airship *Akron* crashed at sea in 1933.

Vice Admiral Joseph M. Reeves. Regarded at the time as the Navy's foremost expert on battleship gunnery, 53-year-old Capt. Reeves assumed the post of Commander, Aircraft Squadron, Battle Fleet in 1925, using *Langley* as his flagship. He is credited with developing the deck park and many of the innovative deck routines that became standardized in carrier operations. Reeves also laid the groundwork for the "Carrier Warfare Model," which determined the tactical role carriers would play within the Battle Fleet. Later, as a Vice Admiral, Reeves was designated Commander-in-Chief, U.S. Fleet, from 1934 to 1936. He died in 1948.

Fleet Admiral Ernest J. King. A submarine officer at the time, Capt. King transferred to Naval Aviation in 1926 at the behest of RADM Moffett and became Naval Aviator No. 3368 in 1927 at age 49. He commanded the seaplane tender *Wright* until 1929 and assumed command of *Lexington* in 1930. Following the unexpected death of Moffett, he became the second chief of BuAer in 1933, being promoted to rear admiral soon afterward. In 1940, as a vice admiral, King was appointed Commander-in-Chief, Atlantic Fleet, then in January 1942, became Chief of Naval Operations (CNO). During his wartime tenure as CNO, he was promoted to fleet admiral. He died in 1956.

Fleet Admiral William F. Halsey. Halsey spent most of his early naval career in torpedo boats and destroyers. In 1934, at age 52, he reported to NAS Pensacola for pilot training and was subsequently designated a Naval Aviator. In 1935, after winning his wings, he assumed command of *Saratoga*. Reaching flag rank in 1938, Halsey took command of Carrier Division One and Carrier Division Two, and in 1940 became Commander Aircraft Battle Force with the rank of vice admiral. Perhaps more than any other high-ranking officer, Halsey exemplified the concept of "aggressive offensive action." As a full admiral during World War II, he commanded South Pacific Forces from late 1942, and in 1944, became Commander-in-Chief, Third Fleet. Halsey was promoted to fleet admiral after the war ended and died in 1959.

Admiral John S. McCain, Sr. After serving mainly on battleships, McCain became a Naval Aviator in 1936 at age 51. From 1937 to 1939, while commanding *Ranger,* he made major contributions to development of aircraft carrier tactics in later Fleet Problems. In early World War II, after being promoted to rear admiral, he served as Commander of Air Forces for the Western Sea Frontier in the South Pacific, then from late 1942 to 1944, acted as chief of BuAer. McCain returned to the Pacific in 1944 as a vice admiral in command of the Fast Carrier Task Force that supported various amphibious operations during 1945. He died in September 1945 and received a posthumous promotion to full admiral. Admiral McCain was the grandfather of Senator John S. McCain, III.

Admiral Marc A. Mitscher. Naval Aviator No. 33, Mitscher served aboard battleships for several years before undertaking flight training in 1916. As pilot of NC-1, he participated in the first transatlantic flight attempt in 1919. During the 1920s Mitscher was instrumental in developing early flight operations from *Langley* and *Saratoga* and in the 1930s, played an active role in the formulation of tactics and carrier doctrine. He became the first captain of *Hornet* in late 1941 and was in command during the Doolittle raid in April 1942 and the Battle of Midway in June. As a rear admiral, Mitscher became Commander Air, Solomon Islands during 1942 and 1943, then after promotion to vice admiral, commanded Task Force 58 in 1944 and 1945. After the war, in 1946, he attained full admiral and was named Commander-in-Chief, Atlantic Fleet. He died in 1947.

General Roy S. Geiger. Known as the "father of Marine Aviation," Geiger joined the Marines in 1907 and received his wings as a Naval Aviator in 1917. After serving with the First Aviation Force in France during World War I and holding various Marine Aviation command positions through the 1920s, he became Officer-in-Charge, Marine Corps Aviation in 1930. After rising to the rank of Colonel in 1935, Geiger was appointed as Commanding Officer, Aircraft One, Fleet Marine Force. In mid–1941, he was promoted to brigadier general when his command was reorganized as the 1st Marine Air Wing. After the 1st MAW arrived at Guadalcanal in 1942, Geiger was given combined command of all Navy, Army Air Force, and Marine air operations in the area and subsequently promoted to major general. He became director of Marine Aviation in 1943 but returned to the Pacific later that year to command the I Amphibious Corps. In mid–1945, as a lieutenant general, he was appointed Commanding General of the Fleet Marine Force, Pacific. He died in 1947 and was posthumously promoted to four-star general.

Emergence of Marine Corps Aviation

Following World War I, the aviation arm of the Marine Corps almost ended before it got off to a good start. When the 2,462-man strong First Aviation Force disbanded in 1919, Marine aviation suddenly found itself with no permanent status within the peacetime Naval Aviation establishment. Given this tenuous state of affairs, Marine officials, most notably its Director of Aviation, Major Alfred A. Cunningham, began actively lobbying the U.S. Congress to mandate a permanent postwar Marine aviation branch. In 1920, due in part to these efforts, Congress established a peacetime Marine manpower level at a 20 percent ratio (i.e., 26,380 officers and men) of the Navy, which included 1,020 personnel allocated to aviation operations as well as establishing permanent Marine air stations (MCAS) at Quantico, Parris Island, and San Diego.

From this point forward, Marine Aviation was entirely reformed in terms of both organization and mission. During World War I, the First Aviation Force had operated without any organic connection to Marine ground forces; however, under the 1920 plan, it was reorganized into four groups of squadrons or detachments having the prime mission of supporting Marine operations on the ground. Marine Aviation did not actually become an official part of the Naval Aviation establishment until early 1925, from which point procurement of virtually all Marine aircraft, with minor exceptions, was tied to the BuAer system and likewise, prospective Marine pilots were trained pursuant to the Student Naval Aviator curriculum at NAS Pensacola. By the late 1920s, Marine fighter and observation squadrons had been reequipped with carrier-capable aircraft and routinely underwent carrier qualification as an operational training requirement, and from 1932 to 1934, two Marine squadrons were detached for permanent duty aboard *Lexington* and *Saratoga*.

In 1927 Marine Aviation reorganized itself into the East Coast Expeditionary Force (Quantico) and West Coast Expeditionary Force (San Diego), with squadrons detached to support ground operations in China, Haiti, and Nicaragua. During this timeframe Marine Aviation is generally credited with having developed the first combat-tested dive-bombing techniques while providing close air support to ground forces during the Nicaraguan campaign. Commencing with the establishment of the Fleet Marine Force (FMF) in 1933, Marine Aviation, with an inventory of 92 aircraft at the time, was reclassified between FMF Aircraft One on the West Coast (three squadrons) and FMF Aircraft Two on the East Coast (four squadrons), and this scheme of organization, with its emphasis on support of amphibious and ground operations, remained in force into the World War II–era and afterward. From 1930, in addition to regular frontline squadrons, Marine Aviation's pool of pilots and trained personnel was augmented by establishment of reserve units, having grown to 10 squadrons by 1940, and the reserve pilot training system (Navy and Marine both) received another boost in 1935 with the passage of the Naval Aviation Cadet Program. During 1941, Marine Aviation grew to a strength of 6,467 officers and men with 659 rated pilots, but the process of bringing new units to operational readiness went much slower, so that as of December 6, 1941, frontline operational strength consisted of just 227 combat aircraft in two air wings with five frontline squadrons each. In the four years that followed (1942–1945), these numbers increased to an incredible 116,648 officers and men with 10,049 pilots, organized into five air wings, 31 air groups, and 103 squadrons.

Emergence of Coast Guard Aviation

The U.S. Coast Guard came into being in 1915 as a result of a merger of the Revenue Cutter Service (armed maritime law enforcement) and Life-Saving Service (assistance to ships in distress). From its initial organization, the Coast Guard functioned an agency of the U.S. Treasury Department until November 1941, from which point operational control was vested in the Navy Department. In 1916 and 1917, with the objective of establishing an aviation group within the Coast Guard, a number of its officers underwent pilot training at NAS Pensacola, but as events transpired, they were subsequently assigned to serve in various Navy aviation units for the duration of World War I. The first actual Coast Guard Aviation operations commenced in 1920 when six Curtiss flying boats on loan from the Navy were used to evaluate the practicality of aerial search and rescue missions from a base established at Morehead City, North Carolina; however, operations ceased in 1921 due to lack of funding. In 1926, after five years of inactivity, Coast Guard Aviation finally received funding to acquire five single-engine seaplanes to be operated from new bases established at Gloucester, Massachusetts, and Cape May, New Jersey, for the purpose of assisting Coast Guard vessels in the detection and apprehension of Prohibition Act violators (i.e., liquor smugglers).

But the most significant expansion of Coast Guard Aviation came in the early and mid–1930s as search and rescue capabilities were added to augment its law enforcement duties. Between 1931 and 1935, over 40 aircraft were added to the Coast Guard air fleet, including 19 twin-engine seaplanes (i.e., Douglas RDs and General Aviation PJs) billed as "flying life boats" and 15 single-engine amphibians (i.e., Grumman JFs) that could be used for either law enforcement or rescues missions. Coast Guard Aviation continued to grow through the late 1930s, establishing new operating bases on both coasts, and by late 1941, when it officially came under the Navy Department, numbered 90 pilots and 56 aircraft divided between 10 bases. Although the Coast Guard adopted the naval designation system for its aircraft, it appears that procurement was made through the Treasury Department rather than BuAer until 1941. The exact numbers of aircraft serving with the Coast Guard during World War II is not reported anywhere, but some references suggest that up to 300 aircraft, most under Navy bureau numbers but some under AAF serials, were allocated to Coast Guard units between 1942 and 1945. Coast Guard aircraft flew armed antisubmarine patrols off both coasts and the Gulf of Mexico during the wartime period, but search and rescue operations, including ships sunk or in distress and downed aircraft, remained their prime mission. Control of the Coast Guard reverted back to the Treasury Department in 1946.

PART I

Heavier-Than-Air Development

ATTACK AIRCRAFT

Synopsis of Attack Aircraft Procurement

The first decade following World War I marked a dramatic shift in emphasis by Naval Aviation from shore-based aerial attack toward aircraft launched from carriers operating within the Battle Fleet. As the United States' first carrier, USS *Langley* (CV-1), joined the fleet in 1922, the Navy possessed no made-for-purpose carrier aircraft and had yet to develop any practical criteria upon which new aircraft requirements could be issued, and even after the first true fleet carriers, *Lexington* and *Saratoga* (CV-2 and -3), entered service in late 1927, budgetary constraints obliged the newly established carrier air groups to make due with a variegated mix of aircraft, many of which had been adapted from obsolescent floatplane and landplane designs. Thus, from its inception in 1921, one of the U.S. Naval Bureau of Aeronautics' (BuAer) principal aims in procuring new aircraft—for obvious logistical and financial reasons—was to combine as many functions as practical into one airframe-engine combination. What the new carrier air groups needed were more fighters to improve air superiority around the Battle Fleet and more dedicated attack aircraft to extend the reach of the fleet's offensive striking power.

During the mid and late 1920s, the aerial torpedo was viewed as Naval Aviation's principal anti-ship weapon, so that early procurement efforts were focused mainly on carrier-based torpedo planes like the Martin T3M and T4M. At the same time, to preserve some shore-based torpedo and bombing capability, BuAer commenced development of the twin-engine Naval Aircraft Factory TN/Douglas T2D; however, after Air Corps criticism, the Navy was officially restricted from maintaining land-based bombardment operations, and these aircraft were subsequently reconfigured as floatplanes for patrol duties. As Naval Aviation moved into the decade of 1930s, rapid progress made in dive-bombing tactics influenced a shift toward procurement of purpose-built bomber and bomber-fighter types like the Martin BM, Great Lakes BG, and Curtiss BFC/BF2C to such extent that the Navy's fourth carrier, USS *Ranger* (CV-

4), was launched in 1933 with no provision for torpedo stowage.

By 1935, however, further refinements of tactics led BuAer to narrow the field to two basic attack classifications: two-seat scout-bombers (SB) combining the functions of scouting and dive-bombing into one airplane and three-seat torpedo bombers (TB) capable of either launching torpedoes or making level bombing runs. Renewed interest in torpedo-carrying aircraft had been spurred by the prospect of developing new aircraft types for the larger *Yorktown* class carriers planned. Carrier air groups, from this point, typically comprised four squadrons of 15 to 22 aircraft, consisting of one fighter unit (VF), two scout-bomber units (normally one VS and one VB), and one torpedo-bomber unit (VT), and this would form the basic air group pattern for fleet carriers until the middle of World War II. This rule-of-thumb did not apply, at least initially, to the two fleet carriers built without provision for torpedo stowage, *Ranger* (CV-4) and *Wasp* (CV-7), which both carried an extra VS unit instead of a VT.

While BuAer made considerable progress in establishing the functional criteria for carrier-based attack aircraft, it was decidedly slow in taking advantage of certain advances seen in the aeronautical state-of-the-art during the 1930s. Chief among its concerns was the higher operating speeds and unforgiving stall characteristics exhibited by newer all-metal monoplane designs, with the result that all of the fleet's operational attack aircraft were biplanes until the first monoplane types began entering service in late 1937. This conservative approach to innovation was nowhere more apparent than in 1934 and 1935 when simultaneous requirements were issued for new monoplane and biplane torpedo and scout-bombers as a hedge against the possibility that the monoplane types might fail to work out. However, as events transpired, new monoplanes like the Douglas TBD and Vought SB2U measurably out-performed the biplanes while still demonstrating acceptable approach speeds and wave-off characteristics. Although the first monoplane scout and torpedo-bombers began reaching fleet squadrons in late 1937, the re-equipping process was lethargic and did not keep pace with the formation of new air groups necessitated by new carriers coming into commission (i.e., *Yorktown* in 1937, *Enterprise* in 1938, *Wasp* in 1940, and *Hornet* in 1941).

The outbreak of war in Europe in 1939, coupled with serious concerns over Japan's intentions in the Pacific, induced U.S. policy-makers to lay plans for an unprecedented expansion of Naval Aviation. In 1940 the U.S. Congress authorized a massive carrier construction program, encompassing not only a new class of fleet carriers but providing for light carriers (CVLs) and escort carriers (CVEs) as well. To equip the emergent carrier force, BuAer pressed aircraft companies hard to develop new types of attack aircraft (i.e., Brewster SB2A, Curtiss SB2C, Grumman TBF, and Vought TBU) and simultane-

ously announced plans to order them in unheard of quantities. But the effect was far from instantaneous, so that by December 1941 the Navy's inventory of dedicated attack aircraft stood at only 809 torpedo and scout-bombers. During the course of World War II this figure grew exponentially, rising to 10,038 attack aircraft on hand by the middle of 1945.

Airco DH-4B/4M (O2B)—1918

TECHNICAL SPECIFICATIONS (DH-4B)

Type: Two-place observation, bomber, and general purpose.
Manufacturer: Dayton-Wright Co., Dayton, Ohio; Standard Aircraft

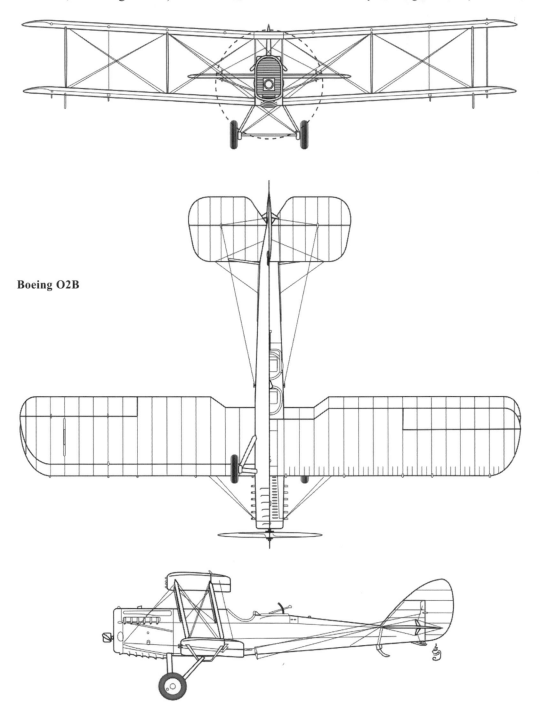

Boeing O2B

Corp., Patterson, New Jersey; Fisher Body Div. of General Motors, Cleveland, Ohio; Boeing Airplane Co., Seattle, Washington; and Naval Aircraft Factory, Philadelphia, Pennsylvania.

Total produced: 222 (USN/USMC)

Powerplant: One 400-hp (various auto mfrs.) Liberty 12-cylinder water-cooled inline engine driving a two-bladed fixed-pitch wooden propeller.

Armament: Two fixed forward-firing .30-cal. machine guns, two flexible .30-cal. machine guns in rear cockpit, and up 322 lbs. of bombs carried on wing racks.

Performance: Max. speed 123 mph at s.l.; ceiling 14,000 ft.; combat range 550 mi.

Weights: 2,939 lbs. empty, 4,595 lbs. loaded.

Dimensions: Span 42 ft. 5½ in., length 29 ft. 11 in., wing area 440 sq. ft.

Based on Geoffrey de Havilland's British design for Airco, a total of 4,846 DH-4s powered by American-designed and made Liberty engines were license-built in the U.S. during 1918 and 1919. From 1919 to 1923, to improve crash protection and crew communication, 1,538 DH-4s were completed or converted to DH-4B standard, which entailed moving the main fuel tank forward and the cockpit aft, repositioning the landing gear, and skinning the entire fuselage with plywood. In the interval, the Navy received 92 DH-4Bs from the War Department, including 50 DH-4B-1s with increased fuel capacity, plus another 80 rebuilt by the Naval Aircraft Factory. Starting in 1923 as an Army program, 147 DH-4s were remanufactured by Boeing as the DH-4M with new welded, steel tube fuselages, and

This Marine DH-4B-1 was attached to VO-8M out of San Diego in 1927, one of 80 DH-4Bs rebuilt from War Department stocks by the Naval Aircraft Factory during the early 1920s. Replaced by OC-1s in 1928.

30 were delivered to the Marine Corps in 1925 under the new designation O2B-1. DH-4Bs and O2Bs serving with Marine Expeditionary Forces in Nicaragua during 1927 were credited with developing the first combat-tested dive-bombing techniques. The Navy operated DH-4Bs until 1927, while the last O2Bs remained in Marine service until 1929.

Curtiss R-6L—1919

TECHNICAL SPECIFICATIONS (R-6L)

Type: Two-place observation and torpedo floatplane.

Manufacturer: Curtiss Aeroplane Co., Buffalo, New York.

An R-6L seen on beaching dolly about 1920. Retrofitting of a 400-hp Liberty engine gave it the ability to take off with a 1,063-pound aerial torpedo. Two squadrons were maintained until 1922.

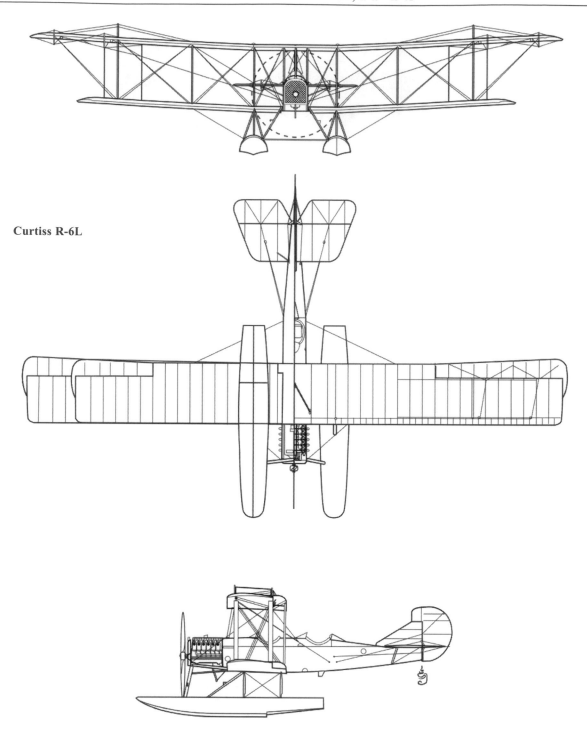

Curtiss R-6L

Total produced: 40 (USN)

Powerplant: One 400-hp (various auto mfrs.) Liberty 12-cylinder water-cooled inline engine driving a two-bladed fixed-pitch wooden propeller.

Armament: One 1,036-lb. torpedo carried between the floats.

Performance: Max. speed 104 mph at s.l.; ceiling 9,900 ft.; combat range 368 mi.

Weights: 3,513 lbs. empty, 5,662 lbs. loaded.

Dimensions: Span 57 ft. 1 in., length 33 ft. 5 in., wing area 613 sq. ft.

Introduced in 1915 with a 150-hp Curtiss V-X engine, the Curtiss R Series was subsequently produced as an observation aircraft in both landplane and float-equipped versions for the Army, Navy, and Britain's Royal Naval Air Service. The last 40 of 76 Navy R-6s built in 1918 became R-6Ls when they were modified to accept installation of 400-hp Liberty 12 engines. With the added power, the R-6L was the first Navy aircraft capable of lifting a torpedo. After carrying out successful tests in the spring of 1919, the Navy established two R-6L torpedo squadrons, one in San Diego, California, and another in Hampton Roads, Virginia. Not very well suited to the stresses of torpedo-carrying operations, all R-6Ls were replaced by newer aircraft types in 1921 and 1922.

Martin MBT/MT-1 (TM) — 1920

TECHNICAL SPECIFICATIONS (MT-1)

Type: Three or four-place torpedo bomber.
Manufacturer: Glenn L. Martin Co., Cleveland, Ohio.
Total produced: 10 (USN/USMC)
Powerplant: Two 400-hp (various auto mfrs.) Liberty 12-cylinder water-cooled inline engine driving two-bladed fixed-pitch wooden propellers.
Armament: Two flexible .30-cal. machine guns in the nose, two flexible .30-cal. machine guns in the rear cockpit, and one 1,618-lb. torpedo carried under the fuselage.
Performance: Max. speed 105 mph at s.l.; ceiling 9,900 ft.; combat range 400 mi.
Weights: 7,150 lbs. empty, 12, 076 lbs. loaded.

Dimensions: Span 74 ft. 2 in., length 42 ft. 8 in., wing area 1,121 sq. ft.

Intended as a land-based bomber and torpedo plane, the twin-engine MBT was a three-bay biplane of wood and fabric construction, essentially identical to Martin's Army MB-1 of 1918. Martin delivered a total of ten of these big aircraft to the Navy during 1920, two MBTs followed by eight MT-1s built to the same specification as the longer wing Army MB-2. The Navy retained four of these aircraft at its San Diego, California base and the remaining six were transferred to the Marine Corps. When the Navy adopted a standardized system for identifying its aircraft in 1922, MBTs and MT-1s were re-designated

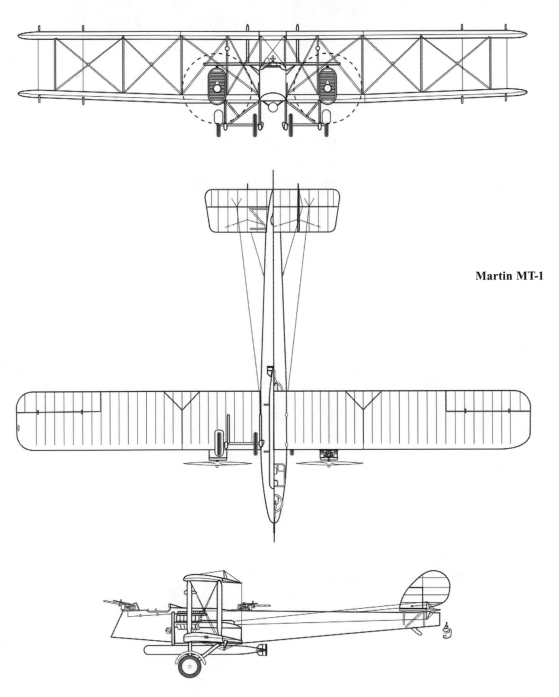

Martin MT-1

One of four Navy MT-1s based at NAS San Diego in 1922 or 1923. Used for land-based bombing or torpedo attack. Note aerial torpedo mounted between the landing gear.

TM-1. The last Marine example was withdrawn from service sometime in 1928.

Naval Aircraft Factory PT—1921

TECHNICAL SPECIFICATIONS (PT-2)

Type: Two-place patrol and torpedo floatplane.
Manufacturer: Naval Aircraft Factory, Philadelphia, Pennsylvania.

Total produced: 33 (USN)
Powerplant: One 330-hp (various auto mfrs.) Liberty 12-cylinder water-cooled inline engine driving a two-bladed fixed-pitch wooden propeller.
Armament: One 1,446-lb. torpedo carried between the floats.
Performance: Max. speed 100 mph at s.l.; ceiling 6,100 ft.; combat range 334 mi.
Weights: 4,231 lbs. empty, 7, 075 lbs. loaded.
Dimensions: Span 74 ft. 0 in., length 34 ft. 5 in., wing area 808.5 sq. ft.

A PT-2 with torpedo loaded between floats is seen in 1922 on beaching dolly. This type combined a Curtiss R-6 fuselage with HS-2L wings and was used primarily to evaluate torpedo attack tactics in early 1920s.

To overcome the shortcomings of the R-6L and make use of surplus parts on hand, NAF created the PT-1 by combining the fuselage of the R-6 with the wings of a Curtiss HS-1L flying boat (see, below) and enlarging the vertical tail surfaces to offset increased wing area. After delivering 15 PT-1s in 1921, NAF produced a further 18 in 1922 as the PT-2, which differed in having the larger wing of the HS-2L. PTs were used by the Navy primarily to evaluate tactics for torpedo attack, and in 1922, conducted the first mass attack on a real target when they launched

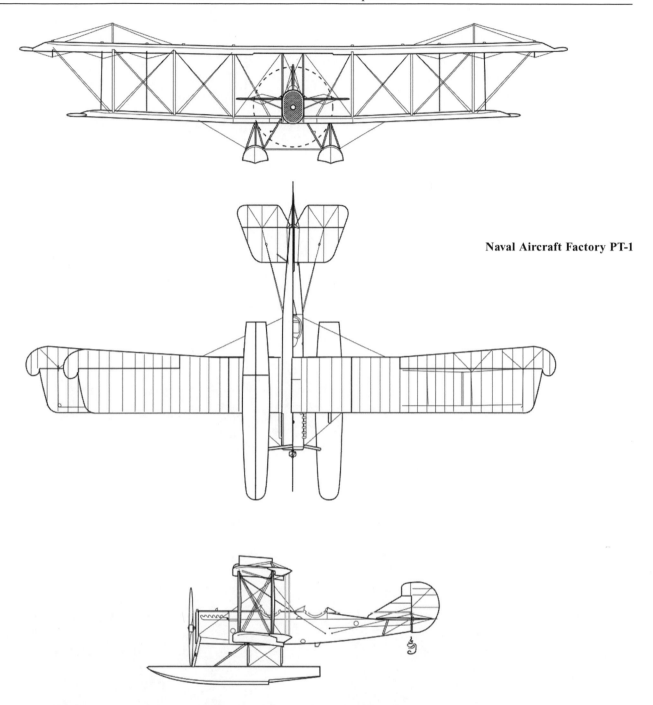

Naval Aircraft Factory PT-1

live torpedoes against an old, mothballed battleship. PTs were only in service briefly, being replaced within a couple of years by newer types such as the Douglas DT.

Curtiss CT—1921

TECHNICAL SPECIFICATIONS (CT-1)

Type: Three-place torpedo floatplane.
Manufacturer: Curtiss Aeroplane and Motor Co., Buffalo, New York.
Total produced: 1 (USN)
Powerplants: Two 350-hp Curtiss D-12 (V-1145) 12-cylinder water-
 cooled inline engine driving two-bladed fixed-pitch wooden pro-
 pellers.

Armament: One flexible .30-cal. machine gun in the rear cockpit and
 one 1,835-lb. torpedo carried between the floats or wheels.
Performance: Max. speed 107 mph at s.l.; ceiling 5,200 ft.; combat
 range 350 mi.
Weights: 7,684 lbs. empty, 11,208 lbs. loaded.
Dimensions: Span 65 ft., length 52 ft., wing area 830 sq. ft.

In an effort to find a better torpedo plane, the CT-1 was one of two twin-engine monoplanes considered by the Navy in 1921 and 1922. Constructed entirely of wood, the CT-1 emerged with a very thick, fully cantilevered wing and a tailplane supported by booms running from the rear of the engine nacelles and the afterbodies of the floats. The prototype was initially flown in March 1921 with two 300-hp Wright Hispano V-8 en-

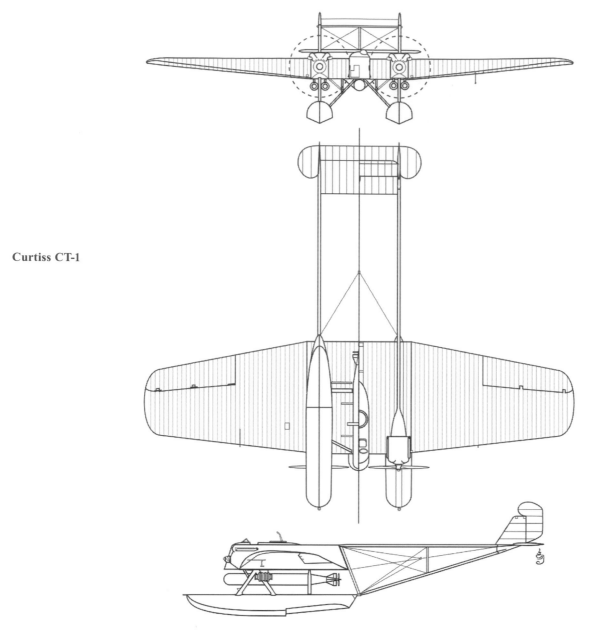

Curtiss CT-1

A CT-1 is shown during tests in 1921 with original Wright Hispano engines. The serial number appears on the side of floats. The Navy ultimately abandoned the idea in favor of single-engine designs.

gines, but was found to be underpowered for its weight. After substituting 350-hp Curtiss D-12 engines, the CT-1 was re-delivered to the Navy for testing in 1922. Once testing was completed, the Navy placed an order for eight production CT-1s, however, after a decision was made to procure single-engine types in quantity, the contract was cancelled before any further examples had been built.

Douglas DT—1921

TECHNICAL SPECIFICATIONS (DT-2 SEAPLANE)

Type: Two-place torpedo landplane and floatplane.

Manufacturer: Douglas Aircraft Co., Santa Monica, California; L.W.F. Engineering Co., Long Island, New York; and Naval Aircraft Factory, Philadelphia, Pennsylvania.

Total produced: 67 (USN, USMC)

Powerplant: One 420-hp Liberty 12A 12-cylinder water-cooled inline engine driving a two-bladed fixed-pitch wooden propeller.

Armament: One flexible .30-cal. machine gun in the rear cockpit and one 1,835-lb. torpedo carried between the floats or wheels.

Performance: Max. speed 99 mph at s.l.; ceiling 7,400 ft.; combat range 275 mi.

Weights: 4,528 lbs. empty, 7,293 lbs. loaded.

Dimensions: Span 50 ft. 0 in., length 37 ft. 8 in., wing area 707 sq. ft.

The DT was the first aircraft to be produced in quantity by Douglas Aircraft and one of the most important Navy combat types of the early and mid–1920s. Based largely on the design of Douglas's first plane, the Cloudster, the DT was a two-bay biplane featuring a welded, steel tube fuselage, with wings and tail surfaces of built-up wooden construction. Like most naval aircraft of the period, it could be rigged as either a landplane or seaplane, and the wings could be folded rearward for stowage. In November 1921, the Navy took delivery of the first of three single-seat DT-1s ordered, then after trials concluded in early 1922, directed that the remaining two be completed as two-seaters. Soon afterward, the Navy gave Douglas an order to produce 38 two-seat types as the DT-2 and also contracted with L.W.F. to build 20 and with NAF to build another six.

As deliveries proceeded, DT-2s began entering operational service in late 1922 with VT-2 in San Diego, California, and during 1923 and 1924, at least six were transferred to the Marine Corps. Two NAF DT-2s became DT-4s when they were fitted with 525-hp Wright TA-2 engines, and another modified as a testbed with the installation of a 400-hp Wright P-1 air-cooled radial engine was re-designated DT-6. Three L.W.F. DT-2s rebuilt by Dayton-Wright with deeper fuselages to carry more fuel returned to service as SDW long-range scouts. All DTs had been withdrawn from Navy and Marine service by the end of 1927.

Top: **DT, based on the Douglas Cloudster, was the first Navy aircraft built from the ground up as a torpedo plane. This example, an early production DT-2, is seen serving with VT-2 in the early 1920s.** *Bottom:* **Same aircraft as previous photograph, seen in 1923 while rigged with floats. Last examples withdrawn in 1927.**

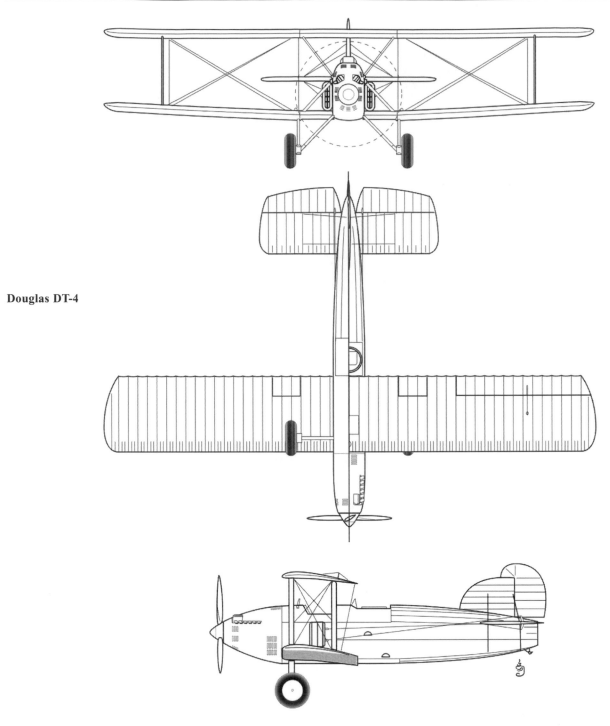

Douglas DT-4

Stout ST—1922

TECHNICAL SPECIFICATIONS (ST-1)

Type: Two-place torpedo landplane and floatplane.
Manufacturer: Stout Metal Airplane Co., Dearborn, Michigan.
Total produced: 1 (USN)
Powerplant: Two 330-hp Packard V-1237 12-cylinder water-cooled inline engines driving two-bladed fixed-pitch wooden propellers.
Armament: One flexible .30-cal. machine gun in the rear cockpit and one 1,835-lb. torpedo carried between the floats or wheels.
Performance: Max. speed 110 mph at s.l.; ceiling 10,000 ft.; combat range 385 mi.

Weights: 6,557 lbs. empty, 9,817 lbs. loaded.
Dimensions: Span 60 ft., length 37 ft., wing area 790 sq. ft.

Another torpedo-carrying twin-engine monoplane type evaluated by the Navy, the Stout ST-1 presented an early American example of the all-metal construction methods previously developed in Germany by Junkers. The use of fully cantilevered structures skinned in corrugated duraluminum produced an exceptionally clean design for its day. In 1921, the Navy made plans to acquire at least five of these aircraft, but soon after its first flight on April 25, 1922, the ST-1 prototype inexplicably crashed and the order was cancelled. Stout went on to become

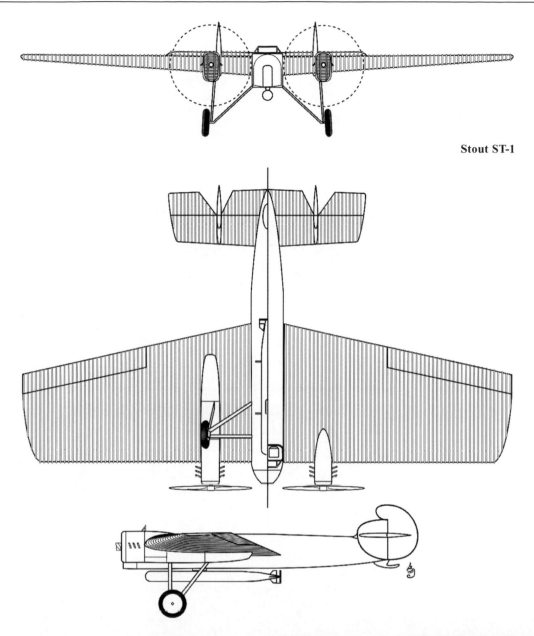

Stout ST-1

The sole example of ST-1 before delivery in 1922. The Navy ordered five aircraft, but cancelled the contract after the prototype crashed. It was intended as a shore-based torpedo plane.

a division of Ford Motor Co. and produce the well-known line of Tri-Motor transports.

Curtiss CS and Martin SC (T2M)—1924

TECHNICAL SPECIFICATIONS (SC-2 SEAPLANE)

Type: Three-place scout and torpedo landplane or floatplane.
Manufacturer: Curtiss Aeroplane and Motor Co., Buffalo, New York; and Glenn L. Martin Co., Cleveland, Ohio.

Total produced: 78 (USN)
Powerplant: One 540-hp Wright T-3 12-cylinder water-cooled inline engine driving a two-bladed fixed-pitch wooden propeller.
Armament: One flexible .30-cal. machine gun in the middle cockpit and one 1,618-lb. torpedo carried between the floats or wheels.
Performance: Max. speed 101 mph at s.l.; ceiling 5,430 ft.; combat range 335 mi.
Weights: 5,908 lbs. empty, 9,323 lbs. loaded.
Dimensions: Span 56 ft. 6 in., length 41 ft. 9 in., wing area 856 sq. ft.

Intended as a replacement for the DT, the Curtiss CS arose from a standard Naval Bureau of Aeronautics (BuAer) design

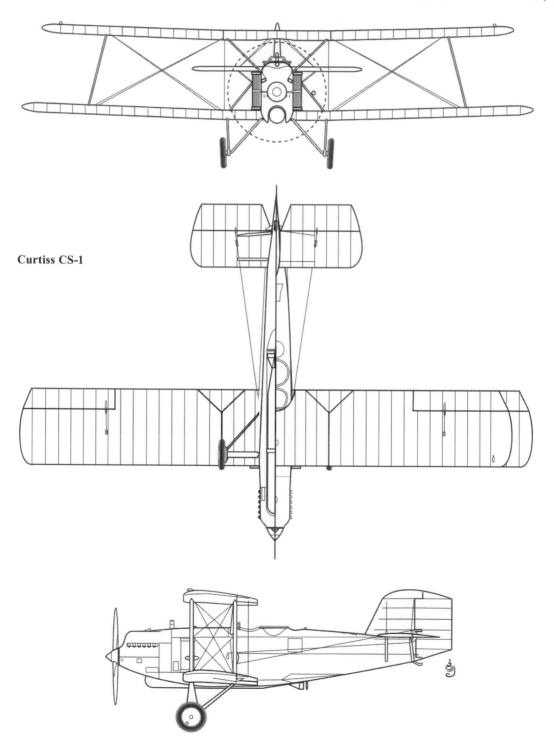

Curtiss CS-1

that would be contracted out to various manufacturers on a bid basis if placed in production. It appeared as a single-bay biplane of fabric-covered, wooden construction, characterized by an upper wing having about six feet less span than the lower, and as typical with naval types of the era, could be operated on either wheels or floats and had foldable wings. Curtiss received the initial construction contract, delivering the first CS-1 in November 1923, followed in January 1924 by two CS-2s powered with 585-hp geared Wright T-3 engines. In June 1924, however, after coming in as the low bidder at $20,000 per aircraft, Martin obtained the production order under two separate contracts: 35 examples powered by T-2 engines delivered as the SC-1 between February and August 1925, and 40 powered by T-3s delivered as the SC-2 by the end of the year.

A float-equipped CS-1 as seen in 1924. It was designed to a multi-role function as a scout, bombing, or torpedo plane, either on wheels or floats. All but three were ultimately produced by Martin as the SC-1 and -2.

As they arrived to equip frontline units, SC-1s and 2s served with two scout and two torpedo squadrons, and under the new designation scheme, they became the T2M-1 and -2. Like many military aircraft developed during the 1920s, the service life of the SC/T2M was relatively brief, and all had been replaced by newer aircraft by the end of 1928.

Martin T3M—1926

TECHNICAL SPECIFICATIONS (T3M-2)

Type: Three-place scout and torpedo landplane or floatplane.
Manufacturer: Glenn L. Martin Co., Cleveland, Ohio.
Total produced: 126 (USN)
Powerplant: One 710-hp Packard 3A-2500 12-cylinder inline driving a three-bladed
Hamilton Standard fixed-pitch propeller.
Armament: One flexible .30-cal. rear machine gun in rear cockpit and one torpedo or up to 1,500 lbs. of bombs carried externally.
Performance: Max. speed 109 mph at s.l.; ceiling 7,900 ft.; combat range 634 mi.
Weights: 5,814 lbs. empty, 9503 lbs. loaded.
Dimensions: Span 56 ft. 7 in., length 41 ft. 4 in., wing area 883 sq. ft.

The T3M originated in late 1925 as a development of the SC/T2M with a welded, steel tube fuselage structure and a 575-hp Wright T-3B engine. After Martin had delivered 26 examples in 1926 as the T3M-1, BuAer asked for a more powerful derivative having greater wing area, redesigned crew locations, and arresting gear, giving it the distinction of becoming the first type of attack aircraft intended specifically for carrier operations. The resulting T3M-2, flown in early 1927, had equal span wings (unlike the short upper wing of the T3M-1), a 135-hp increase in power, three individual cockpits in tandem for the pilot, bombardier, and gunner/observer, plus a tailhook to engage arresting wires. After acceptance, Martin was given a contract to built 100 of the type.

A float-equipped T3M-2 of VT-9S attached to the seaplane tender Wright. Note small "s" on fuselage side marking, indicating that the aircraft was serving with the Scouting Fleet.

Deliveries of T3M-2s to active service units began in mid–1927, and by the end of the year they were equipping VT-1S aboard the newly commissioned *Lexington* and VT-2B of *Langley*, the Navy's first carrier. T3M-2s also were assigned to shore-based squadrons, where they served as the Navy's stan-

dard single-engine torpedo plane. As typical of naval aircraft developed in the mid–1920s, the T3M-2 was rapidly overtaken by newer types and began to be replaced in frontline service as early as mid–1928 and had been relegated to utility status by 1930.

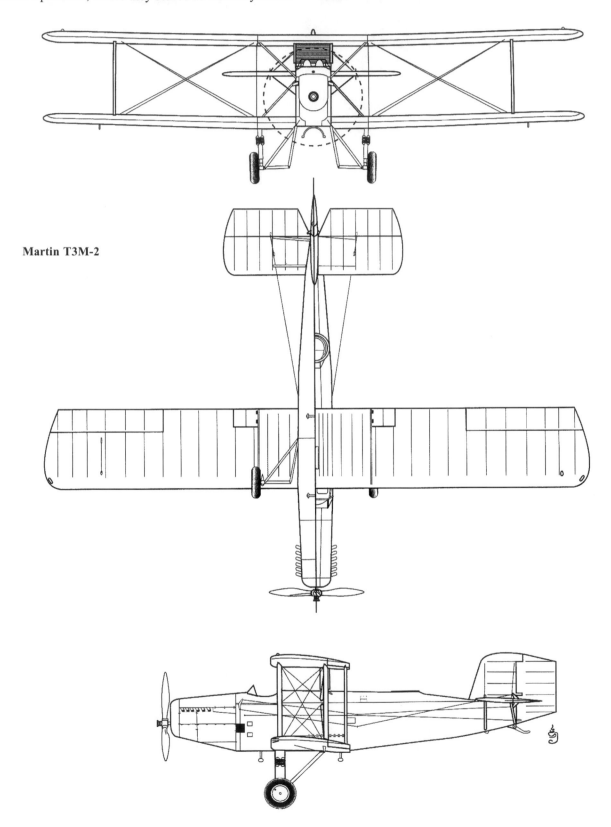

Martin T3M-2

The first carrier-based attack aircraft: This T3M-2 is seen dropping parachutists while serving with VT-2B aboard *Langley* in 1927. The squadron moved to the *Saratoga* Air Group during 1928.

Boeing TB—1927

TECHNICAL SPECIFICATIONS (TB-1)

Type: Three-place scout and torpedo landplane or floatplane.

Manufacturer: Boeing Airplane Co., Seattle, Washington.

Total produced: 3 (USN)

Powerplant: One 730-hp Packard 1A-2500 12-cylinder inline driving a three-bladed Hamilton Standard fixed-pitch propeller.

Armament: One flexible .30-cal. rear machine gun in rear cockpit and one torpedo or up to 1,500 lbs. of bombs carried externally.

Performance: Max. speed 106 mph at sea level.; ceiling 11,750 ft.; combat range 850 mi.

Weights: 6,298 lbs. empty, 10,537 lbs. loaded.

Dimensions: Span 55 ft., length 42 ft. 7 in., wing area 868 sq. ft.

Another BuAer-inspired design, the TB-1 was ordered from Boeing in May 1925 to be considered alongside the Martin T3M-1, however, the first of three aircraft ordered did not reach the Navy until May 1927, by which time the T3M-2 had already been placed in production. The landplane version featured an unusual four-wheeled landing gear arrangement, but apparently was never equipped with arresting gear for carrier operations. The TBs were the last non-indigenous aircraft designs to be built by Boeing until the advent of World War II.

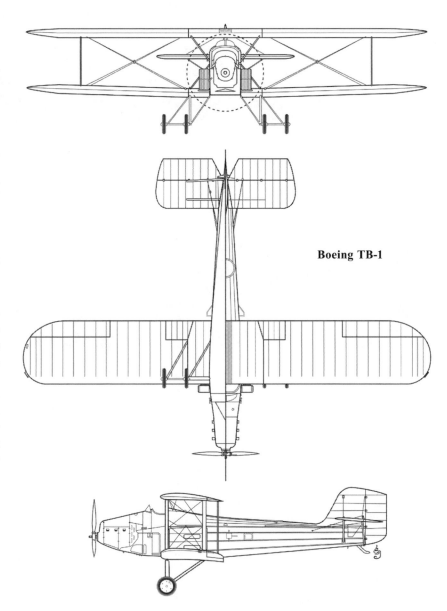

Boeing TB-1

Based on an internal BuAer design, the TB-1 was originally intended to be considered with the Martin T3M-1, but by the time it arrived for evaluations in mid–1927, the T3M-2 had already been ordered.

ary 27, 1927, several months ahead of NAF's XTN-1. After official acceptance, all three T2D-1s were assigned to VT-2 out of San Diego, and after embarking aboard the *Langley* in mid–1927, earned the distinction of being first type of twin-engine aircraft to be operated from an aircraft carrier.

Later the same year, BuAer officials were sufficiently encouraged to order nine more T2D-1s, but by the time deliveries commenced, official Army criticism of the Navy's land-based bomber operations caused them to be configured as floatplanes and shifted to patrol duties with VP-1 out of Pearl Harbor. In 1930, Douglas received a follow-up order for an improved patrol variant, which differed in having twin rudders, ring cowls, and upgraded engines. After the last of 18 examples had been delivered in 1932, P2D-1s served with VP-3 in the Panama Canal Zone until replaced by PBY-1s in 1937.

Naval Aircraft Factory TN and Douglas T2D/P2D—1927

TECHNICAL SPECIFICATIONS (T2D-1 [P2D-1])

Type: Four-place torpedo landplane or floatplane; three-place patrol bomber.

Manufacturer: Naval Aircraft Factory, Philadelphia, Pennsylvania; and Douglas Aircraft Co., Santa Monica, California.

Total produced: 31

Powerplant: Two 525-hp Wright R-1750 [575-hp Wright R-1820] *Cyclone* 9-cylinder air-cooled radial engines driving two-bladed [three-bladed] Hamilton Standard fixed-pitch propellers.

Armament: One flexible .30-cal. rear machine gun in front cockpit, one flexible .30-cal. rear machine gun in rear cockpit, and one torpedo or up to 1,835 lbs. of bombs carried externally.

Performance: Max. speed 124 mph [135 mph] at s.l.; ceiling 14,400 ft. [12,100 ft.]; combat range 454 mi. [1,010 mi.].

Weights: 6,298 lbs. empty, 10,537 lbs. loaded.

Dimensions: Span 55 ft., length 42 ft. 7 in., wing area 868 sq. ft.

The TN and T2D offer an interesting example of naval aircraft procurement practices prior to the Great Depression. In this case, after creating the basic design concept in early 1925, BuAer assigned NAF the task of initial development. While construction of NAF's XTN-1 prototype was still in progress, BuAer contracted with Douglas to produce three essentially identical aircraft as the T2D-1. Whether by accident or design, BuAer's concept for a twin-engine torpedo plane bore a close resemblance to the land-based biplane bombers being developed around the same time for the Army Air Corps (e.g., Curtiss B-2 and Keystone B-3). Despite getting a later start, Douglas flew its first T2D-1 in a landplane configuration on Janu-

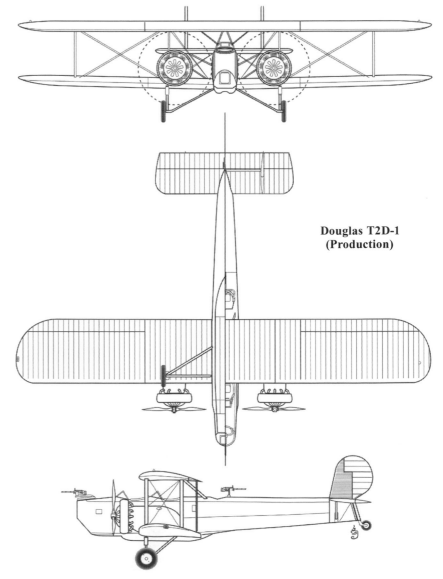

Douglas T2D-1 (Production)

Top: **The second T2D-1 was delivered in early 1927. This T2D-1 with two others embarked aboard *Langley* in mid–1927 where they earned the distinction of being the first twin-engine aircraft to operate from a carrier.** *Bottom:* **This P2D-1 served with VP-3 in the Panama Canal Zone from 1932 until 1937, when the unit started receiving PBY-1s. All had been withdrawn from service by the end of that year.**

Martin T4M and Great Lakes TG—1927

TECHNICAL SPECIFICATIONS (T4M-1)

Type: Three-place torpedo plane
Manufacturer: Glenn L. Martin Co., Cleveland, Ohio; Great Lakes Aircraft Corp., Cleveland, Ohio.
Total produced: 153 (USM, USMC)
Powerplant: One 525-hp Pratt & Whitney R-1690-24 9-cylinder radial driving a three-bladed Hamilton Standard fixed-pitch propeller.
Armament: One flexible .30-cal. rear machine gun in rear cockpit and one torpedo or up to 1,500 lbs. of bombs carried externally.

Performance: Max. speed 114 mph at s.l.; cruise 98 mph; ceiling 10,150 ft.; combat range 363 mi.
Weights: 3,931 lbs. empty, 8,071 lbs. max. loaded.
Dimensions: Span 53 ft., length 35 ft. 7 in., wing area 656 sq. ft.

The T4M/TG biplane was the Navy's principal carrier-based torpedo aircraft from 1928 until it was replaced during 1937 by Douglas TBD monoplanes. When BuAer began expressing a preference for aircraft equipped with air-cooled engines, Martin, in early 1927, modified the first T3M-2 prototype to accept installation of an R-1690 *Hornet* radial and delivered

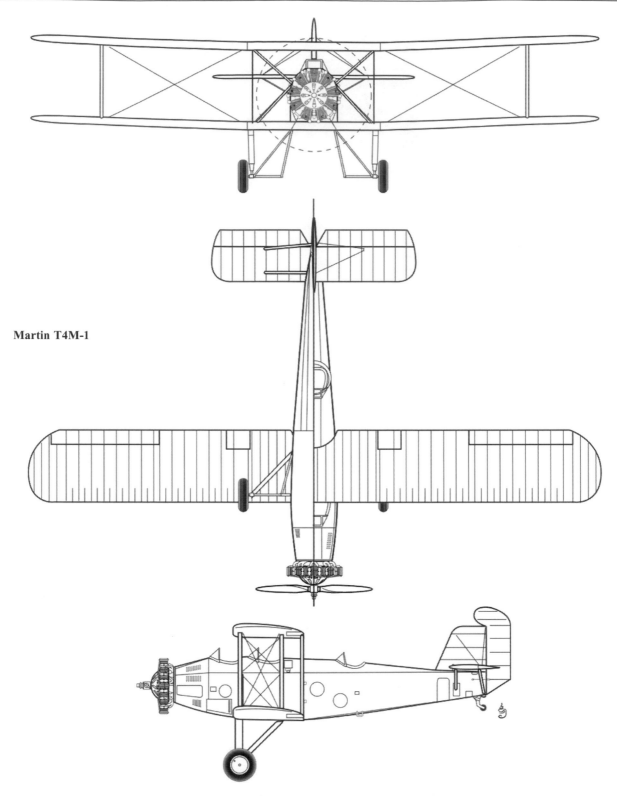

Martin T4M-1

it for tests as the XT3M-3. Experimental trials were sufficiently encouraging that BuAer ordered an improved *Hornet*-powered prototype from Martin under the designation XT4M-1. When the XT4M-1 arrived for testing in April 1927, it had smaller, narrow-chord wings, a balanced rudder, and many other refinements to the overall fuselage design. Like the T3M-2, it was convertible to floatplane operations. Martin was awarded a pro-

duction contract for 102 T4M-1s in June 1927 and deliveries to fleet units began in mid–1928. Great Lakes acquired Martin's Cleveland plant and production rights to the T4M in late 1928, and it produced a further 18 aircraft delivered in early 1930 as the TG-1. In July 1930 Great Lakes received an order for 32 additional aircraft to be equipped with Wright R-1820-86 *Cyclone* engines under the designation TG-2. Delivered from mid–1931,

Top: **Identical to the T4M-1, this TG-1 of VT-2B was one of 18 produced by Great Lakes in 1930. After being replaced by TG-2s in 1931 and 1932, all T4M-1s and TG-1s were assigned to shore stations or reserve units.** *Bottom:* **This reserve T4M-1 is shown serving with VN-12RD2 at NRAB Robertson in St. Louis, Missouri, during the late 1930s. Seven T4Ms and TGs remained on the naval inventory at the end of 1941.**

the TG-2 offered a 10 mph increase in top speed and improved rate-of-climb.

VT-2B of *Saratoga*'s air group received its first T4M-1s in August 1928, followed by VT-1B aboard *Lexington* later in the year, and both units were augmented with deliveries of TG-1s in 1930. When TG-2s began arriving in June 1931, the T4M-1s/TG-1s of VT-2B were transferred to shore-based utility or reserve units; those with VT-1B experienced a similar fate when

the unit converted to Martin BM-1 dive-bombers in 1932. BuAer's efforts to find a T4M/TG replacement in the early 1930s were not successful, with the result that TG-2s remained active with VT-2B until the first TBD-1s began arriving in October 1937. Many T4Ms/TGs saw service in Navy and Marine reserve units up through the late 1930s, and six remained on the naval inventory as of December 1941.

Naval Aircraft Factory T2N and Martin BM (T5M)—1930

TECHNICAL SPECIFICATIONS (BM-2)

Type: Two-place dive-bomber.

Manufacturer: Naval aircraft Factory, Philadelphia, Pennsylvania; and Glenn L. Martin Co., Baltimore, Maryland.

Total produced: 34 (USN)

Powerplant: One 625-hp. Pratt & Whitney R-1690-44 9-cylinder radial driving a two-bladed Hamilton Standard fixed-pitch propeller.

Armament: One fixed forward-firing .30-cal. machine gun and one flexible .30-cal. machine gun in rear cockpit, and up to 1,000 lbs. of bombs (or one torpedo) carried externally.

Performance: Max. speed 146 mph at 6,000 ft.; ceiling 16,800 ft.; combat range 413 mi.

Weights: 3,662 lbs. empty, 6,219 lbs. loaded.

Dimensions: Span 41 ft., length 28 ft. 9 in., wing area 436 sq. ft.

The first Navy aircraft designed to a dive-bomber specification, the T2N and BM were virtually identical except for powerplants. The BM-1 pictured served with VB-3B aboard *Langley* in 1934.

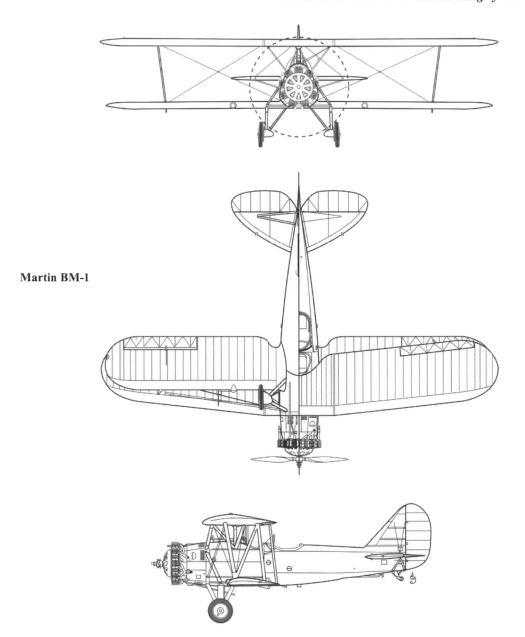

Martin BM-1

The NAF T2N and Martin T5M/BM occupy the distinction of being the first made-for-purpose dive-bomber aircraft ordered by the Navy. Successful naval experiments with dive-bombing and recent Marine combat experience using the tactic in Nicaragua inspired BuAer in 1928 to issue a requirement for a new biplane dive-bomber type capable of lifting a bomb heavy enough (i.e., 500 lbs.+) to damage or sink an armored warship. The general aerodynamic and structural design for the new type was laid down by BuAer itself and contracts for single prototypes were issued in June 1928 to Naval Aircraft Factory for an R-1750-powered version, designated XT2N-1, and to Martin for an R-1690-powered version, designated XT5M-1. Both aircraft featured the newly invented bomb crutch, a tubular metal device that swung the bomb past the propeller arc during steep (i.e., 70 to 80 deg.) dives. The XT2N-1 and XT5M-1 prototypes made their first flights close together in March 1930 and were thereafter delivered to NAS Anacostia for testing and evaluations.

In April 1931 Martin received a contract to manufacture 12 aircraft, re-designated BM-1 under the new bomber (B) category. Later, in October 1931, the Navy ordered 16 additional examples as BM-2s, which differed only in small details, then in 1932 Martin was directed to produce five more examples to be completed as BM-1s. The active service of BM-1s and -2s was primarily with two carrier units: VT-1S (later VB-1S) aboard *Lexington* beginning in 1932 and VB-3B aboard *Langley* in 1934. All BMs were withdrawn from fleet service during 1937 but continued to be used at shore stations for miscellaneous test and utility duties until the last example was scrapped in 1940.

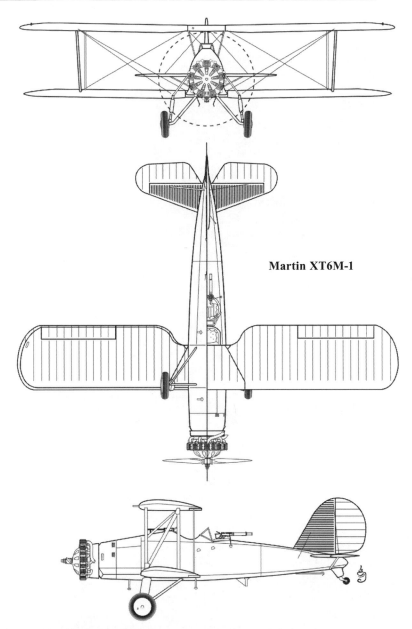

Martin XT6M-1

Martin T6M—1930

TECHNICAL SPECIFICATIONS (XT6M-1)

Type: Three-place torpedo plane
Manufacturer: Glenn L. Martin Co., Baltimore, Maryland.
Total produced: 1 (USN)
Powerplant: One 575-hp Wright R-1820-58 9-cylinder radial driving a two-bladed Hamilton Standard fixed-pitch propeller.
Armament: Two flexible .30-cal. rear machine guns in rear cockpit and one torpedo or up to 1,500 lbs. of bombs carried externally.
Performance: Max. speed 124 mph at s.l.; ceiling 11,600 ft.; combat range 323 mi.
Weights: 3,500 lbs. empty, 6,841 lbs. max. loaded.
Dimensions: Span 42 ft. 3 in., length 33 ft. 8 in., wing area 502 sq. ft.

Ordered by BuAer in mid–1929, the T6M represented one of several unsuccessful

The single XT6M-1 as it appeared for trials in early 1931. BuAer's efforts to replace its aging fleet of T4Ms and TGs would not be realized until the advent of the TBD monoplane in 1937.

attempts to generate a replacement for the T4M/TG series of torpedo planes. The XT6M-1 prototype, the first torpedo plane to feature a metal-skinned fuselage and tail group, was delivered to Anacostia for official evaluations in December 1930. However, flight testing indicated that the type's general performance was no better than, and in some instances inferior to, the TG-2, thus, no production was ordered.

Douglas T3D—1931

TECHNICAL SPECIFICATIONS (XT3D-2)

Type: Three-place torpedo plane
Manufacturer: Douglas Aircraft Co., Santa Monica, California.
Total produced: 1 (USN)
Powerplant: One 800-hp Pratt & Whitney R-1830-54 14-cylinder radial driving a two-bladed Hamilton Standard fixed-pitch propeller.
Armament: One fixed forward-firing .30-cal. machine gun, one flexible .30-cal. rear machine gun, and up to 1,000 lbs. of bombs or one torpedo carried externally.
Performance: Max. speed 142 mph at s.l.; ceiling 13,800 ft.; combat range 748 mi.
Weights: 4,876 lbs. empty, 8,543 lbs. loaded.
Dimensions: Span 50 ft., length 35 ft. 6 in., wing area 649 sq. ft.

Ordered in June 1930, the Douglas XT3D-1 signified another attempt by BuAer to find a torpedo plane replacement for the T4M/TG series. When the prototype was delivered to NAS Anacostia for testing in October 1931, it featured such innovations as a metal wing structure covered by fabric and a townsend drag ring around a single-row R-1690B *Hornet* engine; however, because the new type's overall performance was only marginally better than the TG-2, it was returned to the factory for modifications. The prototype reappeared in February 1933 as the XT3D-2, with a twin-row R-1830

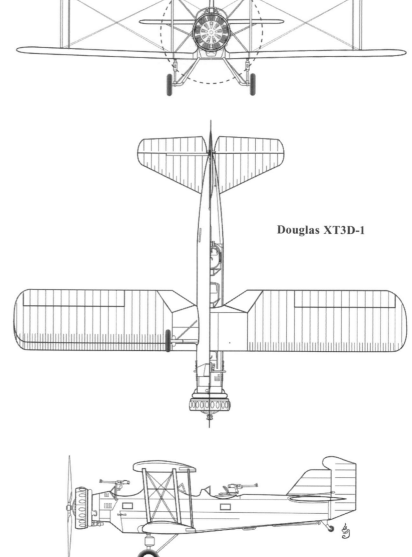

Douglas XT3D-1

engine, NACA-type cowling, and wheel spats on the landing gear. Although trials revealed some improvement in speed and range, it was not judged to be good enough to justify placing the type in production, and further development was abandoned.

Consolidated BY—1932

TECHNICAL SPECIFICATIONS (XBY-1)

Type: Two-place dive-bomber
Manufacturer: Consolidated Aircraft Co., Buffalo, New York.
Total produced: 1 (USN)
Powerplant: One 600-hp Wright R-1820-78 9-cylinder radial driving a two-bladed Hamilton Standard propeller.

The XT3D-1 as delivered for trials in fall of 1931. Although this aircraft was returned to the factory and reappeared in early 1933 with a more powerful engine, new cowling, and spatted landing gear, no production was ordered.

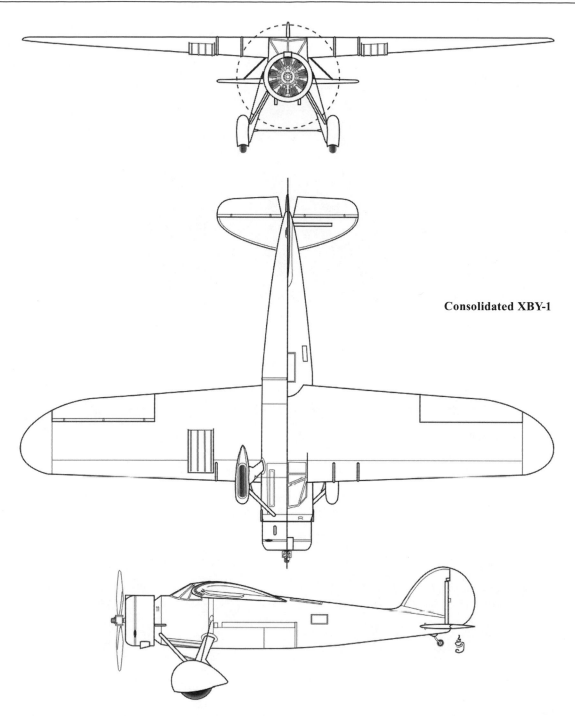

Consolidated XBY-1

Armament: One flexible .30-cal. rear machine gun fired from sliding rear dorsal hatch, and up to 1,000 lbs. of bombs (est.) carried in two internal wing bays.
Performance: Max. speed 181 mph; ceiling 22,700 ft.; range not specified.
Weights: 3,800 lbs. empty, 6,547 lbs. loaded.
Dimensions: Span 50 ft., length 33 ft. 8 in., wing area 361 sq. ft.

The monoplane XBY-1 stands out as an anomaly among the various biplane dive-bomber types considered by BuAer during the early 1930s. The airplane materialized as a direct development of Consolidated's Model 17 *Fleetster* 5-passenger monoplane transport, which first flown in 1930. BuAer ordered a naval bomber variant prototype in April 1931 as the XBY-1 and the aircraft was delivered for testing in September 1932. The design featured a high-mounted, cantilevered wing supported by a large, spatted undercarriage, and in general appearance was reminiscent of the well-known Lockheed *Vega*, though, unlike the wooden *Vega*, the XBY-1 was all-metal except for fabric-covered control surfaces. The two bomb bays, located at about 30 percent span, were enclosed by an unorthodox system of orange-peel-type doors. Despite being faster than existing biplane types, trials completed in early 1933 revealed that the XBY-1 was not suited for dive-bombing and too large for carrier stowage, thus no production was forthcoming.

turned to *Ranger* in 1937 as VB-4, and in 1938, began exchanging its BG-1s for monoplane SB2U-1s. Two Marine squadrons received BG-1s, VB-4M (later VMB-2) in 1935 and VB-6M (later VMB-1) in 1936, where they remained in active service until 1940. Once released from frontline squadrons, Navy and the Marine BG-1s were used for utility duties at shore bases, and 22 still remained on the naval inventory as of December 1941.

A military adaptation of the *Fleetster* five-passenger transport, the one and only XBY-1 appeared for Navy trials at Anacostia in late 1932. Bombs were carried in wing bays enclosed by orange-peel doors.

Great Lakes BG—1933

TECHNICAL SPECIFICATIONS (BG-1)

Type: Two-place dive-bomber
Manufacturer: Great Lakes Aircraft Corp., Cleveland, Ohio.
Total produced: 60 (USN,USMC)
Powerplant: One 750-hp Pratt & Whitney R-1535-82 14-cylinder radial driving a two-bladed Hamilton Standard variable-pitch propeller.
Armament: One fixed forward-firing .30-cal. machine gun, one flexible .30-cal. rear machine gun, and up to 1,000 lbs. of bombs carried externally.
Performance: Max. speed 188 mph at 8,900 ft.; ceiling 20,100 ft.; combat range 549 mi.
Weights: 3,903 lbs. empty, 6,347 lbs. loaded.
Dimensions: Span 36 ft., length 28 ft. 9 in., wing area 384 sq. ft.

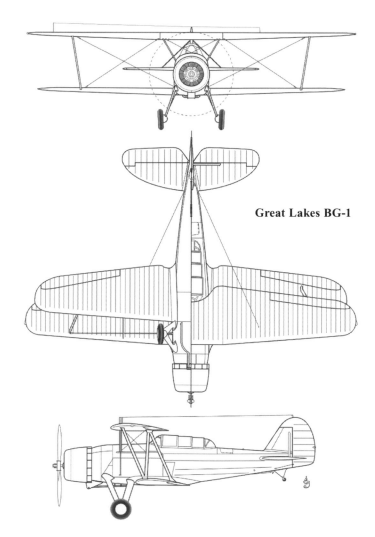

Great Lakes BG-1

The BG holds the distinction of being the only indigenous design of the short-lived Great Lakes Aircraft Corporation (1928–1936) to have been built in any quantity for the Navy and Marine Corps. Designed in response to a mid–1932 BuAer requirement for a two-place, biplane dive-bomber capable of carrying a 1,000-lb. bomb, the XBG-1 made its first flight in June 1933, and soon afterward was delivered to the Navy for service trials. A competitive fly-off conducted in late 1933 resulted in the XBG-1 being selected for production over the rival Consolidated XB2Y-1. Sixty aircraft under three contracts were manufactured by Great Lakes during 1934–1935, half of that number being assigned to the Marine Corps. Production BG-1s, which began reaching operational units in October 1934, differed from the prototype in having an enclosed canopy over the pilot and gunner/observer position.

The only frontline Navy squadron to equip with BG-1s was VB-3A. This unit initially formed part of *Ranger*'s new air group but was later transferred to *Lexington.* The squadron re-

A BG-1 serving with Marine squadron VMB-2 (formerly VB-4M) while attached to FMF One in San Diego. Half (30 aircraft) of all BG production was allocated to the Marine Corps. The last examples were retired in 1940.

Consolidated B2Y — 1933

TECHNICAL SPECIFICATIONS (XB2Y-1)

Type: Two-place dive-bomber
Manufacturer: Consolidated Aircraft Co., Buffalo, New York.
Total produced: 1 (USN)
Powerplant: One 700-hp Pratt & Whitney R-1535-64 14-cylinder radial driving a two-bladed Hamilton Standard fixed-pitch propeller.
Armament: One fixed forward-firing .30-caliber machine gun, one flexible .30-cal. machine gun in rear cockpit, and up to 1,000 lbs. of bombs carried externally.
Performance: Max. speed 182 mph at 8,900 ft.; ceiling 21,000 ft.; combat range 487 mi.
Weights: 3,538 lbs. empty, 6,010 lbs. loaded.
Dimensions: Span 36 ft. 6 in., length 27 ft. 10 in., wing area 362 sq. ft.

After a failed effort with the BY, Consolidated's B2Y represented a more serious attempt to compete in the Navy's newest dive-bomber contest. It began in mid–1932

when Consolidated and Great Lakes were both invited to build prototypes according to BuAer plans and specifications for an R-1535-powered biplane dive-bomber capable of delivering a 1,000-lb. bomb. Great Lakes' XBG-1 was delivered to the Navy in June 1933 and Consolidated's XB2Y-1 arrived in September. Both came in an open cockpit configuration and were extremely similar in appearance, differing in small details like the cowling, shape of the fin and rudder, and landing gear struts. Instead of the more conventional belly crutch, the XB2Y-1 featured a wing-shaped bomb displacement device in front of the main gear struts. During service trials that lasted into November, the XBG-1 revealed itself to be the better bombing platform of the two, and as a consequence, was selected as winner of the competition.

The XB2Y-1 as delivered for trials in September 1933. The unusual wing-shaped bomb displacement device, attached to a 1,000-pound bomb, is clearly visible. The XB2Y-1 and XBG-1 both were built to the same BuAer plan.

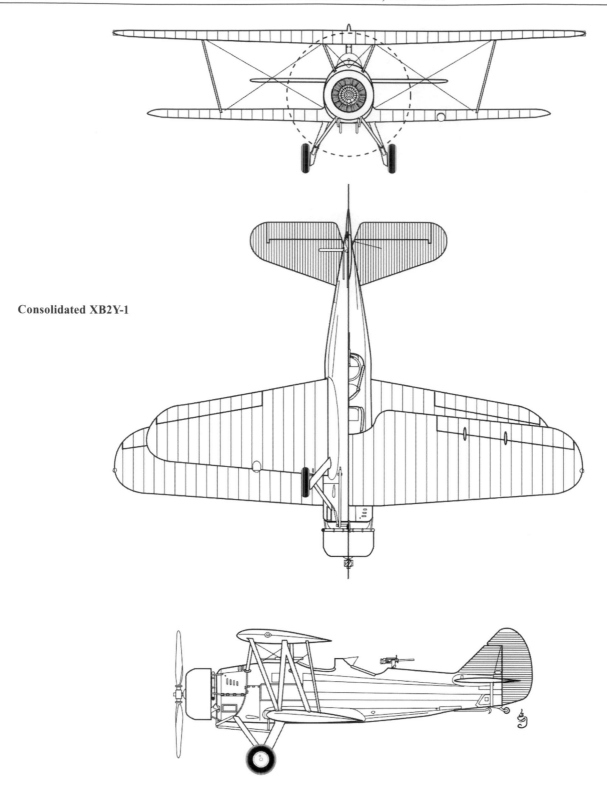

Consolidated XB2Y-1

Curtiss SBC (F12C, S4C) Helldiver—1933

TECHNICAL SPECIFICATIONS (SBC-4)

Type: Two-place dive-bomber
Manufacturer: Curtiss-Wright Corp., Curtiss Aeroplane Division, Buffalo, New York.
Total produced: 270 (USN, USMC)
Powerplant: One 950-hp Pratt & Whitney R-1820-34 9-cylinder radial

driving a three-bladed Hamilton Standard variable-pitch propeller.
Armament: One fixed forward-firing .30-caliber machine gun and one flexible .30-cal.machine gun in rear cockpit and up to 1,000 lbs. of bombs carried externally.
Performance: Max. speed 237 mph at 15,200 ft.; cruise, 127 mph; ceiling 27,300 ft.; combat range 590 mi. (500-lb. bomb)
Weights: 4,841 lbs. empty, 7,141 lbs. loaded.
Dimensions: Span 34 ft., length 28 ft. 4 in., wing area 317 sq. ft.

The Curtiss SBC not only became the last combat biplane in the active Navy and Marine Corps inventory, but was the last combat biplane of any type to be manufactured in the U.S. Arising from requirements for a retractable-gear, two-seat fighter similar to Grumman's FF/SF series, the Curtiss design was originally completed in late 1933 as a parasol-wing monoplane under the designation XF12C-1. Because of evolving naval requirements, the fighter designation was changed briefly to XS4C-1, and in early 1934, to XSBC-1. During dive-bombing tests conducted in mid–1934, the prototype was destroyed in a crash attributed to failure of the parasol wing.

In April 1935 BuAer ordered a second prototype built in a biplane configuration as the XSBC-2, and the new aircraft arrived for testing in December of the same year. The XSBC-2 was in effect a complete redesign, with revisions to the cowling, fuselage, and entire tail group. After a change to the 825-hp R-1535 engine and successful competitive trials against the XSBF-1 and XB2G-1, Curtiss received a contract in August 1936 to produce 83 aircraft as the SBC-3, and deliveries to fleet units commenced in mid–1937. In early 1938 Curtiss introduced the improved SBC-4, which, equipped with a 950-hp R-1820 engine plus other refinements, doubled bomb load to a more lethal 1,000 lbs. Curtiss thereafter received a production order for 174 SBC-4s in January 1938, with deliveries commencing in March 1939. When 50 SBC-4s were diverted to France in 1940, production of the Navy and Marine order extended into 1941.

Starting in July 1937 and continuing into 1938, SBC-3s were delivered to VS-5 (*Yorktown*), VS-3 (*Saratoga*), and VS-6 (*Enterprise*). The Marines received only one SBC-3 in 1938. SBC-4s initially equipped VS-2 aboard *Lexington* in 1939 and later VS-8 and VB-8 of the *Hornet* air group in 1941. In 1939–1940, SBC-4s were allocated in threes or fours to

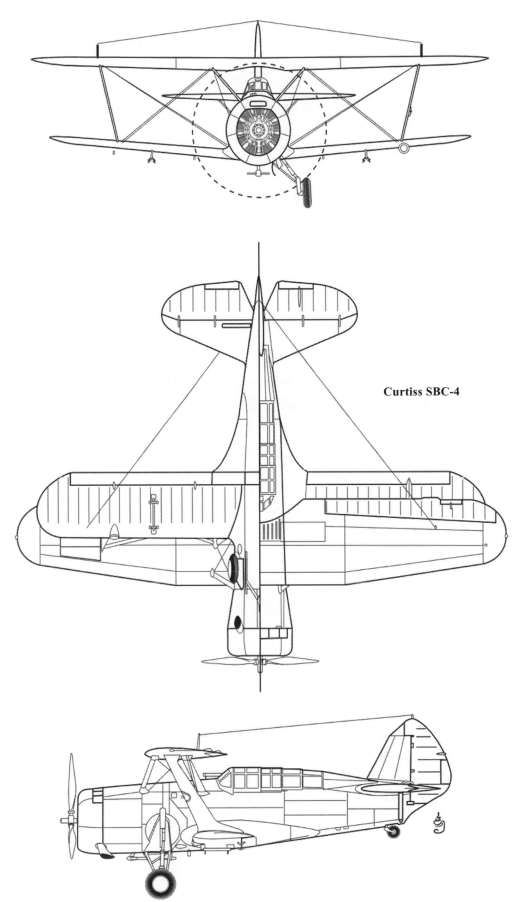

Curtiss SBC-4

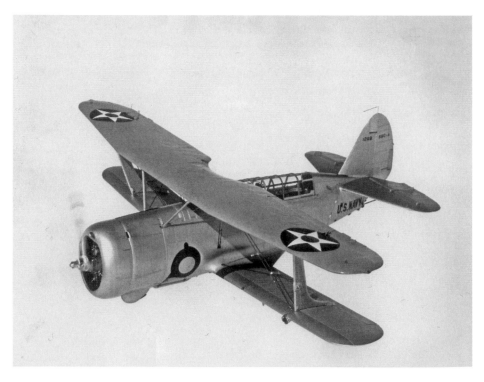

eleven different Naval Reserve units. The Marine Corps received its first SBC-4 in 1940, and the type was equipping VMO-151 and VMO-155 by mid–1941. At the time of the Japanese attack on Pear Harbor, in December 1941, some 69 SBC-3s and 117 SBC-4s remained in the Navy and Marine active inventories, though none ever saw combat. After active service, a number of SBCs were thereafter used as trainers.

Vought SBU (F3U)—1933

TECHNICAL SPECIFICATIONS (SBU-1)

Type: Two-place dive-bomber
Manufacturer: Chance Vought Division of United Aircraft Corp., Stratford, Connecticut.
Total produced (all models): 125 (USN, USMC)
Powerplant: One 700-hp Pratt & Whitney R-1535-80 14-cylinder radial driving a two-bladed Hamilton Standard variable-pitch propeller.
Armament: One fixed forward-firing .30-cal. machine gun and one flexible .30-cal. machine gun in rear cockpit and up to 500 lbs. of bombs carried externally.
Performance: Max. speed 205 mph at 8,900 ft.; cruise 122 mph; ceiling 23,700 ft.; range 548 mi. loaded.
Weights: 3,645 lbs. empty, 5,618 lbs. max. loaded.
Dimensions: Span 33 ft. 3 in., length 27 ft. 9 in., wing area 327 sq. ft.

The Vought SBU was the first of the new SB-types to enter operational service and the last type of combat aircraft with fixed-gear to be placed in production by the Navy. It began life in June 1932 under the designation XF3U-1 as a two-seat fighter laid down in accordance with BuAer Design 113. When the XF3U-1 prototype arrived at Anacostia for testing in June 1933, the Navy was in the process of abandoning the two-seat fighter concept, and the aircraft was returned to the factory to be reworked as a scout-bomber with the offer that it would most likely be placed in production. Revisions to the basic design included enlarging and strengthening

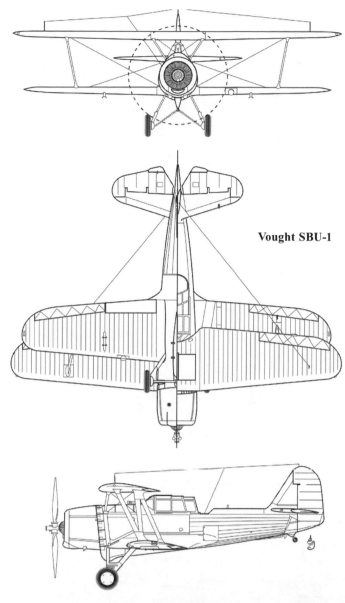

Vought SBU-1

the wings, increasing fuel capacity, and adding dive-bombing apparatus. Under the new designation XSBU-1, the prototype was returned to the Navy in June 1934, and after changes to the vertical tail surfaces and cowling, Vought received a production order for 84 SBU-1s in January 1935 and deliveries began the following November. A second batch of 40 aircraft was ordered in November 1936 as SBU-2s with R-1535-98 engines and minor detail changes.

VS-3B of *Lexington*'s air group received the first production SBU-1s in November 1935, followed by VS-2B aboard *Saratoga* and VS-1B aboard *Ranger*. Most SBU-2s never saw frontline service but were delivered new to Navy and Marine reserve units during 1937. All SBU-1s had been retired from fleet squadrons by the end of 1940, and SBU-2s were withdrawn from reserve units during 1941. Some 83 remaining SBUs finished their career as trainers at NAS Pensacola and NAS Corpus Christi.

Great Lakes B2G—1935

TECHNICAL SPECIFICATIONS (XB2G-1)

Type: Two-place dive-bomber
Manufacturer: Great Lakes Aircraft Corp., Cleveland, Ohio.
Total produced: 1 (USN, USMC)
Powerplant: One 750-hp Pratt & Whitney R-1535-82 14-cylinder radial driving a two-bladed Hamilton Standard variable-pitch propeller.
Armament: One fixed forward-firing .50-cal. machine gun, one flexible .30-cal. rear machine gun, and up to 1,000 lbs. of bombs carried in internal bomb bay.
Performance: Max. speed 198 mph at 8,900 ft.; ceiling 19,500 ft.; combat range 582 mi.
Weights: 4,248 lbs. empty, 6,802 lbs. loaded.
Dimensions: Span 36 ft., length 28 ft. 9 in., wing area 384 sq. ft.

In 1934 BuAer issued nearly simultaneous requirements for new biplane and monoplane scout-bomber designs to be equipped with retractable landing gear. Great Lakes Aircraft, having previously achieved moderate success with its fixed-gear BG, went back and revised the basic airframe by deepening the belly to incorporate a Grumman-type, inward-retracting landing gear and adding an internal bomb bay. The single forward-firing gun was increased to .50-caliber, but other features of the previous BG design were retained. BuAer ordered one prototype in June 1934 under the designation XB2G-1. After initial testing at the factory in late 1935, the aircraft was delivered to the Navy for competitive trials.

Interestingly, Great Lakes' chief competition was not the monoplanes but two

Most SBU-2s, like this example seen at NRAB New York in 1940, went directly to reserve units. SBU-1s served in carrier air groups aboard *Lexington*, *Saratoga*, and *Ranger* from 1935 until 1940.

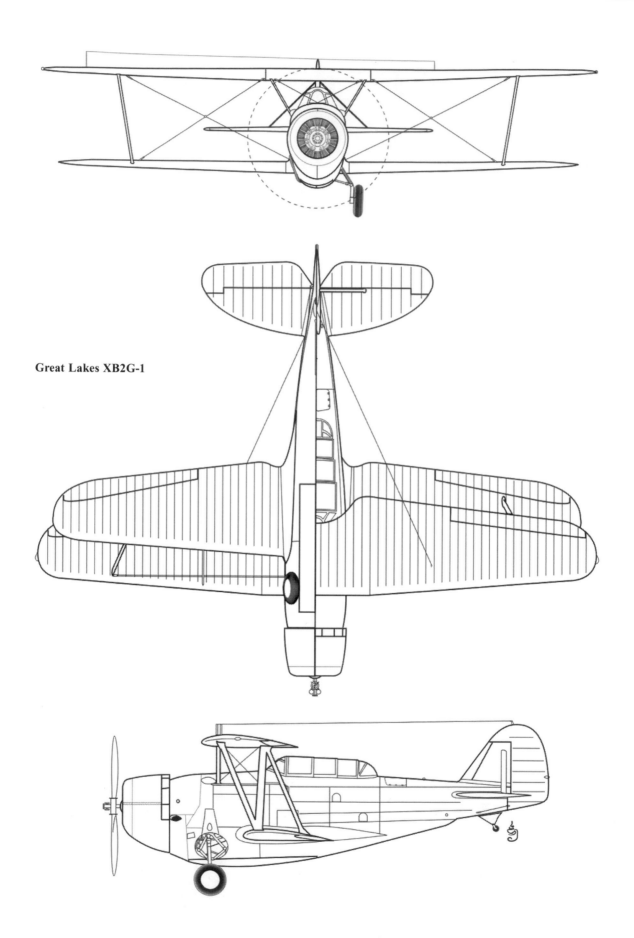

Great Lakes XB2G-1

The sole example of XB2G-1 in 1938 after it had been reassigned to the Marines to be used as a command plane to tour bases. Great Lakes was out of business by the end of 1936.

other biplane designs, the Grumman XSBF-1 and the Curtiss XSBC-2. A fly-off between the three prototypes conducted from late 1935 to early 1936 ultimately resulted in the selection of the XSBC-2 for production. However, the Navy did purchase the single XB2G-1 prototype, and it was eventually transferred to the Marine Corps, where it was used as a command plane to tour reserve bases until 1938. When Great Lakes went out of business in 1936, Bell Aircraft acquired its manufacturing rights, but no effort was made to continue development of the former company's dive-bomber series.

Grumman SBF—1936

TECHNICAL SPECIFICATIONS (XSBF-1)

Type: Two-place dive-bomber
Manufacturer: Grumman Aircraft Engineering Corp., Bethpage, New York.
Total produced: 1 (USN)
Powerplant: One 700-hp Pratt & Whitney R-1535-72 14-cylinder radial driving a two-bladed Hamilton Standard variable-pitch propeller.
Armament: One fixed forward-firing .30-cal. machine gun, one flexible .30-cal. machine gun in rear cockpit, and up four 500 lbs. of bombs carried externally.
Performance: Max. speed 215 mph at 15,000 ft.; ceiling 26,000 ft.; range 688 mi.

Weights: 3,395 lbs. empty, 4,442 lbs. max. loaded.
Dimensions: Span 31 ft. 6 in., length 25 ft. 9 in., wing area 310 sq. ft.

The Grumman SBF was one of three retractable-gear biplane designs built for the newly created scout-bomber (SB) requirement issued by BuAer in 1934. Ordered from Grumman

The sole XSBF-1 as delivered in early 1936. The aerodynamic configuration was very similar to Grumman's FF/SF series. The Curtiss XSBC-2 was selected for production over the XSBF-1 and the Great Lakes XB2G-1.

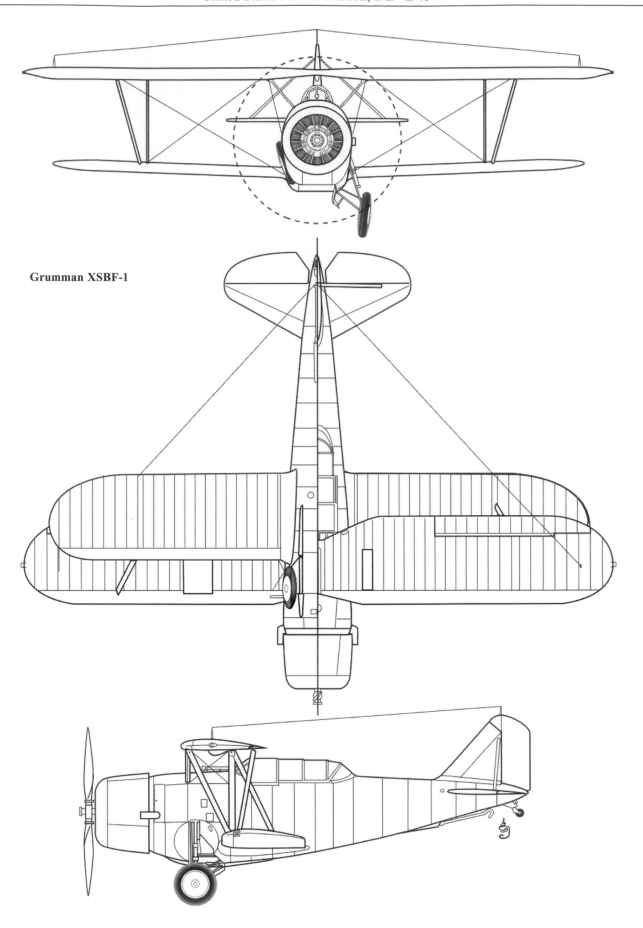

Grumman XSBF-1

in March 1935, the XSBF-1 was essentially a re-engined development of the basic SF-2 airframe having a somewhat shorter, broader-chord wing and dive-bombing apparatus. After the XSBF-1 prototype was delivered for testing in February 1936, it was subjected to competitive trials against the Great Lakes XB2G-1 and Curtiss XSBC-2. In August, when the Navy announced that the Curtiss entry had been selected for production, no further development of the XSBF-1 was undertaken.

Douglas TBD Devastator—1935

SPECIFICATIONS (TBD-1)

Type: Three-place torpedo-bomber
Manufacturer: Douglas Aircraft Co., El Segundo Division, El Segundo, California.
Total produced: 130 (USN)
Powerplant: One 900-hp Pratt & Whitney R-1830-64 14-cylinder radial driving a three-bladed Hamilton Standard variable-pitch propeller.
Armament: One fixed forward-firing .30-cal. machine gun, one flexible .30-cal. rear machine gun, and up to 1,000 lbs. of bombs or one torpedo carried externally.
Performance: Max. speed 206 mph at s.l.; cruise 128 mph; ceiling 19,700 ft.; range 716 mi. (with 1,000-lb. payload).
Weights: 6,182 lbs. empty, 10,194 lbs. loaded.
Dimensions: Span 50 ft., length 35 ft., wing area 422 sq. ft.

The TBD was the first type of monoplane combat aircraft to be placed in production and enter service with the Navy. In mid–1934, to keep pace with new carrier construction and also replace its aging fleet of T4M/TG torpedo planes, BuAer issued a completely new requirement for a torpedo-bomber (TB) type and authorized two prototypes: a monoplane from Douglas designated the XTBD-1 and a biplane from Great Lakes designated the XTBG-1. Both aircraft were to be powered by an R-1830 engine, have retractable landing gear, and carry a crew of three. The XTBD-1 prototype was test flown on April 15, 1935, and delivered to Anacostia just nine days later. Flight trials conducted through the balance of 1935 indicated not only superior performance over the rival XTBG-1 biplane, but far better stability and overall handling characteristics. Douglas received a contract in

February 1936 for 114 TBD-1 production models, which differed in having an uprated engine, a raised canopy enclosure, more vertical fin area, and a revised cowling. In mid–1938, after the type had joined the fleet, 15 more TBD-1s were added to the original order.

Deliveries of TBD-1s began in early October 1937 and the first squadron to receive the type was VT-3 of *Saratoga*'s air group. From mid–1938 onwards, TBD-1s equipped VT-2 of *Lexington*, VT-5 of *Yorktown*, and VT-6 of *Enterprise*, and finally, in late 1941, VT-8 of *Hornet*. TBDs were the Fleet's standard torpedo-bomber when the U.S. entered World War II and were

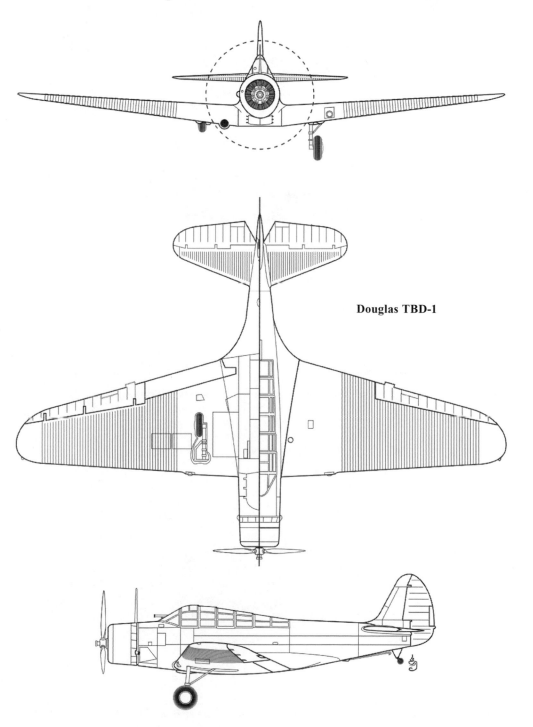

Douglas TBD-1

Above: **The first Navy monoplane to enter carrier service in late 1937, this TBD-1 was assigned to VT-6 of the newly formed *Enterprise* Air Group. All 130 had joined the fleet by the end of 1938. *Below:* TBD-1 of VT-2 in the *Lexington* Air Group, circa late 1940. The tail color was bright yellow. During 1941, the colorful orange-yellow and silver paint scheme on fleet aircraft was changed to overall light gray.**

involved in the very earliest carrier actions of 1942 against land-based Japanese targets in the Marshall and Gilbert Islands. However, in the carrier-to-carrier engagements which followed, TBDs proved to be highly vulnerable to both enemy antiaircraft fire and fighters, and during the Battle of Midway on June 4–5, 1942, 41 of 47 TBDs launched were lost. After being replaced by Grumman TBFs in mid–1942, surviving TBDs served a while longer as advanced trainers.

Great Lakes TBG—1935

TECHNICAL SPECIFICATIONS (XTBG-1)

Type: Three-place torpedo-bomber
Manufacturer: Great Lakes Aircraft Corp., Cleveland, Ohio.
Total produced: 1 (USN)
Powerplant: One 800-hp Pratt & Whitney R-1830-60 14-cylinder radial driving a three-bladed Hamilton Standard variable-pitch propeller.
Armament: One fixed forward-firing .30-cal. machine gun, one flexible .30-cal. rear machine gun, and up to 1,000 lbs. of bombs or one torpedo carried in internal bay.
Performance: Max. speed 185 mph at 7,000 ft.; ceiling 16,400 ft.; combat range 586 mi.
Weights: 5,323 lbs. empty, 9,275 lbs. loaded.
Dimensions: Span 42 ft., length 35 ft. 1 in., wing area 547 sq. ft.

The TBG was the last type of torpedo-carrying biplane to be considered by the Navy and the final product of Great Lakes before that company ceased operations. In June 1934, BuAer selected Great Lakes to build a retractable-gear biplane torpedo-bomber prototype under the designation XTBG-1 in what was to be a biplane versus monoplane fly-off. The design was essentially a fifteen percent scale-up of the basic BG/B2G blueprint, adding a bombardier's station beneath a low-profile canopy located forward of the cabane struts. Following delivery of the XTBG-1 prototype to Anacostia in August 1935, testing revealed not only poor stability, but levels of performance that were generally inferior to Douglas's rival XTBD-1 monoplane. Development was abandoned in early 1936 and Great Lakes, lacking any production prospects, closed its doors soon afterward.

Northrop BT—1935

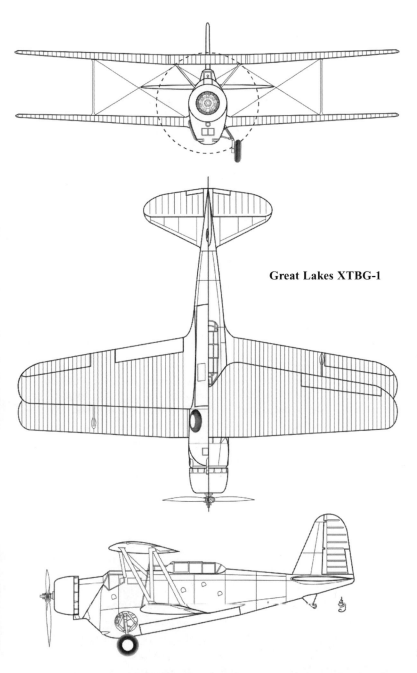

Great Lakes XTBG-1

TECHNICAL SPECIFICATIONS BT-1

Type: Two-place dive-bomber

Manufacturer: Northrop Aircraft Corp. (subsidiary of Douglas Aircraft), El Segundo, California.

Total produced: 56 (USN)

Powerplant: One 825-hp Pratt & Whitney R-1535-94 14-cylinder radial driving a two-bladed Hamilton Standard variable-pitch propeller.

Armament: One fixed forward-firing .50-cal. machine gun, one flexible .30-cal. rear machine gun, and up to 1,000 lbs. of bombs carried externally.

Performance: Max. speed 222 mph at 9,500 ft.; cruise 192 mph; ceiling 25,300 ft.; range 550 mi. loaded, 1,150 mi. max.

Weights: 4,606 lbs. empty, 7,197 lbs. loaded.

Dimensions: Span 41 ft. 6 in., length 31 ft. 8 in., wing area 319 sq. ft.

The Northrop BT is recognized as being the direct precursor to the legendary SBD Dauntless series. When BuAer issued a 1934 requirement for a retractable-gear, monoplane scout-bomber, Northrop responded with a slightly scaled-down version of its Army A-17 attack airplane, which itself had been derived from the Gamma transport of 1932. Unlike the fixed, spatted landing gear of production A-17s, the Navy design retained the semi-retractable gear arrangement seen on Gamma 2F demonstrator. It also introduced a perforated, split-type dive brake that would reduce buffeting at high diving speeds. BuAer gave Northrop a contract in November 1934 for one prototype as the XBT-1, and the aircraft made its first flight on August 19, 1935. Following completion of official trials in October 1936, the Navy awarded Northrop a contract for 54 BT-1s. While production was underway, the company commenced development of an XBT-2 variant having a bigger engine and fully flush, inward-retracting landing gear (first developed for the Army A-17A). After the company was renamed Douglas Aircraft, El Segundo Division in 1938, the XBT-2 was ultimately placed in production as the SBD-1.

Production BT-1s first entered service in April 1938 with VB-5, becoming part of *Yorktown*'s air wing, and in early 1939, began equipping VB-6 of the recently commissioned *Enterprise*. The service career of the BT was comparatively brief, however, the phase-out

The XTBG-1 as delivered to Anacostia in mid–1935. BuAer ordered it as a hedge against the possibility that the monoplane Douglas TBD would be too "hot" for carrier operations. Note bombardier's station forward.

commencing in early 1941 as new SBD-2s and -3s began arriving to take their place.

Brewster SBA and Naval Aircraft Factory SBN—1936

TECHNICAL SPECIFICATIONS (SBN-1)

Type: Two-place dive-bomber
Manufacturer: Brewster Aeronautical Corp., Long Island City, New York; and Naval Aircraft Factory, Philadelphia, Pennsylvania.
Total produced: 31 (USN)
Powerplant: One 950-hp Wright R-1820-38 9-cylinder radial driving a three-bladed Hamilton Standard variable-pitch propeller.
Armament: One fixed forward-firing .50-cal. machine gun, one flexible .30-cal. rear machine gun, and one 500-lb. bomb carried in internal bay.
Performance: Max. speed 254 mph at 15,200 ft.; cruise 117 mph; ceiling 28,300 ft.; range 1,110 mi. max.
Weights: 4,503 lbs. empty, 6,759 lbs. loaded.
Dimensions: Span 39 ft., length 27 ft. 8 in., wing area 259 sq. ft.

The SBA was the first original aircraft design of the controversial Brewster Aeronautical Corp. Though Brewster's roots were traceable to a 19th century horse carriage business, the company in truth had been completely restructured in 1932 with the principal aim of obtaining Navy aircraft contracts. Having no business of its own at the time, Brewster commenced operations by performing subcontract work for Vought and Grumman. When BuAer circulated a requirement for a new monoplane scout-bomber (SB) in mid–1934, Brewster was invited to submit a proposal based upon a somewhat different specification. Unlike Vought's XSB2U-1 and Northrop's XBT-1, Brewster's XSBA-1 would be a mid-wing design incorporating an internal bomb bay and using the larger diameter R-1820 powerplant. Brewster received a contract to construct a single prototype in October 1934 and the completed aircraft was delivered to the Navy for tests in April 1936.

Early trials revealed less than expected performance, causing the prototype to be returned to the factory for modifications. When the XSBA-1 reappeared in 1937 with an uprated engine, revised cowling, three-bladed propeller, and raised canopy, top speed had risen to 263 mph, the fastest of any monoplane SB type thus far tested. BuAer awarded a contract to manufacture 30 airplanes in September 1938, not to Brewster however, but

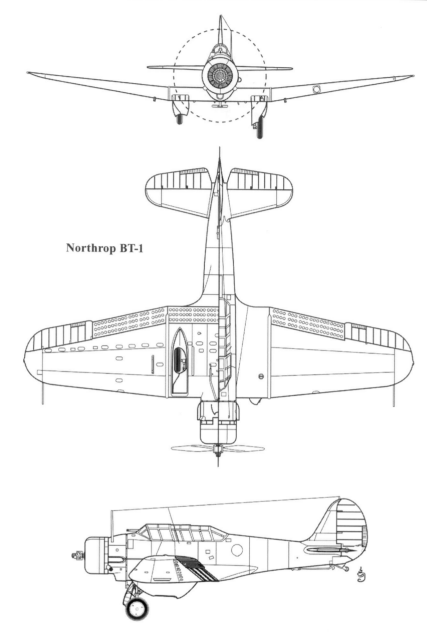

Northrop BT-1

A BT-1 of VB-5 attached to *Yorktown* in 1938. Detail of split-type dive brakes shows to good advantage. A more powerful engine, flush-folding landing gear, plus other improvements turned the BT into the legendary SBD.

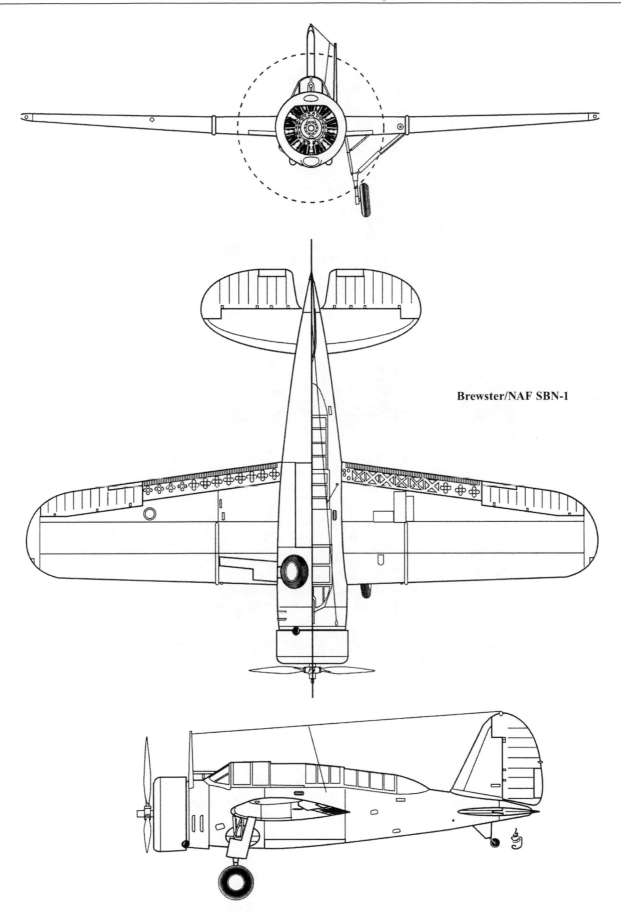

Brewster/NAF SBN-1

Top: **A Brewster XSBA-1 prototype seen at Anacostia in 1937 following modifications. Production, as the SBN-1, was given to the Naval Aircraft Factory because of Brewster's limited plant capacity.** *Bottom:* **One of thirty SBN-1s built by the Naval Aircraft Factory from 1939 to 1942. The type was virtually obsolete by the time it reached operational units. Served very briefly with VB-3 of the *Saratoga* Air Group.**

not delivered until late 1940 and the balance of the contract was not completed until early 1942, by which time the type was already obsolete. SBN-1s served briefly with VB-3 of *Saratoga*'s air group and were later used as trainers by VT-8 aboard *Hornet.*

Vought SB2U Vindicator—1936

TECHNICAL SPECIFICATIONS (SB2U-1)

Type: Two-place dive-bomber

Manufacturer: Chance Vought Division of United Aircraft Corp., Stratford, Connecticut.

Total produced: 170 (USN, USMC)

Powerplant: One 825-hp Pratt & Whitney R-1535-96 14-cylinder radial driving a two-bladed Hamilton Standard variable-pitch propeller.

Armament: One fixed forward-firing .50-cal. machine gun and one flexible .30-cal. machine gun in rear cockpit and up to 1,000 lbs. of bombs carried externally.

Performance: Max. speed 250 mph at 9,500 ft.; cruise 143 mph; ceiling 27,400 ft.; range 635 mi. (1,000-lb. payload).

Weights: 4,676 lbs. empty, 7,278 lbs. max. loaded.

Dimensions: Span 42 ft., length 34 ft., wing area 305 sq. ft.

Following the Douglas TBD by two months, the Vought SB2U was the first monoplane scout-bomber to join the fleet. Ordered by BuAer in October 1934, the XSB2U-1 was one of *seven* scout-bomber prototypes authorized that year (i.e., the XBT-1 and XSBA-1 monoplane designs, plus the XB2G-1, XSBC-2, XSBF-1, and XSB3U-1 biplane designs). By doing this, BuAer hoped to solve two problems at once: find out whether or not monoplanes could be safely operated from carriers; and regardless of outcome, obtain new airplanes to equip the Navy's growing carrier force. The design of the XSB2U-1 mixed newer aerodynamic ideas with older construction methods, appearing with fabric covering on the aft fuselage and on the wings aft of the main spars. The prototype made its first flight on January 4, 1936 and was delivered to Anacostia three months later.

to the government-owned NAF plant as the SBN-1. Since by that time Brewster was heavily occupied with the F2A-1 fighter project, BuAer reasoned that the company lacked plant capacity to produce the XSBA-1 in quantity. Ironically, NAF's production proceeded at such a lethargic rate that the first SBN-1s were

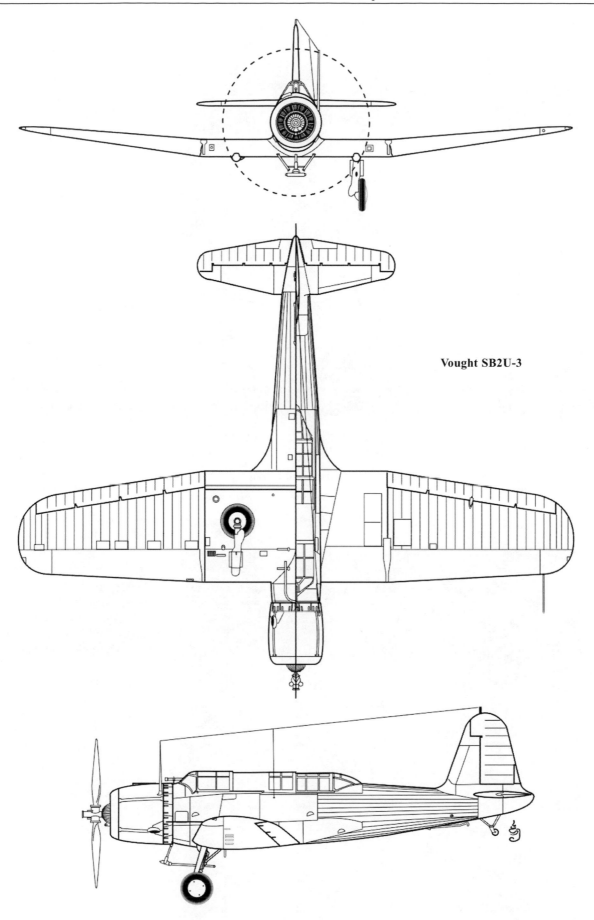

Vought SB2U-3

Above: **The Fleet's first monoplane dive-bomber, these SB2U-1s are seen serving with VB-3 in the *Saratoga* Air Group in 1938. Most had been replaced by SBDs by the time the United States entered World War II.** *Below:* **An overall gray Marine SB2U-3 seen in June 1941 in VMS-1 markings just before the change to VMSB-131. The only unit to employ SB2U-3s in combat was Midway-based VMSB-231 in 1942.**

In trials conducted through the summer of 1936, the monoplanes clearly outperformed the biplanes in terms of speed (and thus time to target) and climb, while still demonstrating acceptable approach speeds and wave-off characteristics.

In October 1936, Vought received a production order for 54 SB2U-1s, and deliveries to fleet units began in December 1937. A second batch of 58 aircraft was ordered in January 1938 as the SB2U-2, with changes in equipment and a small increase in gross weight, and entered service later the same year. The final version, ordered in September 1939 as the SB2U-3, came with an uprated R-1535-102 engine, increased fuel capacity, and a .50-cal. gun in the rear position. Nearly all of the 57 SB2U-3s produced were allocated to the Marine Corps in 1940–1941. One SB2U-1 was modified as a floatplane but no production was undertaken. Vought also built two export versions, 20 to the French in 1939 as the V-156-F3 and 50 to the Royal Navy under Lend-Lease in 1941 as the V-156-B1.

The first production SB2U-1s equipped VB-3 of the *Saratoga* air group, followed by *Lexington*'s VB-2. By early 1940, SB2U-1s and -2s were also serving with VB-4 (*Ranger*) and VS-72 (*Wasp*, commissioned April 1940). Although SB2Us were still equipping the *Ranger* and *Wasp* air groups when the war broke out in December 1941, none were ever involved in combat actions. VMSB-231, one of two Marine squadrons operating SB2U-3s, flew combat sorties against the Japanese fleet from Midway Island in June 1942, but the type was soon replaced by SBDs in frontline units. After active service, a number of SB2Us were used in the Advanced Carrier Training Groups (ACTGs).

Vought SB3U—1936

TECHNICAL SPECIFICATIONS (XSB3U-1)

Type: Two-place dive-bomber
Manufacturer: Chance Vought Division of United Aircraft Corp., Stratford, Connecticut.
Total produced: 1 (USN)
Powerplant: One 750-hp Pratt & Whitney R-1535-82 14-cylinder radial driving a two-bladed Hamilton Standard variable-pitch propeller.
Armament: One fixed forward-firing .50-cal. machine gun and one flexible .30-cal. machine gun in rear cockpit and up to 500 lbs. of bombs carried externally.
Performance: Max. speed 215 mph at 8,900 ft.; ceiling 26,500 ft.; range 590 mi.
Weights: 3,876 lbs. empty, 5,837 lbs. max. loaded.
Dimensions: Span 33 ft. 3 in., length 28 ft. 2 in., wing area 327 sq. ft.

Produced in parallel to the monoplane SB2U, the biplane SB3U was perhaps the most extreme

The sole XSB3U-1 prototype as seen at Anacostia in 1936, delivered the same month as the XSB2U-1. This probably represents one of the best examples of official Navy reluctance toward monoplane carrier aircraft.

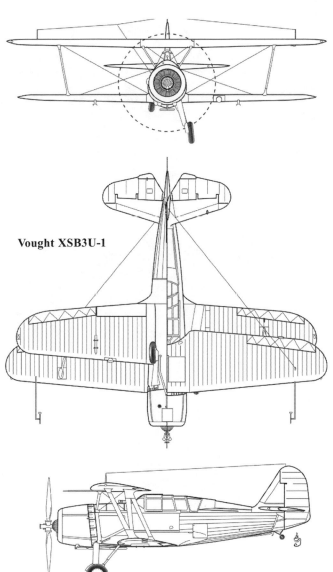

Vought XSB3U-1

example of BuAer's official ambivalence toward the suitability of monoplanes for carrier operations. In February 1935, four months after authorizing three scout-bomber monoplane prototypes, BuAer ordered a retractable-gear biplane from Vought under the designation XSB3U-1. Utilizing the same basic airframe and engine as the SBU-2, the XSB3U-1 incorporated a rearward-folding landing gear and a somewhat longer chord cowling. It is noteworthy that the XSB2U-1 and XSB3U-1 prototypes were completed and delivered to Anacostia at the same time. Trials held between the two types unquestionably confirmed the superiority of the monoplane's aerodynamics: though 500 lbs. heavier and dimensionally larger than the XSB3U-1, the monoplane XSB2U-1, equipped with an identical power plant, was nonetheless faster by 15 mph, had similar range, and could carry twice the bomb load, while exhibiting the same 66 mph stall speed. The sole XSB3U-1 prototype was retained at Anacostia for test purposes until 1938.

Douglas SBD Dauntless—1938

TECHNICAL SPECIFICATIONS (SBD-2)

Type: Two-place dive-bomber
Manufacturer: Douglas Aircraft Company, El Segundo Division, El Segundo, California.
Total produced: 4,899 (USN, USMC)
Powerplant: One 1,000-hp Wright R-1820-32 9-cylinder radial driving a three-bladed Hamilton Standard variable-pitch propeller.
Armament: Two fixed forward-firing .30-cal. machine guns, two flexible .30-cal. rear machine guns, and up to 2,000 lbs. of bombs carried externally.
Performance: Max. speed 252 mph at 16,000 ft.; cruise 148 mph; ceiling 26,000 ft.; range 1,370 mi. max., 1,225 mi. loaded.
Weights: 6,293 lbs. empty, 10,360 lbs. loaded.
Dimensions: Span 41 ft. 6 in., length 33 ft., wing area 325 sq. ft.

Although BuAer viewed the SBD as a stopgap design when it entered service in 1940, it was destined to become, in terms of tactical success, the most important Navy and Marine

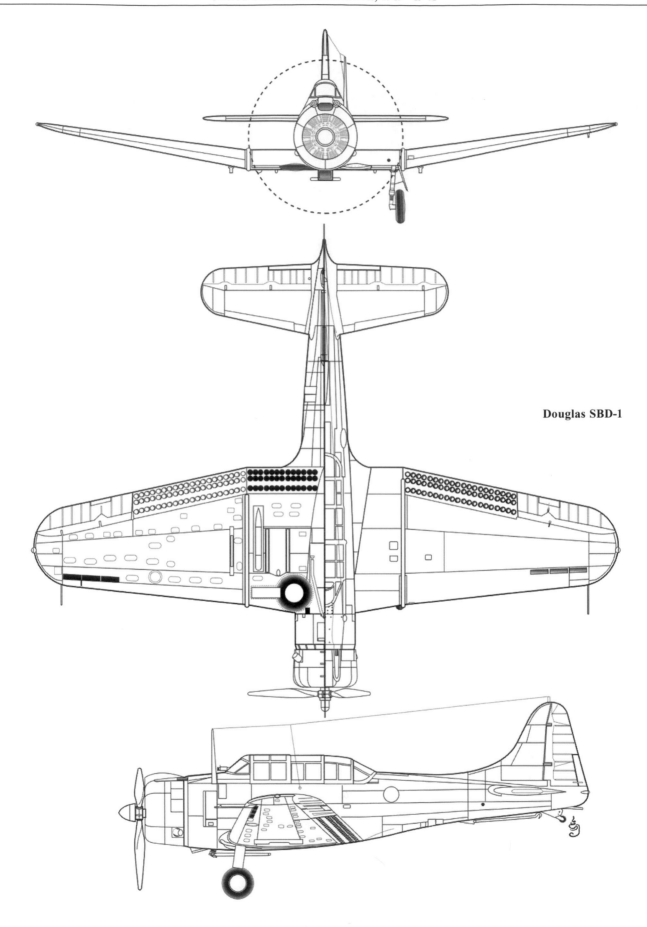

Douglas SBD-1

Top: **The first Marine monoplane combat aircraft of any type. In early 1941, these SBD-1s replaced the BG-1s of MCAS Quantico-based VMB-1 (reclassified VMSB-132 in late 1941).** *Bottom:* **An overall light gray SBD-3 seen at the Douglas plant in the summer of 1941. As they entered service, SBD-3s replaced SBC-3s and -4s, BT-1s, and SB2U-1s in six carrier squadrons before the end of 1941.**

Corps dive-bomber type of World War II. The origins of the SBD relate back to BuAer's 1934 requirement for a monoplane scout-bomber, which resulted, among other things, in a production contract being given to Northrop in late 1936 for its BT-1. At the time Northrop's name changed to Douglas Aircraft, El Segundo Division in 1938, the firm was about to complete work on its XBT-2, an improved derivative having a 1,000-hp. R-1820-32 engine and a redesigned landing gear that retracted flush into the wing roots. The plane made its first flight in April 1938, and further refinements such as a reshaped fin/rudder and a new canopy enclosure created a new model that was ordered into production in 1939 as the SBD-1.

BuAer had originally contemplated terminating SBD production in early 1942 at 174 (i.e., 57 SBD-1s, 87 SBD-2s, and 30 SBD-3s) but the intervention of World War II kept the assembly line moving until mid–1944, resulting in a further 470 SBD-3s, 780 SBD-4s, 3,025 SBD-5s, and finally, 450 SBD-6s. Another 953 were completed for the AAF as the A-24 (SBD-3), A-24A (SBD-4), and A-24B (SBD-5). The SBD series was continually improved during its production life: the SBD-2 included hydraulically actuated landing gear; the SBD-3, self-sealing tanks, protective armor, and forward guns increased from .30-caliber to .50-caliber; the SBD-4, a 24-volt electrical system; the SBD-5, 1,200-hp. R-1820-60 engine, reshaped cowling, and reflector-type gun/bombsight; and SBD-6, 1,350-hp. R-1820-66 engine.

All SBD-1s were assigned to the Marine Corps (VMB-2 in 1940 and VMB-1 in 1941) and in 1941, SBD-2s first equipped VB-6 and VS-6 aboard *Enterprise* and VB-2 aboard *Lexington*. SBD-3s began arriving in mid–1941 and by December, were replacing SBCs and

SB2Us in air groups aboard *Lexington, Saratoga, Yorktown,* and *Enterprise.*

Curtiss SB2C Helldiver—1940

TECHNICAL SPECIFICATIONS (XSB2C-1)

Type: Two-place dive-bomber

Manufacturer: Curtiss-Wright Corp., Airplane Division, Columbus, Ohio

Total produced: 7,203 (USN, USMC)

Powerplant: One 1,700-hp Wright R-2600-8 14-cylinder radial driving a three-bladed Curtiss Electric fully reversible, constant-speed propeller.

Armament: Two fixed forward-firing .50 cal. machine guns in the nose, two flexible .30-cal. machine guns in rear cockpit, and up to 1,000 lbs. of bombs carried in an internal bay.

Performance: Max. speed 322 mph at 14,600 ft.; cruise, 155 mph; ceiling 29,975 ft.; combat range 996 mi. (1,000-lb. payload).

Weights: 7,122 lbs. empty, 10,859 lbs. loaded.

Dimensions: Span 49 ft. 9 in., length 35 ft. 4 in., wing area 422 sq. ft.

The Curtiss SB2C, after a protracted development period, became the Navy's chief scout-bomber from late 1943 until the

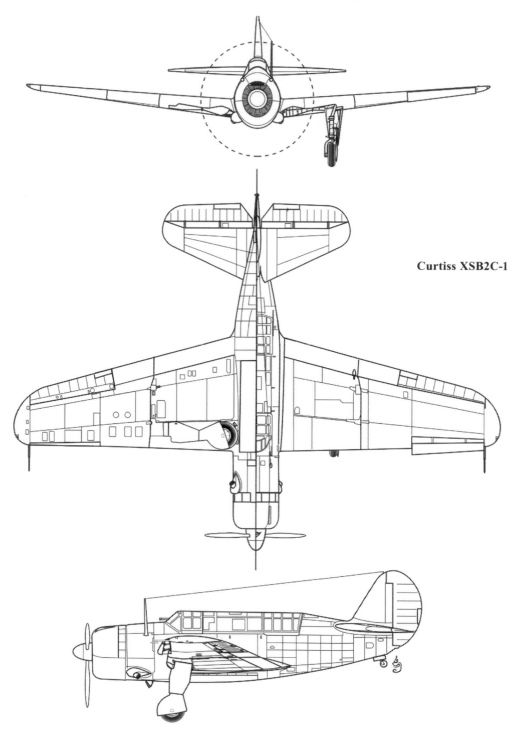

Curtiss XSB2C-1

The XSB2C-1 prototype made its first flight in December 1940. Already ordered into production, 800 design changes were made before the first production model flew in July 1942.

end of World War II, replacing Douglas SBDs in carrier-based combat operations. In May 1939, under requirements comparable to Brewster's XSB2A-1, BuAer ordered an R-2600-powered scout-bomber prototype from Curtiss under the designation XSB2C-1. As part of the general naval expansion triggered by the European war and increasing friction with Japan, the SB2C-1 was ordered into large-scale production in November 1940 even before a prototype had flown. In order to increase plant capacity, Curtiss established a new factory for SB2C production at Columbus, Ohio.

The program received a severe setback when the XSB2C-1 was destroyed in a crash only days after its first flight on December 18, 1940. Due to extensive revisions to the basic design, which included enlarging the vertical tail surfaces, lengthening the fuselage, and adding armor protection and self-sealing fuel tanks, the first production model did not fly until June 1942. And with more than 800 design changes required, the Columbus plant fell seriously behind on its production schedule, so that deliveries of the first SB2C-1s to operational units was delayed until December 1942 and the type not did enter combat until late 1943. To keep up with wartime demand, SB2Cs were ultimately license-produced by Canadian Car & Foundry (as the SBF) and Fairchild of Canada (as the SBW). The type remained in frontline Navy service until 1949.

Brewster SB2A Buccaneer—1941

TECHNICAL SPECIFICATIONS (XSB2A-1)

Type: Two-place dive-bomber
Manufacturer: Brewster Aeronautical Corp., Johnsville Division, Johnsville, Pennsylvania.
Total produced: 301 (USN, USMC)
Powerplant: One 1,700-hp Wright R-2600-8 14-cylinder radial driving

a three-bladed Curtiss Electric fully reversible, constant-speed propeller.
Armament: Two fixed forward-firing .50-cal. machine guns in fuselage, two fixed forward-firing .30-cal. machine guns in wings, two flexible .30-cal. machine guns in rear cockpit, and one 1,000-lb. bomb in internal bay.
Performance: Max. speed 311 mph at 15,000 ft.; cruise 157 mph; ceiling 27,000 ft.; range 1,570 mi. max., 980 mi. loaded.
Weights: 6,935 lbs. empty, 10,982 lbs. loaded.
Dimensions: Span 47 ft., length 38 ft., wing area 379 sq. ft.

Despite having three new types of monoplane scout-bombers in production, BuAer had determined by early 1939 that larger, more powerful designs would be needed to equip the Navy's emerging carrier force. In April 1939, Brewster was selected to build a prototype of its proposed Model 340 under the designation XSB2A-1. Taking much from its SBA predecessor, the XSB2A-1 evolved as a mid-wing design having inward-retracting landing gear, an internal weapons bay, and provision for an enclosed dorsal turret. In December 1940, to speed preparations, BuAer authorized Brewster to proceed with production of 140 SB2A-1s before the prototype had flown. The company also obtained orders from Great Britain and the Netherlands for 912 export models as the *Bermuda* and Model 340D, respectively. Mass production of the new type was to take place at Brewster's new plant in Johnsville, Pennsylvania.

The XSB2A-1 flew for the first time on June 17, 1941, appearing with a dummy dorsal turret aft of the cockpit. New combat requirements and testing necessitated lengthening the fuselage one foot two inches, replacing the turret with a flexible gun mount, revising the canopy, increasing fin area, and installing armor and self-sealing tanks, which upped empty weight nearly 3,000 lbs. and seriously degraded expected performance in terms of speed, range, and payload. Meanwhile,

An XSB2A-1 as seen in its original configuration with dummy turret in mid–1941. A combination of design changes and corporate mismanagement delayed deliveries until 1943. The plane was never used in combat.

mismanagement problems led to a Navy takeover (by Presidential order) of all Brewster plants in April 1942. Although some 80 SB2A-2s, 60 SB2A-3s and 162 SB2A-4s were delivered to the Navy and Marines during 1943 and 1944, none was ever used in combat.

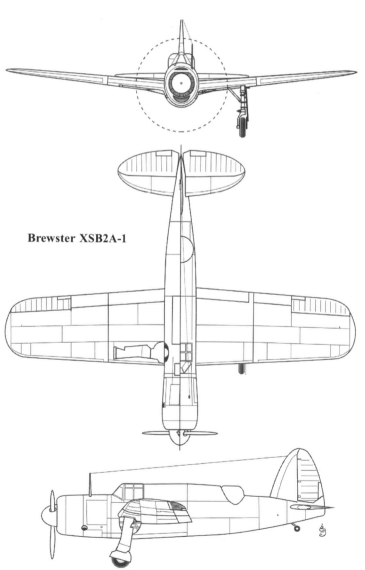

Brewster XSB2A-1

Grumman TBF (TBM) Avenger—1941

TECHNICAL SPECIFICATIONS (XTBF-1)

Type: Three-place torpedo-bomber
Manufacturer: Grumman Aircraft Engineering Corp., Bethpage, New York.
Total produced: 8,810 (USN, USMC)
Powerplant: One 1,700-hp Wright R-2600-8 14-cylinder radial driving a three-bladed Hamilton Standard fully reversible, constant-speed propeller.
Armament: One fixed forward-firing .30-cal. machine gun in nose, one flexible .50-cal. machine gun in dorsal power turret, one flexible .30-cal. machine gun in ventral position, one torpedo or up to 2,000 lbs. of bombs carried in an internal bay.
Performance: Max. speed 271 mph at 12,000 ft.; cruise 145 mph; ceiling 22,400 ft.; range 1,450 mi. max., 1,215 mi. loaded.
Weights: 10,080 lbs. empty, 15,905 lbs. loaded.
Dimensions: Span 54 ft. 2 in., length 40 ft., wing area 490 sq. ft.

The TBF series (later produced by General Motors as the TBM) is universally regarded as having been the most successful Navy and Marine Corps torpedo-bomber design of the World War II era. Its origins can be traced to a BuAer requirement issued in early 1940 for a TBD replacement having more horsepower, improved speed, range, and payload, plus much better defensive protection. To eliminate the drag of external stores, particularly torpedoes, BuAer also specified that the new type be designed with an internal bomb bay. Proposals were received from Grumman and Vought, and in April 1940 prototypes for both were ordered as the XTBF-1 and XTBU-1, respectively. The Navy was in such a hurry to obtain new torpedo-bombers that 286 TBF-1s were ordered before the first prototype had flown.

The XTBF-1 made its first flight on August 1, 1941, and service trials were completed by December. In early January 1942, the war emergency generated an order for an additional 1,600 TBF-1s, and added to that, a contract was given to the Eastern Aircraft Division of General Motors to build many

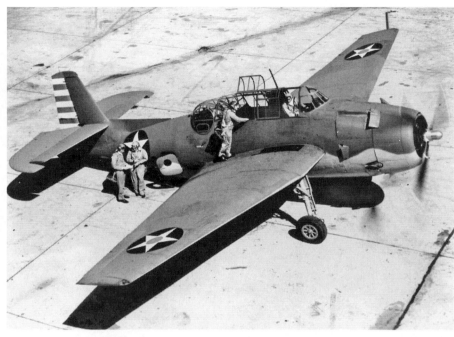

more under license as the TBM-1 (and later as the improved TBM-3). Production TBF-1s began replacing Douglas TBDs in frontline torpedo squadrons during the spring of 1942, but not in time to participate in the battles of Coral Sea and Midway. Later TBM variants remained in service until 1954.

Vought TBU (TBY) Sea Wolf—1941

TECHNICAL SPECIFICATIONS (XTBU-1)

Type: Three-place torpedo-bomber
Manufacturer: Chance Vought Division of United Aircraft Corp., Stratford, Connecticut.
Total produced: 182 (USN)
Powerplant: One 2,000-hp Pratt & Whitney R-2800-20 18-cylinder radial driving a three-bladed Hamilton Standard fully reversible, constant-speed propeller.
Armament: One fixed forward-firing .50-cal. machine gun, one .50-cal machine gun in power-operated dorsal turret, one flexible .30-cal. machine gun in ventral tunnel, and up to 2,000 lbs. of bombs or one torpedo carried in an internal bay.
Performance: Max. speed 311 mph at 14,700 ft.; cruise 165 mph; ceiling 27,900 ft.; range 1,400 mi. loaded.
Weights: 10,504 lbs. empty, 16,247 lbs. loaded.
Dimensions: Span 57 ft. 2 in., length 39 ft., wing area 439 sq. ft.

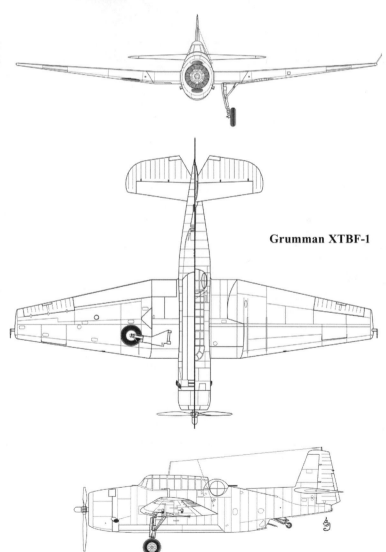

Grumman XTBF-1

But for the aircraft production priorities dictated by America's sudden entry into World War II, the TBU might have shared billing with Grumman's famous TBF as one of the Navy's top combat aircraft of the wartime period. By 1940 the Navy was planning a massive expansion of its carrier force and needed many aircraft to equip new air groups, and its standard torpedo-bomber, the Douglas TBD, was rapidly approaching obsolescence. Early the same year, BuAer had issued requirements for a new torpedo-bomber having better speed, payload, and defensive armament and in April, authorized prototypes to be built by both Grumman and Vought as the XTBF-1 and XTBU-1, respectively.

As the design evolved, the XTBU-1 shared the mid-wing over bomb bay layout of the XTBF-1 while possessing a smaller fuselage cross-section and 10 percent less wing area. After the XTBU-1 prototype flew on December 22, 1941 (six months after the XTBF-1), testing revealed general performance equal to or better than the TBF; however, due to the priority placed upon F4U production, Vought lacked plant capacity to mass-produce another aircraft. Therefore, in September 1943, license-production

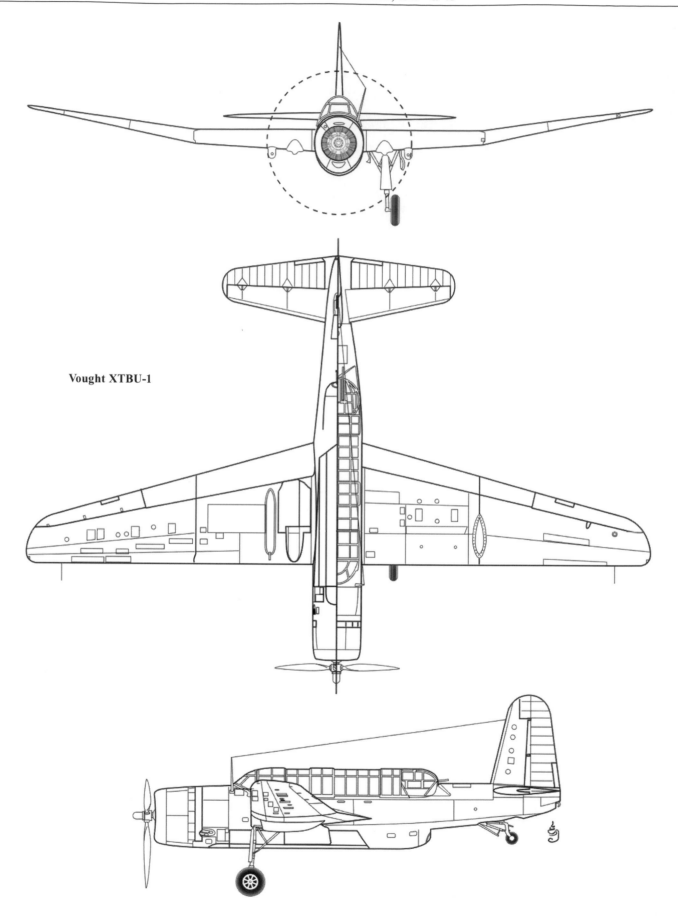

Vought XTBU-1

An XTBU-1 seen at the Vought plant in December 1941, delivered to NAS Anacostia in March 1942. Production was eventually shifted to Consolidated as the TBY-2.

rights were transferred to Consolidated-Vultee, including a contract to manufacture 1,100 aircraft as the TBY-2, though only 180 had been delivered by the time the war ended and the balance of the order was cancelled. The last examples were withdrawn in 1947.

Douglas BD (XF-3)—1941

TECHNICAL SPECIFICATIONS (BD-1 [XF-3])

Type: Four-place landplane light bomber
Manufacturer: Douglas Aircraft Company, El Segundo Division, El Segundo, California.
Total produced: 9 (USN/USMC)
Powerplants: Two turbo-supercharged 1,700-hp Wright R-2600-7 *Double Cyclone* 14-cylinder radials driving three-bladed Hamilton Standard fully reversible, constant-speed propellers.
Armament: Four forward-firing .30-cal. machine guns, two flexible .30-cal machine guns in dorsal mount, one flexible .30-cal. machine gun in ventral tunnel (bomb racks removed to allow installation of T-3A cameras in bomb bay).
Performance: Max. speed 388 mph at 20,000 ft.; cruise 218 mph; ceiling 31,500 ft.; range 767 mi. loaded, 1,100 mi. max.
Weights: 15,051 lbs. empty, 20,329 lbs. loaded.
Dimensions: Span 61 ft. 4 in., length 47 ft. 7 in., wing area 464 sq. ft.

Whether or not the Douglas BD-1 was actually in the Navy's possession before the end of 1941 may be conjectural, however, it does appear on the year-end inventory as Bureau Number 4251, assigned to the Naval Proving Ground in Dahlgren, Virginia. This aircraft was one of three Army Model, turbo-supercharger-equipped A-20 prototypes modified during 1940 for high-speed photo-reconnaissance under the AAC

The XF-3 still in Air Corps markings. The plane was acquired by Navy in late 1941 as the BD-1 to be evaluated for shore-based Marine combat operations. Eight A-20Bs were later transferred to the Marines as the BD-2 and employed as target tugs.

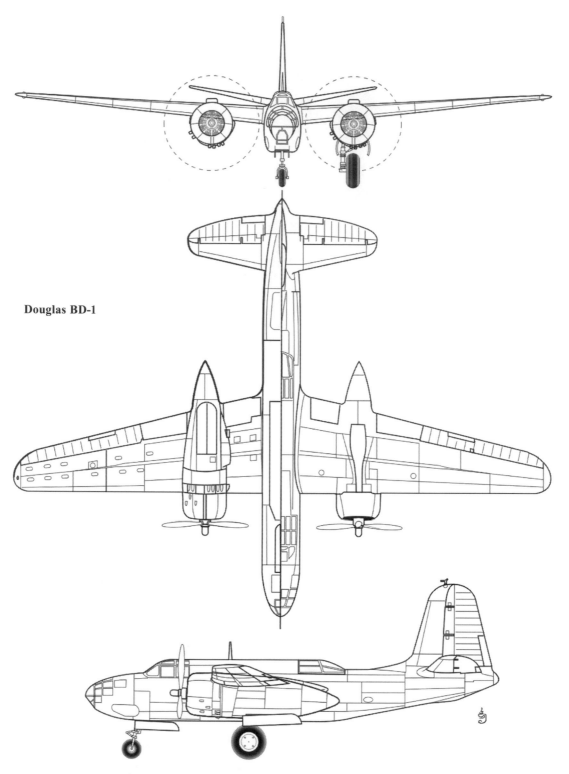

Douglas BD-1

designation XF-3. One historical source indicates that the plane had originally been procured with the aim of evaluating its potential as a Marine Corps land-based bomber. In late 1942 and early 1943, the Navy also acquired eight ex–AAF A-20Bs with non–turbo-charged R-2600-3 engines as the BD-2, which, as they were delivered, transferred into Marine service and subsequently employed as high-speed target tugs in the Base Aviation Detachment at MCAS Cherry Point, North Carolina. Al-

though multiple variants of the A-20 saw wide combat use during World War II with the AAF, RAF, British Commonwealth Nations, and Soviet Air Force, the type was never used in such capacity by the Navy or the Marines. From 1943 onwards, however, the Navy did procure some 706 North American B-25s in five different variants, with most being assigned to Marine bombing squadrons in the southwest and central Pacific combat theaters of the war.

FIGHTER AIRCRAFT

Synopsis of Fighter Aircraft Procurement

Although single-seat fighters had seen some use with land-based Marine Corps forces, their air superiority role—protecting the fleet from air attack—did not become relevant until they had been adapted to deploy from ships, either float-equipped variants carried by capital ships or wheeled types launched from aircraft carriers. From 1927 onwards, once *Langley*'s participation in early fleet problems had established the tactical efficacy of carrier-based fighters over floatplane fighters, virtually all of BuAer's fighter procurement efforts became focused on acquiring wheeled types equipped with arresting gear. Within the same timeframe, BuAer refined its carrier fighter specifications to require air-cooled radial engines and include the ability to carry bombs in a light attack role.

As Naval Aviation moved into the decade of the 1930s, BuAer was faced with the dilemma that its biplane carrier fighters would soon be obsolete in light of recent aeronautical advances. At the same time, the higher takeoff and landing speeds of new monoplanes like the Army's Boeing P-26 were seen as posing serious problems for carrier operations. A loaded aircraft, even a small fighter, required relatively light wing loading in order to safely fly off the deck in moderate winds, and more to the point, aviation officials believed that the higher approach and stall speeds of monoplanes would produce dangerous wave-off and go-around characteristics. The Navy did go so far as to evaluate four different monoplane fighter prototypes between 1930 and 1935—Boeing F5B, Boeing F7B, Curtiss F13C, and Northrop FT—but none were rated as satisfactory for operational use.

From 1932 to 1936, instead of monoplanes, BuAer ordered new biplanes with better streamlining and retractable landing gear such as the Grumman FF/SF, Curtiss BF2C, Grumman F2F and F3F. Almost out of desperation, two Army monoplane fighter types—the Curtiss H75B (Y1P-36) and Seversky NF-1 (P-35)—were acquired for testing in 1936 and 1937, however, both were rejected. BuAer did not move forward with definite plans to acquire any type of monoplane fighter for operational duty aboard carriers until June 1938 when it awarded Brewster a production contract for 54 F2A-1s. This move was followed quickly in February 1939 by an order for another production batch of monoplane fighters, this time to Grumman for 78 F4F-3s. But the reequipping process proved to be very slow, Brewster and Grumman both being hindered by commitments to divide production of new aircraft between the Navy and foreign air arms (e.g., primarily Great Britain, France, and the Netherlands).

But even before testing of the F2A and F4F proceeded very far, BuAer officials were already at work formulating more ambitious plans to acquire yet a second generation of monoplane fighters for the anticipated expansion of the carrier fleet. During 1938 contacts were issued to Grumman for the

XF5F, to Vought for the XF4U, and to Bell for the XFL, and all three prototypes were flying by the spring of 1940. Meanwhile, naval planners had scrutinized intelligence reports of air fighting in Europe and the Far East which strongly suggested that these new fighters would be highly vulnerable in combat. To survive against the most modern adversaries (e.g., Messerschmitt bf 109E, Mitsubishi A6M1), fighters needed better overall performance, heavier gun armament, self-sealing fuel tanks, and armor protection in vital places. Ironically, the only one of the three selected for production, Vought's F4U, was forced to undergo design changes of such extent that its introduction to carrier-based combat operations was delayed, ultimately, until mid–1944, by which time Grumman's F6F, ordered in June 1941 and flown in June 1942, had already established itself as the fleet's standard shipboard fighter.

Thomas-Morse MB-3 (1919)

TECHNICAL SPECIFICATIONS

Type: Single-place landplane fighter
Manufacturer: Thomas-Morse Aircraft Corp., Ithaca, New York.
Total produced: 11 (USMC)
Powerplant: One 300-hp Wright-Hispano 8-cylinder water-cooled in-line engine driving a two-bladed fixed-pitch wooden propeller.
Armament: Two fixed forward-firing .30-cal. machine guns.
Performance: Max. speed 152 mph at s.l.; ceiling 24,900 ft.; range 288 mi.

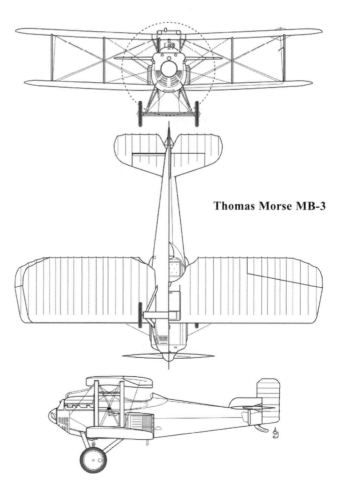

Thomas Morse MB-3

Weights: 1,506 lbs. empty, 2,094 lbs. gross.

Dimensions: Span 26 ft., length 20 ft., wing area 250 sq. ft.

Developed for the Army and flown for the first time in 1919, the Thomas-Morse MB-3 was a two-bay biplane of fabric-covered wooden construction whose general structural design had been derived from the French Spad VII and XIII. Performance of the Army's MB-3 was shown to be superior to that of various foreign-built fighter types evaluated by the Navy shortly after World War I (e.g., Hanriot HD-1, Nieuport 28, R.A.F S.E.5a, and Sopwith Camel). Eleven ex–Army MB-3s transferred to the Navy Department in 1921 were assigned to the Marine Corps in January 1922, and thereafter formed the earliest Marine fighter unit at Quantico, Virginia, where they served until being replaced by Boeing FB-1s in late 1925 and early 1926.

Eleven MB-3As transferred to the Navy from the Army Air Service in 1921 and formed the earliest Marine fighter unit (Third Air Squadron) at Quantico, Virginia.

Naval Aircraft Factory TF—1920

TECHNICAL SPECIFICATIONS

Type: Three-place escort fighter.

Manufacturer: Naval Aircraft Factory, Philadelphia, Pennsylvania.

Total produced: 4 (USN)

Powerplant: Two 300-hp Wright-Hispano H-3 8-cylinder water-cooled inline engines driving four-bladed wooden fixed-pitch propellers.

Armament: Two flexible Lewis .30-cal. machine guns in the bow and one flexible Lewis .30-cal. machine gun in the rear cockpit.

Performance: Max. speed 95 mph; ceiling 13,000 ft; range 650 mi.

Weights: 5,575 lbs. empty, 8,846 lbs. loaded.

Dimensions: Span (upper) 60 ft., length 44 ft., wing area 930 sq. ft.

The origins of the TF (Tandem Fighter) can be traced to a 1918 requirement issued by the British Technical Committee for a long-range sea-borne fighter to escort patrol aircraft (H-16s, F-5s, etc.) on maritime sorties.

After the armistice, Navy officials retained sufficient interest in the idea to authorize NAF to proceed with design proposals. After reviewing various options, the Navy approved a twin-tandem engine design that incorporated a hull and tailplane boom arrangement nearly identical to the larger NC series and authorized construction of four prototypes. Originally, the TF was to have been powered by Curtiss-built 400-hp Kirkham engines, however, me-

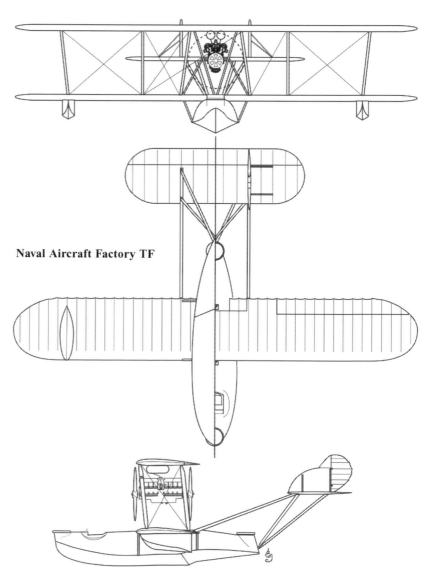

Naval Aircraft Factory TF

chanical problems with the powerplants led to a decision to substitute less powerful Wright-Hispanos. Construction of the first prototype commenced in August 1919 and the first flight took place on October 1, 1920. Testing revealed poor handling characteristics plus a marked tendency of the engines to overheat at high RPM settings. Although three more prototypes were completed and tested during 1921 and 1922, results were still rated as unsatisfactory, and the program was formally cancelled in January 1923. The fourth prototype was reportedly completed with 400-hp Packard 1-A V-12 engines, but no performance data on it was reported.

One of four TFs seen at the Naval Aircraft Factory in Philadelphia. The concept behind the design originally envisaged escorting larger flying boats like the H-16 and F-5L on maritime patrol.

Naval Aircraft Factory/ Curtiss TS (F4C)—1922

TECHNICAL SPECIFICATIONS

Type: One-place landplane and seaplane fighter.
Manufacturer: Naval Aircraft Factory, Philadelphia, Pennsylvania; and Curtiss Aeroplane and Motor Co., Buffalo, New York.
Total produced: 45 (USN)
Powerplant: One 200-hp Lawrence J-1 (later Wright J-4) 9-cylinder air-cooled radial engine driving a two-bladed fixed-pitch metal propeller.
Armament: One fixed forward-firing .30-cal. machine gun.
Performance: Max. speed 123 mph at s.l.; ceiling 16,250 ft; range 482 mi.
Weights: 1,240 lbs. empty, 2,133 lbs. loaded.
Dimensions: Span 25 ft., length 22 ft. 1 in., wing area 228 sq. ft.

The TS is noteworthy in having been the first Navy fighter actually designed to a naval specification. In 1921, while employed by the newly established Naval Bureau of Aeronautics, engineer Rex Beisel (who later rose to fame designing aircraft for Curtiss and later still, Vought) laid down a design for a compact fighter to be powered by the new Lawrence air-cooled radial engine and convertible to wheels or floats as with most naval aircraft of the period. The design was characterized by a lower wing slung below the fuselage on cabane struts and the use of W-type interplane struts in place of rigging wires. Another interesting feature was the location of the fuel tank in a deep lower wing center-section. BuAer assigned construction to both NAF and Curtiss, and the first of 24 Curtiss-built TS-1s was flown on May 9, 1922. (Note, TS was apparently used as a one-time designation for "convertible fighter.") Of the five aircraft completed by NAF the same year, four were used as engine testbeds, two TS-2s with 240-hp Aeromarine inlines and two TS-3s with 180-hp Wright-Hispano inlines, and one TS-3 was further modified as the TR-3 Navy racer of 1923.

In late 1922, after being outfitted with arresting gear, the first Curtiss TS-1 commenced operational trials aboard the car-

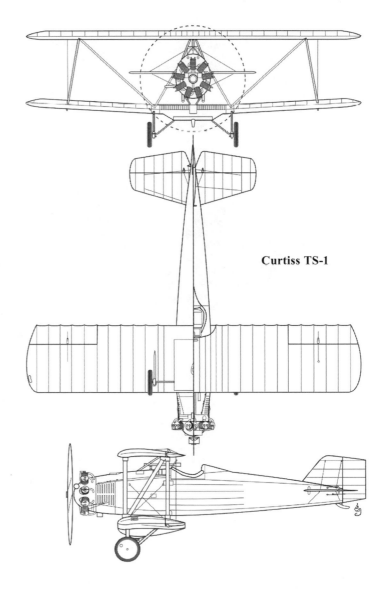

Curtiss TS-1

Top: **The first fighter type actually designed to a naval specification. Float equipped TS-1s served aboard battleships while wheeled variants formed VF-1, the Navy first carrier-based fighter contingent.** *Bottom:* **The F4C-1 was an all-metal derivative of the TS-1 designed by Charles W. Hall to provide comparative data on the performance, strength, and cost of metal airframe structures.**

rier *Langley*, and production TS-1s afterward formed VF-1, the Navy's first carrier-based fighter squadron. Float-equipped TS-1s also operated from various battleships as detachments of VO-1. In early 1924, Curtiss received a contract to build an improved TS variant that featured an all-metal, fabric-covered airframe designed by Charles W. Hall (who later founded Hall Aluminum Aircraft Co.) and a more conventional, bottom-mounted lower wing configuration. Two of the new types, designated F4C-1 (note, preceding number sequence assigned to

the RC, R2C, and R3C racers), were delivered to the Navy for testing in late 1924, but no production was ordered. The Navy began phasing-out its TS-1s during 1925 as newer fighters came into service (e.g., Boeing FB and Curtiss F6C), and the last examples were withdrawn from frontline units during 1926 but served in four different reserve units until 1928.

Boeing FB—1925

TECHNICAL SPECIFICATIONS (FB-5)

Type: One-place landplane and carrier fighter.
Manufacturer: Boeing Airplane Co., Seattle, Washington.
Total produced: 40 (USN, USMC)
Powerplant: One 525-hp Packard 2A-1500 12-cylinder water-cooled inline engine driving a two-bladed fixed-pitch metal propeller.
Armament: One .50-cal. and one .30-cal. fixed forward-firing machine guns.
Performance: Max. speed 169 mph at s.l.; ceiling 20,200 ft; range 323 mi.

Weights: 2,416 lbs. empty, 3,196 lbs. loaded.
Dimensions: Span 32 ft., length 23 ft. 8 in., wing area 241 sq. ft.

Appearing as a navalized version of the PW-9 first tested by the Army in 1923, BuAer ordered 16 aircraft from Boeing in late 1924 to be delivered under the designation FB-1, although the contract was later limited to the 10 examples accepted in December 1925. Virtual duplicates of PW-9s powered by 435-hp Curtiss D-12 inline engines, all FB-1s were all allocated to the Marine Corps following delivery, initially serving with VF-1M, VF-2M, and VF-3M. In 1927, nine of the fighters were as-

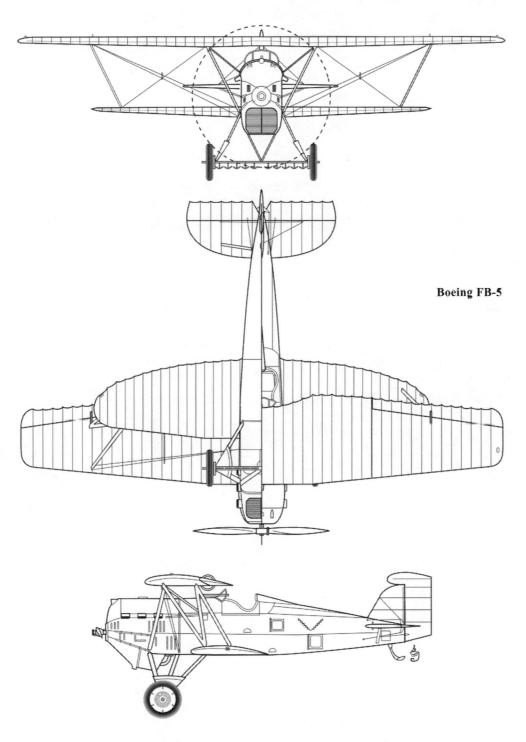

Boeing FB-5

Top: **Essentially identical to the Army PW-9, all FB-1s were allocated to the Marines. This photograph depicts an FB-1 serving with Quantico-based VF-2M in 1926. The circle around the "F" distinguished a Marine unit.** *Bottom:* **One of 13 FB-5s assigned to VF-6B aboard *Langley* in 1927. Interestingly, Boeing delivered the new aircraft to *Langley* via barge, and their first flights were made from the carrier's deck.**

signed to the newly formed VF-10M, where they served with the Marine Expeditionary Force in China, and the tenth went to VO-8M in San Diego. Boeing modified two FBs with strengthened airframes, cross-axle landing gear, and carrier arresting equipment, which were delivered for testing as FB-2s, followed by three FB-3s powered by 525-hp Packard engine and having fittings for floats. One FB airframe served as an engine testbed for air-cooled radial engines, initially as the FB-4

with a 450-hp Wright, then later, as the FB-6, with a 400-hp Pratt & Whitney R-1340.

The next true production version was the FB-5, flown for the first time on October 7, 1926. In addition to the improvements of the Packard-powered FB-3, the FB-5 possessed a balanced rudder and increased wing stagger with the top wing having been moved forward and the lower wing aft. Following acceptance trials, BuAer ordered 27 more of the type, and the method of delivery, made about a year later on January 21, 1927, was very unusual: Boeing, whose Seattle plant abuts Puget Sound, loaded all 27 planes onto barges and moved them out to the carrier *Langley* waiting nearby, where they were hoisted aboard and made their first flights from the carrier's deck. FB-5s initially joined VF-1B and VF-6B of *Langley*'s Air Group, but some later served with VF-3B aboard the new carrier *Lexington*. After leaving active Navy service during 1928, at least six FB-5s continued with Marine Squadron VF-6M until sometime in 1929.

Curtiss F6C—1925

TECHNICAL SPECIFICATIONS (F6C-3 [F6C-4])

Type: One-place landplane and carrier fighter.
Manufacturer: Curtiss Aeroplane and Motor Co., Buffalo, New York.
Total produced: 79 (USN, USMC)
Powerplant: One 400-hp Curtiss D-12 12-cylinder water-cooled in-line engine [410-hp Pratt & Whitney R-1340 *Wasp* 9-cyliner air-cooled radial engine] driving a two-bladed fixed-pitch metal propeller.
Armament: Two fixed forward-firing .30-cal. machine guns.
Performance: Max. speed 154 mph [155 mph] at s.l.; ceiling 20,300 [22,900] ft.; range 351 [362] mi.
Weights: 2,161 lbs. [1,980 lbs.] empty, 3,349 lbs. [3,171 lbs.] loaded.
Dimensions: Span 31 ft. 6 in., length 22 ft. 10 in. [22 ft. 6 in.], wing area 252 sq. ft.

Competing head-to-head with Boeing, Curtiss gained status during the 1920s as a leading supplier of fighter aircraft to both the Army and the Navy.

In January 1925, only a month after the company had delivered the PW-8B prototype to the Army (subsequently ordered into production as the P-1), BuAer awarded it a contract to manufacture nine very similar aircraft under the designation F6C-1 (note, F5C not used). The F6C-1s, when they arrived in mid–1925, were convertible to floats but not equipped for carrier operations, however, the four F6C-2s that followed in late 1925, possessed straight-axle landing gear, stronger wing bracing, and carrier arresting equipment, and were thus assigned to VF-2 aboard *Langley*. Following successful carrier trials with the F6C-2s, BuAer awarded Curtiss a production contact for 35 nearly identical F6C-3s, with deliveries starting in January 1927. F6C-3s first entered service with VF-2B of *Langley*'s Air Group, then later equipped VF-5S in two detachments aboard the new carriers *Lexington* and *Saratoga*, and the type also went into service with Marine squadron VF-8M at Quantico in 1928.

In 1926, BuAer adopted a policy of specifying air-cooled radial engines for all new naval aircraft, thus one F6C-1 became the F6C-4 prototype after being re-worked for installation of Pratt & Whitney's new *Wasp* engine (note, experimental X prefix was not adopted until 1927). While the change in overall performance

over water-cooled engines was negligible, naval officials nonetheless considered the new radials to be far more reliable and easier to maintain. Following acceptance trials, Curtiss received an order for 31 *Wasp*-powered F6C-4s that were delivered from February through June 1927. F4C-4s initially equipped VF-2B embarked on *Langley*; however, due to newer fighter types then coming into service (e.g., Boeing F2B-1 in 1927 and F3B-1 in 1928), most were assigned to VN-4D8, the advanced fighter-training unit at NAS Pensacola; and another 15 equipped two Marine squadrons, VF-4M at Quantico and VF-10M at San Diego. Several F6Cs underwent conversions: an F6C-4 became the XF6C-5 when modified for test purposes to accept installation of a 525-hp Pratt & Whitney R-1690 *Hornet* engine; the XF6C-6 (see Appendix 2) was an F6C-3 converted into a parasol monoplane configuration for the 1929 National Air Races; and another F6C-4, re-designated XF6C-7, was briefly used as a testbed for a 250-hp Ranger V-770 air-cooled inline engine. All F6C variants had been replaced in active service units by the end of 1932.

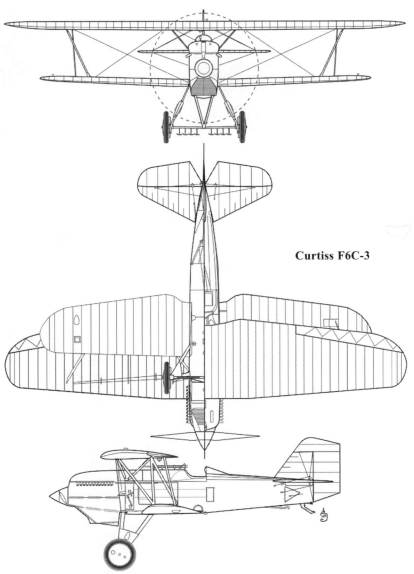

Curtiss F6C-3

Above: The nine F6C-1s, essentially identical to the Army P-1, were convertible to floats, as seen here, but lacked carrier arresting gear. One F6C-1, after being reworked, became the prototype for the radial-engined F6C-4. *Right:* First carrier-capable version F6C-2s were assigned to VF-2 and began operating from *Langley* in 1926. *Below:* One of eight F6C-4s serving with VF-10M at San Diego in the summer of 1931. The insignia on the tail is a winged devil. All F6C variants were phased out of active service during 1932.

Wright F3W—1926

TECHNICAL SPECIFICATIONS (XF3W-1)

Type: One-place landplane and floatplane fighter.

Manufacturer: Wright Aeronautical Corp., Dayton, Ohio.

Total produced: 1 (USN)

Powerplant: One 450-hp Pratt & Whitney R-1340B *Wasp* 9-cyliner air-cooled radial engine driving a two-bladed fixed-pitch metal propeller.

Armament: None installed.

Performance: Max. speed 162 mph at s.l.; ceiling 33,400 ft.; range (not reported).

Weights: 1,414 lbs. empty, 2,180 lbs. loaded.

Dimensions: Span 27 ft. 4 in., length 22 ft. 1 in., wing area 215 sq. ft.

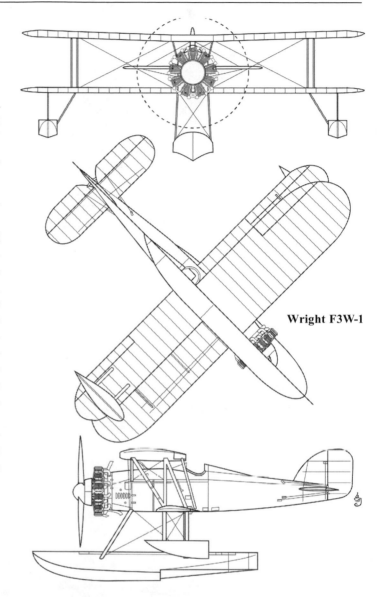

Wright F3W-1

After developing the NW-1, -2, and F2W-1 in 1922 and 1923 for racing (see Appendix 2), BuAer gave Wright a contract sometime in 1925 to develop a fighter around the company's experimental P-1 (R-1300) radial engine as the F3W-1. However, the engine project faltered, so that the aircraft was ultimately completed with a Pratt & Whitney *Wasp* engine and flown in May 1926. Smaller and lighter than the contemporaneous Boeing FB and Curtiss F6C, Wright's F3W-1 (redesignated XF3W-1 in 1927) emerged as a conventional single-bay biplane that utilized a fabric-covered, steel tube fuselage and built-up wooden wings. BuAer never considered the F3W-1 for production but used it instead for various test purposes. At one time it was rigged in a single, centerline float configuration to evaluate the concept of basing floatplane fighters aboard battleships, and later still, used to establish altitude records.

The F3W-1 as delivered to NAS Anacostia in 1926. Evaluated with centerline float as a battleship fighter, then used afterward for experimental purposes.

Boeing F2B—1926

TECHNICAL SPECIFICATIONS (F2B-1)

Type: One-place carrier fighter.

Manufacturer: Boeing Airplane Co., Seattle, Washington.

Total produced: 33 (USN)

Powerplant: One 450-hp Pratt & Whitney R-1340B *Wasp* 9-cylinder air-cooled radial engine driving a two-bladed fixed-pitch metal propeller.

Armament: One .50-cal. and one .30-cal. fixed forward-firing machine guns and 125 lbs. of bombs carried on belly and wing racks.

Performance: Max. speed 158 mph at s.l.; ceiling 21,500 ft.; range 317 mi.

Weights: 1,989 lbs. empty, 2,805 lbs. loaded.

Dimensions: Span 30 ft. 1 in., length 22 ft. 11 in., wing area 243 sq. ft.

Flown for the first time on November 3, 1926, Boeing's model 69 appeared as an unsolicited private venture developed in response to BuAer's new policy of specifying air-cooled radial engines. It represented a fairly straightforward adaptation of the FB-5 airframe to a Pratt & Whitney *Wasp* engine

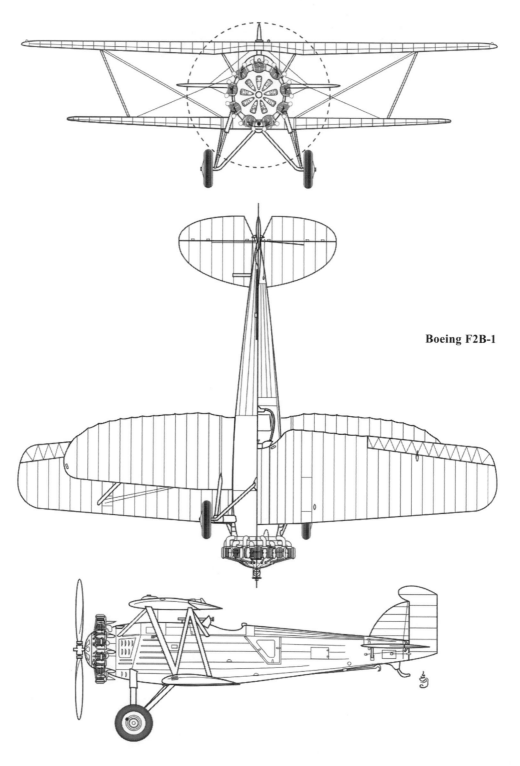

Boeing F2B-1

with the additional provision for carrying five 25-lb. bombs on racks.

Boeing's prototype was subsequently accepted by the Navy as the XF2B-1, the first aircraft tested at NAS Anacostia, Maryland to carry the experimental X prefix in its designation. Following trials, BuAer ordered 32 F2B-1s which, in definitive form, came without a spinner and incorporated the balanced rudder of the FB-5. Deliveries of production aircraft began in January 1928, equipping VF-1B (fighter) and VB-2B (bombing) of the *Saratoga* Air Group. In the fall of 1928, three F2B-1s flown by members of VB-2B formed the "Three Sea Hawks," the Navy's first aerial demonstration team. The service career of F2Bs was brief, being withdrawn from active units by 1931.

One of 15 F2B-1s assigned to *Saratoga's* VF-1B "Top Hats" in 1928. Having an airframe very similar to the FB-5, F2B-1s gained fighter-bomber capability with wing racks that carried five 25-lb. bombs.

Eberhart FG and F2G—1926

TECHNICAL SPECIFICATIONS (FG-1)

Type: One-place Navy carrier/floatplane fighter.
Manufacturer: Eberhart Steel Products Co., Buffalo, New York.
Total produced: 1 (USN)
Powerplant: One 425-hp Pratt & Whitney R-1340C *Wasp* 9-cylinder air-cooled radial engine driving a two-bladed fixed-pitch metal propeller.
Armament: (none installed).
Performance: Max. speed 154 mph at s.l.; ceiling 18,700 ft.; range (not reported).
Weights: 2,145 lbs. empty, 3,208 lbs. loaded.
Dimensions: Span 28 ft. 9 in., length 27 ft. 3 in., wing area 241 sq. ft.

This little-known company got its start in aviation license-manufacturing 50 examples of the R.A.F. S.E.5a for the Army in the early 1920s. The *Wasp*-powered prototype FG-1, a single-bay biplane having a welded, steel-tube fuselage and fabric-covered wings of duralumin structure, was delivered to the Navy in November 1926. It exhibited an unusual wing layout having 7 degrees of sweepback in the upper span and 6 degrees forward sweep in the lower. In 1927, Eberhart fitted the

prototype with a single, centerline float and increased the span of the upper wing to 32 feet, following which it was evaluated as a floatplane fighter under the designation F2G-1. Soon af-

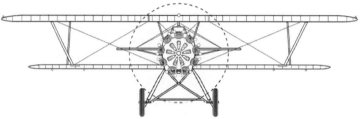

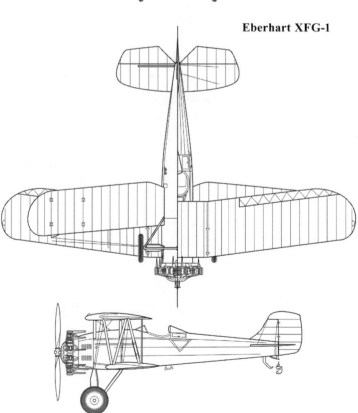

Eberhart XFG-1

The aircraft depicted was tested with wheels as the XFG-1 in late 1927, then with lengthened wings and a center float, as the XF2G-1 in early 1928. Development was abandoned after a crash of the sole prototype.

terward, the prototype was destroyed in testing, and further development was abandoned.

Vought FU—1927 see Vought UO under OBSERVATION AND SCOUT AIRCRAFT

Boeing F3B—1927

TECHNICAL SPECIFICATIONS (F3B-1)

Type: One-place carrier fighter.
Manufacturer: Boeing Airplane Co., Seattle, Washington.
Total produced: 74 (USN, USMC)
Powerplant: One 450-hp Pratt & Whitney R-1340-80 Wasp 9-cylinder air-cooled radial engine driving a two-bladed fixed-pitch metal propeller.
Armament: One .50-cal. and one .30-cal. fixed forward-firing machine guns and 125 lbs. of bombs carried on belly and wing racks.
Performance: Max. speed 157 mph at s.l.; ceiling 20,900 ft.; range 340 mi.
Weights: 2,179 lbs. empty, 2,945 lbs. loaded.
Dimensions: Span 33 ft., length 24 ft. 10 in., wing area 275 sq. ft.

Delivered to NAS Anacostia in March 1927 as another Boeing private venture, the model 74 initially differed little from the F2B-1 other than having the fittings required for a centerline float rig. After brief testing by the Navy as the XF3B-1, it was deemed unacceptable and returned to the factory for modifications. When redelivered in early 1928, the revised XF3B-1 featured an all-new constant-chord upper wing with sweepback, a lengthened fuselage, plus aluminum-skinned ailerons and tail surfaces. Satisfactory trials led to an order for 74 production F3B-1s, which were all delivered between August and September of 1928. The type initially entered service with VB-2B of *Saratoga* and went on to equip VF-3B and VB-1B on the *Lexington*. All F3Bs had been replaced in active carrier squadrons by the end of 1932, though a few survived as command planes (i.e., flown by senior officers not attached to squadrons) and utility hacks until 1937. One was also transferred to the Marines in 1934 for command and utility duties.

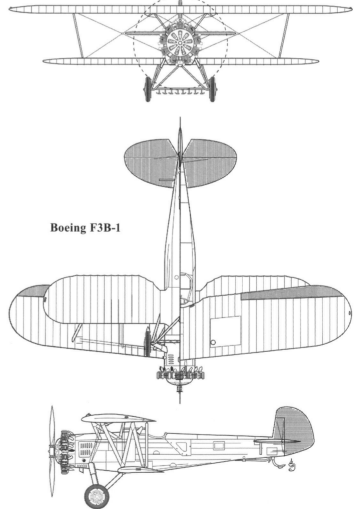

Boeing F3B-1

Top: **An F3B-1 of VF-2B operating from *Langley* in 1929. This aircraft was assigned to the staff of Air Battle Force at the time of the photograph. Note "Flying Chiefs" emblem below cockpit.** *Bottom:* **Seen in a command plane paint scheme during 1936, this F3B-1 assigned to VJ-5D11 served as the personal aircraft of NAS San Diego's commanding officer.**

Curtiss F7C—1927

TECHNICAL SPECIFICATIONS (F7C-1)

Type: One-place carrier and landbased fighter.
Manufacturer: Curtiss Aeroplane and Motor Co., Buffalo, New York.
Total produced: 18 (USN, USMC)
Powerplant: One 450-hp Pratt & Whitney R-1340B *Wasp* 9-cyliner air-cooled radial engine driving a two-bladed fixed-pitch metal propeller.

Armament: Two fixed forward-firing 30-cal. machine guns.
Performance: max. speed 151 mph at s.l.; ceiling 23,350 ft.; range 330 mi.
Weights: 2,038 lbs. empty, 2,782 lbs. loaded.
Dimensions: span 32 ft. 8 in., length 22 ft. 2 in., wing area 276 sq. ft.

Designed for carrier service by Rex Beisel, who was then working for Curtiss, the F7C differed from the F6C-4 mainly in having new constant-chord wings with sweepback in the

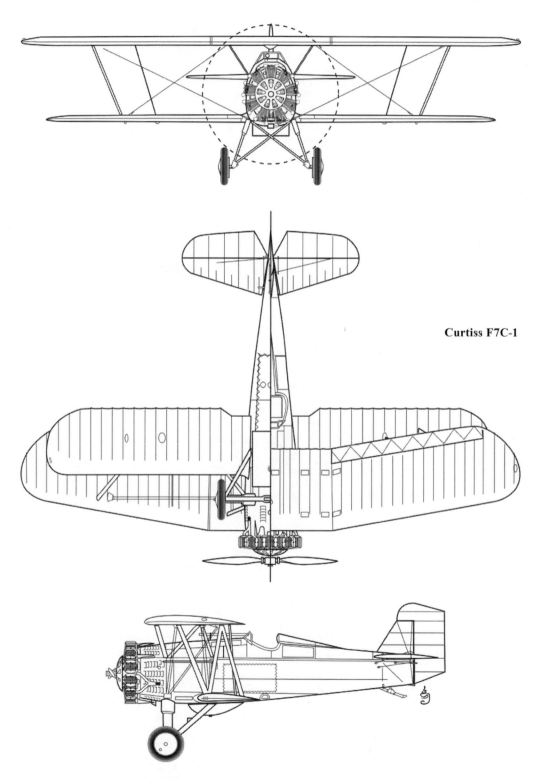

Curtiss F7C-1

upper span. Navy evaluations of the XF7C-1 commenced in February 1927, followed shortly by a contract for 18 production examples. As delivered between November 1928 and January 1929, production F7C-1s came without spinners and featured strengthened landing gear. All F7C-1s were afterward assigned to the Marine Corps, where they served with VF-5M (later VF-9M) at Quantico until 1933.

The first of 18 F7C-1 production models as seen after delivery in late 1928. Since they lacked arresting gear, most were assigned to Marine land-based units. The Navy used several for experimental purposes.

Curtiss F8C (OC/O2C)
Helldiver—1927

TECHNICAL SPECIFICATIONS (F8C-5)

Type: Two-place carrier and landplane fighter-bomber, ground attack.
Manufacturer: Curtiss Aeroplane and Motor Co., Buffalo, New York.
Total produced: 110 (USN, USMC)
Powerplant: One 450-hp Pratt & Whitney R-1340-4 *Wasp* 9-cylinder radial engine driving a two-bladed fixed-pitch metal propeller.
Armament: Two fixed forward-firing .30-caliber machine guns, one flexible .30-caliber machine gun in rear cockpit, and up to 474 lbs. of bombs carried externally.

A Marine OC-2 (F8C-3) serving with VJ-7M out of San Diego in 1933. The F8C/OC series, an adaptation of the Army A-3, arose from a Marine requirement for a multi-role fighter, bomber, and observation type.

Performance: Max. speed 146 mph at s.l.; ceiling 16,050 ft.; combat range 560 mi.
Weights: 2,520 lbs. empty, 4,020 lbs. loaded.
Dimensions: Span 32 ft., length 25 ft. 8 in., wing area 308 sq. ft.

Another Rex Biesel design, the F8C arose from a 1927 Marine Corps requirement for a multi-purpose airplane that could fulfill the roles of fighter, dive-bomber, and observation platform in one airframe. Curtiss responded by adapting its two-seat Army O-2/A-3 *Falcon* design, normally powered by a water-cooled V-12, to an air-cooled radial engine approved by BuAer. In early 1928, two aircraft designated XF8C-1s were delivered to the Marine Corps and four more production F8C-1s soon followed; and a year later, the Marines took delivery of one very similar XF8C-3 and 21 more F8C-3 production variants. In service use, the Marines re-designated F8C-1s as the OC-1 and F8C-3s as the OC-2. They replaced World War I–era DH-4B/O2Bs in many Marine units and saw combat service in Nicaragua with VO-7M.

In early 1929 BuAer authorized the improved XF8C-2 having new equal-span wings, a strengthened and redesigned fuselage, and a balanced rudder. After the flight of the first prototype in mid–1929, 25 aircraft were ordered as F8C-4s for

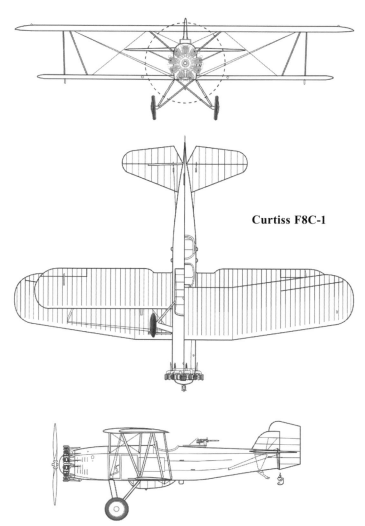

Curtiss F8C-1

the Navy and another 63 as F8C-5s for the Marine Corps. In 1931, two F8C-5s equipped with engine superchargers and wings slots were re-designated XF8C-6, and one F8C-4 airframe, fitted with an R-1820 engine and an enclosed canopy, was delivered to the Navy as the XF8C-7, however, neither version was ordered into production. F8C-4s served initially with VF-1B aboard *Saratoga* but were transferred from active status to the reserves beginning in 1931. Marine F8C-5s were re-designated O2C-1s and remained active with VO-6M and VO-7M until they were replaced during 1936–1937; a few remaining examples were retained for utility duties until 1938.

In Marine service, the F8C-5 became the O2C-1. This example, seen at MCAS Quantico in 1935, was assigned to VJ-6M as a hack after having been withdrawn from frontline service.

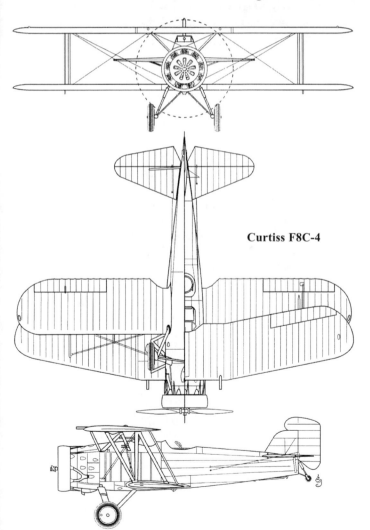

Curtiss F8C-4

Boeing F4B—1928

TECHNICAL SPECIFICATIONS (F4B-1 [F4B-4])

Type: One-place carrier and landplane fighter
Manufacturer: Boeing Airplane Co., Seattle, Washington.
Total produced: 190 (USN, USMC)
Powerplant: One 450-hp Pratt & Whitney R-1340-8 [550-hp R-1340-16] *Wasp* 9-cylinder radial engine driving a two-bladed fixed-pitch metal propeller.
Armament: Two fixed forward-firing .30-caliber machine guns and up to 232 lbs. of
bombs carried on external racks.
Performance: Max. speed 176 mph [188 mph] at 6,000 ft.; ceiling 27,700 [26,900] ft.; combat range 371 [370] mi.
Weights: 1,950 lbs. [2,354 lbs.] empty, 2,750 lbs. [3,611 lbs.] loaded.
Dimensions: Span 30 ft., length 20 ft. 1 in. [20 ft. 5 in.], wing area 227.5 sq. ft.

Boeing F4Bs, produced in four major variants, comprised most of the fleet's fighter force up through the mid–1930s. It arose as an unsolicited private venture when Boeing delivered two prototypes, company models 83 and 89, to NAS Anacostia in early August 1928, both of which were accepted for trials as the XF4B-1. The two prototypes differed in landing gear, the model 83 having a split-axle type and arresting gear, while the model 89 came with a cross-axle type and fittings to carry a 500-lb. bomb under its belly. Though a biplane of conventional design, the compact and highly maneuverable F4B represented the culmination of Boeing's experience as a Navy and Army fighter contractor throughout the 1920s. After satisfactory trials, BuAer purchased both prototypes and awarded Boeing a contract to produce 27 F4B-1s.

Production F4B-1s, as they began arriving during the spring of 1929, all featured cross-axle gear, bomb fittings, and

Left: **An F4B-2 of VF-6B serving aboard *Saratoga* in 1931. Note the distinctive "Felix the Cat" squadron emblem. F4B-2s differed from -1s in having ring cowls and split-axle landing gear.** *Right:* **The F4B-3 was the first version to feature an all-aluminum, semi-monocoque fuselage. Only 21 were delivered before being superceded in production by the F4B-4.**

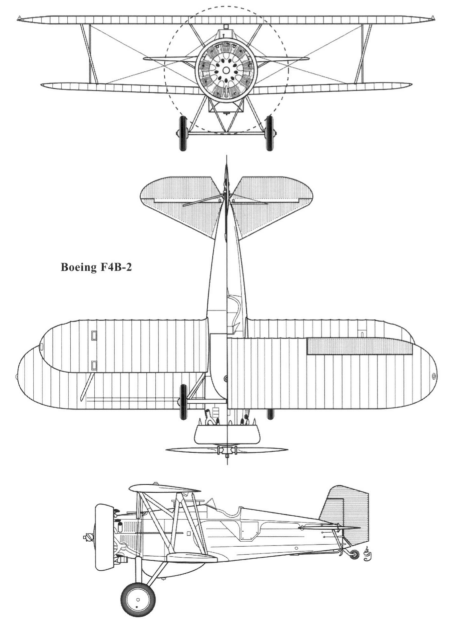

Boeing F4B-2

carrier arresting equipment. In this time period, Boeing also sold 90 very similar aircraft to the Army as the P-12B. F4B-1s were first assigned to VF-2B aboard *Langley,* replacing F2Bs, and VB-1B (later VF-5B) of *Saratoga,* replacing its F3Bs and FUs. In later service, most F4B-1s were retrofitted with ring cowls and F4B-4-type fins and rudders. In June 1930, following development of the analogous P-12C for the Army, Boeing received an order for 46 F4B-2s having ring cowls, Frise-type ailerons, spit-axle gear, and a tailwheel. Deliveries of -2s began in early 1931, initially equipping VF-5B of *Lexington* and VF-6B of *Saratoga.* After an unsuccessful venture with the monoplane XF5B-1 (see below), Boeing adapted the type's all-metal, semi-monocoque fuselage and reshaped tailplane to the biplane model 218, which it offered to the Navy in late 1930 as the F4B-3 and to the Army as the P-12E. In April 1931, following trials conducted at Anacostia, BuAer placed an order for 75 F4B-3s, however, 54 of these were ultimately delivered as F4B-4s, and a second contract in 1932 added 45 more F4B-4s, totaling 130 aircraft.

The 21 F4B-3s completed began entering service in December 1931 with *Saratoga*'s VF-1B where they replaced Curtiss F8C-4s, then during 1933, most were reassigned to Marine squadron VB-4M in San Diego. Except for their larger fins and rudders and uprated R-1340-16 engines, the first 54 F4B-4s, delivered from mid–1932, were otherwise identical to the -3 while the last 45, arriving toward the end of the year, came with enlarged headrests. By the middle of 1933, F4B-4s were equipping the fighter squadrons of the Air Groups aboard all three carriers, as well as two Marine fighter squadrons. The type remained in frontline service with the fleet until 1937, when they were replaced by Grumman F3Fs, and continued with Marine units until 1938. Upon release from active service, a number of F4Bs were retained for utility duties, and in 1940, 23 ex–Army P-12Es were taken into Navy service as F4B-4As and thereafter used as radio-controlled target drones. As of December 1941, some three F4B-3s and 18 F4B-4s were still carried on the naval inventory.

This aircraft was flown by the section leader of VF-2B from *Lexington* in 1934. F4Bs remained in frontline Navy and Marine service until the end of 1938.

Hall FH—1929

TECHNICAL SPECIFICATIONS (XFH-1)

Type: One-place carrier fighter
Manufacturer: Hall Aluminum Aircraft Co., Buffalo, New York.
Total produced: 1 (USN)
Powerplant: One 450-hp Pratt & Whitney R-1340-B *Wasp* 9-cylinder radial engine driving a two-bladed fixed-pitch metal propeller.
Armament: (not installed).
Performance: Max. speed 153 mph at s.l.; ceiling 25,300 ft.; range 275 mi.
Weights: 2,038 lbs. empty, 2,514bs. loaded.
Dimensions: Span 32 ft., length 22 ft. 6 in., wing area 255 sq. ft.

After having received a contract to build the PH-1, an NAF-designed flying boat (see under *Patrol Aircraft*), Charles Hall's

The XFH-1 as delivered to NAS Anacostia in June 1929 for trials. It was unique in having a watertight fuselage for flotation in the event of ditching, but it did not compare favorably with the contemporaneous F4B-1.

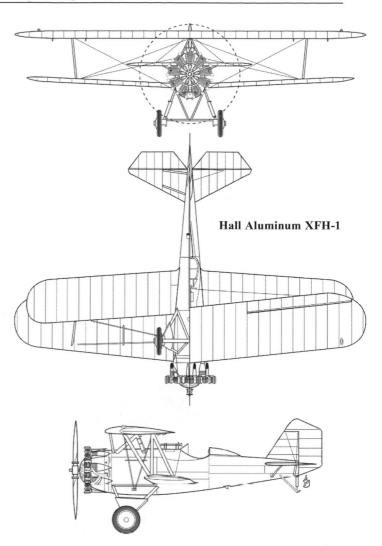

Hall Aluminum XFH-1

new company tried to interest the Navy in an original fighter design that utilized Hall's all-aluminum structural methods. Completed and delivered to Anacostia in June 1929, the XFH-1 featured a semi-monocoque fuselage advertised as being watertight, an unorthodox wing layout reminiscent of the XFG-1 (reported above) in which the upper span swept back and the lower forward, plus landing gear that could be jettisoned in the event of ditching. During testing, however, BuAer rated the XFG-1's performance as substandard, then in early 1930, after the prototype was destroyed in a crash, the program was discontinued.

Vought F2U—1929

TECHNICAL SPECIFICATIONS (XF2U-1)

Type: Two-place carrier fighter
Manufacturer: Chance Vought Corp., Long Island City, New York.
Total produced: 1 (USN)
Powerplant: One 450-hp Pratt & Whitney R-1340C *Wasp* 9-cylinder radial driving a two-bladed fixed-pitch metal propeller.
Armament: Two fixed forward-firing .30-caliber machine guns, one flexible .30-caliber machine gun in rear cockpit, and up to 474 lbs. of bombs carried externally.

Performance: Max. speed 146 mph at s.l.; ceiling 18,700 ft.; combat range 495 mi.
Weights: 2,539 lbs. empty, 4,208 lbs. loaded.
Dimensions: Span 36 ft., length 27 ft., wing area 318 sq. ft.

Ordered under a BuAer contract issued in 1928, the XF2U-1 represented an attempt by Vought to offer the Navy a design that would be competitive against the Curtiss F8C-4/-5 two-seat fighter/dive-bomber. Like Curtiss during this period, Vought was a major Navy contractor, having delivered over 400 aircraft (huge volume in those days) since 1918. Sharing many aerodynamic and structural characteristics with Vought's successful O2U series (see *Observation and Scout Aircraft*), the XF2U-1 prototype emerged with an NACA-type cowling and slightly larger overall dimensions than the rival F8C. The prototype was delivered to the Navy for trials in June 1929,

Intended to compete with the Curtiss F8C, the XF2U-1 emerged in 1929 with an innovative NACA cowling. Aerodynamic characteristics were similar to Vought's successful series of O2U float and observation planes.

however, BuAer afterward declined production on the basis that the type's performance offered no advantage over existing F8Cs.

Berliner-Joyce FJ—1930

TECHNICAL SPECIFICATIONS (XFJ-2)

Type: One-place carrier fighter
Manufacturer: Berliner-Joyce Co., Baltimore, Maryland.
Total produced: 1 (USN)
Powerplant: One 500-hp Pratt & Whitney R-1340-C *Wasp* 9-cylinder radial driving a two-bladed fixed-pitch metal propeller.
Armament: (none installed).
Performance: Max. speed 193 mph at 6,000 ft.; ceiling 24,700 ft.; range 520 mi.
Weights: 2,102 lbs. empty, 3,116 lbs. loaded.
Dimensions: Span 28 ft., length 20 ft. 10 in., wing area 179 sq. ft.

Appearing as the first of three aircraft built to BuAer's "small carrier fighter" requirement (see also, Curtiss F9C and General Aviation FA), Berliner-Joyce received a contract in May 1929 to construct a single prototype as the XFJ-1. The design called for by the specifications was unusual: a biplane having a metal-skinned, semi-monocoque fuselage and metal tail group with shoulder-mounted upper wings and a lower wing underslung on cabane-type struts. The prototype arrived at NAS Anacostia for testing in May 1930, but after incurring damage to the lower wing and landing gear, was returned to the factory for repairs and modifications. When redelivered in May 1932 as the

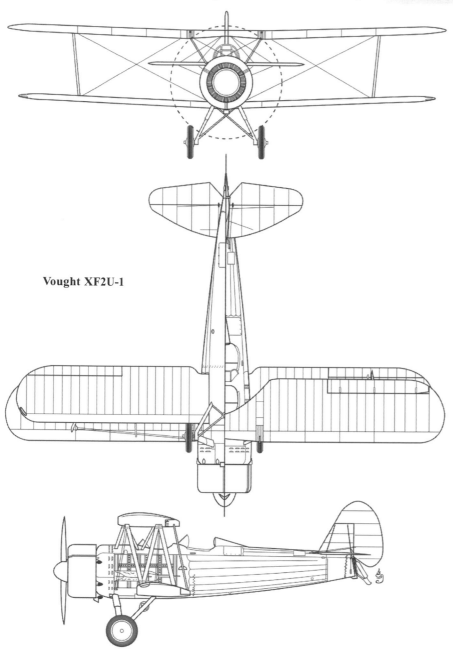

Vought XF2U-1

One of three prototypes built to a 1929 "small carrier fighter" requirement. Following an engine change plus addition of a ring cowl and wheel pants, the XFJ-1 returned to NAS Anacostia in 1932 as the XFJ-2.

qualities. BuAer purchased the prototype but by this time had decided to order the competing F9C as a dirigible fighter, with the result that further development of the XFJ-2 was discontinued.

Boeing F5B—1930

TECHNICAL SPECIFICATIONS (XF5B-1)

Type: One-place carrier fighter
Manufacturer: Boeing Airplane Co., Seattle, Washington.
Total produced: 1 (USN)
Powerplant: One 500-hp Pratt & Whitney R-1340D *Wasp* 9-cylinder radial engine driving a two-bladed fixed-pitch metal propeller.
Armament: (none installed).
Performance: Max. speed 183 mph at 6,000 ft.; ceiling 27,100 ft.; range (not reported).
Weights: 2,091 lbs. empty, 2,848 lbs. loaded.
Dimensions: Span 30 ft. 6 in., length 21 ft., wing area 157 sq. ft.

The F5B was the first monoplane fighter design to be evaluated by the Navy since the Dornier-Wright WP-1 of 1923 (see Appendix 1). In early 1930, as an unsolicited private venture,

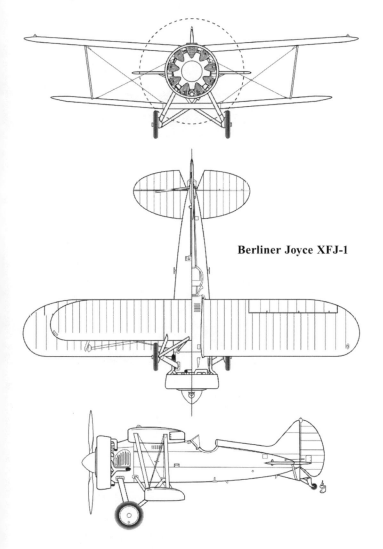

Berliner Joyce XFJ-1

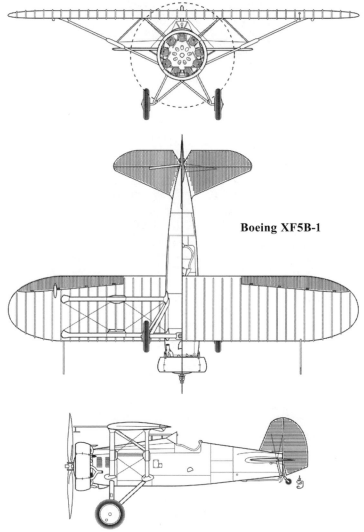

Boeing XF5B-1

XFJ-2, the aircraft had been revised to include enlarged vertical tail surfaces, a ring cowl, spinner, and large wheel pants. Subsequent flight-testing, though indicating a 15 mph increase in top speed, revealed poor stability and unacceptable handling

Boeing offered to deliver its model 205 for testing, and sometime after the prototype arrived at NAS Anacostia, BuAer purchased it under the designation XF5B-1. Though similar in some respects to Boeing's highly successful F4B series, the XF5B-1 introduced a new type of metal-skinned, semi-monocoque fuselage and a parasol-mounted wing of about fifty percent greater area than a standard F4B upper wing. Following trials, naval officials rated the type as unsatisfactory, presumably due to its higher landing speeds (i.e., 12 mph higher than the F4B-1). Instead, BuAer gave Boeing contract to produce the F4B-3, a biplane derivative that incorporated similar structural improvements. The Army also evaluated the type as the XP-15, but, again, no production was forthcoming.

This was the first type of monoplane fighter to be evaluated by the Navy in 1930. Though rated as unsatisfactory, its aluminum-clad fuselage structure was incorporated into the F4B-3 and -4.

Curtiss F9C Sparrowhawk—1931

TECHNICAL SPECIFICATIONS (F9C-2)

Type: One-place dirigible/carrier fighter
Manufacturer: Curtiss Aeroplane and Motor Co., Garden City, New York.
Total produced: 8 (USN)
Powerplant: One 438-hp Wright R-975-E3 9-cylinder radial driving a two-bladed fixed-pitch metal propeller.
Armament: Two fixed forward-firing 30-cal. machine guns.
Performance: Max. speed 177 mph at 4,000 ft.; ceiling 19,200 ft.; combat range 366 mi.
Weights: 2,089 lbs. empty, 2,770 lbs. loaded.
Dimensions: Span 25 ft. 5 in., length 20 ft. 7 in., wing area 173 sq. ft.

Though originally designed to fulfill BuAer's "small carrier fighter" requirement, the Curtiss F9C went on to achieve distinction as the only type of naval aircraft ever intended for combat operations from a rigid airship. Ordered in June 1930 and making its first flight on February 12, 1931, the XF9C-1 was the last Curtiss aircraft to be completed at its Garden City facility. As required in the specifications, the XF9C-1 emerged with a metal-skinned fuselage, metal tailplane, and upper wings mounted directly to the top of the fuselage. While undergoing

acceptance trials at NAS Anacostia during the spring of 1931, BuAer determined that the XF9C-1's small size would permit to fit through the bottom-mounted hangar doors of the two large rigid airships, ZRS-4 *Akron* and ZRS-5 *Macon*, then under construction by Goodyear. "Dirigible fighters," as they were termed, were seen as a means of defending the airship from outside fighter attack and also forming a scouting screen ahead of it.

An apparatus for launching and recovering aircraft aboard airships was successfully tested when the XF9C-1 made its first hook-on with the ZR-3 *Los Angeles* on October 27, 1931. The system consisted of a "trapeze," a half ring suspended from a derrick lowered by the airship, which, in turn, was engaged by a "skyhook" mounted on struts above the aircraft's upper wing. As a result of design changes recommended by BuAer, the XF9C-2, delivered in April 1932, featured a slightly more pow-

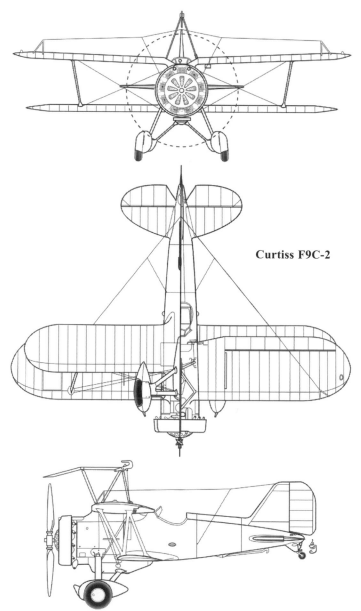

Curtiss F9C-2

erful engine, upper wings raised four inches, wheel pants, and larger, reshaped vertical tail surfaces, and following brief trials, Curtiss received a contract to manufacture six production examples. On June 29, 1932, soon after the first F9C-2 entered service, the first hook-on was made with the airship *Akron*. When the final example was delivered the following September, all six F9Cs were attached to *Akron*. Fortunately, none were aboard when the airship was lost at sea in April 1933, and they were reassigned to the *Macon* upon its commissioning in June 1933. Once airship operations were underway, the Sparrowhawks, to increase speed, often flew from the airship with their landing gear removed, depending solely on skyhooks for launch and recovery. But when the *Macon* was itself destroyed off the California coast in February 1935, four of the F9C-2s perished with it. The three remaining Sparrowhawks operated briefly as utility aircraft but had been withdrawn by 1936.

F9C-2s, equipped with "skyhooks" as seen here, formed the heavier-than-air fighter and scouting force aboard the large rigid airships Akron and Macon from 1933 to 1935.

Grumman FF/SF—1931

TECHNICAL SPECIFICATIONS (FF-1)

Type: Two-place carrier fighter
Manufacturer: Grumman Aircraft Engineering Corp., Bethpage, New York.
Total produced: 63 (USN)
Powerplant: One 700-hp Wright R-1820-78 9-cylinder radial driving a two-bladed Hamilton Standard variable-pitch propeller.
Armament: One fixed forward-firing .30-cal. machine gun, two flexible .30-cal. machine guns in rear cockpit, and up four 112-lb. bombs on wing racks.
Performance: Max. speed 207 mph at 4,000 ft.; ceiling 22,000 ft.; combat range 685 mi.
Weights: 3,098 lbs. empty, 4,888 lbs. loaded.
Dimensions: Span 34 ft. 6 in., length 24 ft. 6 in., wing area 310 sq. ft.

The FF/SF was not just the Navy's first retractable-gear combat aircraft but was the airplane that literally got the brand new Grumman company off the ground. Soon after Leroy Grumman started an aeronautical engineering business in 1929, he obtained a Navy contract to build a new type of seaplane float that incorporated retractable landing wheels for land op-

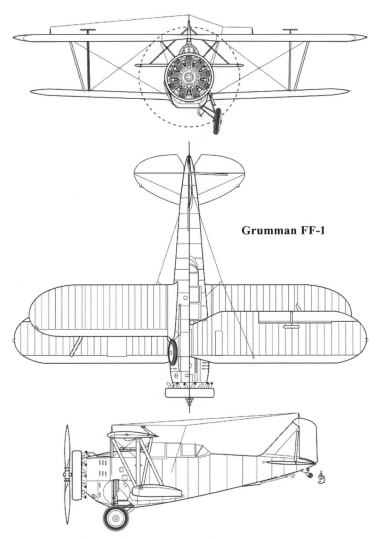

Grumman FF-1

erations. From this beginning, the company received a contract in April 1931 to build an airplane of its own design—a two-seat-fighter designated the XFF-1—that utilized the landing gear retraction system developed for pontoons. The landing gear was manually raised and lowered by operating a hand-crank linked to a pair of long jackscrews. The XFF-1 was the first naval fighter designed around the new Wright R-1820 *Cyclone* engine and included other innovations such as an all-metal fuselage and fully enclosed canopies for the pilot and gunner/observer.

After the XFF-1 made its first flight in December 1931, testing revealed that it was faster than any single-seat Navy fighter of the day (i.e., a top speed of 195 mph versus 186 mph for the F4B-2). A second prototype, differing mainly in equipment carried, was completed as the XSF-1. In December 1932 the Navy ordered 27 production examples of the FF-1 fighter and 33 more as SF-1 scouts. Installation of R-1820-78 and -84 engines boosted top speed to over 200 mph. As deliveries commenced in 1934, FF-1s were assigned to VF-5B and SF-1s to VS-3B, both serving in *Lexington*'s Air Group. FF-1s and SF-1s were phased-out of active service during 1936 and transferred to the reserves, where they continued to operate until 1940. In

Top: **The FF-1 and the nearly identical SF-1 were the first retractable-gear combat aircraft evaluated by the Navy. Both types were assigned only to Lexington's Air Group, FF-1s to VF-5B and SF-1s to VS-3B.** *Bottom:* **One of the 18 SF-1s that served with VS-3B aboard *Lexington* during 1935. VS-3B were reequipped with SBU-1s in 1936.**

1934 Canadian Car & Foundry obtained a license from Grumman to build FF-1s as the G-23, and 57 examples were manufactured between 1935 and 1937, fifteen of them going to the RCAF, one each to Nicaragua and Japan, and forty to the Spanish Republican forces.

General Aviation FA—1932

TECHNICAL SPECIFICATIONS (XFA-1)

Type: One-place dirigible/carrier fighter
Manufacturer: General Aviation Mfg. Corp., Hasbrouk Heights, New Jersey.
Total produced: 1 (USN)
Power plant: One 450-hp Pratt & Whitney R-1340C *Wasp* 9-cylinder radial driving a three or two-bladed Hamilton Standard fixed-pitch propeller.
Armament: Two fixed forward-firing .30-cal. machine guns.

Performance: Max. speed 170 mph at s.l.; ceiling 20,200 ft.; combat range 375 mi.

Weights: 1,837 lbs. empty, 2,508 lbs. loaded.

Dimensions: Span 25 ft. 6 in., length 22 ft. 2 in., wing area 175 sq. ft.

XFA-1, seen here at NAS in early 1932, at Anacostia, was the last of three aircraft evaluated under the "small carrier fighter" specification. It was similar in layout to the Curtiss F9C.

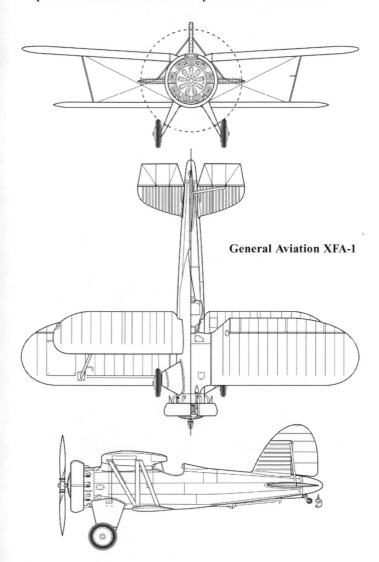

General Aviation XFA-1

The FA appeared during early 1932 as the last of three aircraft designed to BuAer's "small carrier fighter" requirement. General Aviation, before being acquired by General Motors in 1929, had been the Atlantic Aircraft Division of Fokker Aircraft Corp. of America. Similar in many respects to the F9C, the XFA-1 featured an all-metal fuselage and gull-mounted upper wings but could be distinguished by large landing gear fairings that were strut-braced to the wings. The prototype was delivered to NAS Anacostia on March 5, 1932 with a three-bladed propeller installed which was later exchanged for a two-bladed type. As BuAer had already made the decision to procure the F9C-2 for the small numbers of dirigible fighters needed, development of the XFA-1 was short-lived and no production orders resulted.

Curtiss F10C—1932 see *Curtiss S3C under* OBSERVATION AND SCOUT AIRCRAFT

Curtiss F11C (BFC, BF2C) Goshawk—1932

TECHNICAL SPECIFICATIONS (F11C-2 [BF2C-1])

Type: One-place carrier fighter/bomber-fighter

Manufacturer: Curtiss-Wright Corp., Curtiss Aeroplane Div., Buffalo, New York.

Total produced: 56 (USN)

Powerplant: One 700-hp Wright R-1820-78 [R-1820-04] *Cyclone* 9-cylinder radial driving a two-bladed Hamilton Standard variable-pitch propeller.

Armament: Two fixed forward-firing .30-caliber machine guns and up to 474 lbs. of bombs carried externally.

Performance: Max. speed 205 mph [228 mph] at 8,000 ft.; ceiling 24,300 [27,000] ft.; combat range 560 [797] mi.

Weights: 3,037 lbs. [3,329 lbs.] empty, 4,638 lbs. [5,086 lbs.] loaded.

Dimensions: Span 31 ft. 6 in., length 25 ft. [23 ft.], wing area 262 sq. ft.

Curtiss, after being reorganized as Curtiss-Wright Corp. in 1929, continued to be a major supplier of naval aircraft through the 1930s. In April 1932, BuAer ordered two biplane fighter prototypes from Curtiss based upon the company's *Hawk II* model, a radial engine design incorporating the aerodynamic and structural improvements of the Army's P-6E. The XF11C-1 was to be powered by a twin-row R-1510 and the XF11C-2 (actually the company's existing *Hawk II* demonstrator) by a single-row R-1820. Both aircraft were to possess light dive-bombing capability, configured to carry either a 474-lb. bomb on the centerline or four 112-lb. bombs under the wings. The XF11C-2 was delivered for trials in June 1932 and the F11C-1 a year later. Curtiss received an order in October 1932 for 28 F11C-2s and deliveries began the following February. In 1934 these aircraft were re-designated BFC-2s and later retrofitted with half sliding canopies mounted to a raised rear turtledeck that housed a life raft. The fifth production F11C-2 was reworked to accept a Grumman-type, inward-retracting landing gear assembly and re-designated F11C-3, and the Navy

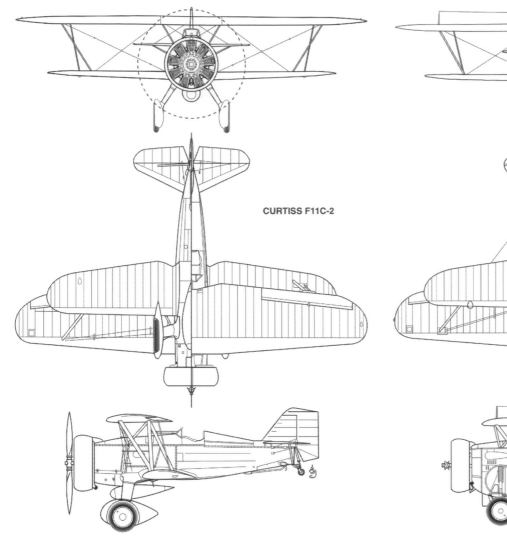

CURTISS F11C-2

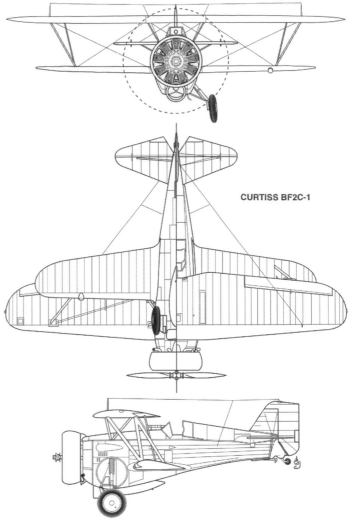

CURTISS BF2C-1

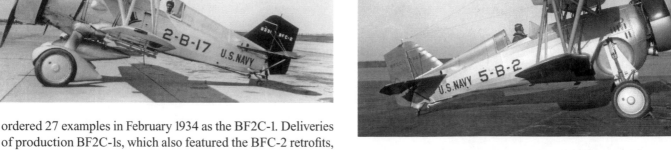

ordered 27 examples in February 1934 as the BF2C-1. Deliveries of production BF2C-1s, which also featured the BFC-2 retrofits, commenced in late 1934.

All F11C-2s/BFC-2s served with VF-1B (later renamed VB-2B, and later still, VB-3B) aboard *Saratoga* from early 1933 until the type was withdrawn from active service in early 1938. Retractable-gear BF2C-1s, starting in late 1934, were assigned to VB-5B of the Air Group formed for the newly commissioned

Left, bottom: The F11C was essentially a radial engine, a naval-ized variant of the Army P-6E. All F11C-2s became BFC-2s in 1934. The photograph depicts a BFC-2 serving with VB-2B aboard *Lexington* in 1934. *Above:* The retractable-gear F11C-3 prototype was placed in production as the BF2C-1. All served with VB-5B of the *Ranger* Air Group from late 1935 until unexpectedly with-drawn in 1937 due to structural problems in the wings.

Ranger, but after less than three years in the fleet, had to be withdrawn from service due to a serious flutter problem attributed to the metal structure of the upper wing, which, in one reported case, had resulted in a complete wing separation during a dive-bombing run. These were the last Curtiss-built fighters in regular Navy service.

Berliner-Joyce F2J—1933

TECHNICAL SPECIFICATIONS (XF2J-1)

Type: Two-place carrier fighter.
Manufacturer: Berliner-Joyce Aircraft Corp., Baltimore, Maryland.
Total produced: 1 (USN)
Powerplant: One 625-hp Wright R-1510-92 14-cylinder radial driving a two-bladed Hamilton Standard fixed-pitch propeller.
Armament: One fixed forward-firing .30-cal. machine gun, one flexible .30-cal. rear machine gun, and up to 500 lbs. of bombs carried externally.
Performance: Max. speed 193 mph at 6,000 ft.; ceiling 21,500 ft.; combat range 522 mi.
Weights: 3,211 lbs. empty, 4,851 lbs. loaded.
Dimensions: Span 36 ft., length 28 ft. 10 in., wing area 304 sq. ft.

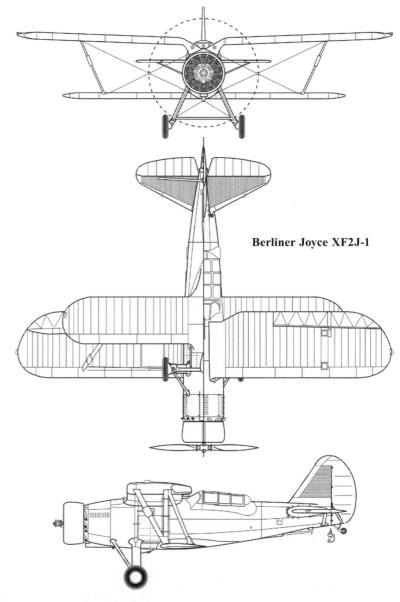

Berliner Joyce XF2J-1

A product of the relatively short-lived Berliner-Joyce Aircraft Corporation (1929–1935), the F2J was built to fulfill the same multi-role biplane fighter requirement as the contemporaneous FD and F3U (see below, and Vought SBU, above), but, unlike them, was not tied to a specific BuAer design pattern. Following the unsuccessful effort with its single-seat XFJ-1 and -2, Berliner-Joyce received a contract in June 1931 to construct a two-seat fighter prototype under the designation XF2J-1. Much of its general design concept was borrowed from the company's two-seat Army Y1P-16 fighter, whose chief characteristic was upper wings that gulled into the fuselage instead of being supported by conventional cabane struts. Like the rival FD and F3U, the XF2J-1 featured fixed landing gear, a metal-clad fuselage, and fabric-covered wings. Sometime after delivery, a fully enclosed cockpit canopy was also installed. Completion of the prototype extended over a two-year period, however, and delivery to Anacostia did not occur until mid–1933. Testing of the prototype subsequently revealed poor visibility (presumably due to the wing configuration) and sub-standard performance compared to other

The short-lived XF2J-1 while at Anacostia for trials during 1933. The two-seat scout and fighter concepts ultimately merged into the new scout-bomber requirement in 1934.

new scout and fighter types, thus no further development was undertaken.

Douglas FD—1933

TECHNICAL SPECIFICATIONS (XFD-1)

Type: Two-place carrier fighter
Manufacturer: Douglas Aircraft Co., Santa Monica, California.
Total produced: 1 (USN)
Powerplant: One 700-hp Pratt & Whitney R-1535-64 14-cylinder radial driving a two-bladed Hamilton Standard fixed-pitch propeller.
Armament: One fixed forward-firing .30-cal. machine gun, one flexible .30-cal. rear machine gun, and up to 500 lbs. of bombs carried externally.
Performance: Max. speed 204 mph at 8,900 ft.; ceiling 23,700 ft.; combat range 576 mi.
Weights: 3,227 lbs. empty, 5,000 lbs. loaded.
Dimensions: Span 31 ft. 6 in., length 25 ft. 4 in., wing area 295 sq. ft.

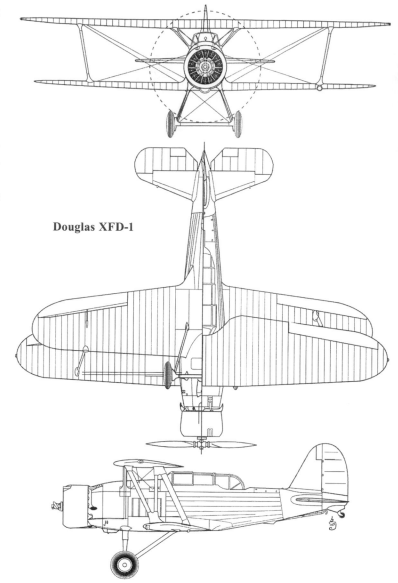

Douglas XFD-1

The FD was a continuation of the two-seat fighter concept that had originated with the F8C series, in which the functions of fighter, scout, and dive-bomber were combined in one airframe. A 1932 requirement listed as BuAer Design 113 called for a conventional two-seat biplane layout, fixed landing gear, 500-lb. bomb load, and an R-1535 powerplant. In June 1932, contracts for construction of single prototypes under this requirement were given to Douglas as the XFD-1 and Vought as the XF3U-1. When both prototypes arrived for testing at NAS Anacostia in June 1933 (within four days of each other), the chief differences between them was a spreader bar between the main gear struts on the XFD-1 and minor aerodynamic details. Ironically, by the time the XFD-1 had been delivered, the Navy had already moved away from the two-seat fighter idea in favor of scout-bomber (SB) types, which it planned to operate in conjunction with single-seat fighters. As a consequence, no further development of the XFD-1 was undertaken after 1933.

The sole XFD-1 running up at Anacostia in 1933. Ordered along with the Vought XF3U-1, the Navy was already moving away from the two-seat fighter concept by the time this prototype arrived for testing.

Vought F3U—1933 see *Vought SBU under*
ATTACK AIRCRAFT

Curtiss F12C—1933 see *Curtiss SBC under*
ATTACK AIRCRAFT

Boeing F6B (BFB)—1933

TECHNICAL SPECIFICATIONS (XBFB-1)

Type: One-place carrier fighter/bomber-fighter.
Manufacturer: Boeing Airplane Co., Seattle, Washington.
Total produced: 1 (USN)
Powerplant: One 625-hp Pratt & Whitney R-1535-44 14-cylinder
    radial driving a two-bladed Hamilton Standard variable-pitch
    propeller.
Armament: Two fixed forward-firing .30-caliber machine guns
    and up to 474 lbs. of bombs carried externally.
Performance: Max. speed 195 mph at 6,000 ft.; ceiling 20,700
    ft.; combat range 437 mi.
Weights: 2,823 lbs. empty, 3,705 lbs. loaded.
Dimensions: Span 28 ft. 6 in., length 22 ft. 2 in., wing area 252
    sq. ft.

Boeing XBFB-1

The F6B/BFB was the second installment of the
Navy's short-lived, single-seat bomber-fighter concept. In
1931, while Boeing was making preparations to
manufacture the F4B-3 and F4B-4 in quantity, BuAer indicated interest in a related design that would possess improved light dive-bombing capability, and thus in June of
1931, authorized the company to construct a single
prototype as the XF6B-1. But as a consequence of Boeing's
concurrent involvement in other military projects (i.e.,
F4B-3 and -4, P-12E, B-9, and P-26) completion and delivery of the XF6B-1 to NAS Anacostia was delayed until
February 1933, by which time Curtiss had already flown
two prototypes (i.e., F11C-1 and -2) built to the same requirements. After commencing flight trials, the prototype
received the new bomber-fighter designation XBFB-1.
While having many aerodynamic and structural characteristics in common with the F4B-3 and -4, the
XBFB-1 came with ten percent more wing
area, more horsepower, and fully cantilevered
main gear legs allowing clearance for ordnance on the centerline. The aircraft was retained for testing but no production was ordered. It was the last type of biplane to be
built by Boeing at Seattle.

**The sole XBFB-1 (XF6B-1) evaluated at Ana-
costia during 1933. Similarity to Boeing's successful F4B series is evident. By the time the
XBFB-1 arrived, the Navy had decided to purchase the Curtiss BFC-2 (F11C-2).**

Grumman F2F—1933

TECHNICAL SPECIFICATIONS (F2F-1)

Type: One-place carrier fighter.

Manufacturer: Grumman Aircraft Engr. Corp., Bethpage, New York.

Total produced: 55 (USN)

Powerplant: One 700-hp Pratt & Whitney R-1535-44 14-cylinder radial driving a two-bladed Hamilton Standard variable-pitch propeller.

Armament: Two fixed forward-firing .30-caliber machine guns.

Performance: Max. speed 231 mph at 7,500 ft.; ceiling 27,100 ft.; range 985 mi. max.

Weights: 2,691 lbs. empty, 3,847 lbs. loaded.

Dimensions: Span 28 ft. 6 in., length 21 ft. 5 in., wing area 230 sq. ft.

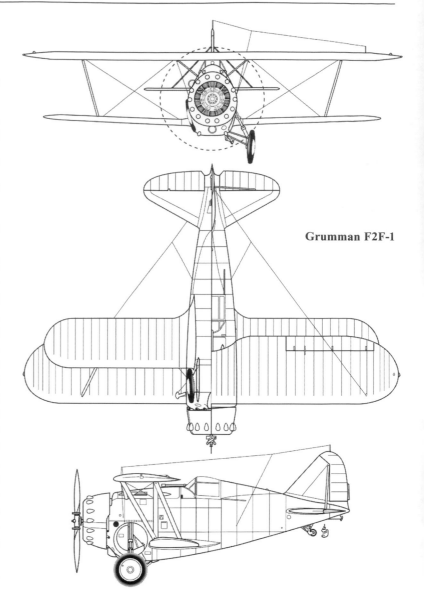

Grumman F2F-1

In the wake of Grumman's success with the FF-1 in 1931, BuAer awarded the company a contract in November 1932 to design and construct a prototype for the Navy's most recent single-seat fighter competition (i.e., one of two retractable-gear biplanes considered along with the Curtiss XF11C-3/BF2C-1, reported above). When flown for the first time on October 18, 1933, the XF2F-1 epitomized the stubby, "beer-barrel" appearance associated with all Grumman biplane fighters. Using many of the structural and aerodynamic features seen on the FF-1, the XF2F-1 introduced improved streamlining with a very tightly cowled engine having bumps for cylinder-head clearance. During acceptance trials, the prototype showed itself to be highly maneuverable and fast, posting a top speed of 229 mph and a rate-of-climb exceeding 3,000 feet-per-minute. On the negative side, flying the XF2F-1 proved to be tricky, with a predisposition to spin, but the trait was not judged serious enough to require aerodynamic changes.

In May 1934, Grumman received a contract to produce 54 aircraft as the F2F-1, and deliveries to the fleet commenced in early 1935. By mid-year, the type was equipping VF-2B on *Lexington* and VF-3B aboard the *Ranger*. When VF-3B was changed to VF-7B on the new *Yorktown*, then later, to VF-5 on the even newer *Wasp*, the F2Fs went with the unit. All F2F-1s had been replaced by F3Fs in carrier squadrons before the end of 1940 but remained in service as gunnery and fighter trainers. As of December 1941, 16 F2F-1s were still flying at NAS Miami and another seven at NAS Pensacola.

A brand-new F2F-1 in front of Grumman's factory in mid–1934, just before delivery. The aircraft is depicted in the markings of *Lexington*'s VF-2B, the first squadron to become operational with the type.

Boeing F7B—1933

TECHNICAL SPECIFICATIONS (XF7B-1)

Type: One-place carrier fighter.
Manufacturer: Boeing Airplane Co., Seattle, Washington.
Total produced: 1 (USN)
Powerplant: One 550-hp Pratt & Whitney R-1340-30 *Wasp* 9-cylinder radial driving a two-bladed Hamilton Standard variable-pitch propeller.
Armament: Two fixed forward-firing .30-caliber machine guns.
Performance: Max. speed 239 mph at 10,000 ft.; ceiling 26,900 ft.; range 824 mi. max.
Weights: 2,697 lbs. empty, 3,579 lbs. loaded.
Dimensions: Span 31 ft. 11 in., length 27 ft. 7 in., wing area 213 sq. ft.

The first of three monoplane fighter prototypes to be tested at NAS Anacostia during the early and mid–1930s, the F7B represented an ultimately unsuccessful effort by Boeing to maintain its place as a major supplier of Navy fighters. Though sharing the same powerplant and some design characteristics with the Army's monoplane P-26, the XF7B-1 differed in having 30 percent more wing area, an enclosed canopy, and per requirements, landing gear that retracted rearward into the wings. The prototype made its first flight on September 14, 1933, and was delivered for military trials two months later. Despite having a top speed 10 mph higher (239 mph) than the rival biplanes (i.e., XF11C-3 and XF2F-1), the XF7B-1 suffered from excessive takeoff runs, high landing speeds, and general instability to the extent that the Navy returned it to the factory for modifications in the spring of 1934. When the prototype arrived back at Anacostia for testing in early 1935 without the canopy and flaps installed on the wings, landing speed was 12 mph lower, however, the added weight of the improvements effectively cancelled any speed advantage over the biplanes. Soon afterward, the plane was rendered non-flyable after being overstressed in dive tests and the project was cancelled.

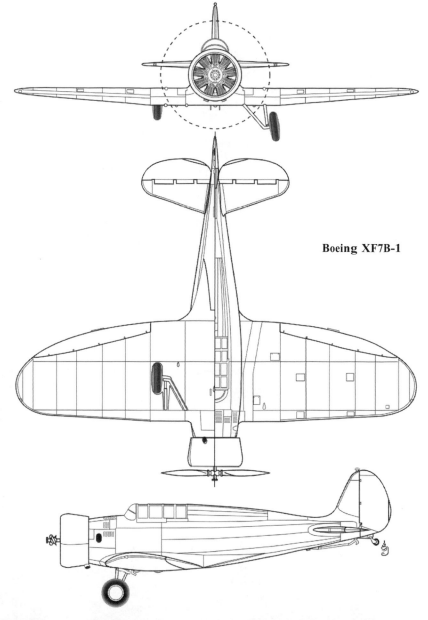

Boeing XF7B-1

The F7B-1, seen here at Anacostia in 1934, was one of three monoplane fighter prototypes being tested by the Navy. It was ultimately rejected in favor of improved biplanes (e.g., Curtiss BF2C-1 and Grumman F2F-1).

Berliner-Joyce F3J—1934

TECHNICAL SPECIFICATIONS (XF3J-1)

Type: One-place carrier fighter/bomber-fighter.
Manufacturer: Berliner-Joyce Co., Baltimore, Maryland.
Total produced: 1 (USN)
Powerplant: One 625-hp Wright R-1510-26 14-cylinder radial driving a two-bladed Hamilton Standard variable-pitch propeller.
Armament: Two fixed forward-firing .30-caliber machine guns and up to 474 lbs. of bombs carried externally.
Performance: Max. speed 209 mph at 6,000 ft.; ceiling 24,500 ft.; range 719 mi. max.
Weights: 2,717 lbs. empty, 4,016 lbs. loaded.
Dimensions: Span 29 ft., length 22 ft. 11 in., wing area 240 sq. ft.

The XF3J-1, pictured here in 1934, was the last of three "bomber-fighter" prototypes to be tested at Anacostia. Although the Curtiss BFC and BF2C had achieved limited production, the BF concept was on its way out.

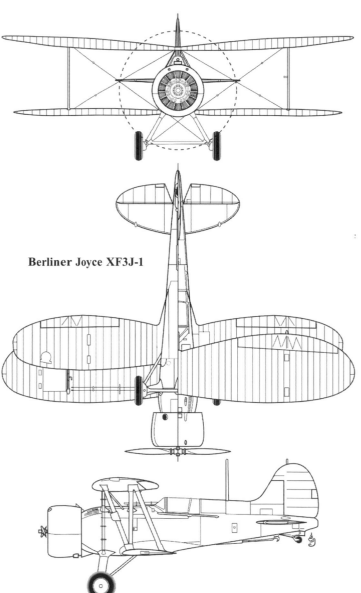

Berliner Joyce XF3J-1

The last type of fixed-gear biplane fighter to be considered by the Navy and the final product of Berliner-Joyce before that company ceased operations, the F3J was one of three aircraft ordered to evaluate the Navy's short-lived bomber-fighter concept (see also Curtiss F11C and Boeing F6B, above). BuAer authorized construction of an XF3J-1 prototype in June 1932, but delivery was not forthcoming until April 1934, by which time the competing F11C-2/BFC-2 had already entered service and the retractable-gear BF2C-1 had been ordered into production. After remaining at Anacostia for a year, the XF3J-1 was stricken from the Navy inventory.

Curtiss F13C—1934

TECHNICAL SPECIFICATIONS (XF13C-3)

Type: One-place carrier fighter.
Manufacturer: Curtiss-Wright Corp., Curtiss Aeroplane Div., Buffalo, New York.
Total produced: 1 (USN, USMC)
Powerplant: One 700-hp Wright R-1510-12 14-cylinder radial driving a two-bladed Hamilton Standard variable-pitch propeller.
Armament: Two fixed forward-firing .30-caliber machine guns.
Performance: Max. speed 232 mph at 7,000 ft.; ceiling 24,100 ft.; range 726 mi. max.
Weights: 3,499 lbs. empty, 4,721 lbs. loaded.
Dimensions: Span 35 ft., length 26 ft. 3 in., wing area 205 sq. ft.

Perhaps the most interesting contender in the Navy's mid–1930s fighter competition, the Curtiss F13C offered a two-for-one approach in which the aircraft could be rigged as either a monoplane or a biplane. The monoplane version included a broader chord high wing that utilized a combination of flaps and retractable leading-edge slats to bring takeoff and landing speeds within acceptable limits (i.e., 65 to 70 mph). First flown in monoplane configuration on January 7, 1934, then delivered to Anacostia a month later, the XF13C-1 subsequently posted a top speed of 236 mph and exhibited generally good flying characteristics but was hampered by poor visibility, faulty slat operations, and problems with the experimental twin-row R-1510 engine.

When flown as the XF13C-2 in a biplane rig, the plane's performance did not compare favorably against competing biplanes such as the F2F-1 and BF2C-1. The prototype was returned to Curtiss for a reshaped fin a rudder to permit easier carrier stowage, and as the XF13C-3, rigged again as a monoplane, it arrived back at Anacostia in the spring of 1935 to resume testing. In the interval, BuAer had decided against production, and the prototype was transferred to N.A.C.A. where it was used as a flying testbed briefly during 1937; after leaving N.A.C.A., the XF13C-3 served as a Marine command plane at Quantico until late 1938.

Northrop FT—1934

TECHNICAL SPECIFICATIONS (XFT-1)

Type: One-place carrier fighter.
Manufacturer: Northrop Corp., El Segundo, California.
Total produced: 1 (USN)
Powerplant: One 625-hp Wright R-1510-26 14-cylinder radial driving a two-bladed Hamilton Standard variable-pitch propeller.
Armament: Two fixed forward-firing .30-caliber machine guns and 232 lbs. of bombs carried on external racks.
Performance: Max. speed 235 mph at 6,000 ft.; ceiling 26,500 ft.; range 976 mi. max.
Weights: 2,469 lbs. empty, 4,003 lbs. loaded.
Dimensions: Span 32 ft., length 21 ft. 1 in., wing area 177 sq. ft.

Coming as Northrop's first endeavor to obtain a Navy contract, the FT appeared as the only fixed-gear participant in the Navy's first monoplane fighter com-

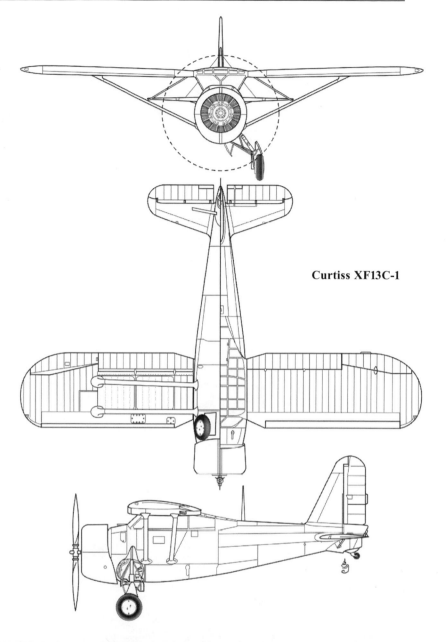

Curtiss XF13C-1

Left: **The XF13C-1 in original monoplane configuration as delivered to Anacostia in February 1934. Testing revealed faulty leading-edge slats, engine problems, and restricted pilot visibility.** *Right:* **The same aircraft, rigged as a biplane, after arriving back at Anacostia in the spring of 1935. In this configuration, its performance did not compare favorably with the F2F or BF2C.**

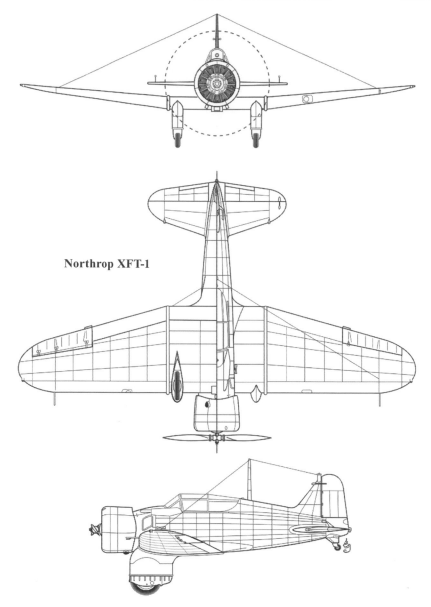

Northrop XFT-1

petition. As delivered to NAS Anacostia for trials in March 1934, the XFT-1 was powered by an experimental twin-row R-1510 engine and bore a strong aerodynamic resemblance to Northrop's successful Gamma series. The 235 mph top speed attained in flight-testing was slightly better than the biplanes but engine problems, coupled with dangerous spin characteristics, caused the prototype to be returned to the factory for modifications. Northrop thereafter exchanged the engine for a more reliable Pratt & Whitney R-1535, installing a longer-chord cowling, but other than small revisions to the wheel covers, the airframe was left unchanged. After the aircraft was returned to Anacostia in April 1936 as the XFT-2, its spin characteristics were still unacceptable and the aircraft was grounded. Soon afterward, when a Northrop test pilot attempted an unauthorized flight back to the factory, the prototype crashed en route, and the program was terminated.

Grumman F3F—1935

TECHNICAL SPECIFICATIONS (F3F-2)

Type: One-place carrier fighter.
Manufacturer: Grumman Aircraft Engr. Corp., Bethpage, New York.
Total produced: 163 (all versions)
Powerplant: One 950-hp Wright R-1820-22 *Cyclone* 9-cylinder radial driving a three-bladed Hamilton Standard variable-pitch propeller.
Armament: One .50-cal. and one .30-cal. fixed forward-firing machine gun and 232 lbs. of bombs carried on external racks .

Performance: Max. speed 260 mph at 17,250 ft.; ceiling 32,300 ft.; range 1,030 mi. max.
Weights: 3,254 lbs. empty, 4,750 lbs. loaded.
Dimensions: Span 32 ft., length 23 ft. 2 in., wing area 260 sq. ft.

In late 1934, in order to correct the shortcomings of the F2F-1, BuAer authorized Grumman to proceed with an XF3F-1 prototype incorporating a one foot nine inch extension to the fuselage and adding three and half feet to wingspan while retaining the F2F's R-1535 powerplant and other structural features. Right after the prototype's first flight on

One of several monoplane fighters being evaluated, the XFT-1 with Wright R-1510 engine is shown at NAS Anacostia in the spring of 1934. Flight testing indicated dangerous spin characteristics.

March 20, 1935, it failed to recover from a terminal dive, killing Grumman test pilot Jimmy Collins; then only two months later, the second XF3F-1 was lost when the pilot was forced to bail out during an uncontrolled spin. Despite the inauspicious start, the third XF3F-1 was delivered to NAS Anacostia for military testing the following June and performed well enough during acceptance trials that, in August 1935, Grumman received a contract to manufacture 54 production examples as the F3F-1. Deliveries began in March 1936, and by the end of the year, the type had reequipped VF-5B aboard *Ranger* and VF-6B on *Saratoga*. After being released from frontline squadrons in 1940, F3F-1s served as fighters trainers at NAS Norfolk and NAS Miami, 39 still remaining active as of December 1941.

The last biplane fighters produced for the Navy, the F3F-2 and -3, were the outcome of a desire on the part of BuAer to achieve better all-around performance from an already proven airframe. Ordered from Grumman in July 1936, the XF3F-2 was redesigned for installation of a 950-hp Wright R-1820, receiving in the process a larger diameter, shorter-chord cowling along with a three-bladed propeller. Internal fuel was increased to 130 gallons, extending range by 10 percent. When tested at Anacostia during January 1937, the prototype reached a maximum speed of 260 mph and showed a 30 percent increase in rate-of-climb (2,800 feet-per-minute). As a result of trials, the canopy was revised and the rudder enlarged to offset increased torque. BuAer placed an order for 81 F3F-2s in March 1937, followed a year later by a contract for 27 F3F-3s, identical except for water-injection systems added to the engine (which were later removed). Deliveries to the fleet began in late 1937, initially to VF-6 of the newly commissioned *Enterprise,* then later to VF-5 on *Yorktown.* As production continued, F3F-2s and -3s went on to equip two more Navy and two Marine squadrons.

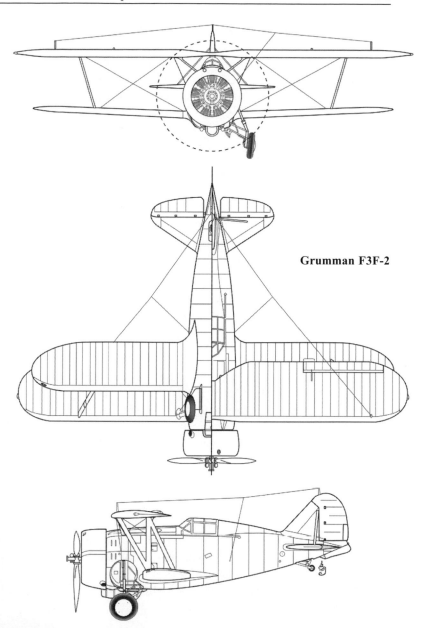

Grumman F3F-2

Left: **A VF-3 F3F-1 from the *Saratoga* Air Group in 1938. The unit operated F3F-1s and F2A-1s side-by-side from mid–1939 until mid–1941, when both were replaced by F4F-3s.** *Right:* **One of 17 F3F-2s that began equipping San Diego–based VMF-2 (later VMF-211) in 1938. A small number of these aircraft remained active with VMF-111 and -211 right up to the end of 1941.**

They remained in frontline service until replaced by monoplanes (i.e., Grumman F4Fs and Brewster F2As) during the middle of 1941, and by December, a small number were still active in Marine squadrons (VMF-111 and -211) while 77 had been transferred to shore bases for fighter training.

Curtiss H75B (Y1P-36)—1936

TECHNICAL SPECIFICATIONS (H75B)

Type: One-place landplane fighter.
Manufacturer: Curtiss-Wright Corp., Curtiss Aeroplane Div., Buffalo, New York.
Total produced: 1 (USN)
Powerplant: One 850-hp Wright R-1820-39 *Cyclone* 9-cylinder radial driving a three-bladed Curtiss Electric variable-pitch propeller.
Armament: (none installed).
Performance: Max. speed 280 mph at 10,000 ft.; ceiling 32,500 ft.; range 730 mi. max.
Weights: 4,049 lbs. empty, 5,075 lbs. loaded.
Dimensions: Span 37 ft. 4 in., length 28 ft. 1 in., wing area 236 sq. ft.

In mid–1936, after disappointing trials with the Boeing F7B, Curtiss F13C, and Northrop FT monoplane fighters, BuAer asked Curtiss to fly its H75B to NAS Anacostia to be considered as a potential naval variant. The H75B, a company-owned demonstrator carried under civil registration NX17Y, had already been tested at Wright Field in Dayton, Ohio, and was being developed for the Army Air Corps as the service test Y1P-36. Little is known about the Navy trials following delivery of the aircraft other than the fact that BuAer ultimately determined that the H75B was unsuited for carrier operations. Evaluating officials probably concluded that with the extra weight of carrier arresting gear and armament, the H75B would offer little or no performance advantage over the proven F3F.

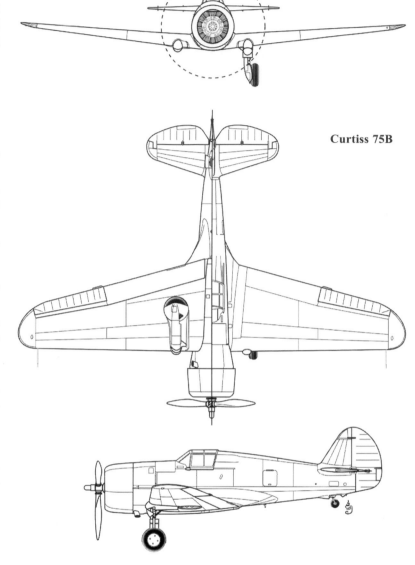

Curtiss 75B

Left: **The Curtiss H75B (Y1P-36) company demonstrator flown to Anacostia for evaluations in mid–1936. With the extra weight of arresting gear and armament, the plane was seen as offering little advantage over the F3F-2.**

Seversky NF-1 (SEV-1XP)— 1937

TECHNICAL SPECIFICATIONS (NF-1)

Type: One-place carrier fighter.
Manufacturer: Seversky Aircraft Corp., Farmingdale, New York.
Total produced: 1 (USN)
Powerplant: One 950-hp Wright R-1820-22 *Cyclone* 9-cylinder radial driving a three-bladed Hamilton Standard variable-pitch propeller.
Armament: Two fixed forward-firing 30-cal. machine guns.

Right: Essentially a navalized version of the Army P-35, the NF-1 was deemed as not showing much improvement in performance over the F3F-2 when tested at NAS Anacostia in late 1937.

Performance: Max. speed 267 mph at 15,000 ft.; ceiling 30,700 ft.; range 1,100 mi. (est.).
Weights: 4,020 lbs. empty, 5,231 lbs. loaded.
Dimensions: Span 36 ft., length 25 ft. 2 in., wing area 220 sq. ft.

In September 1937, a year after the Navy had rejected the Curtiss H75B as a monoplane fighter candidate, Seversky's NF-1 (Naval Fighter One) prototype reached NAS Anacostia for official acceptance trials. Unlike the H75B, the NF-1 carried armament and was equipped with carrier arresting gear. Seversky had also enlarged the windshield to permit better over-the-nose visibility during carrier approaches. The reason why BuAer specified a *Cyclone*-powered variant instead of the R-1830 *Twin Wasp* powerplant that equipped the Army's P-35 production model is not made clear. In any case, testing of the NF-1 subsequently revealed it to be only marginally faster than the F3F-2 and possess a similar rate-of-climb. Though never receiving an official naval designation, the NF-1 reportedly stayed at Anacostia for several more years where it was evaluated against new fighter designs such as the Brewster F2A and Grumman F4F.

Brewster F2A Buffalo—1937

TECHNICAL SPECIFICATIONS (F2A-2)

Type: One-place carrier fighter.
Manufacturer: Brewster Aeronautical Corp., Long Island City, New York.
Total produced: 163 (USN/USMC)
Powerplant: One 1,200-hp Wright R-1820-42 *Cyclone* 9-cylinder radial driving a three-bladed Curtiss Electric variable-pitch propeller.
Armament: Four fixed forward-firing 50-cal. machine guns, two in the nose and one in each wings.
Performance: Max. speed 323 mph at 16,500 ft.; ceiling 34,000 ft.; range 1,105 mi. combat, 1,670 mi. max.
Weights: 4,576 lbs. empty, 6,890 lbs. loaded.
Dimensions: Span 35 ft., length 26 ft. 2 in., wing area 209 sq. ft.

The Brewster F2A, although much criticized, still deserves recognition as the first type of monoplane fighter to enter service aboard Navy carriers. Toward the end of 1935, after having rejected all of

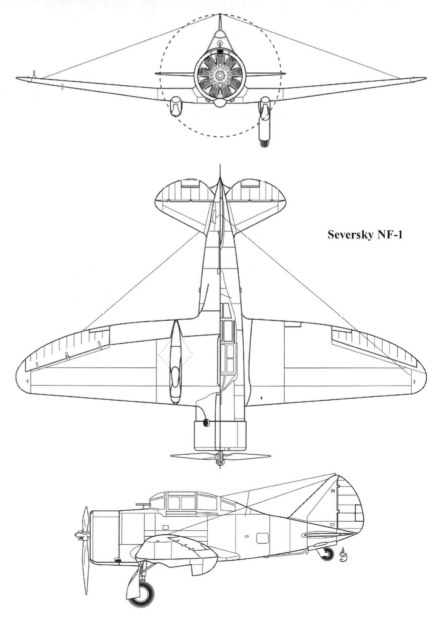

Seversky NF-1

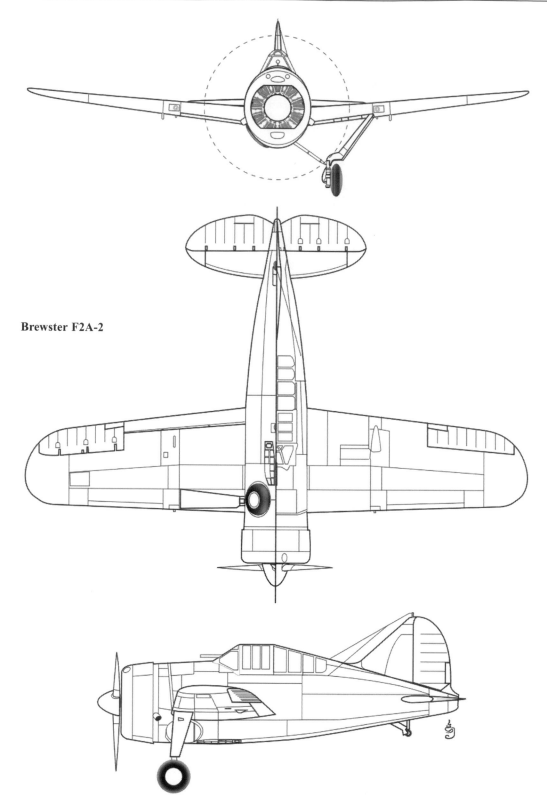

Brewster F2A-2

the monoplane fighters previously tested (i.e., Boeing F7B, Curtiss F13C, and Northrop FT), BuAer asked Brewster, a new-comer to the military aviation scene, and Grumman to both conceive new fighter designs that would eventually replace F2Fs and F3Fs. At this point in its history, Brewster had performed some sub-contract work for Grumman and Vought but

was still in the process of building its first airplane—the XSBA-1—for the Navy's current scout-bomber competition. In response to BuAer's latest request, the company design team, led by chief engineer Dayton Brown, came forward with the model 139, a mid-wing monoplane concept resembling a scaled-down version of the company's XSBA-1 prototype (see above), and soon afterward, in June 1936, Brewster received a contract for construction of a single prototype as the XF2A-1, with completion expected before the end of 1937. Originally, the aircraft was to have been powered by the smaller-diameter Pratt & Whitney R-1535 twin-row engine, however, before the final design had been fixed, BuAer changed the specification to the 950-hp Wright XR-1820-22 (the same powerplant specified for the XF3F-2). As a consequence, the final design of the XF2A-1 emerged with the very rotund fuselage profile that would become the plane's most distinctive feature, and as events would later prove, limit the design's development potential. Other design characteristics in common with the XSBA-1 included elliptical tail surfaces and a levered gear system that retracted the wheels into the belly of the fuselage.

The XF2A-1 prototype was rolled out for its first flight sometime in December 1937 and delivered to NAS Anacostia in early 1938 to participate in a fly-off against Grumman's XF4F-2. As testing of the two aircraft proceeded, the XF4F-2 proved to be 10 mph faster, but in comparison, the XF2A-1 exhibited superior handing qualities and performed better in carrier deck landing trials. In mid–

Top, right: **The first monoplane fighter to enter fleet service, F2A-1s began replacing VF-3's F3F-1s aboard** *Saratoga* **in mid–1939. Only 11 F2A-1s were accepted in anticipation of the improved F2A-2.** *Middle:* **The XF2A-2 as delivered to Anacostia in July 1939. Its nose had been shortened eight inches to compensate for added engine weight. The plane ultimately reached service with VF-2 on** *Lexington* **and VF-3 on** *Saratoga. Bottom:* **A factory-new F2A-3 in 1941, painted in overall light gray. By the end of the year, F4Fs had replaced F2As in all combat units except for VF-2, VS-201, and VMF-221. Some were delivered directly to training centers.**

June 1938, after a forced landing caused Grumman's prototype to be returned to the factory for repairs, BuAer declared Brewster interim winner of the competition and awarded the company a contract to produce 54 aircraft as the F2A-1. Delivery of the first 11 F2A-1 production models, featuring larger fins and raised canopy enclosures, commenced in June 1939, with ten joining VF-3 of the *Saratoga* Air Group, augmenting the unit's existing F3F-1s. However, during this time-frame, reports of air fighting from Spain and other parts of the world strongly indicated that American fighters needed to be faster and better armed, and with this in mind, BuAer directed Brewster to forego future deliveries of F2A-1s to await development of the improved F2A-2. (Note, the undelivered 44 F2A-1s were ultimately exported to Finland, where they went on to achieve an impressive combat record against the Soviet Air Force).

The XF2A-2, fitted with a 1,200-hp R-1820-40 engine and a Curtiss Electric propeller, was delivered to Anacostia in July 1939. To compensate for the weight added forward, the fuselage had been shortened eight inches between the firewall and the leading edge of the wing. Once testing revealed a 25 mph increase in top speed and improved rate-of-climb (3,100 feet-per-minute), BuAer authorized Brewster to manufacture a further 43 F2A-2s. Political events, however, namely production of similar export models for Great Britain and Belgium, caused deliveries of Navy F2A-2s to be delayed until the fall of 1940, when they began reequipping VF-2 aboard *Lexington*. And starting with the 30th production model, the type came with self-sealing fuel tanks and a .50-caliber machine gun added to each wing. The final batch of F2A-2s, received before year-end, entered service with VF-3 on *Saratoga*.

But after receiving the Navy's first monoplane fighter production contract, Brewster's fortunes dwindled rapidly. Even before 1940 ended, BuAer had decided to limit development of the F2A, which, according to some, had more to do with the company's management problems and unpredictable production schedules than the attributes of its airplanes, and in January 1941, Brewster received its final fighter order from BuAer. The 108 F2A-3s, delivered from July to December 1941, differed from the -2s in having 400 lbs. of armor plating added around the cockpit and provision for 80 more gallons of fuel. The extra weight necessitated a ten-inch fuselage extension between the firewall and wing leading edge to regain balance. With no corresponding increase in power to offset extra weight, overall performance suffered, and the shift in center-of-gravity degraded maneuverability. F2A-3s initially equipped VF-2, VF-3, and VS-201 (aboard *Long Island*, CVE-1) in fleet squadrons and replaced the F3F-2s of Marine squadron VMF-221. By the end of 1941, however, VF-3 had reequipped with F4F-3s, and many F2A-2s and -3s were being reassigned to non-combat duties with shore-based fighter training establishments in Miami, Norfolk, and San Diego. VF-2 received F4F-3s in early 1942, prior to the Battle of the Coral Sea,

leaving VMF-221 as the only combat unit still equipped with the type. When the Japanese struck Midway in June, Marine F2A-3s defending the island proved to be no match for the superior firepower and maneuverability of attacking Zeros, with the consequence that 13 of 19 were shot down during the first day of the battle; surviving F2As were withdrawn from VMF-211 immediately afterward.

Grumman F4F Wildcat—1937

TECHNICAL SPECIFICATIONS (F4F-3)

Type: One-place carrier fighter.
Manufacturer: Grumman Aircraft Engr. Corp., Bethpage, New York.
Total produced: 1,977 (USN, USMC)
Powerplant: One 1,200-hp Pratt & Whitney R-1830-76 *Twin Wasp* 14-cylinder radial driving a three-bladed Curtiss Electric controllable propeller.
Armament: Four fixed forward-firing .50-cal. machine guns and two 100-lb. bombs carried on external racks.

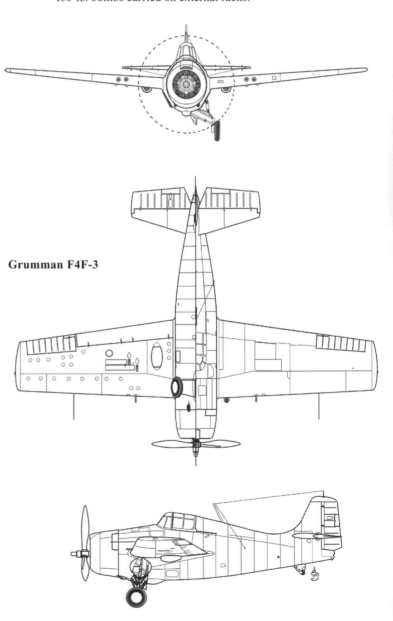

Grumman F4F-3

Performance: Max. speed 328 mph at 21,000 ft.; ceiling 37,500 ft.; combat range 845 mi. combat, 1,690 mi. max.
Weights: 5,342 lbs. empty, 7,002 lbs. loaded.
Dimensions: Span 38 ft., length 28 ft. 9 in., wing area 260 sq. ft.

Originally, in early 1936, BuAer had authorized Grumman to proceed with the XF4F-1 as an improved biplane to be powered by either a Wright XR-1670 or a Pratt & Whitney R-1535 engine, but in August the same year, a month after ordering Brewster's XF2A-1 monoplane, it cancelled Grumman's biplane project in favor of a monoplane design that would become the XF4F-2. In a move that was to have important consequences, BuAer departed from its usual policy of specifying the same engines for competing prototypes, directing Grumman instead to develop the XF4F-2 around the new 1,050-hp Pratt & Whitney R-1830 twin-row powerplant. Grumman, working fast to catch up with Brewster, had the XF4F-2 flying by September 1937 and on its way to NAS Anacostia two months ahead of the rival XF2A-1. Bearing a strong family resemblance to the F2F and F3F, the XF4F-2 emerged as a stubby, mid-wing design with rounded wingtips and tail surfaces, and used the proven inward-retracting gear system seen on Grumman biplanes. But the competitive fly-off held in the spring of 1938 proved to

Top: **An XF4F-2 in early 1938 during trials held at NAS Anacostia. While marginally faster than the rival XF2A-1, the XF4F-2's flying characteristics did not compare as favorably.** *Middle:* **The original configuration of the XF4F-3 as seen in early 1939. A combination of 1,200-hp XR-1830-76 engine and aerodynamic refinements boosted performance and improved overall handling and maneuverability.** *Bottom:* **A lineup of VF-3 F4F-3s from *Saratoga*'s Air Group during 1941 war games. Note "white cross" markings. VF-3 had only recently traded its F2A-1s and F3F-1s for new F4Fs.**

be disappointing: though faster (288 mph vs. 277 mph), the XF4F-2's general flying characteristics did not compare favorably with the XF2A-1, then, before the fly-off could be completed, it was damaged in a forced landing caused by an engine failure. As a consequence, in June 1938, Brewster received the initial production contract while the XF4F-2 was returned to Grumman for repairs.

BuAer, determining that the XF4F should remain under development as a second fighter option, approached Grumman to make some far-reaching modifications which, among other things, included installation of a 1,200-hp XR-1830-76 engine with a two-stage supercharger. The follow-on XF4F-3, featuring a fuselage lengthened by two feet, squared-off wings having increased span and area, plus enlarged and reshaped tail surfaces, was flown in February 1939 and delivered to Anacostia soon afterward. Other than cooling problems with the new engine, trials of the XF4F-3 exceeded expectations: both performance and maneuverability had improved significantly, top speed (335 mph) having increased having by 50 mph. Grumman's efforts were decisively rewarded in August 1939 when BuAer awarded a contract for 78 F4F-3s. And further refinements such as raising the tailplane, moving the cowling intakes, and relocating all armament to the wings, resulted in the definitive F4F-3 production variant.

Like Brewster and a number of other American military aircraft contractors, Grumman's ability to deliver new F4F-3s to the Navy was shaped by the start of World War II in Europe: priority on the first production models, 81 G-36As, had been promised to the French *Aéronavale*, then after France fell to the Germans in June 1940, production (subsequently increased to 90) was reallocated to Great Britain. The British G-36As, known as Martlet Is, differed from the F4F-3 in having a single-row Wright R-1820-S3C engine and six .50-cal wing guns (in place of the six 7.5-mm guns of the original French prototype). After entering service with the Fleet Air Arm during the fall of 1940, two Martlet Is scored the type's first combat victory in December when they shot down a Junkers Ju88 off Scapa Flow. The first U.S. Navy F4F-3s reached the fleet in December 1940, replacing the F3Fs of VF-41 (formerly VF-4) of *Ranger*'s Air Group, and all 78 had been received by February 1941. During this interval, BuAer ordered another 237 F4F-3s, including 61 aircraft redesignated as the F4F-3A (originally tested in November 1940 as the XF4F-6), which, due to production shortages, came with R-1830-90 engines having single-stage superchargers.

Grumman had begun work on the XF4F-4, a folding wing version armed with six .50-cal. wing guns, as early as March 1940, but other priorities—i.e., delivery of 130 *Twin-Wasp*–powered Martlet IIs and IIIs to Great Britain—delayed its first flight until April 1941. (Note, the Martlet IIIs, originally ordered by Greece as the F4F-3A, were taken over by Britain prior to delivery.) Two aircraft equipped with 1,200-hp Wright R-1820-40 engines were tested as the XF4F-5 in June of 1940, but since their performance did not compare favorably to the F4F-3, no production was undertaken. Grumman resumed deliveries of F4F-3s and -3As, now known as Wildcats, during the spring of 1941, and by the end of the year, the type was equipping seven Navy squadrons (VF-3, *Saratoga*; VF-5 and VF-41, Ranger; VF-6, *Enterprise*; VF-71 and -72, *Wasp*; and VF-8, *Hornet*) plus two Marine squadrons (VMF-121, Quantico; and VMF-211, then detached from Ewa to Wake Island).

The first five of 1,169 F4F-4s ordered by BuAer during 1941 were delivered in November of that year, and by the spring of 1942, sufficient numbers had reached fleet squadrons in time to participate in the Battle of Midway the following June. Twenty-one F4F-7 photo-reconnaissance versions ordered in 1941, essentially unarmed F4F-3s having greater fuel capacity, were also delivered in 1942. And before World War II ended, another 6,027 Wildcats would be licensed and produced by General Motors, 1,150 FM-1s similar to the F4F-4 and 4,777 FM-2s, the production version of the XF4F-8, powered by a 1,350-hp Wright R-1820-56 engine and having a taller fin. One F4F-3 fitted with twin floats was tested in early 1942 as the F4F-3S, but no production resulted.

Grumman F5F Skyrocket—1940

TECHNICAL SPECIFICATIONS (XF5F-1)

Type: One-place carrier fighter.

Manufacturer: Grumman Aircraft Engr. Corp., Bethpage, New York.

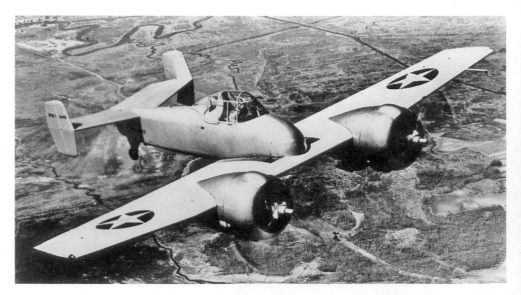

The first twin-engine carrier fighter, the XF5F-1, as flown in April 1940. The design objective was to fit two engines on the most compact airframe possible. This was superceded by the XF7F-1 design proposal in mid–1941.

Total produced: 1 (USN)
Powerplants: Two 1,200-hp Wright R-1820-40 *Cyclone* 9-cylinder air-cooled radial engines driving three-bladed Curtiss Electric controllable propellers.
Armament: Four fixed forward-firing .50-cal. machine guns.
Performance: Max. speed 383 mph at s.l.; ceiling 34,500 ft.; combat range 780 mi. combat, 1,170 mi. max.
Weights: 7,990 lbs. empty, 10,138 lbs. loaded.
Dimensions: Span 42 ft., length 28 ft. 11 in., wing area 303 sq. ft.

Even as the Brewster XF2A-1 and Grumman XF4F-2 were in the midst of trials during early 1938, BuAer was making preparations to initiate a far more ambitious set of new monoplane fighter requirements. Development contracts were issued simultaneously on June 30, 1938, one to Grumman for its twin-engine model G-34, to be delivered as the XF5F-1, and a second to Vought for its model V-166B as the XF4U-1. Although Grumman's XF5F-1 twin-engine concept was unorthodox, it potentially offered a means of doubling available horsepower in an airframe still compact enough to fit aboard existing carriers. Keeping length to a minimum, the design of the XF5F-1 was arranged so that the leading edge of the wing actually extended forward of the fuselage, with the two engine nacelles protruding ahead of the wing. In order to enhance directional stability, twin fins and rudders were located in the airflow behind the engines.

With Grumman test pilot G. A. Gilles at the controls, the XF5F-1 made its first flight from the Bethpage plant on April 1, 1940, but engine cooling problems, requiring modifications to the oil cooling ducts, delayed commencement of official military trials. Before delivery to Anacostia, BuAer directed Grumman to lower the height of the canopy and install four .50-cal. machine guns in place of the two 23-mm Madsen cannon originally planned. Navy testing of the XF5F-1 continued until February 1941, at which point the prototype was returned to the factory for extensive modifications. To improve airflow, large spinners were added to the props, the nose lengthened, and the engine nacelles extended past the trailing edge of the wing. Testing of the XF5F-1 resumed in July 1941, but soon afterward, BuAer decided against production of the type in favor of Grumman's newer twin-engine model G-51, which had been ordered in June as the XF7F-1.

Once the official testing program ended, the XF5F-1 remained at Anacostia where it was used for various test purposes until late 1944, when it was damaged beyond repair as the result of a belly landing.

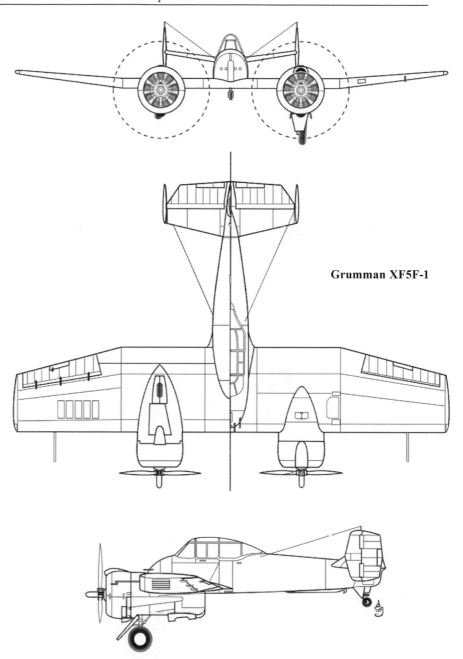

Grumman XF5F-1

Bell FL Airabonita—1940

TECHNICAL SPECIFICATIONS (XFL-1)

Type: One-place carrier fighter.
Manufacturer: Bell Aircraft Corp., Buffalo, New York.
Total produced: 1 (USN)
Powerplant: One 1,150-hp Allison V-1710-6 12-cylinder water-cooled inline engine driving a three-bladed Curtiss Electric controllable propeller.
Armament: (none installed).
Performance: Max. speed 338 mph at 11,000 ft.; ceiling 30,900 ft.; combat range 965 mi. combat, 1,475 mi. max.
Weights: 5,161 lbs. empty, 6,651 lbs. loaded.
Dimensions: Span 35 ft., length 29 ft. 9 in., wing area 232 sq. ft.

In November 1938, only five months after ordering new fighter prototypes from Grumman (XF5F-1) and Vought

(XF4U-1), BuAer gave Bell a contract to build yet another fighter contestant as the XFL-1. Bell, a fairly new military contractor at the time, was already at an advanced stage of construction on the similar XP-39 prototype, a mid-engine, tricycle gear fighter being developed for the Army. The naval variant, though retaining the same Allison V-12 powerplant mounted aft of the cockpit, differed in having arresting gear, underwing coolant radiators, a conventional (tailwheel) landing gear configuration, and a taller fin. Other changes included a

The XFL-1 as seen upon delivery in early 1941. Carrier landing trials revealed that its aft center-of-gravity caused poor pitch stability. Cancelled in 1942.

raised canopy to improve over-the-nose visibility and an airframe strengthened to withstand the rigors of carrier operations. Armament, when installed, would be the heaviest yet specified for a naval fighter, consisting of a 37-mm cannon firing through the propeller hub, plus two synchronized .30-caliber machine guns in the nose.

The XFL-1 prototype was rolled out and made its first flight on May 13, 1940, but a series of problems encountered with its Allison engine prevented delivery to NAS Anacostia until February 1941. Carrier deck trials subsequently revealed poor pitch stability due to the aft center-of-gravity and landing gear too weak for sustained operations. The XFL-1 was returned to Bell for modifications in December 1941, but before the prototype could be redelivered to Anacostia, BuAer determined that the aircraft lacked further development potential and cancelled the program.

Bell XFL-1

Vought F4U Corsair—1940

TECHNICAL SPECIFICATIONS (XF4U-1)

Type: One-place carrier fighter.

Manufacturer: Chance Vought Div. of United Aircraft Corp., Stratford, Connecticut.

Total produced: 1 (USN; 14,346 ultimately produced in seven major versions).

Power plant: One 1,850-hp Pratt & Whitney R-2800-4 *Double Wasp* 18-cylinder air-cooled radial engine driving a three-bladed Hamilton Standard constant-speed propeller.

Armament: Two fixed forward-firing .30-cal. machine guns in the nose, one .50-cal.

Performance: Max. speed 405 mph at 20,000 ft.; ceiling 35,200 ft.; range 1,070 mi. max.

Weights: 7,505 lbs. empty, 9,357 lbs. loaded.

Dimensions: Span 41 ft., length 31 ft. 11 in., wing area 314 sq. ft.

Probably the best-known aircraft to be designed by Rex Beisel, the Vought F4U was the first American fighter to exceed 400 mph in level flight, and though universally regarded as one of the most outstanding air superiority fighters of World War II, its prowess as a ground attack platform kept it in production longer (1942–1952) than any other type of Navy or Marine propeller-driven fighter. Its origins can be traced to January 1938 when Vought tendered two new fighter proposals to BuAer, one for a model V-166A to be powered by a Pratt & Whitney R-1830 engine and another for a larger model V-166B to be designed around Pratt & Whitney's as yet untested XR-2800 18-cylinder, twin-row powerplant. On June 30, 1938, on the premise that the experimental engine would be ready in time (note, the engine was in fact successfully bench-tested in 1939), BuAer gave Vought a contract to develop the more speculative V-166B as a single prototype under the designation XF4U-1. As work proceeded, partly out of an effort to provide adequate ground clearance for the large-diameter propeller (i.e., 13 ft., 4 in.), Beisel's team created the XF4U-1's most noticeable characteristic — inverted gull wings that not only reduced the length of the main landing gear legs and the corresponding ground angle, but also produced the optimum angle for minimum drag at the wing-fuselage junction. Other low-drag features included spot-welded skin assemblies and oil cooler and air intakes buried in the wing roots. The main gear system was innovative, pinioning 90 degrees while retracting rearward so that the wheels lay flush within the wings under wheel doors. Forty five-pound bombs, enclosed in two underwing bays, were intended to be dropped onto a bomber formation from above, with the pilot aiming through a small window on the belly of the fuselage (a feature not incorporated on production models).

The XF4U-1 made its first flight from the Stratford plant on May 29, 1940, piloted by Lyman A. Bullard, Jr., and just four months later, between Stratford and Hartford, attained 404 mph in level flight, the first American-built fighter to do so. But despite its stunning speed, recent intelligence reports from the European air war indicated that, as designed, the new fighter would be deficient in combat. To survive the conditions reported, the XF4U-1 would need heavier gun armament, more armor protection, and self-sealing fuel tanks. The revisions re-

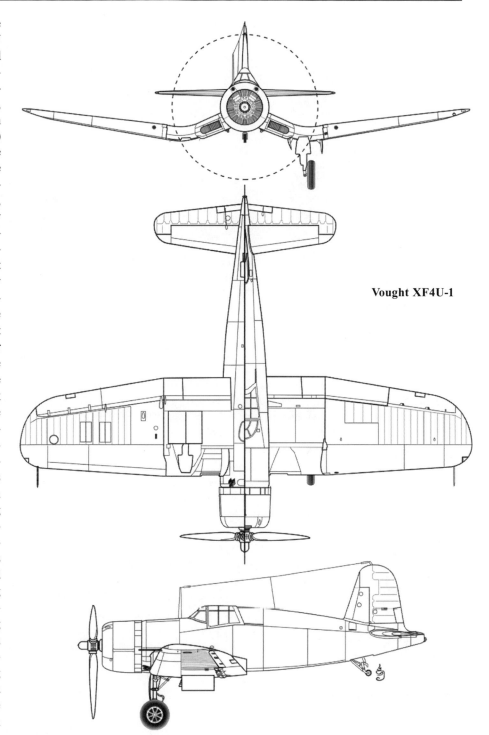

Vought XF4U-1

quired to correct the basic design were drastic: the fuel tanks would have to be moved from the wings to the fuselage to make room for four more .50 caliber guns, and in order to place the new fuselage tank over the center of gravity, it would be necessary to move the cockpit three feet aft. In June 1941, after approving the proposed changes, BuAer gave Vought a contract to produce 585 aircraft as the F4U-1. The first production model, dubbed the Corsair, was flown on June 25, 1942, followed by initial deliveries of aircraft for operational trials in late July.

The XF4U-1 as seen in 1940. It was the first American fighter to exceed 400 mph in level flight. Revisions to basic design due to new combat requirements were drastic.

But the Navy's quest for an unequaled fighter was not to be realized: in carrier trials conducted aboard *Sangaman* (CVE-26) during September 1942, the F4U-1 failed to pass deck qualifications. Restricted visibility from the aft-located cockpit during the approach, combined with poor handling characteristics at low airspeeds, caused the type to be rated unsuitable for further carrier operations. As a direct consequence, F4U-1s were issued to Marine land-based units, the first being VMF-124. After numerous improvements, Corsairs were finally cleared for carrier operations in mid–1944, however, as events transpired, F4U-1Ds did not actually embark aboard Navy carriers for combat duties until January 1945.

OBSERVATION AND SCOUT AIRCRAFT

Synopsis of Observation and Scout Aircraft Procurement

As with attack and fighter types, the real potential of observation and scout aircraft in Navy service was not realized until they had been adapted to operate from ships, starting in 1922 with the assignment of World War I–era Vought VE-7 floatplanes (see page 103) to battleships. At practically the same time, wheeled versions of the VE-7 were among the first aircraft to be used for experiments aboard the USS *Langley* (CV-1), the Navy's first carrier. When attempts to develop larger, three-place Martin MO and Naval Aircraft Factory NO/Martin M2O floatplanes for shipboard use in 1923 and 1924 proved unsuccessful, the Vought UO, basically an improved derivative of the

VE-7, became the next standard observation type. After problematic trials conducted from 1923 to 1926 with two small floatplanes, the Cox-Klemin XS and Martin MS, naval officials concluded that the idea of operating scout aircraft from submarines was not practical.

The observation role grew to include ship-to-shore utility duties as the first shipboard amphibians, Loening OLs, began entering service in 1925. Because of different operational requirements, ex–Army Airco DH-4s, which could carry bombs, were supplied to Marine observation units from 1921 to 1925. The Vought O2U, the first naval aircraft actually designed from the ground up for observation, began reaching service in 1927, with float-equipped variants assigned to battleships and cruisers and wheeled versions to carriers and land-based Marine units. From 1928, Marines began the process of replacing their outdated DH-4s with new two-place Curtiss F8Cs, assigning them new observation designations as the OC (F8C-1 and -3) and O2C (F8C-5).

In late the 1920s and early 1930s, as the fleet's need for more diverse types of aircraft became more apparent, BuAer began evolving observation and scout requirements that were tailored to more narrow operational conditions. The "light observation" requirement of 1929, ultimately leading to procurement of the Berliner-Joyce OJ for duty aboard light cruisers, represented an attempt to gain range without increasing catapult weight. BuAer took matters a step further in 1931 when it specified distinct versions of Vought's new O3U: a lighter "observation" variant for battleships and cruisers (O3U-1 and -3) and a more powerful and heavily armed "scout" for carriers and land-based Marine units (initially O3U-2 and -4 but later changed to SU-1, -2, and -3). The Navy revived the submarine scout concept in 1931 with the Loening SL, but abandoned the project again after two years of trials. From 1932 to 1934, with the aim of procuring a long-range, armed scout for carriers, trials were carried out with the Bellanca SE, Curtiss S2C (a navalized version of the Army's A-8), and Curtiss S3C (essentially an improved O2C-2), but none proved to be acceptable, and in any event, the armed-scout concept soon afterward became absorbed into an all-new "scout-bomber" requirement, which is discussed in more detail in the preceding section on Attack Aircraft.

Commencing in 1931, BuAer acquired several Pitcairn autogyros as the XOP to assess their suitability for the carrier and land-based observation role and in 1934, also tested the float-equipped Pennsylvania Aircraft Syndicate XOZ, but discontinued all autogiro experiments in 1936. The advent of hangars on new heavy cruisers kindled a fresh string of aircraft developments, the first being issued in 1931 as an "amphibious cruiser scout" requirement. However, evaluations of three boat-hulled amphibians during 1932 and 1933—Great Lakes SG, Loening S2L, and Sikorsky SS—failed to produce a satisfactory aircraft, prompting BuAer to initiate a second round of competition in 1934 that ultimately ended with the procurement of the Curtiss SOC as the fleet's standard cruiser floatplane. Thereafter, aircraft specialized for cruiser service were classified as "scout-observation" types or SO, whereas those destined for battleships became "observation-scout" or OS. The first new OS requirement appeared in 1936 with the goal of finding a modern replacement for obsolescent O3Us and to obtain additional floatplanes for the first new battleships planned since adoption of the Washington Naval Treaty in 1922 (i.e., BB-55 and -56). After evaluating the Naval Aircraft Factory XOSN, Stearman XOSS, and Vought XOS2U during 1938, BuAer selected Vought's candidate for quantity production, which, as the OS2U-1, was the first float-equipped monoplane to be accepted for fleet service.

But even before the first OS2U had flown, naval officials were already moving forward with plans to obtain a new type of floatplane for the heavy and light cruisers under construction (12 ships at the time), and in 1937, issued a detailed SO specification calling for a monoplane to be powered by an experimental, air-cooled V-12 engine (i.e., 500-hp Ranger XV-770). Development contracts were subsequently issued for two prototypes, the Curtiss XSO3C and Vought XSO2U, and flight trials between them began in early 1940. Curtiss received the production contract later that year, not because its XSO3C was a better aircraft, but due to the fact that Vought, faced with a large backlog of OS2U and F4U orders, simply lacked the plant capacity to mass-produce another type of aircraft. And as events turned out, persistent operational difficulties with production SO3C-1s caused the type to be declared unfit for shipboard service in mid–1942, with the consequence that the older biplane SOCs (together with license-built NAF SONs) remained in service aboard cruisers for most of the duration of World War II.

Vought VE-7 and -9—1919

TECHNICAL SPECIFICATIONS (VE-7H)

Type: Two-place landplane/floatplane trainer, observation, and fighter.
Manufacturer: Chance Vought Corp., Long Island City, New York; and Naval Aircraft Factory, Philadelphia, Pennsylvania.
Total produced : 140 (USN, USMC)
Powerplant: One 180-hp Wright-Hispano E-2 8-cylinder water-cooled inline engine driving a two-bladed fixed-pitch wooden propeller.
Armament (none VE-7, -7H, -9): one fixed forward-firing .303-cal. Vickers machine gun (VE-7S, SF) and one flexible .30-cal. Lewis machine gun in the rear cockpit (VE-7G,GF).
Performance: Max. speed 110 mph at s.l.; ceiling 14,800 ft.; range 250 mi.
Weights: 1,505 lbs. empty, 2,100 lbs. loaded.
Dimensions: Span 34 ft. 1 in., length 31 ft. 1 in., wing area 285 sq. ft.

Although listed here under observation, the VE-7 and -9 served in a variety of roles through most of the 1920s. A two-bay biplane of wooden construction, powered by a license-built 150-hp Hispano-Suiza engine (E-1), the VE-7 was initially eval-

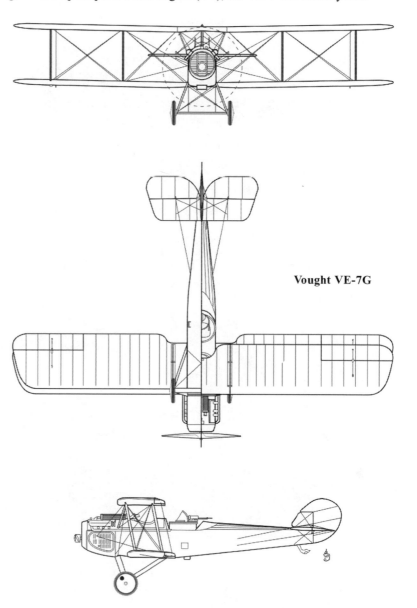

Vought VE-7G

uated during 1918 by the Army as an advanced trainer, then in 1919, the Navy ordered 20 standard VE-7s that entered service as landplane trainers. This transaction marked the beginning of a relationship with Vought—as a major naval aircraft contractor—that would continue for over 60 years. From 1919 to 1922, Vought delivered another 20 VE-7s and NAF completed a further 79 examples in four different versions. Twenty NAF VE-7G/GFs (F denoted addition of flotation gear) used for training and observation, emerged in 1920 with an uprated E-2 engine and a Lewis machine gun mounted on a scarf ring in the rear cockpit. The 50 NAF-built VE-7S/SF variants delivered in 1921 and 1922 were single-place fighters armed with a fixed Vickers machine gun and served with VF-2 and the Marine's First Aviation Group at Quantico. NAF also built nine float-equipped, unarmed VE-7Hs stressed for catapulting that operated as gun spotters aboard battleships. VE-7Hs could be distinguished by the larger tail fin needed to offset the side area of the float.

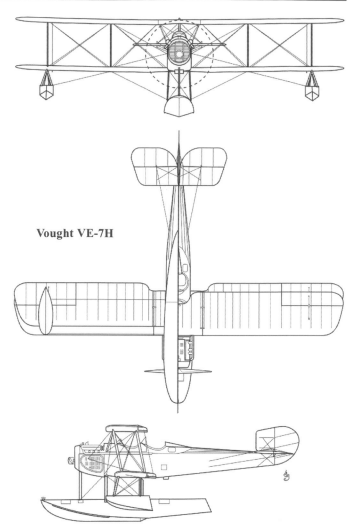

Vought VE-7H

The Standard version VE-7 seen in 1928, the last example of the type to be operated by VO-8M out of San Diego. It was replaced the same year by the new Curtiss F8C-1s (re-designated OC-1s).

The float-equipped VE-7H, also stressed for catapulting, became the first standard shipboard type. The aircraft depicted is one of nine VE-7Hs built by the Naval Aircraft Factory in 1922. Vought built 21 more in 1923.

After installation of an 180-hp Wright-Hispano engine and larger tailfin, one NAF-built VE-7 became the first VE-9, and 21 identical examples were subsequently built by Vought and accepted into service during 1922 and 1923. VE-9s typically carried no armament and could be rigged as either landplanes or floatplanes. Both VE-7s and VE-9s were phased out of active Navy service from 1925 to 1927, but one or two examples remained operational with the Marines until mid–1928.

Loening/Naval Aircraft Factory M-8 Series (LS)—1919

TECHNICAL SPECIFICATIONS (M-8-1)

Type: Two-place, land-based observation.
Manufacturer: Loening Aeronautical Engr. Co., New York, New York; Naval Aircraft Factory, Philadelphia, Pennsylvania.
Total produced : 43 (USN)
Powerplant: One 300-hp Wright-Hispano H-3 8-cylinder water-cooled inline engine driving a two-bladed fixed-pitch wooden propeller.
Armament: Two flexible .30-cal. Lewis machine guns in the rear cockpit.
Performance: Max. speed 125 mph at s.l.; ceiling 13,750 ft.; range 550 mi.

Weights: 1,623 lbs. empty, 2,742 lbs. loaded.
Dimensions: Span 32 ft. 9 in., length 24 ft. 2 in., wing area 229 sq. ft.

After organizing his own company in 1918, aeronautical engineer Grover C. Loening sold the War Department on the idea of developing a two-seat monoplane fighter that he claimed would deliver performance superior to that of the RFC's biplane Bristol F.2b Fighter. The first M-8, apparently flown sometime in late 1918, emerged with broad-chord wings attached to the upper fuselage edge, each braced by a pair of airfoil-shaped struts that added aerodynamic lift. It also introduced a tunnel-type radiator below the engine, which provided better streamlining than the more common flat-nosed types. Performance was good enough that Loening received a provisional War Department order for 5,000 M-8s, but as a result of the armistice in November 1918, the entire contract was terminated before any aircraft could be built. Then in June 1919, Loening obtained the first of many Navy contracts when six M-8-0s were ordered initially as two-seat fighters.

The first Navy M-8-0 was damaged beyond repair on its delivery flight in September 1919, however, the other five later arrived without mishap and were placed into service as observation types rather than fighters, and in 1920 and 1921, NAF built a further 36 to the same pattern as the M-8-1. In operational use, M-8s (compared to biplane observation types) were very unpopular with aircrews due to the restricted visibility over their wide wings, so that most were withdrawn after only two or three years of service. One M-8-1 fitted with a smaller set of wings participated as a Navy entry in the 1920 Pulitzer race. An additional M-8 airframe completed by Loening in 1921 as the LS-1 seaplane featured a five-foot increase in wingspan and an unusual Richardson pontoon system that could be rigged as a single float or split along the centerline to form twin floats. The LS-1 was not successful, but Loening managed to sell a further 14 M-8 types to the Army in 1921 and 1922 as the PW-2 and -2A.

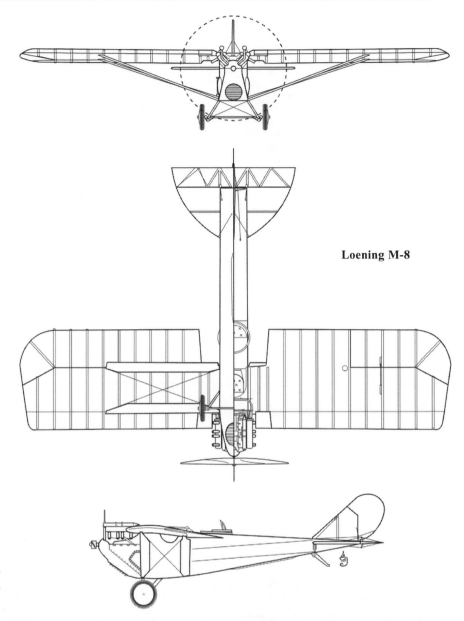

Loening M-8

One of 36 M-8-1s built by the Naval Aircraft Factory in 1920. High-mounted wings served to seriously restrict the downward visibility of the observer. The plane was withdrawn after only three years of service.

Martin K-IV—1921

TECHNICAL SPECIFICATIONS (K-IV)

Type: Single-place trainer submarine scout floatplane.

Manufacturer: James V. Martin Aeroplane Co.,
Elyra, Ohio.

Total produced : 3 (USN)

Powerplant: one 60-hp Lawrence L-4 3-cylinder
air-cooled radial engine driving a two-bladed
fixed-pitch wooden propeller.

Performance: Max. speed 82 mph at s.l.; ceiling
11,400 ft.; range 150 mi. (est.).

Weights: 646 lbs. empty, 940 lbs. loaded.

Dimensions: Span 24 ft. 2 in., length 17 ft., wing
area 100 sq. ft. (est.).

Also known as the "Kitten Floatplane,"
the K-IV was not a product of the well-known
Glenn L. Martin Co. but a design of the short-
lived James V. Martin Aeroplane Co. of
Elyra, Ohio. The K-IV appeared as an en-

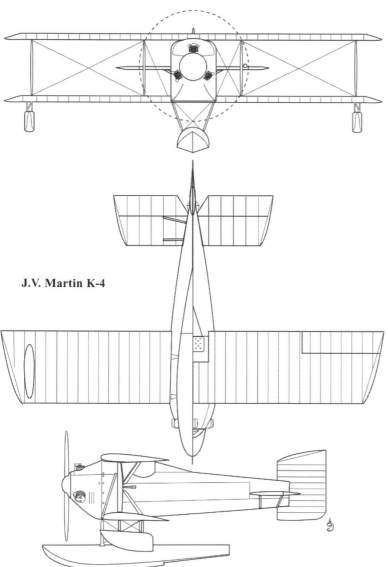

J.V. Martin K-4

Three of these diminutive J. V. Martin "Kitten Floatplanes" were tested in 1921 for the submarine scout role. Development was discontinued in favor of the Cox-Klemin XS and Martin MS.

larged floatplane development of Martin's smaller K-III
(15-foot span), which had been unsuccessfully offered to
the Army in 1918. Three K-IVs were procured by the Navy
Department in 1921 to be evaluated for the submarine
scout role alongside the Macchi M.16 and Heinkel-Caspar
U.1 (see Appendix 1). Development was dropped in favor
of the Cox-Clemin XS and Martin MS.

Aeromarine AS—1922

TECHNICAL SPECIFICATIONS (AS-2)

Type: Two-place observation floatplane.

Manufacturer: Aeromarine Plane and Motor Corp., Keyport,
New Jersey.

Total produced : 3 (USN)

Powerplant: One 300-hp Wright-Hispano E 8-cylinder water-
cooled inline engine driving a two-bladed fixed-pitch
wooden propeller.

Armament: One flexible .30-cal. Lewis machine gun in the rear
cockpit.

Performance: Max. speed 117 mph at s.l.; ceiling 19,300 ft.; range
500 mi.

Weights: 2,933 lbs. empty, 3,916 lbs. loaded.

Dimensions: Span 37 ft. 6 in., length 30 ft. 6 in., wing area 380
sq. ft.

Designed by Charles Willard and inspired by the layout of the German Hansa-Brandenburg twin-float
seaplane of 1917, the Navy Department contracted with
Aeromarine in 1921 to build three similar aircraft billed
as "fighting ship machines" under the designation AS-1.
The design was characterized by two bays of metal N-
type interplane struts and an underslung fin and rudder

that gave the gunner a unobstructed field of fire to the rear. After the first AS-1 appeared in 1922 with an under-mounted radiator, the next two examples were completed and delivered as AS-2s with front-mounted radiators. Though evaluated for the armed observation role, no operational details about the aircraft were recorded.

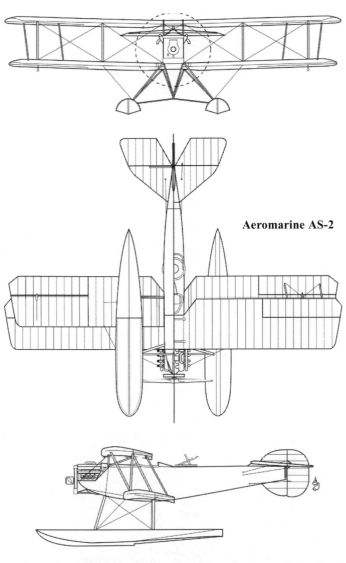

Aeromarine AS-2

Elias EM/EO—1922

TECHNICAL SPECIFICATIONS (EM-2)

Type: Two-place multi-purpose landplane or floatplane.
Manufacturer: G. Elias and Brother, Buffalo, New York.
Total produced : 7 (USN, USMC)
Powerplant: One 400-hp Liberty 12-cylinder water-cooled inline engine driving a two-bladed fixed-pitch wooden propeller.
Armament: One flexible .30-cal. Lewis machine gun in the rear cockpit.
Performance: Max. speed 111 mph at s.l.; ceiling 19,300 ft.; range 500 mi.
Weights: 2,933 lbs. empty, 3,916 lbs. loaded.
Dimensions: Span 39 ft. 8 in., length 28 ft. 6 in., wing area 382 sq. ft.

The EM stands as having been the first airplane designed solely to a Marine Corps specification. The requirement, originally issued in 1919, called for a multi-purpose expeditionary

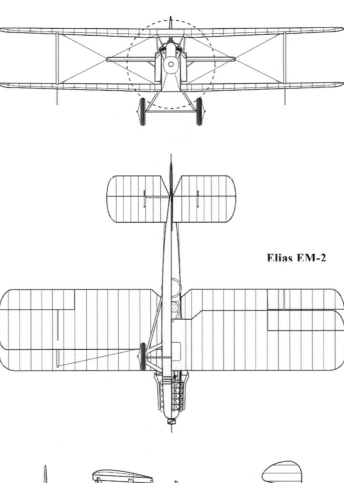

Elias EM-2

Left: **The Aeromarine AS was evaluated during 1921 and 1922 for the armed observation role. Fin and rudder were mounted ventrally to give the rear gunner an unobstructed field of fire. No production was undertaken.**

aircraft that would be readily convertible to wheels or floats. The EM-1, completed in 1922 with a 300-hp Wright-Hispano engine and unequal span wings, posted a top speed of only 90 mph and was deemed unacceptable. A second aircraft powered by a Liberty 12 engine and having equal span wings and a larger rudder was evaluated by the Marines later the same year as the EM-2. After showing a 21 mph increase in speed, five more EM-2s were ordered, but by the time they were delivered Marine units had decided instead to equip expeditionary units with less expensive DH-4Bs, and the five EM-2s went into to Navy service as observation types. One EM-2 converted to a center float configuration was subsequently re-designated EO-1. Elias also built several TA-1 trainers and one twin-engine NBS-3 bomber for the Army, but the company apparently ceased operations during the late 1920s.

This EM-2, pictured in 1922, was the first of five originally procured for the Marines but subsequently allocated to Navy observation units after the Marines decided to equip with less expensive DH-4Bs.

Vought UO/FU—1922

TECHNICAL SPECIFICATIONS
(UO-1 SEAPLANE [FU-1])

Type: Two-place observation [one-place fighter] landplane or floatplane.
Manufacturer: Chance Vought Corp., Long Island City, New York.
Total produced : 141 (USN, USCG)
Powerplant: One 200-hp Lawrence (later Wright J-3) [220-hp Wright J-5] 9-cylinder air-cooled radial engine driving a two-bladed fixed-pitch wooden [metal] propeller.
Armament: None [two fixed forward-firing .30-cal. machine guns].
Performance: Max. speed 124 mph at s.l. [147 mph at 13,000 ft.]; ceiling 18,000 [26,500] ft.; range 398 [410] mi.
Weights: 1,494 lbs. [2,074 lbs.] empty, 2,305 lbs. [2,774 lbs.] loaded.
Dimensions: Span 34 ft. 4 in., length 24 ft. 4 in. [28 ft. 4in.], wing area 290 [270] sq. ft.

One of the most widely used naval aircraft of the 1920s, the UO first appeared in 1922 as a direct development of Vought's VE-7. The type was originally to have been powered by a 250-hp Aeromarine U-873 water-cooled engine but a decision was made to switch to a Lawrence J-1 radial before the first example had flown. While similar in structure to the VE-7,

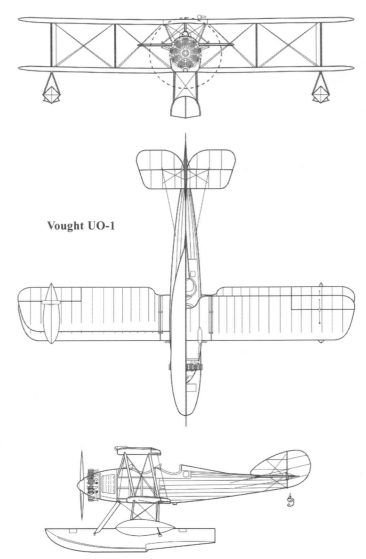

Vought UO-1

A UO-1 of VO-3 is seen in 1924 being hoisted aboard the recently commissioned light cruiser Richmond (CL-9). It became the standard battleship and cruiser floatplane until replaced by O2U-1s in 1927 and 1928.

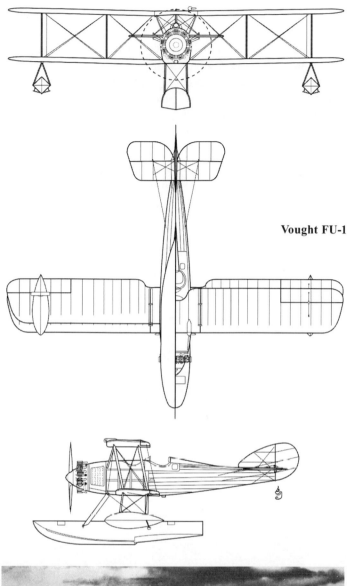

Vought FU-1

An armed, single-seat FU-1 of VF-2B while assigned to Battleship Division four in 1927. It was re-rigged with wheels and transferred to *Langley* the next year.

the UO-1 came with a new, rounded fuselage cross-section and re-shaped tail surface, plus cheek-type fuel tanks and redesigned cabane strut rigging that improved cockpit access and visibility. UO-1s were built and delivered under a series of contracts running from the early to mid–1920s and a majority, as floatplanes, attached to various battleship and cruiser units throughout the fleet. At least twelve, rigged as landplanes, were fitted with arresting gear and used for utility duties aboard all three of the Navy's carriers. The Navy began phasing out UO-1s from battleships and cruisers as new Vought O2Us arrived to replace them in 1927 and 1928, though some remained in service a few years longer at shore bases and with reserve squadrons. One UO-1 stripped down and fitted with the original Aeromarine engine by NAF in 1922 was, as the UO-2, entered in the Curtiss Marine Trophy race the same year but was damaged at the start of the race.

Twenty aircraft ordered from Vought in mid–1926 as UO-3 single-seaters were intended to meet an interim BuAer requirement for floatplane fighters aboard battleships. The UO-3 differed in having a 220-hp Wright J-5 engine with a Rootes integral supercharger, narrower-chord wings with a thicker N-9 airfoil and rounded tips, a four-foot fuselage extension aft of the cockpit, two fixed machine guns, and a smaller vertical fin. When initially delivered in January 1927 under the new designation FU-1, it became the first type of naval aircraft to achieve its maximum speed above sea level. Float-equipped FU-1s were deployed in one or two-plane detachments aboard battleships in 1927 and 1928; then, rigged with wheels and arresting gear, assigned to VF-2B aboard *Langley,* where they served until being replaced by Boeing F3Bs during 1929. Some FU-1s were converted to a two-seat configuration as FU-2s and served aboard all three carriers as utility aircraft until 1932. In 1926, two UOs built with FU-1 wings and J-5 engines were delivered to the Coast Guard as the UO-4 and remained in active service until 1935.

Martin MO—1923

TECHNICAL SPECIFICATIONS (MO-1 SEAPLANE VERSION)

Type: Three-place observation landplane or floatplane.
Manufacturer: Glenn L. Martin Co., Cleveland, Ohio.
Total produced : 36 (USN)
Powerplant: One 435-hp Curtiss D 12-cylinder water-cooled inline engine driving a two-bladed fixed-pitch wooden propeller.
Armament: One flexible .30-cal. Lewis machine gun in the rear cockpit.
Performance: Max. speed 102 mph at s.l.; ceiling 10,000 ft.; range 467 mi.
Weights: 3,440 lbs. empty, 4,945 lbs. loaded.
Dimensions: Span 53 ft. 1 in., length 38 ft. 2 in., wing area 488 sq. ft.

The MO originated in response to a BuAer requirement issued in 1922 for a single-engine, three-place observation type, stressed for catapulting, that would be convertible to wheels or floats. Martin, proposing a monoplane with an all-metal, fabric-covered structure that had been designed by a former Junkers

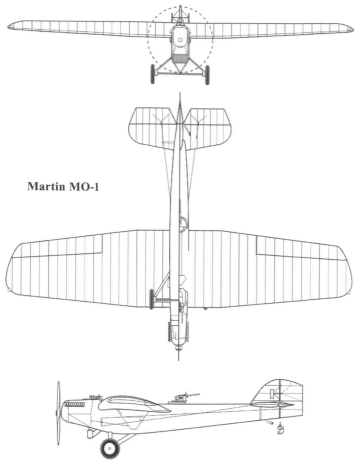

Martin MO-1

Float-equipped MO-1s during their brief tenure aboard *Mississippi* (BB-41) in late 1924. Trials revealed that the type, when loaded, was seriously underpowered in catapult operations.

engineer, received a contract to build 36 aircraft as the MO-1. The first example, rigged as a landplane, was apparently flown sometime in 1923, and the next six, with twin floats, were delivered to VO-6 at Hampton Roads in early 1924 for service evaluations. Once testing revealed that the type was too underpowered for ship-borne catapult operations, they were replaced by smaller and lighter Vought VE-7Hs and UO-1s. MO-1s, rigged as landplanes apparently, were afterward used at various shore stations for utility duties until 1926.

Cox-Klemin XS and Martin MS—1923

TECHNICAL SPECIFICATIONS (XS-1)

Type: One-place submarine scout floatplane.
Manufacturer: Cox-Klemin Aircraft Corp., College Point, New York; Glenn L. Martin Co., Cleveland, Ohio.
Total produced : 12 (USN, USMC)

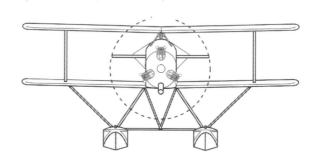

Cox-Klemin XS-1

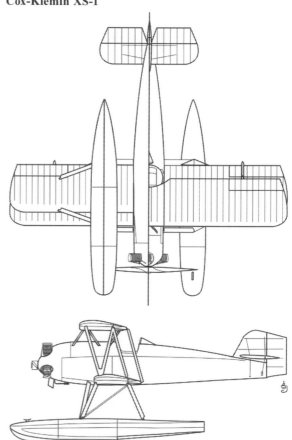

Powerplant: One 60-hp Lawrence 3-cylinder air-cooled radial engine driving a two-bladed fixed-pitch wooden propeller.
Armament: None.
Performance: Max. speed 103 mph at s.l.; ceiling 11,300 ft.; range (not reported).
Weights: Empty (not reported), 1,030 lbs. loaded.
Dimensions: Span 18 ft. 0 in., length 18 ft. 2 in., wing area 108 sq. ft.

Following demonstrations of the tiny Sperry M-1 Messenger biplane before the Army, officials at BuAer conceived the idea of designing a similarly small aircraft to be used as a scout that could be dismantled and stored in a waterproof container aboard submarines. The design materialized as a twin-float biplane using struts in place of rigging wires to facilitate quick assembly and disassembly. Contracts were awarded to Cox-Klemin to build six aircraft of wooden construction as the XS-1, and to Martin for six more with fabric-covered, aluminum airframes and metal floats as the MS-1. All 12 of the submarine scouts were delivered to the Navy for initial trials during 1923 and operational testing and evaluations with submarines continued into late 1926, after which the program was terminated and the aircraft scrapped. In 1923, when refitted with an 84-hp Kinner 5-cylinder radial, one XS-1 was tested as the XS-2. The Marines operated one XS-1 in San Diego in 1926 and 1927. The submarine scout program was reactivated in 1931 with the Loening XSL-1, reported below.

One of six MS-1s delivered for trials in 1923. MS-1 and XS-1 were identical except for type of airframe materials. Exercises with submarine S-1 continued until late 1926, when further testing was deemed impractical.

Naval Aircraft Factory NO and Martin M2O—1923

TECHNICAL SPECIFICATIONS (NO-1)

Type: Three-place observation landplane or floatplane.
Manufacturer: Naval Aircraft Factory, Philadelphia, Pennsylvania; Glenn L. Martin Co., Cleveland, Ohio.
Total produced : 6 (USN)
Powerplant: One 350-hp Curtiss D 12-cylinder water-cooled inline engine driving a two-bladed fixed-pitch wooden propeller.
Armament: One flexible .30-cal. Lewis machine gun in the rear cockpit.

Performance: Max. speed 103 mph at s.l.; ceiling 11,200 ft.; range 490 mi.
Weights: 3,337 lbs. empty, 4,842 lbs. loaded.
Dimensions: Span 43 ft. 6 in., length 31 ft. 10 in., wing area 462 sq. ft.

A more conservative approach to the three-place observation requirement than the preceding Martin MO-1, the NO arose

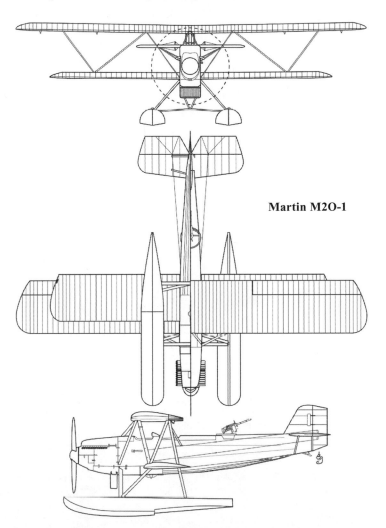

Martin M2O-1

The NAF NO-1 in pictured in 1923 or 1924. M2O and NO were both powered by Curtiss D-12 engines and identical except for small details. Note W-types struts in place of usual rigging wires.

from a BuAer design in which construction contracts were assigned to both NAF and Martin during 1923 for three aircraft each. While the identity of the designer is not recorded anywhere, the NO/M2O incorporated a structural design using W-type and N-type struts very similar to those of the TS fighter designed by Rex Beisel in 1921. Martin's M2O-1 was the first to fly, sometime in 1923, and all of six ordered had been delivered before the end of 1924. The chief differences between the NAF and Martin versions appear to have been a spinner, individual exhaust stacks, and a slightly taller fin and rudder appearing on the M2O-1. One NAF aircraft retrofitted with a 440-hp Packard 1A-1500 engine was tested as the NO-2, but no performance details were reported. Not placed in quantity production, the type served at various shore detachments until withdrawn in 1926 and 1927.

Loening OL, HL—1923

TECHNICAL SPECIFICATIONS (OL-2 [OL-9])

Type: Three-place military observation and utility amphibian.

Manufacturer: Loening Aeronautical Engineering Co., New York, New York

Total produced: 160 (USN, USMC, USCG)

Powerplant: one 400-hp Liberty 12-cylinder water-cooled engine driving a four-bladed wooden fixed-pitch propeller [one 450-hp Pratt & Whitney R-1340-4 *Wasp* 9-cylinder air-cooled radial engine driving a three-bladed ground-adjustable propeller].

Armament: one flexible .30-caliber Lewis machine gun in the rear cockpit, [one fixed .30-caliber machine in the upper wing; and four 114-lb. bombs on wing racks].

Performance: max. speed 121 mph [122 mph]; ceiling 12,100 ft. [14,300 ft.]; range 405 mi. [625 mi.].

Weights: 3,540 lbs. [3,469 lbs.] empty, 5,010 lbs. [5,404] loaded.

Dimensions: span 45 ft. 0 in., length 33 ft. 10 in. [34 ft. 19 in.], wing area 500 sq. ft. [502 sq. ft].

When the first examples appeared in 1923, Grover C. Loening's "shoehorn" series of observation and utility planes were really flying boat–floatplane hybrids in which the upper fuselage faired into a main float that extended all the way aft to support the tail group. This novel configuration, similar in many respects to that of his civil Flying Yacht of 1921, was conceived by Loening out of an desire to offer an amphibian whose performance would match a landplane having an engine of similar horsepower. The manually operated

landing gear used a system of sprockets and chains to retract into the main float. The original prototype was delivered to the Army in 1923 as the XCOA-1 (the C was later dropped) and nine production models followed in 1924. A Navy prototype powered by a 440-hp Packard engine and having a third cockpit was delivered in 1925 as the XOL-1. The same year, the Navy acquired five Liberty-powered OA-1s, placing them in service as OL-2s to be used in the 1925 Arctic Expedition, and four essentially identical aircraft were purchased from Loening as OL-3s. The first of six OL-4s, which differed in having a reshaped and balanced rudder, revised cowling, and three-bladed metal pro-

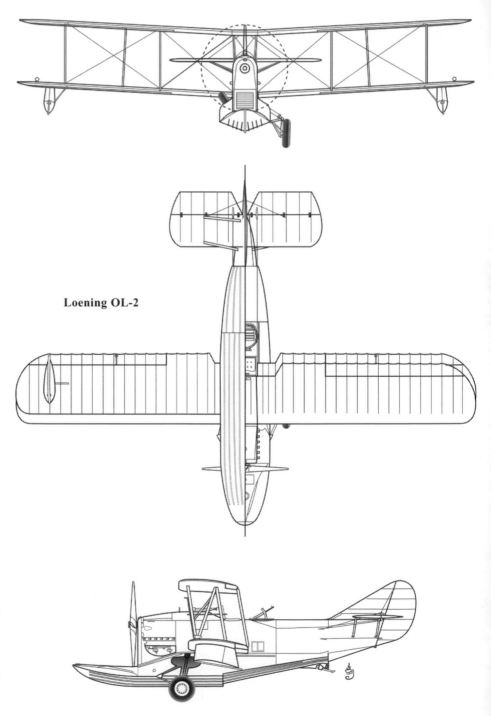

Loening OL-2

peller was delivered in early 1926. These were followed by three very similar OL-5s, which bore the distinction of being the first aircraft ordered specifically for use by the Coast Guard.

Flown in late 1926, the OL-6 came with a 475-hp Packard V-12 engine and a third cockpit, and twenty-six production examples were delivered from early to mid–1927. During the same timeframe, twenty-four very similar OA-1As and Bs were also produced for the Army, followed by ten OA-1Cs with reshaped tails. As the wingspan of the OLs was too large to enable them fit onto the deck elevators of the Navy's new aircraft carriers, one OL-6 modified in mid–1927 with a smaller wing and a thicker airfoil section was tested in mid–1927 as the XOL-7, but its performance proved to be disappointing and no production resulted. In late 1927, after BuAer specified that all future naval aircraft would be equipped with air-cooled engines, Loening modified the Last OL-6 to accept installation of an R-1340 *Wasp* radial engine and delivered it as the XOL-8. After trials, twenty production models were delivered during 1928 as the OL-8, followed in 1929 by twenty nearly identical OL-8As. Eight OA-2s, similar to OL-8As except for 480-hp Wright V-1640 V-12 water-cooled engines, were delivered to the Army the same year.

The final version, the OL-9, which differed from the OL-8

in having a fixed .30-caliber machine in the upper wing and underwing racks for four 114-lb. bombs, was produced during 1931 and 1932 after Loening had been acquired by Keystone, and the last of 26 built accepted by the Navy in March 1932. Two airframes similar to the OL-8, completed as ambulance

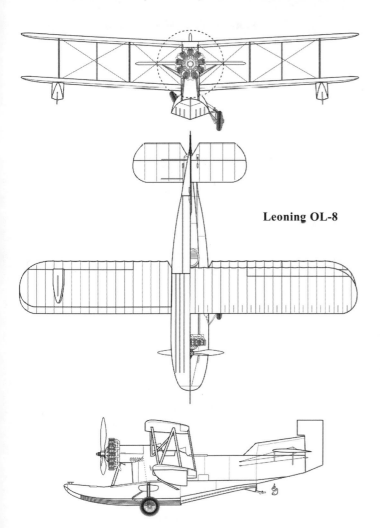

Leoning OL-8

Top: An OL-2, one of five Army OA-1s transferred to the Navy in 1925 to be used in the Arctic Expedition. The novel "shoehorn" configuration and gear-fold mechanism made OLs one of the first practical military amphibians. *Middle:* Introduced in 1926, the OL-6 featured a third cockpit and a 475-hp Packard engine driving a three-bladed propeller. Most were assigned to battleships for utility and observation duties. *Bottom:* All OL-9s were built between 1931 and 1932 after Loening had been acquired by Keystone. This aircraft is depicted in its later career serving in the Naval Reserve at NRAB Oakland, California, in 1937.

planes with a cabin occupying the space behind the pilot's cockpit, were delivered to the Navy in 1929 as XHL-1s, with one assigned to the Marines. As newer Grumman JF Ducks began arriving during the mid–1930s, OL-8s and 9s were phased out of active service, with the final OL-9 being withdrawn by the end of 1937.

Douglas OD—1926

TECHNICAL SPECIFICATIONS (OD-1)

Type: Two-place observation landplane.
Manufacturer: Douglas Aircraft Co., Santa Monica, California.
Total produced : 2 (USMC)
Powerplant: One 439-hp Liberty V-1650-1 12-cylinder water-cooled inline engine driving a two-bladed fixed-pitch wooden propeller.
Armament: One flexible .30-cal. Lewis machine gun in the rear cockpit.
Performance: Max. speed 126 mph at s.l.; ceiling 12,275 ft.; range 606 mi.
Weights: 2,941 lbs. empty, 4,630 lbs. loaded.
Dimensions: Span 39 ft. 8 in., length 29 ft. 6 in., wing area 411 sq. ft.

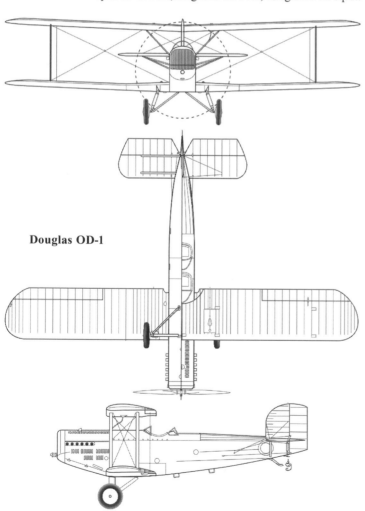

Douglas OD-1

Two OD-1s were procured for the Marines in 1926 and served alongside the DH-4Bs and O2B-1 of VO-8M until replaced by OC-2s in 1929. The plane was similar to the Army's O-2 and was used briefly as utility hacks.

As the O-2, a single-bay biplane of mixed construction that utilized a surplus Liberty powerplant, this aircraft became the Army's standard observation type during the mid– and late 1920s. In 1926, two O-2Cs, which differed from earlier versions in having a nose-mounted radiator and split-axle landing gear, were delivered to the Marine West Coast Expeditionary Force in San Diego and taken into service as the OD-1. Both examples operated with VO-8M until being replaced by Curtiss OC-2s (F8C-3s) in early 1930, and were used for utility duties until withdrawn from service altogether in 1931.

Vought O2U—1926

TECHNICAL SPECIFICATIONS (O2U-1 SEAPLANE)

Type: Two-place observation landplane or floatplane.
Manufacturer: Chance Vought Corp., Long Island City, New York.
Total produced : 291 (USN, USMC, USCG)
Powerplant: One 450-hp Pratt & Whitney R-1340-88 *Wasp* 9-cylinder air-cooled radial engine driving a two-bladed ground-adjustable Hamilton-Standard metal propeller.
Armament: One fixed forward-firing .30-cal. machine gun and one flexible .30-caliber machine gun in the rear cockpit.
Performance: Max. speed 127 mph at s.l.; ceiling 18,700 ft.; range 571 mi.
Weights: 2,600 lbs. empty, 3,893 lbs. loaded.
Dimensions: Span 34 ft. 6 in., length 28 ft. 7 in., wing area 320 sq. ft.

The first of the "Corsair" series, the O2U represented a serious effort by the Navy to upgrade its observation fleet with a newer aircraft that incorporated recent structural and aerodynamic improvements. After issuing requirements, BuAer awarded Vought a contract in mid–1926 to design and build two aircraft for evaluation as the O2U-1. In line with recent BuAer policy, the new type was developed around Pratt & Whitney's new 450-hp R-1340 *Wasp* engine, and though no arresting gear had been specified, overall dimensions were small enough to enable it to fit onto the deck elevators of the new carriers. The first prototype, flown on November 2, 1926, featured a spinner and straight-axle landing gear, but the second prototype, with no spinner and split-axle gear, formed the basis for 130 O2U-1 production models ordered in early 1927.

As deliveries proceeded, O2U-1s became the fleet's standard floatplane aboard battleships, serving as detachments of VO-3B, VO-4B, and VO-5B, and a small number, rigged as landplanes and fitted with arresting gear, served with VS-1B aboard *Langley*. Ten O2U-1 landplanes also were assigned to Marine units, six to VO-7M in Nicaragua and four to VO-9M in Haiti. Thirty-seven O2U-2s completed in 1928 with an 18-inch increase in upper wingspan and factory-installed arresting gear served exclusively in VS units aboard the Navy's three carriers. The fleet's growing need for floatplanes generated new orders for 80 O2U-3s and 42 O2U-4s (minor differences in equipment) delivered in 1929 and 1930, which both featured revised tail surfaces and the larger upper wing of the O2U-2. The

The Vought O2U was the first aircraft designed from the ground up as a ship-based floatplane. As deliveries proceeded during 1927, O2U-1s became standard throughout the fleet.

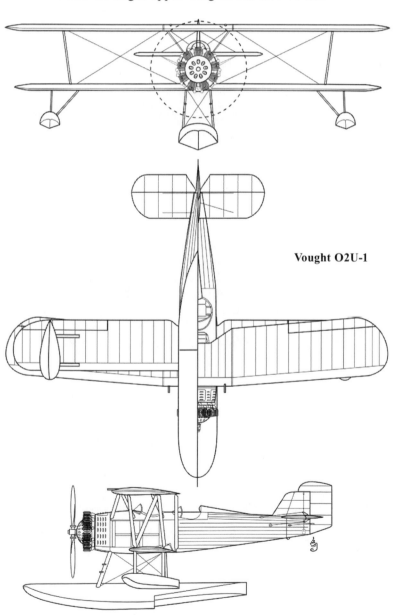

Vought O2U-1

phase-out of O2U floatplanes with newer types began as early as 1931, but many continued in various utility roles until the last examples were withdrawn from Navy service during 1937. Nine ex–Navy O2U-2s allocated to the Coast Guard in 1934 and 1935 served longer, the last not being withdrawn until 1941.

Curtiss OC/O2C—1928 see Curtiss F8C under FIGHTER AIRCRAFT

Viking OO—1930

TECHNICAL SPECIFICATIONS (OO-1)

Type: Four-place general purpose flying boat.
Manufacturer: Viking Flying Boat Co. (subsidiary of Stearman-Varney, Inc.), New Haven, Connecticut.
Total produced: 5 (USCG)
Powerplant: One 250-hp Wright R-760 *Whirlwind* 9-cylinder air-cooled radial engine driving a two-bladed, fixed-pitch wooden propeller.
Performance: Max. speed 104 mph, cruise 88 mph; ceiling 15,300 ft.; range 390 mi.
Weights: 4,200 lbs. empty, 5,900 lbs. loaded.
Dimensions: Span 42 ft. 4 in., length 29 ft. 4 in., wing area 250 sq. ft.

In 1930, after importing three 17HT-4 flying boats manufactured in France by Schreck Hydroavions FBA, Viking completed and certified a license-built, Wright J-6-powered U.S. version as the model V-2. Though efforts to market V-2s in the U.S. civil market were generally unsuccessful, the company did sell one of its Schreck 17HT-4s to the Coast Guard in 1931. While a comparatively outdated biplane design, the small wooden-hulled and framed aircraft nevertheless exhibited good open-sea handling qualities needed in Coast Guard operations. After the 17HT-4 was accidentally destroyed in a fire in 1934, the Coast Guard entered into a contract with Viking to license-build five examples under the new designation OO-1, and all were delivered

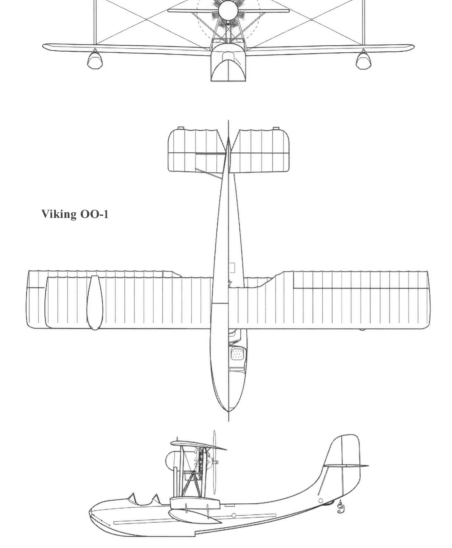

Viking OO-1

The second OO-1 (V152), but the first to be completed by Viking, as delivered to the Coast Guard in 1936. An identical French-built Schreck 17HT-4 (V107) had been destroyed in 1934. This type remained in active service until 1941.

between October and December 1936. Once in service, the OO-1s operated from stations at Biloxi, Mississippi; Cape May, New Jersey; Charleston, South Carolina; and Miami and St. Petersburg, Florida. Their active career was relatively brief, however, the last example being retired in April 1941.

Vought O3U/SU (O4U-2, O5U, and OSU)—1930

TECHNICAL SPECIFICATIONS (O3U-3 [SU-4])

Type: Two-place observation floatplane and carrier and landplane scout.

Manufacturer: Chance Vought Division of United Aircraft, Inc., East Hartford, Connecticut.

Total produced: 328 (USN, USMC)

Powerplant: one 550-hp Pratt & Whitney R-1340-12 *Wasp* [600-hp R-1690-42 *Hornet*] 9-cylinder air-cooled radial engine driving a two-bladed, fixed-pitch [variable-pitch] metal propeller.

Armament: One fixed forward-firing .30-cal. machine gun and two flexible .30-caliber machine guns in the rear cockpit

Performance: max. speed 156 mph [168 mph] at s.l.; ceiling 16,600 ft. [18,600 ft.]; range 650 mi. [680 mi.].

Weights: 2,938 lbs. [3,312 lbs.] empty, 4,451 lbs. [4,765 lbs.] loaded.

Dimensions: span 36 ft. 0 in., length 27 ft. 3 in. [27 ft. 11 in.], wing area 337 sq. ft.

The O3U-1, ordered by BuAer in January 1930 and tested later the same year, was essentially an O2U-4 airframe incorporating several degrees of sweepback and dihedral to the lower wing. After completion of official trials, 87 production O3U-1s were delivered to the fleet from mid–1930 to mid–1931, most replacing older O2Us in battleship divisions and carrier utility units. In May 1931, one O3U-1 was used as a testbed for Grumman's new amphibious float and 15 of the floats were later procured.

Commencing in early 1931, BuAer issued a new requirement directing Vought to split future O3U production between two types: in addition to *Wasp*-powered floatplanes, it called for a heavier carrier and land-based version to be powered by a 600-hp *Hornet* engine encased in a ring cowling. The first *Hornet*-powered variants, 29 O3U-2s delivered from late 1931 to early 1932, were placed in service with VS-1B on *Langley* and VS-2B on *Lexington* and Marine squadrons VS-14M and VS-15M then stationed aboard *Lexington* and *Saratoga*. In 1932 and 1933 Vought produced a further 63 *Hornet*-powered O3U-4s (differing from -2s in small details), which entered service with VS-1B on *Langley*, VF-2B, VF-5B, VS-3B, and VS-15M on *Lexington*, VF-1B, VF-6B, VS-2B, and VS-14M

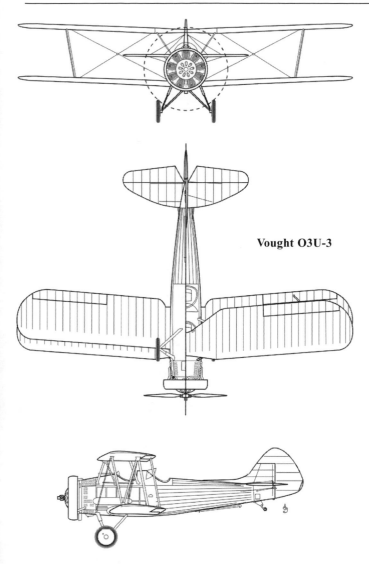

Vought O3U-3

on *Saratoga*, VO-8M in San Diego, and VO-9M in Haiti. When BuAer added a new scout designation in 1933, O3U-2s became SU-1s, 44 O3U-4s became SU-2s, and 20 camera-equipped O3U-4s became SU-3s.

From mid–1932 to mid–1934, Vought manufactured 76 *Wasp*-powered O3U-3 floatplanes featuring a new, rounded vertical tail shape and drag rings, which replaced older aircraft in battleship and cruiser divisions, and also delivered 20 similar *Hornet*-powered SU-4s that all entered service with VS-1B aboard *Langley*. One O3U-4/SU-2 became the sole XO3U-5 prototype when modified in mid–1932 to test installation of an R-1535 *Twin Wasp Junior* engine. The final production variant, the *Wasp*-powered O3U-6, appeared in early 1935 with an NACA-type cowling and a partial canopy, and 32 were delivered to the Marines during 1935, being equally split between VO-7M and VO-8M.

In addition to production models, several modified O3U airframes were tested under different designations: the XO4U-2, flown in June 1932 (not to be confused with the XO4U-1 reported below), featured the rounded fin and rudder of the O3U-3, an all-metal wing structure, plus a cowled R-1535 *Twin*

Top: **A rare picture of an O3U-1 fitted with a Grumman B-type amphibious float, probably in 1933. The O3U-1 combined improvements of the O2U-4 with sweepback to the upper wing. This replaced older O2Us in the fleet.** *Middle:* **Featuring revised tail group and drag ring, 76 O3U-3s joined the fleet between 1932 and 1934. This picture shows the no. 3 plane at the Naval Academy in 1940. Thirty-five were still on inventory as of December 1941.** *Bottom:* **Hornet-powered SU-2s (initially designated O3U-2s) began equipping carrier units and Marine land-based units in late 1931. This SU-2 was one of six assigned to VX-4D5 at NAS Anacostia in 1937.**

Wasp Junior engine; the XO5U-1, tested during 1934 and 1935, came with folding wings to be evaluated as a cruiser scout in competition with the Curtiss XO3C-1 (later SOC) and Douglas XO2D-1; and the XOSU-1, flown in October 1936, was an

O3U-3 modified to test an experimental system of upper and lower wing flaps. Although the Navy and the Marines began retiring O3Us and SUs from frontline duties during the late 1930s, some 141 of the type were still being employed in a of variety training, utility, and reserve roles as of December 1941.

The XO5U-1 seen in its original configuration with amphibious float during 1934 VSO trials. It featured folding wings for stowage in cruiser hangars. Curtiss won the competition with the XO3C-1 (produced as the SOC-1).

Keystone OK—1931

TECHNICAL SPECIFICATIONS (XOK-1 FLOATPLANE)

Type: Two-place lightweight observation floatplane.

Manufacturer: Keystone Aircraft, Corp. (a subsidiary of Curtiss-Wright), Bristol, Pennsylvania.

Total produced: 1 (USN)

Powerplant: One 400-hp Wright R-975C *Whirlwind* 9-cylinder air-cooled radial engine driving a two-bladed, fixed-pitch metal propeller.

Armament: One fixed forward-firing .30-cal. machine gun and one flexible .30-caliber machine gun in the rear cockpit

Performance: Max. speed 139 mph at s.l.; ceiling 19,900 ft.; range 330 mi. (est.).

Weights: 2,219 lbs. empty, 3,395 lbs. loaded.

Dimensions: Span 34 ft. 8 in., length 29 ft. 10 in., wing area 293 sq. ft.

The origins of the OK stemmed from a 1929 BuAer requirement calling for a "lightweight" observation floatplane destined for service aboard *Omaha* class light cruisers refitted with catapults. BuAer Design No. 86 specified a single-bay biplane, powered by a 400-hp Pratt & Whitney or Wright radial engine, readily convertible to wheels or floats, and light enough (less than 4,000 lbs. loaded) to operate from the CL-type catapult. On June 28, 1929, BuAer ordered single prototypes from both Keystone and Berliner-Joyce as the XOK-1 and XOJ-1, respectively. While these two aircraft were under construction, BuAer authorized Vought to built a third lightweight candidate as the XO4U-1.

Keystone's XOK-1 prototype, appearing with an all-metal, semi-monocoque fuselage and tail group and an engine enclosed by a drag ring, made its first flight on January 5, 1931.

Initial factory testing in a wheeled configuration resulted in the enlargement of the tail surfaces and replacement of the drag ring with an NACA-type cowling. On April 15, 1931, during a demonstration before naval officials, the XOK-1 broke up in flight after the cowling detached itself and smashed into the wings and tailplane. The test pilot managed to get out and para-

Built to a 1929 "lightweight" observation requirement for duty aboard light cruisers, the XOK-1 competed against similar Berliner-Joyce and Vought prototypes at NAS Anacostia in 1931.

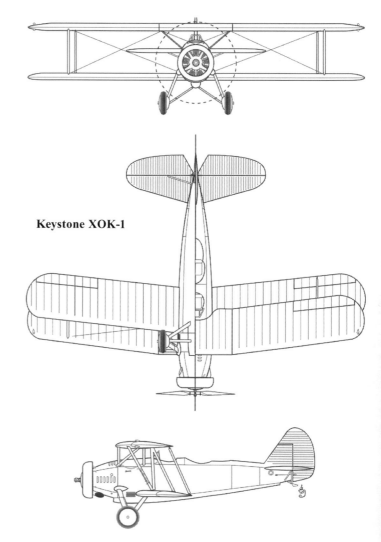

Keystone XOK-1

chute to safety. With the Berliner-Joyce and Vought prototypes nearly ready for trials, BuAer elected to discontinue further development of the XOK-1.

Berliner-Joyce OJ—1931

TECHNICAL SPECIFICATIONS (OJ-2 FLOATPLANE)

Type: Two-place lightweight observation floatplane.
Manufacturer: Berliner-Joyce Co., Baltimore, Maryland.
Total produced: 40 (USN, USMC)
Powerplant: One 400-hp Pratt & Whitney R-985-88 *Wasp Junior* 9-cylinder air-cooled radial engine driving a two-bladed, fixed-pitch metal propeller.
Armament: One fixed forward-firing .30-cal. machine gun and one flexible .30-caliber machine gun in the rear cockpit
Performance: Max. speed 149 mph at s.l.; ceiling 13,500 ft.; range 679 mi.
Weights: 2,520 lbs. empty, 3,851 lbs. loaded.
Dimensions: span 33 ft. 8 in., length 29 ft. 1 in., wing area 284 sq. ft.

One of the more successful designs of the short-lived Berliner-Joyce Co., BuAer ordered the XOJ-1 on June 28, 1929, to fulfill the same "lightweight" observation floatplane requirement as the rival Keystone XOK-1 and Vought XO4U-1. While

built to BuAer Design No. 86 like the XOK-1, the XOJ-1 differed in having a fabric-covered, metal-framed fuselage and tailplane. After being tested at NAS Anacostia in May 1931 (date of first flight not known), the XOJ-1 was returned to the factory for installation of a full-span "Zap" flap system on the upper and lower wings which was designed to provide more lift with less specific wing area. Following new trials conducted in 1932, BuAer deemed the flap system to be unsatisfactory, but awarded Berliner-Joyce a contract to produce 39 production aircraft lacking the flap system as the OJ-2.

As OJ-2s reached the fleet during 1933, they began serving in two-plane detachments of VS-5B and VS-6B aboard the ten *Omaha* class light cruisers that had been retrofitted with catapults. One OJ-2 modified in early 1934 with an NACA-type cowling and canopy enclosure was redelivered to NAS Anacostia for trials as the XOJ-3, but after a crash, was rebuilt and returned to service as an OJ-2. The active service life of OJ-2s was brief, and the type had been completely replaced by newer Curtiss SOC-1s by mid–1936. After that, 35 OJ-2s continued to operate with various Navy and Marine reserve units as trainers until the final examples were scrapped in 1941.

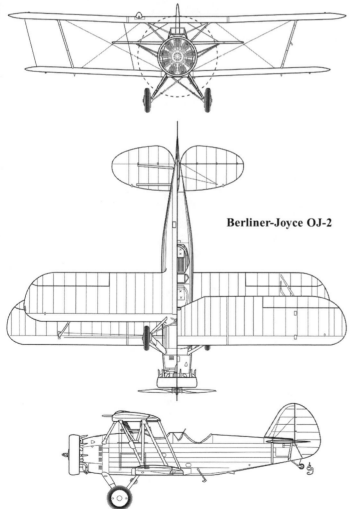

Berliner-Joyce OJ-2

Top: **One of 39 OJ-2s delivered in 1933. They served in two-plane detachments aboard *Omaha* class light cruisers until replaced by Curtiss SOC-1s during 1935 and 1936. *Bottom:* After being replaced aboard light cruisers, most OJ-2s were converted to wheels and transferred to reserve units. Final examples withdrawn in 1941.**

Vought O4U—1931

TECHNICAL SPECIFICATIONS
(XO4U-1 RIGGED WITH WHEELS)

Type: Two-place lightweight observation floatplane.

Manufacturer: Chance Vought Division of United Aircraft, Inc., East Hartford, Connecticut.

Total produced: 1 (USN)

Powerplant: One 500-hp Pratt & Whitney R-1340D *Wasp* 9-cylinder air-cooled radial engine driving a two-bladed, fixed-pitch metal propeller.

Armament: One fixed forward-firing .30-cal. machine gun and one flexible .30-caliber machine gun in the rear cockpit.

Performance: Max. speed 143 at s.l.; ceiling 21,200 ft.; range 539 mi.

Weights: 2,178 lbs. empty, 3,696 lbs. loaded.

Dimensions: Span 37 ft., length 27 ft. 9 in., wing area 335 sq. ft.

The XO4U-1 seen at Vought's plant after its first flight in February 1931. Note deep fuselage and shoulder-mounted upper wing. The prototype crashed soon after this picture and development was discontinued.

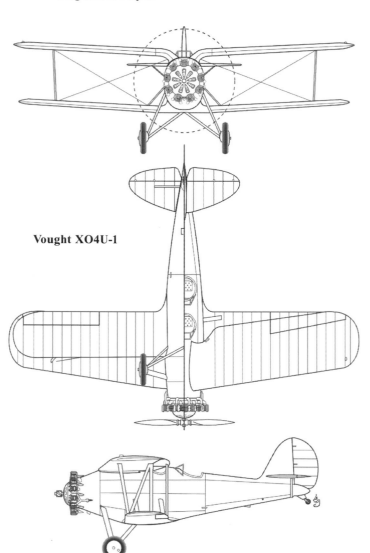

Vought XO4U-1

Ordered in May 1930 as the third type of "lightweight" observation to be considered as a candidate along with the Keystone XOK-1 and Berliner-Joyce XOJ-1, the Vought XO4U-1 was completed to a somewhat different specification. The design was characterized by a deep, metal-clad fuselage, a swept upper wing mated to the top of the fuselage, and a rounded tailplane. When the aircraft crashed right after its maiden flight on February 28, 1931, BuAer discontinued development. The XO4U-2 (see above), though flown in June 1932 under the same Bureau Number, was actually an O3U-3 airframe fitted with an R-1535 *Twin Wasp Junior* engine.

Loening (Keystone) SL—1931

TECHNICAL SPECIFICATIONS (XSL-1)

Type: One-place submarine scout.

Manufacturer: Loening Aeronautical Div. of Keystone Aircraft Corp. (a subsidiary of Curtiss-Wright), East River, New York.

Total produced: 1 (USN)

Powerplant: One 110-hp Warner *Scarab* 7-cylinder air-cooled radial engine driving a two-bladed fixed-pitch metal propeller.

Performance: Max. speed 101 mph; ceiling 13,000 ft.; range (not reported).

Weights: 1,114 lbs. empty, 1,512 lbs. loaded.

Dimensions: Span 31 ft., length 27 ft. 2 in., wing area 148 sq. ft.

The Loening SL was the last type of aircraft used in a series of Navy experiments, conducted intermittently from 1923 to 1933, to develop a small seaplane scout that could be deployed from a submarine. The aircraft had to be designed so that it could easily be dismantled and stowed in a watertight, eight-foot-diameter tube carried on the deck of the submarine. The earliest experiments had been carried out with diminutive float-equipped biplanes (e.g., Cox-Klemin XS-1 and -2, Martin MS-1) and actual submarine trials conducted in 1926, but these small aircraft were deemed unsatisfactory. Four years later,

BuAer decided to reinstate the idea with a small monoplane flying boat, and in June 1930, awarded Loening a contract to construct a single prototype as the XSL-1. The design emerged with a semi-cantilevered monoplane wing which attached to the top of a single-step metal boat hull. The Warner engine, mounted on struts in a pusher configuration, featured a ring cowl and a small bullet-shaped nacelle. Stowage in the deck tube was accomplished by simply detaching the wings and stabilizing floats. The prototype, date of first flight unknown, was delivered to NAS Anacostia for trials February 1931. When testing revealed the XSL-1 to be underpowered with the Warner engine, it was returned to the factory for installation of a 160-hp Menasco B-6 and a more streamlined engine mount. The revised aircraft, re-designated

The XSL-1, shown in its original configuration in 1931, was underpowered with the Warner engine. The Navy abandoned the program in 1933 after the modified XSL-2 was damaged during exercises with a submarine.

XSL-2, resumed testing at Anacostia in early 1933, but these trials indicated only a nominal improvement in performance. Soon afterward, the Navy abandoned the entire program when the XSL-2 suffered serious damage during exercises with a submarine.

Pitcairn OP—1931

TECHNICAL SPECIFICATIONS (XOP-1)

Type: Two-place observation autogyro.
Manufacturer: Pitcairn-Cierva Autogyro Co., Willow Grove, Pennsylvania.
Total produced: 3 (USN, USMC)
Powerplant: One 300-hp Wright R-975 Whirlwind 9-cylinder air-cooled radial engine driving a two-bladed fixed-pitch metal propeller.
Performance: Max. speed 123 mph; ceiling 16,400 ft.; range (not reported).
Weights: 2,250 lbs. empty, 2,807 lbs. loaded.
Dimensions: Rotor diameter 45 ft. 0 in., length 23 ft. 1 in.

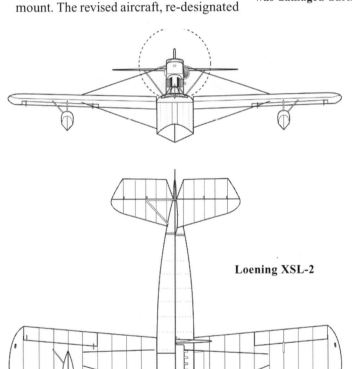

Loening XSL-2

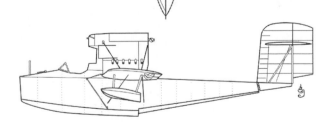

The XOP-1, the first of three Pitcairn PCA-2 autogyros evaluated by the Navy for the observation role starting in 1931. Landing trials were conducted aboard *Langley* in the fall of 1931.

In 1931 the Navy acquired three Pitcairn autogyros for evaluation purposes under the designation XOP-1. All three were essentially similar to the civil model PCA-2 having 30-foot monoplane wings with upturned tips and a freewheeling rotor mounted on struts. Both the airframe and rotor consisted of metal structures covered in fabric. The type commenced official trials aboard the *Langley* in the fall of 1931 but was apparently never employed operationally. One XOP-1 was transferred to the Marines in 1933, where it served with VJ-6M in Nicaragua for less than a year. Another XOP-1 was re-designated and presumably test flown as the XOP-2 in 1936 when it was modified by removing the wings, installing a new 50-foot rotor, and adding a full-chord cowling. All three were withdrawn from service sometime in 1937.

Douglas O-38—1931

TECHNICAL SPECIFICATIONS (O-38C)

Type: Two place observation landplane.
Manufacturer: Douglas Aircraft Corp., Santa Monica, California.
Total produced : 1 (USCG)
Powerplant: One 525-hp Pratt & Whitney R-1690-7 Hornet 9-cylinder

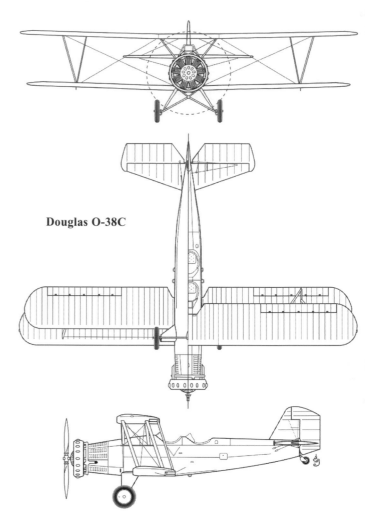

Douglas O-38C

Pitcairn XOP-1

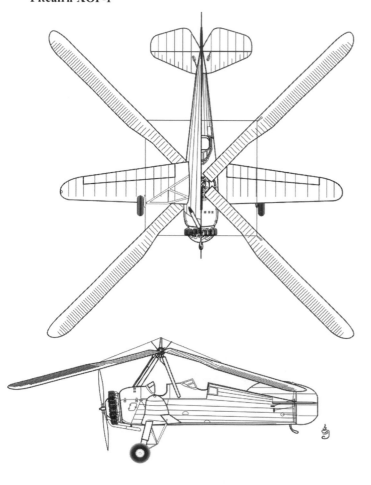

The single Douglas O-38C, a standard Army observation type, purchased by the Coast Guard in 1931, apparently for training purposes. It was withdrawn in 1934 after being damaged beyond repair.

air-cooled radial engine driving a two-bladed fixed-pitch metal propeller.
Performance: Max. speed 147 mph at s.l.; ceiling 20,700 ft.; range 600 mi.
Weights: 3,050 lbs. empty, 4,350 lbs. loaded.
Dimensions: Span 40 ft., length 31 ft. 3 In., wing area 371 sq. ft. (est.).

The Douglas O-38, a standard Army observation type produced in several variants between 1931 and 1934, served with Air Corps and the National Guard until 1941. One unarmed example, originally procured in 1931 under an Army contract an O-38B, was fitted with dual controls and assigned to the Coast Guard the same year as the O-38C. The aircraft operated under call number V108 until mid–1934, when it was damaged beyond repair in an accident.

Bellanca SE—1932

TECHNICAL SPECIFICATIONS (XSE-2)

Type: Three-place long-range scout.
Manufacturer: Bellanca Aircraft Corp., New Castle, Delaware.
Total produced: 1 (USN)
Powerplant: One 650-hp Wright R-1510-98 *Twin Whirlwind* 14-cylinder air-cooled radial engine driving a two-bladed fixed-pitch metal propeller.
Armament: Two fixed forward-firing .30-cal. machine guns and one flexible .30-caliber machine gun in the rear cockpit.
Performance: Max. speed 173 mph at s.l.; ceiling 18,800 ft.; range 1,455 mi.
Weights: 3,570 lbs. empty, 6,042 lbs. loaded.
Dimensions: Span 49 ft. 9 in., length 29 ft. 8 in., wing area 411 sq. ft.

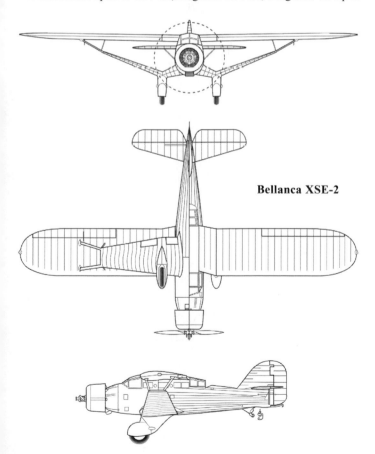

Bellanca XSE-2

The modified second prototype, the XSE-2, running up at Anacostia in 1934. The airfoil-shaped lift strut was characteristic of Bellanca's high-wing designs. No production was ordered.

The XSE-1 was ordered by BuAer on October 19, 1931, to be evaluated as a carrier or land-based long-range scout. Its design concept, similar to Bellanca's P-200 Airbus, was characterized by a high-wing that utilized large, airfoil-shaped lift and landing gear struts as auxiliary wing surfaces. To fulfill BuAer requirements for carrier stowage, the wings and lift struts were hinged to fold rearward along the fuselage. In its original configuration, the prototype was powered by a 650-hp Wright R-1820 *Cyclone* F and mounted an arrester hook forward of the tailwheel. The XSE-1 commenced initial factory flight-testing in December 1932 but was destroyed in a crash before it could be delivered to the Navy for scheduled trials. The second prototype, designated XSE-2, emerged in late 1934 with a twin-row Wright R-1510 engine, plus a redesigned rear fuselage, enlarged vertical tail surfaces, and a stronger tail hook positioned aft of the tailwheel. By this time, however, BuAer was making plans to procure a new generation of bomber (B) and scout bomber (SB) types to fulfill the scouting role (e.g., BG, SBU, and SBC) and Bellanca's contract was terminated.

Loening (Keystone) O2L—1932

TECHNICAL SPECIFICATIONS (XO2L-1)

Type: Three-place observation/utility amphibian.
Manufacturer: Loening Aeronautical Div. of Keystone Aircraft Corp. (a subsidiary of Curtiss-Wright), East River, New York.
Total produced: 1 (USN)
Powerplant: One 450-hp Pratt & Whitney R-1340-4 *Wasp* 9-cylinder air-cooled radial engine driving a three-bladed fixed-pitch metal propeller.
Performance: Max. speed 132 mph, cruise 110 mph; ceiling 16,200 ft.; range 350 mi.
Weights: 2,742 lbs. empty, 4,053 lbs. loaded.
Dimensions: Span 37 ft. 0 in., length 29 ft. 10 in., wing area 348 sq. ft.

The O2L represented the ultimate evolution of the design series that had begun in 1925 with the Liberty-powered OL-1.

In 1931, while deliveries of the OL-9 were still underway, Loening received a contract to design and build a substantially revised prototype under the designation XO2L-1. Though sharing many similarities with the OL-9, including the *Wasp* powerplant, the XO2L-1 made extensive use of semi-monocoque construction techniques that improved streamlining of the fuselage and main pontoon; and a 30-percent decrease in weight allowed smaller wings supported by a single bay of struts. Directional stability problems encountered soon after the prototype's first flight in early 1932 led to the addition of finlets on the horizontal stabilizers. But when performance and handling still fell below Navy expectations, the prototype was returned to the factory and subjected to modifications which included installation of a 550-hp R-1340D engine, lengthening the fuselage and pontoon three and a half feet, and enlarging the fin and rudder. Under the new designation XO2L-2, trials continued into late 1932, but Navy officials judged that the small performance improvement over the OL-9 did not merit production. BuAer then turned to Grumman for a new amphibian, ultimately resulting in the creation of JF/J2F Duck series.

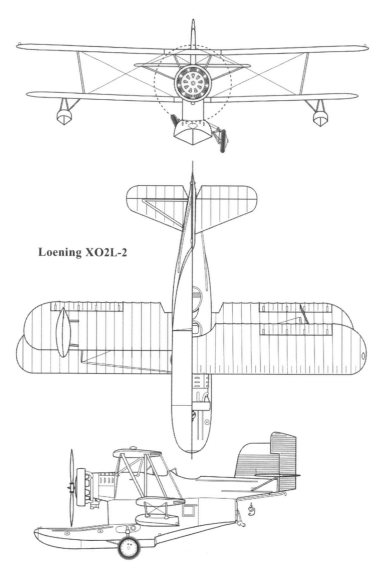

Loening XO2L-2

Curtiss S2C—1932

TECHNICAL SPECIFICATIONS (XS2C-1)

Type: Two-place landplane scout.
Manufacturer: Curtiss-Wright Corp., Curtiss Aeroplane Division, Buffalo, New York.
Total produced: 1 (USN)

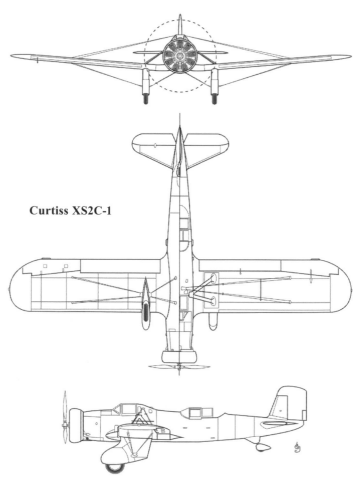

Curtiss XS2C-1

The sole prototype at NAS Anacostia in 1932, re-designated XO2L-2 after installation of a larger fin and rudder. The plane was fleet tested aboard battleships with VO-1B but not placed in production.

Powerplant: One 650-hp Wright R-1510-28 *Twin Whirlwind* 14-cylinder air-cooled radial engine driving a three-bladed fixed-pitch metal propeller.

Armament: Four fixed .30-cal. machine guns, one flexible .30-cal. rear machine gun, and up to 464 lbs. of bombs carried on external racks.

Performance: Max. speed 186 mph at s.l.; ceiling 18,900 ft.; range 640 mi. (combat).

Weights: 3,677 lbs. empty, 5,180 lbs. loaded.

Dimensions: Span 44 ft., length 31 ft. 3 in., wing area 285 sq. ft.

The XS2C-1 came as a direct development of the Curtiss YA-10, which itself was a radial-engine offshoot of the Army's inline-powered A-8 *Shrike* of 1931. After specifying delivery with a Wright R-1510 twin-row engine, BuAer purchased the XS2C-1 from Curtiss in December 1932, apparently not for assessment as a potential operational aircraft, but to test and evaluate the type's innovative slot and flap system. In any case, the XS2C-1 was not suited for carriers operations due to the size of its non-folding, wire-braced wings and absence of arresting gear. The aircraft is known to have been tested at Anacostia during 1933, but its ultimate disposition was not reported.

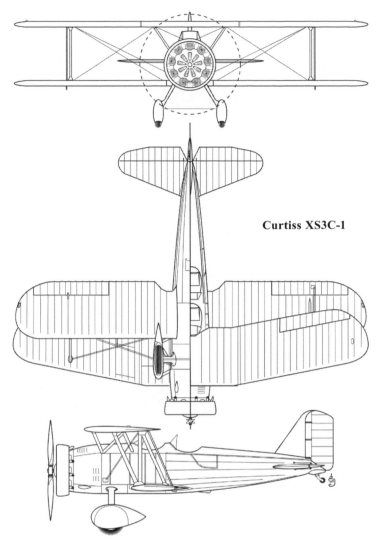

Curtiss XS3C-1

A radial-engine derivative of the Army A-8, the XS2C-1 was tested in 1932 and 1933 to evaluate its innovative slot and flap system. It was never equipped with arresting gear.

Curtiss S3C (F10C)—1932

TECHNICAL SPECIFICATIONS (XS3C-1)

Type: Two-place carrier scout.

Manufacturer: Curtiss-Wright Corp., Curtiss Aeroplane Division, Buffalo, New York.

Total produced: 1 (USN)

Powerplant: One 620-hp Wright R-1820-E *Cyclone* 9-cylinder air-cooled radial engine driving a two-bladed fixed-pitch metal propeller.

Armament: Two fixed .30-cal. machine guns, one flexible .30-cal. machine in the rear, an up to 500 lbs. of bombs carried on external racks.

Performance: Max. speed 178 mph at s.l.; ceiling 19,800 ft.; range 696 mi.

Weights: 3,387 lbs. empty, 4,959 lbs. loaded.

Dimensions: Span 32 ft., length 25 ft. 8 in., wing area 308 sq. ft.

Initially designated XF10C-1, the Curtiss XS3C-1 was basically an O2C-2 (see above) airframe which had been adapted to a new low-drag, cantilevered landing gear arrangement and

Basically an improved O2C-1, the only prototype of the S3C, shown here at Anacostia in early 1932, was destroyed only weeks later when it lost its elevators during dive testing.

a reshaped fin and rudder. It flew from the Buffalo factory for the first time on January 29, 1932, then was delivered to NAS Anacostia for trials in early February. But only several weeks later, the XS3C-1 project came to an abrupt end when the sole example was destroyed after shedding its elevators in a dive.

Great Lakes SG—1932

TECHNICAL SPECIFICATIONS (XSG-1)

Type: Two-place amphibian scout.
Manufacturer: Great Lakes Aircraft Corp., Cleveland, Ohio.
Total produced: 1 (USN)
Powerplant: One 400-hp Pratt & Whitney R-985-38 9-cylinder air-cooled radial engine driving a two-bladed, ground-adjustable metal propeller.
Armament (proposed): One flexible .30-caliber machine gun in the observer's position.
Performance: Max. speed 124 mph; ceiling 8,400 ft.; range 695 mi.
Weights: 2,707 lbs. empty, 4,218 lbs. loaded.
Dimensions: Span 35 ft., length 32 ft. 7 in., wing area 347 sq. ft.

The sole prototype XSG-1, probably off the Maryland coast near NAS Anacostia in 1933. Its unusual configuration is evident in this side view. The Navy eventually abandoned the idea of an amphibious cruiser scout.

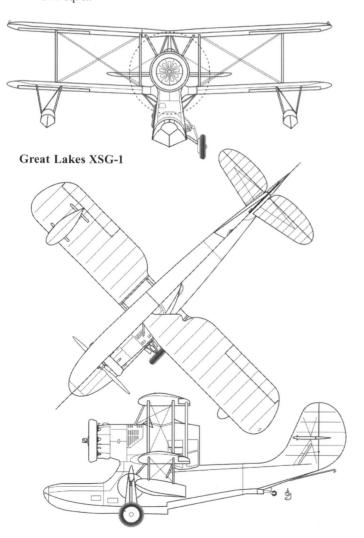

Great Lakes XSG-1

The Great Lakes XSG-1 was one of three aircraft (see Loening XS2L-1 and Sikorsky XSS-2) ordered by the Navy and tested during 1932 and 1933 as part an ultimately unsuccessful effort to find a scout amphibian as a replacement for the conventional floatplanes then serving aboard cruisers. The BuAer specification called for a single-engine amphibian stressed for catapult launches that, with wings folded, would be small enough to fit into the hangar space aboard Navy cruisers. The Great Lakes entry, designated the XSG-1, was delivered to Naval Air Station Anacostia for trials in November 1932. Its design presented a curious two-story layout: two-bays of biplane wings resting on a main pontoon, with the engine and pilot being situated in a separate nacelle between the upper and lower wings. The gunner/observer's position was located down in the pontoon aft of the wings. When, following brief trials, the XSG-1 failed to meet BuAer's performance expectations, further development was cancelled.

Loening (Keystone) S2L—1933

TECHNICAL SPECIFICATIONS (XS2L-1)

Type: Two-place amphibian scout.
Manufacturer: Loening Aeronautical Div. of Keystone Aircraft Corp. (a subsidiary of Curtiss-Wright), East River, New York.
Total produced: 1 (USN)
Powerplant: One 400-hp Pratt & Whitney R-985-28 *Wasp Junior* 9-cylinder air-cooled radial engine driving a two-bladed, ground-adjustable metal propeller.
Armament: One flexible .30-caliber machine gun in the observer's position.
Performance: Max. speed 130 mph; ceiling 12,400 ft.; range 633 mi.
Weights: 2,833 lbs. empty, 4,317 lbs. loaded.
Dimensions: Span 34 ft. 6 in., length 30 ft. 7 in., wing area 355 sq. ft.

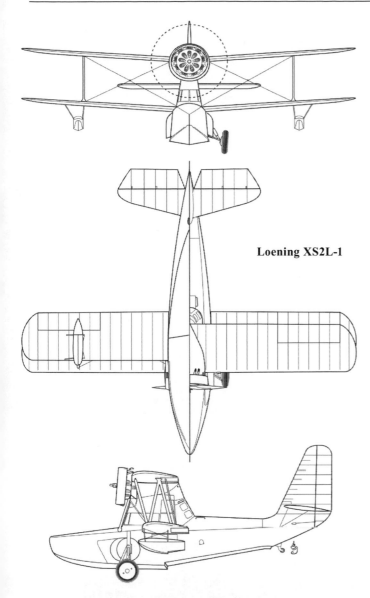

Loening XS2L-1

The XS2L-1 prototype was part of an unsuccessful experiment to replace floatplanes aboard Navy cruisers with boat-hulled amphibian. Development discontinued in 1933.

The Loening XS2L-1 was the second of three amphibian designs (see Great Lakes XSG-1 and Sikorsky XSS-1) to be considered as possible replacements for conventional float-planes aboard Navy cruisers. The Navy had previously experimented with the idea of adding fully amphibious floats to existing observation types, but the resulting weight penalty had degraded performance unacceptably. A designed-for-purpose amphibian, however, was viewed as a potentially better solution to the current problem of periodically re-rigging floatplanes to wheeled undercarriage, then back to floats again. After receiving a contract in 1932 to construct a single amphibian prototype, Loening proceeded to conceive a conventional biplane design that appeared to derive features from both its Navy OL-9 and the civilian K-85 Air Yacht. A rather odd-looking cockpit area resulted from glazed panels being placed around the interplane struts below the engine and wing center-section. By the time the XS2L-1 arrived at NAS Anacostia for official trials in February 1933, the Great Lakes entry had already been graded as unsatisfactory. Although the aircraft exhibited marginally better performance than its rival, it still did not compare favorably with existing cruiser-based floatplanes like the Vought O3U-3 and Berliner-Joyce OJ-2, and no production resulted.

Sikorsky SS—1933

TECHNICAL SPECIFICATIONS (XSS-2)

Type: Two-place amphibian scout.
Manufacturer: Sikorsky Div. of United Aircraft Corp., Bridgeport, Connecticut.
Total produced: 1 (USN)
Powerplant: One 550-hp Pratt & Whitney R-1340-12 *Wasp* 9-cylinder air-cooled radial engine driving a two-bladed, ground-adjustable metal propeller.
Armament: One flexible .30-caliber machine gun in the observer's position.
Performance: Max. speed 159 mph; ceiling 22,600 ft.; range 618 mi.
Weights: 3,274 lbs. empty, 4,790 lbs. loaded.
Dimensions: Span 42 ft., length 33 ft. 1/2 in., wing area 285 sq. ft.

The Sikorsky XSS-2 appeared as the last of three amphibian designs (see Great Lakes XSG-1 and Loening XS2L-1) to be considered as possible replacements for conventional float-planes aboard Navy cruisers. In addition to adequate scouting range, the requirement specified that the aircraft be stressed for catapult launches and small enough, with wings folded, to fit within the confines of existing cruiser hangars (i.e., a width of 14 feet, 6 inches). Compared to his rivals, Sikorsky emerged with a remarkably modern aeronautical concept: a very stream-lined two-step hull of all-metal semi-monocoque construction with monoplane wings that were raised above the spray in a gull configuration. The single *Wasp* engine, contained in a clean cowling-nacelle combination, was strut-mounted between the V of the wings. In stowed position, the wings folded back from the gull break to rest against the tail fin. The aircraft employed a Grumman-type amphibious landing gear and per specification, came with a tailhook to permit arrested landings aboard carriers. Sikorsky delivered the XSS-1 prototype to Anacostia

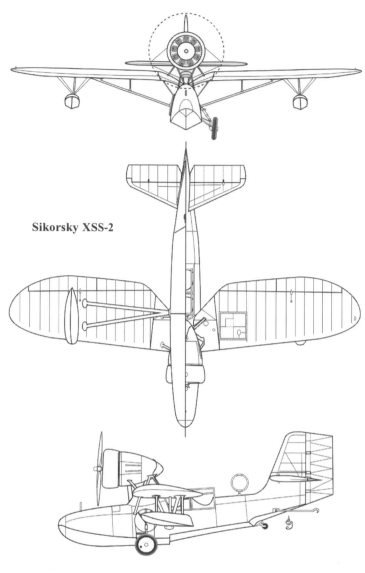

Sikorsky XSS-2

sometime in 1933, and following modifications, was subsequently evaluated as the XSS-2. Though its range was similar to the XSG-1 and XS2L-1, the XSS-2 demonstrated itself to be 50 mph faster with a much better rate-of-climb. In the interval, however, the Navy had decided to abandon the small flying boat idea in favor of new types of cruiser-based floatplanes, and thus no production of the XSS-2 was ordered.

Pennsylvania Aircraft Syndicate
OZ—1934

TECHNICAL SPECIFICATIONS (XOZ-1)

Type: Two-place observation autogyro.
Manufacturer: Pennsylvania Aircraft Syndicate Ltd., Philadelphia, Pennsylvania.
Total produced: 1 (USN)
Powerplant: One 155-hp Kinner R-490 (R-5) 5-cylinder air-cooled radial engine driving a two-bladed fixed-pitch metal propeller.
Performance: Max. speed 107 mph; ceiling (not reported); range 150 mi.

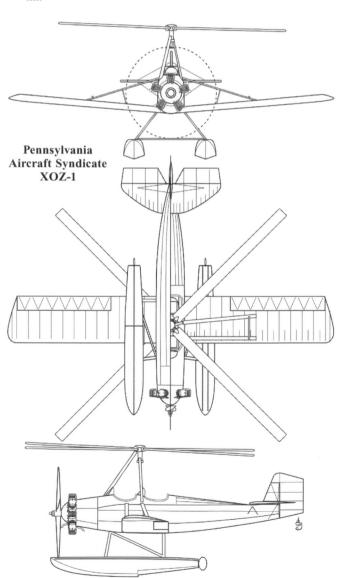

**Pennsylvania
Aircraft Syndicate
XOZ-1**

The XSS-2 was the last of the three amphibious cruiser scouts evaluated by the Navy in 1932 and 1933 and the only monoplane. All were ultimately deemed unsatisfactory.

Weights: 1,455 lbs. empty, 1,985 lbs. loaded.
Dimensions: Rotor diameter 32 ft., length 21 ft. 4 in.

A very rare photograph of the float-equipped XOZ-1 autogyro in 1934. Wilford rotor system was adapted to fuselage, lower wing, and tail group of Consolidated N2Y-1.

Constructed to BuAer specifications in 1934 from the fuselage, lower wings, and tail group of a Consolidated N2Y-1 trainer, the XOZ-1 was the second autogyro to be designed by E. Burke Wilford. Unlike the Pitcairn-Cieva arrangement (see Pitcairn OP), where the blades were hinged to the rotor head at a fixed pitch angle, the Wilford system used rigid rotors that automatically adjusted their pitch angle in response to changes in angle-of-attack. Little is known about the XOZ-1 other than the fact that Navy conducted tests with it during 1934 in both a wheeled and twin float configuration.

Curtiss SOC (O3C, SO2C, and SON) Seagull—1934

TECHNICAL SPECIFICATIONS (SOC-3)

Type: Two-place scout-observation (VSO) floatplane.
Manufacturer: Curtiss-Wright Corp., Curtiss Aeroplane Division, Buffalo, New York; Naval Aircraft Factory, Philadelphia, Pennsylvania.
Total produced: 309 (USN, USMC, USCG)
Powerplant: One 550-hp Pratt & Whitney R-1340-22 *Wasp* 9-cylinder air-cooled radial engine driving a two-bladed, ground-adjustable metal propeller.
Armament: One fixed .30-cal. machine gun, one flexible .30-cal. machine gun in the observer's position, and up to 650 lbs. of bombs carried on external racks.
Performance: Max. speed 164 mph ar s.l.; ceiling 14,400 ft.; range 1,025 mi.
Weights: 3,633 lbs. empty, 5,305 lbs. loaded.
Dimensions: Span 36 ft., length 32 ft. 3 in., wing area 342 sq. ft.

Beginning in the early 1930s, BuAer reclassified cruiser and battleship-based floatplanes into two distinct types: heavier-than-air scout-observation (VSO) for cruisers and heavier-than-air observation-scout (VOS) for battleships. VSO types, scout-

ing ahead of the cruiser screen, needed more range and the ability to communicate from longer distances; and for maintenance and protection in rough seas, they also needed to fit within the confines of existing cruiser hangars (i.e., length varied but a width of 14 feet, 6 inches was standard). Requirements for new VSO types were circulated in mid–1933 to Curtiss, Douglas, and Vought, with the expectation that prototypes would be delivered for trials in early 1934. In addition to biplane folding wings and performance factors, the specification called for each prototype to be equipped with an R-1340 *Wasp* powerplant and an amphibious center float. The Curtiss prototype, designated XO3C-1, made its first flight from the Buffalo plant on March 5, 1934 and was delivered to NAS Anacostia for official testing shortly thereafter. Though retaining open cockpits for the pilot and observer, the XO3C-1 featured a highly innovative system of full-span flaps on the upper wings and automatic leading-edge slats that kept takeoff and landing speeds within the required

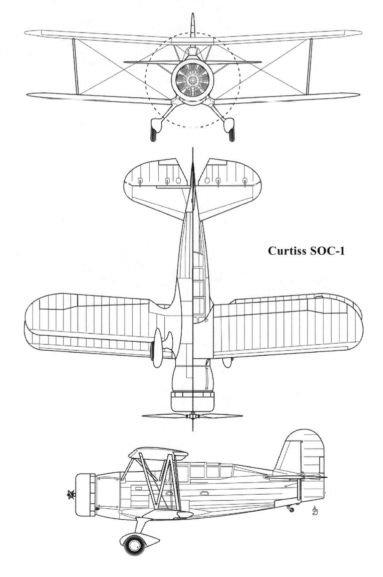

Curtiss SOC-1

60 mph range. Competitive trials between the XO3C-1, the Douglas XO2D-1, and the Vought XO5U-1 started in June 1934, but while still in progress, BuAer abandoned the notion of amphibious floats after deciding that the extra weight imposed by

Top: **The first floatplane built to new VSO requirement, the prototype XO3C-1 seen in 1934 with original amphibious main float. The weight of the gear mechanism was ultimately judged to unacceptably limit performance.** *Middle:* **The** *Cincinnati* **Detachment SOC-1 of VCS-3 is seen in 1938. While a ship was in port, its scout aircraft would often be converted to wheels for shore operations.** *Bottom:* **One of three SOC-4s acquired by the Coast Guard in 1938. The -4 was essentially identical to the SOC-3 except for different equipment carried.**

the landing gear reduced performance to an unacceptable extent, and ordered all three prototypes to be refitted with conventional pontoons.

In March 1935, once VSO trials had ended, Curtiss was declared the winner and given a contract for 135 production aircraft under the new scout-observation designation SOC-1, and at some point the factory name "Seagull" was applied. Notably, this was the Navy's single largest floatplane order since the O2U-1 of 1926, and though no comparative cost data was reported, the performance between the three prototypes was so similar that unit price must have been an important factor. SOC-1 production models, which began reaching the fleet in late 1935, differed from the prototype in having a redesigned cowling with moveable flaps and a full canopy enclosure ending in a raised turtledeck behind the cockpit area. As deliveries continued, SOC-1s were assigned to VS-5S, -6B, -9S, -10S, and -12S in detachments assigned to various cruisers within the fleet.

While nearly identical to the SOC-1, the 40 SOC-2s produced in late 1936 came with wheeled undercarriage only (though some were later reportedly adapted to floats). The XSO2C-1, an experimental variation tested in early 1937, featured a five-foot fuselage extension and flaps on the lower wings, but production was declined in favor of 83 SOC-3s ordered in May, which differed from previous SOCs in having interchangeable wheel and float undercarriage and were the first of the type to be assigned to battleships. The last four Curtiss-built examples, four SOC-4s (identical to SOC-3s), were delivered to the Coast Guard in early 1938. Twelve SOC-3s were delivered to Marine squadron VMS-2 during 1939 and 1940. SOC-2s and -3s subsequently retrofitted with carrier arresting gear were re-designated SOC-2A and -3A, respectively. Apparently due to production scheduling priorities at Curtiss, a further 44 SOC-3s were license-built by the Naval Aircraft Factory between late 1938 and mid–1939 and accepted into service as the SON-1. Over 250 SOCs/SONs were still on the active naval inventory as of December 1941, and many remained in service until the conclusion of hostilities in 1945.

Douglas O2D—1934

TECHNICAL SPECIFICATIONS (XO2D-1)

Type: Two-place scout-observation (VSO) floatplane.
Manufacturer: Douglas Aircraft Co., Santa Monica, California.
Total produced: 1 (USN)
Powerplant: One 550-hp Pratt & Whitney R-1340-12 *Wasp* 9-cylinder air-cooled radial engine driving a two-bladed, ground-adjustable metal propeller.
Armament: One fixed .30-cal. machine gun, one flexible .30-cal. machine gun in the observer's position, and up to 650 lbs. of bombs carried on external racks.
Performance: Max. speed 162 mph at s.l.; ceiling 14,300 ft.; range 798 mi.

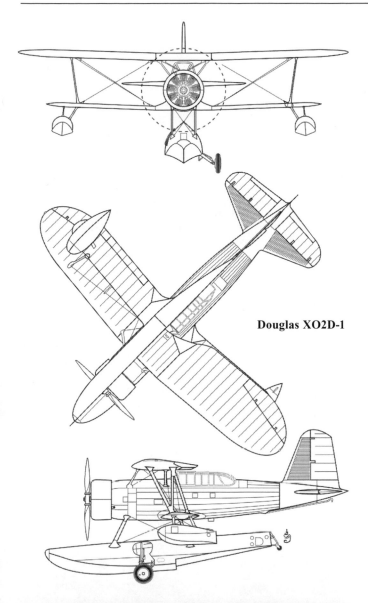

Douglas XO2D-1

Weights: 3,460 lbs. empty, 5,109 lbs. loaded.
Dimensions: Span 36 ft., length 32 ft., wing area 303 sq. ft.

Ordered by BuAer in June 1933, the Douglas XO2D-1 was one of three prototypes built in response to the Navy's VSO (heavier-than-air scout-observation) requirement. The specification was aimed at finding one type of aircraft to replace Vought O2Us and O3Us then serving aboard heavy cruisers and Berliner-Joyce OJs on light cruisers. After initial factory testing in early 1934, the XO2D-1 was delivered to NAS Anacostia in March 1934 just a few weeks before the rival Curtiss XO3C-1. Compared to the XO3C-1, the XO2D-1 was marginally lighter and came with a fully enclosed cockpit and a conventional trailing edge flap system on the upper wing. The official fly-off between competing prototypes commenced with the arrival of the Vought XO5U-1 (see Vought O3U, above, for more details) in June 1934.

Per specifications, the VSO types were initially equipped with amphibious center floats, but after deducing that the weight of the landing gear imposed serious limitations on range, BuAer ordered all three prototypes to be refitted with conventional pontoons. In March 1935, despite a very close competition, BuAer announced Curtiss as the winner and ordered its prototype into production as the SOC-1. After only 86 hours of flying time, the XO2D-1 was stripped of its engine and equipment and sent to the Naval Aircraft Factory for static structural tests.

Bellanca SOE—1936

TECHNICAL SPECIFICATIONS (XSOE-1)

Type: Two-place scout-observation (VSO) floatplane.
Manufacturer: Bellanca Aircraft Corp., New Castle, Delaware.
Total produced: 1 (USN)
Powerplant: One 725-hp Wright R-1820-84 *Cyclone* 9-cylinder air-cooled radial engine driving a two-bladed, variable-pitch metal propeller.
Armament: none installed.
Performance: Max. speed 176 mph at s.l.; ceiling 21,400 ft.; range 1,104 mi.
Weights: 4,508 lbs. empty, 6,552 lbs. loaded.
Dimensions: Span 41 ft., length 34 ft. 7 in., wing area 398 sq. ft.

In October 1934, while the VSO fly-off between the XO3C-1, XO2D-1, and XO5U-1 (see above) was ongoing, BuAer ordered two larger cruiser scouts, the Bellanca XSOE-1 and the Fairchild XSOK-1 (prototype cancelled prior to completion). The specification was broad, calling for a non-amphibious, folding-wing seaplane having an empty weight of not more than 3,800 lbs. Bellanca evolved a sesquiplane concept characterized by gulled upper wings that blended into a long-greenhouse canopy and a very broad center float joined to the fuselage with a streamlined fairing in lieu of struts. The design employed trailing edge flaps on both upper and lower wings to keep takeoff and landing speeds within acceptable limits. Construction of the XSOE-1 was somewhat protracted, however, and when finally rolled out for factory flight testing in March 1936, its completed weight exceeded design

Built to the 1933 VSO requirement, the XO2D-1 appeared with an amphibious main float. After the SOC-1 was selected for production, this aircraft was sent to the Naval Aircraft Factory for static structural tests.

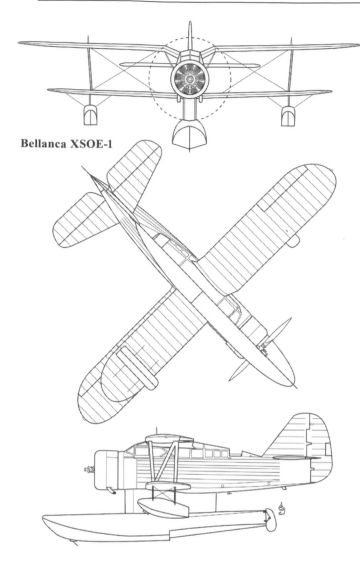

Bellanca XSOE-1

limitations by a factor of 20 percent, leading Navy officials to determine that catapult speeds would be unacceptably high. The prototype was delivered to NAS Philadelphia in August but was eventually dismantled without ever having been flown.

Vought OS2U Kingfisher—1938

TECHNICAL SPECIFICATIONS (OS2U-1)

Type: Two-place observation-scout (VOS) floatplane.
Manufacturer: Chance Vought Division of United Aircraft, Inc., Stratford, Connecticut.
Total produced: 1,518 (USN, USMC, USCG)
Powerplant: One 450-hp Pratt & Whitney R-985-48 *Wasp Junior* 9-cylinder air-cooled radial engine driving a two-bladed, variable-pitch metal propeller.
Armament: One fixed .30-cal. machine gun and one flexible .30-cal. machine gun in the rear cockpit.
Performance: Max. speed 175 mph at 5,500 ft.; ceiling 19,000 ft.; range 1,015 mi.
Weights: 3,432 lbs. empty, 5,077 lbs. loaded.
Dimensions: Span 35 ft. 11 in., length 33 ft. 7 in., wing area 262 sq. ft.

In 1936, out of a mutual desire to replace the Navy's aging fleet of O3Us and equip two new battleships planned (1936 pro-

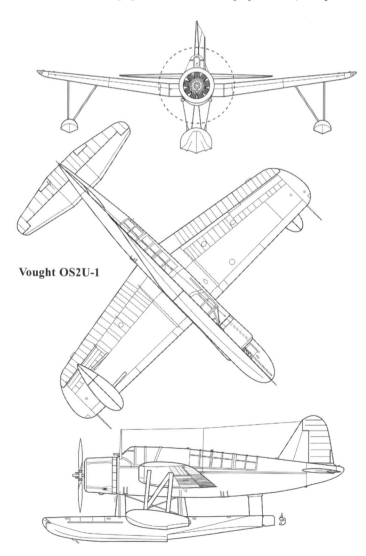

Vought OS2U-1

The XSOE-1 prototype as delivered to NAS Philadelphia in August 1936. It exceeded specified catapult weigh by 20 percent and was dismantled without ever having been flown by the Navy.

gram), BuAer announced a new VOS (heavier-than-air observation-scout) requirement calling for a floatplane, readily convertible to wheel undercarriage, that would be small enough to operate from battleships without need of folding wings. Initially, in May 1936, two biplane ideas were authorized: a Vought O3U-3 refitted with an experimental flap system as the XOSU-1 and a new design from the Naval Aircraft Factory as the XOSN-1. Whether the XOSU-1, tested in late 1936, represented a bona fide candidate is not clear, but its performance, in any event, was apparently deemed to offer too little advantage over the O3U-3. In early 1937, with the goal of making a production decision by late 1938 or early 1939, BuAer ordered two more VOS prototypes, the biplane XOSS-1 from Stearman and the monoplane XOS2U-1 from Vought.

Vought's XOS2U-1 completed its first flight with wheels on March 1, 1938, and with floats on May 19, arriving at NAS Anacostia mid-summer, and all three prototypes were ready to commence a competitive fly-off by the fall of 1938. Whereas the XOSN-1 and XOSS-1 biplanes both showed incremental improvements over the O3U series, the XOS2U-1 established a new state-of-the-art in floatplane design. With 30 percent less wing area, 25 percent less horsepower, and 15 percent less gross weight, Rex Beisel's pioneering concept out-performed the competition in every category of flight—speed, ceiling, and range—while posting a similar landing speed (56 mph). The XOS2U-1's wide operating speeds were made possible by utilizing a broad-chord wing design that incorporated large, full-span flaps for slow flight and spoilers for roll control. It was also the first American military aircraft to employ spot-welding in its primary airframe structures. During evaluations, a third centerline strut was added on the pontoon afterbody for extra bracing and a small step incorporated in the wing floats.

In May 1939, after less than a year of official evaluations, Vought received a contract for 54 production OS2U-1s, which all entered service with the fleet between May and November of 1940. Departing from the Corsair tradition, Vought named the new type "Kingfisher." BuAer placed a new order in December 1939 for 158 improved OS2U-2s having armor protection, self-sealing tanks, and the newer R-985-50 engine. As deliveries proceeded into 1940 and 1941, 45 OS2U-2s were completed as floatplanes and 113 as landplanes accompanied by 70 extra sets of Edo floats. Many of the Kingfisher landplanes went to shore stations where they equipped the Navy's new Inshore Patrol squadrons. Starting in July 1941, the first of 1,006 OS2U-3s, identical to the -2 except for an R-985-AN2 engine, began rolling off Vought's assembly lines. By December 1941, some 446 OS2U-1s, -2s, and -3s were active in ship and shore stations, with another 90 awaiting assignment in the fleet. In order to relieve the wartime demand on Vought's plant capacity, a further 300 OS2U-3s were manufactured by the Naval Aircraft Factory between May and October of 1942 as the OS2N-1. OS2Us/OS2Ns remained in frontline service until they began to be replaced by Curtiss SC-1s in mid–1944.

Top: **The XOS2U-1, seen during acceptance trials in 1938, represented a quantum leap in floatplane design. Innovations included full-span flaps with spoilers for roll control and spot-welded airframe assembles.** *Bottom:* **An OS2U-1 rigged with wheels seen in 1941 while serving in the VO detachment aboard** *Mississippi* **(BB-41). By the end of the year, all Battleship VOS had replaced their SOCs with OS2Us.**

Naval Aircraft Factory OSN—1938

TECHNICAL SPECIFICATIONS (XOSN-1)

Type: Two-place observation-scout (VOS) floatplane.
Manufacturer: Naval Aircraft Factory, Philadelphia, Pennsylvania.
Total produced: 1 (USN)
Powerplant: One 550-hp Pratt & Whitney R-1340-36 *Wasp* 9-cylinder air-cooled radial engine driving a two-bladed, ground-adjustable metal propeller.
Armament: One fixed .30-cal. machine gun and one flexible .30-cal. machine gun in the rear cockpit.
Performance: Max. speed 160 mph at 6,000 ft.; ceiling 14,900 ft.; range 925 mi.
Weights: 3,771 lbs. empty, 5,516 lbs. loaded.
Dimensions: Span 36 ft., length 34 ft., wing area 378 sq. ft.

Authorized on May 11, 1936, the Naval Aircraft Factory XOSN-1 was the first all-new aircraft design to be ordered under the Navy's new VOS (heavier-than-air observation-scout) requirement. As with existing battleship-based floatplanes, the VOS type's primary role would be spotting for the big guns rather than long-range scouting. Design and construction of the XOSN-1 proceeded over the next two years, the prototype

The XOSN-1 prototype competed against the XOSS-1 and XOS2U-1 in 1938. Though having advanced features for a biplane, its performance did not match the more innovative XOS2U-1.

being delivered to NAS Anacostia for official trials in May 1938. Though of biplane design, the XOSN-1 featured such innovations as an all-metal airframe clad entirely in aluminum, large, automatic slats on the upper wing, and an I-strut bracing system that eliminated the need for interplane bracing wires. In December 1939, after Vought's XOS2U-1 had been slated for production as the winning VOS candidate, the XOSN-1 was assigned to the Naval Academy at Annapolis where it was used as a trainer as part of VD-8D5 until finally stricken in mid–1944.

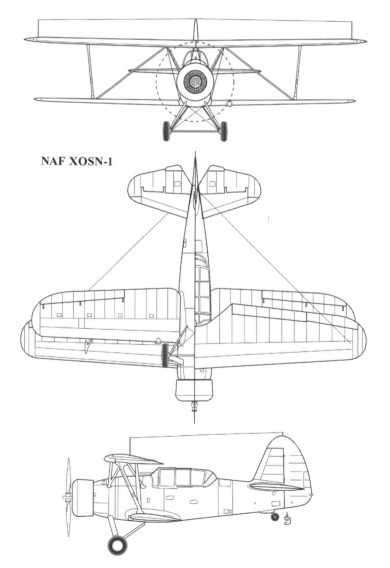

NAF XOSN-1

Stearman OSS—1938

TECHNICAL SPECIFICATIONS (XOSS-1)

Type: Two-place observation-scout (VOS) floatplane.
Manufacturer: Stearman Aircraft Div., Boeing Airplane Co., Wichita, Kansas.
Total produced: 1 (USN)
Powerplant: One 550-hp Pratt & Whitney R-1340-36 *Wasp* 9-cylinder air-cooled radial engine driving a two-bladed, ground-adjustable metal propeller.
Armament: One fixed .30-cal. machine gun and one flexible .30-cal. machine gun in the rear cockpit.
Performance: Max. speed 162 mph at 6,000 ft.; ceiling 16,600 ft.; range 986 mi.
Weights: 3,826 lbs. empty, 5,612 lbs. loaded.
Dimensions: span 36 ft., length 34 ft. 7 in., wing area 378 sq. ft.

Ordered by BuAer on May 6, 1937, Stearman's XOSS-1, along with the Naval Aircraft Factory XOSN-1 and Vought XOS2U-1, was one of three prototypes to be considered in the Navy's quest to find a new VSO (heavier-than-air observation-scout) type for duty aboard battleships. When delivered to NAS Anacostia for trials in July 1938, Stearman's entry appeared as an all-metal biplane having fabric covered wings and control surfaces which, for slow flight, used Junkers-type trailing-edge flaps that ran the full span of the upper wing. A year later, after

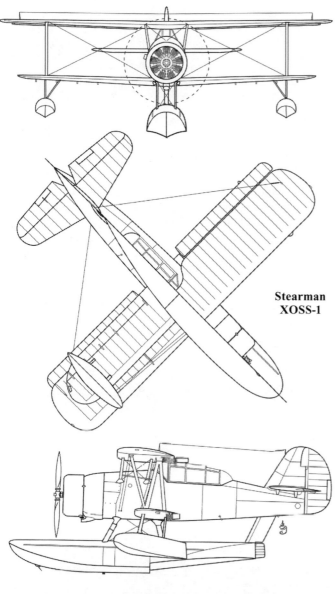

**Stearman
XOSS-1**

the XOS2U-1 had been declared winner of the VSO competition, the XOSS-1 was sent to the Naval Aircraft Factory in Philadelphia, where, as part of VX-3D4, it was used to perform various tests until July 1941, at which point it was scrapped after having flown a total of 396 hours.

Vought SO2U—1939

TECHNICAL SPECIFICATIONS (XSO2U-1)

Type: Two-place scout-observation (VSO) floatplane.

Manufacturer: Chance Vought Division of United Aircraft, Inc., Stratford, Connecticut.

Total produced: 1 (USN)

Powerplant: One 500-hp Ranger XV-770-4 12-cylinder air-cooled inline engine driving a two-bladed, variable-pitch metal propeller.

Armament: One fixed .30-cal. machine gun, one flexible .30-cal. machine gun in the rear cockpit, and up 650 lbs. of bombs or depth-charges carried on wing racks.

Performance: Max. speed 190 mph at 9,000 ft.; ceiling 22,200 ft.; range 984 mi.

Weights: 4,016 lbs. empty, 5,634 lbs. loaded.

Dimensions: Span 38 ft. 2 in., length 37 ft. 1 in., wing area 300 sq. ft.

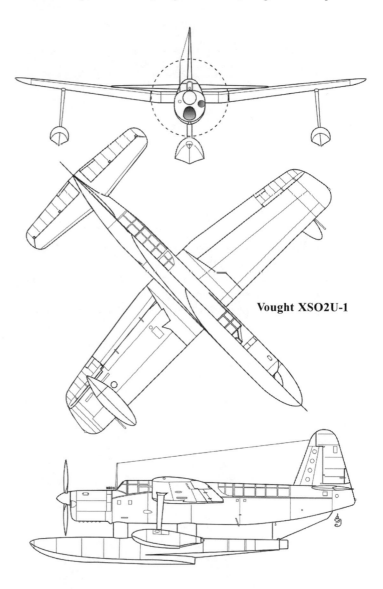

Vought XSO2U-1

The XOSS-1 as delivered to NAS Anacostia for testing in mid–1938. Note Junkers-type flaps on upper wing. While more advanced than the O3U, it could not match the performance parameters of the XOS2U.

In an effort analogous to the VOS competition, the Navy hoped to obtain a more modern VSO floatplane that would eventually replace the SOC biplanes serving the cruiser divisions. Thus, in 1937 BuAer issued a new requirement calling for a monoplane designed around the experimental Ranger XV-770-4, inverted V-12 powerplant being developed especially for the Navy. Detailed specifications listed a wingspan of 38 feet that folded to a width of 14-feet, six-inches to permit stowage in cruiser hangars, a maximum catapult weight of 6,350 lbs., a 56 mph landing speed, provision for long-range radio equipment, widely spaced pilot and observer position for optimal visibility, and an airframe stressed to 7.5-Gs for dive-bombing. In the late spring of 1938, after considering design proposals, BuAer awarded contracts to construct single prototypes to Curtiss and Vought, respectively as the XSO3C-1 and XSO2U-1.

The Vought monoplane VSO contender, the XSO2U-1, was delivered to NAS Anacsotia in early 1940. Vought by that time lacked the plant capacity to put another type of aircraft into production.

Resembling a longer, more streamlined Kingfisher, Vought's XSO2U-1 made its first flight with wheels in July 1939 and with floats later in the year. It arrived at NAS Anacostia for trials in February 1940, just weeks after the XSO3C-1. Even though both prototypes were very similar in appearance due to the precise nature of the specifications, the XSO2U-1 exhibited slightly better performance and better overall stability than its Curtiss counterpart. However, by mid–1940, Vought's Stratford facilities were already at capacity with the OS2U and planned production of the F4U-1 and as a result, the XSO3C-1 was selected for production. The sole XSO2U-1 was transferred to the Ranger Engine Corp. in Farmingdale, New York, and served there as an engine testbed until stricken from the Navy inventory in 1944.

Curtiss SO3C Seagull (Seamew)—1939

TECHNICAL SPECIFICATIONS (SO3C-2)

Type: Two-place scout-observation (VSO) floatplane.
Manufacturer: Curtiss-Wright Corp., Curtiss Aeroplane Division, Buffalo, New York.

Total produced: 801 (USN, USCG)
Powerplant: One 530-hp Ranger V-770-8 12-cylinder air-cooled inline engine driving a two-bladed, variable-pitch metal propeller.
Armament: One fixed .30-cal. machine gun, one flexible .50-cal. machine gun in the rear cockpit, and up 650 lbs. of bombs or depth-charges carried on wing racks.
Performance: Max. speed 172 mph at 8,100 ft.; ceiling 15,800 ft.; range 1,150 mi.
Weights: 4,785 lbs. empty, 7,000 lbs. loaded.
Dimensions: Span 38 ft., length 35 ft. 8 in., wing area 293 sq. ft.

In 1937 BuAer circulated a new VSO requirement with the aim of finding a new cruiser-based scout that would incorporate the aerodynamic advances recently seen in Vought's XOS2U-1, and it is not surprising that construction of prototypes was narrowed in May 1938 to the two airframe contractors having the most up-to-date experience with ship-based floatplanes. Both entries, the Curtiss XSO3C-1 and the Vought XSO2U-1, were to be monoplanes built to very detailed specifications governing size (with wings folded), weight, performance, armament, and cockpit arrangement. In a parallel project, Ranger Engine Corp. was developing an inverted V-12 inline, air-cooled engine that would power both.

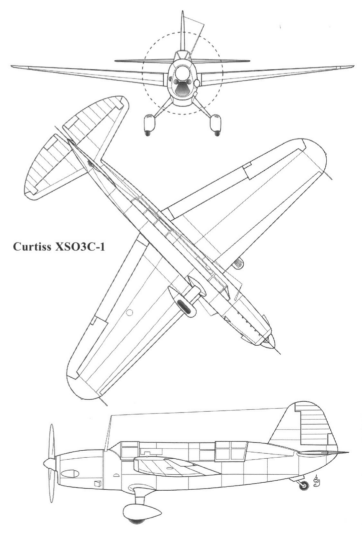

Curtiss XSO3C-1

Although the completed prototypes emerged with a similar appearance, Vought's XSO2U-1 borrowed many elements of its proven OS2U design, while Curtiss was forced to develop the XSO3C-1 almost from scratch. Curtiss employed a more conservative wing layout, using a conventional aileron and trailing-edge flap arrangement, with only a few degrees of dihedral. The tail group was located slightly above the thrust line. But soon after the XSO3C-1 made it first flight on October 6, 1939, the aircraft exhibited serious control problems with regard to roll and yaw stability. Curtiss attempted to remedy the defects by adding upturned endplates on the wingtips to compensate for insufficient dihedral and increasing vertical fin area through a long fillet that extended over the observer's cockpit. Complicating matters further, BuAer was by mid–1940 moving to a wartime procurement schedule that effectively ruled out production of a new aircraft type by Vought. In October 1940, as a consequence, Curtiss received a production contract for 300 aircraft as the SO3C-1. In addition to the aerodynamic changes, production models featured a deepened engine cowling to permit better cooling, a V-770-6 engine rated at 530-hp, plus armor plating and self-sealing fuel tanks. Rear armament was upgraded to a 50-cal. machine gun.

Service trials of the first production SO3C-1s during the spring of 1942 revealed that the type was too underpowered to operate from cruisers, causing them to be replaced with either OS2Us or SOCs. After 141 SO3C-1s had been completed in mid–1942, they were superceded on the production line by 150 SO3C-2s, which came with a centerline bomb rack and arresting gear and were intended mainly for wheeled operations from escort carriers. These were followed, starting in December 1942, by 309 SO3C-2Cs, with 650-hp V-770-8 engines, 24-volt electrical systems, and upgraded radios, 250 of which were delivered to Great Britain as the *Seamew*. Although the type's U.S. Navy name was officially Seagull, it is most commonly referred to as the Seamew. The 200 SO3C-3s produced between June 1943 and January 1944 lacked arresting gear and were used as trainers and target drones. Forty-five SO3C-3 landplanes were assigned to the Coast Guard in 1943 for coastal patrol. Plans

for Ryan to produce the aircraft under license as the SOR-1 were cancelled.

PATROL AIRCRAFT

Synopsis of Patrol Aircraft Procurement

Patrol aircraft, all single or twin-engine biplane flying boats, were the most numerous type of combat aircraft in the Navy's inventory at the close of World War I. Flying boats, due to their superior range and ability to operate from distant shore bases, were ideally suited to maritime patrol and reconnaissance, which included offensive bombing attacks against hostile submarines. Wartime contracts, with deliveries continuing into 1919, accounted for acceptance of 350 Curtiss H-16s, 1,100 Curtiss HS-1s and -2s, and 227 Naval Aircraft Factory (NAF) F-5s, many of which continued to serve up through the late 1920s. During the first decade after the war, NAF functioned as a clearing-house for many patrol boat developments, testing new designs such as the PN-7, -8, -9, 10, and -12, and from 1927 to 1929, BuAer initiated the largest postwar flying boat order when it awarded contracts to Douglas, Hall, Martin, and Keystone to build 122 aircraft based upon NAF's PN-12 design.

From the late 1920s onward, the Navy's desire to maintain its reach in two oceans kept patrol boat procurement at the forefront. At the same time, budgetary constraints on spending, imposed by the onset of the Depression, caused BuAer to shift emphasis on design and development from government-sponsored NAF programs to private contractors. In 1928, BuAer embarked upon a program to procure the Navy's first monoplane patrol boat, awarding the initial development contract to Consolidated for the PY, but as a result of a competitive bidding process, gave Martin a contract in 1929 to produce ten nearly identical examples as the P2M and P3M. In 1931, when BuAer solicited bids for an extensive redesign of the PY, Consolidated landed a production contract this time for 47 P2Ys that were delivered from 1933 to 1935. Experiments conducted in 1932 and 1933 with the smaller Sikorsky XP2S and larger Hall XP2H patrol boat prototypes did not yield any new production contracts, however, officials at BuAer were hard at work on a plan to replace all of the Navy's older biplane patrol boat force with a modern monoplane having improved range and superior offensive capabilities. Development contacts were issued in 1934 for the Douglas XP3D and Consolidated XP3Y which, followed by trials between both prototypes during 1935, culminated in a production order being awarded to Consolidated for 60 aircraft that began entering service in 1936 as the PBY-1, the change in designation denoting a new naval emphasis on the "patrol bomber" (PB) aspect of the aircraft's overall mission. This initial contract was followed over the next five years by a succession of new PBY orders: 50 PBY-2s and 66 PBY-3s delivered in 1937 and 1938, 33 PBY-4s in 1938 and 1939, and 164 PBY-5s and 33 PBY-5As (amphibious) by the end of 1941.

The XSO3C-1 prototype as delivered in late 1939. Curtiss received the production contract because of Vought's backlog on other aircraft. This type was ultimately deemed unsuited for cruiser operations.

BuAer's quest for new patrol boats during the mid– and late 1930s did not stop with procurement of PBYs but encompassed even bolder plans to acquire different twin-engine types, plus a four-engine concept that would bring forth several of the largest military flying boats ever built in the U.S. The Hall XPTBH provides an interesting example of an ultimately unsuccessful twin-engine idea. Its 1934 specification, the one and only "patrol-torpedo-bomber" requirement ever issued, contemplated a large twin-float aircraft carrying two Mk. 13 torpedoes, which could be launched from the shore to attack approaching enemy capital ships. However, by the time the XPTBH-2 underwent trials in early 1937, naval officials had reached the conclusion that, from a tactical perspective, building more carrier-launched torpedo-bombers (i.e., Douglas TBDs) was far more practical than the PTB concept. An unsolicited proposal received from Martin resulted in the mid–1937 contract for the prototype XPBM, followed later in the year with an order for 20 more production models. When it flew for the first time in February 1939, the XPBM-1 was arguably the most advanced twin-engine flying boat in the world, and as deliveries of new PBM-1s proceeded in 1940 and 1941, BuAer added a series of contacts for 379 PBM-3s to be delivered in 1942. Consolidated's bid to offer the Navy a militarized variant of its highly innovative civil Model 31 twin-engine flying boat did not materialize into a P4Y production order until early 1942, however, the type never actually achieved production due to unavailability of R-3350 engines.

The Navy's most ambitious program during this period was perhaps the so-called "Sky Dreadnaughts"—huge, four-engine flying boats that could assume a long-range bombardment role in case America ever found itself cutoff from access to overseas land bases. Development contracts for the four-engine prototypes were issued to Sikorsky in 1935 for the XPBS, to Consolidated in 1936 for the XPB2Y, and finally, to Martin in 1938 for the XPB2M. Competitive trials between the XPBS-1 and XPB2Y-1 ended in early 1939 when Consolidated received a limited production contract for six PB2Y-2s. Naval officials still had serious reservations over the four-engine program in terms of cost: since three PBYs could be procured for the cost of one PB2Y, the same amount of ocean area could be patrolled by simply buying more PBYs for less money. In due course, the passage of the Naval Expansion act in late 1940 led BuAer to contract for 210 PB2Y-3s in addition to the PBY-5s and PBM-3s already on order. Martin's XPB2M-1, massing over twice the weight of the PBS or PB2Y, was damaged during taxi tests in late 1941 and did not fly until mid–1942, by which time the entire Sky Dreadnaught concept had been abandoned in favor of other wartime priorities. All of the production PB2Ys and the sole XPB2M ended up as over-ocean transports in 1942 and 1943.

A shift in the post–World War I military policy, one which had barred the Navy from maintaining any type of land-based bomber force, opened the door to acquisition of 20 lend-lease Lockheed *Hudsons* in April 1941 as the PBO-1. As they entered Navy service during late 1941 and early 1942, PBOs were chiefly intended to conduct antisubmarine patrols off the U.S. Coast. After December 1941, the Navy ended up procuring huge numbers of Army land-based bombers under the PB or P designation: 1,713 Consolidated PB4Ys (AAF B-24), 706 North American PBJs (AAF B-25), and 2,133 Lockheed PVs (AAF B-34). Between 1927 and 1932 BuAer also assigned patrol designations to five Sikorsky twin-engine amphibians as the PS-1, -2, and -3, later reclassifying them as utility transports, and to five "flying life boats" acquired for the Coast Guard as the General Aviation PJ-1 and -2.

Curtiss H-16 (Large America)—1917

TECHNICAL SPECIFICATIONS

Type: Four- to five-place patrol flying boat.
Manufacturer: Curtiss Aeroplane & Motor Co., Garden City, New York; Naval Aircraft Factory, Philadelphia, Pennsylvania.
Total produced: 349 (USN)

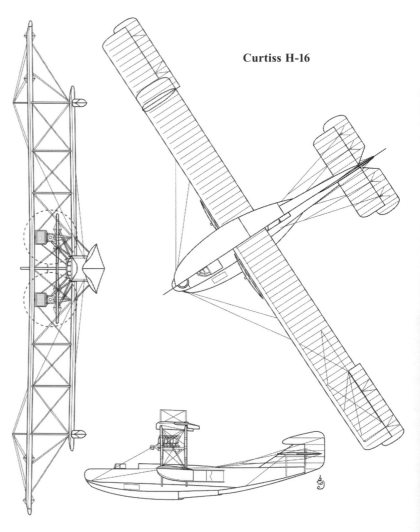

Curtiss H-16

Powerplants: Two 400-hp Liberty 12-cylinder water-cooled engines driving four-bladed wooden fixed-pitch propellers.

Performance: Max. speed 95 mph; ceiling 9,950 ft.; range 378 mi.

Armament: Two .30-caliber Lewis machine guns in the bow, one .30-caliber Lewis machine gun on each side in waist positions, and one .30-caliber Lewis machine gun in the rear cockpit; and one 230-lb. bomb carried under each wing.

Weights: empty 7,400 lbs., 10,900 lbs. loaded.

Dimensions: Span (upper) 95 ft. 1 in., length 46 ft. 2 in., wing area 1,164 sq. ft.

The Curtiss H series of flying boats, beginning with the H-4 "America" in 1914, followed by the H-8 in 1915 and the H-12 in 1916, have the distinction of being the first type of combat-capable aircraft to be mass-produced in the United States during World War I. With the help of the Royal Naval Air Service facility in Felixstowe, England, the H series progressively improved over time, resulting by late 1917 in the introduction of the H-16 with larger wings in four bays of struts, a Porte two-step sponson hull, heavier armament, and more powerful V-12 engines. Like most aircraft of the period, construction was primarily wood with fabric-covered wings and tail surfaces.

The first operational H-16 was accepted by the Navy in February 1918 and 199 production models followed, with 72 being allocated to the RNAS. U.S. versions were equipped with 400-hp Liberty engines, whereas RNAS types, designated Felixstowe F.2As, were powered by 345-hp Rolls-Royce Eagles. Wartime demand for H-16s grew to such a great extent that license-production was awarded to the new Naval Aircraft Factory at Philadelphia, which completed a further 150 examples between March and October 1918. Curtiss tested an H-16 reconfigured with pusher engines and wing sweep to compensate for the change in center of gravity, but no production of the type resulted. After the armistice, many H-16s continued in Navy service, and the final examples were not withdrawn until 1929.

The H-16, along with the NAF F-5L, remained in service as the Navy's standard maritime patrol type from 1918 up through the late 1920s. The final example was retired in 1929.

Curtiss HS—1917

TECHNICAL SPECIFICATIONS (HS-2L)

Type: Three-place patrol flying boat.

Manufacturer: Curtiss Aeroplane & Motor Co., Garden City, New York; Standard Aero Corp., Plainfield, New Jersey; Lowe, Willard and Fowler Co., College Point, New York; Gallaudet Aircraft Corp., Norwich, Connecticut; Boeing Airplane Co., Seattle, Washington; and Loughead Aircraft Mfg. Co., Santa Barbara, California.

Total produced: 1,151 (USN, USMC, USCG)

Powerplant: One 350-hp Liberty 12-cylinder water-cooled engine driving a four-bladed wooden fixed-pitch propeller.

Performance: Max. speed 83 mph; ceiling 5,200 ft.; range 517 mi.

Armament: One flexible .30-caliber Lewis machine gun in the bow; and one 230-lb. bomb under each bottom wing.

Weights: 4,300 lbs. empty, 6,432 lbs. loaded.

Dimensions: Span (upper) 74 ft. ½ in., length 39 ft., wing area 803 sq. ft.

Designed in response to a Navy requirement for a smaller coastal patrol flying boat, the HS-1 (initially developed as the twin-engine H-14) appeared in early 1917 as a one-third scale-down of the H-16 having a single pusher-mounted powerplant. The HS-1 was conceived as a 3-bay biplane, and like the H-16, incorporated the refinements of the Porte-type hull. The first HS-1 proved to be underpowered with the original 200-hp Curtiss VXX V-8 engine, but performance dramatically improved when the aircraft was refitted with a 350-hp Liberty V-12 in October 1917. Designated the HS-1L, the Liberty-powered type was ordered into large-scale production in such great numbers

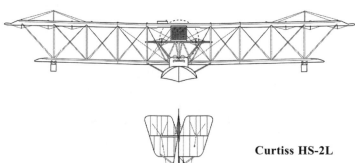

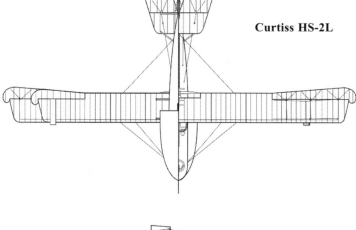

Curtiss HS-2L

that, in addition to the Curtiss order for 664 examples, license contracts were given to Standard Aircraft Corp. (250), Lowe, Willard and Fowler Co. (200), Gallaudet Aircraft Corp. (60), Boeing Airplane Co. (50), and Loughead Aircraft Co. (2), for

An HS-2L shown in World War I–era markings. A total of 1,152 were produced by five manufacturers between 1918 and 1919. This type remained in Navy service until 1926.

1,226 aircraft total. When the war ended, however, these orders were cut back to 1,101 aircraft, while another twenty to twenty-five were reportedly assembled at various naval stations from spare parts available. To boost armament payload, the HS-2L appeared in mid–1918 with an eleven foot one inch increase in wingspan and an additional bay of struts, and all pending HS production was thereafter bought up to the 2L standard. The final version, the HS-3L featuring an improved hull design, did not fly until 1919, and only five had been completed by Curtiss and two by NAF when all HS production ceased.

The HS claimed the honor of being the first type of American-designed and -built aircraft to be received by U.S. forces in France, when, in late May 1918, the first eight HS-1Ls were taken into service by the Navy station at Pauillac and, as deliveries proceeded, another 174 HS-1Ls and 2Ls equipped nine more stations in France by the time of the armistice in November. After the war, the HS-2L remained the Navy's standard single-engine patrol and flying boat trainer until the last examples were retired in 1926. Four HS-2Ls were loaned to the Coast Guard in 1920 and 1921 to conduct the first search and rescue experiments and six operated with the Marines from 1922 to 1926 in the expeditionary detachment at Guam.

Naval Aircraft Factory/ Curtiss F-5L (PN-5, -6)—1918

Type: Four- to five-place patrol flying boat.
Manufacturer: Naval Aircraft Factory, Philadelphia, Pennsylvania; Curtiss Aeroplane & Motor Co., Garden City, New York; Canadian Aeroplanes, Ltd., Toronto, Ontario.
Total produced: 227 (USN, USMC)
Powerplants: Two 420-hp Liberty A 12-cylinder water-cooled engines driving four-bladed wooden fixed-pitch propellers.
Armament: Two .30-caliber Lewis machine guns in the bow, one .30-caliber Lewis machine gun on each side in waist positions, and one .30-caliber Lewis machine gun in the rear cockpit; and one 230-lb. bomb carried under each wing.
Performance: Max. speed 90 mph; ceiling 5,500 ft; range 830 mi.
Weights: 8,720 lbs. empty, 13,600 lbs. loaded.
Dimensions: Span (upper) 103 ft. 9 in., length 49 ft. 4 in., wing area 1,397 sq. ft.

Coming as the ultimate evolution of the Curtiss Large Americas that began with the H-8, the F-5L incorporated improvements of the Felixstowe F.5 such as removal of the enclosed cockpit, increased fuel capacity, enlarged wing area, more powerful engines, straight-balanced ailerons, and a taller,

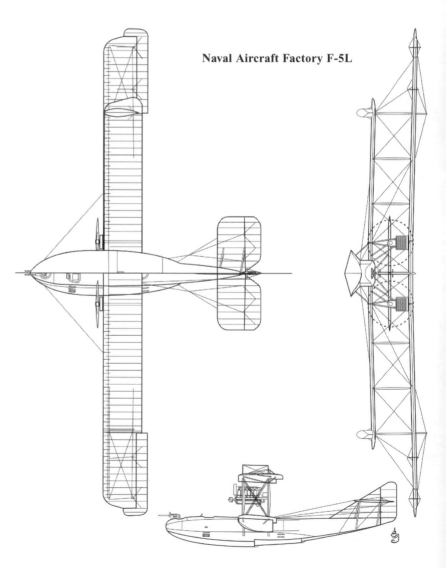

Naval Aircraft Factory F-5L

balanced rudder. Though slightly slower than the H-16, the F-5 enjoyed a significant improvement in range. Powered by Liberty uprated 12A engines, the first F-5L, built by NAF, was de-

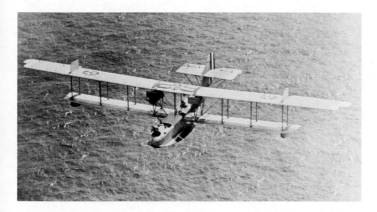

This NAF-built F-5L is shown in postwar markings. Derived from the Curtiss H-16, the F-5L incorporated the increased wing area and greater fuel capacity of the Royal Navy's Felixstowe F.5. It served until the late 1920s.

livered to the Navy for trials in September 1918, too late to see action. Production continued after the war, however, with 136 more F-5Ls being completed by NAF, 60 by Curtiss, and 30 by Canadian Aeroplanes, Ltd. The last two, completed by NAF as F-6Ls, featured improvements to the hull and a reshaped fin and balanced rudder, and most F-5Ls remaining in service during the early 1920s were subsequently brought up to this standard. When the Navy adopted a standardized designation system in 1922, the F-5Ls became PN-5s and the two F-6Ls became PN-6s. PN-5s/-6s, together with H-16s, continued to form the mainstay of the Navy's flying patrol boat force until replaced by newer types during the late 1920s. Four F-5Ls are known to have operated with the Marine detachment in Haiti during the early 1920s.

Navy-Curtiss NC-1 to NC-10—1918

TECHNICAL SPECIFICATIONS (NC-4)

Type: Five-place patrol flying boat.
Manufacturer: Curtiss Aeroplane & Motor Co., Garden City, New York; Naval Aircraft Factory, Philadelphia, Pennsylvania, and various sub-contractors.
Total produced: 10 (USN)
Powerplants: Four 420-hp Liberty A 12-cylinder water-cooled engines driving two-bladed wooden fixed-pitch propellers.
Performance: Max. speed 90 mph; ceiling 4,500 ft.; range 1,470 mi.
Armament: (None installed).

Weights: 15,874 lbs. empty, 28,000 lbs. loaded.
Dimensions: Span (upper) 126 ft., length 68 ft. 3 in., wing area 2,380 sq. ft.

The NC-4 completed the first crossing of the Atlantic Ocean by any aircraft when it reached England on May 31, 1919, following a 51 hour, 31 minute flight which had originated from Rockaway Beach, New York. Popularly known as "Nancy Boats," the NC (Navy-Curtiss) class stemmed from a mid–1917 Navy requirement for a flying boat that possessed transatlantic range for extended submarine patrols. The initial development contract was issued to Curtiss in November 1917, and following a study of several different design concepts by naval officials, a three-engine layout was adopted. Because the NCs were classified as a research and development project, the four aircraft ordered were not to be built at the main Curtiss plant in Garden City but sub-contracted out to eight different companies for various parts and sub-assemblies.

The NC-1 was completed in late September 1918 and made its first flight on October 4. Despite lifting a record payload of 51 passengers and crew in November, the three-engine layout

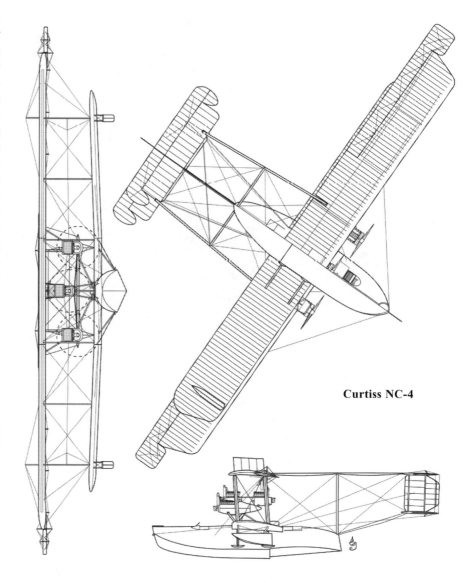

Curtiss NC-4

was determined insufficient to lift the takeoff weight (i.e., 28,000 lbs.) to carry enough fuel for transatlantic range, as a result of which the NC-2 was completed in April 1918 with four engines mounted in a tandem configuration. But when performance with the tandem engines proved to be unsatisfactory, the NC-3 and -4, which both flew in early 1919, were completed with two engines mounted in tandem between the wings on the centerline and two tractor engines mounted outboard; the NC-2 was thereafter cannibalized so that the NC-1 could be modified to the NC-3/-4 standard. The NC transatlantic flight plan called for 3,875-mile, five-leg journey from Rockaway Beach: 540 miles to Halifax, Nova Scotia; 460 miles to Trepassey Bay, Newfoundland; 1,300 miles to the Azores; 800 miles to Lisbon, Portugal; and finally, 775 miles to Plymouth, England. After departing on May 8, 1919, the NC-1 and -3 both were subsequently damaged upon landing in the Azores, the NC-1 being abandoned, while the NC-3 jury-rigged sails to make it as far as Sao Miguel Island. The NC-4 was left to ultimately complete its journey twenty-three days after departing the U.S. coast.

Six more aircraft, NC-5 through -10, were built by NAF during 1918 and 1919, the NC-5 and -6 being completed in a three-engine configuration and NC-7, -8, -9, and -10 in the four-engine NC-4 pattern. The NCs still in service in 1922 were redesignated P2N. Upon completion of a publicity tour in 1919, the hull of the NC-4 was placed on display by the Smithsonian Institution. After obtaining the remaining components from storage, a total restoration of the NC-4 was completed as a joint Navy-Smithsonian project in 1969, and it was loaned to the Navy in 1974 for exhibition in the Naval Aviation Museum in Pensacola, Florida, where it remains today.

The NC-4 became the most famous of the series when it completed the first flight across the Atlantic Ocean on May 31, 1919. It is preserved today at the Naval Aviation Museum in Pensacola, Florida.

Naval Aircraft Factory
PN-7, -8, -9, -10, and -12 — 1924

TECHNICAL SPECIFICATIONS (PN-7 [PN-12])

Type: Five to six-place patrol flying boat.
Manufacturer: Naval Aircraft Factory, Philadelphia, Pennsylvania.
Total produced: 8 (USN)
Powerplants: Two 525-hp Wright T-2 12-cylinder water-cooled engines driving two-bladed wooden fixed-pitch propellers [two 525-hp Wright R-1750D 9-cylinder air-cooled engines driving three-bladed ground-adjustable metal propellers].
Armament: One flexible .30-caliber machine gun in the bow, one flexible .30-caliber machine gun amidships, and up to four 230-lb. bombs carried under lower wing.
Performance: Max. speed 105 mph [114 mph]; ceiling 9,200 ft. [10,900 ft.]; range 655 mi. [1,310 mi.].
Weights: 9,637 lbs. [7,699 lbs.] empty, 14,203 lbs. [14,122 lbs.] loaded.
Dimensions: span (upper) 72 ft. 10 in., length 49 ft. 1 in. [49 ft. 2in.], wing area 1,217 sq. ft.

The PN series represented a cumulative effort on the part of NAF and BuAer from 1924 to 1928 to develop and test concepts for a new type of patrol flying boat that would replace the Navy's World War I–era fleet of wooden-hulled PN-5s and PN-6s. Construction of the first of the series, the PN-7, was begun during 1923; the first was completed in January 1924 and the second in June. While it retained the wooden hull of the PN-5, the PN-7 incorporated an entirely new set of single-bay biplane wings of fabric-covered, metal construction that utilized

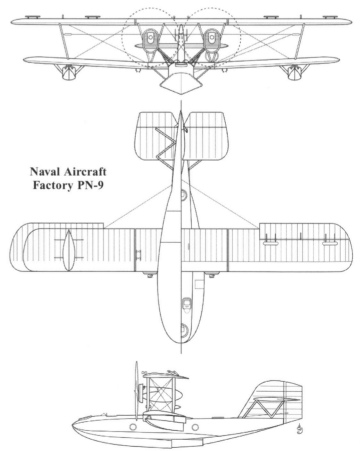

Naval Aircraft Factory PN-9

a much thicker section USA 27 airfoil in place of the RAF 6 of the PN-5. The increase in lift permitted a significant reduction in both wingspan and area, plus the strength resulting from the deeper wing spars required only one bay of struts outboard the engines. In place of the old Liberty engines, experimental Wright T-2 powerplants were tractor-mounted in neat, streamlined nacelles with the water radiators slung under the upper wing center section. Trials conducted during 1924 indicated vastly improved performance over the PN-5; however, the Wright engines proved to be unreliable, and BuAer officials expressed concerns over the long-term durability of the wooden hull.

Based upon experience gained with the PN-7, the first of two PN-8s ordered was delivered in January 1924 with a duraluminum hull identical in shape to the Porte-type sponson hull and was flown with Wright T-3 engines. Other changes included a longer-chord fin and rudder, plus horizontal tail surfaces possessing a thicker airfoil section. The second example, delivered in May 1925 as the PN-9, was tested with 480-hp geared Packard 1A-2500 V-12 engines behind large water radiators; soon afterward, the PN-8 was converted to the Packard engines and re-designated PN-9. In company with the metal-hulled Boeing XPB-1 (see below), the Navy planned to use both PN-9s to attempt the first flight from the California coast to Hawaii. As events turned out, however, only the second PN-9 was deemed ready for the 2,410-mile flight, and it departed San Francisco on August 31, 1925. Twenty-eight and a half hours and 1,841 miles into the flight, the PN-9 was forced to land in the ocean approximately 560 miles from Hawaii due to fuel exhaustion. The seaworthiness of its metal hull was aptly demonstrated after the crew, using fabric panels detached from the lower wings, sailed the aircraft the remaining distance to the islands. De-

Left, top: **Although the hull was similar to H-16/F-5L, the PN-7 introduced a shorter span, single-bay wing having a much thicker airfoil section, and new engines producing 25 percent more power.** *Middle:* **PN-9 no. 1 after being forced to land at sea between California and Hawaii due to fuel exhaustion in August 1925, used fabric from the wings and sailed the remaining 560 miles to Pearl Harbor over a 10-day period.** *Bottom:* **The Wright** *Cyclone-* **powered, metal-hulled PN-12 depicted in this photograph became the patrol boat pattern for the Douglas PD, Hall PH, Keystone PK, and Martin PM.**

spite the shortfall, the flight still attained recognition for a new seaplane distance record.

Given the success of the PN-9s, BuAer ordered four essentially identical PN-10s, two of which were delivered in late 1926. During trials carried out during 1927, the two PN-10s went on to establish new seaplane records for distance, speed, and payload. Due to the air-cooled engine policy implemented by BuAer in 1927, NAF was directed to complete the other two PN-10s with different radial engine types under the new designation PN-12. The first, equipped with Wright R-1750 *Cyclone* engines, was delivered in December 1927 and the second, with Pratt & Whitney R-1690 *Hornets*, arrived in June 1928. In May 1928 the first PN-12 set a new seaplane record when it carried a payload of 2,205 lbs. (1,000 kg) over a distance of 1,242 miles (2000 km) at an average speed of 80.5 mph (130 kph). Once BuAer settled on the Wright-powered PN-12 as the pattern for the Navy's new generation of patrol boats, aircraft companies were invited to submit proposals and, over a two year interval, contracts awarded to four different airframe contractors. (See Douglas PD, Hall PH, Martin PM, and Keystone PK, below.)

Boeing PB—1925

TECHNICAL SPECIFICATIONS (XPB-1)

Type: Five-place patrol flying boat.
Manufacturer: Boeing Airplane Co., Seattle, Washington.
Total produced: 1 (USN)
Powerplants: Two 800-hp Packard 2A-2540 12-cylinder water-cooled engines driving four-bladed wooden fixed-pitch propellers.
Armament: (None installed.)
Performance: Max. speed 125 mph, cruise 80 mph; ceiling 3,300 ft.; range 2,230 mi.
Weights: 12,742 lbs. empty, 26,822 lbs. loaded.
Dimensions: span 87 ft. 6 in., length 59 ft. 5 in., wing area 1,823 sq. ft.

Ordered by BuAer in 1925, the XPB-1 was essentially a scale-up of the NAF PN-7 (see above) incorporating an all-metal two-step, aluminum hull together with a unique tandem arrangement for its two Packard engines. Originally, the Navy had contemplated using the XPB-1 to lead two NAF PN-9s on the first flight attempt between the California coast and the Hawaiian Islands. Although the XPB-1 made it first flight on August 31, 1925, persistent problems with the Packard engines caused its participation in the California-Hawaii trip to be cancelled. The XPB-1 was thereafter retained by NAF as a testbed, and during 1928, once BuAer had officially switched to a preference for air-cooled engines in Navy aircraft, it was re-designated XPB-2 after being modified and tested with 500-hp Pratt & Whitney R-1690 *Hornet* radial engines, also mounted in tandem, but no production was undertaken.

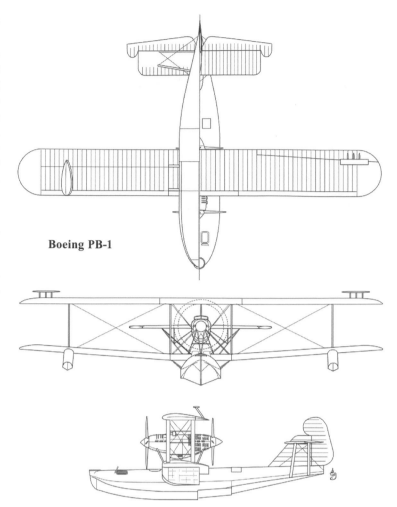

Boeing PB-1

The PB-1, when it appeared in mid–1925, was the first type of naval patrol boat to be built with an all-metal hull. The single prototype spent most of its career with NAF as a flying testbed.

Sikorsky PS-1 (S-36)—1927

TECHNICAL SPECIFICATIONS

Type: Eight-place patrol amphibian.
Manufacturer: Sikorsky Aero Engr. Co., Bridge-
   port, Connecticut.
Total produced: 5 (USN)
Powerplants: Two 225-hp Wright J-4 9-cylinder
   air-cooled engines driving two-bladed
   ground-adjustable metal propellers.
Performance: Max. speed 110 mph; ceiling 15,000
   ft. (est.); range 200 mi.
Weights: Empty (not reported); 6,000 lbs. loaded.
Dimensions: Span 56 ft., length 34 ft., wing area
   (not reported).

The first Sikorsky amphibian tested by the Navy in 1928, the S-36 was initially evaluated in the armed patrol role as the XPS-1.

Sikorsky's second flying boat design, the
company model S-36, was flown and tested
during 1927 with far better success than the
short-lived S-34 of 1926. While sharing the
S-34's general design concept, the S-36 possessed more wing area and featured a sesquiplane layout having the wing floats mounted below the bottom
wings. Another difference was an upper wing positioned higher
over the fuselage to permit the engines and nacelles to be
mounted below it. The first S-36 was flown with open cockpits
but subsequent versions came with a raised cockpit enclosure
and cabin that blended into the rear of the hull. Of five S-36s
known to have been built, one was sold to the Navy for evaluation purposes in 1927 or 1928 as the XPS-1.

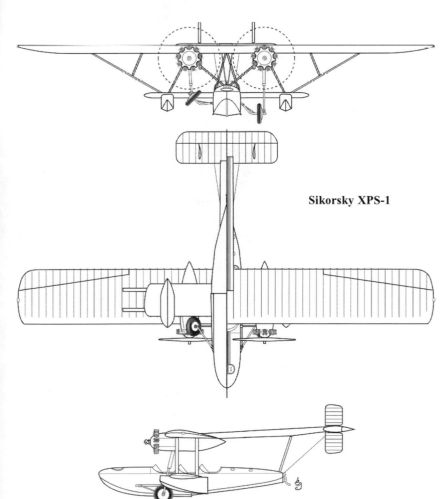

Sikorsky XPS-1

Sikorsky PS/RS-2 and -3 (S-38), and RS-1 (S-41)—1928

TECHNICAL SPECIFICATIONS (RS-3 [RS-1])

Type: Ten- to twelve-place patrol and utility amphib-
   ian.
Manufacturer: Sikorsky Aero Engr. Co. (later Sikorsky
   Aviation Div. of United Aircraft Corp.), Bridge-
   port, Connecticut.
Total produced: 9 (USN, USMC)
Powerplants: Two 420-hp Pratt & Whitney R-1340
   Wasp [575-hp Pratt & Whitney R-1690-34 *Hornet*] 9-cylinder water-cooled engines driving two-
   bladed ground-adjustable metal propellers.
Performance: Max. speed 124 mph [133 mph], cruise
   109 mph [115 mph]; ceiling 18,000 ft. [13,500 ft.];
   range 600 mi. [575 mi.].
Weights: 6,548 lbs. [8,100 lbs.] empty, 10,479 lbs.
   [13,800 lbs.] loaded.
Dimensions: span 71 ft. 8 in. 78 ft. 9 in.], length 40 ft.
   5 in. [45 ft. 2 in.], wing area 720 sq. ft. [790 sq.
   ft.].

Sikorsky's first real commercial success, the
amphibious S-38, made its first flight on June 25,
1928. It was a thirty percent scale-up of the S-36
having twice the horsepower and three times the
range. In order to maintain similar proportions,
the engines were suspended from the upper wing
on struts and the wing floats were lowered. After
11 civil versions had been sold as the S-38A, two
examples were acquired by the Navy in late 1928
to be evaluated as the XPS-2.

Left: RS-2 and -3 were derived from the S-38. This RS-3, assigned to the Marine Corps in 1931, was based in Quantico and saw service with expeditionary forces in Nicaragua. *Right:* The RS-1 was based upon the slightly larger S-41. Photo depicts one of three RS-1s delivered to the Navy in 1933. Note cowl rings and absence of lower sesquiplane wing.

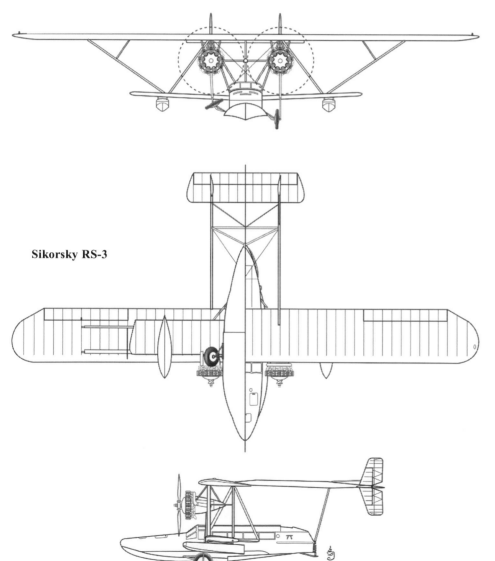

Sikorsky RS-3

The major production variant, the S-38B, was introduced in late 1928 with slightly more powerful *Wasp* engines and greater fuel capacity, and over 100 had been delivered to civil operators by end of 1932. Four S-38Bs were procured by the Navy between 1929 and 1932 and taken into service under the designation PS-3. In 1933, after removing the gun positions in the bow and stern, BuAer reclassified the PS-2s and -3s as transports under the designations RS-2 and -3, respectively. One RS-3 was assigned to the Marine Corps and used at Quantico and in Nicaragua until 1935.

Though outwardly resembling the S-38, the S-41 of 1931 was actually ten percent larger and could lift an almost 50 percent greater useful load. Besides a five-foot lengthening of the hull plus bigger, fully cowled *Hornet* engines, the S-41 discarded the lower sesquiplane layout of the S-38 for a single upper wing having ten percent more area. The first three went to commercial users, then in 1933, three were acquired by the Navy as RS-1 utility amphibians, one subsequently being assigned to Marine Corps squadron VO-9M in Haiti. All RS-1s, -2s, and -3s were phased out of service during the mid–1930s.

Naval Aircraft Factory P4N (PN-11)—1928

TECHNICAL SPECIFICATIONS (XP4N-1)

Type: Five-place patrol flying boat.

Manufacturer: Naval Aircraft Factory, Philadelphia, Pennsylvania.

Total produced: 5 (USN)

Powerplants: Two 575-hp Wright R-1820-64 *Cyclone* 9-cylinder air-cooled radial engines driving three-bladed, ground adjustable metal propellers.

Armament: One flexible .30-caliber machine gun in bow, one flexible .30-caliber machine gun in rear cockpit, and up to 920 lbs. of bombs in underwing racks.

Performance: Max. speed 115 mph; ceiling 9,000 ft.; range 1,930 mi. max.

Weights: 9,770 lbs. empty, 20,340 lbs. loaded.

Dimensions: Span 72 ft. 10 in., length 54 ft., wing area 1,154 sq. ft

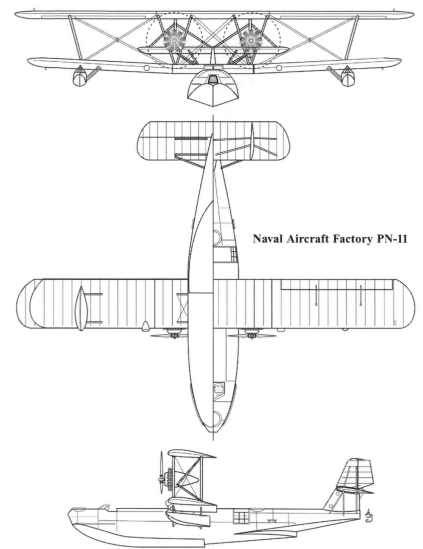

Naval Aircraft Factory PN-11

The PN-11 and P4N represented an effort to achieve better performance by combining a more streamlined hull with the biplane wings and powerplants of the PN-12. (The PN-12 actually preceded the PN-11 by a year.) Since its introduction on the Curtiss H series in 1915, nearly every large Navy flying boat had been designed with some variation of the Porte sponson-type hull. Comparatively, the new hull was longer, deeper in profile, and approximately thirty percent narrower in beam. The chief advance expected was not speed but improved hydrodynamic efficiency allowing higher takeoff weights, which corresponded to more fuel and range. The new hull also introduced a new empennage arrangement featuring twin fins and rudders on top of a high-mounted horizontal stabilizer. In 1927 BuAer ordered two aircraft with the new hull as the PN-11, and the first, powered by 525-hp Pratt & Whitney R-1690 *Hornet* engines, was flown in October 1928, and the second, with 525-hp Wright *Cyclones*, in June 1929. Trials indicated that the PN-11, with the same takeoff power as the PN-12, had picked up a 2,500-lb. increase in useful load that could be translated to a 600-mile improvement in range.

BuAer placed an order in mid–1929 for three similar aircraft as the XP2N, but changed the designation to XP4N-1 before the first example was accepted in December 1930. The XP4N-1 was virtually identical to the PN-11, while the other two, both completed in March 1932 as the XP4N-2s, carried an extra 150 gallons of fuel that raised takeoff weight by 1,250 lbs. Although the PN-11s and

The PN-11/XP4N-1 was a hybrid design, incorporating a narrower hull and twin-fin empennage with the biplane wings of the PN-12. The new hull shape became a key element in the designs of the PY/P2Y and P2M/P3M.

P4Ns never served operationally, the new hull became a key element of new monoplane patrol boats like the XPY/ P2Y and P2M/P3M.

Douglas PD—1929

TECHNICAL SPECIFICATIONS

Type: Five-place patrol flying boat.

Manufacturer: Douglas Aircraft Co., Santa Monica, California.

Total produced: 25 (USN)

Powerplants: Two 525-hp Wright R-1750 *Cyclone* (later 575-hp R-1820) 9-cylinder air-cooled radial engines driving three-bladed, ground-adjustable metal propellers.

Armament: One flexible .30-caliber machine gun in bow, one flexible .30-caliber machine gun in rear cockpit, and up to 920 lbs. of bombs in underwing racks.

Performance: max. speed 114 mph, cruise 94 mph; ceiling 10,900 feet; range 1,309 mi.

Weights: 8,319 lbs. empty, 14,988 lbs. loaded.

Dimensions: span 72 ft. 10 in., length 49 ft. 2 in., wing area 1,162 sq. ft.

The first of four flying boat types to be manufactured to the specification of the Naval Aircraft Factory–designed PN-12,

Shown from the rear quarter, the Douglas PD-1 appeared in 1929 as the first production derivative of the NAF PN-12 and was part of a broad Navy effort to replace older patrol boats like the H-16 and F-5L.

Douglas received a contract from BuAer on December 27, 1927, to build twenty-five aircraft under the designation PD-1. It was the first Navy flying boat to be manufactured in quantity since World War I and also the first flying boat of any type to be completed by Douglas Aircraft. Other than engine nacelles with flat top and bottom profiles, PD-1s were constructed according to the PN-12 specification without variation. The actual date of the first flight was not reported, but the first production PD-1s were listed as having been accepted and placed into service with San Diego–based VP-7 in June 1929. As deliveries proceeded, the type also equipped both VP-4 and VP-6 at Pearl Harbor, Hawaii. Like most of the Navy's second generation of biplane patrol boats, the career of the PD-1 was relatively brief, and all had been withdrawn from active service by the end of 1936.

Hall PH—1929

TECHNICAL SPECIFICATIONS (PH-3)

Type: Four to five-place patrol and rescue flying boat.

Manufacturer: Hall Aluminum Aircraft Corp., Buffalo, New York and Bristol, Pennsylvania.

Total produced: 24 (USN, USCG)

Powerplants: Two 875-hp Wright R-1820-F51 *Cyclone* 9-cylinder air-cooled radial engines driving three-bladed, variable-pitch metal propellers.

Armament: (PH-1 and -2 only) four flexible .30-caliber machine guns in bow and waist positions and up to 1,000 lbs. of bombs or depth charges carried under the wings.

Performance: Max. speed 159 mph, cruise 136 mph; ceiling 21,350 ft.; range 2,300 mi. max.

Weights: 9,614 lbs. empty, 17,679 lbs. loaded.

Dimensions: span 72 ft. 10 in., length 51 ft., wing area 1,170 sq. ft.

The longest-lived of the series derived from the design of the Naval Aircraft Factory PN-12, the Hall PH was the last type of biplane flying boat in American military service. Hall Aluminum became the second of four companies ultimately selected to manufacture the NAF design,

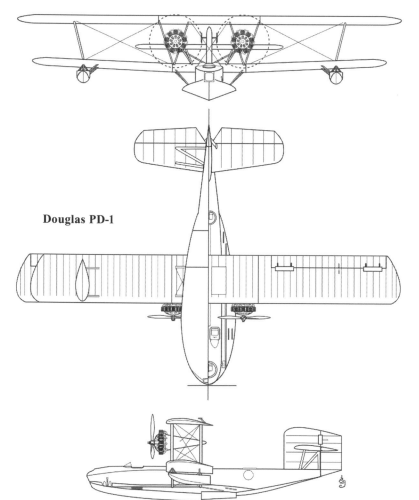

Douglas PD-1

receiving a contract in December 1927 to build a prototype under the designation XPH-1. While all of the patrol boats based on the PN-12 were very similar in general layout, they differed in details according to the manufacturer. The XPH-1, when delivered to Anacostia for trials late in 1929, appeared with a raked forward hull having a more blended sponson, a taller elephant-ear rudder, and full-chord cowlings that faired into the engine nacelles. In its test program, the XPH-1 demonstrated superior aerodynamic efficiency by posting better speed and range than the similarly equipped PN-12. BuAer awarded Hall a contract in June 1930 to produce nine examples as the PH-1, and deliveries started late in 1931. Production models differed in having enclosed cockpits, uprated R-1820-86 engines, and ring-type cowlings. All nine PH-1s were subsequently assigned to VP-8 operating out of Pearl Harbor, Hawaii, and remained in service until replaced by PBYs during 1937.

As the Navy trended toward larger and more complex monoplane patrol boats in the mid–1930s, the Coast Guard still needed a smaller aircraft to operate in the search and rescue role. The biplane planform, allowing lower landing and takeoff speeds, was also better suited to the rough sea conditions likely to be encountered. Thus, nearly five years after last PH-1 had been completed, Hall received a new contract in June 1936 to manufacture seven aircraft for the Coast Guard as the PH-2. Built to a slightly revised specification, PH-2s featured special rescue equipment that included facilities for as many as twenty survivors plus air-to-ship and direction-finding radio systems. As the PH-2s entered service

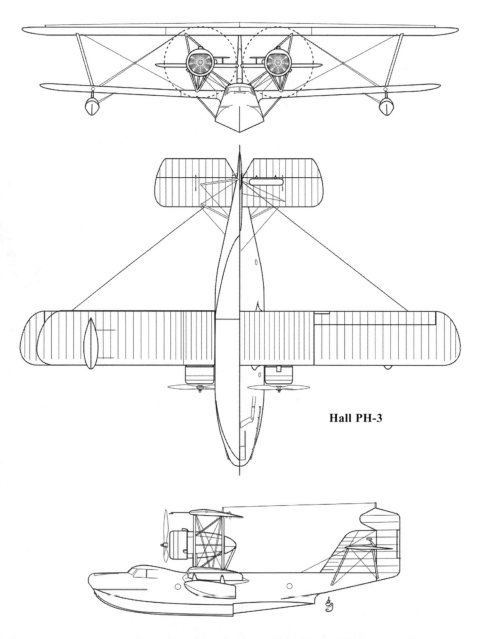

Hall PH-3

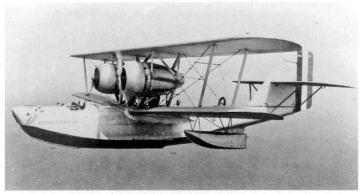

Left: **XPH-1, first of the Hall-built flying boats, as seen in late 1929. The nine production PH-1s, delivered through 1932, came with ring cowlings and enclosed cockpits. All served with VP-8 out of Pearl Harbor.** *Right:* **One of 7 PH-3s ordered by the Coast Guard in 1939. This aircraft is shown in its wartme paint scheme on the ramp at CGAS San Francisco in 1942. The last PH-3s were removed from active service in 1944.**

on both coasts during 1938, they effectively doubled (i.e., 750 miles) the Coast Guard's operational radius in search and rescue operations.

To keep pace with Coast Guard expansion and attrition of the existing PH-2 fleet, Hall received an order in early 1939 for seven more aircraft to be completed as the PH-3, with deliveries scheduled to begin in the spring of 1940. The PH-3 differed in having a revised cockpit enclosure, no gun armament, NACA-type cowlings, and a 1,300-lb. increase in useful load. After the United States entered World War II, the PH-2s and -3s were repainted in non-spectacular intermediate blue over gray schemes, but continued to operate primarily in the search and rescue role. The last examples, replaced by newer types such as Consolidated PBYs and Martin PBMs, were retired from Coast Guard service during 1944.

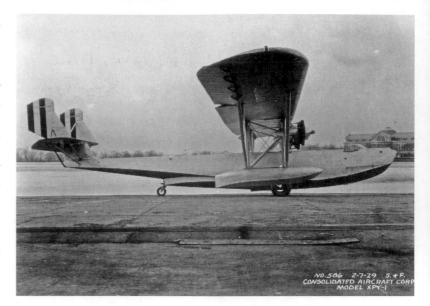

The first of Isaac Laddon's famous flying boat designs, the XPY-1 shown in 1929 on beaching gear. The type was ultimately produced by Martin as the P2M and P3M.

Consolidated PY—1929

TECHNICAL SPECIFICATIONS (XPY-1)

Type: Four to five-place patrol flying boat.
Manufacturer: Consolidated Aircraft Corp., Buffalo, New York.
Total produced: 1 (USN)

Powerplants: Two (or three) 450-hp Pratt & Whitney R-1340-38 *Wasp* 9-cylinder air-cooled radial engines driving two-bladed, ground-adjustable metal propellers.
Armament: One flexible .30-caliber machine gun in the bow and one flexible .30-caliber machine gun in the waist position.
Performance: Max. speed 118 mph, cruise 110 mph; ceiling 15,300 ft.; range, 2,629 mi. max.
Weights: 8,369 lbs. empty, 16,492 lbs. loaded.
Dimensions: Span 100 ft., length 61 ft. 9 in., wing area 1,110 sq. ft.

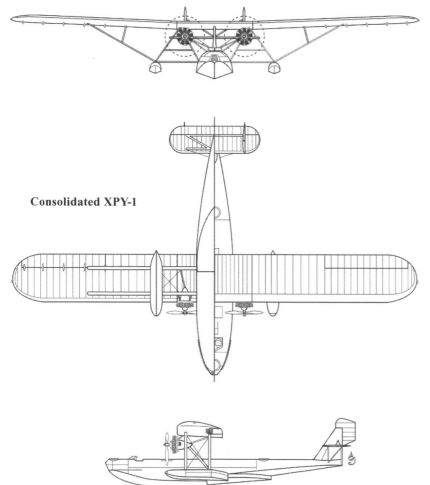

Consolidated XPY-1

Ordered in early 1928 as the Navy's first monoplane flying boat, the Consolidated XPY-1 was designed to a BuAer specification calling for a twin-engine aircraft having a single, parasol-mounted wing, mated to a metal hull and empennage similar to that of the NAF PN-11 (see above). The task of developing the design was given to Consolidated's Isaac M. "Mac" Laddon, who served as the firm's chief engineer on large aircraft projects. In order to create the aerodynamic proportions dictated by the larger monoplane wing, Laddon and his team first lengthened the PN-11 hull by seven feet nine inches, then positioned the wing overhead with W-struts from which the two engines were suspended. Horizontal spars below the W-struts were used to brace the wing structure and also served as outriggers for the stabilizing floats. As with the earlier PN series, the wings and tail surfaces were of fabric-covered metal construction, and the cockpit and crew accommodations were left open. According to standard naval procurement practices of the day, once the design was fixed, production rights were assigned to BuAer.

Construction of the XPY-1 was completed over a ten-month period and its first flight made on January 10, 1929. Consolidated assigned the factory name "Admiral" to the project, but it was never adopted by the Navy. While testing was underway, to boost speed and climb performance, BuAer ordered Consolidated to add a third R-1340 engine above the wing center-section. In early 1929, BuAer invited manufacturers to submit proposals for production of the new design and, ironically, the Glenn L. Martin Co., which came in as low bidder, received a contract June to build nine examples (see Martin P2M, P3M, below). Consolidated then turned to the civil airline market, ultimately selling 14 in three variants known as the "Commodore" model 16, 16-1, and 16-2.

Martin PM—1930

TECHNICAL SPECIFICATIONS (PM-2)

Type: Five-place patrol flying boat.

Manufacturer: Glenn L. Martin Co., Baltimore, Maryland.

Total produced: 55 (USN)

Powerplants: Two 575-hp Wright R-1820-64 *Cyclone* 9-cylinder air-cooled radial engines driving three-bladed, ground-adjustable metal propellers.

Armament: One flexible .30-caliber machine gun in the bow, one flexible .30-caliber machine gun in the rear cockpit, and 920 lbs. of bombs carried under the wings.

Performance: Max. speed 119 mph, cruise 100 mph; ceiling 10,900 ft.; range 1,347 mi. max.

Weights: 9,919 lbs. empty, 19,062 lbs. loaded.

Dimensions: span 72 ft., length 49 ft., wing area 1,236 sq. ft.

Martin's first flying boat, the PM, also became the most numerous of the patrol boat

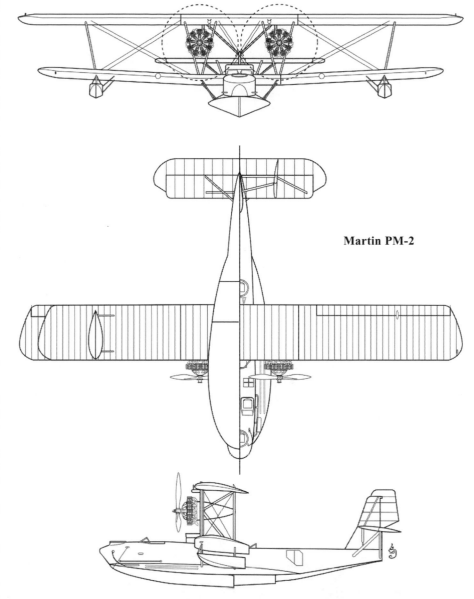

Martin PM-2

Left: A PM-1 serving with VP-9, based in Norfolk, Virginia, in the mid–1930s, the very first of a long line of flying boats to be produced by Martin over a 30-year interval. Enclosed cockpit and cowl rings were added later. *Right:* The reshaped bow and twin-fin empennage distinguishes this factory-new PM-2. The 55 PM-1s and -2s, as the most numerous PN-12 derivatives, equipped five patrol units from 1930 to 1938.

types derived from the design of the Naval Aircraft Factory PN-12. In May 1929, when Martin received a contract to build twenty-five aircraft as the PM-1, the company already enjoyed a well-deserved reputation as one of the Navy's most reliable airframe contractors. The following October, after construction had started, BuAer added five more of the flying boats to the order. Listed as the company model 117, PM-1s were virtual duplicates of the PN-12, varying only slightly in finished weight. Deliveries of the new aircraft to fleet units started right on schedule in July 1930, but before the process could be completed, three of the PM-1s were diverted to the Brazilian government to assist it in putting down a rebellion; in an ironic turnabout, the rebels, who staged a successful coup while the planes were still en route, ultimately took delivery of them when they arrived. After entering Navy service, all PM-1s were later upgraded with ring cowlings and fully enclosed cockpits.

In June 1930, Martin received a third contract for twenty-five improved PM-2s (Model 122), which differed from -1s in having a reshaped forward hull profile and the twin fin empennage of the PN-11. Deliveries of all PM-2s were completed between June and September of 1931, making Martin-built patrol boats the most numerous types in Navy service at the time. Replacing T4M-1 floatplanes, PM-1s and -2s were assigned to the Navy's two large seaplane tenders, VP-2 and -7 aboard the *Wright* based in the Canal Zone and VP-8, -9, and -10 aboard the *Argonne* in Pearl Harbor. The phase-out of PM-1s and -2s began in the late 1930s as they were replaced by P2Ys and PBYs, with the last examples being retired in early 1938.

Keystone PK—1931

TECHNICAL SPECIFICATIONS (PK-1)

Type: Five-place patrol flying boat.
Manufacturer: Keystone Aircraft Corp., Bristol, Pennsylvania.
Total produced: 18 (USN)
Powerplants: Two 575-hp Wright R-1820-64 *Cyclone* 9-cylinder air-cooled radial engines driving three-bladed, ground-adjustable metal propellers.
Armament: One flexible .30-caliber machine gun in bow, one flexible .30-caliber machine gun in the rear cockpit, and 920 lbs. of bombs carried under the wings.

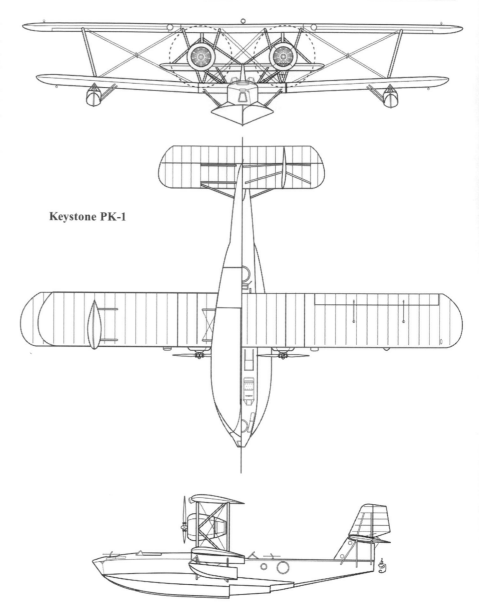

Keystone PK-1

A PK-1 as seen from the rear. In late 1929, Keystone became the last of four manufacturers selected to build derivatives of the NAF PN-12. All of the 18 built were assigned to patrol squadrons operating out of Pearl Harbor.

Performance: Max. speed 120 mph, cruise 100 mph;
ceiling 9,700 ft.; range 1,355 mi. max.
Weights: 9,387 lbs. empty, 17,074 lbs. loaded.
Dimensions: span 72 ft., length 48 ft. 11 in., wing area
1,226 sq. ft.

In November 1929, BuAer selected Keystone as the fourth and last airframe contractor to manufacture a derivative of the Naval Aircraft Factory PN-12. It was the only type of flying boat ever produced at the Bristol plant. Though not an established Navy contractor, Keystone had a proven record of building and delivering large aircraft to the Army. As built, the PK-1 (no experimental prototype) differed from other PN-12 types in having the twin-fin tail group seen on the PN-11 (see P4N, below) and engines in NACA-type engine cowlings mounted in a slightly lower position. The only variation from the standard, sponson-type hull was a flattened bow having an access hatch. While the date of the first flight was not recorded, all of the eighteen PK-1s ordered were known to have been delivered to the Navy by September 1931. PK-1s were assigned to VP squadrons based at Pearl Harbor, Hawaii and remained active until being retired in July 1938. They were the last biplane patrol boats to serve in the Navy.

Martin P2M and P3M—1931

TECHNICAL SPECIFICATIONS (P3M-2)

Type: Five-place patrol flying boat.
Total produced: 10 (USN)
Powerplants: Two 525-hp Pratt & Whitney R-1690-32

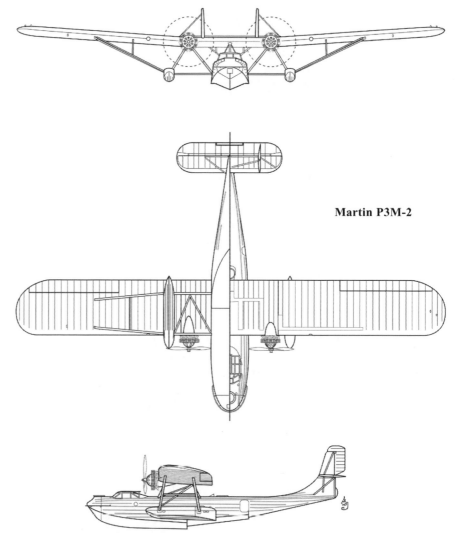

Martin P3M-2

Left: One-of-a-kind XP2M-1 as seen at NAS Anacostia in mid–1931. Because of the additional weight and drag, the third engine (as with the XPY-1) was deemed impractical. *Right:* One of nine *Hornet*-powered P3M-2s. The first three P3M-1s were underpowered with two *Wasp* engines, while the remaining six came with 525-hp *Hornets* as P3M-2s.

Hornet 9-cylinder air-cooled radial engines driving three-bladed, ground-adjustable metal propellers.

Armament: One flexible .30-caliber machine gun in the bow and one flexible .30-caliber machine gun in the rear cockpit (no bomb load listed).

Performance: Max. speed 115 mph, cruise 100 mph; ceiling 11,900 ft.; range 1,570 mi. max.

Weights: 10,032 lbs. empty, 17,977 lbs. loaded.

Dimensions: Span 100 ft., length 61 ft. 9 in., wing area 1,119 sq. ft.

As direct developments of the Consolidated XPY-1 of 1929 (see above), the P2M and P3M were both byproducts of a naval aircraft procurement system which permitted one manufacturer's design to be produced by an altogether different company according to a competitive bidding process. In this case, Martin underbid Consolidated, receiving two contracts in June 1929 to build one development aircraft as the XP2M-1 plus nine others as the P3M-1. With the XP2M-1, Martin was given considerable leeway in making certain engineering changes, while the XP3M-1s were to be exact copies of the XPY-1, including its original two-engine layout. The first of three P3M-1s, powered by 450-hp R-1340 *Wasp* engines and having an open cockpit, was delivered in January 1931; however, when overall performance fell substantially below expectations, BuAer directed Martin to complete the six remaining aircraft to a revised specification under the designation P3M-2 and modify the three P3M-1s to the same standard. The upgrade included installation of 525-hp *Hornet* engines encased in ring cowlings, plus fully enclosed cockpits. But even after trials with the new engines, the P3M's performance was still substandard, causing them to be replaced in frontline service within a year and reassigned to NAS Pensacola as trainers, and three remained on the naval inventory as of December 1941.

The one-of-a-kind XP2M-1 was rolled-out for its first flight in June 1931. It differed from the P3Ms in having three 575-hp Cyclone engines, two mounted directly to the wings in nacelles and a third on top. The wing itself was positioned lower in relation to the fuselage. Shortly after the XP2M-1 commenced flight trials, Navy officials determined that the extra weight and drag of the third engine effectively offset any advantage in speed and climb, and ordered it removed. However, by the time the aircraft resumed testing later in the year as the XP2M-2, the Navy had decided to award Consolidated a construction contract for the very similar P2Y-1. The wing-mounted nacelle arrangement was later adopted on the P2Y-3.

Sikorsky P2S—1932

TECHNICAL SPECIFICATIONS (XP2S-1)

Type: Three-place patrol flying boat.

Manufacturer: Sikorsky Aviation Div. of United Aircraft Corp., Bridgeport, Connecticut.

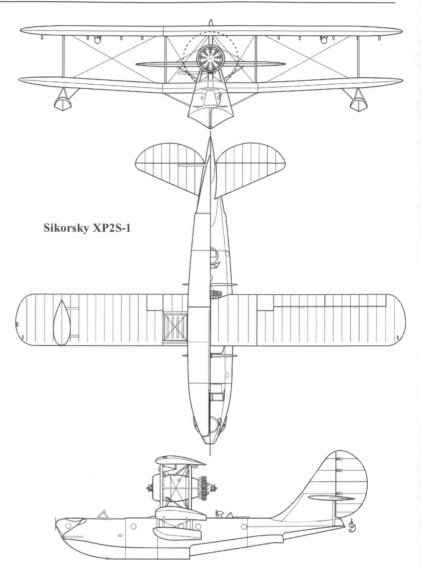

Sikorsky XP2S-1

The sole prototype of XP2S-1, delivered to NAS Anacostia in June 1932. After a year of trials, the Navy decided not to pursue the small patrol boat concept and cancelled development.

Total produced: 1 (USN)

Powerplants: Two 450-hp Pratt & Whitney R-1340-88 *Wasp* 9-cylinder air-cooled radial engines driving two-bladed, ground-adjustable metal propellers.

Armament: One flexible .30-caliber machine gun the bow, one flexible .30-caliber machine gun the rear cockpit, and up to 1,000 lbs. of bombs carried under the wings.

Performance: Max. speed 124 mph; ceiling 13,900 ft.; range (not reported).

Weights: 6,040 lbs. empty, 9,745 lbs. loaded.

Dimensions: Span 56 ft., length 44 ft. 2 in., wing area 762 sq. ft.

After selling the XPS-1 and four PS-2s to the Navy between 1927 and 1929, Sikorsky endeavored to interest BuAer in a pure flying boat patrol type that looked more like scaled-down PN-12 instead of the company's usual amphibian designs. Sikorsky received a development contract in mid–1930 to build one prototype as the XP2S-1, but did not deliver a completed aircraft to NAS Anacostia, Maryland for testing until June of 1932, nearly two years later. Using an all-metal hull similar in shape to that of the Hall PH-1, the XP2S-1 appeared as a two-bay, equal-span biplane with its two *Wasp* engines mounted in a tandem configuration. Overall performance was on a par with the larger biplane patrol boats of that era, though its range was not revealed. After approximately one year of official trials, the Navy cancelled the project.

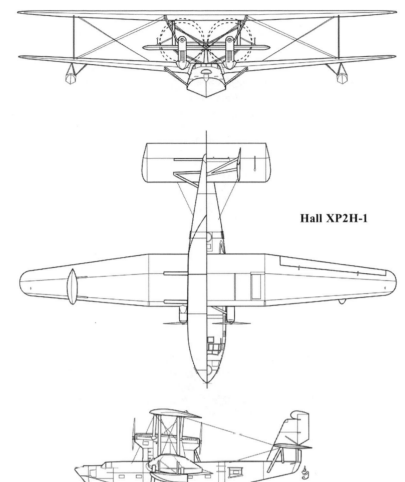

Hall XP2H-1

Hall P2H—1932

TECHNICAL SPECIFICATIONS (XP2H-1)

Type: Six-place patrol flying boat.

Manufacturer: Hall Aluminum Aircraft Corp., Buffalo, New York.

Total produced: 1 (USN)

Powerplants: Four 600-hp Curtiss V-1670-54 *Conqueror* 12-cylinder water-cooled inline engines driving three-bladed, ground-adjustable metal propellers.

Armament: Five flexible .30-caliber machine guns in bow, waist, and tail positions and up to 2,000 lbs. of bombs or depth charges carried under the wings.

Performance: max. speed 139 mph, cruise 120 mph; ceiling 10,900 ft.; range 3,350 mi. max.

Weights: 20,856 lbs. empty, 43,193 lbs. loaded.

Dimensions: span 112 ft., length 70 ft. 10 in., wing area 2,742 sq. ft.

The largest Navy flying boat to be built since the Curtiss NC-4, the Hall P2H represented an experimental effort to enlarge both the range and offensive capabilities of a naval patrol flying boat. Notably, it became the last biplane patrol type to be completed to a Navy specification and the first to feature tail gun armament. When ordered in June 1930 as the XP2H-1, BuAer departed from standard practice by specifying water-cooled Curtiss engines, apparently due to the inherent problem of cooling rear-mounted radial engines in a tandem arrangement. Hall

Massing over twice the weight of the PH, the XP2H-1 was built to evaluate long-range patrol missions. By the time trials were concluded in 1933, BuAer had decided to pursue monoplane designs instead.

evolved a design in which the dimensions of the PH-1 were increased by a factor of approximately fifty percent, yielding over twice the wing area and interior hull volume. The four engines, mounted at the lower wing roots, sat on wide, raised pylons that also contained the radiators. The XP2H-1 was flown for the first time on November 15, 1932, and was accepted by the Navy soon afterward. By mid–1933, however, BuAer had reached a decision to concentrate instead on more modern monoplane designs like the Consolidated XP3Y-1 and Douglas XP3D-1, and as a consequence, development of the XP2H-1 was discontinued.

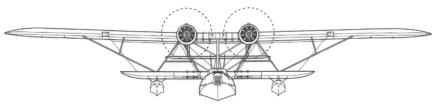

Consolidated P2Y-2

Consolidated P2Y—1932

TECHNICAL SPECIFICATIONS (P2Y-3)

Type: Five-place patrol flying boat.

Manufacturer: Consolidated Aircraft Corp., Buffalo, New York.

Total produced: 47 (USN)

Powerplants: Two 750-hp Wright R-1820-90 *Cyclone* 9-cylinder air-cooled radial engines driving three-bladed, ground-adjustable metal propellers.

Armament: One flexible .30-caliber machine gun in the bow, two flexible .30-caliber machine guns in the waist positions, and up to 2,000 lbs. of bombs carried on underwing racks.

Performance: Max. speed 139 mph, cruise 117 mph; ceiling 16,100 ft.; range 2,050 mi. max.

Weights: 12,769 lbs. empty, 21,291 lbs., 25,266 lbs. loaded.

Dimensions: Span 100 ft., length 61 ft. 9 in., wing area 1,514 sq. ft.

In May 1931 BuAer gave Consolidated a development contract for the XP2Y-1, a redesign of the XPY-1 which involved the addition of sesquiplane wings to the upper hull. The sequis-

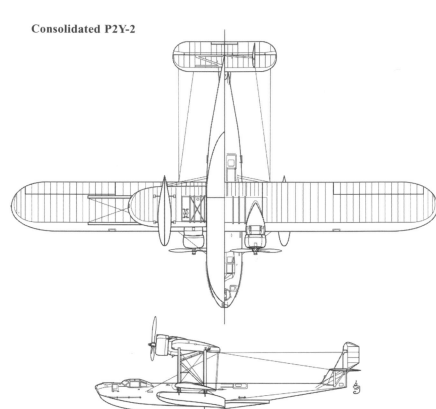

Left: A P2Y-1 serving with VP-10 over Norfolk, Virginia, in late 1933. The lower sesquiplane wing not only provided extra lift but also added space for fuel tankage and weapons storage. *Right:* One of 23 P2Y-3s, seen in 1935. Twenty-one P2Y-1s were subsequently modified to incorporate the P2Y-3 improvements and returned to service as P2Y-2s. Used as trainers during World War II.

plane layout, adding 404 square feet of wing area, not only reduced wing loading and improved payload but also supplied additional space for fuel storage and bomb racks. Other enhancements included a fully enclosed cockpit and more powerful R-1820 engines equipped with ring cowlings. In June 1931, after reviewing competitive proposals, BuAer awarded Consolidated a contract to produce a further twenty-three examples as the P2Y-1, with deliveries scheduled to start in early 1933. The XP2Y-1 made its first flight on March 26, 1932, in the three-engine configuration originally specified, but following two months of trials, the third engine was removed, and a two-engine layout was adopted as the production standard.

The first production P2Y-1s began entering service with VP-10 at Naval Air Station Norfolk, Virginia in February 1933, and by the end of the year were also equipping VP-5 in the Panama Canal Zone. Demonstrating the capabilities of their new aircraft, these two units made some notable long-distance flights: non-stop from Norfolk to Coco Solo, Canal Zone in late 1933; then non-stop from San Francisco to Pearl Harbor in mid–1934. The last P2Y-1 on the production line became the XP2Y-2 in August 1933 when modified to have its engines re-mounted on the upper wing in nacelles, together with full-chord engine cowlings having moveable cowl-flaps. In December 1933, following trials of the XP2Y-2, Consolidated received a contract to manufacture twenty-three more aircraft to be delivered as the P2Y-3. San Diego–based VP-7 received its first P2Y-3 in January 1935, and all had been delivered to Navy units by the end of May. Starting in 1936, at least twenty-one P2Y-1s underwent modifications that brought them up to the P2Y-3 standard and were thereafter returned to service as the P2Y-2. While on active service, P2Y-1s, -2s and -3s also served at various times with VP-4, VP-14, VP-15, VP-19, VP-20, and VP-21. The Navy began the process of replacing P2Ys with new PBYs in frontline units during the late 1930s, but many continued afterward in service at NAS Pensacola as flying boat trainers, and 41 were still on hand in December 1941.

General Aviation PJ/FLB Flying Lifeboat—1932

TECHNICAL SPECIFICATIONS (PJ-1)

Type: Seven-place search and rescue flying boat.
Manufacturer: General Aviation Manufacturing Corp. (later North American Aviation, Inc.), Dundalk, Maryland.
Total produced: 5 (USCG)
Powerplants: Two 420-hp Pratt & Whitney R-1340C-1 *Wasp* 9-cylinder air-cooled radial engines driving two-bladed, ground-adjustable metal propellers.
Performance: Max. speed 120 mph; ceiling 15,000 ft. (est.); range 1,150 mi.
Weights: 7,000 lbs. empty, 11,200 lbs. loaded.
Dimensions: span 74 ft. 2 in., length 55 ft., wing area 754 sq. ft.

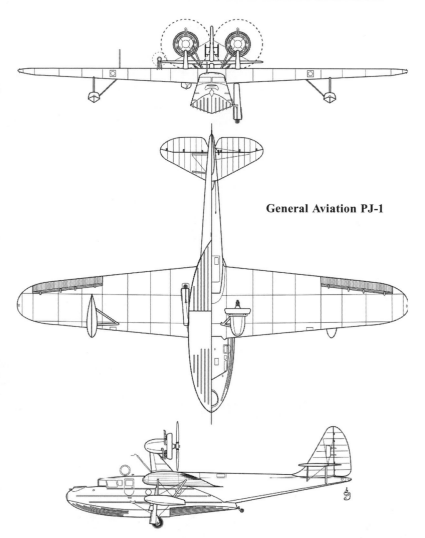

General Aviation PJ-1

Designed to a U.S. Coast Guard specification calling for a twin-engine aircraft to be used primarily in open-sea search and rescue operations, The General Aviation PJ started life in 1930 as the company Model AF-15. After reviewing competitive proposals from several manufacturers, the Coast Guard selected General Aviation's (formerly Fokker Corp. of America) proposal as the winning entry and initially identified the new aircraft as the flying life boat (FLB) without assigning a specific military designation. Though fifteen percent larger and better streamlined, the general layout of the FLB was similar to the company's earlier Fokker F-11A flying boat, also designed by Alfred A. Gassner. The date of the first flight is not a matter of record, however, the first aircraft was evidently completed sometime in late 1931 and accepted by the Coast Guard in January 1932 as FLB-8. Shortly after General Aviation was merged into North American, FLB-8, and the four production examples that followed it, received the designation PJ-1. As completed, the PJ-1 featured an all-metal hull reinforced with numerous external strakes on the sides and bottom so it could withstand the stresses of landing and taking off in heavy seas. The two *Wasp* pusher engines, encased in ring cowls behind conical nacelles, were mounted atop the wing on streamlined pylons. For beaching, small wheels enclosed in fairings could be folded-down from the wings.

As all five PJ-1s entered operational service during 1932, they were assigned the following USCG serial numbers and names: FLB-51 (formerly FLB-8) *Antares*, FLB-52 *Altair*, FLB-53 *Acrux*, FLB-54 *Acamar*, and FLB-55 *Arcturus*. Three of the PJs were based at the Coast Guard station at Cape May, New Jersey, and the other two, Miami, Florida. In 1933, FLB-51 was sent to the Naval Aircraft Factory in Philadelphia to be fitted with new 500-hp Pratt & Whitney R-1690 *Hornet* engines that would be remounted in a tractor configuration. When the aircraft reappeared as the PJ-2, its engines rested on struts rather than pylons and featured tight-fitting NACA-type cowlings that blended into the nacelles. Although the PJ-2 proved to be 15 mph faster and had slightly better range, the four PJ-1s were never modified. In their role as flying lifeboats, the five aircraft began accumulating a very impressive record, making many noteworthy rescues in the open ocean that would have otherwise been impossible. But as a consequence of the tremendous wear and tear on the airframes due to operations in heavy seas, the Coast Guard was forced to start retiring them after less than ten years of service: FLB-54 *Acamar* was withdrawn in mid–

1937; FLB-52 *Altair* in early 1940; FLB-53 *Acrux* in late 1940; and finally, both FLB-51 *Antares* and FLB-55 *Arcturus* by the end of 1941.

Douglas P3D—1935

TECHNICAL SPECIFICATIONS (XP3D-2)

Type: Seven-place patrol flying boat.
Manufacturer: Douglas Aircraft Co., Santa Monica, California.
Total produced: 1 (USN)
Powerplants: Two 900-hp Pratt & Whitney R-1830-64 *Twin Wasp* 14-cylinder air-cooled radial engines driving three-bladed, variable-pitch metal propellers.
Armament: One .30-caliber machine gun in a bow turret, two flexible .30-caliber machine guns on each side of the dorsal position, and up to 4,000 lbs. (est.) of bombs, depth charges, and torpedoes carried on underwing racks.
Performance: Max. speed 183 mph; ceiling 18,900 feet; range 3,380 mi. max.
Weights: 15,120 lbs. empty, 22,909 lbs. normal gross, 27,946 lbs. max. takeoff.
Dimensions: Span 95 ft., length 69 ft. 7 in., wing area 1,295 sq. ft.

The P3D and its amphibious Army counterpart, the OA-5, represented a serious but ultimately unsuccessful attempt by Douglas to gain a share of the growing military flying boat

Top: **Flying Life Boat 53,** *Acrux,* **shown later in its career when the Coast Guard had gone to an overall silver paint scheme.** *Acrux* **was one of the last PJs retired, in late 1940.** *Bottom:* **The first FLB delivered in early 1932 as FLB-8, it became the PJ-2, FLB-51 (V116)** *Antares,* **after being converted to tractor engines by the Naval Aircraft Factory in 1933. This was the only example to be modified.**

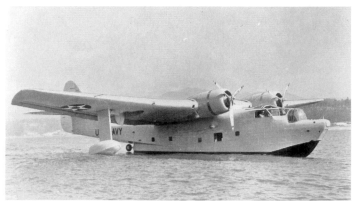

Top: **The chief contender against Consolidated's XP3Y-1 (later XPBY-1) in the Navy's 1935 patrol boat fly-off, the XP3D-1 reportedly lost the competition because of its higher unit cost.** *Bottom:* **The modified XP3D-2 as seen during new patrol boat trials conducted in mid–1936. Despite the improvement in speed, the Navy elected instead to acquire 50 PBY-2s.**

market during the early and mid–1930s. The process actually began as far back as 1932 when the Navy and Army both expressed interest in a large, twin-engine flying boat that could be utilized for either patrol or bombing missions. In December 1932 the Army gave Douglas a contract to proceed with design work on an amphibious flying boat under the designation XB-11, but after inspection of the mockup in April 1933, the designation was changed to YO-44. Only a month later, in an analogous project designated the XP3D-1, BuAer authorized Douglas to perform engineering studies with the option to order construction of a prototype. The Navy exercised its option in February 1934, and construction of the Army prototype was apparently approved around the same time, so that the two aircraft were built almost side-by-side. Whereas the YO-44 was essentially an experimental Army project, the XP3D-1 would be competing directly with the Consolidated XP3Y-1 (see below) for a sizeable Navy production contract.

Apart from the engines specified and amphibious landing gear, the XP3D-1 and YO-44 were almost identical. As the shared design emerged, it featured a two-step metal hull and a fully cantilevered, shoulder-mounted wing having the two engines mounted above on twin pylons. Stabilizing floats were fixed below the wings on struts. Positioned in front of the windscreen behind the mooring hatch, the bow turret was the first to appear on any type of military flying boat. The single fin empennage resembled a scale-up of the arrangement seen on the Dolphin. On February 6, 1935, the *Twin Wasp*–powered XP3D-1 was rolled out for its first flight; the *Cyclone*-powered YO-44, under the new designation YOA-5 (observation-amphibian), followed just eighteen days later.

Competitive trials between the XP3D-1 and the XP3Y-1, conducted at Naval Air Station Anacostia, Maryland during the spring of 1935, revealed acceptable performance and handling qualities from both aircraft. The selection of the XP3Y-1 for production over the XP3D-1 was apparently based on unit cost more than any other single factor. Soon afterward, the XP3D-1 returned to the factory to be readied for yet another round of patrol boat competition scheduled for the next year. When it reemerged in May 1936 as the XP3D-2, the engines had been upgraded to 900-hp R-1830-64s and moved down to nacelles on the wing, plus the floats now folded into the wings. These enhancements increased top speed by 22 mph and gave some improvement in range, but were not sufficient to gain the production contract, which BuAer subsequently awarded to Consolidated for fifty PBY-2s. While the YOA-5 underwent extensive evaluations with the U.S. Army Air Corps, no production was ever ordered.

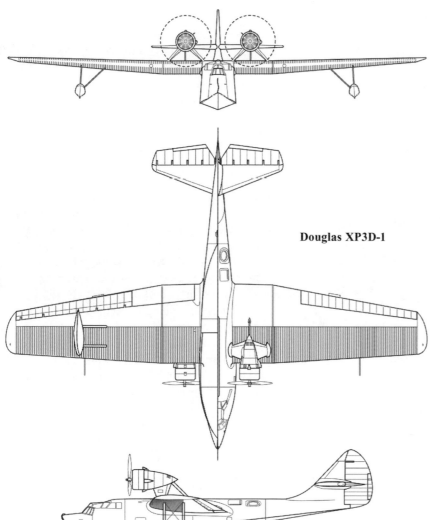

Douglas XP3D-1

Consolidated PBY (P3Y) Catalina—1935

TECHNICAL SPECIFICATIONS
(PBY-1 [PBY-5])

Type: Seven- to nine-place patrol-bomber flying boat (amphibian).

Manufacturer: Consolidated Aircraft Co., San Diego, California.

Total produced: 1,713 (USN, USMC, USCG)

Powerplants: Two 900-hp [1,200-hp] Pratt & Whitney R-1830-64 [-92] *Twin Wasp* 14-cylinder, twin-row air-cooled radial engines driving three-bladed, variable-pitch [constant-speed] metal propellers.

Armament: One [two] .30-caliber machine guns in a nose turret, two flexible .30-caliber [.50-caliber] machine guns in the waist [blister] positions, [one flexible .30-caliber machine gun in the tunnel], and up to 4,000 lbs. of bombs, depth charges, or torpedoes carried on underwing racks.

Performance: Max. speed 177 mph [195 mph]; ceiling 20,900 ft. [17,700]; range 4,042 mi. [2,860 mi.] max.

Weights: 14,576 lbs. [18,790 lbs.] empty, 28,447 lbs. [34,000 lbs.] loaded.

Dimensions: Span 104 ft., length 65 ft. 2 in. [63 ft. 10 in.], wing area 1,400 sq. ft.

A PBY-1 shown serving with Pearl Harbor-based VP-6 in 1937. The order of 100 PBY-1s and -2s in 1935 and 1936 represented an across-the-fleet upgrade of the Navy's patrol boat force.

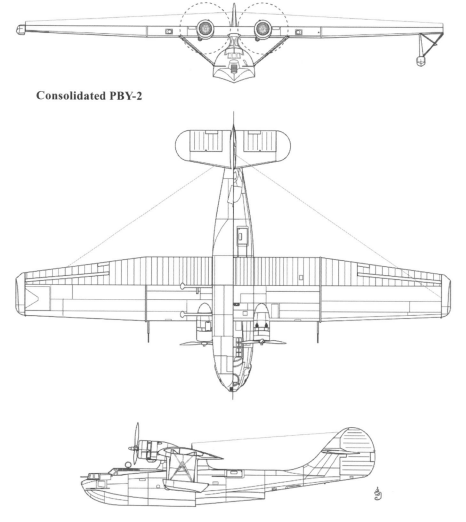

Consolidated PBY-2

In terms of sheer numbers, longevity, and versatility, the Consolidated PBY Catalina was destined to become the most famous and most widely used flying boat in the history of aviation. The origins of the PBY can be traced to a requirement issued by BuAer during 1933 soliciting proposals for a new type of patrol boat that would eventually replace the Navy's existing fleet of P2Ys and P3Ms. Consolidated received a development contract in October 1933 to build a flying prototype of its proposed Model 28 under the designation XP3Y-1, and a similar contract was given to Douglas in February 1934 to build the rival XP3D-1 (see above). Both aircraft were scheduled to arrive at Anacostia for competitive trials in early 1935.

Taking the experience accumulated with the PY and P2Y, Isaac M. Laddon and Consolidated's engineering staff evolved the design of the XP3Y-1 as an all-metal monoplane to be powered by newly available 850-hp Pratt & Whitney *Twin Wasp* engines. Special emphasis was placed on drag-reducing features such as a streamlined pylon supporting a broad, semi-cantilevered wing that dispensed with all but a pair of diagonal lift struts on each side, together with stabilizing floats that retracted flush into the wings to form the tips and a fully cantilevered cruciform tailplane. The entire airframe was to be clad in metal except for fabric-covered control surfaces and wing section aft of the main spar.

Top: **A PBY-3 with double tail bars. The 176 PBY-1s, -2s, and -3s represented an across-the-board replacement of the Navy's maritime patrol force during the late 1930s.** *Bottom:* **A PBY-4 with VP-3 in 1939. The "13" preceding the "P" on the nose indicated Patrol Wing One, Third Squadron. This was the first PBY variant to feature gun blisters and reshaped rudder.**

Construction of the prototype was completed at Consolidated's Buffalo plant in early 1935 just prior to the company's move en masse to San Diego. On March 21, 1935, after being shipped by rail to NAS Anacostia, the XP3Y-1 made its first flight. Trials carried out afterward demonstrated a significant improvement in performance over earlier patrol boat types, and while the Douglas XP3D-1 compared favorably, Consolidated bid a lower unit cost ($90,000 each) and consequently received a contract to produce sixty aircraft as the P3Y-1. During the fall

of 1935, the prototype was returned to the factory for changes that included lengthening the nose eighteen inches to accommodate an enclosed gun turret, redesigned vertical tail surfaces, and installation of 900-hp R-1830-64 engines. In the interval, the designation was changed to PBY-1, denoting new naval emphasis on the bombing role of the overall patrol mission.

Shortly after being redelivered and test flown on May 19, 1936, the revised XPBY-1 posted a record non-stop flight of 3,443 miles. As deliveries of production aircraft proceeded,

PBY-1s began entering service with Pearl Harbor squadrons during the fall of 1936, initially with VP-11, then with VP-12. In mid–1936, BuAer held yet a second competition between the XPBY-1 and the substantially modified Douglas XP3D-2, with the result that Consolidated prevailed again, receiving a contract in July 1936 to manufacture fifty more aircraft as the PBY-2, which differed from the PBY-1 only in small details. As production continued, the first PBY-2s reached VP units in mid–1937, with the last being delivered by February 1938.

In a move designed to upgrade substantially all of the Navy's old patrol boat fleet, BuAer awarded Consolidated another contract in November 1936 to manufacture sixty-six PBY-3s, which would be powered by 1,000-hp R-1830-66 engines. PBY-3s began entering service in late 1937, and by August 1938, when the last had been delivered, fourteen Navy patrol squadrons were equipped with PBY-1s, -2s, and -3s, including five based at Pearl Harbor and two in the Panama Canal Zone. In December 1937, as part of its plan to replace older aircraft, BuAer ordered thirty-three PBY-4s to be powered by 1,050-hp R-1830-72 engines, with the first examples reaching operational service during 1938. The last three PBY-4s were competed with blister-type enclosures over the waist gunner's position, a feature that became standard on future models. In order to expand mission versatility, BuAer directed that the last PBY-4 be returned to the factory and converted to an amphibian having tricycle retractable landing gear. This aircraft was flown on November 22, 1939, as the XPBY-5A.

In December 1939, in connection with a general expansion of naval aviation prompted by the start of World War II in Europe and increasing tensions with Japan in the Far East, BuAer ordered 200 PBY-5s, the largest Navy procurement of a single type of aircraft since World War I. PBY-5s featured a squared off rudder, 1,200-hp R-1830-82 engines (using 100-octane fuel), plus an upgrade to .50-caliber guns in the waist blisters. During the same time period, Consolidated received additional orders for 174 essentially similar Model 28-5Ms to be delivered to Great Britain, France, Australia, and Canada, the French order, following the German conquest, being eventually absorbed by Great Britain. The first Navy PBY-5 was accepted in September 1940 and the second delivered to the Coast Guard shortly afterward. Taken into RAF service as the *Catalina I*, the British Model 28-5Ms differed in having R-1830-S1C3G engines, six .303-caliber guns with twin mounts in the blisters, self-sealing fuel tanks, and 225 lbs. of extra armor plating around the gunner's positions. By December 1941, the Navy had a total of 362 PBYs in service, which included 164 PBY-5s and 33 amphibious PBY-5As.

Wartime contracts resulted in orders being placed with Consolidated for an additional 1,533 PBY-5s and -5As, which, besides Navy production, included 54 to the USAAF as the OA-10, 225 to Great Britain under Lend Lease, and 12 to Dutch forces in the East Indies. To keep pace with PBY demand, Consolidated opened a second assembly line in 1943 at a new plant located in New Orleans, Louisiana. Another 731 PBY-5/-5A variants were manufactured in Canada by Canadian-Vickers and Boeing of Canada. PBY-5/-5A production in the U.S. terminated in January 1945, and the final Consolidated variant, 167 PBY-6As, was produced at New Orleans from January to September 1945, at which point all PBY production ceased.

Hall PTBH—1937

TECHNICAL SPECIFICATIONS (XPTBH-2)

Type: Four-place patrol-torpedo-bomber floatplane.
Manufacturer: Hall Aluminum Aircraft Corp., Bristol, Pennsylvania.
Total produced: 1 (USN)
Powerplants: Two 800-hp Pratt & Whitney R-1830-60 *Twin Wasp* 14-

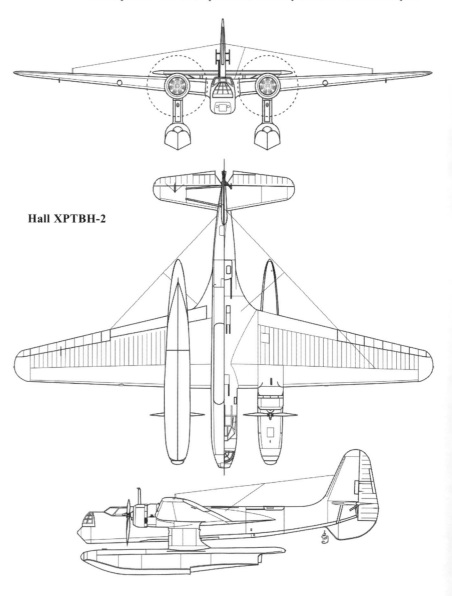

Hall XPTBH-2

cylinder air-cooled radial engines driving three-bladed, variable-pitch metal propellers.
Armament: One .30-cal. machine gun in bow turret, one flexible .50-cal. machine gun in waist position, one .30-cal. machine gun in

The one-of-a-kind XPTBH-1 seen over the Maryland coast in the spring of 1937. By the time the prototype arrived for testing, naval policy had shifted back toward carrier-based torpedo bombers like the TBD.

ventral tunnel, and one 1,850-lb. torpedo or 2,000 lbs. of bombs carried beneath the fuselage.
Performance: Max. speed 182 mph; ceiling 19,200 ft.; range 850 mi.
Weights: 11,992 lbs. empty, 21,414 lbs. loaded.
Dimensions: span 79 ft. 4 in., length 55 ft. 11 in., wing area 828 sq. ft.

The Hall PTBH was the only Navy aircraft to ever receive the patrol-torpedo-bomber designation. Its origins can be traced to a BuAer requirement issued in early 1934 for a torpedo-armed seaplane that would be launched to attack enemy capital ships (i.e., battleships and battlecruisers). The initial specification contemplated a twin-engine, twin-float seaplane with a maximum takeoff weight of 25,000 lbs. which could carry two 1,927-lb. Mk. 13 aerial torpedoes. A development contract was awarded to Hall on June 30, 1934 to construct a single prototype under the designation XPTBH-1; however, as detailed design work proceeded to the mockup stage later that year, it became evident that the anticipated speed and range could not be achieved carrying two torpedoes, thus BuAer reduced the specification to one torpedo and a takeoff weight of 20,000 lbs. The designation changed from XPTBH-1 to XPTBH-2 when the engine requirement was changed from Wright *Cyclones* to Pratt & Whitney *Twin Wasps*.

Completion of the prototype fell behind schedule due to Hall moving its operations from Buffalo, New York to its new plant in Bristol, Pennsylvania. The XPTBH-2 finally made its first flight from the factory on January 30, 1937, and was delivered to Anacostia the following April.

Although the prototype was accepted and briefly tested, naval officials had in the interval deemed the PTB concept to be impractical and decided instead to concentrate on single-engine, carrier-based torpedo-bombers like the Douglas TBD.

Sikorsky PBS—1937

TECHNICAL SPECIFICATIONS (XPBS-1)

Type: Ten-place long-range patrol-bomber flying boat.
Manufacturer: Sikorsky Aviation Div. of United Aircraft Corp., Bridgeport, Connecticut.
Total produced: 1 (3 JR2S-1)
Powerplants: Four 1,050-hp Pratt & Whitney R-1830-68 *Twin Wasp* 14-cylinder air-cooled radial engines driving three-bladed, variable-pitch metal propellers.
Armament: One 50-caliber machine in a bow turret, one flexible . 30-caliber machine gun in each waist position, and one 50-caliber machine in a tail turret (presumed to carry bomb load similar to PB2Y but no information available).
Performance: Max. speed 227 mph; ceiling 23,100 ft.; range 3,170 mi. (normal), 4.545 mi. (max.).
Weights: 26,407 lbs. empty, 48,541 lbs. loaded.
Dimensions: span 124 ft., length 76 ft. 2 in., wing area 1,670 sq. ft.

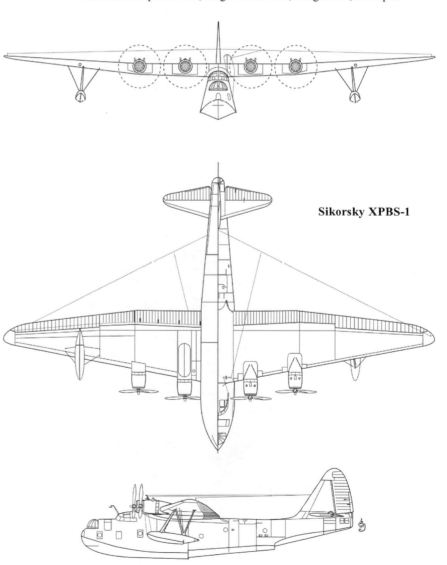

Sikorsky XPBS-1

The PBS, as the Sikorsky model S-44, came into being as one of three "Flying Dreadnoughts" to be considered by the Navy between 1937 and 1942 (see also Consolidated PB2Y and Martin PB2M, below). When BuAer requested proposals for its ambitious four-engine project in early 1935, the competition was limited to Consolidated and Sikorsky initially, Martin being invited to submit a proposal three years later. From the start, because of the enormous expense involved (i.e., $300,000+ per aircraft, not including development cost), the Navy viewed the Flying Dreadnoughts as an experimental program, limited to single prototypes. Production, if undertaken, would be based upon extensive testing and operational evaluation. After receiving a development contract in June 1935 to construct one prototype as the XPBS-1, Sikorsky and his staff began evolving a very modern design that was both functional and elegant. While sharing some similarities with the S-34 airliner, the XPBS-1 eliminated the need for supporting pylons or struts by employing a very deep, two-step hull that curved upward from the second step to raise the tail group clear of the sea-spray. Equally as innovative, the tapered, fully cantilevered wing smoothly blended into the top of the hull and incorporated fully articulated trailing flaps over 55 percent of the span.

After a two-year construction period, the XPBS-1 prototype completed its maiden flight on August 13, 1937. Initial testing revealed a top speed of 227 mph and a loaded range well within design specifications (i.e., 3,000 miles+). A stability problem traced to turbulence generated by the wings was corrected by adding dihedral to the horizontal stabilizers. After being delivered to the Navy in October 1937, the XPBS-1 was joined by the Consolidated XPB2Y-1 in mid–1938, and extensive trials between the competing prototypes followed throughout the balance of the year. Even though the Navy officially accepted the XPBS-1 in January 1939, BuAer announced

that Consolidated's entry had narrowly won the competition on a point basis and would be selected for limited production as the PB2Y-2. The XPBS-1 was thereafter assigned to Patrol Wing Five at NAS Norfolk, Virginia, where it was used to evaluate long-range patrol-bomber operations until late 1941. Early in the new year, the aircraft was reassigned to VR-2 out of NAS Alameda, California, for transport duties between the West Coast and the Hawaiian Islands, and on June 30, 1942, while returning from Pearl Harbor, the XPBS-1 struck a log in San Francisco Bay and sank. Included among the passengers and crew, all of whom safely escaped, was Admiral Chester W. Nimitz, commander of the Pacific Fleet.

Efforts to offer a 32-passenger civil version of the XPBS-1 resulted in the sale to American Export Airlines in late 1939 of three aircraft as the VS-44A (denoting a name change to Vought-Sikorsky Div. of United Aircraft). In mid–1942, shortly after all three VS-44As had begun airline operations, they were impressed into naval service under the designation JR2S-1. One VS-44A was destroyed in a takeoff accident in October 1943, but in late 1944, the other two were returned to airline ownership.

Consolidated PB2Y Coronado—1937

TECHNICAL SPECIFICATIONS (PB2Y-2)

Type: Ten-place long-range patrol flying boat.
Manufacturer: Consolidated Aircraft Co., San Diego, California.
Total produced: 217 (USN, USCG)
Powerplants: Four 1,200-hp Pratt & Whitney R-1830-78 *Twin Wasp* 14-cylinder, twin-row air-cooled radial engines driving three-bladed, constant-speed metal propellers outboard and four-bladed, fully reversible propellers inboard.
Armament: One .50-cal. machine gun in a nose turret, one flexible .50-cal. machine gun in a dorsal blister, one flexible .50-cal. machine gun in each waist position, one flexible .50-cal. machine gun in a ventral tunnel, and one .50-cal. machine gun in a tail turret, plus up to 8,000 lbs. of bombs, depth charges, and/or torpedoes carried in wing bays.
Performance: max. speed 255 mph; ceiling 24,100 ft.; range 4,275 mi. max.
Weights: 40,495 lbs. empty, 68,000 lbs. loaded.
Dimensions: span 115 ft., length 79 ft. 3 in., wing area 1,780 sq. ft.

The Consolidated PB2Y was one of several large, four-engine flying boats (see Sikorsky PBS, above, and Martin PB2M, below) conceived to fulfill the Navy's "Sky Dreadnought" concept, which envisaged a very long-range aircraft that not only fulfilled the traditional maritime patrol function but could also operate as a heavy bomber from widely dispersed sea bases. Originally proposed to BuAer as the company Model 29, Consolidated received a contract on July 27, 1936 to built one flying prototype under the designation XPB2Y-1. While sharing some characteristics in common with the PBY, such as folding wing floats, a cruciform tail group with a single fin and rudder, and a bow projecting in front of the nose turret, the design of the XPB2Y-1, by comparison, offered a much deeper hull having fully cantilevered wings mounted directly atop the fuselage without any supporting pylon. Its higher aspect-ratio

The first of the "Sky Dreadnoughts," the XPBS-1 as delivered in August 1937. In June 1942, after being assigned to transports duties, this aircraft was lost when it struck a log in San Francisco Bay and sank.

wing, swept from the leading edge, carried a load factor (i.e., 30 lbs. per sq. ft.) approximately 30 percent higher than that of the contemporaneous PBY-2. Except for moveable control surfaces, the entire structure was skinned in stressed aluminum. A very clean overall configuration was achieved by housing all droppable munitions in flush bays under the wings.

After a construction period of slightly less than eighteen months, the XPB2Y-1 made its first flight from San Diego on December 17, 1937. Serious problems with directional stability were immediately encountered, with the result that finlets were added to the horizontal stabilizers after the third flight. Further testing revealed continuing stability problems together with the need to improve the hydrodynamic characteristics of the hull planing surfaces. The prototype returned to the factory and emerged in mid–1938 with totally redesigned empennage in which twin circular fins and rudders had been end-mounted to a new horizontal stabilizer that possessed about six degrees of dihedral. To enhance hull performance, the rear step had been lengthened to extend nearly halfway to the tail. The Navy accepted the XPB2Y-1 following suitability trials, but no production was ordered at that time. The aircraft was thereafter assigned to the Aircraft Scouting Force as the admiral's "flagship."

In March 1939, after what amounted to a virtual redesign of the hull, BuAer authorized Consolidated to proceed with the construction of six PB2Y-2s. The hull of the -2 was deepened to such an extent that the wing was moved down to a shoulder position on the fuselage. Both streamlining and hydrodynamics were improved by fairing the bow smoothly into a reshaped nose turret. Enlarged fins and rudders now resembled those of the Model 31 (see P4Y, below), and available horsepower was boosted fifteen percent by an upgrade to R-1830-78 engines. New gunner's positions appeared as a dorsal blister behind the wing and circular windows on each side in the waist. In November 1940, even before the first PB2Y-2 had been accepted, Consolidated received a contract for 210 production aircraft, 177 to be delivered to the Navy as the PB2Y-3 under a revised production standard that included heavier armament, armor protection, and self-sealing fuel tanks, plus 33 similar aircraft to Great Britain as the PB2Y-3B.

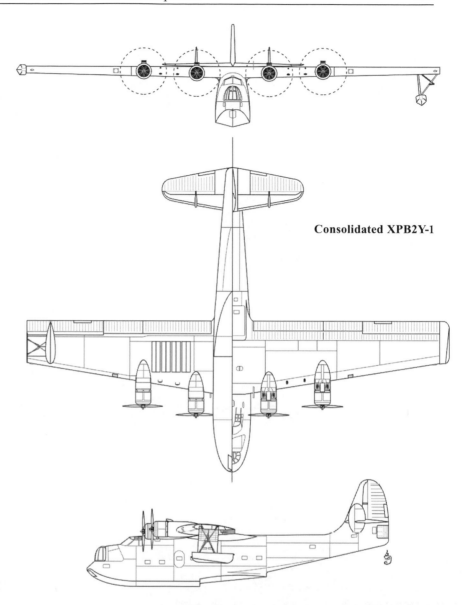

Consolidated XPB2Y-1

Right: **An XPB2Y-1 shown in original configuration in front of Consolidated's plant in San Diego, California, in late 1937. Directional control problems resulted in the addition of finlets and later, twin fins.**

One of five PB2Y-2s delivered in 1940 and 1941. The sixth became the PB2Y-3 template for mass production. All PB2Y-s were initially assigned to VP-13, a West Coast transition training squadron (TTS).

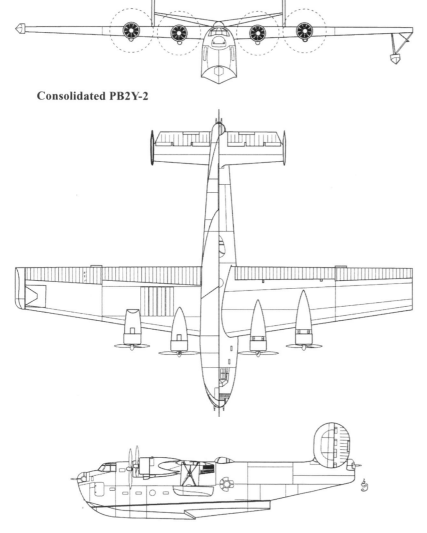

Consolidated PB2Y-2

Named "Coronado" by the factory, the first PB2Y-2 was delivered to the Navy on December 31, 1940, and four more had been accepted by mid–1941. While empty weight had risen 7,500 lbs., top speed increased to 255 mph at 19,000 feet and normal range was nearly twice that of the PBY-5. Following delivery, the Navy used the five PB2Y-2s mainly for operational training and evaluation. The sixth PB2Y-2, modified to the new production standard, flew in December 1941 as the XPB2Y-3. However, once the war started, the Navy abandoned the Sky Dreadnought notion in favor of fast carriers using smaller aircraft to bomb targets, and as a result, virtually all of the PB2Ys were thereafter converted or completed as unarmed cargo versions to be used as over-ocean transports (PB2Y-3R and -5R) or for medical evacuation (PB2Y-5H). Five PB2Y-3s and -5s were assigned to Coast Guard West Coast operations in 1944.

Lockheed PBO/R4O—1938

TECHNICAL SPECIFICATIONS (PBO-1)

Type: Four-place land-based patrol-bomber, transport.
Manufacturer: Lockheed Aircraft Corp., Burbank, California.
Total produced: 21 (USN)
Powerplants: Two 1,200-hp Wright R-1820-40 *Cyclone* 9-cylinder air-cooled engines driving three-bladed Hamilton Standard constant-speed propellers.
Armament: Two fixed .30-cal. machine guns in nose, one flexible .50-caliber machine gun in a dorsal position, up to 1,400 lbs. of bombs (or depth charges) carried in an internal bomb bay.
Performance: Max. speed 253 mph at 15,000 feet; ceiling 26,500 ft.; range 2,800 mi. max.
Weights: 12,825 lbs. empty, 20,500 lbs. loaded.
Dimensions: Span 65 ft. 6 in., length 44 ft. 4 in., wing area 551 sq. ft.

The Lockheed Model 14 "Super Electra" initially entered service as a 12-passenger airliner in September 1937, only two months after making its first flight. Its design embodied the state-of-the-art, presenting a very sleek, elliptical-section fuselage mated to a mid-wing having compound taper at the trailing edge. To offset high wing-loading (31.5 lbs. per sq. ft.), Lockheed introduced a system of tracked Fowler-type trailing-edge flaps and fixed leading-edge slots that kept landing speeds in the 70 mph range. The first militarized versions, Model 14Ls reconfigured for armed coastal patrol, were ordered by the British government in June 1938 and began entering service with RAF Coastal Command the next year as the *Hudson I,* then from 1939 onwards, approximately 2,000 more were delivered to Britain and its Commonwealth Nations in six variants (*Hudson I, II, III, IV, V,* and *VI*).

The Navy acquired its first Super Electra in late 1938, a civil Model 14H2 powered by Pratt & Whitney

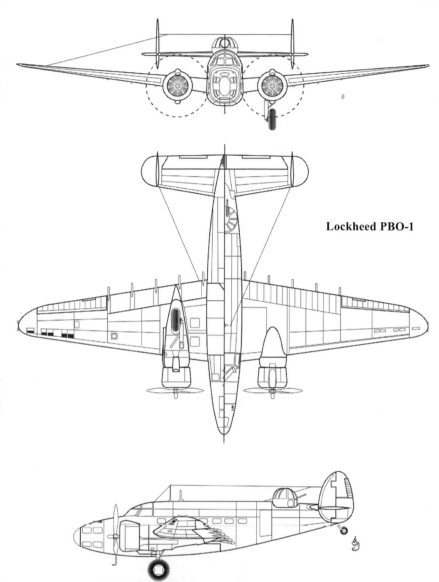

Lockheed PBO-1

R-1690-52 *Hornet* engines, which was placed in service under the designation XR4O-1 and based at NAS Anacostia to be used as a fast VIP transport. In May 1941, as American war preparations intensified, the U.S. Government ordered Lockheed to deliver 416 *Cyclone*-powered *Hudson IIIAs* to the Army Air Corps as the A-29; however, the first 20 were diverted to the Navy for the purpose of flying convoy escort and antisubmarine patrol missions from coastal stations. This marked a sudden shift in the prevailing military policy that restricted the Navy from maintaining any type of land-based bomber force (see Douglas T2D/P2D under Attack Aircraft, above). Under the assigned naval designation PBO-1, the first Lockheeds began entering service with VP-82 at NAS Quonset Point, Rhode Island in October 1941, and the unit had 14 on hand by year's end. Within the same timeframe, four more PBO-1s were received at NAS Norfolk to be used for transition training and as spares.

The first sinking of an enemy submarine credited to U.S. forces occurred on March 1, 1942, when a PBO-1 of VP-82 engaged and sank U-656 off Cape Race (southeast Newfoundland). PBOs remained in frontline service until being replaced by newer Lockheed PV-1s during the fall of 1942 and were afterward used in PV transition training units at NAS Deland and NAS Sanford in Florida.

Martin PBM Mariner — 1939

TECHNICAL SPECIFICATIONS (PBM-1)

Type: Seven- to ten-place patrol-bomber flying boat (amphibian).
Manufacturer: Glenn L. Martin Co., Baltimore, Maryland.
Total produced: 1,366 (USN, USCG)
Powerplants: Two 1,600-hp Wright R-2600-6 *Twin Cyclone* 14-cylinder air-cooled radial engines driving three-bladed, electric controllable-pitch metal propellers.
Armament: One .50-cal. machine gun in powered nose, dorsal, and tail turrets, one .50-cal. machine gun in each waist position, one .30-cal. machine gun firing downward in aft tunnel position, and up to 4,000 lbs. of bombs, torpedoes, or depth charges carried in nacelle bays.
Performance: Max. speed 200 mph; ceiling 20,200 ft.; range 3,424 mi. max.
Weights: 24,143 lbs. empty, 56,000 lbs. loaded.
Dimensions: Span 118 ft., length 77 ft. 2 in., wing area 1,400 sq. ft.

The Martin PBM, in terms of general design and structure, was arguably the most advanced twin-engine flying boat of its day. But the real impetus behind the design had been economic: faced with financial losses on its M130 airliner and dismal prospects for commercial sales, Martin had little choice but return to the highly competitive arena of military patrol boat contracts. Since Consolidated commanded such a strong position

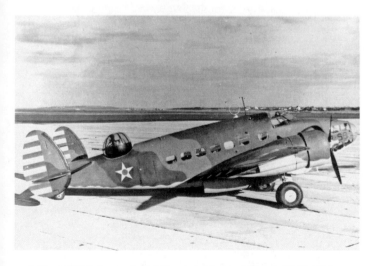

A Navy PBO-1 seen in AAF paint scheme in early 1942. This was the first land-based Navy bomber since the T2D-1 of 1927. A PBO-1 of VP-82 scored first American sinking of an enemy submarine on March 1, 1942.

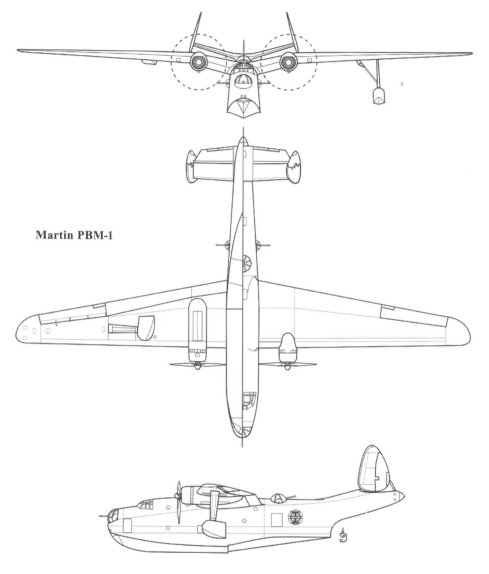

Martin PBM-1

in the twin-engine market with its PBY, Martin sought to interest the Navy in a proposal for the four-engine model 160. Coincidentally, BuAer had already contracted for two other four-engine flying boat prototypes (see Consolidated XPB2Y-1 and Sikorsky XPBS-1), and Martin hoped to insert itself into the eventual competition for a production contract. As an unsolicited private venture, however, Martin would be obliged to fund development of a prototype, which it was in no position to do; instead the company planned to build a one-fourth (25 percent) scale flying demonstrator that would validate the main characteristics of the design. When BuAer declined to consider another four-engine project, Martin went back to the drawing boards and returned in early 1937 with an all-new proposal for the twin-engine model 162, which the company promised would deliver substantially better speed, range, and payload than the twin-engine PBY. Consolidated's president, Reuben Fleet, disputed Martin's performance claims and threatened the Navy with political repercussions if his company lost a production contract. As a compromise, BuAer awarded Martin a development contract the following June for a single XPBM-1 prototype with the understanding that future production plans would hinge on test results.

Timing was critical: construction of the XPBM-1 prototype would take eighteen months or longer, and Martin feared this interval might give Consolidated the oppor-

Above: A Martin XPBM-1 in original configuration, as seen in 1939 with straight horizontal stabilizer. Testing revealed a tail flutter problem remedied by adding a dihedral to the horizontal stabilizers, thus producing the "pinwheel" tail. *Right:* The Martin M162A "Tadpole Clipper" parked under the port wing of the XPBM-1. This three-eighths (37.5 percent) scale flying testbed was intended to prove the design concept upon which the full-size aircraft would be based.

tunity to introduce an altogether new twin-engine prototype (i.e., Consolidated Model 31/P4Y). To speed progress, Martin's engineering staff reworked the plan for the M160 demonstrator into a three-eighths scale (37.5 percent) replica of the XPBM-1, and as the M162A, had it flying before the end of the year. Despite receiving a production contract for twenty-one PBM-1s in late December 1937, which had achieved the main purpose of a demonstrator, Martin continued the M162A test program and in doing so, obtained much valuable data subsequently incorporated into the final arrangement of the XPBM-1 hull.

When rolled-out for its first flight on February 18, 1939, the XPBM-1 represented a state-of-the-art flying boat concept. The design attained new levels of aerodynamic efficiency by mounting the fully cantilevered wings to the upper hull in a gull configuration which raised the engines well above the sea-spray without need for drag-inducing struts or pylons. Aft of the rear step, the hull curved upward to support a high-mounted twin-fin empennage designed to provide adequate directional stability and single-engine control when needed. To keep the airframe clean, droppable munitions were housed in enclosed nacelle bays and the stabilizing floats folded into the wings so that only one side remained exposed to the slipstream. A tail flutter problem revealed in early testing was cured by adding an amount of dihedral to the horizontal stabilizers that matched the gull angle of the inner wings, thereby giving the type its distinctive "pinwheel" tail. Performance trials indicated a 17 mph increase in top speed over the PBY-4, but the real difference was that the PBM-1 would go 30 percent further carrying twice the load of bombs or depth charges. And defensive armament was the most formidable yet seen on any twin-engine patrol boat: powered nose and dorsal turrets each armed with a .50-caliber machine gun, flexible .50-caliber guns in two waist positions and in the tail, plus a .30-caliber tunnel gun firing downward in the aft fuselage.

PBM-1s initially became operational during the fall of 1940

with VP-55 and VP-56, based at Norfolk, Virginia, then after combining as VP-74 in mid–1941, moved to a new base in Bermuda. But even as deliveries of the first PBM-1s started, the Navy was making plans for unheard of levels of aircraft production and between November 1940 and August 1941, as part of the buildup, Martin received a series of contracts for 379 aircraft to be delivered as the PBM-3. The sole XPBM-2, a long-range version with increased fuel tankage and stressed for catapult launches, was tested during 1941 but never placed in production. As of December 1941, the Navy had the XPBM-1 and XPBM-2, plus 20 operational PBM-1s on hand. Deliveries of PBM-3s commenced in the spring of 1942, and ultimately, 1,344 more of the type were manufactured, consisting of 581 PBM-3s in four sub-variants, 729 PBM-5s (upgraded to Pratt & Whitney R-2800 engines), and 34 PBM-5A amphibians, the final examples being delivered in 1949. Twenty-seven PBM-3s were assigned to the Coast Guard in 1943, followed by 41 PBM-5s in 1944.

Consolidated P4Y (Model 31) Corregidor—1940

TECHNICAL SPECIFICATIONS (XP4Y-1)

Type: Ten-place patrol flying boat.
Manufacturer: Consolidated Aircraft Co., San Diego, California.
Total produced: 1 (USN)
Powerplants: Two 2,300-hp Wright R-3350-8 *Double Cyclone* 18-cylinder, twin-row air-cooled radial engines driving three-bladed, constant-speed metal propellers.
Armament: one 37-mm cannon in a nose turret, two .50-caliber machine guns in a powered dorsal turret, two .50-caliber machine guns in a powered tail turret, plus up to 4,000 lbs. of bombs, depth charges, and/or torpedoes carried externally.
Performance: Max. speed 247 mph, cruise 136 mph; ceiling 21,400 ft.; range 3,280 mi. max.
Weights: 29,334 lbs. empty, 48,000 lbs. loaded.
Dimensions: Span 110 ft, length 74 ft. 1 in., wing area 1,048 sq. ft.

The origins of the Consolidated Model 31 can be traced to mid–1937, when aeronautical engineer David R. Davis approached Reuben H. Fleet, company president, and Isaac M. Laddon, chief engineer, with the idea of incorporating his patented wing design (i.e., the "Davis wing") to large flying boats. The Davis wing comprised a narrow-chord, high-aspect-ratio planform that utilized a relatively thick airfoil section at the center of pressure. Davis claimed that his design would generate lift at very low angles-of-attack and thereby eliminate much of the induced drag of the wing. A series of wind tunnel tests (financed by Consolidated) conducted afterward at Cal Tech exceeded even the most optimistic expectations, demonstrating that the Davis wing produced greater aerodynamic efficiency that any wing yet tested.

In 1938, with the aim of producing an experimental demonstrator that could potentially be offered on either commercial or military markets, Fleet authorized Laddon to proceed with a new flying boat design that would integrate the Davis wing with a hull similar in configuration to that of the PB2Y. The

A production PBM-1 delivered to Norfolk-based VP-55 in late 1940. The prototype's tail flutter problem was corrected by adding dihedral to the horizontal stabilizers, giving the type its distinctive "pinwheel" tail.

structure utilized the advanced technique of flush-riveting the aluminum skins to the metal framework of the wings and fuse-lage. Moveable control surfaces were of fabric-covered metal construction. To accommodate the narrow chord of the wings, the floats were made to fold inward against the wing undersur-faces. The engines selected, experimental Wright R-3350s, were the most powerful American-made aircraft engines in ex-istence but had yet to be tested on a flying aircraft. Though not actually built to military requirements, the decision to adopt a twin-engine (instead of a four-engine) layout was undoubtedly influenced by BuAer's recent procurement of the Martin PBM (see above). The shape and arrangement of the Model 31's twin fin tail group benefited from Consolidated's previous experi-

ence with the PB2Y, and together with the Davis wing, would be seen again in the design of the Model 32 (XB-24). Soon after making its first flight on May 5, 1939 under civil registra-tion number NX21731, the Model 31 established itself as the fastest flying boat in the world and was also the first aircraft to fly with R-3350 engines.

After no commercial orders for the Model 31 materialized, Consolidated embarked upon a campaign in 1940 and 1941 to sell the Navy a military variant that would be completed to a patrol-bomber specification. Although BuAer evinced no in-terest in the project at the start, Consolidated nonetheless con-tinued the test program at its own expense. Revisions to the prototype during almost two years of testing included raising

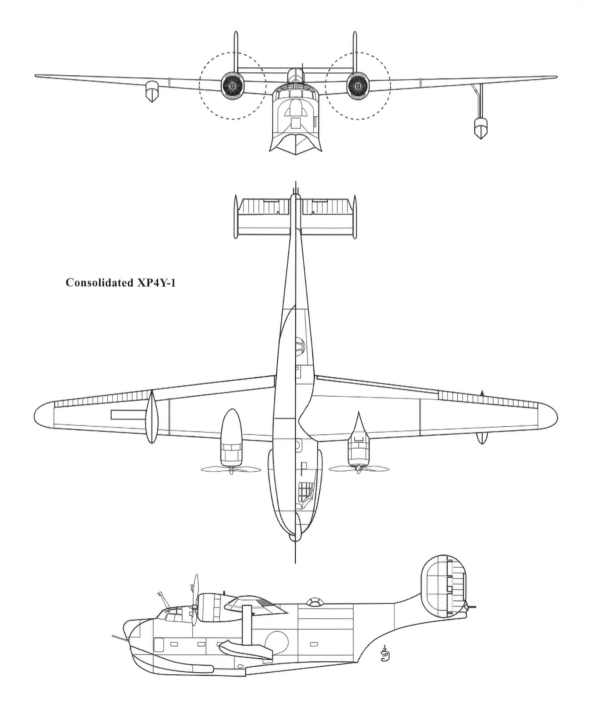

Consolidated XP4Y-1

the empennage to accommodate a tail turret, adding a cuff that widened the planing surfaces of the forward hull, and installation of dummy gun turrets. In April 1942, the Navy finally purchased the Model 31 under the designation XP4Y-1, and soon

An XP4Y-1 depicted in wartime colors. Retractable tip floats and bow skirt are evident in this photograph. Allocation of all R-3350 engine production to the B-29 program caused P4Y production to be cancelled.

Dimensions: Span 200 ft. 0 in., length 117 ft. 3 in., wing area 3,683 sq. ft

Though technically not a pre–1942 aircraft, the PB2M would most likely have flown sometime in late 1941 had it not been damaged in the middle of taxi tests. Martin started preliminary design work on its Model 170 in 1937 while the Navy already had two other four-engine flying boat prototypes under construction (see Sikorsky PBS and Consolidated PB2Y, above). Under the unofficial heading "Sky Dreadnought," naval policy makers were studying the feasibility of using very large flying boats for long-range bombardment as well as maritime patrol. On August 23, 1938, after considering Martin's proposal, BuAer was sufficiently impressed to award the company a development contract for a single prototype as the XPB2M-1. While much larger and heavier, the XPB2M-1's structural, aerodynamic, and hull design shared many characteristics with the XPBM-1, and its final configuration owed much to the data accumulated during the XPBM-1's test program. Instead of nacelle bays, munitions were to be stored in two hull compartments located just below the wings from which weapons would be deployed on sliding racks.

Because of unforeseen production priorities (i.e., B-26 bombers for the Army

afterward, ordered the type placed into production as the P4Y-1 at a new plant to be established in New Orleans, Louisiana. The factory name "Corregidor" was assigned but never officially adopted. In mid–1943, before the P4Y-1 assembly line had been tooled-up, production was cancelled due to the fact that all R-3350 engines were being allocated to the B-29 program for an indefinite time. The New Orleans plant was instead used to open a second assembly line of PBYs.

Martin PB2M Mars—1942

TECHNICAL SPECIFICATIONS (XPB2M-1)

Type: Eleven-place long-range patrol-bomber flying boat.
Manufacturer: Glenn L. Martin Co., Baltimore, Maryland.
Total produced: 1 (USN)
Powerplants: Four 2,200-hp Wright R-3350-8 *Double Cyclone* 18-cylinder air-cooled radial engines driving three-bladed, electric controllable-pitch laminated wooden propellers.
Armament: One .30-caliber machine gun each in nose, dorsal, waist, and tail turrets and up to 10,000 lbs. of bombs, torpedoes, or depth charges carried in two upper hull bays.
Performance: Max. speed 221 mph, cruise 149 mph; ceiling 14,600 ft.; range 4,375 mi. max.
Weights: 75,573 lbs. empty, 144,000 lbs. loaded.

Martin XPB2M-1 in 1942, soon after its first flight. Taxiing accident in November 1941 delayed first flight until July 1942, by which time the "Sky Dreadnought" concept had been abandoned in favor of more carriers.

Martin XPB2M-1

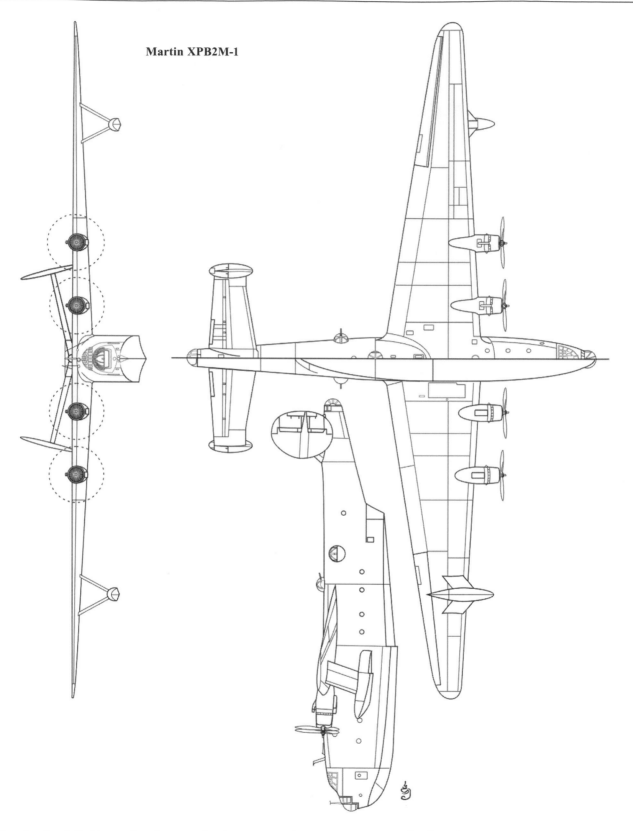

and *Maryland* and *Baltimore* bombers on foreign contracts), Martin did not start construction of the XPB2M-1 prototype until mid–1940. As it neared completion in the fall of 1941, the giant aircraft was christened "Mars" in line with the company's practice of choosing names beginning with the letter M. The

XPB2M-1 was finally rolled out of the factory and launched in the Middle River the first week of November 1941, however, while conducting taxi tests, the number three engine threw a propeller blade and caught fire. By the time the aircraft could be towed to shore, the starboard wing and number three nacelle had been seriously damaged by the fire and the hull where the propeller blade penetrated. Martin spent over six months making repairs, and the first flight of the XPB2M-1 did not occur until July 2, 1942. It was the largest flying boat to have ever flown and the second largest aircraft in the world (the Douglas XB-19 of 1941 being fractionally larger). But by that time, the Navy had discarded the Sky Dreadnought idea and the Mars was eventually disarmed and converted to a transport configuration as the XPB2M-1R.

TRAINER, TRANSPORT, AND UTILITY AIRCRAFT

Synopsis of Trainer, Transport, and Utility Aircraft Procurement

Trainer Aircraft: By the time World War I ended, the Naval Aviation Training Establishment boasted a force of over 1,000 training aircraft, consisting mainly of Aeromarine 39s, Burgess N-9s, and Curtiss F Boats and JN-4s. While some of these aircraft would serve on into 1920s, the Naval Bureau of Aeronautics (BuAer), after being formed in 1921, nonetheless believed that the Navy's future training needs would be better served by one aircraft combining the functions of landplane, seaplane, and aerial gunnery into one airframe. Evaluations of no less than six different trainer types took place between 1923 and 1925, with two of the entries being ordered into production, 73 Boeing NB-1s and -2s and, initially, 76 Consolidated NY-1s (naval version of the Army PT-1). Then from 1926 to 1929, BuAer ordered a further 186 NY-2s (the largest trainer order since 1918), 25 NY-2As, and 20 NY-3s, making it the most important aircraft in the Navy's flight training program at NAS Pensacola. A second trainer competition held between 1928 and 1930 resulted in the purchase of 51 Curtiss N2Cs to equip reserve units, six Consolidated (Fleet) N2Ys for use in the lighter-than-air program, 16 Keystone NKs (eventual application unknown), and six New Standard NTs subsequently assigned to NAF.

BuAer commenced an across-the-board trainer replacement program in 1934 when it acquired three Consolidated N4Y-1s (Navy variant of the Army PT-11) for evaluation purposes, but before any could be ordered in quantity, due to recent legislative initiatives (i.e., Vinson-Trammel Naval Act of 1934), directed the Naval Aircraft Factory (NAF) to build its own prototype XN3N-1. In a series of contracts issued in 1936, NAF received orders for a total of 180 N3N-1s, but at virtually the same time, BuAer ordered 61 Boeing NS-1s to relieve NAF's production backlog. Of even greater import, new Naval Expansion Acts passed in 1938 and 1940 served to produce an explosion of trainer orders: 816 N3N-3s in 1939 and 1940, plus 616 Boeing N2S-1s, -3s (Army PT-17) and -2s (Army PT-13) in 1940 and 1941. BuAer also procured 201 Spartan NPs in 1940 expressly for Naval Reserve Primary Flying Schools, then in 1941,

purchased 100 Ryan NRs (Army PT-22) to be used at a new training facility at NAS Jacksonville. Continuing trainer orders from 1942 onwards accounted for delivery of 3,821 more N2S variants, turning it into the Navy's most numerically important primary trainer of the wartime era.

Through most of the interwar period, if it used them at all, the Navy typically employed older operational aircraft (e.g., Vought O2U, Curtiss O2C, Martin T4M, etc.) for advanced training purposes, however, by the mid–1930s, significant improvements in aircraft performance dictated the need for advanced trainers to provide an incremental transition from primary types into new frontline aircraft, especially fighter and attack types. Toward this end, 40 North American NJ-1s (based on the Army BT-9) delivered in 1937 were incorporated into flight training at NAS Pensacola, followed in 1938 by procurement of 16 retractable-gear versions as the SNJ-1. An urgent need to upgrade equipment in reserve units motivated a follow-up North American contact in 1939 for 61 SNJ-2s. The huge naval expansion that commenced in 1940 ultimately resulted in additional orders for 545 SNJ-3s, 2,400 SNJ-4s, 1,568 SNJ-5s, and 411 SNJ-6s, and to supplement SNJs already on order, Curtiss received contracts in 1940 and 1941 for 305 SNC-1s. The need to introduce "intermediate" pilot training between primary and advanced levels led to a contract award to Vultee in 1940 for 1,350 SNV-1s (Army BT-13), with initial deliveries beginning in mid–1941. Altogether, efforts begun in 1938 had added 2,247 training aircraft of all types to the naval inventory by the end of 1941.

Transport and Utility Aircraft: Unlike the aircraft types discussed in the preceding categories, most of the transport and utility aircraft procured during the interwar period were not built to any identifiable naval requirements but acquired as off-the-shelf civil aircraft that had been designed for either private or commercial purposes. Moreover, BuAer's assignment of designations to these aircraft was somewhat perplexing, inasmuch as the delineation between "transport" (initially T, later R) and "utility" (J) types and sub-types appears to have been almost random. The designation system began following a better rule-of-thumb in the late 1930s when BuAer assigned R (transport) to larger multi-engine landplanes, JR (utility-transport) to multi-engine seaplanes and smaller twin-engine landplanes, and G (transport, single-engine) to single-engine landplanes, but even so, J (utility) was still occasionally assigned to some seaplanes and landplanes.

Availability of the first American multi-engine commercial airliners in the mid–1920s prompted acquisition between 1927 and 1932 of seven Atlantic (Fokker) F.VII tri-motors (as TA/RA) and nine Ford 4-AT and 5-AT tri-motors (as JR/RR). Used primarily by Navy and Marine command staff personnel, these aircraft could also move high-priority cargos when the need arose. In this timeframe, to be used as smaller staff transports, BuAer also purchased one Fairchild FC-2 (as JQ/RQ), one Lockheed Altair (as RO), one Curtiss Kingbird (as JC/RC), and three Bellanca CH-400 Skyrockets (as RE/JE). To improve the amphibious transportation capabilities in Navy, Marine, and

Coast Guard operations, Douglas received contracts to manufacture 59 twin-engine RDs which were placed in service between 1931 and 1934. Representing a major effort to replace older single-engine amphibians in the ship-to-shore utility role, BuAer awarded a series of contracts to Grumman from 1933 to 1935 to produce 46 JF "Ducks," with almost half being allocated to Marine, Coast Guard, and Naval Reserve units. Revisions to the Duck plus a change of designation to J2F in 1936 generated even more orders: 20 J2F-1s delivered in 1937; 21 J2F-2s, nine J2F-2As, 20 J2F-3s, and 32 J2F-4s all delivered in 1939; and 144 J2F-5s, of which 68 had been received by the end of 1941. A further 406 J2F-5s and -6s (built by Columbia) were delivered during World War II.

Efforts to upgrade older Atlantic and Ford transports came in 1934 and 1935 with the procurement of two Curtiss AT-32E Condors (as R4C) and five Douglas DC-2s (as R2D). Two Waco UBF biplanes (as JW) acquired in 1934 were fitted with skyhook arresting systems for duties with Macon (ZRS-5). Additionally, BuAer purchased an assortment of single-engine, executive-type transports between 1934 and 1936 for both Navy and Coast Guard use: two Stinson SR-5s (as R3Q [RQ]), one Northrop Delta (as RT), three Kinner Envoys (as RK), one Fairchild 45A (as JK), four Fairchild 24Cs (as J2K), and three Waco EQC cabin biplanes (as J2W). A parasol-wing Fairchild 22C-7 (as R2K) acquired in 1936 under naval registration was used by NACA to test a "Zap" flap system. Two twin-engine Lockheed Model 10 Electras joined the inventory as the R2O and R3O in 1936, one for use by the Secretary of the Navy and the other for the Coast Guard, followed in 1937 by six Lockheed Model 12 Electra Juniors as the JO, three of which were assigned to the Marines, and a seventh fixed tricycle-gear example in 1938, as the XJO-3, delivered to NAS Anacostia for experimental purposes.

The Navy substantially upgraded its twin-engine utility amphibian fleet from 1937 to 1939 with procurement of 17 Sikorsky S-43s (as JRS-1) and 11 Grumman G-21s (as JRF-1). More Grumman Amphibians were ordered during the 1940 and 1941 expansions: seven JRF-2s and three JRF-3s for the Coast Guard, 10 JRF-4s equipped with bomb racks, and finally, 185 JRF-5s, of which 16 had been delivered by the end of 1941. BuAer purchased two Stearman-Hammond Y-1Ss in 1937 as the XJH-1, to be used as target drones.

One single-engine Beech C17R Staggerwing (as JB-1) joined the inventory in 1937 as a staff transport, then ten D17S models (as GB-1) were added in 1939 to be used by Naval Attachés in foreign embassies. Beech received an additional order in 1941 for 271 D17S models, with six reaching service by the end of the year as the GB-2. A single civil Lockheed Model 14 was acquired in 1939 as a fast staff transport as the XR4O-1, followed by militarized versions coming into service in 1941 and 1942 as the PBO-1.

The first Navy transports actually completed to any particular military requirement were four of the seven twin-engine Douglas DC-5s procured in 1940 (as R3D-1, -2, and -3), which, as R3D-2s, came with cargo doors, reinforced cabin floors, and smaller fuel tanks (for increased payload) for use by the Marines in paratrooper operations. In mid–1940 BuAer awarded Beech a contract for 11 twin-engine Model 18S executive transports modified as target drone controllers (as JRB-1), followed later the same year with an order for 15 transport versions (as JRB-2), with all in service by the end of 1941. Another 1,400 naval Beech 18 variants would be produced during World War II (571 JRB-3s and -4s and 829 SNB-1s and -2s). BuAer commandeered all initial production of Grumman's G-44 twin-engine civil amphibian in 1941, allocating the first 25 to the Coast Guard as the J4F-1; and from 1942 to 1945, a further 131 were accepted under Navy Bureau Numbers as the J2F-2. Although originally ordered in 1940 and eventually acquired in substantial numbers during World War II (571 R4Ds in seven variants), the only examples of the legendary Douglas DC-3 to actually reach Navy service during 1941 were two stock civil models requisitioned from Eastern Airlines (as R4D-2). The last type of single-engine civil transport entering service before the end of 1941 was six (of 34 ordered) Howard DGA-15Ps as the GH-1; wartime orders would account for 451 more as the GH-2, -3, and NH-1.

The two types of gliders procured during the interwar period are mentioned in this category only for the purpose of organization. Six one-place Franklin PS-2s were assigned to NAS Pensacola in 1934 to see whether gliders should be incorporated into the pilot training program and 13 Schweizer SGC 2-8s (LNS-1, same as AAF TG-2) went into service with the Marines in 1941 (possibly later) to train pilots for a planned assault glider program.

Curtiss/Burgess N-9—1916

TECHNICAL SPECIFICATIONS (N-9H)

Type: Two-place floatplane trainer.
Manufacturer: Curtiss Aeroplane & Motor Co., Garden City and Buffalo, New York; the Burgess Co., Marblehead, Massachusetts.
Total produced: 560 (USN, USMC)
Powerplant: One 150-hp Wright-Hispano A 8-cylinder water-cooled engine driving a two-bladed wooden fixed-pitch propeller.
Performance: Max. speed 80 mph at s.l.; ceiling 9,850-ft.; range 179 mi.
Weights: 2,140 lbs. empty, 2,765 lbs. loaded.
Dimensions: Span 53 ft. 4 in., length 30 ft. 10 in., wing area 496 sq. ft.

Conceived as a floatplane derivative of the Army's popular JN trainer series, the Navy Department gave Curtiss an initial contract in August 1916 for 30 aircraft as the N-9, and the first examples appeared later the same year. It differed from the basic JN-4 series in having 10 feet of additional wingspan, larger tailplane, and a more powerful (100-hp) OXX-6 engine, which was needed to compensate for the extra weight and drag of the floats. Even so, early experience revealed that the type was still underpowered, leading to the introduction in 1917 of the N-9H with the 150-hp Wright-Hispano A (a licensed copy of the French Hispano-Suiza A). By the time of the armistice in November 1918, 560 of the type, primarily N-9Hs, had been

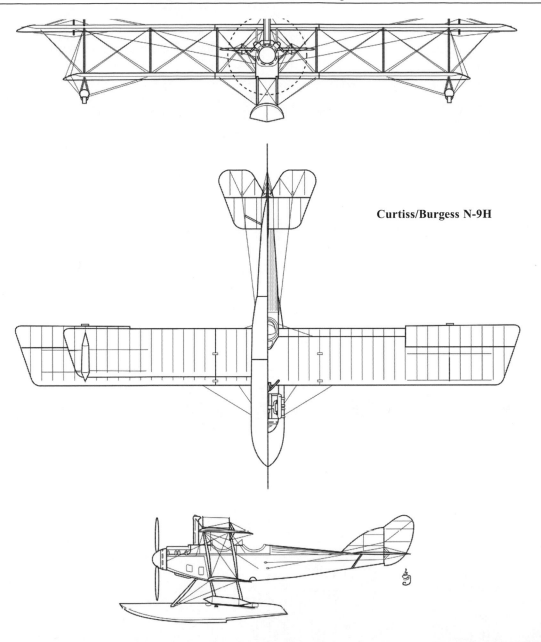

Curtiss/Burgess N-9H

delivered to the Navy, 460 of them having been completed under license by the Burgess Co. (a Curtiss subsidiary). N-9s continued to be extensively used in training and utility roles after the war, and the final examples were not withdrawn from service until 1927.

An N-9H standard World War I Navy trainer, basically a Jenny with a more powerful engine, an extra bay of struts, and enlarged fin and rudder. The last examples were not withdrawn until 1927.

Aeromarine 39—1917

TECHNICAL SPECIFICATIONS (39-B)

Type: Two-place landplane/floatplane trainer.
Manufacturer: Aeromarine Plane & Motor Co., Keyport, New Jersey.
Total produced: 200 (USN).
Powerplant: one 100-hp Curtiss OXX-6 8-cylinder water-cooled engine driving a two-bladed wooden fixed-pitch propeller.
Performance: Max. speed 73 mph at s.l.; ceiling 8,200 ft.; range 273 mi.
Weights: 1,467 lbs. empty, 2,017 lbs. loaded.
Dimensions: span 43 ft. 8 in., length 27 ft. 4 in., wing area 353 sq. ft.

On October 22, 1922, an Aeromarine 39-B piloted by Lt. Cdr. Geoffrey DeChevalier became the first aircraft to land on the *Langley* (CV-1), the U.S. Navy's first aircraft carrier. In mid–1917, as a result of a successful bid on Navy Department specifications issued for a training aircraft convertible to land or sea operations, Aeromarine received a contract for 50 Model 39-As, conventional two-bay biplanes of fabric-covered wooden construction that were initially powered by 100-hp Hall-Scott 6-cylinder engines. Early evaluations with twin floats fitted led to an increase in the upper wingspan to reduce wing loading

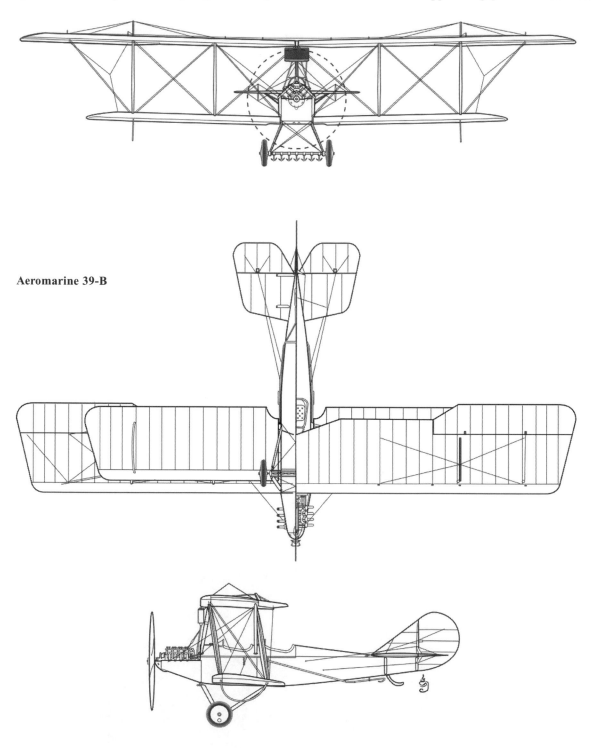

Aeromarine 39-B

for easier water takeoffs. The 100 Model 39-Bs, delivered in 1918, introduced refinements to the basic design that included enlarged tail surfaces, a centerline float for seaplane operations, and an OXX-6 V-8 powerplant. In the period following the war, the Navy continued to operate the 39-Bs as one of its standard primary trainers.

The Curtiss "Jenny" was the most produced American aircraft of the World War I era. The Navy procured 30 JN-4Hs in 1918 for advanced pilot training, followed by 83 more in 1919. It was withdrawn in 1926.

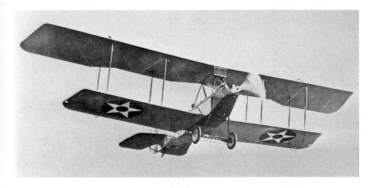

On final approach, this 39-B is seen just before making the first landing aboard the carrier Langley on October 22, 1922. Docile handling qualities made it a good choice for early carrier experiments.

Because of its excellent low airspeed handling qualities, the 39-B was selected for the earliest carrier experiments. The aircraft was fitted with a rear-mounted arrestor hook to engage cross-deck cables in combination with alignment hooks on the spreader bar between the main wheels to engage lengthwise wires intended to keep the plane running straight. Starting in early 1923, after successful experiments, a unit of 39-Bs began operating aboard *Langley* to test and develop deck procedures for handling larger numbers of aircraft. The last examples were withdrawn in 1926.

Curtiss JN-4 and -6—1918

TECHNICAL SPECIFICATIONS (JN-4H)

Type: Two-place landplane advanced and gunnery trainer.
Manufacturer: Curtiss Aeroplane & Motor Co., Garden City and Buffalo, New York.
Total produced: 261 (USN, USMC).
Powerplant: One 150-hp Wright-Hispano A 8-cylinder water-cooled engine driving a two-bladed wooden fixed-pitch propeller.
Armament (JN-4HG): One .30-cal. machine gun on scarf ring in rear cockpit.
Performance: Max. speed 93 mph at s.l.; ceiling 10,525 ft.; range 268 mi.
Weights: 1,467 lbs. empty, 2,017 lbs. loaded.
Dimensions: span 43 ft. 8 in., length 27 ft. 4 in., wing area 353 sq. ft.

The Curtiss "Jenny," achieved fame as the Army's most important primary trainer during the World War I era and later, as a civil aircraft, after hundreds had been sold surplus. Although the Navy acquired small numbers of early Jenny variants, JN-1s, JN-1Ws (float-

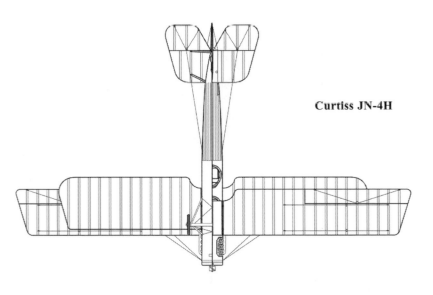

Curtiss JN-4H

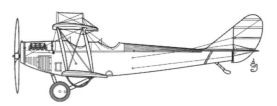

equipped), and JN-4Bs in 1916 and 1917, the Wright-Hispano-powered JN-4H and -4HG became the principal naval versions. Thirty JN-4Hs were procured in 1918 for advanced pilot training, followed by 90 JN-4HGs outfitted as gunnery trainers. The Navy also purchased 10 JN-6Hs, which were distinguished by having ailerons on both upper and lower wings. A final batch, 113 JN-4H advanced trainers, was accepted by the Navy during the early post-war era. A number of JN-4Hs/-4HGs were transferred to the Marines, where they were used for training and observation duties. The Navy and Marines began phasing out their Jennies in the mid–1920s as newer aircraft came into service, the final examples being withdrawn in 1926.

Curtiss/Naval Aircraft Factory MF—1918

TECHNICAL SPECIFICATIONS

Type: Two-place flying boat trainer.
Manufacturer: Curtiss Aeroplane & Motor Co., Garden City and Buffalo, New York; Naval Aircraft Factory, Philadelphia, Pennsylvania.
Total produced: 96 (USN, USCG)

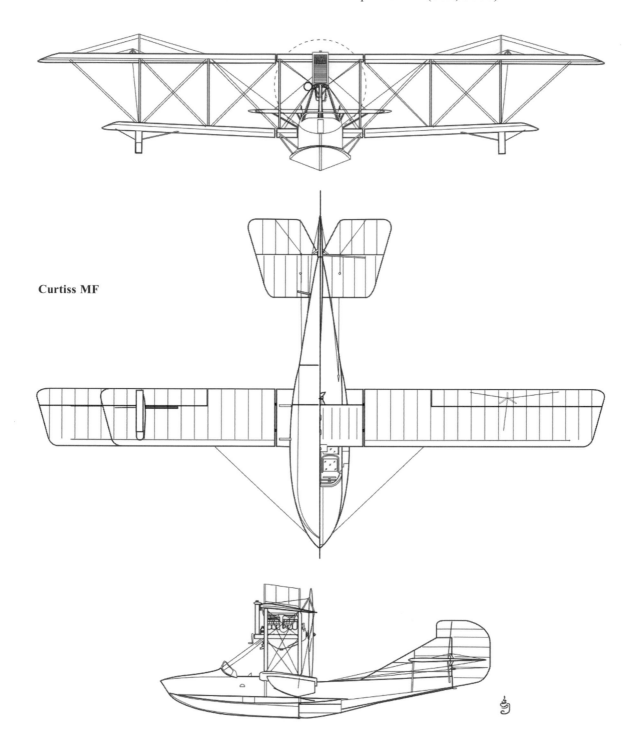

Curtiss MF

Powerplant: One 100-hp Curtiss OXX-3 8-cylinder water-cooled engine driving a two-bladed wooden fixed-pitch propeller.
Performance: Max. speed 72 mph; ceiling 4,100 ft.; range 345 mi.
Weights: 1,850 lbs. empty, 2,488 lbs. loaded.
Dimensions: span (upper) 49 ft. 9 in., length 28 ft. 10 in., wing area 402 sq. ft.

The MF (or modified F) was introduced in 1918 as the successor to the Navy's F Boat trainers. Although a three-bay bi-

Production of the MF was foreshortened by the end of World War I. Most of 96 built were completed by the Naval Air Factory after the war. Several were transferred to the Coast Guard in 1920 and 1921.

plane of wooden construction like the F, it was actually an entirely new design that utilized the sponson-type hull of the H-16, new wings having trailing-edge ailerons on the upper span, along with a reshaped fin and balanced rudder. The Navy gave Curtiss an order for 47 MFs, but only 16 had been delivered when the contract was cancelled following the World War I armistice in late 1918. Eighty more examples built by NAF were delivered to the Navy after the war, and the type remained in service as a trainer until the mid–1920s. Several MFs transferred to the Coast Guard were used in 1920 and 1921 to develop aerial search and rescue methods.

Aeromarine 40—1919

TECHNICAL SPECIFICATIONS (40F)

Type: Two-place flying boat trainer.
Manufacturer: Aeromarine Plane & Motor Co., Keyport, New Jersey.
Total produced: 50 (USN)
Powerplant: One 100-hp Curtiss OXX-6 8-cylinder water-cooled engine driving a two-bladed wooden fixed-pitch propeller.
Performance: Max. speed 71 mph at s.l.; ceiling 3,500 ft.; range 250 mi. (est.).
Weights: 2,061 lbs. empty, 2,592 lbs. loaded.
Dimensions: span 48 ft. 6 in., length 28 ft. 11 in., wing area (not reported).

The Model 40, following the model 39 trainer, was designed and built in response to a 1918 Navy Department requirement for a two-seat seaplane trainer. Though similar in general layout to the Curtiss Model MF (see above), which it was intended to augment, it appeared as a two-bay biplane of fabric-covered wooden construction, characterized by a single-step hull having a more rounded bow and less-pronounced sponsons than those seen on the Curtiss types. The Navy originally contracted for 200 as the Model 40F, but the order was reduced to only 50 after the November armistice, and the first deliveries did not occur until 1919. Some Model 40Fs were reportedly fitted with 150-hp Wright-Hispano engines to improve performance and

Model 40 was intended to augment Curtiss Fs and MFs in the training role, however, the contract was cut short by the end of World War I. Fifty were delivered in 1919.

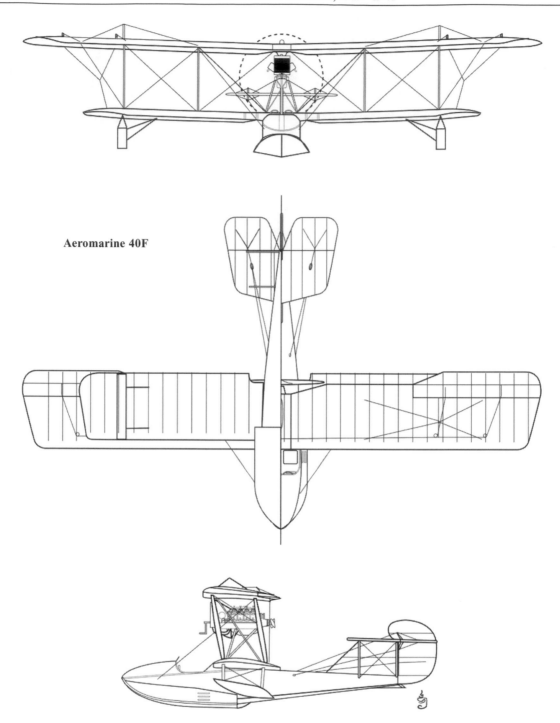

Aeromarine 40F

payload. All had been withdrawn from service by the mid–1920s.

Huff-Daland HN/HO— 1923

TECHNICAL SPECIFICATIONS (HN-1)

Type: Two-place landplane/floatplane trainer, observation.
Manufacturer: Huff-Daland Airplane Co., Bristol, Pennsylvania.
Total produced: 9 (all versions)
Powerplant: One 180-hp Wright-Hispano E-2 8-cylinder water-cooled engine driving a two-bladed wooden fixed-pitch propeller.
Armament (HO-1): one .30-cal. machine gun on scarf ring in rear cockpit.

Performance: Max. speed 114 mph at s.l.; ceiling 13,700 ft.; range (not reported).
Weights: 2,020 lbs. empty, 2,545 lbs. loaded.
Dimensions: span 33 ft. 6 in., length 28 ft. 6 in., wing area (not reported).

Huff-Daland, organized in 1920, is noteworthy as having been one of the first American aircraft manufacturers to adopt the German Fokker-inspired construction techniques of welded, steel tube fuselages and thick semi or fully cantilevered wings. In 1923, the Navy ordered a total of six essentially identical aircraft, three as trainers under the designation HN-1 and three for observation as the HO-1, the latter having provision for a

.30-cal. Lewis gun mounted in the rear cockpit. Huff-Daland's semi-cantilevered biplane wing configuration closely resembled that of the Fokker D.VII. Specifications called for both types to be powered by surplus Wright-Hispano engines and convertible to wheeled or twin float undercarriage. Three additional trainer versions equipped with the new 200-hp Lawrance J-1 radial engine were produced for the Navy in 1925 as the HN-2. Huff-Daland was absorbed into Keystone Aircraft Corp. sometime in the late 1920s.

An HN-1, one of three ordered, is seen taking off from the Washington Monument reflecting pool in 1923 or 1924. Note similarities to the Fokker D.VII, which inspired much of its design.

Naval Aircraft Factory N2N—1923

TECHNICAL SPECIFICATIONS

Type: Two-place landplane/floatplane trainer.
Manufacturer: Naval Aircraft Factory, Philadelphia, Pennsylvania.
Total produced: 3 (USN)
Powerplant: One 200-hp Lawrance J-1 R-787 9-cylinder air-cooled radial engine driving a two-bladed wooden fixed-pitch propeller.
Performance: Max. speed 106 mph at s.l.; ceiling 16,900 ft.; range (not reported).
Weights: 2,100 lbs. empty (est.), 2,640 lbs. loaded.

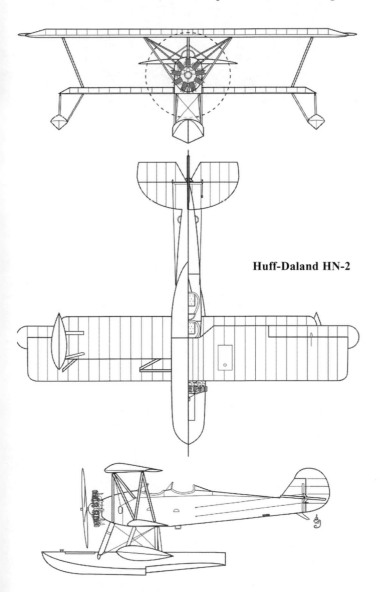

Huff-Daland HN-2

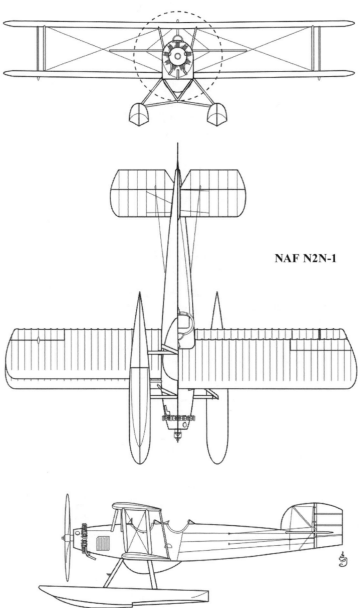

NAF N2N-1

One of three N2N-1s tested in 1923, primarily to evaluate a trainer powered by a Lawrance J-1 engine. Though not ordered into production, all three subsequently served as trainers at Pensacola.

The N2M-1 was another Lawrance-powered trainer that Martin adapted from its Model 66 Mail Plane design. Only one was built in 1924, and it was later used as a trainer at Pensacola.

Dimensions: span 33 ft. 8 in., length 26 ft. 11 in., wing area 260 sq. ft. (est.).

The N2N-1 (NN designation not used) flew for the first time in 1923 as a Naval Aircraft Factory project to develop and evaluate a float-equipped trainer powered by the new air-cooled radial engine recently introduced by the Lawrance Aero Engine Co. Its all-wood construction and general aerodynamic design were very similar to the contemporaneous TS-1 fighter (see above), which had been designed by Rex Beisel while employed by BuAer. The three N2N-1s completed by NAF were briefly used for training at NAS Pensacola.

Martin N2M—1924

TECHNICAL SPECIFICATIONS

Type: Two-place landplane/floatplane trainer.
Manufacturer: Glenn L. Martin Co., Cleveland, Ohio.
Total produced: 1 (USN)
Powerplant: One 200-hp Lawrance J-1 R-787 9-cylinder air-cooled radial engine driving a two-bladed wooden fixed-pitch propeller.
Performance: Max. speed 112 mph at s.l.; ceiling 19,000 ft.; range (not reported).
Weights: (not reported).
Dimensions: span 41 ft., length 27 ft. 10 in., wing area (not reported).

In 1924 Martin offered the Navy another Lawrance-powered trainer which was based largely on the design of its Wright-Hispano–powered Model 66 Night Mail Plane of 1923. The sole example, taken into service as the N2M-1 (NM-1 had apparently been assigned to Packard for a racer), emerged as a one-bay, wood and fabric biplane characterized by low-aspect ratio wings braced by single interplane struts. After acceptance trials, the aircraft saw limited service as a trainer at NAS Pensacola until the mid–1920s.

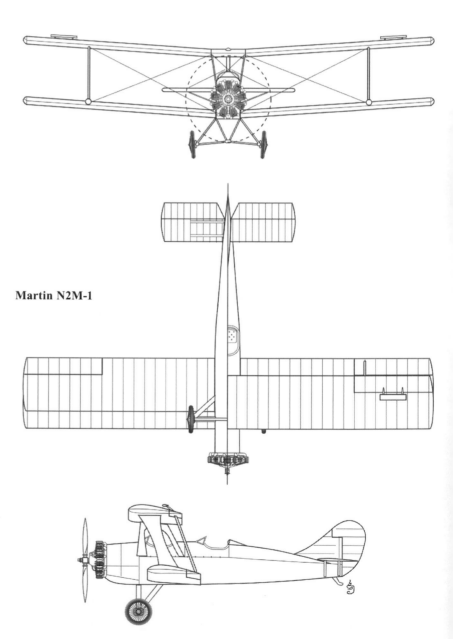

Martin N2M-1

Naval Aircraft Factory TG—1924

TECHNICAL SPECIFICATIONS (TG-2)

Type: Two-place floatplane gunnery trainer.
Manufacturer: Naval Aircraft Factory, Philadelphia, Pennsylvania.
Total produced: 5 (USN)
Powerplant: One 200-hp Liberty L 6-cylinder water-cooled engine driving a two-bladed wooden fixed-pitch propeller.
Armament: One .30-cal. machine gun on scarf ring in rear cockpit.

Performance: Max. speed 97 mph at s.l.; ceiling 13,140 ft.; range (not reported).
Weights: 2,400 lbs. empty (est.), 2,800 lbs. loaded.
Dimensions: span 36 ft. 0 in., length 30 ft. 10 in., wing area 340 sq. ft. (est.).

The Naval Aircraft Factory built five float-equipped gunnery trainers in 1924 as TG-1 through -5. They were conventional two-bay biplanes of wood and fabric construction, iden-

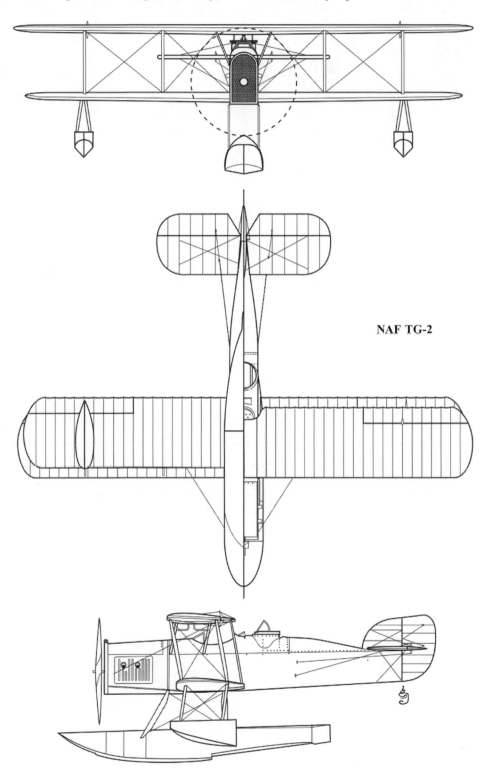

NAF TG-2

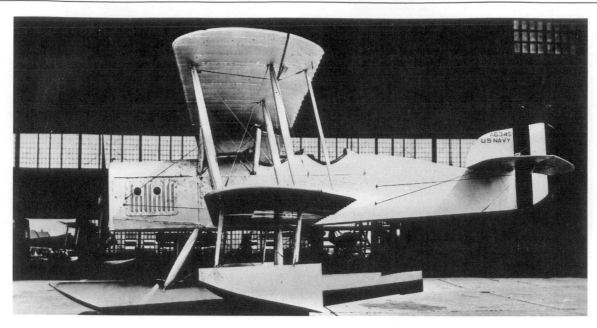

A Liberty 6-powered TG-2 in 1924. Five were built with various powerplants as gunnery trainers, but none were listed as active after 1925.

tical except for the powerplants installed (i.e., TG-1 and -2, 200-hp Liberty 6; TG-2 and -3, 200-hp Aeromarine T-6; and TG-5, 180-hp Wright Hispano E). The type apparently was not very successful, as none were listed as active after 1925.

Boeing NB—1924

TECHNICAL SPECIFICATIONS (NB-1)

Type: Two-place landplane/floatplane trainer.
Manufacturer: Boeing Airplane Co., Seattle, Washington.
Total produced: 73 (USN, USMC)
Powerplant: One 200-hp Lawrance J-1 9-cylinder air-cooled radial engine driving a two-bladed wooden fixed-pitch propeller.
Armament (on some): One .30-cal. machine gun on scarf ring in rear cockpit.

The Boeing NB-1, the first type of post-war trainer to be ordered in quantity. Note the hand crank right behind engine. Like all Navy trainers of this era, it could be rigged for floats or wheels as needed.

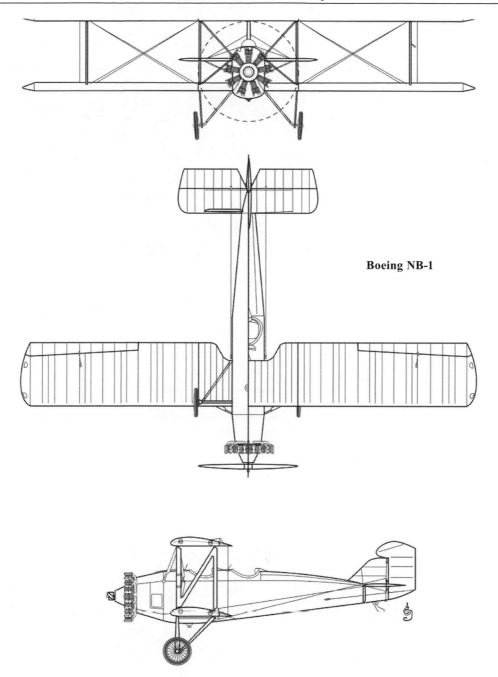

Boeing NB-1

Performance: Max. speed 100 mph at s.l.; ceiling 15,500 ft.; range 300 mi.

Weights: 2,136 lbs. empty, 2,837 lbs. loaded.

Dimensions: span 36 ft. 10 in., length 25 ft. 5 in., wing area 344 sq. ft.

One of the first Navy trainers to be purchased in double-digit quantities following World War I, the Boeing Model 21 originated as the prototype NB-1 delivered in mid–1924. After Initial testing revealed that the aircraft was actually too docile for training purposes, showing a marked reluctance to spin, it was given modifications that made it more maneuverable. After satisfactory trials, BuAer awarded Boeing a contract for 42 NB-1 production aircraft, and deliveries commenced before the end of the year. The design was characterized by such innova-tions as a welded, steel tube fuselage structure, single-bay wings braced by metal N-type struts, and a balanced rudder. In 1925 Boeing received a follow-on order for thirty NB-2s powered by 180-hp Wright-Hispano E-4 water-cooled engines, which, like the -1s, could be rigged with either wheels or a cen-terline float.

Most NB-1s and -2s were assigned to NAS Pensacola with VN-1D8 and VN-1D4, while some served with VN-6D5 at NOB Hampton Roads and VN-7D11 at NAS North Island in San Diego. One NB-2 modified for crop dusting served with Marine squadron VO-6M during 1929 to spray the mosquito-infested swamps around Santo Domingo, Nicaragua. One NB-2 was re-designated NB-4 after the fuselage was lengthened.

Consolidated NY (N3Y)—1925

TECHNICAL SPECIFICATIONS (NY-2)

Type: Two-place landplane/floatplane trainer.
Manufacturer: Consolidated Aircraft Corp., Buffalo, New York.
Total produced: 307 (USN, USMC)
Powerplant: One 220-hp Wright R-790-8 J-5 *Whirlwind* 9-cylinder air-cooled radial engine driving a two-bladed fixed-pitch metal propeller.
Armament (NY-1A/-2A): One flexible .30-cal. machine gun in the rear cockpit.
Performance: Max. speed 98 mph at s.l.; ceiling 15,200 ft.; range 300 mi.

Weights: 1,801 lbs. empty, 2,627 lbs. loaded.
Dimensions: span 40 ft., length 27 ft. 11 in., wing area 370 sq. ft.

Originating as a navalized development of the Army's PT-1, the NY represented a serious effort by BuAer to upgrade the Navy's variegated mix of training aircraft. Consolidated Aircraft Corp., founded in 1923 by Reuben H. Fleet, launched itself as a major military aircraft supplier in 1924 with a contract to produce 221 PT-1 trainers to replace the Army's aging fleet of Curtiss JN-4Ds. Though powered by a surplus Wright-Hispano powerplant in order to minimize unit cost, the PT-1 nonetheless offered other advanced features such as a welded

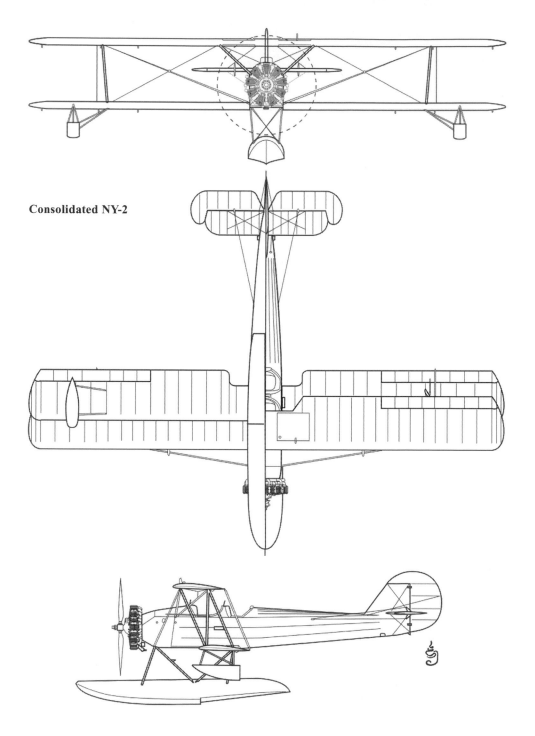

Consolidated NY-2

Top: The Navy's most important trainer from the mid–1920s to the mid–1930s, this NY-1 is seen while attached to NAS Hampton Roads in 1929. The basic design of the NY was derived from the Army's PT-1. *Bottom:* The NY-2 had added wingspan and a more powerful J-5 engine. Most were assigned to NAS Pensacola. Note the Gosport tube connected to the face of the flight instructor in the front cockpit.

A Wright R-790 engine was the chief difference between the XN3Y-1 and the NY-2. Only one was built.

fuselage framework of chrome-molydbenum steel tubing, wooden-framed wings using the new Clark Y thick-section airfoil, and metal N-type cabane and interplane struts. The result—a durable and easy to maintain airframe with excellent flight characteristics—was ideal for a trainer.

In 1925 BuAer asked Consolidated to adapt the PT-1 to naval specifications that included an air-cooled Wright J-4 powerplant and the ability to convert to either a wheeled or centerline float undercarriage. Fin and rudder area were increased accordingly to offset the side area of the floats. After the Navy awarded a contract for 76 aircraft as the NY-1, the first production model (no experimental prototype) was flown on November 12, 1925 and deliveries commenced in May 1926. In service, a number of these were re-designated NY-1A when retrofitted with a flexible .30-cal. machine gun mount and used for gunnery training. Early operational experience with the NY-1 revealed that in a float configuration, at gross weight, the aircraft suffered from excessive wing-loading. In late 1926, to overcome these shortcomings, Consolidated introduced the NY-2 having a 5-foot 6-inch increase in wingspan and more power from a 220-hp J-5 engine. Following completion of successful trials in 1927, the Navy ordered 186 NY-2 production models (the largest trainer order since 1918), all having been delivered by the end of 1928.

A further 25 NY-2s specifically outfitted for gunnery training were ordered in 1928 as the NY-2A. The final 20 variants built, NY-3s with 240-hp Wright R-760-94 7-cylinder engines, went directly to various Navy and Marine reserve units as they were delivered in 1929. In later service, NY-1s receiving the larger wings of the -2 and 220-hp J-5 engines were returned to duty as the NY-1B. A single NY-2 airframe fitted with a Wright R-790-A engine was tested in 1929 as the XN3Y-1 but not placed in production. From the late 1920s onward, NY variants not only established themselves as the Navy's most important trainer for primary flight instruction and gunnery, but also formed a vital training component within the ten Navy and Marine reserve units organized during 1928. NY-1Bs, -2s, and -2Bs continued in service as the Navy's most numerous type of primary trainer until Naval Aircraft Factory N3N-1s began arriving in quantity during 1936. All NY variants had been replaced at training centers by the end of 1937, but the very last NY-3s were not withdrawn from the reserves until 1939.

Atlantic (Fokker) TA/RA—1927

TECHNICAL SPECIFICATIONS (TA-1)

Type: Ten- to fourteen-place landplane transport.
Manufacturer: Atlantic Aircraft Div., Fokker Aircraft Corp. of America, Hasbrouck Heights, New Jersey.
Total produced: 7 (USN,USMC).
Powerplants: Three 220-hp Wright J-5 R-790 *Whirlwind* 9-cylinder air-cooled radial engine driving two-bladed (2 outboard) and three-bladed (1 center) metal fixed-pitch propellers.
Performance: Max. speed 116 mph at s.l.; ceiling 12,050 ft.; range 720 mi.
Weights: 5,400 lbs. empty, 9,000 lbs. loaded.
Dimensions: span 63 ft. 4 in., length 49 ft. 1 in., wing area 630 sq. ft.

In the mid–1920s the Navy began evaluating the desirability of acquiring large commercial aircraft to be used as staff transports and cargo carriers. Fokker, a company based in the Netherlands, was marketing its F.VII/3M, a tri-motor transport which had attracted much attention in the 1925 Ford Reliability Tour and had also been selected by Cdr. Richard E. Byrd for the North Pole over flight. Designed by Walter Rethel in 1924, the F.VII series were high-wing mono-planes featuring a welded, steel tube fuselage and tailplane structure covered in fabric with built-up wooden wings skinned in a plywood veneer. The basic airframe could be ordered in either single or three-engine versions. So as to avoid Fokker's wartime association with Germany, the company created an American-registered subsidiary under the name Atlantic Aircraft to reassemble and deliver aircraft sold in the United States.

Following a 1926 Army order for three F.VIIa/3Ms with widened fuselages and Wright J-5 engines as the C-2, the Navy contracted for three identical aircraft under the transport designation TA-1. When delivered in late 1927 and early 1928, all three TA-1s were subsequently assigned to VO-6M as part of the Second Marine Brigade in Nicaragua. VO-6M also received two TA-2s in 1928 which differed in having 9 feet 6 inches added to wingspan. Sometime in 1930, the three TA-1s and two TA-2s were modified to accept installation of 300-hp Wright J-6-9 engines and all returned to service as the TA-3. When Navy adopted the "R" for transport designation in 1931, the TA-3s became RΛ-3s. In late 1930 and early 1931, as the RA-4, the Navy evaluated an Atlantic F.Xa that came with an 18-inch nose extension and three 450-hp Pratt & Whitney *Wasp* engines encased in ring cowls, but ultimately judged the aircraft as unsuitable for service. The RA-3s do not appear on Marine records after 1932 and presumably had been withdrawn.

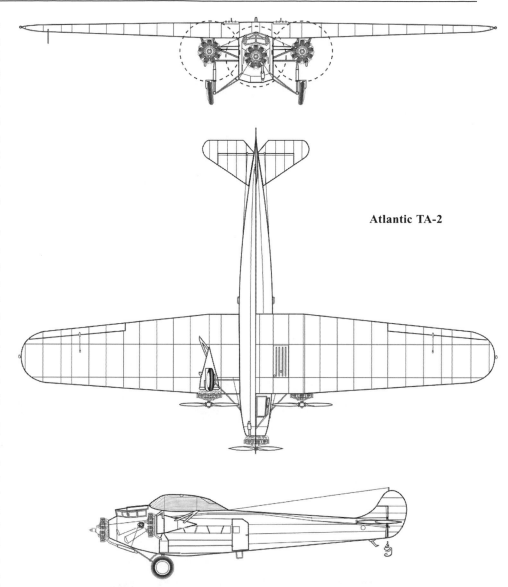

Atlantic TA-2

The Navy procured three examples of the TA-1 for the Marines in 1927, all serving with VJ-6M in Nicaragua. Atlantic was an American-based subsidiary of Fokker, and the design was based on the Fokker V.VIIa/3m airliner.

Atlantic (Fokker) JA—1928

TECHNICAL SPECIFICATIONS (XJA-1)

Type: Eight-place landplane transport.

Manufacturer: Atlantic Aircraft Div., Fokker Aircraft Corp. of America, Hasbrouck Heights, New Jersey.

Total produced: 1 (USN)

Powerplant: One 450-hp Pratt & Whitney R-1340B *Wasp* 9-cylinder air-cooled radial engine driving a two-bladed fixed-pitch metal propeller.

Performance: Max. speed 134 mph at s.l.; ceiling 16,900 ft.; range 720 mi.

Weights: 3,250 lbs. empty, 5,500 lbs. loaded.

Dimensions: span 50 ft. 7 in., length 36 ft. 7 in., wing area 370 sq. ft.

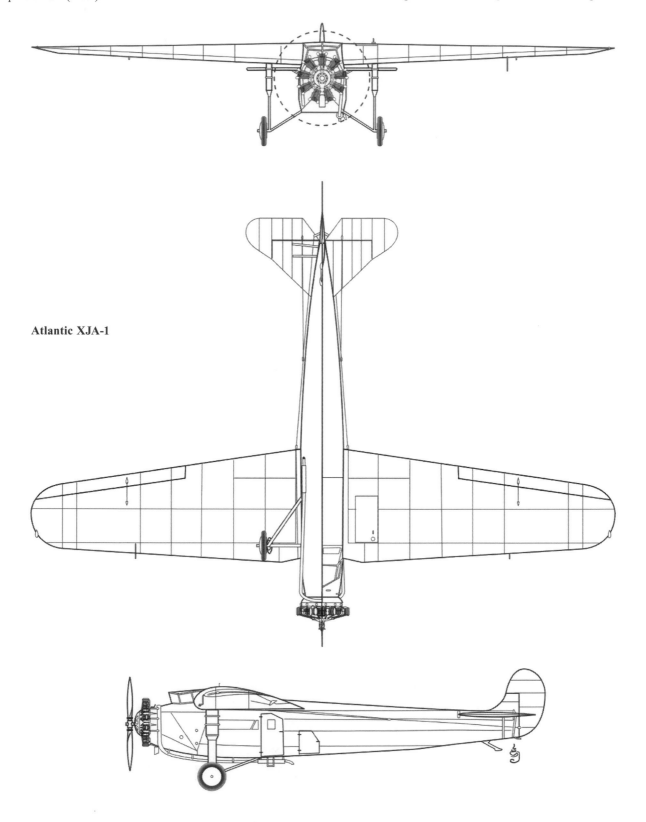

Atlantic XJA-1

The Fokker "Super Universal," designated XJA-1, as seen at NAS Anacostia in 1928. Following brief trials, the aircraft was returned to the manufacturer.

Another type of Atlantic-assembled, Fokker-designed transport to be considered by the Navy, one single-engine F.VIII "Super Universal" was delivered for evaluation in 1928 as the XJA-1. Other than having a 20 percent smaller airframe, the F.VIII was basically the same in design and construction as the F.VII series. Following brief trials, naval officials decided against procurement and returned the aircraft to the manufacturer.

Ford JR/RR—1928

TECHNICAL SPECIFICATIONS (JR/RR-3)

Type: Eleven- to seventeen-place landplane transport.

Manufacturer: Stout Metal Airplane Div. of Ford Motor Co., Dearborn, Michigan.

Total produced: 9 (USN, USMC)

Powerplants: Three 450-hp Pratt & Whitney R-1340-88 *Wasp* 9-cylinder air-cooled radial engine driving two-bladed fixed-pitch metal propellers.

Performance: Max. speed 135 mph at s.l.; ceiling 18,000 ft.; range 505 mi.

Weights: 8,149 lbs. empty, 13,499 lbs. loaded.

Dimensions: span 77 ft. 10 in., length 50 ft. 3 in., wing area 835 sq. ft.

The origins of the famous Ford Trimotor date to 1925, when automaker Henry Ford and a group of investors acquired the Stout Metal Airplane Co. Using methods developed in Germany by Prof. Hugo Junkers, William B. Stout pioneered the use of fully cantilevered, all-metal airframe structures that were skinned in corrugated duraluminum (see Stout ST, above).

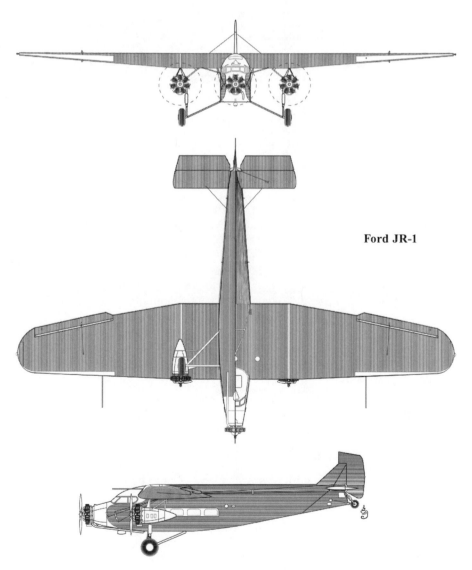

Ford JR-1

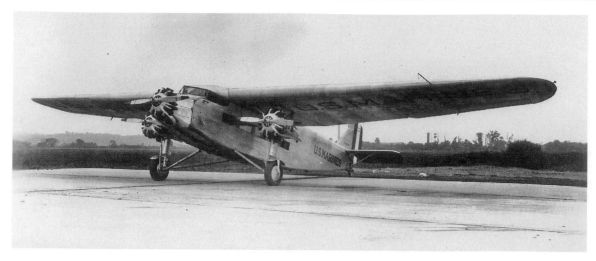

Top: **One of two JR-2s, improved Ford 4-AT-Es, ordered by the Navy in 1928 and assigned to Marine squadron VJ-6M when delivered in 1929. Re-designated RR-2 in 1931 and withdrawn from service in 1935.** *Bottom:* **A Navy RR-3, one of three 5-AT-Cs acquired in 1930 and re-designated RR-3 in 1931. This RR-3 served as a staff transport at NAS Pensacola while the other two were allocated to the Marine squadron VJ-6M.**

The new company's first product, the 8-passenger Ford 4-AT, powered by three 200-hp Wright J-4 engines, made its first flight in June 1926. Its high-wing aerodynamic configuration closely resembled that of the Fokker F.VII/3M. On March 9, 1927, following acceptance of the 4-AT into U.S. airline service, BuAer contracted to purchase the fourth aircraft on Ford's production line under the designation XJR-1. The aircraft arrived at NAS Anacostia In April 1928 and after about a year of testing, the Navy ordered two improved 4-AT-Es, equipped with 300-hp Wright J-6-9 engines, as the JR-2, which were both assigned in 1929 to VJ-6M with the Second Marine Brigade in Nicaragua.

Three Ford 5-AT-Cs, featuring a 3-foot 10-inch increase in span, 450-hp Pratt & Whitney Wasp engines, and a 30 percent improvement in useful load over the 4-AT-E, were purchased in 1930, one being retained by the Navy to be used as a staff transport at Pensacola and the other two going to VJ-6M. In 1931, when the Navy adopted the "R" for transport designation, the type became RR-2s (note, the XJR-1 was damaged beyond

repair in 1930), the remaining Marine JR-3, the RR-3 (one JR-3 crashed in Nicaragua), and the Navy JR-2, the RR-4. Two Ford 5-AT-Ds, having uprated *Wasp* engines, entered service in 1932 as RR-5s, one to the Navy and one to Marine squadron VJ-6M (later VMJ-1). All RRs were withdrawn from the naval inventory service by the end of 1937.

Fairchild JQ/ J2Q and R2Q—1928

TECHNICAL SPECIFICATIONS (XJQ-1)

Type: Five-place landplane utility transport.
Manufacturer: Fairchild Aircraft Mfg. Co., Farmingdale, New York.
Total produced: 1 (USN)
Powerplant: One 200-hp Wright R-790 J-5 *Whirlwind* 9-cylinder air-cooled radial engine driving a two-bladed fixed-pitch metal propeller.
Performance: Max. speed 122 mph at s.l.; ceiling 11,500 ft.; range 700 mi.
Weights: 2,160 lbs. empty, 3,600 lbs. loaded.
Dimensions: span 44 ft. 0 in., length 31 ft. 0 in., wing area 290 sq. ft.

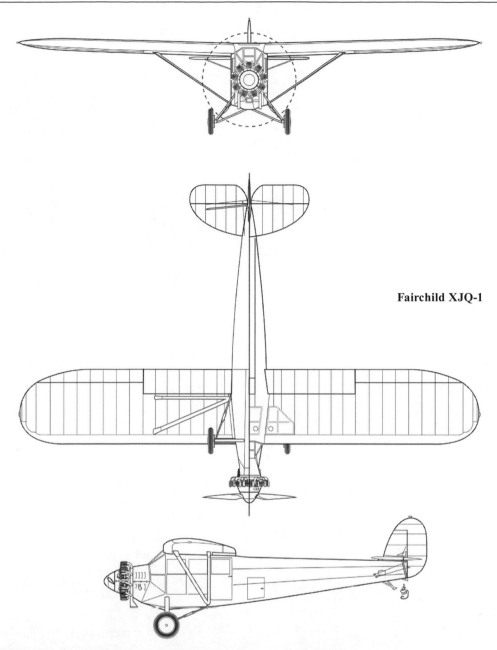

Fairchild XJQ-1

The XJQ-1 as seen at NAS Anacostia in 1928 with original Wright J-5 engine. When fitted with a P&W Wasp engine in 1929, it became the XJ2Q-1, then the XR2Q-1 in 1931 under a new designation scheme.

The JQ and J2Q/R2Q were the same aircraft with different engines. As part of its evaluation of civil transports, the Navy acquired one Fairchild Model FC-2 in early 1928 as the XJQ-1. The FC-2 was a high-wing, fabric covered monoplane design that utilized a steel tube fuselage and strut-braced, built-up wooden wings, and the first type of aircraft to be produced by Fairchild in quantity. After a year of trials at Anacostia, the aircraft was refitted with a 450-hp Pratt & Whitney Wasp engine (though apparently not with the larger wings of the FC-2W) and re-evaluated as the XJ2Q-1. In 1931, it was re-designated XR2Q-1.

The FC-2 series evolved into the Model 71 manufactured by Fairchild Aircraft Ltd. of Canada, which went to gain wide popularity during the 1930s as a small transport and bush plane.

XN2B-1, after installation of more conventional Wright R-540 engine, was returned to Anacostia in 1929 for a new series of trials, but no production resulted. Aircraft was sold back to Boeing.

Boeing N2B—1928

TECHNICAL SPECIFICATIONS (XN2B-1)

Type: Two-place landplane/floatplane trainer.
Manufacturer: Boeing Airplane Co., Seattle, Washington.
Total produced: 1 (USN)
Powerplant: One 125-hp Fairchild-Caminez R-447 4-cylinder (crankless) air-cooled radial engine driving a four-bladed fixed-pitch wooden propeller.
Performance: Max. speed 104 mph at s.l.; ceiling 13,500 ft.; range 335 mi.
Weights: 1,652 lbs. empty, 2,178 lbs. loaded.
Dimensions: span 35 ft. 0 in., length 25 ft. 8 in., wing area 259 sq. ft.

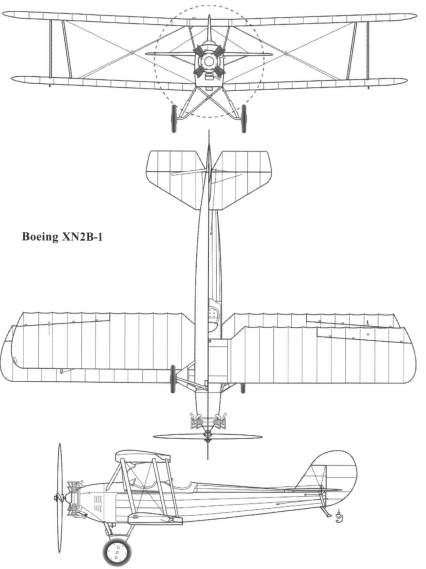

Boeing XN2B-1

A trainer competition conducted by BuAer in 1928 resulted in delivery of prototypes by Boeing, Curtiss, and Keystone. Boeing's entry, designated the XN2B-1, had originated in 1926 as the Wright J-3-powered Model 64, then reappeared in 1928 as the Model 81 with a Fairchild-Caminez powerplant. This unorthodox 4-cylinder engine was a crankless air-cooled radial that developed its peak horsepower at only 1000 RPM and employed a high-pitched, four-bladed propeller to deliver thrust. The XN2B-1's fabric-covered construction was mixed, consisting of a welded, steel tube fuselage and all-wood biplane wings using an NACA M-12 airfoil section. Initial Navy trials were unsatisfactory, however, and the prototype returned to Boeing to be fitted with a more conventional 165-hp Wright J-6-5 (5-cylinder R-540) engine. Despite better performance in 1929 Navy trials, no production was ordered, and the sole XN2B-1 eventually sold back to Boeing for use in its school of aeronautics.

Curtiss N2C Fledgling—1928

TECHNICAL SPECIFICATIONS (N2C-2)

Type: Two-place landplane/floatplane trainer.
Manufacturer: Curtiss Aeroplane Co., Buffalo and Garden City, New York.
Total produced: 52 (USN, USMC)
Powerplant: One 240-hp Wright R-760-94 7-cylinder air-cooled radial engine driving a two-bladed fixed-pitch metal propeller.
Performance: Max. speed 116 mph at s.l.; ceiling 17,800 ft.; range 384 mi.
Weights: 2,138 lbs. empty, 2,860 lbs. loaded.
Dimensions: Span 39 ft. 5 in., length 27 ft. 5 in., wing area 368 sq. ft.

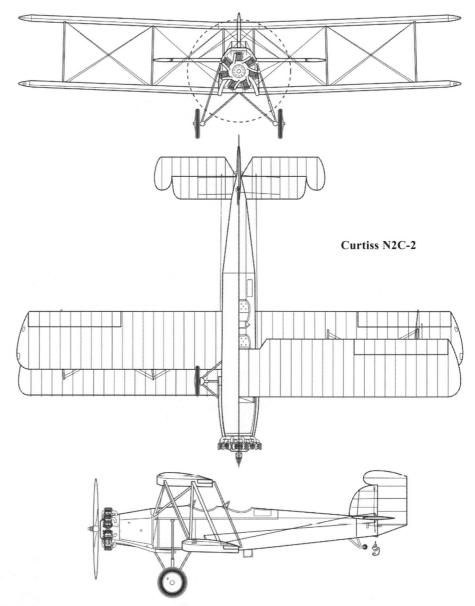

Curtiss N2C-2

Winner of BuAer's 1928 trainer competition, the Curtiss XN2C-1 (Model 48) began as a joint project with the Model 51 Fledgling to develop both a military prototype and a civil trainer to be used in the nationwide schools operated by Curtiss-Wright Flying Service. The new Curtiss *Challenger* twin-row, 6-cylinder radial was to power the civil model, while BuAer specified a more conventional Wright J-5 engine for its prototype. Construction consisted of a welded, steel tube fuselage and tailplane with built-up wooden wings. Its aerodynamic design was somewhat behind the times, appearing with thin-section wings that were braced by two bays of struts. Following evaluations in both landplane and floatplane configurations, Curtiss received a contract to build 31 production models as the N2C-1. In 1929, shortly after production of the J-5 engine had been discontinued, the Navy gave Curtiss a follow-up order for 20 aircraft to be powered by the 240-hp Wright J-6-7 (R-760-94) under the designation N2C-2.

As deliveries were completed in 1928 and 1929, most N2C-1s and -2s went directly to recently formed Navy and Marine reserve units as training aircraft. From 1931 to 1933, three N2C-2s served with Marine squadron VJ-6M in Nicaragua and Quantico and another with VJ-7M at San Diego. By

The original XN2C-1 prototype seen in the mid–1930s serving with the reserves at NRAB New York. This type saw use in reserve pilot training up to 1940.

mid–1937, a total of 37 N2C-1s and -2s were still listed as operating with 11 different Navy and Marine reserve units, however, all had been withdrawn from service by the end of 1939. At the very end of their career, two N2C-2s were modified with tricycle landing gear and used as radio-controlled drones to simulate dive-bombing attacks on ships.

Keystone NK—1928

TECHNICAL SPECIFICATIONS (NK-1)

Type: Two-place landplane/float-plane trainer.

One of three XNK-1s delivered to NAS Anacostia in 1928, to be considered along with the XN2B-1 and XN2C-1. Although 16 more were purchased in 1930, they were not assigned to the training establishment.

Manufacturer: Keystone Aircraft Corp., Bristol, Pennsylvania.
Total produced: 19 (USN)
Powerplant: One 220-hp Wright J-5 R-790 9-cylinder air-cooled radial engine driving a two-bladed fixed-pitch metal propeller.
Performance: Max. speed 115 mph at s.l.; ceiling 13,200 ft.; range 375 mi.
Weights: 2,050 lbs. empty, 2,658 lbs. loaded.
Dimensions: span 37 ft., length 26 ft. 6 in., wing area (not reported).

Developed in parallel with the civil model "Pup," Keystone delivered three essentially identical XNK-1 trainer prototypes to NAS Anacostia in 1928 to be evaluated alongside the XN2B-1 and XN2C-1 (see above). BuAer subsequently gave Keystone a contract for 16 NK-1 production models, but the expected delivery in 1929 was delayed due to modifications suggested by continued testing of the XNK-1s. When delivered in 1930, the production NK-1s differed in having an enlarged and reshaped fin and rudder, plus a small amount of dihedral added to the horizontal stabilizer. Eventual use and disposition of these trainers is not clear, but they were apparently never assigned to any regular training or reserve units.

Keystone XNK-1

Consolidated (Fleet) N2Y—1929

TECHNICAL SPECIFICATIONS (N2Y-1 PRODUCTION)

Type: Two-place landplane trainer.
Manufacturer: Fleet Div. of Consolidated Aircraft Corp., Buffalo, New York.
Total produced: 6 (USN)
Powerplant: One 115-hp Kinner K-5 R-372 5-cylinder air-cooled radial engine driving a two-bladed fixed-pitch metal propeller.

Performance: Max. speed 105 mph at s.l.; ceiling
    12,200 ft.; range 350 mi.
Weights: 1,072 lbs. empty, 1,637 lbs. loaded.
Dimensions: span 28 ft., length 21 ft. 5 in., wing
    area 194 sq. ft.

In 1929 and 1930, the Navy evaluated
two "lightweight" biplane trainers that were
both based on preexisting civil designs. The
first, delivered in 1929 as the Consolidated
XN2Y-1 with a 110-hp Warner *Scarab* engine,
was the initial production version of the Fleet
Model 1, which itself had been derived from
the Consolidated Model 14 "Husky Junior"
of 1928. Fleet had been created in 1929 as a
division of Consolidated to manufacture
small sport planes and trainers and in 1930,
expanded its operations into Ontario as Fleet

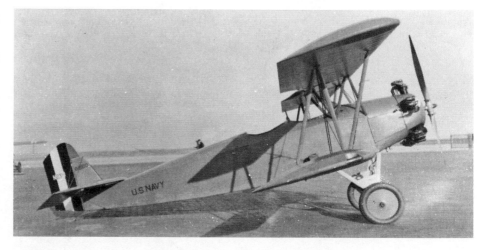

One of five N2Y-1s ordered in 1929 with revised cockpit configuration. N2Y-1s were later fitted with "skyhooks" to be used as familiarization trainers in dirigible hook-on operations.

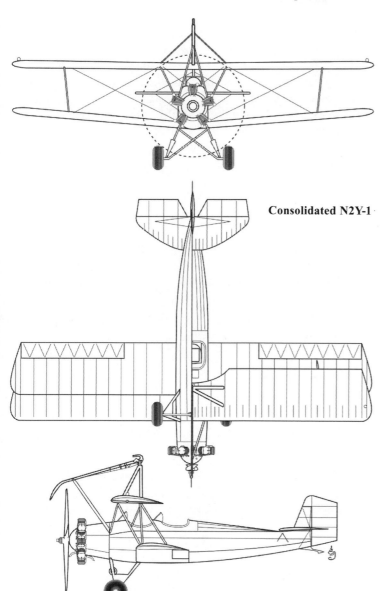

Consolidated N2Y-1

Aircraft of Canada, Ltd. As delivered, the XN2Y-1 possessed
an unusual "bathtub" cockpit having no structure between
the front and rear seats. Construction was comprised of a
welded, steel tube fuselage, built-up wings with wooden
spars and duraluminum ribs, and fabric covering.

Though not selected as a primary trainer, BuAer nevertheless ordered five Kinner-powered Fleet Model 2s as
the N2Y-1 to serve as familiarization trainers for the "skyhook" pilots assigned to the rigid airships *Akron* and *Macon*
(see Curtiss F9C, above). The Army also purchased 16 Fleet
2s as the PT-6. Production N2Y-1s came with separate cockpits and a streamlined fairing over the engine crankcase.
One of these, fitted with a skyhook to engage the airship's
"trapeze" system, was re-designated XN2Y-2. After *Akron*
and *Macon* were lost, two N2Y-1s were placed in storage at
NAF and two others fitted with tailhooks served with the
utility units aboard *Saratoga* and *Ranger* until 1937. The
XN2Y-2 was transferred to the Pennsylvania Aircraft Syndicate in 1934 to become the basis for the XOZ-1 autogiro
(see above).

Loening HL—1930 see Loening OL under
OBSERVATION AND SCOUT AIRCRAFT

New Standard NT—1930

TECHNICAL SPECIFICATIONS (NT-1)

Type: Two-place landplane trainer.
Manufacturer: Standard Aircraft Corp, Paterson, New Jersey.
Total produced: 6 (USN, USCG)
Powerplant: One 100-hp Kinner K-5 R-372 5-cylinder air-cooled
    radial engine driving a two-bladed fixed-pitch metal propeller.
Performance: Max. speed 99 mph at s.l.; ceiling 10,000 ft.; range
    300 mi.
Weights: 1,097 lbs. empty, 1,632 lbs. loaded.
Dimensions: span 30 ft., length 24 ft. 11 in., wing area 248 sq. ft.

The Navy purchased six New Standard D-29As as the NK-1, one of several "lightweight" trainers tested in 1930. Very similar in design to the N2Y-1, they were afterward assigned to NAF.

The second "lightweight" trainer tested, six New Standard Model D-29As acquired by the Navy in 1930 were subsequently taken into the naval inventory as the NT-1. Slightly larger than the N2Y, The NT-1's fabric-covered airframe featured the typical built-up wooden wings and a very robust fuselage fabricated from riveted and bolted duraluminum girders. The six aircraft also came with the odd bathtub-type cockpits, but were later modified with more conventional separate enclosures. After testing, the NT-1s were assigned to the Naval Aircraft Factory, one on flight status with VX-3D4 and the others in storage.

In 1934, two New Standard D-25As that had been confiscated from whiskey smugglers by the Treasury Department were assigned to the Coast Guard under the designation NT-2. They were not derivatives of the NT-1 but a somewhat larger biplane design, with a sesquiplane wing layout and a 225-hp Wright J-6-7 engine. Both aircraft were lost in crashes during 1935.

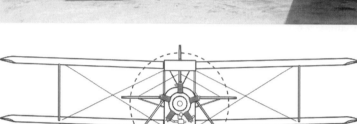

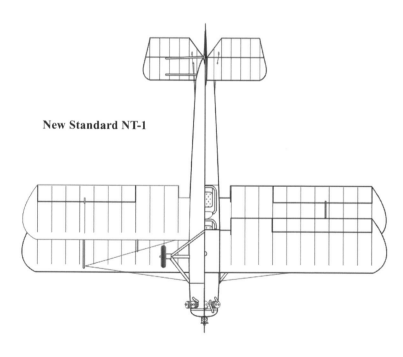

New Standard NT-1

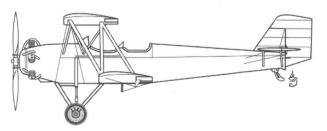

Douglas RD Dolphin—1931

TECHNICAL SPECIFICATIONS (RD-4)

Type: Eight-place utility transport and rescue amphibian.
Manufacturer: Douglas Aircraft Co., Santa Monica, California.
Total produced: 59 (USN, USMC, USCG)
Powerplants: Two 450-hp Pratt & Whitney R-1340-96 *Wasp* 9-cylinder air-cooled radial engines driving a two-bladed, ground-adjustable metal propellers.
Performance: Max. speed 147 mph; ceiling 14,900 ft.; range 660 mi.
Weights: 6,467 lbs. empty, 9,737 lbs. loaded.
Dimensions: span 60 ft. 10 in., length 45 ft. 3 in., wing area 592 sq. ft.

Completed in July 1930 as the non-amphibious Sinbad under civil registration NX145Y, Douglas's first in-house seaplane design was initially conceived as a "flying yacht" to be offered on the civilian market. The Sinbad appeared as a monoplane having an all-metal hull of semi-monocoque construction and a two-spar cantilevered wing covered in plywood that featured slotted, Handley Page-type ailerons. In original configuration, the 300-hp Wright J-5C *Whirlwind* engines were mounted directly above the wing and encased in nacelles that blended in with its upper surface. After flight-testing revealed the need to raise the thrust line, the engines were moved above the wing on struts, along with an auxiliary airfoil mounted between the conical engine nacelles to add

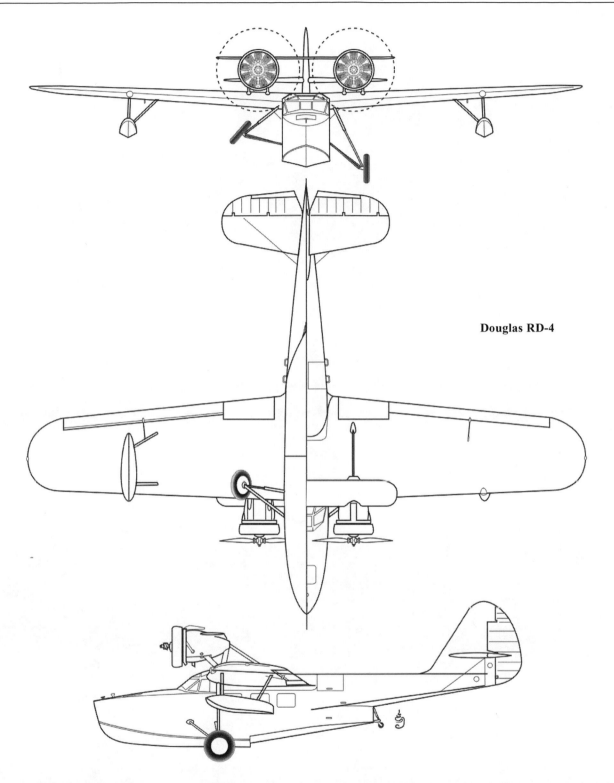

Douglas RD-4

structural support and lift. When no civilian buyers surfaced, the Sinbad was sold to the Coast Guard in March 1931 for $31,500, where it was operated for a period of time as call-sign "24 G" without a military designation but later simply listed as the "RD" with no numeric suffix.

The improved civil Dolphin, equipped with amphibious landing gear, a modified hull, and uprated engines, emerged in early 1931, and later the same year, BuAer purchased one ex-

ample powered by 350-hp Wright R-975-3 *Whirlwind* engines and placed it in service as the XRD-1. Twenty-three more Dolphins variants were procured for the Navy and the Coast Guard between 1932 and 1934: three RD-2s in early 1933, two delivered to the Navy and one to the Coast Guard, powered by 450-hp Pratt & Whitney R-1340-10 engines; six very similar RD-3s in mid–1933 to the Navy; and ten RD-4s in late 1934 to the Coast Guard, powered by 450-hp R-1340-96 engines. One of the Navy

Top: **The Sinbad prototype after being modified and sold to the Coast Guard in 1931. In its original configuration as NX145Y, the engines had been mounted directly above the wings in streamlined nacelles.** *Bottom:* **One of two RD-2s ordered by the Navy in 1932. This example entered service in 1933 with the Utility Unit based at Coco Solo in the Canal Zone.**

RD-2s was specially outfitted for President Franklin D. Roosevelt, but there is no record of it ever having been used for such purpose. Navy RDs were typically assigned to utility squadrons and used primarily as transports, whereas Coast Guard versions saw extensive service in the search and rescue role as flying lifeboats. Two RD-3s were subsequently assigned to the Marine Corps to be used as utility transports. One Dolphin manufactured as an RD-2 but not placed on the naval inventory was used as a government transport by the Secretary of the Treasury until 1937. Two Navy RD-3s and four Coast Guard RD-4s were still listed as active in December 1941.

Lockheed RO—1931

TECHNICAL SPECIFICATIONS (XRO-1)

Type: Three or four-place landplane staff transport.
Manufacturer: Lockheed Aircraft Div. of Detroit Aircraft Corp., Burbank, California and Detroit, Michigan.
Total produced: 1 (USN)
Powerplant: One 645-hp Wright R-1820-E *Cyclone* 9-cylinder air-cooled radial engine driving a two-bladed fixed-pitch metal propeller.
Performance: Max. speed 209 mph at 7,000 ft.: ceiling 23,800 ft.; range 580 mi.
Weights: 3,235 lbs. empty, 4,895 lbs. loaded.
Dimensions: Span 42 ft. 9 in., length 28 ft. 4 in., wing area 293 sq. ft.

In October 1931, under the designation XRO-1, the Navy accepted delivery of one Lockheed Altair to be used as a personal transport for the Assistant Secretary of the Navy (David Ingalls). It was the first Navy aircraft of any type to possess fully retractable landing gear (preceding the Grumman XFF-1, reported above, by a couple of months). Designed by Gerald Vultee, the Altair was a retractable gear development of the fixed-gear Sirius first flown in 1928. Altairs, one of the most aerodynamically clean designs of the period, were typically constructed of wood, however, the DL-2 version sold to the Navy differed in having the all-metal, semi-monocoque fuselage seen on the Sirius 8.

The XRO-1 was based at NAS Anacostia during its term of service.

Curtiss JC/RC—1931

TECHNICAL SPECIFICATIONS (RC-1)

Type: Eight-place landplane utility transport.
Manufacturer: Curtiss Aeroplane and Motor Co., Garden City, New York.

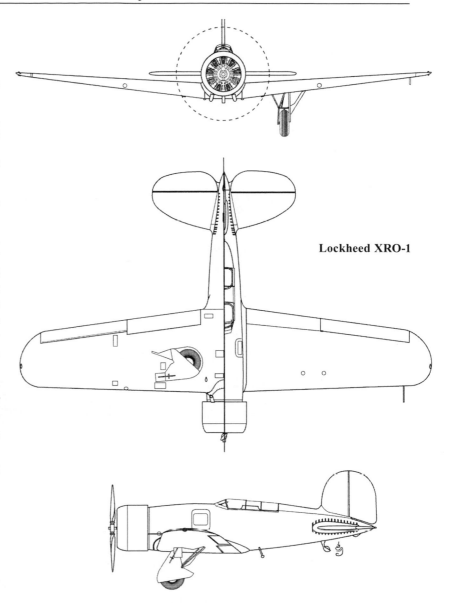

Lockheed XRO-1

The DL-2 version of Altair with a metal fuselage, placed on the inventory in October 1931 as the XRO-1 for the personal use of Assistant Secretary of the Navy David Ingalls.

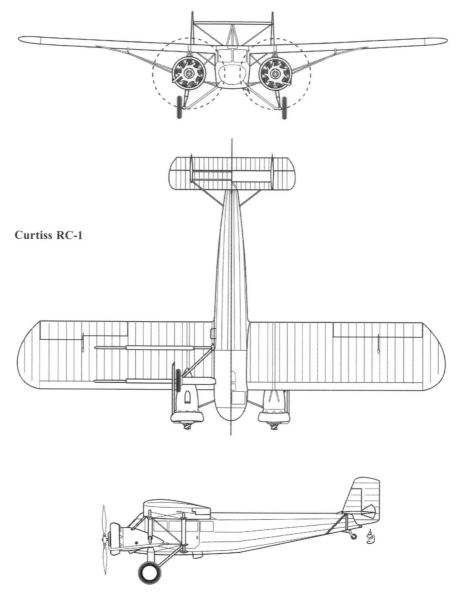

Curtiss RC-1

Only example of a military "Kingbird," the sole RC-1 was delivered to the Marines in 1931 to used as a utility transport and air ambulance. Assigned initially to VF-9M in Quantico, then to VF-7M in San Diego until 1936.

Total produced: 1 (USMC)
Powerplant: Two 300-hp Wright J-6-9 (R-975) *Whirl-wind* 9-cylinder air-cooled radial engines driving two-bladed fixed-pitch metal propellers.
Performance: Max. speed 138 mph at s.l.: ceiling 16,500 ft.; range 455 mi.
Weights: 3,280 lbs. empty, 6,115 lbs. loaded.
Dimensions: Span 54 ft. 6 in., length 34 ft. 10 in., wing area 327 sq. ft.

The Curtiss Model 55 "Kingbird," a twin-engine derivative of the Thrush, initially entered service with Eastern Air Transport in 1929 as a small airliner. Its most noticeable characteristics were a twin-finned, biplane empennage and strut-mounted engine nacelles that placed the propeller arcs in front of the aircraft's blunt nose. The Navy purchased a single Model 55 in March 1931 as the JC-1, but placed it into service as the RC-1. Following delivery, the aircraft was assigned to the Marines, serving with VF-9M at Quantico for two years, then transferring to VJ-7M at San Diego, where it was employed as a transport and air ambulance until the middle of 1936.

Bellanca RE/JE—1932

TECHNICAL SPECIFICATIONS (XRE-1)

Type: Six-place landplane utility transport.
Manufacturer: Bellanca Aircraft Corp., New Castle, Delaware
Total produced: 4 (USN,USMC)
Powerplant: One 420-hp Pratt & Whitney R-1340-C *Wasp* 9-cylinder air-cooled radial engine driving a two-bladed fixed-pitch metal propeller.
Performance: Max. speed 155 mph at s.l.: ceiling 17,300 ft.; range 670 mi.
Weights: 2,702 lbs. empty, 4,710 lbs. loaded.
Dimensions: Span 46 ft. 4 in., length 27 ft. 10 in., wing area 255 sq. ft.

The Navy acquired three civil Bellanca Model CH-400 "Skyrockets" during 1932 that were placed in service as the XRE-1, -2, and -3, respectively. Giuseppe M. Bellanca, beginning with his Air Sedan of 1922, had evolved a successful series of commercial high-wing monoplanes (WB/CH-200, -300, and -400) that

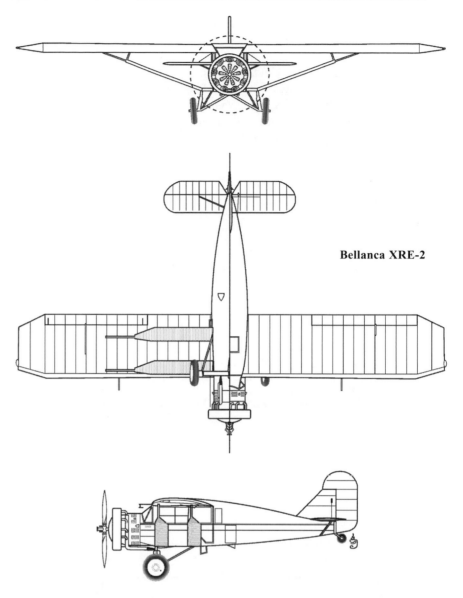

Bellanca XRE-2

This XJE-3, one of three Bellanca CH-400s procured by the Navy in 1933, was assigned to VJ-6M at MCAS Quantico, where it was used as an air ambulance until 1938.

enjoyed reputations as good load carriers with excellent range. The hallmarks of Bellanca's monoplane designs were a boxy, humped fuselage to accommodate passengers or cargo, broad-chord wings with tapered tips, and large, airfoil section wing struts that added to overall lift. Following official acceptance, the XRE-1 and -2 were retained as NAS Anacostia as utility transports and testbeds for radio equipment until being withdrawn during the late 1930s. The XRE-3 was assigned to Marine squadron VJ-6M (later VMJ-1) at Quantico and used there as a two-litter air ambulance until 1938.

In 1938, under the designation JE-1, the Navy procured a single Bellanca Model 31-42 "Super Skyrocket" to serve as a utility transport at NAS Lakehurst in New Jersey. Powered by a 570-hp R-1340-27, the larger JE was characterized by enlarged fin and rudder area, cantilevered landing gear, and a close-fitting bump cowling. This aircraft was listed as still active at NAS New York in December 1941.

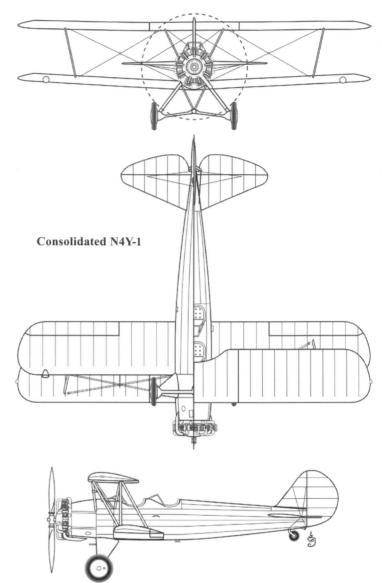

Consolidated N4Y-1

Consolidated N4Y—1932

TECHNICAL SPECIFICATIONS (USN XN4Y-1)

Type: Two-place landplane/floatplane trainer.
Manufacturer: Consolidated Aircraft Corp., Buffalo, New York.
Total produced: 4 (USN/USCG)
Powerplant: One 220-hp Lycoming R-680 7-cylinder air-cooled radial engine driving a two-bladed fixed-pitch metal propeller.
Performance: Max. speed 118 mph at s.l.: ceiling 13,700 ft.; range (not reported).
Weights: 1,918 lbs. empty, 2,585 lbs. loaded.
Dimensions: Span 31 ft. 7 in., length 26 ft. 11 in., wing area 280 sq. ft.

Representing a significant aerodynamic improvement over the earlier NY and PT-1/-3 series, the Consolidated Model 21 first appeared in 1931 as the Army Y1PT-11, powered by a 165-hp Wright J-6-5 (5-cylinder R-540) engine. A single J-6-5-powered Model 21-A purchased by BuAer in 1932 en-

One of three Lycoming-powered XN4Y-1s acquired for evaluation in 1934. After the Navy decided to procure N3N-1s in quantity, the XN4Y-1s were assigned to the training establishment at NAS Pensacola.

tered service with the Coast Guard at Cape May, New Jersey without any assigned designation. This aircraft, used for general training duties until late 1941, was afterward refitted with a 220-hp Lycoming R-680 engine and given the designation N4Y-1. In 1934 BuAer acquired three Lycoming-powered variants (Identical to the Army PT-11D) for evaluation as the XN4Y-1 and assigned them to the VD-2D8 training unit at NAS Pensacola. In the interval, however, naval officials had decided to re-equip the training establishment with NAF-built N3Ns, with the consequence that no further production of the N4Y-1 was ordered.

Grumman JF/J2F Duck—1933

TECHNICAL SPECIFICATIONS (JF-1 [J2F-5])

Type: Four- to five-place utility amphibian.

Manufacturer: Grumman Aircraft Engr. Corp., Bethpage, New York.

Total produced: 626 (USN, USMC, USCG)

Powerplant: One 700-hp Pratt & Whitney R-1830-62 *Twin Wasp* 14-cylinder [850-hp Wright R-1920-50 9-cylinder] air-cooled radial engine driving a three-bladed, ground-adjustable [variable-pitch] metal propeller.

Armament: One (two on J2F-2A) flexible .30-caliber machine gun in the rear cockpit [and one fixed .30-caliber machine gun in the nose] and up to 200 lbs. [650 lbs. (400 lbs. on J2F-2A)] of bombs carried on underwing racks.

Performance: Max. speed 168 mph [188 mph]; ceiling 18,000 ft. [27,000 ft.]; range 686 mi. [780 mi.].

Weights: 3,700 lbs. [4,300 lbs.] empty, 5,399 lbs. [6,711 lbs.] loaded.

Dimensions: Span 39 ft., length 33 ft. [34 ft. 0 in.], wing area 409 sq. ft.

Like the Loening "Shoehorns" with which Grumman had been closely associated, the JF/J2F series were amphibians in which the fuselage structure formed an integral part of the main pontoon. In 1931 BuAer asked Grumman to initiate a study for an amphibian designed to the Navy's new "utility" category, which specified that the aircraft also be capable of operating from an aircraft carrier. After reviewing Grumman's proposal for the model G-7, BuAer awarded the company a contract in late 1932 for construction of a prototype under the designation XJF-1. Not surprisingly, the design combined the shoehorn outline of Loening's OL series with the more modern aerodynamic and structural features of the FF-1. Along with Grumman's already proven gear retraction system, drag was minimized by utilizing all-metal, semi-monocoque construction methods to streamline the junctions between the fuselage and the main float. The single-bay biplane wings and all moveable control surfaces were conventional metal-framed structures with fabric covering.

The first flight of the XJF-1 took place on April 25, 1933, near the Grumman factory in Farmingdale, and it was delivered to Naval Air Station Anacostia in Mary-

land for military trials on May 4. As originally built, the tail group of the XJF-1 was similar in size and shape to that of the FF-1, but after early testing revealed stability problems, all vertical and horizontal tail surfaces were reshaped and enlarged. Following official acceptance, the Navy placed an order for twenty-seven production models to be delivered as the JF-1. The only noticeable difference between the production JF-1 and the prototype was the rounded fin and rudder shape that became standard throughout the series. As JF-1s began entering service in late 1934, they replaced Loening OL-9s aboard the Navy's

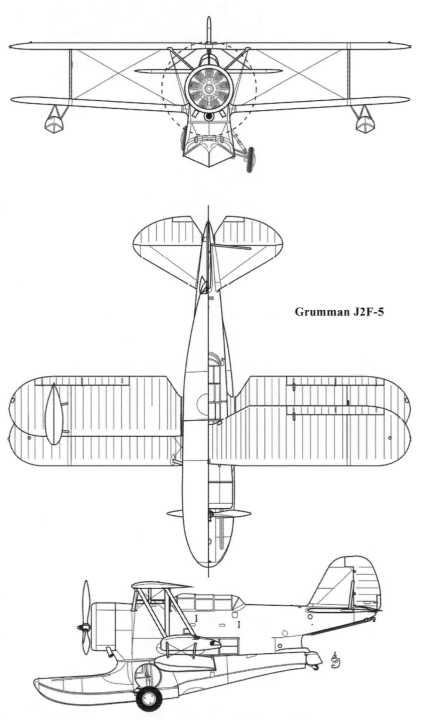

Grumman J2F-5

four carriers, and as deliveries proceeded, began replacing older observation and torpedo types in utility (VJ) squadrons; and between 1936 and 1939, four of these were transferred to the Marine Corps. The fourteen JF-2s ordered by the Coast Guard in early 1934 differed in having single-row 750-hp Wright R-1820-20 *Cyclone* engines that came with ring-type cowlings and a direction-finding loop antenna behind the canopy. Initial deliveries of JF-2s commenced later the same year, and on December 4, 1934, a USGC JF-2 established a new amphibian world speed record of 191 mph. One of the last JF-2s produced was reassigned to the Marines and entered service with VJ-6M at Quantico, Virginia in late 1935. The last of the JF series, five *Cyclone*-powered JF-3s completed in late 1935, came without carrier arresting gear and were delivered directly to naval reserve units.

Grumman began design work on the improved model G-15 in 1935, and in March 1936, BuAer ordered twenty production aircraft as the J2F-1. Powered by the same R-1820-20 engine as the JF-2, changes included a lengthening of the main float with accommodation for an additional crewmember or a medical stretcher in the compartment below the cockpit, removal of the inter-aileron struts, and a strengthening of the airframe to allow catapult launches from ships. The first J2F-1 was flown on April 3, 1937, and all had been delivered to Navy and Marine units by the end of the year. To keep pace with the general expansion of the fleet, BuAer ordered four more batches of J2Fs from Grumman in 1937 and 1938, which all entered service during 1939: twenty-one J2F-2s equipped with 790-hp R-1820-30 engines and one fixed .30-caliber machine gun firing between cylinders; nine J2F-2As for the Marines that featured two additional bomb racks and twin

Left, top: **The XJF-1 prototype in 1933 following enlargement of vertical fin. Production models came with the rounded fin and rudder and a shorter chord cowling.** *Middle:* **One of 14 JF-2s accepted by the Coast Guard in 1934 and 1935. The aircraft shown (V148) was initially based at CGAS Port Angeles in Washington state.** *Bottom:* **The J2F-1 depicted here was delivered to the Marine Corps at MCAS Quantico in June 1938, where it served with utility squadron VMJ-1. The Marines also operated several more JFs and J2Fs at other stations.**

machine gun mounts in the rear cockpit; twenty J2F-3s specially outfitted to serve as VIP transports; and thirty-two J2F-4s that differed from -2s only in minor details.

With war clouds on horizon, BuAer placed an order with Grumman in early 1940 for 144 J2F-5s, and deliveries started before the end of the year. J2F-5s were powered by 850-hp R-1820-50 engines, upping top speed by 10 mph, and could be distinguished by their full-chord cowlings. At some point during J2F-5 production the airplane acquired the name "Duck." As of December 1941, over 200 JF and J2F variants were active with the Navy, Marines, and Coast Guard. During World War II, with Grumman's production lines at capacity producing fighters and torpedo-bombers, license-production of the J2F was shifted to the Columbia Aircraft Corp. at Valley Stream, New York, and from mid–1942 to late 1945, a further 330 Ducks were completed there as the J2F-6 (initially designated JL-1). J2F-6s were identical to -5s except for a 1,050-hp R-1820-54 engines and constant-speed propellers.

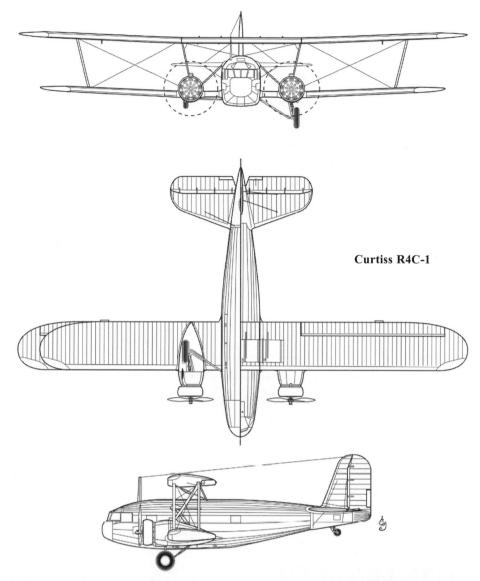

Curtiss R4C-1

Curtiss R4C—1934

TECHNICAL SPECIFICATIONS (R4C-1)

Type: Sixteen-place landplane transport.
Manufacturer: Curtiss Airplane Div. of Curtiss-Wright Corp., St. Louis, Missouri.
Total produced: 2 (USN/USMC)
Powerplants: Two 720-hp Wright R-1820-F *Cyclone* 9-cylinder air-cooled radial engines driving three-bladed variable-pitch metal propellers.
Performance: Max. speed 190 mph; ceiling 23,000 ft.; range 716 mi.
Weights: 12,235 lbs. empty, 17,500 lbs. gross.
Dimensions: Span 82 ft. 0 in., length 48 ft. 7 in., wing area 1,208 sq. ft.

In 1934, for general transportation duties, the Navy acquired two late-production Curtiss AT-32E Condor II airliners, which entered service under the designation R4C-1. The AT-32 differed from the earlier T-32 in having full-chord cowlings rather than drag rings and variable-pitch propellers instead of fixed units, and the number "32" related to the type's 3,200-lb. payload capacity. Despite being biplanes of mixed,

The first of two R4C-1s ordered for the Marines in 1934. This aircraft was assigned initially to VJ-7M in San Diego. In 1940 both R4C-1s were equipped with skis and transferred to the U.S. Antarctic Expedition.

fabric-covered construction in an age of all-metal monoplane airliners like the Boeing 247 and Douglas DC-2, some 30 Condors IIs had been placed in service during 1933 and 1934 by American Airlines and Eastern Air Transport as overnight "sleeper" transports, where the type's spacious, 12-berth cabin was considered more important than its 155 mph cruising speed.

The first R4C-1, delivered in June 1934, was assigned to Marine squadron VJ-6M in Quantico, Virginia. In similar fashion, the second example, arriving the following November, went to VJ-7M in San Diego, California, then in late 1935, when VJ-6M received two Douglas R2D-1s (DC-2s), its R4C-1 transferred to VJ-7M (became VMJ-1 in 1937). After leaving Marine service in 1940, the two aircraft were equipped with skis and attached to the U.S. Antarctic Expedition, and reportedly left behind when the expedition returned in 1941.

Waco JW—1934

TECHNICAL SPECIFICATIONS (XJW-1)

Type: Three-place landplane trainer and utility aircraft.
Manufacturer: Waco Aircraft Co., Troy, Ohio.
Total produced: 2 (USN)
Power plant: One 210-hp Continental R-670 7-cylinder air-cooled radial engine driving a two-bladed fixed-pitch metal propeller.
Performance: Max. speed 132 mph: ceiling (not reported); range 400 mi.
Weights: 1,400 lbs. empty, 2,300 lbs. loaded.
Dimensions: span 29 ft. 6 in., length 20 ft. 9 in., wing area 296 sq. ft.

The last two of 18 UBF-2 sport biplanes built by Waco were purchased by the Navy in 1934 under the designation XJW-1. After being assigned to the rigid airship *Macon* HTA unit, both aircraft were fitted with

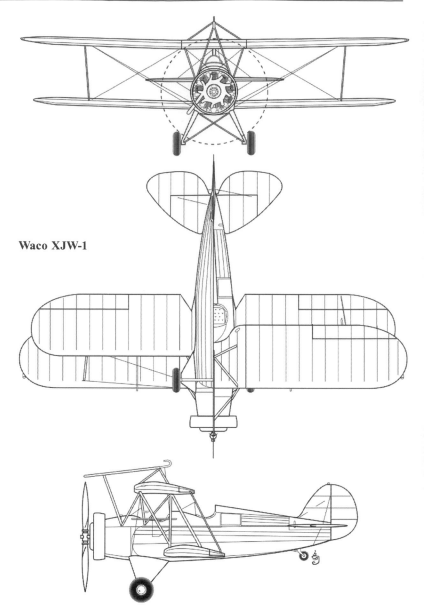

Waco XJW-1

One of two XJW-1s acquired in 1934 as hook-on trainers for the airship *Macon*. They also were used as aerial couriers between the airship and the ground. One was lost with *Macon*, and the survivor was sent to NAS Anacostia.

a "skyhook" arresting system to operate as hook-on trainers for pilots as well as carrying mail and passengers to and from the airship. Following the loss of *Macon* in 1935, the surviving XJW-1 was attached to VX-4D5 at NAS Anacostia and remained in service there until late 1941.

Douglas R2D—1934

TECHNICAL SPECIFICATIONS (R2D-1)

Type: Seventeen-place landplane transport.
Manufacturer: Douglas Aircraft Co., Santa Monica, California.
Total produced: 5 (USN/USMC)
Powerplants: Two 750-hp Wright R-1820-12 *Cyclone* 9-cylinder air-cooled radial engines driving three-bladed variable-pitch metal propellers.
Performance: Max. speed 210 mph: ceiling 22,450 ft.; range 1,200 mi.
Weights: 12,408 lbs. empty, 18,200 lbs. loaded.
Dimensions: span 85 ft., length 61 ft. 9 in., wing area 939 sq. ft.

The Douglas DC-1, flown for the first time in July 1933, followed 10 months later by the definitive DC-2 production model, shifted the paradigm in air travel by offering commercial operators a combination of speed, payload, and range that would enable them—for the first time—to carry passengers at a profit without reliance on air mail contract subsidies. Motivated by the desire to create an aircraft that could effectively compete for airline routes against Boeing's new Model 247, the Douglas engineering team led by Arthur Raymond had evolved a highly advanced low-wing monoplane design that utilized multi-cellular wing construction allowing the main spars to run below the floorboard. Other innovations included a twin-strut, knee-action main landing gear retraction system, split flaps that lowered takeoff and landing speeds, and an all-aluminum alloy structure throughout except for fabric-covered control surfaces. More importantly, compared to the Model 247, the DC-2 cruised 14 mph faster, 500 miles further, with four more passengers.

In 1934, out of a desire to replace its obsolescent Ford RRs (tri-motors) with more up-to-date equipment, BuAer ordered five DC-2s from Douglas in two batches under the designation R2D-1. The first three (DC-2-125s) were accepted in late 1934, two of which were assigned to NAS Anacostia

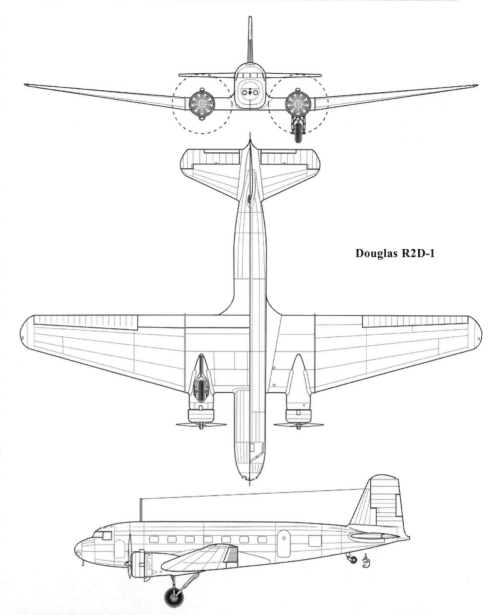

Douglas R2D-1

On of three DC-2-125s accepted during late 1934, this R2D-1 was assigned to VJ-6M at MCAS Quantico to be used as a staff transport. Of the five R2D-1s ultimately procured, three were allocated to the Marines.

as staff transports and the other to Quantico with Marine squadron VJ-6M. Two improved DC-2-142s (increased fin area and small interior variations) were delivered in 1935, one entering service with VJ-5 at NAS San Diego and the second with VJ-6M (became VMJ-2 in 1937). The USMC R2D-1s were later used to conduct the first Marine paratrooper experiments. By the end of 1941, two R2D-1s had been removed from the naval inventory, two were based at NAS Pensacola, and one remained with the Marines at San Diego.

Franklin PS-2

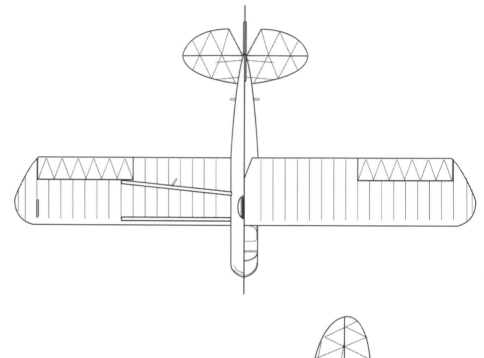

Franklin PS-2—1934

TECHNICAL SPECIFICATIONS (PS-2)

Type: One-place training glider.
Manufacturer: Franklin Glider Co., (location unknown).
Total produced: 6 (USN)
Powerplant: None.
Performance: Max. speed (not reported); glide ratio 15:1.
Weights: Empty (not reported), 400 lbs. loaded.
Dimensions: Span 36 ft., length (not reported), wing area 180 sq. ft.

In 1934 the Navy acquired six one-seat Franklin PS-2 (primary-secondary-two) gliders to evaluate the possibility of incorporating them into the pilot training program. No naval designation was ever assigned. Designed to withstand the rigors of training, the PS-2 featured a welded, steel tube fuselage and tail group, built-up wooden wings braced by struts, and a mono-wheel landing gear. After official evaluations, the gliders were assigned to NAS Pensacola, where they operated until sometime in 1938. At least one PS-2 was transferred to NACA at Langley, Virginia, for ground effect tests.

A very modern glider in its day, the Navy acquired six of these PS-2s and operated them at NAS Pensacola to evaluate the feasibility of using them as part of a pilot training program.

Stinson R3Q (RQ)—1935

TECHNICAL SPECIFICATIONS (XR3Q-1)

Type: Six-place landplane staff transport.
Manufacturer: Stinson Aircraft Corp., Northville, Michigan.
Total produced: 2 (USN, USCG)
Powerplant: One 225-hp Lycoming R-680-6 7-cylinder air-cooled
    radial engine driving a two-bladed fixed-pitch metal propeller.
Performance: Max. speed 133 mph at s.l.: ceiling 15,500 ft.; range 550
    miles.

Weights: 2,250 lbs. empty, 3,550 lbs. loaded.
Dimensions: Span 41 ft., length 27 ft. 3 in., wing area 230 sq. ft

The Navy purchased one Stinson SR-5A in 1934 under the designation XR3Q-1 and thereafter assigned it as a utility transport at NAS Sunnyvale (later renamed Moffett Field) in California. Stinson's SR "Reliant" series, fabric-covered high-wing monoplanes characterized by clean lines, cantilevered landing gear, and close-fitting bump cowlings, had gained wide popu-

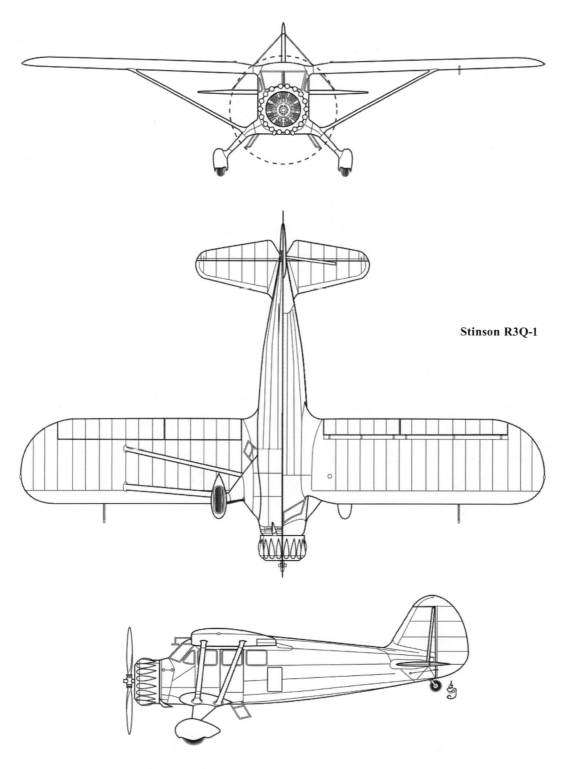

Stinson R3Q-1

larity as personal and executive transports in the United States, with about 250 having been sold by 1934. A second SR-5A acquired in 1935 went into service with the Coast Guard at Floyd Bennett Field in Brooklyn, New York, initially as the RQ-1 but later changed to XR3Q-1 to conform with its Navy counterpart. This aircraft was used to test electronic equipment until 1939, when it was transferred to the Air Patrol Detachment at Cape May, New Jersey. Both XR3Q-1s had been stricken from the inventory by the end of 1941.

This Stinson SR-5A was placed on the Coast Guard inventory in 1935 as the RQ-1 but subsequently changed to XR3Q-1 to conform to the Navy SR-5A acquired in 1934. This aircraft was assigned to Floyd Bennett Field, New York.

Naval Aircraft Factory N3N—1935

TECHNICAL SPECIFICATIONS (N3N-3)

Type: Two-place landplane/floatplane trainer.
Manufacturer: Naval Aircraft Factory, Philadelphia, Pennsylvania.
Total produced: 998 (USN, USMC, USCG)
Powerplant: One 235-hp Wright R-760-2 (J-6-7) 7-cylinder air-cooled radial engine driving a two-bladed fixed-pitch metal propeller.
Performance: Max. speed 126 mph at s.l.: ceiling 15,200 ft.; range 470 miles.
Weights: 2,090 lbs. empty, 2,940 lbs. loaded (with floats).
Dimensions: Span 34 ft., length 25 ft. 6 in., wing area 305 sq. ft.

The N3N was a byproduct of the Vinson-Trammel Act of 1934, which, among other things, directed the Navy to generate at least 10 percent of its aircraft from the government-owned Naval Aircraft Factory. With this in mind, BuAer issued a requirement in October 1934 for NAF to design and develop a primary trainer that would replace the Navy's existing fleet of Consolidated NYs in both training centers and reserve units. The requirement, in addition to being convertible to wheel or float undercarriage, specified that the new aircraft have "maximum ruggedness and ease of maintenance," plus the "general stability for primary training purposes." Soon afterward, BuAer awarded NAF a contract to construct one aircraft as the XN3N-1, to be followed by 45 production models, with the understanding the prototype would be ready for testing by late 1935.

While the general aerodynamic design of the XN3N-1 was typical of open-cockpit, fabric-covered biplanes of the day, its structural features were more innovative: a fuselage built-up of riveted aluminum extrusions rather than welded, steel tubing, an all-aluminum semi-monocoque tail group, and wings made up of extruded aluminum I-beams and stamped aluminum ribs. For ready access to the interior, the left side of the fuselage incorporated three removable panels. On August 23, 1935, several months ahead of schedule, the XN3N-1 was rolled out for its first flight. Early air testing, however, revealed a serious amount of tail heaviness coupled with difficulty recovering from spins. Evaluating officials also expressed concern over the lack of forward crash protection and the danger presented by the midships location of the fuel tanks. As a result, the engine mount was extended to shift the center of gravity forward, the stabilizer revised and rudder area increased to improve spin recovery, and the main fuel tanks relocated to the upper wings. Although the changes did not completely resolve all stability and control problems, BuAer nonetheless increased the order to 85 aircraft, and the first production N3N-1 completed acceptance trials at NAS Anacostia in mid–1936.

Through the course of 1936, as N3N-1 deliveries proceeded, NAF received two more production contracts, the

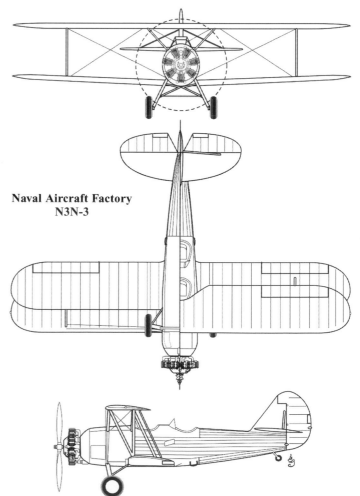

**Naval Aircraft Factory
N3N-3**

Top: **The 180 N3N-1s produced between 1935 and 1938 represented an across-the-board replacement of the Navy's trainer fleet. Full-chord cowling seen on this example was later removed.** *Bottom:* **N3N-3s began displacing -1s in the Naval Training Establishment during 1940, and a total of 816 had been delivered when production ceased in 1942.**

first 25 of which (as with the original 85) were to be powered by 220-hp Wright R-790-8 9-cylinder engines and the remaining 80 by 235-hp Wright R-760-2 7-cylinder engines. Ten aircraft of the original order were subsequently cancelled so that 180 N3N-1s had been accepted when production ended in April 1938. All N3N-1s came with full-chord cowlings that were later removed. Continuing efforts by NAF to remedy the shortcomings of the N3N-1 resulted in the testing of the R-760-powered XN3N-2 during mid–1936. Despite further revisions to the engine mount and the movement of certain equipment forward, the XN3N-2 was judged not to offer much improvement over the -1 and never went into production.

In light of passage of the Naval Expansion Act of 1938 and the unprecedented growth it portended for naval aviation (i.e., 3,000 new aircraft), NAF officials obtained approval from BuAer to initiate a redesign program that would eliminate the N3N-1's most serious flaws, and in June 1939, received a contract to manufacture 50 new aircraft as the N3N-3. One N3N-1 returned to NAF where it was modified to incorporate a completely new tail group consisting of a larger, rounded fin and rudder and a repositioned stabilizer, a single-strut landing gear (on the landplane version), and a new nose contour which dispensed with a cowling. Other less visible improvements included changes to the controls and a strengthening of the airframe. Flight-testing of the XN3N-3, completed by January 1940 in both wheeled and float configurations, demonstrated not only excellent handling qualities but improved levels of performance that exceeded expectations. In May 1940, BuAer ordered the N3N-3 into high-rate production, initially contracting for 500 aircraft and in September, upped the order to 816. NAF thereafter manufactured N3N-3s at a rate of about 50 aircraft per month, delivering the last examples in January 1942.

As N3N-3s arrived for service at NAS Pensacola and NAS Corpus Christi, the two main primary flight-training centers, most N3N-1s were sent to the reserves or attached to bases for utility duties. N3N-3s also began displacing -1s in reserve units, and in 1941, four were assigned to the Coast Guard, and several more as tugs in the Marine glider training program. At the time the U.S. entered World War II in December 1941, a total of 943 N3Ns were listed on the naval inventory. After serving throughout the course of the war, most surviving N3Ns were sold surplus, however, the very last N3N-3s were not retired from operations at the Naval Academy until 1961.

Boeing (Stearman) NS and N2S Kaydet—1935

TECHNICAL SPECIFICATIONS (N2S-3)

Type: Two-place landplane trainer.
Manufacturer: Stearman Aircraft Div. of Boeing Airplane Co., Wichita, Kansas.
Total produced: 4,437 (USN, USMC, USCG)
Powerplant: One 220-hp Continental R-670-5 7-cylinder air-cooled radial engine driving a two-bladed fixed-pitch wooden or metal propeller.
Performance: Max. speed 124 mph at s.l.; ceiling 11,200 ft.; range 505 miles.
Weights: 1,936 lbs. empty, 2,717 lbs. loaded.
Dimensions: Span 32 ft. 2 in., length 24 ft. 3 in., wing area 297 sq. ft.

In terms of numbers, the Stearman "Kaydet" series, became the Navy's most important primary trainer of the wartime period. Though not as versatile as the N3N, the Stearman Division of Boeing nonetheless possessed the plant capacity to produce trainers in far greater numbers than NAF. In 1934, the same year Stearman was acquired as a subsidiary of Boeing, the Model 70 appeared as a private venture in a bid to replace both the Navy's and the Army's aging fleet of Consolidated primary trainers (i.e., NY and PT-1, -3, and -11). BuAer responded first, ordering one example to be powered by a surplus 220-hp Wright R-790-8 J-5 engine, which was delivered in 1935 under the designation XNS-1. Following trials, Stearman received a contract to produce 61 virtually identical aircraft as the NS-1, and nearly all were placed in service at NAS Pensacola during 1935 and 1936 to augment N3N-1s. Mean-

while, from 1937 onwards, the 225-hp Lycoming R-680-powered Stearman Model 75 was placed in large-scale production for the Army as the PT-13, then in 1940, the 220-hp Continental R-670-powered Model A75-N1 as the PT-17.

The next Navy order came in 1940 when BuAer procured 250 Continental-powered PT-17 copies under the designation N2S-1, with deliveries being completed in 1941. Also accepted during 1941 were 125 Lycoming-powered variants specially outfitted as instrument trainers (identical to PT-13C) that entered service as the N2S-2 plus 211 (out of 1,875 ordered) Continental-powered variants (same as PT-17) delivered as the N2S-3. All of these aircraft were assigned to primary training centers, which by that time included NAS Jacksonville, Florida, as well as NAS Pensacola and NAS Corpus Christi. A total of 616 Stearman-built trainers were in naval service by the end of 1941, and a further 3,821 N2S-3s, -4s (Continental R-670-5), and -5s (Lycoming R-680-17) would be delivered before the war

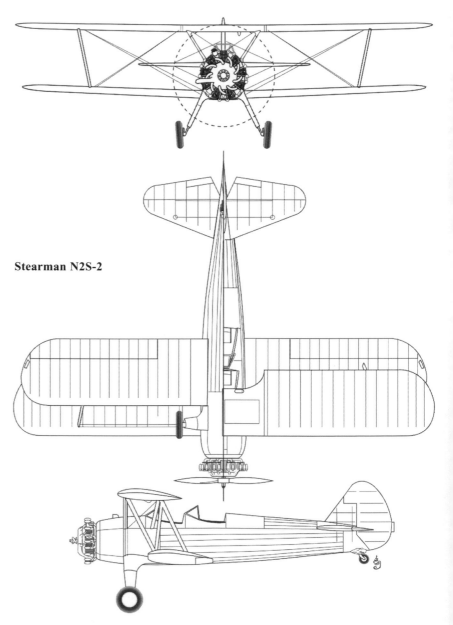

Stearman N2S-2

Top: **The Navy bought 61 NS-1s powered by surplus J-5 engines in 1935 to supplement its primary training fleet at NAS Pensacola, and 42 of them were still on hand at the end of 1941.** *Bottom:* **Burgeoning growth of naval pilot training from 1940 onwards compelled the Navy to order the Army's PT-13 (N2S-2) and PT-17 (N2S-1 through -5). It became the Navy's most numerous wartime primary trainer.**

ended. Eleven N2S-3s were transferred to the Coast Guard for training purposes, and small numbers of different N2S variants also served with the Marines. Like the N3Ns, virtually all of the Navy N2Ss were sold surplus shortly after World War II ended.

Northrop RT—1935

TECHNICAL SPECIFICATIONS (RT-1)

Type: Eight-place landplane staff transport.
Manufacturer: Northrop Corp. (Subsidiary of Douglas Aircraft Co.), Inglewood, California.

Total produced: 1 (USCG)
Powerplant: One 735-hp Wright R-1820-F52 *Cyclone* 9-cylinder air-cooled radial engine driving a three-bladed variable-pitch metal propeller.
Performance: Max. speed 219 mph at 6,300 ft.: ceiling 20,000 ft.; range 1,650 miles.
Weights: 4,540 lbs. empty, 7,350 lbs. loaded.
Dimensions: span 47 ft. 9 in., length 33 ft. 3 in., wing area 363 sq. ft.

A single Northrop Delta 1-D executive transport was procured for the Coast Guard in February 1935 and taken into service as the RT-1. It was an exceptionally clean low-wing monoplane utilizing Northrop's very advanced multi-cellular wing design and all-metal, stressed skin construction. Other noteworthy features included a fixed landing gear encased in streamlined spats and split landing flaps. After introducing the very sleek Delta in 1933, Northrop's plans to market it as a small airliner were effectively frustrated by a 1934 federal regulation requiring multi-engine aircraft for airliner operations at night or over rough terrain. The RT-1, one of eight Delta 1-Ds ultimately completed by Northrop, while technically serving with

This Northrop Delta 1-D was placed on the Coast Guard inventory in 1935 to serve as a personal transport for the secretary of the Treasury. Used in the late 1930s as a USCG VIP transport.

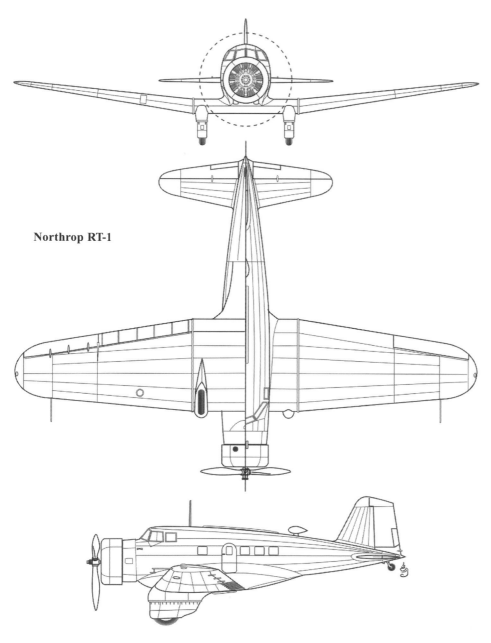

Northrop RT-1

the Coast Guard, had actually been acquired for use as the personal staff transport of then Secretary of the Treasury Henry N. Morgenthau, Jr. The Treasury Department ceased using this aircraft sometime during the late 1930s, after which the Coast Guard continued to operate it as a VIP transport until it was damaged beyond economical repair in late 1940.

Kinner RK—1936

TECHNICAL SPECIFICATIONS (XRK-1)

Type: Four-place landplane utility transport.
Manufacturer: Kinner Airplane & Motor Corp. (owned by Security-National Aircraft Corp.), Downey, California.
Total produced: 3 (USN)
Powerplant: One 300-hp Kinner C-7 (R-1044-2) 7-cylinder air-cooled radial engine driving a two-bladed, variable-pitch metal propeller.
Performance: Max. speed 171 mph; ceiling (not reported); range 700 mi.
Weights: 2,551 lbs. empty, 4,000 lbs. loaded.
Dimensions: Span 39 ft. 9 in., length 28 ft. 7 in., wing area 240 sq. ft.

The Kinner C-7 "Envoy" was flown for the first time in 1934 as four-place outgrowth of the company's earlier two-seat B-2 "Sportster." In general design, like the B-2, it appeared as a fabric-covered, low-wing monoplane with wire-braced wings and spatted undercarriage, with the added features of a close-fitting bump cowling and a noticeably raked forward windscreen. The Navy acquired three of these aircraft in 1936 under the designation XRK-1. One was assigned to the Inspector of Naval Aircraft at Santa Monica, California (where

Douglas was located) and another to VJ-5 as a command transport for the commanding officer of NAS San Diego; disposition of the third is not known. The XRK-1 based at San Diego was later refitted with a 400-hp Pratt & Whitney R-985 engine and given a ring cowl and by the end of 1941, was the only example remaining in naval service.

Fairchild JK—1936

TECHNICAL SPECIFICATIONS (JK-1)

Type: Five-place landplane utility transport.
Manufacturer: Fairchild Engine & Airplane Corp., Hagerstown, Maryland.
Total produced: 1 (USN)
Powerplant: One 320-hp Wright R-760-6 7-cylinder air-cooled radial engine driving a two-bladed, variable-pitch metal propeller.

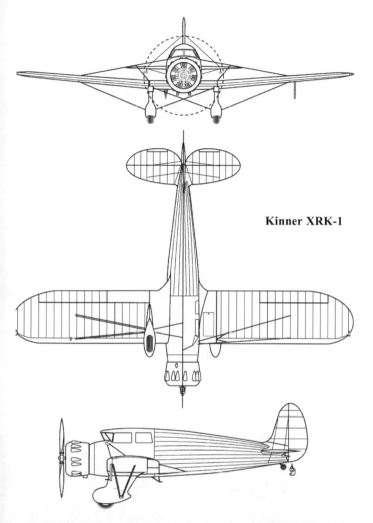

Kinner XRK-1

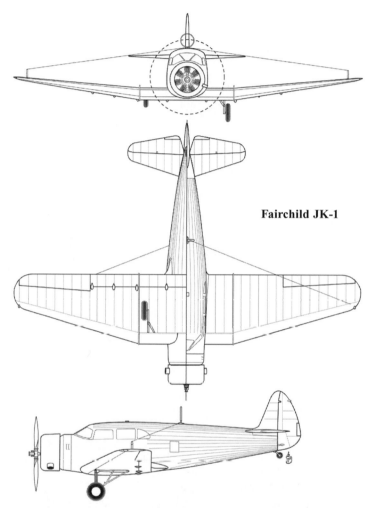

Fairchild JK-1

The Navy procured three Kinner Envoys as the XRK-1 in 1936. The example shown had been assigned to the Inspector of Naval Aircraft at the Douglas Plant in Santa Monica, California.

Sole Fairchild Model 45-A purchased as the JK-1 in 1936, as seen in 1939 at NRAB Oakland, California, after being assigned as a staff transport to serve the new air station under construction in Alameda.

Performance: Max. speed 170 mph; ceiling 18,700
    ft.; range 650 mi.
Weights: 2,512 lbs. empty, 4,000 lbs. loaded.
Dimensions: Span 39 ft. 6 in., length 30 ft. 1 in., wing
    area 248 sq. ft.

    The Navy purchased one Fairchild Model
45-A in 1936 which was taken into service as a
utility transport under the designation JK-1.
Featuring mixed, fabric-covered construction
with a fully cantilevered wing and tail group,
plus retractable landing gear, the Model 45 had
been designed in 1934 as a executive transport
that would be marketed against single-engine
aircraft like the cabin Waco and Stinson
Reliant, however, only a handful sold on the
civil market. Following official acceptance, the
Navy's JK-1 was given a blue-trimmed command paint scheme and assigned to the Admiral's staff at NAS Anacostia. By the time the
U.S. entered World War II in December 1941,
the aircraft had been transferred to general duties at NAS San Diego.

Fairchild R2K—1936

TECHNICAL SPECIFICATIONS (XR2K-1)

Type: Two-place landplane flying testbed.
Manufacturer: Kreider-Reisner Div. of Fairchild En-
    gine & Airplane Corp., Hagerstown, Maryland.
Total produced: 1 (USN)
Powerplant: One 145-hp Warner R-499 *Super Scarab*
    7-cylinder air-cooled radial engine driving a
    two-bladed fixed-pitch metal propeller.
Performance: Max. speed 133 mph; ceiling 20,000
    ft.; range 350 mi.
Weights: 1,102 lbs. empty, 1,750 lbs. loaded.
Dimensions: Span 33 ft. 0 in., length 22 ft. 3 in.,
    wing area 173 sq. ft.

    In 1931, following the acquisition of
Kreider-Reisner Aircraft Corp., Fairchild introduced the two-place Model 22C series, which
were parasol-wing monoplanes of mixed construction, offered with a variety of different inline and radial engines ranging from 75 to 145-
hp. The first of eight Warner *Super Scarab*–
powered 22C-7Fs appeared in 1933, and one
was purchased under USN registry in 1936 as
the XR2K-1 and thereafter used by NACA to
test the full-span "Zap" flap system. The
aircraft was apparently disposed of once the
tests were completed.

**This Fairchild Model 22C-7F was placed on the
naval inventory in 1936 as the XR2K-1 but operated by the National Advisory Committee on
Aeronautics (NACA) to test a full-span Zap flap
system.**

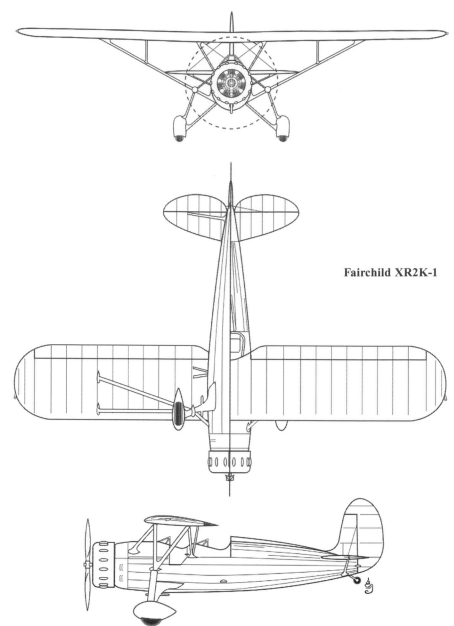

Fairchild XR2K-1

Fairchild J2K and GK— 1936

TECHNICAL SPECIFICATIONS
(J2K-1)

Type: Four-place landplane utility transport.

Manufacturer: Fairchild Engine & Airplane Corp., Hagerstown, Maryland.

Total produced: 17 (USN, USCG)

Powerplant: One 145-hp Ranger 6-410 6-cylinder air-cooled inline engine driving a two-bladed fixed-pitch wooden propeller.

Performance: Max. speed 138 mph; ceiling 16,500 ft.; range 560 mi.

Weights: 1,560 lbs. empty, 2,550 lbs. loaded.

Dimensions: Span 36 ft. 4 in., length 24 ft. 10 in., wing area 173 sq. ft.

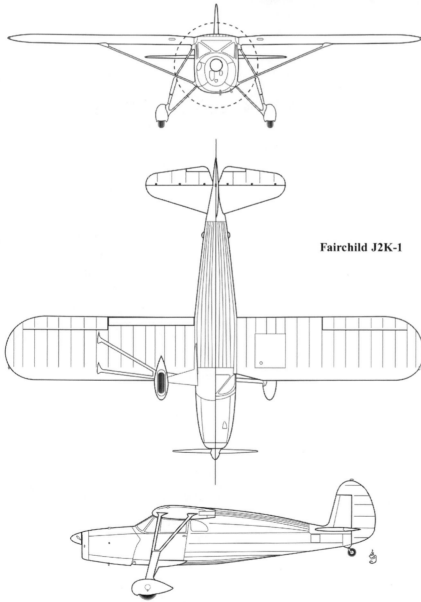

Fairchild J2K-1

One of two Fairchild Model 24-C8Fs purchased by the Coast Guard in 1936 under the designation J2K-1. Both aircraft were based at CGAS St. Petersburg, Florida. Model 24W-40s acquired during the war were GK-1s.

The Fairchild Model 24C originated in 1932 as a two-seat, high-wing cabin adaptation of the parasol-wing Model 22C, and as the type gained popularity (about 200 sold by 1935), evolved into a three-seater powered by either a 145-hp Warner radial (C8E) or 145-hp Ranger inline engine (C8F). Model 24s utilized the fabric-covered construction typical for lightplanes of the day, with a welded, steel tube fuselage and built-up wooden wings and were characterized by a wide-stance main landing gear that tied in to the wing struts. In 1936, two Model 24-C8Fs acquired for the Coast Guard under the designation J2K-1 were assigned as utility transports to the USCG air station at St. Petersburg, Florida, and in 1937, two more Model 24-Hs powered by 150-hp Ranger engines, were added to the Coast Guard inventory as the J2K-2 and assigned to its air station at Charleston, South Carolina. All four of these aircraft were subsequently lost in crashes, the last occurring in mid–1940. In 1941, under the new designation GK-1, BuAer awarded Fairchild contracts for 13 Model 24W-40s (165-hp Warner R-500), three examples having been accepted by the end of the year.

Sikorsky JRS— 1937

TECHNICAL SPECIFICATIONS (JRS-1)

Type: Twenty-one-place utility-transport amphibian.

Manufacturer: Sikorsky Aviation Div. of United Aircraft Corp., Bridgeport, Connecticut.

Total produced: 17 (USN, USMC)
Powerplants: Two 750-hp Pratt &
  Whitney R-1690-52 *Hornet* 9-
  cylinder air-cooled radial engines driving three-bladed,
  variable-pitch metal propellers.
Performance: Max. speed 194 mph,
  cruise 167 mph; ceiling 20,700
  ft.; range 775 mi.
Weights: 12,750 lbs. empty, 19,096
  lbs. loaded.
Dimensions: span 86 ft. 0 in., length
  51 ft. 2 in., wing area 781 sq. ft.

The Sikorsky Model S-43
was originally conceived to fulfill
a Pan American Airways requirement for a twin-engine amphibian
that would operate on secondary
Latin American routes. Flying for
the first time in mid–1935, the S-
43 presented an innovative all-
metal design that employed a
single-step hull and a wing sup-

A Navy JRS-1, probably in 1937, shown before application of unit markings. The 15 Navy and two Marine Corps JRS-1s reportedly remained in service through the end of World War II.

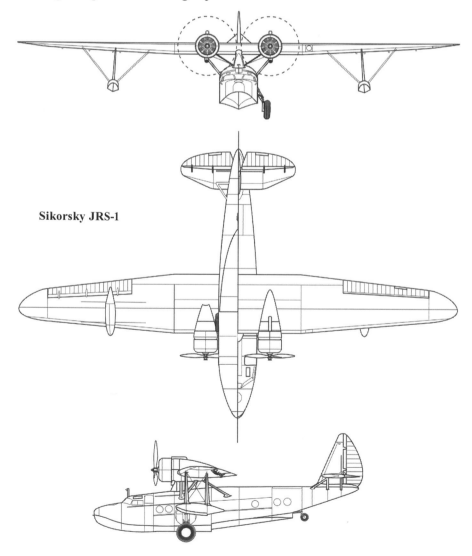

Sikorsky JRS-1

ported by a center pylon and N-struts. Wing
flaps occupying forty-eight percent of the span
reduced stall speed to 65 mph, permitting takeoffs and landings in relatively tight waterways.
In 1937, when Sikorsky had sold over 20 of
these transports to commercial users, BuAer ordered the first of 17 S-43s accepted into service
over the next two years as the JRS-1. Eight JRS-
1s were ultimately assigned to VJ-1 in San Diego
and the remainder to various stations, including
one each to Marine squadron VMJ-1 (became
VMJ-153 in 1941) in San Diego and VMJ-2 (became VMJ-252) in Quantico. At the end of 1941,
four JRS-1s remained active, three with VJ-1,
which saw brief service afterward in coastal patrol, and one with VMJ-252, the only example
to survive the war.

Lockheed R2O and R3O—1936

TECHNICAL SPECIFICATIONS (XR2O-1)

Type: Twelve-place landplane transport.
Manufacturer: Lockheed Aircraft Corp., Burbank,
California.
Total produced: 2 (USN, USCG)
Powerplants: Two 450-hp Pratt & Whitney R-985-13
Wasp Junior 9-cylinder air-cooled radial engines
driving two-bladed, variable-pitch metal propellers.
Performance: Max. speed 202 mph at 5,000 ft.; ceil-
ing 19,400 ft.; range 713 mi.
Weights: 6,454 lbs. empty, 10,500 lbs. loaded.
Dimensions: span 55 ft., length 38 ft. 7 in., wing area
458 sq. ft.

The Model 10 "Electra," designed by Hall
Hibbard and flown for the first time in early

1934, was Lockheed's first all-metal aircraft and came into national attention in July 1937 when the highly modified Model 10-E piloted by aviatrix Amelia Earhart disappeared during an attempted around-the-world flight. Materializing as one of the most advanced aerodynamic concepts of its day, the Electra had been designed to operate on lower capacity airline routes alongside the Boeing 247 and Douglas DC-2. The Navy procured a Model 10-A, the fifty-second built, as the XR2O-1 in February 1936, which was subsequently given a command paint scheme and assigned to NAS Anacostia for use by the Secretary of the Navy and his staff. The aircraft continued in this role through 1941.

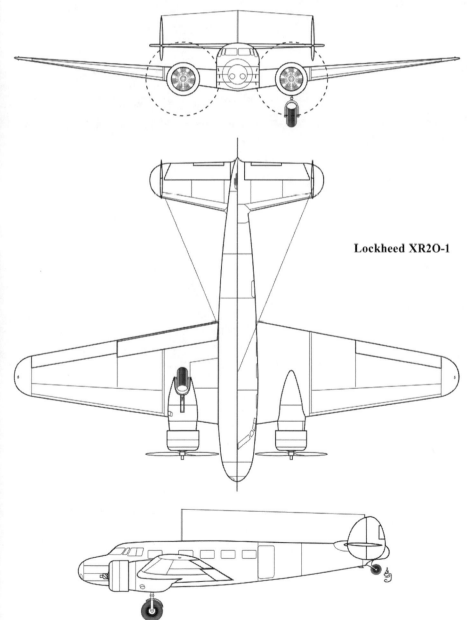

Lockheed XR2O-1

A Lockheed Model 10-A Electra acquired in February 1936 as the XR2O-1. After being painted in a command scheme, the aircraft was assigned to NAS Anacostia for the use of the secretary of the Navy and his staff.

In April 1936, a Lockheed Model 10-B, which differed from the A in having 440-hp Wright R-975-E3 engines, was added to the Coast Guard inventory as the XR3O-1, but like the Northrop RT-1 reported above, placed in service as a personal transport for the Secretary of the Treasury. It served in this capacity until 1939, when it was transferred to the Air Patrol Detachment in Cape May, New Jersey, and later still, to the USCG air station in Biloxi, Mississippi, where it served during World War II.

Waco J2W—1936

TECHNICAL SPECIFICATIONS (J2W-1)

Type: Four-place landplane/floatplane utility transport.
Manufacturer: Waco Aircraft Co., Troy, Ohio.
Total produced: 3 (USCG)
Powerplant: One 320-hp Wright R-760-E2 7-cylinder air-cooled radial engine driving a two-bladed, variable-pitch metal propeller.
Performance: Max. speed 176 mph at s.l.; ceiling (not reported); range 550 mi.
Weights: 2,050 lbs. empty, 3,350 lbs. loaded.
Dimensions: span 35 ft. 0 in., length 25 ft. 9 in., wing area 244 sq. ft.

The Coast Guard acquired three Waco EQC-6s in 1936 under the designation J2W-1. Waco introduced the "Custom Cabin" line in the mid–1930s as a series of sesquiplanes available with a number of powerplant options. The company's unusual alpha-numeric designation system referenced the engine, type, series, and year of manufacture; thus, EQC-6 translated to E = Wright R-760, Q = cabin biplane, C = custom cabin series, and -6 = 1936. Cabin Wacos were fabric-covered biplanes, typically constructed with steel tube fuselage frames and built-up wooden wings. The Coast Guard's three J2W-1s were initially employed for a variety of duties and one (V159) was variously rigged with floats and skis for operations out of Cordova, Alaska. After being assigned to the Air Patrol Detach-

Two of the three Waco EQC-6 cabin biplanes procured by the Coast Guard in 1938 as the J2W-1. After being assigned to various duties, all three were destroyed in crashes during 1939.

ment in El Paso, Texas, all three aircraft were lost in crashes during 1939.

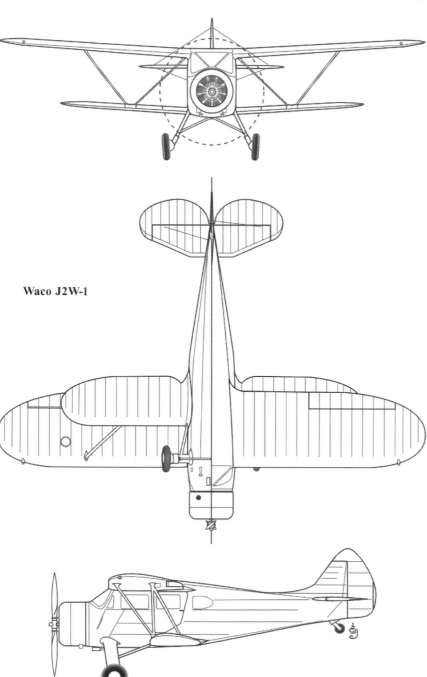

Waco J2W-1

Lockheed JO—1937

TECHNICAL SPECIFICATIONS (JO-2)

Type: Seven- to eight-place landplane utility transport.
Manufacturer: Lockheed Aircraft Corp., Burbank, California.
Total produced: 7 (USN, USMC)
Powerplants: Two 400-hp Pratt & Whitney R-985-48 *Wasp Junior* 9-cylinder air-cooled radial engines driving two-bladed, variable-pitch metal propellers.
Performance: Max. speed 225 mph at 5,000 ft.; ceiling 22,900 ft.; range 800 mi.
Weights: 5,765 lbs. empty, 8,650 lbs. loaded.
Dimensions: span 49 ft. 6 in., length 36 ft. 4 in., wing area 352 sq. ft.

Appearing in mid–1936 as a scaled-down version of the Model 10, the Lockheed Model 12 "Electra Junior" was intended to operate with smaller commercial airline carriers on feeder routes. Designated JO-1, a five-place Model 12-A purchased by BuAer was delivered in August 1937 for use by the Naval Attaché in Rio de Janeiro, Brazil. And from late 1937, BuAer procured five more 12-As, configured for six seats as the JO-2, two of which were assigned to the NAS Anacostia as staff transports and three to the Marines, one to VMJ-1 (later VMJ-152) at Quantico, one to VMJ-2 (later VMJ-252) at San Diego, and the last to Headquarters, USMC. The single XJO-3, delivered to Anacostia in October 1938, was an experimental variant having a fixed tricycle landing gear and an arrestor hook for deck trials conducted aboard *Lexington* to test the new gear arrangement. After completing these tests, the XJO-3 was moved to the

Boston airport in Massachusetts to serve as an airborne radar tesbed.

In August 1941 a civilian 12-A was impressed into naval service as the R3O-2 (the use of this designation rather than JO is an anomaly) and thereafter shipped to London, England for the use of the Naval Attaché there. At the time of the Japanese attack on Pear Harbor on December 7, 1941, the JO-1 and four of the JO-2s were still serving at their original locations, VMJ-252's JO-2 was destroyed on the ground at MCAS Ewa, Hawaii the day of the attack, and the XJO-3 had been transferred to NAS Norfolk.

The Navy acquired six Lockheed 12-As in 1937 and 1938, one as the JO-1 (five-seats) and five as the JO-2 (six-seats). This photograph depicts the first of three JO-2s assigned to the Marines during 1938.

Stearman-Hammond JH—1937

TECHNICAL SPECIFICATIONS (JH-1)

Type: Two-place landplane flying testbed.
Manufacturer: Stearman-Hammond Co., Oakland, California.
Total produced: 2 (USN)
Powerplant: one 150-hp Menasco L-363-C-4S 4-cylinder air-cooled inline engine driving a two-bladed, fixed-pitch wooden propeller.
Performance: max. speed 130 mph at s.l.; ceiling (not reported); range 480 mi.

The Navy purchased two Stearman-Hammond Y-1S "safe airplanes" in 1937 under the designation JH-1. Both were assigned to VJ-1 in San Diego as target drones and written off in late 1938.

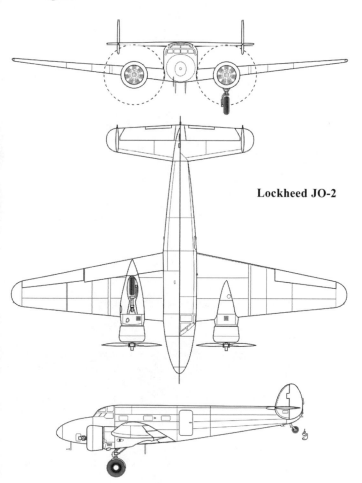

Lockheed JO-2

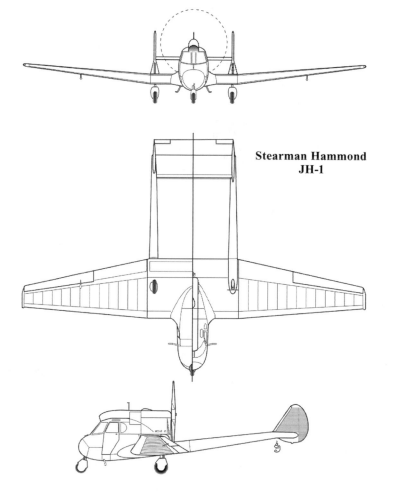

Stearman Hammond
JH-1

Weights: 1,382 lbs. empty, 2,150 lbs. gross.
Dimensions: Span 40 ft. 0 in., length 26 ft. 11 in., wing
    area (not reported).

Designed by Dean B. Hammond in 1934 in
response to the Bureau of Air Commerce "safe
airplane" contest and built by Lloyd Stearman,
the Stearman-Hammond Y-125 (Y-1M), flown in
1936, followed by the improved Y-150 (Y-1S) in
1937, represented an ultimately unsuccessful attempt to introduce a lightplane to the civil market
that would be both easy to fly and relatively af-
fordable. The design—all-metal, tricycle gear in
a twin boom pusher configuration—won the competition, but an eventual price of $5,000 per air-
craft (compared to $1,098 for a Piper J-3 Cub),
turned it into a commercial failure. In 1937,
BuAer purchased two Y-1Ss under the designation
JH-1 and both were placed in service as target
drones with VJ-1 in San Diego. Painted yellow as
trainers in order to hide their identity, they were
the first radio-controlled aircraft to be tested by
the Navy. Although both JH-1s were listed as having "crashed" in late 1938, they are thought to
have been shot down during antiaircraft gunnery
tests.

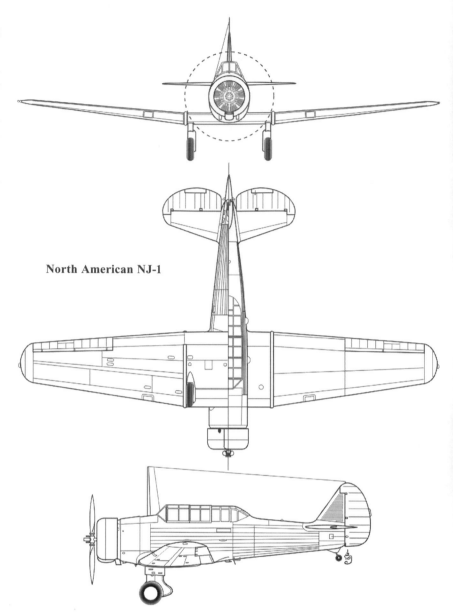

North American NJ-1

North American NJ—1937

TECHNICAL SPECIFICATIONS (NJ-1)

Type: Two-place landplane basic trainer.
Manufacturer: North American Aviation, Inc., Ingle-
    wood, California.
Total produced: 40 (USN)
Powerplant: One 500-hp Pratt & Whitney R-1340-6
    Wasp 9-cylinder air-cooled radial engine driving
    a two-bladed, variable-pitch metal propeller.
Performance: Max. speed 167 mph at s.l.; ceiling
    24,900 ft.; range 944 mi.
Weights: 3,250 lbs. empty, 4,440 lbs. loaded.
Dimensions: Span 42 ft., length 27 ft. 2 in.,
    wing area 248 sq. ft.

The origins of the NJ can be traced to
1934 when the U.S. Army invited aircraft
manufacturers to submit flying prototypes
for a basic trainer that would incorporate
recent advances seen in the aeronautical
state-of-the-art. North American, a relatively new company, tested its NA-16 prototype for the first time on April 1, 1935,
then following a series of improvements
offered it to the Army as the NA-18. Powered by a 400-hp Wright R-975-7 engine,
the NA-18 emerged as a clean monoplane
design that was all-metal in structure with
aluminum-skinned wings, a fabric-covered
fuselage, and fixed landing gear encased

The naval variant of Air Corps BT-9, the 40 NJ-1s featured R-1340 engines and aluminum-clad fuselages. The aircraft pictured had been assigned to command duties in
1938.

in fairings. In 1936, after winning the competition, North American received a contract for 42 production aircraft as the BT-9, then later that year, BuAer ordered 40 naval variants, nearly identical to BT-9s except for 500-hp Pratt & Whitney R-1340 engines, which were taken into service during 1937 under the designation NJ-1. The fortieth NJ airframe was completed with an experimental Ranger V-770-4 inverted V-12 engine and briefly tested as the NJ-2 but afterward refitted with an R-1340 and placed in regular service as an NJ-1. All NJ-1s were assigned to NAS Pensacola for training duties, and 39 still served there in December 1941.

Beechcraft JB and GB—1937

TECHNICAL SPECIFICATIONS (GB-1)

Type: Four-place landplane utility transport.
Manufacturer: Beech Aircraft Co., Wichita, Kansas.
Total produced: 293 (USN, USMC)
Power plant: One 450-hp Pratt & Whitney R-985-50 *Wasp Junior* 9-cylinder air-cooled radial engine driving two-bladed, variable-pitch metal propeller.
Performance: Max. speed 212 mph; ceiling 25,000 ft.; range 670 mi.
Weights: 2,540 lbs. empty, 4,250 lbs. loaded.
Dimensions: span 32 ft., length 26 ft. 10 in., wing area 297 sq. ft.

The legendary Beech Model 17 "Staggerwing" made its debut as a fixed-gear civil aircraft in late 1932, and the retractable-gear B17L of 1934 became the first production model. Of mixed construction, with a welded, steel tube fuselage and built-up wooden wings, all Model 17s were distinguishable by the obvious back stagger of their upper wing and a fuselage that gracefully faired into a rounded fin and rudder. In late 1937, under the designation JB-1, BuAer purchased an off-the-shelf C17R, powered by a 420-hp Wright R-975-E2 engine, which was subsequently employed as a command aircraft from 1937 to 1939.

The next order came in 1939, when the Navy acquired 10 *Wasp Junior*–powered D17S models as the GB-1. The GB-1s served primarily as utility transports attached to various air stations and also with the Naval Attachés in Madrid, Spain and Mexico City, Mexico. During 1941, as part of the war build-up, the first of some 271 GB-2s ordered (historical sources do not agree on the exact number procured by BuAer from 1941 to 1945), identical to -1s with the exception of R-985-AN1 engines,

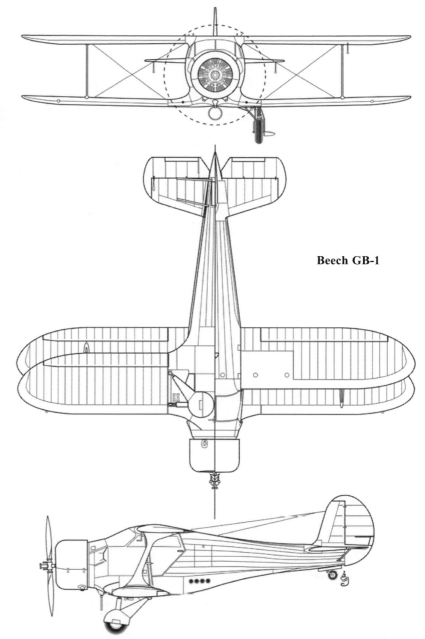

Beech GB-1

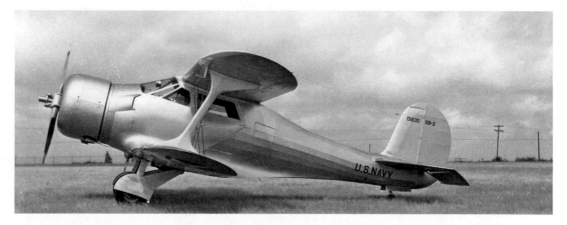

A Navy GB-2 just before World War II, essentially the same as the civil model D17S. Typically they were assigned to various air stations as utility transports.

began entering service as utility transports at both regular and reserve air stations. Twenty-seven GB-1s and -2s were listed as active in December 1941, and a number of civil D17s were reportedly impressed into naval service after the war began.

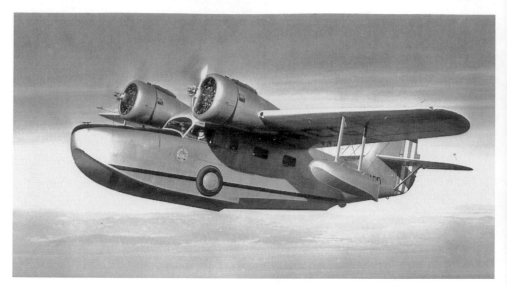

One of seven JRF-2s delivered to the Coast Guard in 1940 and 1941. Coast Guard variants were specially equipped for search and rescue.

Grumman JRF (J3F) Goose—1939

TECHNICAL SPECIFICATIONS (JRF-5)

Type: Eight- to nine-place utility-transport amphibian.

Manufacturer: Grumman Aircraft Engr. Corp., Bethpage, New York

Total produced: 214 (USN, USMC, USCG)

Powerplants: Two 450-hp Pratt & Whitney R-985-AN-12 *Wasp Junior* 9-cylinder air-cooled radial engines driving two-bladed, variable-pitch metal propellers.

Armament (JRF-4, and -5): 250 lbs. of bombs or depth charges.

Performance: Max. speed 201 mph; ceiling 21,300 ft.; range 800 mi.

Weights: 5,245 lbs. empty, 8,000 lbs. loaded.

Dimensions: Span 49 ft., length 38 ft. 6 in., wing area 375 sq. ft.

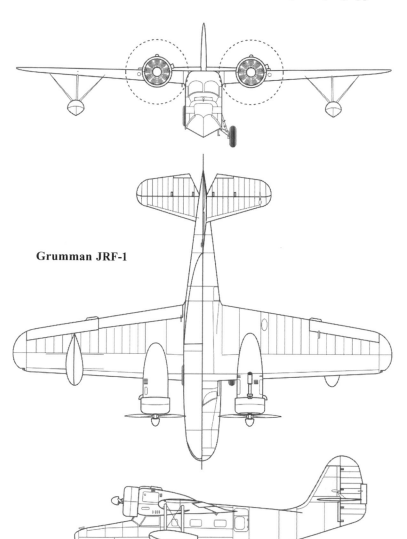

Grumman JRF-1

The well-known Goose amphibian was originally built as a fast executive transport for wealthy businessmen commuting in and out of New York City and is also acknowledged as the very first monoplane to have been designed at Grumman. Known internally as the Model G-21, the design team of William Schwendler as project engineer and Ralston Stalb as hydrodynamicist evolved an exceptionally clean, deep-bodied hull, which joined to a fully cantilevered wing incorporating split-type flaps designed to hold takeoff and landing speeds within acceptable limits. Power came from two tightly cowled *Wasp Junior* engines mounted in streamlined nacelles on the wings Other than fabric-covered control surfaces, the entire airframe consisted of light-alloy aluminum construction. After making its first flight on May 29, 1937, early testing showed the G-21 to possess superb handling qualities along with levels of flight performance that exceeded most twin-engine landplane designs. Refinements to the hull, upgraded SB2 engines, and a 500-lb. increase in takeoff weight resulted in the introduction of the G-21A in 1938 as the standard civil production model.

In late 1938, BuAer acquired one G-21A for evaluation under the designation XJ3F-1, and in early 1939, following brief trials, gave Grumman a contract to produce ten more as the JRF-1. Shortly after entering Navy service, one JRF-1 was transferred to the Marine Corps as a command aircraft and five others, including the original XJ3F-1, after receiving modifications for target-towing and photographic work, were returned to service as the JRF-1A. In 1940 and 1941, 10 JRFs were procured for the Coast Guard, seven as JRF-2s with seats interchangeable with stretchers and three as JRF-3s with autopilots and de-icing equipment, plus 10 for the Navy as JRF-4s equipped with racks that could carry 250 lbs. of ordnance under each wing, either bombs or depth charges. As the United States stepped-up its preparations for war, Grumman received a large-scale contract in 1940 to produce 185 JRF-5s, 16 of which had been delivered by the end of 1941. As the principal production variant, the JRF-5 featured small detail refinements, uprated AN-12 engines, as well as camera equipment. Though most JRFs variants were attached to shore stations for general utility and transportation duties, a number flew armed coastal patrols during the first year of the war.

North American SNJ—1939

TECHNICAL SPECIFICATIONS (SNJ-3)

Type: Two-place landplane advanced trainer.

Manufacturer: North American Aviation, Inc., Inglewood, California and Dallas, Texas.

Total produced: 4,876 (USN, USMC, USCG)

Powerplant: One 600-hp Pratt & Whitney R-1340-AN1 *Wasp* 9-cylinder air-cooled radial engine driving a two-bladed, variable-pitch metal propeller.

Armament (SNJ-3/-4): one fixed .30-cal. machine gun in cowling (plus one fixed .30-cal. machine gun in wing on SNJ-5), provision for one flexible .30-caliber machine gun in the rear cockpit, and up to ten 20-lb. or four 100-lb. bombs carried on wing racks.

Performance: Max. speed 209 mph at 5,100 ft.; ceiling 24,199 ft.; range 750 mi.

Weights: 3,900 lbs. empty, 5,699 lbs. loaded.

Dimensions: Span 42 ft., length 29 ft., wing area 248 sq. ft.

North American's venerable SNJ, in conjunction with its Army AT-6 counterpart, is universally recognized as having been the most important American-made advanced trainer of the wartime period. Since the fixed-gear BT-9/ NJ had been designed from the outset with significant development potential, it is no surprise that North American's Model NA-26, a retractable-gear variant with an uprated R-1340 engine, won the Army's "Basic Combat" trainer competition of 1937, culminating in a contract for 177 aircraft as the BC-1 (production Model NA-36). In 1938, continuing refinements to the basic design such as an all-metal, semi-monocoque fuselage and revised wing tips led to a Navy order for 16 aircraft (production Model NA-52) under the designation SNJ-1, the first naval aircraft to

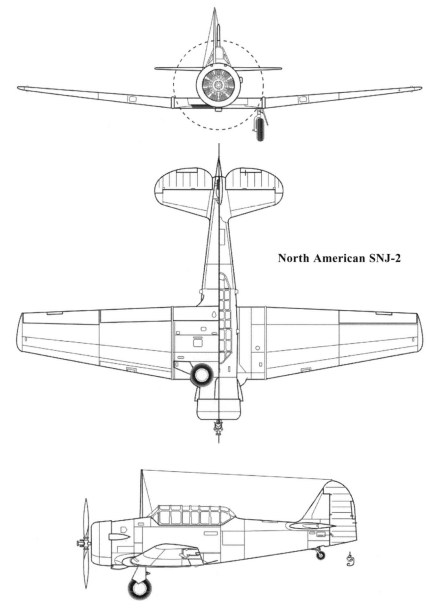

North American SNJ-2

SNJ-1 BuNo 1552, the first of thousands of Navy SNJs, as delivered in 1939. All 16 SNJ-1s went to NAS Pensacola as advanced trainers, and most of the 61 SNJ-2s in 1940 to the reserves as instrument trainers.

use the scout-trainer (SN) designation. In view of the training needed by the Navy's growing pool of reserve pilots, BuAer had originally earmarked all the SNJ-1s for reserve bases but as deliveries began during mid–1939, they were assigned elsewhere, eventually ending up at NAS Pensacola.

The next Navy order came in 1939 for 61 SNJ-2s, which differed in having 550-hp R-1340-56 direct drive engines, the initial batch being delivered in early 1940 to 13 different reserve bases, primarily for instrument training, and as deliveries continued, 19 were assigned to NAS Pensacola, 15 to Anacostia, and a number of others to flag officers as command aircraft. In 1940, due to increasing U.S. war preparations and the anticipated need for thousands of training aircraft, the Navy and the Army agreed upon a standardized SNJ-3/AT-6A version (production Models NA-77, 78, and 85) that would be manufactured at a new North American plant being built in Dallas, Texas, as well as the company's existing facilities in California. Thus, in 1941, the Navy began receiving the first of 420 SNJ-3s ordered, 295 of which were on hand by the end of the year. A majority of these (248) were assigned to flight training centers at Corpus Christi, Jacksonville, Pensacola, and Miami. SNJ-3s/AT-6As were the first of the series to be powered with 600-hp AN1 engines and have the distinctive triangular fin and rudder shape.

During the course of the war, the Navy accepted delivery of a further 125 SNJ-3s, 2,400 SNJ-4s, 1,568 SNJ-5s and 411 SNJ-6s. SNJs retrofitted with arresting gear for carrier qualification training carried a "C" suffix (i.e., SNJ-3C, -4C, and -5C). After the war, up through the late 1950s, large numbers of Navy and Marine SNJs were retained in both the flight-training role and as proficiency and instruments trainers in individuals units, and the very last example was not stricken from the naval inventory until 1968.

Douglas R3D—1940

TECHNICAL SPECIFICATIONS (R3D-1)
Type: Eighteen-place landplane transport.
Manufacturer: Douglas Aircraft Co., El Segundo, California.
Total produced: 7 (USN, USMC)
Powerplants: Two 1,000-hp Wright R-1820-44 *Cyclone* 9-cylinder air-cooled radial engines driving three-bladed, constant-speed metal propellers.
Performance: Max. speed 221 mph at 5,800 ft.; ceiling 19,000 ft.; range 1,440 mi.
Weights: 14,188 lbs. empty, 21,000 lbs. loaded.
Dimensions: Span 78 ft., length 62 ft. 2 in., wing area 824 sq. ft.

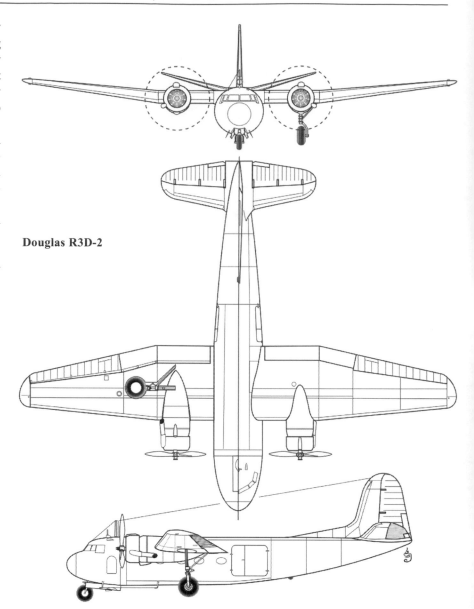

Douglas R3D-2

In mid–1938, while its DB-7 twin-engine, light bomber prototype (Army designation A-20; see Douglas BD, above) was at an advanced stage of construction, the Douglas plant at El Segundo embarked upon the design of the DC-5, a 16-passenger short-haul airliner having a high-wing, tricycle gear layout similar to that of the bomber. The company expected that the plane would be capable of operating out of shorter airfields over shorter routes at the same economy of its DC-3. The design of the DC-5 emerged 25 percent larger than the DB-7, featuring a completely new circular-section fuselage, and wing area was increased chordwise and spanwise in order to create a load factor comparable to that of the DC-3 (i.e., 25.5 lbs. per square foot). In order to operate from shorter airfields, the wings incorporated fully articulated trailing edge flaps running from the wing root to the ailerons. The under-wing position of the circular side windows provided passengers with unsurpassed visibility, and the stance of the tricycle gear gave them easy access through a side door and a level center aisle to walk on. Al-

The only Douglas DC-5s built to a military specification, two R3D-2s were delivered to the Marines in 1940 for planned paratrooper training. The Navy also used three civil versions as the R3D-1 and -3.

though potential airline customers had the option of specifying powerplants, the prototype was equipped with a pair of 900-hp Wright GR-1820-F62 *Cyclones*.

By the time the aircraft was ready to fly, Douglas had received advance orders for 21 civil variants and seven for the Navy. BuAer planned to allocate three to Naval Air Stations as staff transports under the designation R3D-1 and four under a revised specification to the Marines as the R3D-2. The DC-5 prototype made its first flight on February 20, 1939, but the test program ran into immediate difficulties due to a serious tail-buffeting problem encountered during certain phases of flight. While the El Segundo engineering staff worked to solve the problem, all but four of the airline pre-orders were cancelled. The buffeting was traced to turbulence created by engine thrust above the horizontal stabilizers and elevators and eventually corrected by adding fifteen degrees of dihedral to the horizontal tailplane. A dorsal fillet was also added the vertical fin to improve directional stability.

The first R3D-1, completed during the spring of 1940, crashed in June while being tested at the factory. The next two R3D-1s were delivered without incident in July 1940, and both assigned to NAS Anacostia. Between September and November the same year, the four R3D-2s entered service with the Marines, two with VMJ-2 (later VMJ-252) at MCAS Ewa, Hawaii, and two with VMJ-1 (later VMJ-152) at MCAS Quantico, Virginia. The R3D-2s differed from the -1s in having cargo doors on the port side, more seats (22), a reinforced cabin floor, and less fuel capacity in order to increase other payloads. Although the type's aerodynamics problems had been fully resolved, production was ultimately limited to the twelve aircraft completed by the end of 1940 due to new wartime contracts imposed on El Segundo's facilities (i.e., production of SBDs and A-20s). By the end of 1941, both R3D-1s had been transferred to new duty stations, one to NAS San Diego and the

other to NAS New York; the four R3D-2s, which had been used to conduct paratrooper and other combat-related maneuvers, remained in their original assignments. The DC-5 prototype, after being purchased by William E. Boeing as a personal transport, was commandeered by the Navy in February 1942 and placed in service as the R3D-3. This same aircraft was later used to conduct early experiments with the ground controlled approach (GCA) instrument landing system.

Spartan NP—1940

TECHNICAL SPECIFICATIONS (NP-1)

Type: Two-place landplane trainer.
Manufacturer: Mid-Continent Div. of Spartan Aircraft Co., Tulsa, Oklahoma.

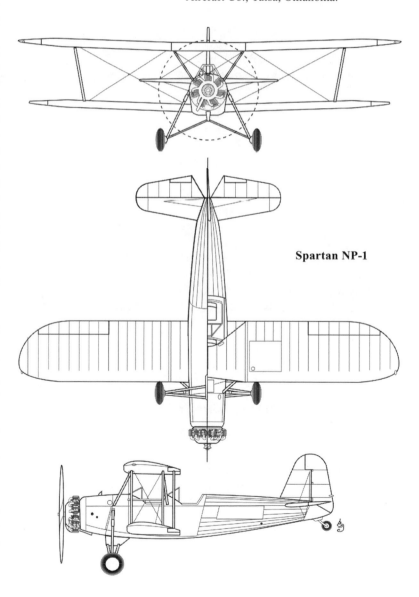

Spartan NP-1

Total produced: 201 (USN)
Powerplant: One 220-hp Lycoming R-680-8 7-cylinder air-cooled radial engine driving a two-bladed, fixed-pitch metal propeller.

One of 75 Spartan NP-1s delivered by the end of 1941. All of these aircraft were earmarked for the new Naval Reserve Primary Flying Schools in Atlanta, Chicago, Dallas, Detroit, Kansas City, New Orleans, and St. Louis.

Performance: Max. speed 108 mph at s.l.; ceiling 13,200 ft.; range 315 mi.
Weights: 2,069 lbs. empty, 2,775 lbs. loaded.
Dimensions: Span 33 ft. 9 in., length 24 ft. 3 in., wing area 301 sq. ft.

The first military aircraft to be produced by Spartan, the Navy accepted delivery of an experimental prototype in 1940 under the designation XNP-1. It emerged as fairly conventional biplane design having an all-aluminum structure with fabric covering on the wings, tailplane, and aft fuselage. The sturdy appearing landing gear was braced by a belly pylon and side oleos. Following official trials, BuAer awarded Spartan an order for 200 more aircraft as the NP-1, with deliveries starting in 1941, 76 of which were on hand by the end of the year. All NP-1s were used to equip the new Naval Reserve Primary Flying Schools in Atlanta, Chicago, Dallas, Detroit, Kansas City, New Orleans, and St. Louis, continuing in this role throughout World War II.

Lockheed R5O—1940

TECHNICAL SPECIFICATIONS (R5O-1)

Type: Eighteen-place landplane transport.
Manufacturer: Lockheed Aircraft Corp., Burbank, California.
Total produced: 67 (USN, USMC, USCG)
Powerplants: Two 1,200-hp Wright R-1820-97 *Cyclone* 9-cylinder air-cooled radial engines driving three-bladed, constant-speed metal propellers.
Performance: Max. speed 246 mph at 7,900 ft.; ceiling 25,400 ft.; range 1,700 mi.
Weights: 11,821 lbs. empty, 17,500 lbs. loaded.
Dimensions: Span 65 ft. 6 in., length 49 ft. 10 in., wing area 551 sq. ft.

Lockheed introduced the Model 18 "Lodestar" in 1939 out of an effort to improve the high seat-mile cost that airlines had experienced with the Model 14 (see Lockheed PBO/R5O, above). Using the general aerodynamic design of the Model 14, the Model 18 appeared with a new fuselage, lengthened five and a half feet, while retaining the same wing planform. As the first production examples began reaching airlines, the Coast Guard procured one Model 18 in May 1940 under the designation XR5O-1, and upon delivery, the aircraft was based at Floyd Bennett Field in New York. A BuAer order later the same year resulted in the delivery of two Model 18s to the Navy as the R5O-1, one assigned one to the Secretary of the Navy and the other to the Chief of the Bureau of Aeronautics, both based at Anacostia. The single R5O-2, a Model 18-07 powered by Pratt & Whitney R-1690-25 *Hornet* engines, entered service at NAS Pensacola in 1940, where it was used as a VIP transport. Two R5O-3s with plush executive interiors and 1,200-hp Pratt & Whitney R-1830-34A powerplants were added to the naval inventory during 1941. Both served as VIP transports at Ana-

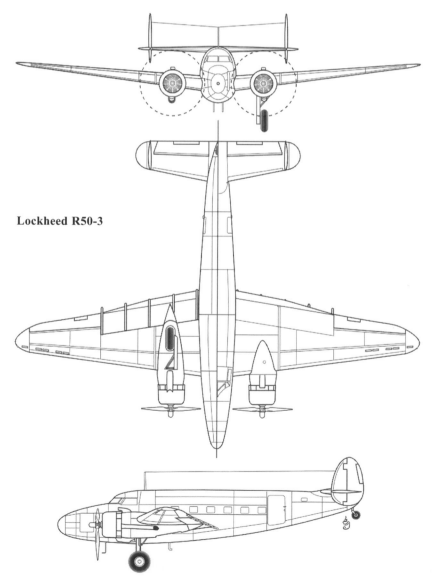

Lockheed R5O-3

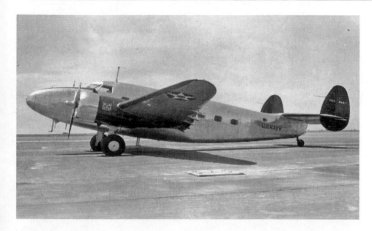

Two Lockheed Model 18 Lodestars were added to the naval inventory in 1940 as the R5O-1. The aircraft depicted served at NAS Anacostia for the use of the secretary of the Navy and his staff.

The Navy received 15 JRB-2s in 1941, which were identical to the Army C-45A. The aircraft depicted was assigned as a flag plane for Commander Air Scouting Forces.

costia, one being assigned to the Commandant of the Marine Corps.

All six R5Os remained in their initial duty stations as of December 1941. Over the course of World War II, the Navy procured another 61 *Cyclone*-powered Model 18s: 26 impressed from the various airlines, which included 12 as the R5O-4 (7–12 seats) and 14 as the R5O-5 (14 seats), plus 35 C-60As originally ordered by the USAAF that were placed in service as the R5O-6. The R5O-4s and -5s were configured as staff transports, six being assigned to the Coast Guard and two to the Marines. The R5O-6s, configured as 18-seat troop carriers, served with various Navy transport and ferry units (VR and VRF), and at least six were assigned to the Marines.

Beechcraft JRB—1940

TECHNICAL SPECIFICATIONS (JRB-2)

Type: Seven-place landplane utility transport, drone controller.
Manufacturer: Beech Aircraft Co., Wichita, Kansas.
Total produced: 374 (USN, USMC, USCG, not including later SNB variants)
Powerplant: Two 450-hp Pratt & Whitney R-985-50 *Wasp Junior* 9-cylinder air-cooled radial engines driving two-bladed, variable-pitch metal propellers.
Performance: Max. speed 225 mph; ceiling 26,000 ft.; range 1,200 mi.
Weights: 5,501 lbs. empty, 7,850 lbs. loaded.
Dimensions: Span, 47 ft. 8 in., length 34 ft. 8 in., wing area 349 sq. ft.

Known over its long history as the "Twin Beech," the maiden flight of the legendary Model 18 took place on January 15, 1937. Powered at first with 350-hp Wright R-760 engines (Model 18A), it emerged as a very clean monoplane constructed of aluminum alloy, with metal-framed, fabric-covered control surfaces,

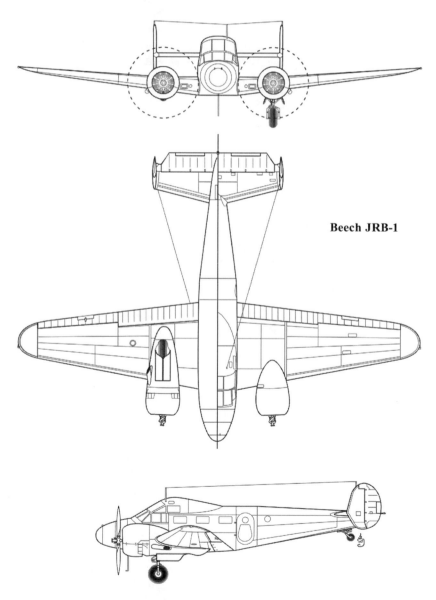

Beech JRB-1

retractable landing gear, and a distinctive twin-fin empennage. Beech initially marketed the type as either a small airliner or business transport which could be ordered in five different powerplant options. Sales were relatively modest, however, until the introduction of the *Wasp Junior*–powered Model 18S in 1939, when Beech began receiving the first military orders, starting with an Army contract for 25 18Ss, 14 of which were to be specially configured for photo-reconnaissance work as the F-2 and the rest as C-45 staff transports.

In June 1940, under naval designation JRB-1, BuAer awarded Beech a contract to produce five aircraft very similar to the Army's F-2, but having an elevated cockpit to accommodate a drone controller directly behind the flight deck as well as the provision for camera installation. Six more were subsequently added to the order, and all 11 JRB-1s had been accepted by the end of the year. Four were assigned to VJ-3 in Anacostia, five to VJ-5 in San Diego, and two to NAF in Philadelphia. Late in 1940, Beech was given a second Navy contract for 15 JRB-2 transport versions (identical to the Army C-45A), with deliveries commencing in 1941. The JRB-2s, all placed in service by the end of the year, received a variety of assignments to various bases and commands, including three examples transferred to the Marines. Once the U.S. entered World War II, all Model 18 naval variants (JRBs and SNBs) were procured from USAAF production orders. By the end of 1945, the Navy, Marine and Coast Guard had taken delivery a further 243 JRB-3s (C-45B), 328 JRB-4s (UC-45F), 320 SNB-1s (AT-11 bombardier trainers), and 509 SNB-2s (AT-7 navigator trainers). As a result of post-war modification and upgrade programs, many JRBs and SNBs were returned to duty as SNB-4s and -5s, and some served well into the 1960s.

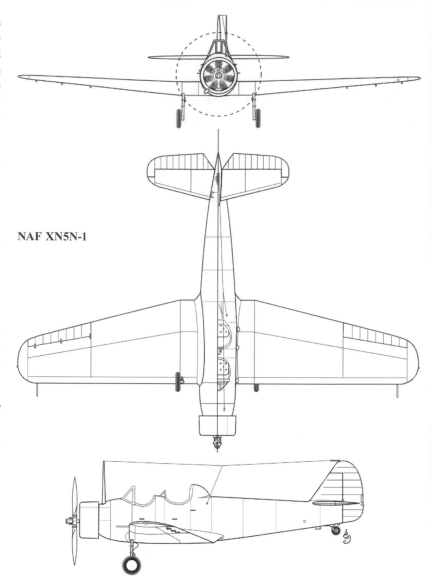

NAF XN5N-1

Naval Aircraft Factory N5N—1941

TECHNICAL SPECIFICATIONS (XN5N-1)

Type: Two-place landplane trainer.
Manufacturer: Naval Aircraft Factory, Philadelphia, Pennsylvania.
Total produced: 1 (USN)
Powerplant: One 240-hp Wright R-760-6 7-cylinder air-cooled radial engine driving a two-bladed, fixed-pitch metal propeller.
Performance: Max. speed 135 mph at s.l.; ceiling 13,900 ft.; range (not reported).
Weights: Empty (not reported), 3,370 lbs. gross.
Dimensions: span 42 ft., length 30 ft. 5 in., wing area 215 sq. ft. (est.).

The sole XN5N-1 seen during World War II with addition of an enclosed cockpit. A backlog of other NAF projects prevented it from reaching production.

In 1938 BuAer authorized NAF to design and build one XN5N-1 prototype with the aim of evaluating a monoplane for potential use as a primary trainer. As work progressed, the design appeared with an all-metal, aluminum-clad airframe and broad-chord, fully cantilevered wings having sufficient area to produce a load factor similar to that of biplane trainers. Other features included split-type flaps and a full engine cowling. The intervention of other NAF projects, however, delayed the first flight of the XN5N-1 until the spring of 1941, by which time the Navy had placed the N3N-3 into high-rate production and contracted for large numbers of Stearman N2Ss to fulfill its long-term primary trainer needs. Even so, testing of the XN5N-1 at NAF continued after 1941, where it was used as a glider tug, and later still, fitted with a fully enclosed cockpit.

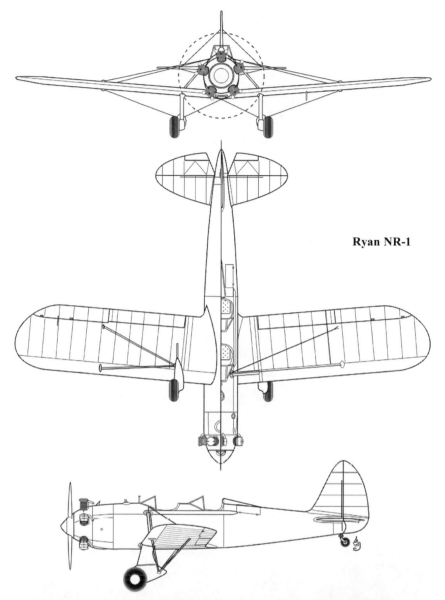

Ryan NR-1

Ryan NR-1—1941

TECHNICAL SPECIFICATIONS (NR-1)

Type: Two-place landplane trainer.
Manufacturer: Ryan Aeronautical Co., San Diego, California.
Total produced: 100 (USN)
Powerplant: One 160-hp Kinner R-5 (R-540-1) 5-cylinder air-cooled radial engine driving a two-bladed, fixed-pitch wooden propeller.
Performance: Max. speed 125 mph at s.l.; ceiling 15,400 ft.; range 297 mi.
Weights: 1,313 lbs. empty, 1,860 lbs. loaded.
Dimensions: Span 30 ft. 1 in., length 22 ft. 8 in., wing area 134 sq. ft.

Better known as the Army PT-22 "Recruit," BuAer ordered 100 Ryan Model STK-3Rs that were accepted into service during 1941 as the NR-1. The STK-3R, featuring an all-metal airframe with fabric covering on the wings, tail group, and aft fuselage, had been conceived as a military development of Ryan's Menasco B-4 inline-powered ST sport plane design of 1934. In addition to the Kinner radial powerplant, the ST-3KR introduced a lengthened fuselage, reshaped fin and rudder, wide-track, knee-action maiin landing gear, plus slight sweepback added to the wings. All NR-1s were assigned to NAS Jacksonville, Florida for primary flight training. The Navy acquired no more after 1941.

In 1941 the Navy procured 100 NR-1s, identical to the Army PT-22. They were all assigned to the newly established base at NAS Jacksonville for primary flight training.

Grumman J4F Widgeon—1941

TECHNICAL SPECIFICATIONS (J4F-1)

Type: Five-place utility and patrol amphibian.
Manufacturer: Grumman Aircraft Engr. Corp., Bethpage, New York.
Total produced: 141 (USN, USCG)
Powerplants: Two 200-hp Ranger L-440-5 6-cylinder air-cooled inline engines driving two-bladed, fixed-pitch wooden propellers.
Armament (J4F-1): One 200-lb. depth charge under right wing.
Performance: Max. speed 153 mph; ceiling 17,500 ft.; range 780 mi.
Weights: 3,240 lbs. empty, 4,525 lbs. loaded.
Dimensions: Span 40 ft., length 31 ft. 1 in., wing area 245 sq. ft.

Originally conceived in 1940 for the civilian market, Grumman's Ranger-powered Model G-44 found itself conscripted into military service by the time it reached production. While utilizing the proven two-step hull configuration, hand-operated landing gear, and all-metal construction of the Model G-21, the smaller G-44 materialized with the squared-off wings and tail surfaces that typified newer Grumman designs (e.g., F4F-3, TBF-1). An all-new wing planform, presenting a constant-chord center-section on which the inline engines were mounted high up out of the spray, featured a sharply tapered trailing edge from mid-chord to the tip and fully articulated trailing-edge flaps. The first flight of the G-44 prototype took place on June 28, 1940 from Grumman's plant at Bethpage, and as flight trials proceeded, the only aerodynamic change consisted of adding mass balance horns to the elevators.

The first twenty-five production G-44s,

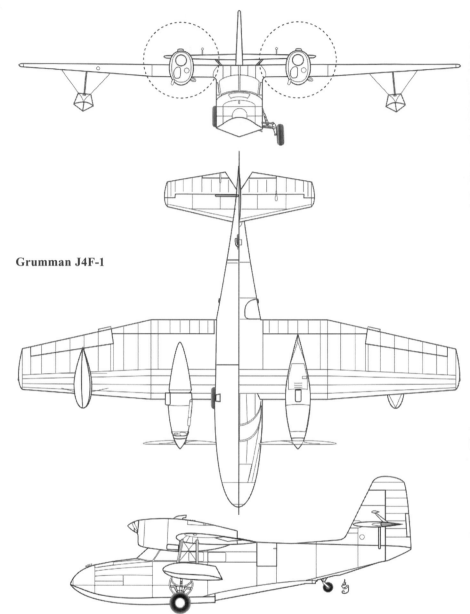

Grumman J4F-1

After the government commandeered G-44 production, the first 25 went to the Coast Guard in 1941 as the J4F-1. They flew armed patrols along the U.S. coast in early World War II.

assigned the naval designation J4F-1, were allocated to the Coast Guard, with deliveries commencing in mid–1941, and the next batch of twenty-six, including ten originally destined for Portugal and sixteen ordered by civilians, were impressed into USAAF service in early 1942 as the OA-14. From 1942 to 1945, Grumman completed another 131 aircraft under Navy contracts as the J4F-2, fifteen of which were subsequently Lend-Leased to Great Britain as the Gosling I (later Widgeon I, which developed into the type's official name), plus several more to the Portuguese Naval Air Service and the Brazilian Air Force. Coast Guard J4F-1s, after being retrofitted to carry a 200-lb. depth charge beneath the right wing between the fuselage and the engine nacelle, began flying antisubmarine missions off the American coast. On August 1, 1942, while operating out of the USCG base at Houma, Louisiana, a J4F-1 flown by Chief Aviation Pilot Henry White was credited with the sinking of *U-166*. (Ironically, following discovery of the wreck by an oil exploration team in 2001, it was determined that the submarine had not been sunk by an aircraft but by PC-556, a Navy coastal patrol ship.) In Navy service, J4F-2s were most often employed as land-based utility transports, though some were also used as instrument trainers.

Douglas R4D—1941

TECHNICAL SPECIFICATIONS (R4D-2)

Type: Twenty-seven-place landplane transport.
Manufacturer: Douglas Aircraft Co., Santa Monica and Long Beach, California.
Total produced: 579 (USN, USMC, USCG, not including post-war R4D-8).
Powerplants: Two 1,200-hp Wright R-1820-71 *Cyclone* 9-cylinder air-cooled radial engines driving three-bladed, constant-speed metal propellers.
Performance: Max. speed 237 mph; ceiling 24,000 ft.; range 1,025 mi.
Weights: 16,600 lbs. empty, 25,200 lbs. loaded.
Dimensions: Span 95 ft. 6 in., length 64 ft. 4 in., wing area 987 sq. ft.

The Douglas DC-3, almost certainly the most famous transport aircraft of all time, had been in regular airline service for over four years at the time BuAer ordered the first 30 Navy examples in September 1940 under the designation R4D-1. Unlike airline versions, the military variant (i.e., the R4D-1 and the Army C-47A were being built to identical specifications), was to be powered by 1,200-hp Pratt & Whitney R-1830-92 *Twin Wasp* engines and come with dual cargo doors and a reinforced floor. In 1941, 71 more R4D-1s were added to the contract, however, ini-

tial deliveries of these aircraft did not commence until early 1942, after the U.S. had entered World War II.

In actual fact, the first two DC-3s placed on naval

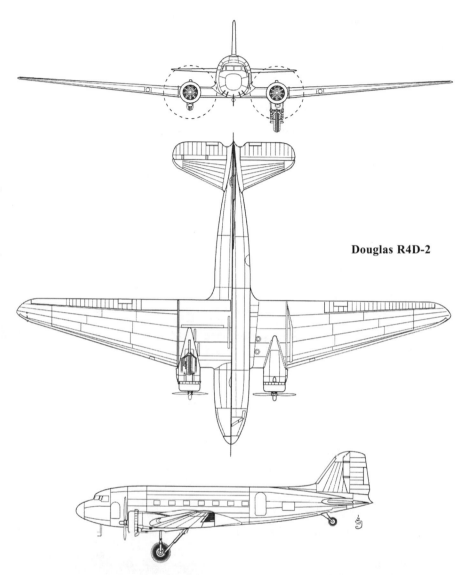

Douglas R4D-2

The Navy impressed two DC-3s from an Eastern Airlines order in 1941 as R4D-2s. The aircraft pictured was assigned to NAS Anacostia as a VIP transport. First production R4D-1s did not arrive until early 1942.

inventory were requisitioned from an Eastern Airlines order in early 1941 and went into to service as the R4D-2. These two aircraft, delivered respectively in March and April 1941, were *Cyclone*-powered variants having standard airline seating and a right-side entry door. Both were assigned as VIP transports, one to NAS Anacostia and the other to NAS Pensacola. From 1942 onwards, R4Ds became the most numerous Navy, Marine, and Coast Guard transport aircraft of the wartime era, which, after delivery of the R4D-1s and -2s, included 20 R4D-3s, 10 R4D-4s, 238 R4D-5s, 157 R4D-6s, and 43 R4D-7s.

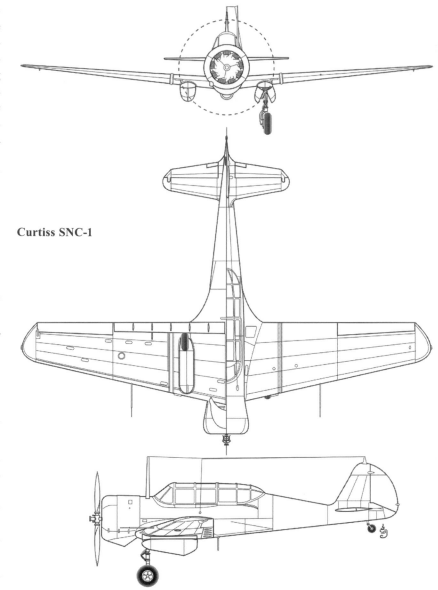

Curtiss SNC-1

Curtiss SNC—1941

TECHNICAL SPECIFICATIONS (SNC-1)

Type: Two-place landplane advanced trainer.
Manufacturer: Curtiss Airplane Div., Curtiss-Wright Corp., St. Louis, Missouri.
Total produced: 305 (USN, USMC)
Powerplant: One 420-hp Wright R-975-E3 *Whirlwind* 9-cylinder air-cooled radial engine driving a two-bladed, variable-pitch metal propeller.
Performance: Max. speed 201 mph at s.l.; ceiling 21,900 ft.; range 515 mi.
Weights: 2,610 lbs. empty, 3,626 lbs. loaded.
Dimensions: Span 35 ft., length 26 ft. 6 in., wing area 174 sq. ft.

In November 1940, to augment the SNJ-3s on order, BuAer awarded Curtiss a contract to build 150 advanced trainers under the designation SNC-1. The Curtiss Model CW-22, advertised as both a light attack aircraft and a trainer, had originally been developed from the CW-21 of 1938, a *Cyclone*-powered, single-place fighter offered to the export market. Sharing the same general dimensions and aerodynamic features of the fighter, the all-metal CW-22 was characterized by a clean, semi-monocoque fuselage structure, wings sharply taped from the leading edges, and a rearward-folding, semi-exposed landing gear arrangement. Deliveries of production aircraft to the Navy commenced during 1941 and at some point, apparently the same year, the order was increased to 305 aircraft. By December the Navy had accepted a total of 148 SNC-1s, 147 of which were serving in training duties at NAS Jacksonville (19) and NAS Corpus Christi (128) and one at NAF for evaluation. Several were assigned to the Marines for liaison duties during the course of the war.

Rapid growth of training in 1940 led the Navy to contract for 150 SNC-1s to augment the SNJ-3s already on order. Most were assigned to NAS Corpus Christi in the advanced phase of pilot training. Another 155 were added in 1941.

Vultee SNV—1941

TECHNICAL SPECIFICATIONS (SNV-1)

Type: Two-place landplane basic trainer.

Manufacturer: Vultee Aircraft, Inc. (later Consolidated-Vultee Corp.), Nashville, Tennessee.

Total produced: 2,000 (USN, USMC, USCG)

Powerplant: One 450-hp Pratt & Whitney R-985-AN1 *Wasp Junior* 9-cylinder air-cooled radial engine driving a two-bladed, variable-pitch metal propeller.

Performance: Max. speed 182 mph at 1,400 ft.; ceiling 21,000 ft.; range 725 mi.

Weights: 2,976 lbs. empty, 3,375 lbs. loaded.

Dimensions: Span 42 ft., length 28 ft. 10 in., wing area 239 sq. ft.

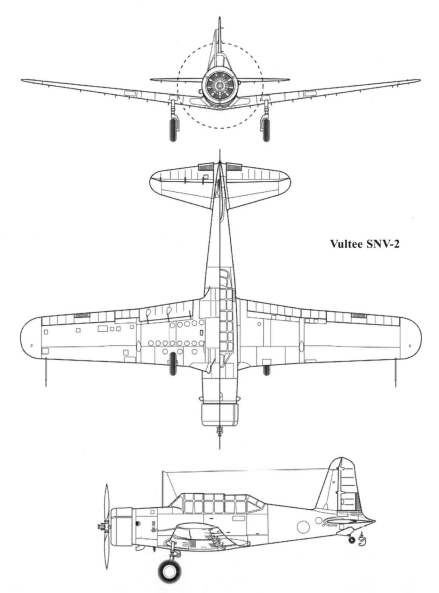

Vultee SNV-2

Similar in concept to the CW-22/SNC discussed above, the SNV had been conceived by designer Richard Palmer as a common airframe which could be adapted to either fighter (Model 48) or trainer (Model 54) variations. Vultee's efforts during early 1939 to sell the Army an R-1340-powered, retractable-gear, advanced trainer version (evaluated as the BC-3) were not successful, but introduction of the Model 54A later the same year, a fixed-gear basic trainer variant with an R-985 engine, resulted in an initial Army production order for 300 aircraft as the BT-13. Slightly lighter than the preceding BT-9/NJ-1, the BT-13 offered a modern, aluminum-clad airframe that could potentially be mass-produced in large quantities for America's growing military training needs. In August 1940, as U.S. war preparations burgeoned, Vultee received contracts for 3,350 improved Model 74s, which combined an Army order for 2,000 BT-13As with a Navy order for another 1,350 under the designation SNV-1. The Model 74 differed from the Model 54A (BT-13) in having a R-985-AN1 powerplant and small detail changes.

The first production SNV-1 arrived at NAS Corpus Christi in August 1941, and 170 more had been placed on the Naval inventory before the year ended, 35 serving at Corpus Christi, 25 at Pensacola, and one at Anacostia, plus a further 100 awaiting assignment. As deliveries continued, SNV-1s were placed in service with major training bases at Miami, Jacksonville, Corpus Christi, and Pensacola. During World War II, the Navy also accepted 650 SNV-2s with AN3 engines and 24-volt electrical systems. During the war, two SNV-1s were assigned to the Coast Guard and small number also served with various Marine squadrons. BuAer declared the type obsolete in mid–1945, and the last SNV-2 was stricken from the inventory in April 1946.

One of the earliest SNV-1s at Corpus Christi in mid–1941. Note the Army BT-14 plus Navy SNJ-3 and JRB-1 in the background. The Navy would accept 170 by the end of the year; another 1,830 were delivered from 1942 onwards.

Howard GH—1941

TECHNICAL SPECIFICATIONS (GH-1)

Type: Four- to five-place landplane utility transport.
Manufacturer: Howard Aircraft, Corp., Chicago, Illinois.
Total produced: 485 (USN, USMC, USCG)
Powerplant: One 450-hp Pratt & Whitney R-985-AN1 *Wasp Junior* 9-cylinder air-cooled radial engine driving a two-bladed, variable-pitch metal propeller.
Performance: Max. speed 201 mph at s.l.; ceiling 21,000 ft.; range 1,260 mi.
Weights: 2,700 lbs. empty, 4,350 lbs. loaded.
Dimensions: Span 38 ft., length 25 ft. 8 in., wing area 210 sq. ft.

In 1941 BuAer initially contracted for 34 Howard civil Model DGA-15s (i.e., DGA = damned good airplane) to be used as single-engine utility transports under the designation GH-1, with six examples reaching service by year-end. The type's general design had been inspired by Howard's Bendix and Thompson Trophy winning DGA-6 *Mr. Mulligan* racer of 1935. Wartime orders accounted for 451 more of the type, 131 as GH-2 utility transports, 115 as GH-3 aerial ambulances, and 205 as NH-1 instrument trainers, a number of which were subsequently assigned duties with the Marines and Coast Guard.

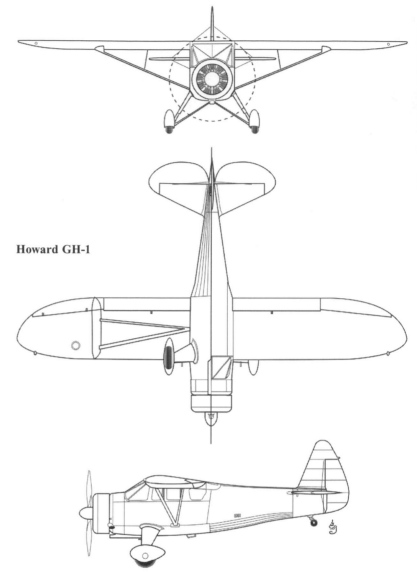

Howard GH-1

Schweizer LNS—1941

TECHNICAL SPECIFICATIONS (LNS-1)

Type: Two-place training glider.
Manufacturer: Schweizer Aircraft Corp., Elmira, New York.
Total produced: 13 (USMC)
Powerplant: (None.)
Performance: Max. speed 72 mph.; glide ratio 18:1 at 42 mph.
Weights: 450 lbs. empty, 860 lbs. loaded.
Dimensions: Span 52 ft., length 25 ft. 9 in., wing area 214 sq. ft.

Whether or not these gliders were actually placed on the naval inventory prior to 1942 is not entirely certain, but they will be reported here in case they were. In early 1941, as part of the U.S. war build-up, the Army and Navy Departments both initiated glider programs to train pilots for future operations using assault-type gliders

One of six Howard GH-1s placed on the naval inventory by the end of 1941. In addition to 16 GH-1s, wartime orders accounted for 131 GH-2 utility transports, 115 GH-3 air ambulances, and 205 NH-1 instrument trainers.

to support paratroopers. The two-seat Schweizer SGS 2-8, intended both for training and sport, first appeared on the civil market in 1938 and was characterized by an all-metal, fabric-covered structure, high aspect-ratio wings mounted at mid-fuselage, and a tandem seating arrangement under a long, greenhouse canopy. After the Army had ordered the type into production as the TG-2, BuAer contracted for 13 examples under the designation LNS-1. The first six, assigned to the Marine Glider Group at Page Field, Parris Island, South Carolina, are thought to have arrived in late 1941. After experimenting with different types of gliders, including larger assault types, the Navy terminated the glider program in 1943.

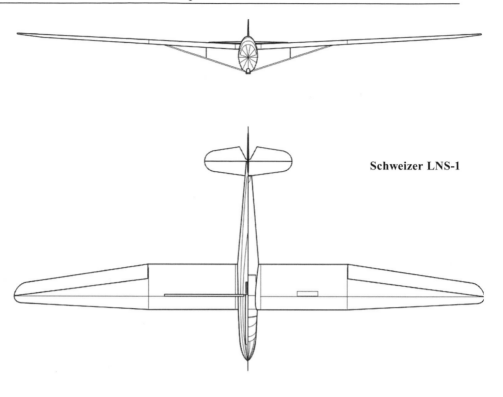

Schweizer LNS-1

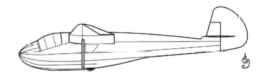

Thirteen of these Schweitzer LNS-1s (same as Army TG-2) were used at Page Field Parris Island to train Marine pilots to fly gliders in projected airborne operations.

PART II

Lighter-Than-Air Development

LTA Program Overview

The Navy's lighter-than-air (LTA) program can be said to have gone full circle during the interwar period, coming out of World War I with a modest fleet of small non-rigid patrol airships (i.e., blimps), then from the early 1920s, focusing practically all emphasis upon construction and operation of huge rigid airships (i.e., dirigibles), and finally, when the rigid program terminated with loss of *Macon* in 1935, redirecting all efforts back to the development of blimps. In any event, all through the 1919–1941 era, LTA represented only a small segment of Naval Aviation as a whole, having no more than two large dirigibles in operation at any given time, and even by the end of 1941, numbered a force of just ten blimps.

RIGID AIRSHIPS (DIRIGIBLES)

Synopsis of Rigid Airship Procurement

Originally, some months after World War I ended, the Navy had planned to obtain several German Zeppelins as war reparations, but in June 1919, before any transfer could take place, the Zeppelins were destroyed in their berths by their German aircrews. Despite this unforeseen turn of events, Navy officials still planned to evaluate the possibility of employing rigid airships within the fleet as long-range scouts, so in August 1919, authorized the Naval Aircraft Factory (NAF) to proceed with construction of ZR-1 (lighter-than-air-rigid-one). Then just three months later, with ZR-1 in the early stages of design, the Navy Department agreed to purchase the partially completed airship R38 from the British Government, which would give the Navy a fully operational rigid airship two years before ZR-1's projected completion date. R38, now classified as ZR-2, began flight-testing in England during the summer of 1921, but on its pre-delivery shakedown run, the airship was completely consumed by fire in a crash subsequently attributed to structural weakness. Taking in the harsh lessons learned from ZR-2,

design officials at NAF resolved that ZR-1 would use non-flammable helium as lifting gas rather than hydrogen. In yet another move, while ZR-1 was still a year away from completion, the Navy concluded negotiations with the German Zeppelin Co. in June 1923 to build a new rigid airship as ZR-3.

The program began in earnest in the fall of 1923, when, following brief flight trials, ZR-1 was commissioned USS *Shenandoah*, and embarked on a series of proving flights that included tactical exercises with the Scouting Fleet and ship-mooring experiments at sea with airship tender USS *Patoka*. A year later, in October 1924, ZR-3 arrived from Germany and was subsequently placed in commission as the USS *Los Angeles*. Helium was in such short supply at the time it became necessary to transfer lifting gas from *Shenandoah* so that *Los Angeles* could begin training its crew. Although *Los Angeles* was one of the world's most advanced airships, international restrictions imposed on the sale of armaments by Germany mandated that it would be used only in non-combat roles such as training and transportation, and before it could be employed in any type of fleet exercise, the Navy would need to obtain clearance from the Allied Control Commission.

By June 1925, *Shenandoah* had been restored to operations and resumed exercises in the Caribbean with the Scouting Fleet until September when it departed NAS Lakehurst on a Midwest promotional tour. On September 25, while transiting over southeastern Ohio, *Shenandoah* came apart in the mist of a violent thunderstorm; 43 of 57 crewmembers managed to survive the disaster by navigating two detached segments of the airship to the ground as free balloons. Undeterred by this setback, LTA advocates within BuAer continued to press ahead, operating *Los Angeles* on a series of proving flights that included a North American cross-country tour and over-water treks to Bermuda and Puerto Rico; concurrently, naval design officials continued work on specifications for an even larger class of new airship having more than twice the lifting capacity of *Los Angeles*. Over the next few years, *Los Angeles* logged some 1,400 hours of flight-time that comprised aircrew training, fleet exercises using *Patoka* as a sea base, and several long-distance trips between the East Coast, Cuba, and Panama Canal Zone. By March 1928, naval officials were sufficiently optimistic about the future of dirigibles in the LTA program to award the Goodyear-Zeppelin consortium a contract to build ZRS-4 and -5, both rigid airships large enough to carry their own complement of small aircraft. To augment the two blimps (L-3 and -4) in the LTA training program, the Navy also took delivery in mid–1929 of ZMC-2, a small airship that featured a rigid aluminum-clad structure.

In late 1929, fitted with a new "trapeze" arresting system, *Los Angeles* completed the first aircraft recovery experiments with a "skyhook"-equipped Vought UO-1, while Goodyear-Zeppelin, at its new facility at Akron, Ohio, had officially begun work on ZRS-4, with construction expected to proceed over the next two years. On September 23, 1931, after being christened USS *Akron*, ZRS-4 commenced initial flight-testing and was officially commissioned at NAS Lakehurst a month later; within the same timeframe, Goodyear-Zeppelin started construction of the nearly identical ZRS-5 in the newly vacated airship dock at Akron. *Los Angeles* maintained a busy schedule of flight operations training personnel for eventual transition to ZRS-4 or -5 until June 1932, after which point it was decommissioned and placed in storage as a static trainer. With the arrival of ZRS-5 forthcoming, the LTA program, as a practical matter, possessed neither the personnel nor the facilities to operate three large rigid airships at once. In fact, a new naval airship base was being built at Sunnyvale, California (near the south end of San Francisco Bay), with the plan that ZRS-4 would be permanently based at NAS Lakehurst and ZRS-5 at Sunnyvale.

Akron flew practice sorties with the Atlantic Scouting fleet during early 1932, and the following spring, with its trapeze installed, initiated aircraft launch and recovery exercises with a Consolidated N2Y-1 and the Curtiss XF9C-1, a fighter prototype designed especially for dirigible operations. After departing on a continental tour, the airship reached the new base at NAS Sunnyvale in June, where it participated with the Pacific Fleet for several weeks, then returned to Lakehurst for the remainder of the year to resume trials with aircraft. The LTA program appeared to be gaining momentum on March 11, 1933, as the nearly complete ZRS-5 was christened *Macon,* but less than a month later, on April 4, *Akron* was caught in a storm off the Jew Jersey coast and plunged into the sea. In the world's largest aviation disaster up to that time, 60 of 63 people aboard perished, including BuAer chief Rear Adm. William A. Moffett.

Commissioned just two months later, *Macon* proceeded with initial crew training and aircraft hook-on experiments at NAS Lakehurst until mid–October, when it made a three-day transit to its permanent base at NAS Moffett Field (formerly Sunnyvale).

By early 1934, with a full complement of three fighters and one utility aircraft aboard (Curtiss F9C-2s and a Waco JW-1), *Macon* was fully operational for the first time. However, its performance in several fleet exercises conducted that spring was rated unsatisfactory overall: in most cases, naval officials scored the airship as having been "destroyed" by carrier-based aircraft before making any measurable contribution to the scouting problem. *Macon* was grounded for repairs in mid–1934 due to damage sustained in severe turbulence; but once back in operation, the airship carried out numerous flights to improve tactics and aircraft deployment methods in preparation for the next year's fleet problems. On February 11, 1935, while en route to a fleet exercise off the California coast, a sudden gust of turbulence ripped away *Macon*'s dorsal fin and punctured three of its aft gas cells. All attempts to save the airship failed, and it settled into the ocean and sank; 81 of 83 crewmembers were rescued. Soon afterward, the rigid airship program ceased operations. Studies of larger rigid designs (i.e., ZRCVs) never got off the drawing board. The program fully and finally ended in late 1939 when *Los Angeles* was stricken from the naval inventory and dismantled.

ZR-2 (R.38)—1921

TECHNICAL SPECIFICATIONS

Type: Long-range reconnaissance and bombardment rigid airship.
Manufacturer: Shorts Brothers, Ltd., Cardington, England.
Total produced: 1 (USN)
Powerplants: Six 350-hp Sunbeam *Cossack III* 12-cylinder water-cooled inline engines driving two-bladed fixed-pitch wooden propellers.
Armament (proposed): One one-pounder gun (top), 24 .30-cal. machine guns in paired positions, and up to 3,920 lbs. of bombs carried internally.
Performance: Max. speed 61 mph at s.l.; ceiling 22,000 ft.; range 144 hours; useful lift 100,000 lbs.
Dimensions: Length 695 ft., diameter 85 ft. 6 in., gas volume 2,724,000 cu. ft.

The origins of the ZR-2 can be traced to mid–1918, when the British Admiralty awarded Shorts Brothers a contract to build an A class rigid airship to be known as the R.38. The A class were designed to be "lightweight" dirigibles capable of

R-38 ZR-2

R.38, now ZR-2, as depicted during its first flight from Cardington, England, on June 23, 1921. Note application of U.S. Navy markings to aft hull and tail fins. Naval officials hoped that the ex–British dirigible would give them a head start in rigid airship operations.

reaching an altitude of 22,000 feet and having a maximum patrol duration of up to six days. However, World War I ended while the R38 was still under construction and the British government announced an intent to abandon the project as a cost-savings measure. At nearly the same time, U.S. Navy plans to acquire several German Zeppelins as wartime reparations had been thwarted when the airships were deliberately destroyed by their crews. Thus, in October 1919, before cancellation of the R.38 could take effect, the Navy Department agreed to purchase the airship for $2,000,000. New specifications called for installation of specialized mooring gear which added a ton of weight forward and had to be offset by an equal amount of ballast aft. Construction consisted primarily of perforated aluminum girders, assembled into frames and longerons, and all connected to an A-frame type keel running the length of the airship. Once the framework was completed and the gas cells installed, an outer covering of linen was sewn into place and doped.

As the ZR-2/R.38 neared completion during the late spring of 1921, 17 U.S. Navy crewmembers arrived at Cardington to be trained by experienced British airship personnel. With U.S. insignia painted on it sides, the ZR-2 was rolled-out for its first flight on June 23, 1921. Initial control problems led to a re-balancing of the control surfaces, then three weeks later, on the

second test flight, severe pitching problems resulted in damage to several of the longitudinal girders. Following repairs, a third test flight was completed without incident. On August 23, with all of the Americans aboard, the ZR-2 embarked on a cross-country test run that was intended to simulate the conditions of an Atlantic crossing. While in the midst of sharp maneuvering, disaster struck as a number of longitudinal girders failed, causing the airship to break up and catch on fire. The flaming wreck ultimately fell into the shallows of the Humber River near Hull in Yorkshire; 16 Americans and 32 Britons perished in the crash. An investigation following the incident revealed the light structure of the ZR-2/R.38 to have been too weak to withstand even normal aerodynamic loads and that the weight added forward and aft had been a contributing factor. Since it was destroyed before delivery, ZR-2 never received an official ship's name.

ZR-1 Shenandoah—1923

TECHNICAL SPECIFICATIONS

Type: Long-range reconnaissance and bombardment rigid airship.
Manufacturer: Naval Aircraft Factory, Philadelphia, Pennsylvania (constructed at NAS Lakehurst, New Jersey).
Total produced: 1 (USN)

Powerplants: Six (later five) 300-hp Packard 6-cylinder water-cooled inline engines driving two-bladed fixed-pitch wooden propellers.
Armament: Six .30-cal. Lewis machine guns in single positions and up to 4,000 lbs. of bombs carried internally.
Performance: Max. speed 68 mph at s.l.; ceiling 13,000 ft.; range 5,000 mi. (approx. 80 hours); useful lift 48,774 lbs.
Dimensions: Length 680 ft., diameter 78 ft. 9 in., gas volume 2,115,000 cu. ft.

The Navy Department authorized NAF to commence work on the ZR-1 in August 1919, two months prior to the purchase of the R.38/ZR-2. It was the first rigid airship to be built in the United States. The general arrangement of the ZR-1 was based upon that of the German Zeppelin L-49 (LZ-96), a high-altitude airship which had been forced down over France in 1917 and carefully dissected afterward. The design was characterized by a high fineness ratio, presenting a very long and slender side aspect with a cylindrical hull center section, and like the L-49 class, the control gondola and engine cars were to be suspended from the hull framework on struts. As detailed engineering work on the ZR-1 proceeded, NAF incorporated many of the structural improvements seen in more recent Zeppelin designs and also selected "duraluminum," an alloy of copper and aluminum recently developed by Alcoa, as the airship's principal structural material. Moreover, in the wake of the ZR-2 disaster, naval officials determined that the ZR-1 would use non-flammable helium rather than hydrogen as a lifting gas, although its lifting value (in payload) was 9.2 percent less. Helium, a byproduct of natural gas wells, was such a rare element at the time that the airship's 2.1 million+ cubic-foot volume accounted for nearly all of the nation's available reserves.

Fabrication of the ZR-1's girders and other structural parts was initially delayed by Alcoa's inability to supply duraluminum in the quantities needed and did not actually begin until mid–1921. Thereafter, structural components were manufactured at NAF's Philadelphia plant, and then shipped by rail and truck to the Navy's construction shed (Hangar No. 1) at NAS Lakehurst for assembly and erection. The ZR-1's 20 individual gas cells were made of goldbeater's skin, a gas-impervious material derived from the outer membrane of bovine large intestine. Assembly of the keel and erection of frames began in June 1922 and continued for over a year. The outer covering consisted of high-quality cotton cloth (i.e., grade "A" fabric), sewn to the duraluminum frame, then sealed with doped-on fabric tapes. Final finish was silver aircraft (nitrate) dope.

The ZR-1's gas cells were inflated with helium for the first time on August 20, 1923 (filled to only 85-capacity to conserve the expensive gas), and on September 4, the airship made its first flight from Lakehurst under the command of Lt. Cdr. Maurice Pierce. A number of proving flights followed to test the ZR-1's airworthiness under various atmospheric conditions such as rain and fog as well as to train its inexperienced air and ground crews in the handling of a large airship. In early October, amid much publicity, the ZR-1 made a 2,200-mile roundtrip flight to and from St. Louis, Missouri to appear at the National Air Races. At a ceremony held at Lakehurst on October 10, 1923, ZR-1 was christened the USS *Shenandoah* and officially commissioned as a Navy ship. Soon afterward, *Shenandoah* completed demonstration flights over New York City, Washington, D.C., and Baltimore and on November 16, for the first time, successfully moored to the new 165-foot-high mast that had been built at Lakehurst for large airship operations. To demonstrate the capabilities of a naval airship, BuAer officials began moving forward with a bold plan to take *Shenandoah* on an Arctic over-flight; however, on January 12, 1924, before any further operations could take place, an unexpected gale-force wind ripped *Shenandoah* from its mooring on the high mast, destroying the forward hull framework and top fin; the resulting damage required the airship to be grounded for repairs until late May. During this time, command changed to Lt. Cdr. Zachary Lansdowne, a highly experienced airship officer who had participated in the first Atlantic crossing by an airship aboard the British R.34 in July 1919. While repairs were underway, *Shenandoah* received structural improvements to the nose, mooring assembly, and fins and the sixth engine was removed from the aft end of the control gondola and replaced with new radio equipment. In a decision that would later be controversial, Lansdowne order the removal of 10 of the airship's 18 automatic gas valves. These valves, as the airship gained altitude, automatically released gas to compensate for the expansion of the cells within the structural framework, and with the modification, *Shenandoah* would be restricted to ascending at no more than 400-feet-per-minute.

When flight operations resumed on May 22, 1924, Lansdowne initiated a series of exercises intended to show the military hierarchy the potential of using large, rigid airships as scouting vessels within the fleet. From midsummer onwards, *Shenandoah* took part in numerous tactical exercises with the Scouting Fleet and reached an important milestone on August 24, when it successfully moored to the USS *Patoka* (AO-9, later AV-6). With the ability to replenish lifting gas, fuel, and supplies at sea, the airship could theoretically operate anywhere with the fleet. Starting in October 1924, *Shenandoah* captured

USS *Shenandoah* ZR-1

Top: ZR-1 is seen moored to the new 165-foot-high mast at NAS Lakehurst in late 1923, soon after commissioning. In January 1924, the airship was damaged when a gale force wind ripped it from the mast. *Bottom:* The general arrangement of *Shenandoah* was based on the design of World War I German Zeppelin LZ-96. The slender aspect (high fineness ratio) of its hull is very evident in this overhead perspective.

national attention by embarking on a 19-day, coast-to-coast tour, which took it from Lakehurst to San Diego (via Fort Worth), up the Pacific coast to Seattle and back to San Diego, then returning to Lakehurst (again via Fort Worth) for a total of 235 flight hours logged. Soon after *Shenandoah*'s return, due to the scarcity of helium on hand, its gas cells were emptied in order to fill those of the newly arrived ZR-3 (*Los Angeles*).

Shenandoah spent the first half of 1925 undergoing an extensive refit and did not return to flight operations until late June of that year. Thereafter, it commenced a new series of summer exercises with the Scouting Fleet, which not only included mooring to *Patoka*'s mast but being taken under tow while the ship was underway. On September 2, 1925, *Shenandoah* departed Lakehurst on a promotional tour, this time to the Midwest with plans to visit 40 cities and moor to a new airship mast erected at Dearborn, Michigan. While en route over southeastern Ohio the next day, *Shenandoah* entered a violent storm containing convection currents (updrafts) that caused it to rise at a rate well above the pressure limits of its helium cells. After a succession of rapid ascents and descents, combined with twisting stresses placed on the hull, *Shenandoah*'s longitudinal girders failed and the airship began to break up. The control gondola separated from the bow and plunged to the ground, while three separate segments of the hull floated away as free balloons. Fourteen crewmen, including Lansdowne, were killed; but 29 managed to survive by riding the free-floating sections to the ground. Unforeseen weather conditions were determined to have been the cause of the crash. Before the flight left, Lansdowne had requested that the entire trip be cancelled due to unpredictable weather this time of year over the planned route but after one postponement, was ordered to depart as planned. Some critics cited Lansdowne's earlier decision to remove the 10 gas relief valves as a major factor. Finally, Karl Arnstein, a German structural engineer employed by the Zeppelin Company who had designed the original L-49 and would later work on the designs of *Akron* and *Macon*, blamed the structural weakness inherent in the ZR-1's general design.

ZR-3 (LZ-126) Los Angeles—1924

TECHNICAL SPECIFICATIONS

Type: Long-range training rigid airship.
Manufacturer: Luftschiffbau Zeppelin GmbH, Friedrichshafen, Germany.
Total produced: 1 (USN)
Powerplants: Five 400-hp Maybach VL-1 12-cylinder water-cooled inline engines driving two-bladed fixed-pitch wooden propellers.
Armament: None.
Performance: Max. speed 65 mph at s.l.; ceiling (not reported); range 5,175 mi. (approx. 86 hours); useful lift 66,970 lbs.
Dimensions: Length 656 ft. 7 in., diameter 90 ft. 6 in., gas volume 2,471,700 cu. ft.

The destruction of the German war-reparation Zeppelins in 1919 combined with the loss of the R.38/ZR-2 in 1921 motivated Navy planners to look to the German Zeppelin Co. as the prospective builder of a new rigid airship. On June 23, 1922, after concluding negotiations, a contract was finalized for construction of 2,471,000 cubic foot airship to be known internally as the LZ-126 and carried under the naval designation ZR-3. Part of the airship's construction cost would be funded as a payment of Germany's wartime reparation debt to the United States. Moreover, due to the military limitations imposed by the post–World War I Versailles Treaty, Germany was restricted to building new airships for "civil purposes" only, with the result that the LZ-126/ZR-3 was to be designed as a commercial-type dirigible having accommodations for 20 to 30 passengers. As Zeppelin's detailed engineering work reached final form, the LZ-126/ZR-3 represented a significant advance in rigid airship design. Unlike *Shenandoah* and earlier Zeppelin designs, the LZ-126/ZR-3 emerged with a lower fineness ratio (7.25:1) and a continuous symmetrical curve along the length of the hull that produced a more resilient structural framework. Streamlining and strength was further enhanced by mounting the control gondola directly to the bottom of the hull envelope and incorporating it into the keel structure.

Construction of LZ-126/ZR-3 at Friedrichshafen, Germany commenced in mid–1922 and proceeded over the next two years. In August 1924, gas cells inflated with hydrogen and static testing satisfactorily completed, the airship emerged from Zeppelin's construction shed and was launched on its first flight, followed, over the next two months, by five more trial runs over Germany that totaled 56 flight hours. In the early hours of October 12, 1924, LZ-126/ZR-3 lifted off from Friedrichshafen en route to North America under the command of Doctor Hugo Eckner (managing director of the Zeppelin Co.), arriving safely at NAS Lakehurst on October 15 after an 82½-hour transatlantic flight. Under the terms of the construction contract, nine German officers and crewmembers remained behind to train the Navy personnel to fly the new airship. After ZR-3 had been berthed in Hangar No. 1 next to *Shenandoah*, the hydrogen was vented from its gas cells and, since helium was in very short supply at the time, ZR-3's cells were refilled with gas pumped from ZR-1. On November 25, commanded by Capt. George W. Steele and fully manned with a Navy aircrew for the first time, ZR-3 departed Lakehurst for NAS Anacostia, where at a ceremony held later the same day the airship was christened USS *Los Angeles* by First Lady Mrs. Calvin Coolidge and commissioned as a naval vessel.

From the beginning, BuAer never envisaged operating *Los Angeles* as a combatant but as a training platform for the larger rigid airships being planned for future naval service (i.e., *Akron/Macon*); indeed, as a consequence of the international restrictions placed on the use of German-made airships, it would be necessary to first obtain permission from the Allied Control Commission before employing ZR-3 in any type of military exercise. During the first half of 1925, operating under the pretext of a "transport," *Los Angeles* completed two long-distance flights to Bermuda and another to Puerto Rico, on two occasions rendezvousing with and mooring to the *Patoka* at sea. Early operations were hindered to some degree by the need to replace the original gas cells, which deteriorated quickly in the North American climate, plus maintenance problems with the Maybach engines compounded by a lack of spares. Command of *Los Angeles* shifted in May 1926 to Lt. Cmdr. Charles E. Rosendahl, the former navigator of the *Shenandoah,* who had survived the crash by flying the bow section down as a free balloon.

Between 1926 and 1929, while most of the 1,400 hours logged by ZR-3 related to aircrew training at Lakehurst, the airship nonetheless managed to accomplish some noteworthy flights, which included: in 1926, a trip to Dearborn, Michigan to moor at the new mast built by Henry Ford; in 1928, a 40-hour flight to the Panama Canal Zone, with a side trip off Cuba to moor with the *Patoka,* the longest flight the airship would record; also in 1928, a Ft. Worth publicity tour by way of Chicago; and then in early 1929, a 40-hour flight out to the Gulf of Mexico to moor again with the *Patoka. Los Angeles* did experience a couple of narrow escapes during this time: one, in August 1927, when an unexpected sea breeze caused the airship to make an 85-degree nose stand on the high mast, but suffering

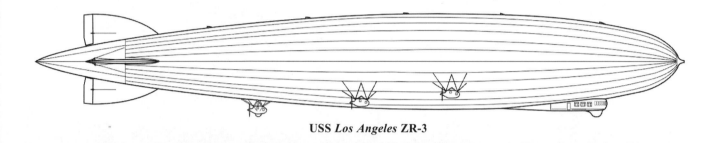

USS *Los Angeles* ZR-3

The *Los Angeles* logged more flight time (4,398 hours) than any other Navy rigid airship. Due it its German origins, post–World War I treaty restrictions prevented it from being used as a combatant.

Handling rigid airships required a huge ground crew as shown by the number of tiny figures surrounding the high mast in this photograph. Scarce manpower was a factor in the decommissioning of ZR-3 in 1932.

only minor damage in the process; and another, off Newport News, Virginia in January 1928, when an attempted landing on the new carrier *Lexington* had to be aborted after the ground crew lost control.

The years 1929 to 1931 were active ones for the *Los Angeles*. In June 1929, it moored for the first time to Lakehurst's new moveable low mast, and during the summer, with its recently installed "trapeze" arresting system, made the first "hook-on" with a specially modified Vought UO-1. *Los Angeles* continued active operations in rigid aircrew training and aircraft recovery techniques in anticipation of the planned arrival of ZRS-4 (*Akron,* 1931) and ZRS-5 (*Macon,* 1933) and in 1931 and 1932, received clearance to participate in the large fleet exercises conducted during that time. Then in June 1932, having by that time logged 4,398 hours over the course of some 331 flights, the Navy, as a cost-cutting measure, decommissioned the *Los Angeles* and stored it in Hangar No. 1 to be used solely for static training. Though briefly reactivated in 1933 following the loss of *Akron,* the airship never flew again. The end came in late

1939, when the *Los Angeles* was officially stricken from the naval inventory and thereafter dismantled inside its hangar.

ZMC-2—1929

TECHNICAL SPECIFICATIONS

Type: Experimental metal-clad hybrid airship.
Manufacturer: Aircraft Development Corp. (later merged into Detroit Aircraft Corp.), Detroit, Michigan.
Total produced: 1 (USN)
Powerplants: Two 220-hp Wright R-790 (J-5) *Whirlwind* 9-cylinder air-cooled radial engines driving two-bladed fixed-pitch metal propellers.
Armament: None.
Performance: Max. speed 70 mph at s.l.; ceiling (not reported); range 863 mi. (approx. 20 hours); useful lift 2,700 lbs.
Dimensions: length 149 ft. 3 in., diameter 52 ft. 7 in., hull volume 202,200 cu. ft.

Whether the hybrid ZMC-2 was a rigid or non-rigid airship might be debatable but is classified rigid here due to the nature of its all-metal hull structure. It was during the early 1920s that Ralph H. Upson, an aeronautical engineer, conceived the possibility of a blimp-like airship using thin plates of "Alclad" (an aluminum alloy developed by Alcoa as an aircraft skin) to contain the gas volume rather than the more conventional rubberized envelope. The design, in theory, would not only minimize seepage of helium (a large concern at that time) but possess considerably more strength than a non-rigid blimp. The company sold the idea to the Navy in 1926, contracting to build a small, blimp-sized airship (200,000 cu. ft.) as a proof of concept demonstrator for a much larger version (750,000+ cu. ft.) that would follow later. BuAer assigned the prototype the non-standard designation ZMC-2 (lighter-than-air/metal-clad; 2 = 200,000 cu. ft. gas volume), and construction took place over an interval of three years inside a hangar at NRAS Grosse Ile, near the company's plant in Detroit, Michigan.

The hull structure consisted of 0.08-inch thick Aclad plates bonded to lightweight duraluminum frames and stringers by

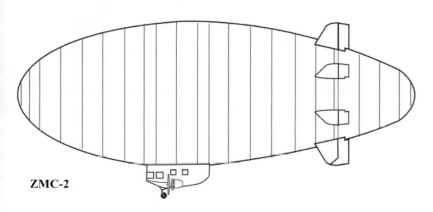

ZMC-2

The very rotund aspect (high fineness ratio) of ZMC-2 is evident in this photograph. Metal cladding made it more durable, but its shape generated handling problems in rough air.

approximately 3,000,000 small rivets. Even so, hull integrity, like that of a blimp, relied upon constant gas pressure, augmented by internal ballonets, to maintain shape. In order to evenly disperse aerodynamic stresses of the hull plating, ZMC-2 emerged with an extremely rotund side aspect, (i.e., a fineness ratio of 2.84:1 compared to 4.36:1 on a J-Type blimp), which, for adequate stability, made it necessary to incorporate eight fins (four with moveable control surfaces) instead of the usual four. ZMC-2 made its first flight at Grosse Ile on August 20, 1929, and arrived at Lakehurst the next month to begin testing. Trials revealed that the airship was more resilient than a standard blimp, however, because of its beamy shape, it proved very difficult to control in rough air conditions. BuAer, in any event, expressed no further interest in procuring a larger MC-type, and Detroit Aircraft went out of business in 1931.

Following official acceptance, ZMC-2 was pressed into active service in the LTA training program at Lakehurst. Known by Navy crews as the "tin bubble" or "tinship," ZMC-2's operational career as a trainer spanned ten years, its last flight occurring in August 1939, when it had logged over 2,250 hours flying time. After it was grounded, the airship remained at Lakehurst as a ground testbed until being broken-up sometime in 1941.

ZRS-4 and -5 Akron/Macon—1931

TECHNICAL SPECIFICATIONS (ZRS-4 [ZRS-5])

Type: Long-range, scouting and aircraft-carrying rigid airship.
Manufacturer: Goodyear-Zeppelin Corp., Akron, Ohio.
Total produced: 2 (USN)
Powerplants: Eight 560-hp Maybach VL-2 12-cylinder water-cooled inline engines driving two-bladed [three-bladed] fixed-pitch, rotable wooden [metal] propellers.
Armament: Seven flexible .30-cal. machine guns in nose, dorsal, ventral, and tail positions and four Curtiss F9C fighter aircraft stowed in an internal hangar.
Performance: Max. speed 79 mph [83 mph]; ceiling 26,000 ft. (both); range 7,349 mi. (approx. 127 hours) [9,143 mi. (approx. 158 hours)]; useful lift 152,644 lbs. [160,644 lbs.].
Dimensions: Length 785 ft., diameter 132 ft. 10 in., gas volume 6,500,000 cu. ft.

ZRS-4 and -5 represented the ultimate (and final) evolution of the rigid airship as a naval weapons system. Spearheaded by figures like Rear Adm. William A. Moffett of BuAer during the early 1920s, Navy policy shifted its emphasis toward large rigid airships (as opposed to blimps) as the future of the LTA program. Encouraged by recent experience with the *Shenandoah*, BuAer pressed forward in 1924 with preliminary design work for a significantly larger fleet-type scout airship capable of carrying its own aircraft. In June 1926, after the unexpected loss of the *Shenandoah*, Congress authorized the Navy's request to move forward with plans to construct two new rigid airships of 6,000,000 cu. ft. capacity (later increased).

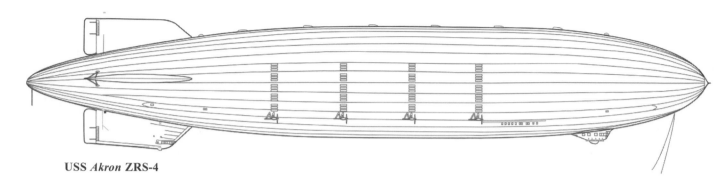

USS *Akron* ZRS-4

Following a design competition, Goodyear-Zeppelin Corp., a consortium of Goodyear Tire & Rubber Co. and the German-based Luftschiffbau Zeppelin GmbH, received contracts on March 2, 1928 to build two airships as ZRS-4 and -5, the letter "S" denoting the importance of the scouting mission they would be expected to undertake. The concept of operating a rigid airship as an airborne aircraft carrier was highly ambitious. Both airships would possess a "trapeze" system for launching and recovering aircraft equipped with a "skyhook" arresting system (first tested on *Los Angeles* during 1929) and could accommodate up to four aircraft in a 60 ft. by 75 ft. hangar located in the bottom of the hull. The aircraft were expected to perform a dual role, functioning either as scouts to extend the airship's effective patrol range or as fighters to protect it from outside air attack.

Construction of ZRS-4 officially started in November 1929 inside Goodyear-Zeppelin's new "airdock" at Akron, and assembly of the structural framework began in March 1930. The new airship's design incorporated a unique "deep ring, three-keel" configuration having sufficient longitudinal rigidity to allow the eight engines to be housed entirely within the hull envelope. This arrangement not only resulted in a dramatic reduction of drag but also provided far better in-flight engine access for inspection and maintenance. The propellers, strut-mounted to the hull and connected to the engines via a system of geared drive shafts, could be vertically rotated through a 90-degree arc to aid close-in maneuvering. An innovative water-recovery system, consisting of vertical condenser panels on the sides of the hull, retrieved water produced by the engine exhaust to compensate for loss of weight as fuel was burned, thereby eliminating the need to valve-off valuable helium. Finishing out proceeded rapidly. On August 8, 1931, at the Goodyear-Zeppelin Airdock, before a crowd of 150,000 people, ZRS-4 was christened USS *Akron* by Mrs. Herbert Hoover, and on September 23, with Lt. Cdr. C. E. Rosendahl in command, left the airdock on its first flight. After ten trial flights totaling 124 hours, *Akron* arrived at NAS Lakehurst on October 22 and was commissioned as a Navy ship one week later. Back in Akron, at virtually the same time, Goodyear-Zeppelin initiated construction of the nearly identical ZRS-5.

Akron began operating with the Scouting Fleet off the East Coast during early 1932, before the trapeze aircraft launch and recovery system had been installed, and made its first at-sea mooring with *Patoka* on January 16. On May 3, with the trapeze in place, successful "hook-ons" were accomplished with both a Consolidated N2Y-1 and the Curtiss XF9C-1 prototype. After

The ZRS-4 *Akron*, intended to be the vanguard of the Scouting Fleet, was launched in summer of 1931. Cruising out of range of naval guns, the airship's onboard aircraft could be used to scout ahead or protect it from air attack.

Top: The *Macon* seen moored to a small mast in Opa Locka, Florida, in spring 1934. Black rectangles above the propellers are condenser panels that recovered water created by engine exhaust. *Bottom:* The *Macon* berthed in its airship shed. Its immense size is apparent from the three people seen standing at the base of the fin. Loss of the *Macon* in early 1935 spelled the demise of the rigid airship program.

making a transcontinental trip to the newly constructed airship base at Sunnyvale, California (later became NAS Moffet Field) in May 1932, *Akron,* without aircraft aboard, participated in West Coast fleet operations during early June. It returned to Lakehurst later the same month, and for the rest of the year, pending delivery of its aircraft complement (F9C-2s), engaged in local flight testing and further hook-on experiments with the N2Ys and XF9C. On April 4, 1933, while proceeding up the Northeast Coast to calibrate its radio direction-finding equipment, *Akron* was caught in a storm and plunged into the sea off New Jersey. In the world's largest aviation disaster up to that time, 60 out of the 63 people aboard perished in the crash, including Rear Adm. Moffett.

On March 11, 1933, just weeks before *Akron* crashed, ZRS-5 was christened USS *Macon* at the Akron airdock. It incorporated a number of structural improvements that produced an empty weight 8,000 lbs. less than that of ZRS-4. Less weight, combined with more efficient three-bladed metal propellers and better streamlining, gave it a 4 mph increase in top speed and extended range by almost 1,800 miles. *Macon* completed its first flight on April 21, 1933, and was commissioned two months later at Akron by the new Chief of BuAer, Rear Adm. Ernest J. King. It was delivered to Lakehurst in late June and over the next several months, continued flight trials and initiated hook-on testing with N2Y-1s and the new F9C-2s. The airship left Lakehurst on October 12, 1933 and made a three-day transit to its new home base at NAS Moffett Field in California. Throughout most of early 1934, with its HTA unit aboard (three F9C-2s and a Waco XJW-1 utility aircraft), *Macon* participated in major fleet exercises on both coasts. In most instances, however, naval officials scored the airship as having been "destroyed" by carrier-based aircraft before it had had the opportunity to make a contribution to the scouting problem. In April 1934, while en route from Moffett Field to Opa Locka, Florida, *Macon* encountered severe turbulence that twisted the frame rings and girders underlying the attachment of the fins. Following repairs, the airship resumed operations, but plans to completely rebuild and strengthen the structure would be delayed until the overhaul period scheduled for early 1935.

Despite the poor showing earlier, *Macon* continued to refine tactics and procedures in the deployment of its HTA unit. From mid–1934 on, the F9Cs flew numerous sorties to rehearse new types of navigational problems and improved their range by operating from the trapeze without landing gear; and by late 1934, scouting results in various fleet problems had measurably improved. On February 11, 1935, a month prior to a planned overhaul, *Macon* left Moffett Field to join a small fleet tactical exercise off the California coast. The next day, while returning to base, disaster struck as a sudden gust of turbulence ripped away the dorsal fin and punctured three of the aft gas cells. After dropping water ballast to correct the extreme up angle, the airship rose above pressure limits and automatically valved-off too much helium. Twenty-four minutes later, *Macon* settled in the ocean and began sinking; the crew abandoned ship and 81 of 83 persons aboard survived. Although BuAer studied

newer designs (i.e., the ZRCV) until 1940, *Macon*'s loss effectively ended further rigid airship operations.

NON-RIGID AIRSHIPS (BLIMPS)
Synopsis of Non-Rigid Airship Procurement

U.S. Navy interest in non-rigid airships arose in 1915 after observing the use of various types by foreign navies in the coastal patrol role. The British termed them "blimps," which is thought to have originally been a contraction of "British B-type airship" and the word "limp." In any event, the first American-made blimp, the Connecticut Aircraft Co. DN-1, was deemed unsatisfactory by the Navy and scrapped soon after being flight-tested in April 1917. But even before DN-1 had flown, the Navy Department issued contracts in early 1917 to Goodyear, B.F. Goodrich, and Connecticut Aircraft for the manufacture of 16 envelopes for a small class of airship similar in design to the British Admiralty's Submarine Scout series. Curtiss received a separate order to built control cars from modified JN-4 trainer fuselages. These airships had been procured to form the first elements of a training fleet for the Navy's newly organized LTA program. By the time the first example arrived for testing in June 1917, it became B-1 under a new alpha-numeric designation system for blimps, although the DN-1 had never been identified as A-1. All 16 B-class blimps were delivered during 1918; Goodyear subsequently rebuilt three with new control cars that returned to service as B-17, -18, and -19, plus Goodyear completed a seventeenth example in 1919 as B-20. The B-class continued in the training role until the last examples were withdrawn in 1924. Thirty larger C-class airships had been ordered in early 1918, but, in the interval, to get blimps into overseas operations faster, the Navy also acquired a number of foreign-built airships: (1) six from Britain—three SST twin-engine Sea Scouts, two single-engine SSZ Sea Scouts, and one twin-engine North Sea type; (2) nine from France—five twin-engine Astra-Torres AT-types, three Zodiac-Vedette VZ-types, and one Zodiac ZDUS-type (delivered in 1919); and (3) one from Italy, a twin-engine semi-rigid (i.e., rigid keel) type listed as O-1. Disposition of most foreign airships after the war is uncertain, however, official Navy records show that O-1 was operated out of Cape May, New Jersey from 1919 to 1921 and the French ZDUS turned over to the Army in 1919.

The 10 C-class airships (out of 30 ordered) delivered between September 1918 and March 1919, were twin-engine types, twice the size of the B-class, and the first American-made blimps that could carry armament; however, due to rapid deterioration of gas envelopes, their service life was brief, and all had been withdrawn by the end of 1922. Two smaller blimps, E-1 delivered in late 1918 and F-1 in early 1919, were used for training and testing until 1923 and 1924. Intended as successors to the C-class, five D-class blimps (out of 20 ordered in 1918) entered service during 1920, four of which were transferred to the Army in 1921 and the fifth (D-6) destroyed the same year in a hangar fire at NAS Rockaway, New York. One very small H-class "pony blimp" procured for evaluation in 1921 was lost in the same the hangar fire with D-6. The first postwar patrol airship design, J-1, was test flown in 1922, but after unsatisfactory trials, the similar J-2 was cancelled, and when J-1 was withdrawn in mid–1924, there were no blimps remaining on the naval inventory. Lack of trainers in the LTA program led BuAer to order two of Army Airship TC-type envelopes from Goodyear in 1925, the first entering service in as J-3 in 1926, followed by the second as J-4 in 1927. In April 1933, J-3 was lost at sea while searching for *Akron* survivors, while J-4 continued in the training role at Lakehurst until stricken in March 1940.

In 1929, BuAer commenced development of K-1, a larger type of blimp that incorporated recent innovations seen on Goodyear's *Defender* class civil airships. K-1 completed its first flight in August 1931 and though plagued by poor handling qualities, served as a trainer until being grounded in 1940. To further augment the LTA training fleet (i.e., ZMC-2, J-4, and K-1), ex–Goodyear *Defender* was taken into service in 1935 as G-1. (Note, the original G-class of 1919 had never been built.) When the Army disbanded its Airship Service in 1937, two of its blimps were transferred to the Navy: TC-14, the newer of the two, entered service in 1938; and TC-13, which needed a new envelope, was delayed until 1940. The Navy added two more blimps to the LTA inventory in 1938: L-1, a small Goodyear *Enterprise* class airship, joined the training fleet in April; and the much larger K-2 arrived in December. Sharing little in common with its K-1 predecessor, K-2 was not only the largest blimp ever placed on the naval inventory up to that time but also the first in over 15 years to be envisaged for a true combat role. Testing and evaluation over the next two years confirmed that K-2 was very well suited for its designed missions of antisubmarine patrol and convoy escort. As part of the general Naval Aviation build-up of 1940, Congress authorized the LTA program to expand to an eventual level of 48 blimps. To start the process, BuAer gave Goodyear a contract in late 1940 to manufacture six new K-2 types for patrol operations (ZP) and two more L-types for training (ZN). Five of the new blimps had been delivered before the end of 1941, L-2 and -3 arriving at NAS Lakehurst in February and June, respectively, while K-3, -4, and -5 all entered service between September and November; K-6, -7, and -8 followed them in early 1942.

As a consequence of wartime programs from 1942 to 1945, the Navy's LTA service took delivery of 146 more blimps: seven G-types (ZNN-G); 19 L-types (ZNN-L), five of which

had been commandeered from Goodyear's civil fleet; 129 K-types (ZNP-K); and in 1943 and 1944, four M-Types (ZNP-M), which were 40 percent larger than the Ks. The very last G and K-types were not withdrawn from active service until 1959.

B-Class—1917

TECHNICAL SPECIFICATIONS (GOODYEAR B-1 THROUGH -9)

Type: Three-place patrol and training non-rigid airship.
Manufacturer: Goodyear Tire & Rubber Co., Akron Ohio; B.F. Goodrich Co., Akron, Ohio; Connecticut Aircraft Co., New Haven, Connecticut: and Curtiss Aeroplane & Motor Co., Garden City, New York (gondolas and engines).
Total produced: 17 (USN)
Powerplant: One 100-hp Curtiss OXX-2 8-cylinder water-cooled V-type engine driving a two-bladed fixed-pitch wooden propeller.
Armament: None.
Performance: Max. speed 47 mph at s.l.; ceiling (not reported); range 927 mi. (approx. 26½ hours); useful lift 1,840 lbs.
Dimensions: Length 163 ft., diameter 31 ft. 6 in., envelope volume 77,000 cu. ft.

The B-class is noteworthy in having been the first airship to enter operational service with the U.S. Navy, even though the DN-1 (A-class, though never officially assigned) was the first type actually procured and tested. About the time the DN-1 was delivered in late 1916, the Navy Department determined that it would also need a number of smaller non-rigid airships for training purposes. The design selected for what would become the B-class was similar in size and configuration to the British Admiralty's Submarine Scout (SS) series, relatively small coastal patrol airships (60,000 to 70,000 cu. ft.) which used an off-the-shelf aircraft fuselage (BE.2) as a combination engine and control gondola. In order to obtain the 16 B-class airships within the time needed, due to the limited production capabilities in the U.S., contracts were issued in early 1917 to three companies for the envelopes—nine from Goodyear, five from Goodrich, and two from Connecticut Aircraft (builder of the DN-1)—plus a separate contract with Curtiss to provide JN-4 fuselages and tractor-mounted OXX-type engines. The modified JN-4 fuselage, like the arrangement seen on SS types, was suspended from cables attached to the envelope with finger patches and used flotation gear in place of wheels.

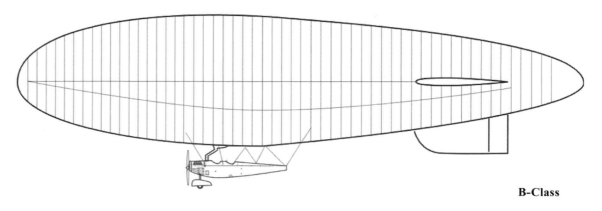

B-Class

The Goodyear-built B-1, first operational blimp in the naval inventory. Note lower twin fin and rudder arrangement. Later Bs had a single lower fin, and envelope shape varied according to manufacturer.

B-1, the first example to be completed by Goodyear, arrived for initial evaluations in June 1917. Thereafter, as deliveries of B-class airships continued, most were placed in service with the newly established LTA training program at bases on the east and southeast U.S. coasts, though some also flew coastal patrol sorties off the East Coast, and on at least one occasion, a B-class operating out of Chatham, Massachusetts is known to have spotted a U-boat and called-in seaplanes for an attack. B-class airships differed according to the manufacturer: some had twin ventral fins and rudders and others only one; the Goodrich built examples (B-10 through -14) were slightly larger (length 167 ft., diameter 33 ft., volume 80,000 cu. ft.); and the two completed by Connecticut Aircraft (B-15 and -16) were shorter and fatter (length 156 ft., diameter 35 ft., volume 75,000 cu. ft.) and powered by 100-hp Hall-Scott A-7 engines. Goodyear rebuilt three of its original Bs with new gondolas as B-17, -18, and -19, and sometime in 1919, built the all-new B-20 featuring a revised gondola and an OXX-3 engine. After World War I, B-class airships continued to serve in the training role until the final examples were withdrawn in 1924.

C-Class—1918

TECHNICAL SPECIFICATIONS (GOODYEAR-BUILT)

Type: Four-place patrol non-rigid airship.

Manufacturer: Goodyear Tire & Rubber Co., Akron Ohio; B.F. Goodrich Co., Akron, Ohio; and Burgess Div. of Curtiss Aeroplane & Motor Co., Marblehead, Massachusetts (gondolas).

Total produced: 10 (USN)

Powerplants: Two 150-hp Wright-Hispano A 8-cylinder water-cooled V-type engines driving two-bladed fixed-pitch wooden propellers.

Armament: One flexible .303-cal. Lewis machine gun and 270 lbs. of bombs.

Performance: Max. speed 60 mph at s.l.; ceiling 8,600 ft.; range 1,440 mi. (approx. 31½ hours); useful lift 4,050 lbs.

Dimensions: Length 196 ft., diameter 42 ft. 0 in., envelope volume 181,000 cu. ft.

Though arriving too late to see action in World War I, the C-class was the first American-built non-rigid airship to possess real combat capability in terms of range and offensive armament and also the first to use helium rather than hydrogen as a lifting gas. To achieve the useful lift needed to carry a

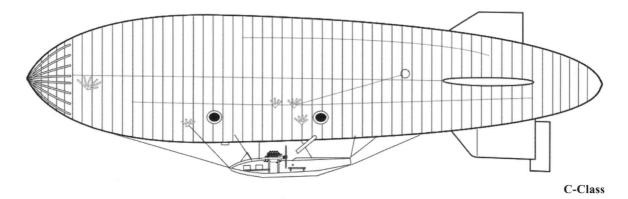

C-Class

much larger payload, the C-class emerged with over twice the gas volume of the preceding B-class. It featured two pusher engines mounted to the sides of a boat-like gondola that housed four crew stations, fuel, and armament. In early 1918, once the design had been finalized, the Navy Department ordered 30 gas envelopes from Goodyear and Goodrich and gave a separate contract to the Burgess Division of Curtiss to build the gondolas and engine mounts.

C-1, the first of the class to be completed, made its first flight from Akron on September 30, 1918, and was delivered to the Navy three weeks later, after flying nonstop to NAS Anacostia. Due to armistice cutbacks, the contract was subsequently limited to 10 airships, and the last C-class was delivered in March 1919. Two were transferred to the recently organized Army Airship Service. In the immediate postwar period, the Navy used the improved capabilities of the Cs to achieve some noteworthy firsts in airship operations, which included the first aircraft release experiment with a Curtiss JN-4, the first at-sea refueling with a submarine chaser, and the first transcontinental flight across the U.S. In May 1919, simultaneous with an attempt by the Curtiss NC-1, -2, and -4

Top: **C-6, erected and flown for the first time at San Diego in March 1920, was the first class of Navy blimp to possess true combat capability. The airship was lost in September 1920 while en route to fleet maneuvers.** *Bottom:* **A later C-class blimp, possibly C-7 before side lettering had been applied. Piloted by Lieutenant Commander Zachary Lansdowne, C-7 made the first flight of a helium-filled airship in December 1921.**

flying boats (see under *Patrol Aircraft*), the Navy planned to make an Atlantic crossing with the airship C-5. The airship completed the first leg of its journey on May 15, a 1,022-mile flight from NAS Montauk, New York to St. Johns, Newfoundland, but while on the ground with no crew aboard, was ripped from the line-handler's hands by high winds, swept out to sea, and lost. Due to deterioration of the envelopes, the operational career of the C-types was relatively brief, the last two examples being deflated and withdrawn in 1922.

E/F-Class—1918

TECHNICAL SPECIFICATIONS (E-1[F-1])

Type: Three-place training and engine-testing non-rigid airship.
Manufacturer: Goodyear Tire & Rubber Co., Akron Ohio.
Total produced: 2 (USN)
Powerplant: One 145-hp Thomas-Morse 8-cylinder V-type [125-hp Union 6-cylinder inline] water-cooled engine driving a two-bladed fixed-pitch wooden propeller.
Armament: None.
Performance: Max. speed 56 mph [52 mph] at s.l.; ceiling 8,000 ft.; range 695 mi. [1,414 mi.] (approx. 20 hours [40 hours]); useful lift 2,050 lbs. [2,300 lbs.].
Dimensions: Length 162 ft. 0 in., diameter 33 ft. 0 in., envelope volume 95,000 cu. ft.

Similar in size and configuration to the B-Class, Goodyear completed three small airships in late 1918, two of which were accepted by the Navy as E-1 and F-1 and one sold to the Army as A-1. Except for small differences in the engine mounts, E-1 and F-1 were identical, both having an open, boat-type control gondola with a single pusher engine mounted at the stern. Unlike earlier non-rigid designs, these two small airships incorporated a fuel tank inside the envelope between the ballonets rather than in the gondola. Delivered to NAS Pensacola in December 1918, E-1 served in the airship training program until mid–1924, when it was removed due to its worn condition; F-1, delivered to NAS Hampton Roads in February 1919, operated as an engine testbed until being deflated and stricken from the inventory in late 1923.

D-Class—1920

TECHNICAL SPECIFICATIONS (D-1 THROUGH D-5)

Type: Four-place patrol non-rigid airship.
Manufacturer: Goodyear Tire & Rubber Co., Akron Ohio; B.F. Goodrich Co., Akron, Ohio; and Naval Aircraft Factory, Philadelphia, Pennsylvania (control gondola on D-6).
Total produced: 6 (USN)

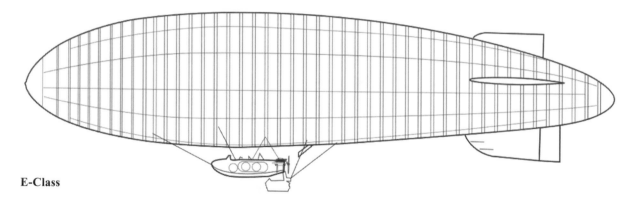

E-Class

Completed by Goodyear in 1918, airship E-1 is seen over Pensacola in the fall of 1920. E-1 and F-1 were identical except for small details. E-1 was used as a trainer until mid–1924, F-1 as an engine testbed until late 1923.

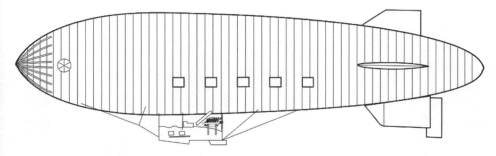

D-Class

and two by Goodrich (D-2 and -5). D-1 was destroyed by fire in Goodyear's hangar before it could be tested and D-3 became the first of the class to fly on July 13, 1920. Testing revealed that the fuel system was unsatisfactory due to leakage in the lines. In 1921, after less than a year of evaluations, all four of the airships were transferred to the Army. D-6, also completed in 1920, differed from the rest of the series in having a C-type Goodyear envelope that used a control gondola designed and built by NAF.

The boat-type gondola was fully enclosed and contained the fuel tanks inside it.

In August 1921, while assigned to NAS Rockaway, New York, D-6 was destroyed in a hangar fire that also included C-1 and H-1.

One of the five D-Class blimps that entered Navy service in 1920. Envelope-mounted fuel tanks are clearly visible.

Powerplants: Two 125 hp Union 6-cylinder water-cooled inline engines driving two-bladed fixed-pitch wooden propellers.
Armament: One flexible .303-cal. Lewis machine gun and 270 lbs. of bombs.
Performance: Max. speed 58 mph at s.l.; ceiling 8,600 ft.; range 1,480 mi. (approx. 37 hours); useful lift 4,340 lbs.
Dimensions: Length 198 ft., diameter 58 ft., envelope volume 190,000 cu. ft.

The Navy Department approved the design of a new D-class armed patrol airship in July 1918 as the successor to the C-Class. Changes included a six-foot extension of the C-type envelope and a re-design of the control gondola which included suspending the fuel tanks from the sides of the envelope and mounting the two pusher engines further aft. Twenty new airships were originally planned, however, due to armistice cutbacks, the order was reduced to three manufactured by Goodyear (D-1, -3, and -4)

H-Class (Pony Blimp)—1921

TECHNICAL SPECIFICATIONS

Type: Two-place observation non-rigid airship.
Manufacturer: Goodyear Tire & Rubber Co., Akron Ohio.
Total produced: 2 (USN)
Powerplant: One 60-hp Laurance (R-223) 3-cylinder air-cooled radial engine driving a two-bladed fixed-pitch wooden propeller.
Armament: None.
Performance: Max. speed 50 mph at s.l.; ceiling 6,000 ft.; range 400 mi. (approx. 7 hours); useful lift 1,146 lbs.
Dimensions: Length 94 ft., diameter 30 ft. 10 in., envelope volume 43,030 cu. ft.

Known variously as the "Pony Blimp" or "Motorized Kite Balloon," the H-class was the smallest non-rigid airship to have been operated by the Navy. The type was envisaged as a tethered observation balloon, capable of navigating from one location to another under its own power. The first of two ordered, H-1 was completed by Goodyear and delivered to NAS Rockaway, New York, by rail in May 1921 and once assembled

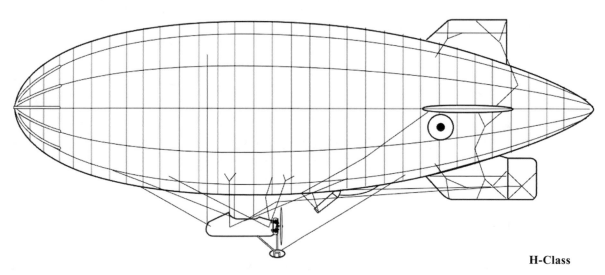

H-Class

Flown in mid–1921, H-1 was the smallest blimp ever placed on the naval inventory. It was destroyed later the same year in a hangar fire at NAS Rockaway, New York.

and inflated, began a series of test flights during the middle of the summer. On August 5, 1921, its seventh flight, engine failure caused a crash landing that pitched both its occupants from the gondola, with the airship drifting away until it settled in a pasture where it was caught and tethered by a farmer. After being deflated and returned to NAS Rockaway for storage, H-1 was destroyed only weeks later in a hangar fire. The second H-Class airship on order was delivered directly to the Army as the OB-1.

J-Class—1922

TECHNICAL SPECIFICATIONS (J-4)

Type: Five- to six-place patrol non-rigid airship.
Manufacturer: Goodyear Tire & Rubber Co., Akron Ohio.
Total produced: 3 (USN)

Powerplants: Two 220-hp Wright J-5 R-790 *Whirlwind* 9-cylinder air-cooled radial engines driving two-bladed fixed-pitch metal propellers.
Armament: None installed.
Performance: Max. speed 60 mph at s.l.; ceiling 8,000 ft.; range 970 mi. (approx. 21 hours); useful lift 4,600 lbs.
Dimensions: Length 196 ft., diameter 44 ft. 6 in., envelope volume 210,600 cu. ft.

The J-class arose out of a joint effort in 1921 between the Navy and Goodyear to incorporate recent experience gained with the C and D-type patrol airships into a new design, resulting in a contract being awarded to build two airships as J-1 and -2. Compared to the C and D-classes, J-1 emerged with a somewhat smaller envelope (175 ft. 6 in. long, 173,00 cu. ft. volume) along with a fully enclosed control gondola, two 150-hp Wright-

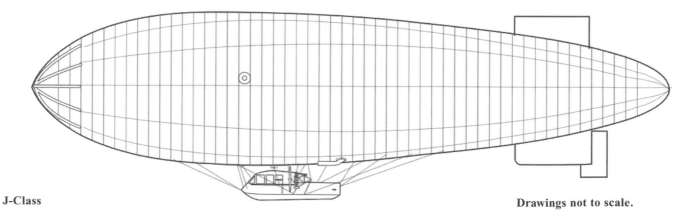

J-Class

Drawings not to scale.

Above: J-4, launched in 1927, combined the unused gondola of J-2 with an Army TC-type envelope. It remained part of the NAS Lakehurst LTA training fleet until 1940. *Below:* The J-4 gondola, built by the Naval Aircraft Factory, featured a planing hull for water landings. It was the last type of gondola to be suspended from the envelope by cables.

Hispano A water-cooled V-8 engines (tractor-mounted for the first time), and a single ballonet arrangement copied from the French *Zodiac* class airships. However, after making its first flight on August 31, 1922, testing of the J-1 revealed serious control and trim problems related to the shortcomings of its single ballonet, which had not been used previously on a helium-filled airship. As a result, the J-2 envelope was cancelled and J-1 was removed from service sometime in 1924, leaving the Navy with no non-rigid airships remaining in its inventory.

To fill the need for a transition trainer in the rigid airship training program at NAS Lakehurst, the Navy acquired Army Airship TC-2 in 1925 and placed it into service as J-3. In addition to a larger envelope (210,600 cu. ft.), J-3 differed from J-1 in having an open control gondola and 150-hp Laurance (later Wright) air-cooled radial engines. Then in 1927, to augment

J-3, the control gondola originally built for J-2 was fitted to another TC-type envelope, upgraded with Wright J-5 engines, and put into operation as J-4. J-3 and -4, together with ZMC-2 after mid–1929, formed the nucleus for training aircrews at

Lakehurst in preparation for duty aboard the much larger rigid airships. In April 1933, J-3 was lost while searching off the New York coast for survivors of the *Akron* (ZRS-4) wreck, with five of its seven crewmembers being ultimately rescued. During the summer of 1933, J-4 transferred to NAS Moffett Field in Sunnyvale, California to support training operations with the newly commissioned *Macon* (ZRS-5), but returned to NAS Lakehurst in May 1935 following the loss of *Macon* and the termination of the rigid airship program, and continued there as a trainer until stricken from the naval inventory in March 1940.

K-1-Class—1931

TECHNICAL SPECIFICATIONS (K-1)

Type: Five- to six-place experimental non-rigid airship.
Manufacturer: Goodyear Tire & Rubber Co., Akron Ohio; Naval Aircraft Factory, Philadelphia, Pennsylvania (control gondola).
Total produced: 1 (USN)
Powerplants: Two 300-hp Wright J-6-9 R-975 *Whirlwind* 9-cylinder air-cooled radial engines driving two-bladed fixed-pitch metal propellers.
Armament: None installed.

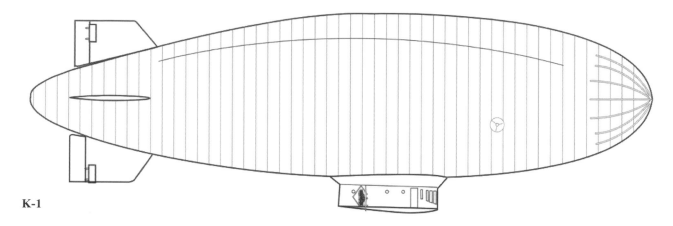

K-1

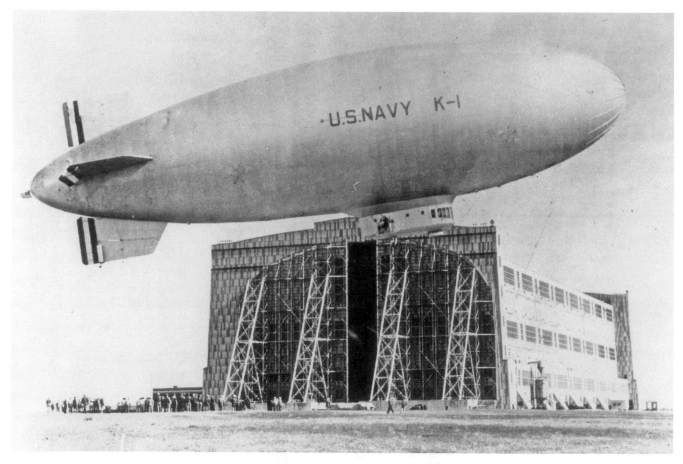

The one-of-a-kind K-1, flown for the first time in August 1931. Sharing many design features with the Goodyear's civil *Defender* class, it served as a trainer and tested various airship design concepts until grounded in 1940.

Performance: Max. speed 63 mph at s.l.; ceiling (not reported); range 1,886 mi. (approx. 41 hours); useful lift 7,684 lbs.
Dimensions: Length 219 ft. 2 in., diameter 53 ft. 11 in., envelope volume 319,000 cu. ft.

BuAer commenced development of the K-1 design during the late 1920s, but with the onset of the Great Depression in 1929, was forced to place construction plans on hold. In the interval since completion of the J-class for the Navy and TC-class for the Army, Goodyear had introduced many design innovations in its growing fleet of civil non-rigid airships (i.e., six new blimps launched by the end of 1929), and by 1930, the Navy was ready to move forward, contracting with Goodyear to manufacture the envelope and with NAF the control gondola. Though twice its size, K-1's envelope was similar in shape to that of Goodyear's civil *Defender* class (see G-class, below) and like it, mated the control gondola directly to the bottom of the envelope by using cables attached to a catenary curtain incorporated within the envelope itself. One of its most noteworthy features was fueling the engines with "blaugas" (similar to propane) instead of gasoline. This enabled fuel to be contained wholly within the envelope in a separate ballonet, and because its weight and density was similar to ambient air, eliminated the need to valve-off helium as fuel burned.

Following assembly of its components, K-1 completed its first flight from NAS Lakehurst on August 31, 1931. Flight trials, while demonstrating a significant increase in range over previous classes, indicated a tendency of K-1 to trim tail low in level flight, which limited speed and affected handling. From late 1931 to mid–1933, K-1 was based at CGAS Cape May, New Jersey (which possessed an airship shed originally built for the ill-fated ZR-2), after which it returned to Lakehurst, serving there until it was grounded in September 1940. K-1 was there-after used for mooring and snow removal experiments until being scrapped in October 1941.

G-Class (ZNN-G)—1935

TECHNICAL SPECIFICATIONS (G-1)

Type: Eight-place training and utility non-rigid airship.
Manufacturer: Goodyear Tire & Rubber Co., Akron, Ohio.
Total produced: 8 (USN)
Powerplants: Two 165-hp Wright J-6-5 R-540 *Whirlwind* 5-cylinder air-cooled radial engines driving two-bladed fixed-pitch metal propellers.
Armament: None installed.
Performance: Max. speed 57 mph at s.l.; ceiling (not reported); range 800 mi. (approx. 17 hours); useful lift 4,115 lbs.

G-1, acquired in 1935 to augment the LTA training fleet at NAS Lakehurst, is shown dropping a parachutist. The airship was destroyed June 1942 in a midair collision with L-1.

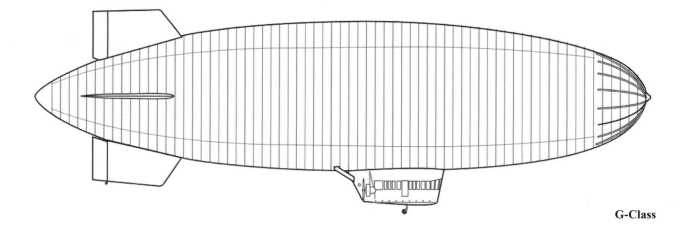

G-Class

Dimensions: Length 186 ft. 8 in., diameter 42 ft. 10 in., envelope volume 183,000 cu. ft.

The original naval G-class, designed in 1919, was never built. In September 1935, after determining the need to acquire another airship for training and utility purposes, BuAer bypassed the normal procurement process by directly purchasing *Defender*, the largest blimp in Goodyear's civil fleet, and placing it on the inventory as G-1. As part of the transaction, *Defender*, which had been first launched in 1929, received a new envelope increasing its volume from 179,000 to 183,000 cubic feet. G-1 was delivered to NAS Lakehurst on October 5, 1935 to operate alongside ZMC-2, J-4, and K-1 in the Navy's scaled back LTA program. Sometime after being placed in operation, G-1 received an upgrade to 225-hp Wright J-6-7 engines, which upped top speed to 62 mph. On June 8, 1942, in the vicinity of Lakehurst at night, G-1 was wrecked in a midair collision with L-1 (see below) in which 12 lives were lost. During the course of World War II, the Navy procured seven more G-types (G-2 through G-8, as ZNN-G under the airship designation system applied after 1940) which differed in having envelope volume increased to 196,700 cubic feet and 220-hp Continental R-670 engines. All of the new G-types were subsequently assigned to ZJ-1 (Airship Utility Squadron One) with detachments serving at NAS Lakehurst and NAS Moffett Field. The last active G-type was retired from naval service in 1959.

TC-13 and -14—1938

TECHNICAL SPECIFICATIONS (TC-14)

Type: Ten-place patrol non-rigid airship.
Manufacturer: Goodyear Tire & Rubber Co., Akron, Ohio.
Total produced: 2 (Army, USN)
Powerplants: Two 375-hp Pratt & Whitney R-985-2 *Wasp Junior* 9-cylinder air-cooled

radial engines driving two-bladed fixed-pitch metal propellers.
Armament: None originally, however, both were later modified to mount one flexible .30-cal. machine forward and aft in the control gondola and provision to carry an unspecified number and weight of depth charges.
Performance: Max. speed 67 mph at s.l.; ceiling (not reported); range 2,000 mi. (approx. 43 hours); useful lift 5,991 lbs.
Dimensions: Length 235 ft. 6 in., diameter 54 ft., envelope volume 374, 850 cu. ft.

TC-13 was originally delivered to the Army in 1932, TC-14 following it in 1934. Both had been designed to a specification for long-range coastal patrol and reconnaissance, and when launched, were the largest type of non-rigid airships then in military service (about 15 percent larger than K-1). Though similar in general outline to the G-class, they were

One of two Army blimps transferred to the Navy in 1937, TC-14 was reassembled and flown in 1938. At the time, it was the largest blimp on the naval inventory and the only one to have combat patrol range.

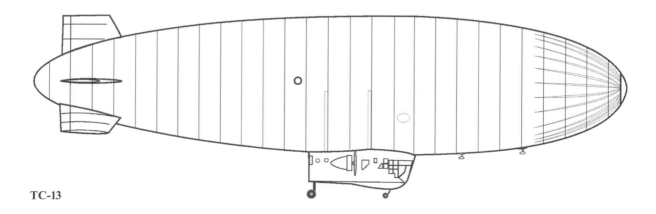

TC-13

readily distinguishable by their twin ventral fins and more angular control gondolas. When the Army decided to disband its Airship Service in 1937, both airships were dismantled and turned over to the Navy. TC-14, which was in the better condition of the two, was reassembled and inflated at NAS Lakehurst during 1938. Until joined by K-2 later in the year, it was the only airship on naval inventory having any long-range patrol capability. TC-13 was placed in storage at NAS Moffett Field pending delivery of a new envelope and as a consequence, not inflated and flown again (at Lakehurst) until 1940. Whether or not TC-13 and -14 ever received a ZN designation (i.e., ZNP-TC) is not reflected in historical references.

Starting in 1940, BuAer directed installation of armament—machine guns and depth charge racks—on both TC-types in preparation for combat patrol duties. In late 1941, TC-13 and -14, together with the four K-2-types, three L-types and G-1, commenced flying patrol missions off the Atlantic Coast; then in January 1942, the two TC-types were deflated and shipped by rail to NAS Moffett Field, where, after being reassembled and inflated, formed the nucleus of ZP-32, the first West Coast LTA combat patrol unit. Both remained on combat status until 1943, when they were replaced by newly arrived K-2-types. Afterward, they were based at Moffett and operated by the LTA school in training and utility roles.

L-Class (ZNN-L)—1938

TECHNICAL SPECIFICATIONS (L-1)

Type: Four-place training non-rigid airship.
Manufacturer: Goodyear Tire & Rubber Co., Akron, Ohio.
Total produced: 22 (USN)
Powerplants: Two 145-hp Warner R-500-2 *Super Scarab* 7-cylinder air-cooled radial engines driving two-bladed fixed-pitch metal propellers.
Armament (added later): Two 234-lb. depth charges.
Performance: Max. speed 60 mph at s.l.; ceiling 9,000 ft.; range 520 mi. (approx. 12 hours); useful lift 2,150 lbs.
Dimensions: Length 149 ft., diameter 39 ft. 10 in., envelope volume 123,000 cu. ft.

The L-class ultimately went on to become the Navy's standard blimp trainer of the wartime period. In 1937, to augment existing blimps in the LTA training program at NAS Lakehurst, BuAer ordered L-1, a small non-rigid design based upon Goodyear's *Enterprise* class of civil airships first launched in 1934. L-1 was completed and delivered to Lakehurst in April

The first in a series of training blimps based on Goodyear's civil *Enterprise* class, L-1 was delivered to NAS Lakehurst in April 1938. The identical L-2 and -3 joined the LTA training fleet during 1941.

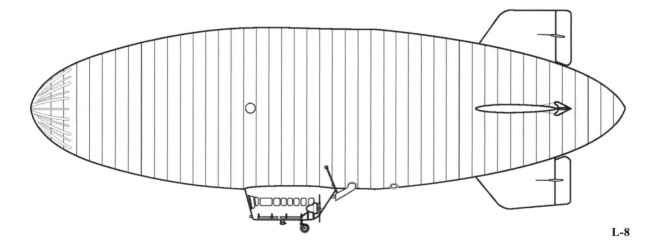

L-8

1938. On September 25, 1940, as part of a general naval expansion following the outbreak of war in Europe, BuAer ordered L-2 and -3 from Goodyear, and both new airships were added to the LTA training program at Lakehurst during 1941 under the new airship designation ZNN-L. Following U.S. entry into World War II in December 1941, the Navy impressed five *Enterprise* class blimps from Goodyear's advertising fleet, which were placed in service as L-4 through L-8. During the early months of the war, L-types at Lakehurst were pulled off training duties, armed with two depth charges, and assigned to fly antisubmarine patrol missions along the eastern seaboard.

One of the great unsolved mysteries of World War II involved L-8 (ex–Goodyear *Ranger*). On the morning of August 16, 1942, after departing NAS Treasure Island to patrol the ocean area west of San Francisco Bay, the airship radioed that it was "investigating a suspicious oil slick." Hours later, L-8 was seen drifting off Fort Funston (near the Golden Gate), then came to rest, fully intact with no one aboard, on a street in Daly City. No trace of its two-man crew was ever found and the cause of their disappearance remains unknown to this day. The next four L-types, L-9 through L-12, were assembled in the shops at NAS Moffett Field, the center of all wartime LTA training, and placed in operation during April 1943. Ten more L-types ordered from Goodyear in February 1943 (L-13 through L-22) were all in service by the end of the year. Once World War II ended, a number of the L-types were returned to Goodyear.

K-2-Class (ZNP-K)—1938

TECHNICAL SPECIFICATIONS (K-2)

Type: Ten- to twelve-place patrol non-rigid airship.
Manufacturer: Goodyear Tire & Rubber Co., Akron, Ohio.
Total produced: 133 (USN)
Powerplant: two 500-hp Pratt & Whitney R-1340-6 *Wasp* 9-cylinder air-cooled radial engines driving three-bladed fixed-pitch metal propellers.
Armament: four 355-lb. depth charges; two flexible .30-cal. machine guns, each mounted forward and aft in the control gondola in K-2 through K-8, and from K-14, one flexible 50-cal. machine gun in the upper forward control gondola.
Performance: max. speed 75 mph at s.l.; ceiling 10,000 ft.; range 1,950 mi. (approx. 34 hours); useful lift 9,400 lbs.

Dimensions: length 246 ft. 0 in., diameter 57 ft. 10 in., envelope volume 404,000 cu. ft.

Procured under the same contract as the L-1 on August 11, 1937, K-2 (which had very little in common with K-1) became the template for the mass-produced K-series of the wartime era (133 delivered by the end of 1945). Over 20 percent larger than K-1, it represented a reversal of BuAer's unofficial bias against procuring non-rigid airships over 200,000 cubic feet in volume. At the time K-2 completed its delivery flight to NAS Lakehurst on December 16, 1938, it was the largest non-rigid airship ever placed on the naval inventory and the first since J-1 to be envisaged for a combat role. Testing and evaluation of K-2 over the next two years not only indicated superior performance and handling compared to K-1, but revealed that it was particularly well-suited for its designed mission of antisubmarine patrol and convoy escort.

As a component of the unprecedented expansion of naval aviation authorized by Congress in mid–1940 (i.e., an eventual buildup to an operational level of 48 non-rigid airships), BuAer awarded Goodyear a contract to manufacture six new K-2-types (K-3 through K-8) under the designation ZNP-K.

They were very similar in details to K-2 except for a switch to 420-hp Wright R-975-28 engines. While all were to be equipped for patrol duties, K-3, -4, -7, and -8 were initially earmarked to serve as transition trainers for the much larger non-rigid fleet envisioned. K-3, -4, and -5 arrived for service between September and November of 1941 and immediately commenced offshore patrols as part of the newly formed ZP-12, but the remaining six were not delivered until early 1942.

As a consequence of wartime contracts issued to Goodyear by the Navy from January 1942 to mid–1943, a total of 130 additional K-2-types were placed on order (K-9 through K-136, though the last four were ultimately cancelled) and by early 1943, Goodyear was producing them at a rate of 11 per month. From K-9 upwards, the production standard changed to 550-hp R-1340-AN2 engines and envelopes enlarged to 416,000 cubic feet. With K-14, envelopes increased again to 425,000 cubic feet and a new upper deck added to the control gondola to include a flexible .50-cal. machine gun mount forward. Other wartime enhancements included radar, sonar buoys, magnetic anomaly detection (MAD) equipment, and long-range

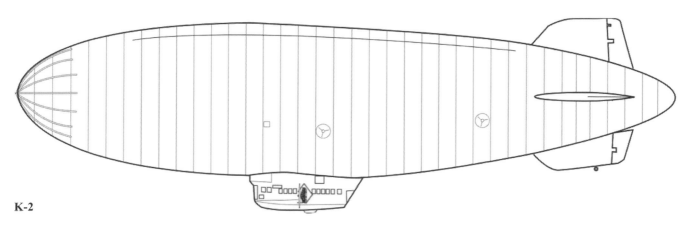

K-2

K-3 seen upon delivery to NAS Lakehurst in September 1941. K-3, -4, and -5, as part of the hastily formed ZP-12, commenced offshore patrols in November 1941. The Navy had taken delivery of 133 K-types by the end of 1945.

(LORAN) radio navigation systems. K-ships performed a vital role in antisubmarine warfare, convoy escort, and search and rescue, operating from nine different stations in the U.S. with overseas detachments in no less than sixteen locations spread throughout the various theaters of the war. Their ability to hover and to operate at low altitudes and airspeeds gave them capabilities unmatched by conventional aircraft. One of the great

legacies of the wartime LTA service was that it never lost a ship in a convoy it was escorting.

Many K-types remained in service following the end of hostilities, some being refitted with 527,000 cubit foot envelopes and further modernized with advanced ASW equipment and weapons. The last K-ship (originally delivered as K-43) was retired from active service in March 1959.

PART III

Aviation-Related Ship Development

AIRCRAFT CARRIERS

Synopsis of Aircraft Carrier Procurement

When the U.S. Congress voted to authorize the Navy's first aircraft carrier in July 1919, it placed Naval Aviation on the steepest of learning curves. Taking inspiration from the flush flight-deck arrangement seen on the British Royal Navy's HMS *Argus*, a converted merchant liner, the Navy Department proceeded with similar plans to convert an existing vessel rather than expend funds on a new ship. USS *Jupiter*, previously a coal collier, underwent a two-year conversion process at the Mare Island Naval Shipyard and returned to commission on March 20, 1922, as the USS *Langley* (CV-1), a 12,700 ton flush-deck aircraft carrier. But even before *Langley* had the chance to commence deck trials with aircraft, the U.S. Government ratified the Washington Naval Treaty, which, among other things, required the Navy to suspend construction of two large battlecruisers, while simultaneously allowing the fleet to add aircraft carriers up to a total displacement of 135,000 tons, including two at 33,000 tons each (actually 36,000 tons standard after allowance for armor protection). On July 1, 1922, as a direct result, the Navy received approval to complete the two battlecruiser hulls as aircraft carriers, and both ships entered service with the fleet in late 1927, USS *Lexington* as CV-2 and USS *Saratoga* as CV-3. These ships were not only significantly larger than *Langley* but more importantly, possessed the speed to maintain formation within the Battle Fleet.

By the time the Navy received authorization to build its fourth carrier in late 1930, major progress had been achieved in air operations, deck handling, tactics, and dedicated aircraft. The design of CV-4, at less than half the displacement of CV-2 and -3, was heavily influenced by the desire to minimize use of tonnage available under the Washington Treaty for future carrier building programs while maximizing the size of its air group (i.e., 76 aircraft versus 80 on CV-2 and -3).

Moreover, recent advances in dive-bombing tactics and availability of aircraft specialized for the role had led designers to omit provision for torpedo-carrying aircraft, with the plan of embarking an extra squadron of bomber-fighter types (BF). CV-4 entered service as USS *Ranger* on July 4, 1934; however, taking part in Fleet Problems from 1935 onwards showed that the weight-saving features of the design produced serious drawbacks in terms of speed and sea-keeping. In any event, by the time design officials received approval in June 1933 to build the next two carriers, CV-5 and -6, BuShips had moved away from the "minimal" carrier concept towards a 20,000 ton vessel accommodating more powerful propulsion machinery and a larger aircraft complement (i.e., up to 96 aircraft). These carriers also restored torpedo-carrying capability to the air group in anticipation of developing more modern torpedo-bomber aircraft types (TB).

In mid–1935, while CV-5 and -6 were at intermediate stages of construction, the Navy began moving forward with plans to build CV-7. The new carrier's size, a displacement of 14,700 tons, was dictated by the tonnage remaining under the Washington Treaty. Its overall design represented a compromise between the features of the CV-5 class and the need to reduce weight, resulting in an 8-percent reduction in length, less powerful propulsion machinery, and no antisubmarine armor belt. CV-7 was laid down in early 1936, and soon afterward, to allow for the additional carrier tonnage, the Navy Department issued a directive for *Langley* to be removed from the fleet as a carrier and converted into a seaplane tender. With completion proceeding on schedule, CV-5 joined the fleet on September 30, 1937, as USS *Yorktown*, followed by CV-6 as USS *Enterprise* on May 12, 1938. Although the size of the Navy's carrier force would be restricted until 1942, when applicable treaties lapsed (i.e., the Washington Treaty plus the follow-on London Naval Treaty of 1936), the Naval Expansion Act of 1938 went ahead to allow a further 40,000 tons of new carrier construction, with funds allocated to start the eighth carrier sometime in 1939. The Navy Department determined that CV-8, expected to enter service around the time the treaty restrictions lapsed, would be a repeat *Yorktown*, whereas CV-9, as soon as funds were appropriated, would be built to a new design being formulated by BuShips. Ironically, in September 1939, the same month CV-8 was laid down, the start of war in Europe effectively ended all shipbuilding limitations imposed by naval treaties. Meanwhile, the smaller CV-7, having already been completed to original specifications, was commissioned as USS *Wasp* on April 25, 1940.

By early 1940, BuShips had finalized design CV-9F as the pattern for the next carrier class: a 27,200 ton vessel, 62 feet longer and 38 feet wider in beam than the *Yorktowns*. Then on July 19, 1940, mere weeks after CV-9 had been ordered, the Navy received its biggest shipbuilding boost since World War I when President Franklin D. Roosevelt signed the Two-ocean Naval Expansion Act into law. In fleet carriers alone, the Act authorized construction of 18 new CV-9 class ships, with sufficient funding being allocated to place orders for eight of them the following September, but this only served to foreshadow an even more massive carrier buildup that began in 1941. Out of an effort to get additional flight-decks into operation faster than the CV-9s could be built (i.e., 24 months+ per ship), the Navy Department began moving forward with plans to convert other ship hull types into an aircraft carrier configuration. The idea of using a smaller type of carrier (i.e., less than 10,000 tons) to replenish fleet carriers and transport aircraft had been studied previously but by 1940 such vessels were seen as potentially functioning in expanded roles such as convoy escort, antisubmarine patrol, support of amphibious operations, and carrier pilot training. With this concept in mind, the Navy Department acquired a C3 cargo vessel in March 1941, which after being modified for installation of a 345-foot flight-deck and hangar space below it, was commissioned just two months later as USS *Long Island*, AVG-1 (auxiliary aircraft carrier; redesignated escort aircraft carrier [CVE] in mid–1943). Sea trials afterward led to a 45-foot deck extension and relocation of the bridge. Another six merchant vessels were earmarked for a similar conversion in late 1941 and altogether, 119 more of these ships (i.e., CVE-2 through -120), variously referred to as "jeep carriers" or "baby flattops," would be completed before the end of 1945.

Even though escort carriers could be built quickly in large numbers, their speed (16 knots) was limited by low-power propulsion systems, and they were completely unarmored. A faster and better-protected type of carrier was still needed to fill the fleet carrier gap until the CV-9 class could begin reaching operational service. Thus, in August 1941, BuShips commenced work on a scheme whereby *Cleveland* class (CL-55) cruiser hulls would be converted into 11,000 ton carriers. Though carrying a reduced air group (i.e., 30 aircraft), the cruiser propulsion system would enable the ship to keep pace with a fast task group. The first such conversion joined the fleet in early 1943 as the USS *Independence* (CV-22), with eight more examples reaching service before the end of the year. All of these ships were later re-classified as light aircraft carriers (CVL). Five CV-9 class fleet carriers (CV-9, -10, -11, -16, and -17) had been laid down by the end of 1941, and the USS *Essex,* name ship of the class, was commissioned on December 31,

1942, and 17 of the 24 ultimately completed would be in service by the time hostilities ended in 1945. CV-8, last of the *Yorktown* class, joined the fleet as USS *Hornet* on October 20, 1941, at which point the Navy possessed five large fleet carriers (CV-2, -3, -5, -6, and -8), two light fleet carriers (CV-4 and -7), and one auxiliary carrier (AVG-1), making it the third largest carrier force in the world. Great Britain, with six large fleet carriers (three previously sunk 1939–1941), two light fleet carriers, and two escort carriers, was second, and Japan, with six fleet carriers, three light carriers, and one training carrier, was first.

Langley CV-1 (AV-3)—1922

TECHNICAL SPECIFICATIONS

Type: Experimental and training aircraft carrier; seaplane tender (1937).
Builder: Mare Island Naval Shipyard, Vallejo, California.
Total built: 1 (USN)
Machinery: 7,000-shp steam turbine with three boilers and a two-shaft General Electric turbo-electric drive.
Displacement: 12,700 tons standard.
Dimensions: Length 534 ft. overall; beam 64 ft., draft 22 ft. (loaded)
Defensive armament: Four 5-in. guns in open mounts.
Performance: Top speed 14 knots; range 14,092 mi.
Aircraft: Six holds accommodating up to 34 fully assembled aircraft.
Crew complement: 350 including aviation personnel.

In July 1919 the U.S. Congress authorized the Navy Department to proceed with conversion of the coal collier *Jupiter* (commissioned AC-3 in 1913) into what would become the first American naval vessel capable of launching and recovering wheeled aircraft at sea. No one at that time, including the most passionate advocates within Naval Aviation, could have appreciated the long-term ramifications of this move. Inasmuch as naval officials were reluctant to devote funds to construction of a new ship, the alteration of an existing auxiliary vessel was seen as the fastest and most cost-effective means of getting an aircraft carrier into operation for purposes of experimentation, training, and tactical evaluation. Moreover, *Jupiter* possessed a minimal superstructure that would permit installation of an almost full-length, flush landing and takeoff deck, together with a hull of sufficient internal volume to allow stowage of aircraft below. The converted ship would not have hangars in the normal sense but store the aircraft in individual cargo holds and move them to and from the flight deck through a large amidships hatch via cranes mounted over the deck edges. In April 1920, while the conversion was underway, *Jupiter* was renamed *Langley* (after aviation pioneer Samuel Pierpont Langley) and reclassified as CV-1 (carrier-heavier-than-air-one). As work progressed, the bridge was left in its forward location, placing it below the wooden-planked flight deck, but the funnels (originally one but a second added later) were repositioned on the port side and articulated to fold down 90 degrees for flight operations, thereby leaving the flight deck completely unobstructed. The initial arresting gear arrangement followed the early British model, using a system of traverse wires, which, when engaged by the aircraft's tailhook, checked its forward

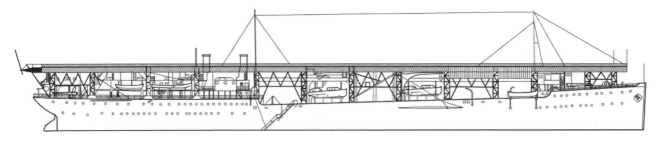

USS *Langley*

motion, in conjunction with fore and aft wires (deleted in 1929), which guided it down the deck in a straight line. Two 60-foot catapults were also installed for launching floatplanes.

Langley was launched in August 1921 and commissioned as a naval ship on March 20, 1922, with Cdr. Kenneth Whiting in command. Flight operations began seven months later and on October 17, Lt. Virgil Griffin completed the first takeoff from its deck in a Vought VE-7 (see under *Scout and Observation Aircraft*, above); then on October 22, an Aeromarine 39-B (see under *Trainer, Transport, and Utility Aircraft,* above) piloted by Lt. Cdr. Geoffrey DeChevalier made the first arrested landing. In early 1923, the ship moved to NOB Norfolk, Virginia, on the East Coast to continue experimental deck operations with aircraft but returned to the West Coast later the same year in order to participate in the Navy's first tactical fleet exercises with an aircraft carrier. By mid–1927, as a result of the experience gained in complex deck operations, combined with noteworthy progress in carrier aircraft procurement, *Langley* could put to sea with an Air Group consisting of 12 fighters, 10 torpedo planes, and 12 scout and utility types. From the late

1920s onward, the ship remained on the West Coast, principally operating out of San Diego, where it continued to refine deck handling procedures and equipment, provide carrier pilot training, and contribute to tactical fleet problems; however, by mid–1936, with three fleet carriers in commission and three more under construction (per Washington Naval Treaty limitations on tonnage), the Navy Department decided to convert the slower and smaller *Langley* into a seaplane tender.

In early 1937, after the forward flight deck had been removed and a large seaplane-handling derrick installed forward, it returned to fleet service under the new classification AV-3. Soon after U.S. entry into World War II, *Langley* moved from its permanent base in Cavite, Philippines to northern Australia where it was employed mainly to transport aircraft on its flight deck area. On February 27, 1942, while en route from Tjilatjap, Java, after dropping off a cargo of 32 Army P-40s, *Langley* was attacked by Japanese aircraft and mortally damaged by five bomb hits. Once its crew abandoned ship, the derelict was sunk by escorting Allied destroyers to prevent it from falling into enemy hands.

The *Langley* **during the summer of 1930 with full complement of 24 aircraft on deck: eight F6C-4s and eight F2B-1s of VF-2B plus one O2U-2 and seven O2U-4s of VS-1B.**

Lexington Class CV-2 and -3—1927

TECHNICAL SPECIFICATIONS

Type: Fleet aircraft carrier.

Builder: Fore River Ship & Engine Bldg. Co., Quincy, Massachusetts (CV-2) and New York Shipbuilding Corp., Camden, New Jersey (CV-3).

Total built: 2 (USN)

Machinery: 180,000-shp steam turbines with 16 boilers and a four-shaft General Electric
turbo-electric drive.

Displacement: 36,000 tons standard.

Dimensions: Length 888 ft. overall; beam 106 ft., draft 32 ft. 6 in. (loaded)

Defensive armament: Eight 8-in. guns in four paired turrets; in 1936, added 24 (36 on CV-2) .50-cal. machine guns in flexible mounts, 16 on side sponsons below flight deck and eight on main turret roofs (and 12 around a funnel platform on CV-2).

Performance: Top speed 33 knots; range 11,500 mi. at 15 knots.

Aircraft: Hangar deck accommodating up to 80 (later 91) fully assembled aircraft.

Crew complement: 1,899 (later 2,122) including aviation personnel.

As a consequence of the limitations placed upon capital ships by the Washington Naval Treaty of 1922, the Navy was required to suspend construction of two 43,500 ton battlecruisers laid down in 1920 and 1921, respectively, as CC-1 and -3. At the same time, however, the Treaty authorized signatories to build a fleet of aircraft carriers up to a combined displaced weight of 135,000 tons, which included two larger examples displacing 36,000 tons standard each. Thus on July 1, 1923, only weeks after the Treaty had been formally approved by the U.S. Government, the two battlecruisers, with their displacements reduced accordingly, were re-authorized as aircraft carriers, CV-2 and -3. As revised, the lines of their original battlecruiser hull plans remained virtually unchanged and most of the underwater armor belt was retained. A flight deck running the entire length of the ship was to be sited above the original main deck line and incorporated directly into the hull structure, a feature not adopted on later carriers. The space between the new flight deck and the old main deck was utilized to create an unobstructed 450 ft. × 70 ft. × 21 ft. aircraft hanger, together with a 105-ft.-long maintenance bay and a 120-ft.-long hold for storing disassembled aircraft. Two deck elevators (30 ft. × 60 ft. forward and 30 ft. × 36 ft. aft) would serve to move aircraft between the hangar and the flight deck. As built, both ships came with a traverse 150-foot catapult forward as well as cranes for handling seaplanes. Unlike *Langley*, the flight deck sited

superstructures on the starboard side, amidships, consisting of an "island" structure with bridge, navigation, and air operation control decks, plus a large single funnel and four traversable turrets (two forward, two aft) each armed twin 8-inch guns, the largest permitted by the Treaty.

Both ships were launched during 1925 and completed over the next two years. On November 16, 1927, CV-3, christened *Saratoga,* became the first commissioned as a naval ship, followed on December 14 by CV-2, christened *Lexington.* At the time, they were the largest aircraft carriers in the world and would retain the distinction until the appearance of *Midway* (CVBs) class carriers in the final months of World War II. In late January 1928, after a brief shakedown, *Saratoga* departed the East Coast via the Panama Canal to join the Battle Fleet at San Pedro (a deep bay adjacent to Long Beach, California that had been used since 1914 as a naval anchorage for capital ships); *Lexington* remained at NOB Norfolk until early April, when it also left for San Pedro. By the end of the summer, the two new carriers were each operating an air group of 56 to 60 aircraft organized into a fighter squadron, a bombing squadron, a scouting squadron (still awaiting aircraft), a torpedo squadron, and a utility unit, namely: VF-1B, VB-2B, VS-2B, and VT-2B on *Saratoga* and VF-3B, VB-1B, VS-3B, and VT-1B on *Lexington.* (Note, the "B" suffix after the squadron number indicated assignment to the Battle Fleet.) The balance of 1928 was devoted to training the carriers' respective air groups, maintenance and deck crews, and ships' companies in preparation for full-scale operations.

In January 1929, *Lexington* and *Saratoga*, in company with *Langley*, left San Pedro to participate in Fleet Problem IX, the first involving a task force which included aircraft carriers fast enough to keep pace with the Battle Fleet. In the fleet problems that followed, the two big carriers were typically assigned to opposing forces, and early difficulties in identification led to a broad black stripe being painted on *Saratoga*'s funnel. Significantly, while not displacing the Battle Line (i.e., battleships grouped by divisions), the new carriers nevertheless assumed a position within the main body of the task force where their aircraft could be used to expand the fleet's offensive striking power. In Fleet Problem X, conducted in the Caribbean during 1930, *Saratoga* and *Langley* were both "disabled" when *Lexington* launched a surprise attack, plainly demonstrating the speed with which air power could change the tactical balance in a naval engagement. The problems also showed the potency

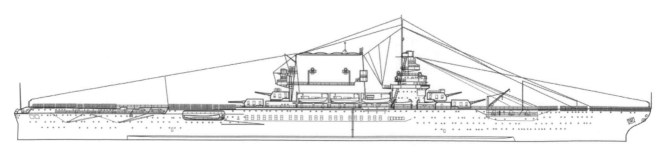

USS *Saratoga*

Top: Lexington **seen in spring of 1928 during shakedown prior to taking aboard her aircraft complement.** *Lexington* **and sister ship** *Saratoga* **were the largest aircraft carriers in the world at the start of World War II.** *Bottom:* **Saratoga in 1936 with 61 aircraft on deck: one command SU-4, 15 SBU-1s of VS-2, 15 F3F-1s of VF-6, 15 BFC-2s of VB-2, and 15 TG-2s of VT-2.**

of ship-based air power (as compared to traditional naval bombardment) against land-based objectives. Ironically, in early 1938 while Fleet Problem XIX was being conducted off the Hawaiian Islands, *Saratoga* launched a successful surprise air attack on Pearl Harbor that was copied to a large degree by the Japanese in December 1941. Later still, similar mock attacks were carried out against Mare Island Naval Shipyard and NAS Alameda in the San Francisco Bay area.

Heavy (.50-caliber) machine gun positions, intended chiefly for antiaircraft defense, were added in 1936 (24 on *Saratoga* and 36 on *Lexington*). In the spring of 1940, the two big carriers participated in Fleet Problem XXI, the last held prior to U.S. entry into World War II. The same year, BuShips determined that the 8-inch gun turrets would be replaced with 5-inch/38-caliber dual-purpose guns which could be used against either surface or aerial targets. Practical experience gained in the fleet problems had shown that the 8-inch guns could not be fired cross-deck, and they were useless against aircraft. The armament refit, scheduled for 1942, also contemplated a significant upgrade in antiaircraft defenses with 1.1-inch (28-mm) "pom-poms" in quad mounts. Both ships underwent extensive overhauls in 1941 during which their flight decks were widened forward and a CAMX-1 search radar installed.

At the time the Japanese struck Pearl Harbor on December 7, 1941, it was fortunate that *Lexington* was at sea delivering aircraft to the Marines at Midway Island (i.e., VMF-211) while *Saratoga*, having just completed its overhaul, was berthed in San Diego. In the weeks immediately following the attack, both carriers took up offensive patrols off Hawaiian waters, including a plan to reinforce the Marines at Wake Island that was recalled on December 22. In January 1942, after sustaining damage from a torpedo fired by a Japanese submarine, *Saratoga* entered the Puget Sound Naval Shipyard for repairs that included the previously scheduled armament refit. Following several skirmishes with the Japanese off New Guinea and Rabaul in the southwest Pacific, *Lexington* docked at Pearl Harbor in March to receive a hasty armament refit which entailed removal of its 8-inch turrets in exchange for 1.1-inch antiaircraft guns in quad mounts. In mid–April, *Lexington* sortied from Pearl Harbor en route to the Coral Sea (between the Solomon Islands and Northeast Australia), joining up on May 1 with *Yorktown* (CV-5) and Task Force 17. On May 8, 1942, after launching a strike against the opposing Japanese force, *Lexington* was attacked by aircraft

from the enemy carriers *Shokaku* and *Zaikaku* during which it suffered hits from two torpedoes and three bombs, plus further damage to the hull from near misses. Several hours after the attack, an explosion of the aviation fuel bunkers rapidly spread fires beyond control, forcing Capt. Frederick Sherman to eventually order an "abandon ship." To foreclose any later attempt at enemy salvage, *Lexington* was deliberately sunk by two torpedoes from the Navy destroyer *Phelps*.

Saratoga was unable to resume combat operations in time to participate in the early carrier battles at Coral Sea and Midway, however, it did open the assault on Guadalcanal in August 1942 and continued in support of Allied combat operations in the southwest and central Pacific areas until coming to Mare Island in late 1943 for a long-overdue overhaul and refit. Returning to combat duty during early 1944, *Saratoga* operated with the British Fleet in the Indian Ocean until June, then spent the balance of the year training carrier pilots out of NAS Bremerton, Washington. In February 1945, the ship joined up with other naval units off Iwo Jima, where it subsequently incurred serious damage from bomb hits and kamikaze strikes while providing air cover to American invasion forces. Following another round of repairs at Puget Sound, *Saratoga* arrived at Pearl Harbor in May 1945 to serve as a training carrier. In the interval following Japanese surrender in September, the ship was used to transport military personnel from the Pacific Theater to the U.S., bringing a total of 29,204 war veterans home, more than any other naval vessel. In early 1946, in the midst of the massive postwar demobilization, *Saratoga* was decommissioned and declared surplus. Having survived over four years of combat, the old carrier—as a stationary target—finally met its end on July 25, 1946 when it was destroyed and sunk during the atomic bomb tests being conducted near Bikini Atoll.

Ranger CV-4—1934

TECHNICAL SPECIFICATIONS

Type: Fleet aircraft carrier.
Builder: Newport News Shipbuilding & Drydock Co., Newport News, Virginia.
Total built: 1 (USN)
Machinery: Two 53,500-shp steam turbines with 6 boilers and a geared, two-shaft drive.
Displacement: 14,000 tons standard.
Dimensions: Length 769 ft. overall; beam 109 ft. 5 in.; draft 22 ft. 6 in. (loaded)

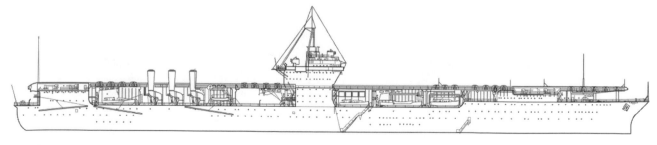

USS *Ranger*

Defensive armament: Four (later increased to eight and moved to sponsons) 5-in./25-cal. dual-purpose guns in open deck-edge mounts on both sides fore and aft.
Performance: Top speed 29.3 knots; range 11,500 mi. at 15 knots.
Aircraft: Hangar deck accommodating up to 76 (later 86) fully assembled aircraft.
Crew complement: 1,788 (later 2,148) including aviation personnel.

The *Ranger*, laid down in September 1931 as CV-4, holds the honor of having been the first Navy ship to be built from the keel up as an aircraft carrier. Its lines and layout bore more resemblance to the general configuration of *Langley* than that of the considerably larger *Lexington* class. The smaller size of the design was dictated by a desire to reserve the tonnage remaining under the Washington Treaty to future carrier building programs (i.e., the *Yorktown* class was already in the early planning stages). The flight deck emerged as a separate structure above the main deck, supported by a light girder latticework, and the space directly below it was utilized for hangars, workshops, and stowage. As originally laid down, CV-4 was to have had an unobstructed flight deck like *Langley*'s; however, prior to the ship being launched in early 1933, the addition of a small island superstructure on the starboard side, amidships, was deemed necessary for command and control. The six funnels, three per side that could be hinged-down 90 degrees for flight operations, were located as far aft as possible for a stern discharge of gases. Hydraulic deck elevators, one sited amidships and one forward of the island, would facilitate movement of

aircraft between decks. One of the new carrier's most conspicuous features was lack of provision for torpedo stowage: CV-4's air group was to consist of a fighter squadron, a scouting squadron, *two* bombing squadrons, and a utility unit. Considerable progress made since 1927 both in refining dive-bombing tactics and procuring new dive-bomber aircraft (see Martin BM, Great Lakes BG, and Curtiss BFC/BF2C) had influenced naval planners to exclude torpedo planes from the aircraft complement. In order to keep weight to a minimum, the ship was unarmored and limited to a defensive armament of only four 5-inch/25-caliber dual-purpose guns in port and starboard deck-edge mounts, forward and aft. As a result of its size and the serious design emphasis on weight-saving, CV-4 materialized at a mere 180 tons displaced per aircraft carried, compared to 450 tons for the *Lexington* class.

On July 4, 1934, CV-4 was commissioned USS *Ranger* with Capt. Arthur Bristol in command. Initial flight operations began in early August, and following a two-month shakedown cruise to South America, the ship engaged in operational training out of NOB Norfolk until March 1935, when it transited the Panama Canal en route to join the Battle Fleet on the West Coast. The fleet anchorage, by this time, had moved from San Pedro to Pearl Harbor, so that over the next four years, *Ranger* participated in various fleet problems between the California coast and the Hawaiian Islands. The design characteristics that gave the new carrier such an efficient aircraft to displacement ratio proved to be shortcomings in operational practice: the

Ranger **was the first Navy ship built from the keel up as an aircraft carrier. This photograph, probably from 1935 or 1936, shows an air group on deck of BM-1s and -2s, SBU-1s, F2F-1s, F3F-1s, and O3U-1s.**

slower top speed (5 knots less than CV-2 and -3) limited its ability to maneuver with the Battle Fleet and poor sea-keeping (rolling and pitching) restricted flight operations to relatively calm conditions. *Ranger* returned to the East Coast in early 1939 and in September, soon after the war broke out in Europe, commenced neutrality patrols along the middle Atlantic between Bermuda, Newfoundland, and the eastern U.S. coast.

Following the Japanese attack on Pear Harbor in December 1941, the ship patrolled the south Atlantic until March 1942, when it entered Norfolk Navy Yard to receive installation of CAMX-1 radar and 16 1.1-inch AA guns in quad mounts forward and aft of the island. Even with the refit, naval officialdom believed *Ranger* to be too slow and too lightly protected for Pacific combat operations.

After leaving the yard, *Ranger* was employed primarily to transport USAAF and Lend-Lease aircraft to West Africa, where they could be ferried to various Allied combat commands. Then in November 1942, leading the naval task force (including four CVEs) that supported Operation Torch, the carrier conducted air strikes against Vichy French targets in Morocco and provided air cover to invading Allied forces. After a stateside overhaul in early 1943, the ship served again as an aircraft transport until August, when it was attached to the British Home Fleet and used to launch air attacks on German shipping in the North Sea. *Ranger* returned to the U.S. later that year and in January 1944, became a training carrier out of NAS Quonset Point, Rhode Island, though it was detached on one occasion to transport USAAF aircraft to the Mediterranean Theater. During the early part of the war, Bu-Ships had planned to subject *Ranger* to an extensive refit and modernization which would have involved lengthening the hull, replacing the flight deck, adding armor plate in vital locations, and installing new propulsion machinery; however, the plan was cancelled in favor of a more modest refit during the spring of 1944 that included strengthening the flight deck, installation of more powerful catapults, plus a radar upgrade. In August 1944 the carrier transferred to the West Coast to support training operations out of Pearl Harbor and San Diego, remaining there until the war's end. After returning to the East Coast and serving briefly at NAS Pensacola, *Ranger* was decommissioned in October 1946 and thereafter sold for scrap.

Yorktown Class CV-5, -6, and -8—1937

TECHNICAL SPECIFICATIONS

Type: Fleet aircraft carrier.
Builder: Newport News Shipbuilding & Drydock Co., Newport News, Virginia.
Total built: 3 (USN)
Machinery: Four 120,000-shp steam turbines with 9 boilers and a geared, four-shaft drive.
Displacement: 20,190 tons standard.
Dimensions: Length 809 ft. 6 in. overall; beam 109 ft. 6 in. [114 ft. on CV-8]; draft 25 ft. 11 in. (loaded).
Defensive armament: Eight 5-in./38-cal. dual-purpose guns and 24 .50-cal. machine guns in open deck-edge mounts on both sides fore and aft (and on CV-8, 16 1.1-inch "pom-poms" in quad mounts forward and aft of the island, retrofitted to CV-6 and -6 in 1941–1942) .
Performance: Top speed 32.5 knots; range 14,375 mi. at 15 knots.
Aircraft: Hangar deck accommodating up to 96 fully assembled aircraft.
Crew complement: 1,890 (later 2,217) including aviation personnel.

As a direct result of passage of the National Recovery Act in June 1933, the Navy received authorization in August to proceed with plans to build two new aircraft carriers, CV-5 and -6. Even before *Ranger* was launched, naval design officials had moved away from the "minimal" carrier concept in favor of a 20,000 ton vessel that would accommodate more powerful propulsion machinery and a larger aircraft complement. Still, as their final designs emerged, CV-5 and -6 had far more in common with *Ranger* than the larger *Lexington* class: a lightly built flight deck above the main deck, with hangars, workshops, and storage areas appearing as a light superstructure rather than being integral to the hull. Although a *Langley*-type flush deck had been considered at first, the design ultimately included a substantial island superstructure on the starboard side that housed bridge, navigation, and air operations decks as well as three fixed funnels. A third deck elevator was positioned near the stern in addition to those at the bow and aft of the island. Besides the two hydraulic catapults located on the forward flight deck, a third catapult firing athwartships was installed in the forward hangar deck to permit launches during deck operations. The new carriers' planned air groups would each consist of 18 fighters, 37 scout/dive-bombers, 36 torpedo-bombers, and five utility types. In the interval since construction of *Ranger*, BuAer had awarded development contracts to Douglas and Great Lakes under a new torpedo-bomber (TB) requirement, and prototypes (i.e., XTBD-1 and XTBG-1) were scheduled to begin evaluations in early 1935. Defensive armament comprised eight of the newly developed 8-inch/38-caliber dual-purpose

USS *Yorktown*

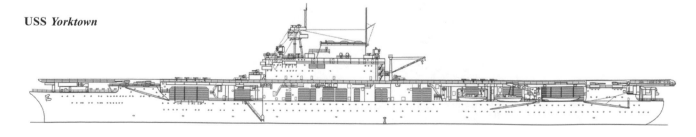

A 1940 photograph showing *Yorktown* with 96 aircraft on deck. Note 16 JRFs parked athwartships, six JRS-1s sans wings, and two JRFs. The air group consisted of F3F-3s, SBC-3s, BT-1s, SB2U-1s, and TBD-1s.

guns in open deck-edge mounts, forward and aft on both sides, plus 24 50-caliber machine guns in flexible mounts. Although the flight deck was unarmored, the design did allow for a 2½-inch to 4-inch waterline belt against torpedoes and armored decking over the propulsion machinery and magazines.

Both ships were laid down in early 1934 and launched during 1936. CV-5, christened *Yorktown*, was commissioned on September 30, 1937, followed by CV-6, *Enterprise*, on May 12, 1938. The new carriers remained on the East Coast to train their new air groups and complete Caribbean cruises until the spring of 1939, when they transited the Panama Canal to join the Pacific Battle Fleet. Although their air groups were comparatively inexperienced, *Yorktown* and *Enterprise* made important contributions to the overall progress made in development of carrier tactics during Fleet Problems XX (1939) and XXI (1940). In early 1941, as the U.S. moved closer to a wartime footing, *Enterprise* was permanently based at Pearl Harbor while *Yorktown* returned to NOB Norfolk as part of the Atlantic Fleet.

After the Washington Treaty's limits on warship tonnage were removed by the follow-on London Treaty of 1936, CV-8, the third carrier of the *Yorktown* class, was authorized in early 1937 and laid down in September 1939. Although the design

for a substantially larger class (i.e., *Essex*) was in the early stages of formulation, naval planners decided that another *Yorktown* could be built and placed in service much faster. CV-8, differing in details from its sister ships, featured a flight deck widened by five feet, plus four batteries of quadruple-mounted 1.1-inch antiaircraft guns and 24 single-mounted .50-calbre machine guns. The new carrier was launched from Newport News in December 1940 and placed in commission as USS *Hornet* on October 20, 1941 and immediately afterward, operated out of NOB Norfolk to train its newly formed air group and complete fitting out. *Yorktown* and *Enterprise* were equipped with new CXAM-1 radar systems during 1941 and *Hornet* in early 1942.

In a fortuitous twist of fate, *Enterprise* and *Lexington* left their berths at Pearl Harbor on December 2, 1941 on a mission to deliver aircraft, personnel (i.e., VMF-211), and military provisions to Wake Island and were still en route back to Hawaii five days later at the time the Japanese struck. The ensuing search for the Japanese carrier force on December 8 and 9 proved to be fruitless, however, an SBD-2 of VS-6 from *Enterprise* did score the first American victory over the Japanese fleet when it attacked and sank submarine I-70 on December

The *Enterprise* is seen in 1940 with an air group consisting of 17 F3F-2s, 17 BT-1s, 18 SBC-3s, 18 TBD-1s, six SUs, one SOC-3, one J2F-1 and one SBC-4 command aircraft. It was the most decorated Navy ship of World War II.

10. Meanwhile, *Yorktown* departed Norfolk for the Pacific on December 16 while *Hornet* remained behind. During the earliest months of 1942, *Yorktown* and *Enterprise*, formed into two separate task forces, initiated the first American offensive operations of the war, carrying out attacks on Japanese shipping and shore bases in the Central and Southwest Pacific. On April 18, 1942, after arriving at NAS Alameda the previous month, *Hornet* launched 16 USAAF B-25s led by Lt. Col. James H. Doolittle in the first American military attack against Tokyo and five other cities on the Japanese mainland (for a more detailed explanation, see http://en.wikipedia.org/wiki/Doolittle_Raid#The_Raid).

On May 8, 1942, with *Lexington* as part of Task Force 17, *Yorktown* fought the first major carrier engagement of the war at the Battle of the Coral Sea. Even though the exchange resulted in the loss of *Lexington* and serious damage to *Yorktown,* the corresponding harm inflicted on enemy carriers *Shokaku* and *Zaikaku* and consequent loss of aircraft was sufficient to stall the Japanese advance into the Southwest Pacific and give U.S. forces time to regroup. Between June 6 and 7, 1942, in what is generally regarded as the most important naval battle of World War II, *Enterprise* and *Hornet* (Task Force 16), along with the hastily repaired *Yorktown* (Task Force 17), engaged and sank four Japanese carriers in the vicinity of Midway Island. Following two waves of enemy air attacks, *Yorktown* had to be abandoned, and while under tow two days later, sank after being torpedoed by a Japanese submarine. During a third carrier engagement, fought off the Santa Cruz Islands (northeast of the Solomons) between October 26 and 27, 1942,

H*ornet* was sunk and *Enterprise* damaged. Though technically a Japanese tactical victory, the extensive repairs required for two of the three IJN carriers involved, combined with large losses of experienced aircrews killed (148 IJN vs. 26 USN) proved to be an irreversible setback to Japanese forces in the Southwest Pacific. *Enterprise*, surviving the war as the Navy's most highly decorated ship, was decommissioned in 1947 and placed in reserve, then following an unsuccessful effort to preserve the ship as a memorial, sold for scrap in 1958.

Wasp CV-7—1940

TECHNICAL SPECIFICATIONS

Type: Fleet aircraft carrier.
Builder: Fore River Ship & Engine Bldg. Co., Quincy, Massachusetts.
Total built: 1 (USN)
Machinery: Two 70,000-shp steam turbines with 6 boilers and a geared, two-shaft drive.
Displacement: 14,700 tons standard.
Dimensions: Length 741 ft. 3 in. overall; beam 109 ft.; draft 24 ft. 6 in. (loaded)
Defensive armament: Eight 5-in./38-cal. dual-purpose guns in open deck-edge mounts on both sides fore and aft; 16 1.1-inch guns in four quad mounts for and aft of the island; and 24 .50-cal. machine guns in deck-edge mounts on both sides.
Performance: Top speed 29.5 knots; range 12,000 mi. at 15 knots.
Aircraft: Hangar deck accommodating up to 76 fully assembled aircraft.
Crew complement: 1,889 including aviation personnel.

Laid down in April 1936, CV-7 emerged as a direct byproduct of the tonnage remaining to the U.S. Navy (i.e., 15,000 tons)

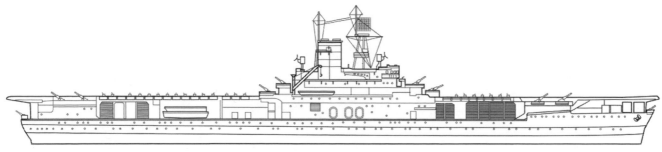

USS *Wasp*

for carrier construction under the Washington Treaty. Overall, its design represented a compromise between displaced weight and the size of the air group to be carried (i.e., 193 tons displaced per aircraft compared to 210 for the CV-5 class). Though having many features in common with the *Yorktowns*, efforts to limit CV-7's weight resulted in a 132-foot decrease in length, reduced-power propulsion machinery, and no anti-submarine armor belt. Its smaller flight deck allowed space for only two elevators, but a moveable deck-edge girder could be rigged to lift aircraft, and to enhance off-deck takeoff capability, provision was made for two hangar-deck catapults firing athwartships. The ship was launched in April 1939 and commissioned USS *Wasp* on April 25, 1940, with Capt. John W. Reeves, Jr., in command.

Upon completion of fitting out, *Wasp* commenced qualifications of its four air group squadrons, two fighter and two scouting (VF-71, VF-72, VS-71, and VS-72). Like *Ranger*, it

had been designed with no provision for torpedo stowage, although a torpedo-bomber complement was in fact added later. Finishing its shakedown in the fall of 1940, *Wasp* was permanently assigned to the Atlantic Fleet at NOB Norfolk, and in March 1941, entered the Norfolk Navy Yard to receive installation of a CAMX-1 radar system, steel splinter shielding around all 1.1-inch and .50-caliber AA batteries, and repairs to the turbines. It subsequently participated in the American occupation of Iceland in August 1941 and while offshore, became the first carrier to launch USAAF aircraft when 30 P-40s and 3 PT-17s left its deck to form the island's initial air defense. During the first months of 1942, after the U.S. declared war, *Wasp* operated in British waters in support of the Royal Navy Home Fleet, then in April and May, sortied into the Mediterranean to assist in the relief of Malta, making two trips to transport approximately 100 RAF *Spitfire* fighters to the besieged island base.

After returning to Norfolk for a hasty refit, *Wasp* embarked

The *Wasp* seen in the Atlantic in early months of 1942, after application of camouflage. Aircraft spotted on rear deck are SB2U-2s of VS-71, still in prewar colors. The carrier moved to the Pacific in the summer of 1942.

for the South Pacific in early June 1942, stopping over in San Diego to exchange its Vought SB2Us for Douglas SBDs (VS-71 and -72) and take on Grumman TBFs for its new torpedo squadron. Once on station, *Wasp* joined forces with *Saratoga* and *Enterprise* in defense of the eastern Solomon Islands and the invasion of Guadalcanal. On September 15, 1942, while escorting troop transports bound for Guadalcanal, the carrier was mortally damaged by three torpedo hits from Japanese submarine I-19. After being abandoned, the ship's demise was hastened by torpedoes fired by American destroyer *Landsdowne*.

Long Island AVG-1 (CVE-1)—1941

TECHNICAL SPECIFICATIONS

Type: Auxiliary (later escort) aircraft carrier.
Builder: Sun Shipbuilding & Drydock Co., Chester, Pennsylvania.
Total built: 1 (USN)
Machinery: One 8,500-bhp Sulzer 7-cyliner diesel engine driving a single shaft.

Displacement: 7,886 tons standard.
Dimensions: Length 492 ft. overall; beam 78 ft.; draft 25 ft. 6 in. (loaded)
Defensive armament: One 4-in./51-cal. gun aft, two 3-in./50-cal. guns forward, and four 50-cal. machine guns (location not reported).
Performance: Top speed 16 knots; range (not reported).
Aircraft: Hangar deck accommodating up to 21 fully assembled aircraft.
Crew complement: 970 including aviation personnel.

Popularly known as "jeep carriers" or "baby flattops," AVG-1 (CVE-1) became the progenitor of 122 escort carriers built in six classes between 1941 and 1945, 84 ultimately serving with the U.S. Navy and 38 lend-leased to Britain. As far back as the early 1930s, naval planners had shown interest in the idea of a small carrier (i.e., less than 10,000 tons) that could function primarily as an auxiliary aircraft transport, either to replenish fleet carriers or move Army aircraft to overseas bases. However, there was little impetus to develop the concept until late 1939, when the U.S. found itself confronted with the outbreak of war

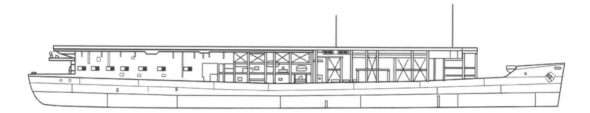

Long Island

The first of 84 escort carriers that would be completed by 1945, *Long Island* is seen underway in July 1941 with two F2A-3s of VS-201 spotted forward. The flight deck was extended 75 feet in late 1941.

in Europe plus increasing concerns over Japanese designs in the Pacific. By this time, in addition to a transport role, smaller types of carriers were also seen as potentially filling the gap in convoy escort, antisubmarine patrol, air support of amphibious operations, and carrier qualification training for new pilots. More importantly, the new ships could be produced very quickly and inexpensively by adapting a flight deck and associated hangar superstructure to an existing merchant vessel hull.

Definite plans were made in early 1941 when the Navy acquired a number of merchant ships to undergo conversion into a carrier configuration. The first example, the former C3 cargo vessel *Mormacmail*, designated AVG-1 (auxiliary aircraft carrier), was commissioned USS *Long Island* on June 2, 1941. As built, the ship appeared with a flight deck running 70 percent of its length (345 feet), a navigating bridge located forward of the deck edge, and no island structure. (The ex–*Mormacland*, second ship of the same class, was delivered to the Royal Navy and commissioned in November 1941 as HMS *Archer* [D78]). Following several months of operational evaluations, *Long Island* left NOB Norfolk and entered the Mare Island shipyard in Vallejo, California to receive modifications that included lengthening the flight deck to 420 feet and relocating the bridge to sponsons on the port and starboard sides.

In early 1942, soon after the U.S. entered the war, *Long Island* escorted a convoy to Newfoundland and returned to NOB Norfolk for pilot training duties. The ship moved to the West Coast in the spring of 1942, then in June, embarked two Marine squadrons at Pearl Harbor and departed for the South Pacific. After leaving Fiji on August 13, it launched the first Marine aircraft to arrive at Henderson Field in defense of Guadalcanal.

From the fall of 1942 to the end of 1943, *Long Island* (redesignated twice, ACV-1 in August 1942, CVE-1 in July 1943) returned to the West Coast and resumed training duties, and from 1944 through the war's end, transported aircraft and personnel to various combat staging areas in the Pacific Theater. After being decommissioned and sold in 1946, the ship reverted to a merchant configuration and remained active until 1966.

Note on CV-9 Class Fleet Carriers. When the Treaty restrictions on carrier tonnage were lifted in 1936, Navy officials began design work on an improved class of fleet carrier to follow the *Yorktowns* into service. New requirements included (1) a 10 percent increase in aircraft complement; (2) a lengthened and widened flight deck to facilitate a faster pace of aircraft takeoff, refueling, rearming, and landing operations; (3) a 25 percent increase in aircraft spares to sustain prolonged combat operations; (4) improved armor protection against bombs and torpedoes; and (5) increased antiaircraft defenses. As finalized in early 1940, design CV-9F emerged as a 27,200 ton ship having a length of 872 feet overall and a beam of 147 feet 6 inches, with 150,000-shp of propulsion machinery driving four shafts. Three ships of the new class had been laid down before the end of 1941, and the first was commissioned as the USS *Essex* on December 31, 1942. From 1943 onwards, *Essex* class carriers formed the backbone of Navy offensive operations in the Pacific, a total of 22 having been placed in commission by the war's end. Six more were completed after the war, and the last active example of the class (i.e., CV-16, the second *Lexington*) was used for training until 1991.

Note on CV-22 Class Light Carriers. In 1941, as it became readily apparent that it would take a period of years for

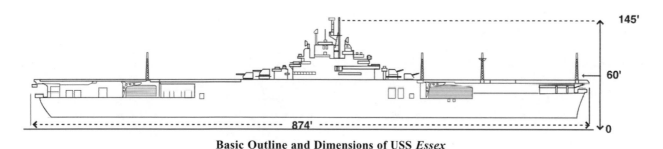

Basic Outline and Dimensions of USS *Essex*

Final arrangement of CV-9 as laid down in 1941.

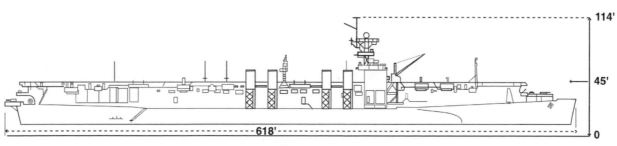

Basic Outline and Dimenions of USS *Independence*

Final arrangement of CV-22 as laid down in 1942.

sizable numbers of CV-9 class fleet carriers to reach combat service, the government instituted an emergency program to convert a number of previously laid down *Cleveland* (CL-55) class light cruiser hulls into a carrier configuration. Leaving the original cruiser propulsion machinery and armor protection essentially unchanged would result in a smaller but well-protected carrier, fast enough to keep up with the main body of the fleet and large enough to support an air group of 30 aircraft comprised into three squadrons (one VF, VB, and VT). The CV-22 class emerged at about half the mass of the *Yorktown*s, displacing 10,833 tons standard, with a small island structure and four stacks offset to the starboard side in order to leave the narrow flight deck (78 feet wide) unobstructed. The first example converted (laid down as CL-59) was launched in August 1942 and commissioned USS *Independence* on January 14, 1943, and by the end of the year, had been joined by eight more carriers of the same class. In mid–1943, as more *Essex* class carrier entered service, the *Independence* class were re-designated as "light" carriers (CVL).

SEAPLANE AND AIRSHIP TENDERS

Synopsis of Seaplane and Airship Tender Procurement

Navy vessels specifically designed to support seaplane operations did not appear until just prior to World War II. Given the fact that the naval demobilization following World War I had generated a multitude of surplus warships and auxiliaries, it was seen as far more practical to refit existing vessels for aviation duties than build new ones. Although several obsolete warships had been used in connection with seaplane experiments and training from 1914 to 1917, there were no dedicated ships on record as serving at the time of the armistice in late 1918. Three ships underwent conversions for the seaplane support role during 1919: USS *Arroostook* (CM-3) and USS *Shawmut* (CM-4), both 3,800 ton ex–passenger steamers that had been requisitioned during the war and reconfigured as minelayers; and USS *Sandpiper* (AM-51), a new 1,350 ton *Lapwing* class minesweeper commissioned directly into service with the aviation branch. One destroyer, USS *Harding* (DD-91), acted as a plane guard in 1919 for the transatlantic flight of the Curtiss NC boats, then after minimal modifications, served from 1920 to 1922 as a support ship in the seaplane training program at NAS Pensacola.

While still under construction, a 11,500 ton fleet auxiliary was initially finished out as an airship and balloon tender, entering service in late 1921 as the USS *Wright* (AZ-1), but after being reequipped for seaplane operations in 1925, was reclassified as AV-1, the first Navy ship to receive the seaplane tender designation. A 16,800 ton fleet oiler, USS *Patoka* (AO-9), be-

came the primary support vessel for the Navy's rigid airship program in 1924 after being fitted with a mooring mast and airship repair and storage facilities. Two more *Lapwing* minesweepers were reassigned to seaplane duties, USS *Pelican* (AM-27) in 1922 and USS *Heron* (AM-10) in 1924. USS *Jason* (AC-12), a 19,550 ton coal collier, began supporting Asiatic Fleet seaplane operations in 1925 and though unmodified, was re-designated AV-2 in 1930. As the patrol and floatplane force grew, four *Lapwing*s were added to the aviation branch in 1931, *Avocet* (AM-19), *Teal* (AM-23), *Swan* (AM-34), and *Gannett* (AM-41); another in 1932, *Lapwing* (AM-1); and the last in 1935, *Thrush* (AM-18). These small vessels had been carried on the naval inventory as "minesweeper for duty with aircraft" but were reclassified in 1936 as small seaplane tenders in hull number order (i.e., AVP-1 through -9).

The aircraft carrier *Langley* (CV-1), after undergoing conversion into a seaplane tender, rejoined the fleet in 1937 as AV-3. With Naval Aviation extending its patrol reach during the mid– and late 1930s (e.g., 409 Consolidated PBYs delivered or ordered by the end of 1939), with particular emphasis on more widespread Pacific operations, it became obvious that a new type of purpose-built heavy seaplane tender would be needed to provide maintenance and logistical support, as well as command and control of VP units. To this end, the Navy received congressional approval in 1937 for construction of the 8,671 ton AV-4, then a year later, the Naval Expansion Act of 1938 appropriated additional funds to build sistership AV-5. The Act likewise authorized the first two ships in a planned series of small seaplane tenders (less than 2,500 tons) that would over time replace the *Lapwing*s. These new AVPs would be specifically designed to support seaplane operations in forward combat areas and have the additional capability, in terms of speed and armament, to act as an escort for heavy tenders and auxiliaries. Construction of AV-4 began in March 1938; AV-5 and the first two small tenders, AVP-10 and -11, were all scheduled to be laid down in 1939.

But even as the shipbuilding efforts moved forward, it became apparent to naval planners that new patrol aircraft would be deployed for ocean operations at rate much faster than these ships could reach service. As an interim solution, the Navy Department initiated a program in early 1938 to convert a number of World War I–era *Clemson* class destroyers into small seaplane tenders and in June 1938, USS *Childs* (DD-241) entered the Philadelphia Naval Shipyard as first to undergo the conversion. Ultimately, 14 of these destroyers were selected for conversion: two entered service in early 1939, ex–DD-241 and -244; and twelve by the end of 1940, ex–DD-196, -186, -188, -342, -344, -251, -255, -267, -270, -260, -266, and -237. The converted destroyers had initially been classified as AVPs, however, in mid–1940, all were re-designated "aviation tender destroyer" (AVD-1 through -14). The massive growth of the patrol aircraft fleet portended by the Two-Ocean Naval Expansion Act of 1940 made it apparent that greater numbers of heavy seaplane tenders would needed in service faster than the AV-4 class could be built. Thus, in mid–1940, the Navy Department acquired two incomplete C3-type merchant vessels to be set aside for conversion into a heavy seaplane tender configuration. On schedule, AV-4 joined the fleet on November 15, 1940, as USS *Curtiss*, followed by AV-5 on December 20 as USS *Abermarle*.

Construction of the first two purpose-built small seaplane tenders commenced in late 1939, and both ships were commissioned the same day on July 3, 1941, USS *Barnegat* (AVP-10) and *Biscayne* (AVP-11), with three more reaching service before the end of 1941: *Casco* (AVP-12), *Humbolt* (AVP-21), *Matagorda* (AVP-22). (Note, hull numbers 14 through 20 had previously been assigned to the *Childs* class.) The two heavy seaplane tender C3 conversions also joined the fleet in mid–1941, USS *Tangier* as AV-8 and *Pocomoke* as AV-9. (Note, hull number AV-6 had provisionally been assigned to *Patoka* [AO-9] in 1939 and AV-7 reserved for a repeat *Curtiss*). As of December 1941, the Navy's fleet comprised a total of 34 ships dedicated to seaplane operations, consisting of six heavy tenders (AV-1, -3, -4, -5, -8, and -9) and 28 small tenders (AVP-1 through -9, AVD-1 through -14, and AVP-10, -11, -12, -21, and -22). Through the course of World War II, 30 more *Barnegat* class and five more *Tangier* class tenders were placed in commission. The repeat *Curtiss*, after a partial redesign, became the *Currituk* class, with four ships (AV-10 through -13) reaching service by the end of 1945.

Aroostook Class CM-3 and -4—1919

TECHNICAL SPECIFICATIONS

Type: Ex–passenger steamer modified as a minelayer and seaplane tender.
Builder: Cramp & Sons Shipyard, Philadelphia, Pennsylvania.
Total built: 2 (USN)
Machinery: two 7,000-shp vertical triple expansion steam engines with eight boilers and a geared, two-shaft drive.
Displacement: 3,800 tons standard (approx.).
Dimensions: Length 395 ft. overall; beam 52 ft. 2 in. ft.; draft 16 ft. (loaded)
Defensive armament: One 5-in./51-cal. and two 3-in./50-cal. guns in open mounts, two flexible .30-cal. machine guns, and provision for 300 mines.
Performance: Top speed 20 knots; range 5,000 mi.
Aircraft: One flying boat or up to 6 floatplanes embarked for repairs.
Crew complement: 200

Aroostook and sistership (very similar but marginally smaller) *Shawmut* were possibly the first Navy ships to be modified specifically for the seaplane support role. Built in 1907 as coastal passenger steamers, both were acquired in 1917 and converted as minelayers under designations ID# 1256 (*Aroostook*) and 1255 (*Shawmut*). In early 1919, *Aroostook* became the first example refitted for aviation duties, followed later the same year by *Shawmut*. Modifications included removing mine rails

Seaplane tender *Aroostook* seen in mid–1920s with one PN-type flying boat on deck aft and another in the water visible beyond the no. 2 funnel. The ship was decommissioned in 1931.

to create deck space, fitting aircraft hoisting booms, and adding new facilities for aircraft repair and servicing. Apparently because they retained much of their original minelaying equipment, the two ships received mine-carrier designations, CM-3 and -4, respectively, and in 1928, *Shawmut* was re-named *Oglala* to avoid confusion with another Navy ship.

Aroostook played a major role in the transatlantic flight of the Curtiss NC boats (see page 141) during the spring of 1919, initially taking station in Trepassy Bay, Newfoundland as a base, and later met the NC-4 in England where the aircraft was dismantled, taken onboard, and ultimately returned to the U.S. Throughout the 1920s, *Aroostook* and *Shawmut* (*Oglala*) principally supported seaplane operations on the West Coast but occasionally took part in Caribbean fleet maneuvers. Both were decommissioned in 1931.

Lapwing Class AVP-1 through -9—1919

TECHNICAL SPECIFICATIONS

Type: Minesweeper refitted as small seaplane tender.
Builder: Various U.S. shipyards; lead ship built by Todd Shipyard, Brooklyn, New York.
Total built: 9 (USN)
Machinery: One 1,400-shp vertical triple expansion steam engine and a geared, single-shaft drive.
Displacement: 1,350 tons standard (as modified).
Dimensions: Length 187 ft. 10 in. overall; beam 35 ft. 6 in.; draft 13 ft. 1 in. (loaded)
Defensive armament: Two 3-in./50-cal. dual-purpose guns in open mounts.

Performance: Top speed 13.5 knots; range (not reported).
Aircraft: One floatplane embarked.
Crew complement: 78

Over a 16-year interval following World War I, the Navy assigned nine *Lapwing* class minesweepers for use as small seaplane tenders. Ordered in 1917 as the first type of naval ship dedicated to minesweeping, the 49 *Lapwings* completed between 1918 and 1920 had been designed around an ocean-going tug hull and came with booms for towing and hoisting. One of the last examples built, USS *Sandpiper* AM-51 (later AVP-9), was the first actually assigned to the aviation branch when it was directly commissioned as a seaplane support ship in October 1919. Eight more of the class followed: *Pelican* AM-27 (later AVP-6) in 1922; *Heron* AM-10 (later AVP-2) in 1924; *Avocet* AM-19 (later AVP-4); *Teal* AM-23 (later AVP-5), *Swan* AM-34 (later AVP-7), and *Gannet* AM-41 (later AVP-8), all in 1931; *Lapwing* AM-1 (later AVP-1) in 1932; and finally, *Thrush* AM-18 (AVP-2) in 1935. Conversion typically involved removing the minesweeping equipment to clear the aft deck for seaplane servicing. Existing booms were used for handling aircraft. The ships were initially classified as "minesweeper for duty with aircraft" but re-designated "small seaplane tender" (AVP) in early 1936 in original hull number order. From 1936 to 1941, USS *Owl* AM-2 was assigned to aviation duties on the East Coast but never reclassified as an AVP.

Throughout the 1920s and 1930s, the *Lapwings* served with seaplane and patrol units based on both coasts, including Hawaii and the Panama Canal Zone, and frequently worked in conjunction with the larger seaplane tenders. During World War II, as more of the new *Barnegat* class AVPs (see below)

The *Gannet* AM-41 (later AVP-8) depicted in 1927 with aviation insignia on bow. *Gannet* and the other *Lapwings* comprised most of the Navy's small seaplane tender fleet up to World War II.

came into service, many of the *Lapwings* were relegated to other duties such as towing, salvage, transport, and training. All were decommissioned and either sold or scrapped after 1945.

Harding DD-91—1920

TECHNICAL SPECIFICATIONS

Type: Destroyer modified as a seaplane tender.
Builder: Union Iron Works, San Francisco, California.
Total built: 1 (USN)
Machinery: 27,000-shp steam turbines with four boilers and a geared, two-shaft drive.
Displacement: 1,060 tons standard.
Dimensions: Length 314 ft. 5 in. overall; beam 31 ft. 8 in., draft 8 ft. 6 in. (loaded)
Defensive armament: Four 4-in./50-cal. guns in open mounts and four triple 21-in. torpedo tubes.
Performance: Top speed 35 knots; range (not reported).
Aircraft: None embarked.
Crew complement: 100

Harding began life as one of 111 *Wickes* class destroyers ordered in 1917. Shortly after being commissioned in early 1919, it served as a guide ship for the transatlantic flights of the Curtiss NC boats (see page 141), then following a permanent assignment to seaplane operations, underwent a brief refit at the Philadelphia Navy Yard. Conversions details are unknown but possibly included removal of torpedo tubes and associated equipment. From mid–1920 until mid–1921, *Harding* served in conjunction with the seaplane training program at NAS Pensacola and was detached during the summer of 1921 to observe the sinking of the ex–German battleship *Ostfriesland* and other

obsolete warships by Brig Gen. Billy Mitchell's First Air Brigade. The ship was decommissioned in mid–1922.

Wright AV-1 (AZ-1)—1921

TECHNICAL SPECIFICATIONS

Type: Auxiliary vessel completed as airship and balloon tender, then became a seaplane tender.
Builder: American International Shipbuilding Corp., Hog Island, Pennsylvania.
Total built: 1 (USN)
Machinery: One 6,000-shp GE steam turbine with six boilers and a geared, single-shaft drive.
Displacement: 11,500 tons standard.
Dimensions: Length 448 ft. overall; beam 58 ft.; draft 23 ft. (loaded)
Defensive armament: Two 5-in./51-cal. and two 3-in/50-cal. guns in open mounts and two flexible .30-cal. machine guns.
Performance: Top speed 15 knots; range (not reported).
Aircraft: Large enough to embark an F-5L or NC-type flying boat.
Crew complement: 228

Originally laid down in early 1919 as a fleet auxiliary, the ship was subsequently finished out as an airship and balloon tender under the hull designation AZ-1 and commissioned USS *Wright* on December 16, 1921. While *Wright* did subsequently conduct some trials with kite balloons, most of its early service related to seaplane operations. Following an extensive refit at the Norfolk Navy Yard in 1925, in which all balloon and airship handling equipment was removed and replaced by aircraft hoisting booms and repair facilities, the ship, re-designated AV-1, became the first Navy vessel actually classified as a seaplane tender. From 1925 onwards, *Wright* remained on the East Coast as the flagship for the Air Squadron Scouting Fleet, providing

The *Wright*, seen here at Guantanamo Bay, Cuba, in 1927 while serving as the flagship for Air Scouting Fleet, was the first Navy ship to be designated as a seaplane tender (AV).

tender service to seaplanes operating out of Norfolk, Key West, the Caribbean, and the Panama Canal Zone. The ship moved to NAS North Island in San Diego in early 1932 and from there, supported seaplane operations all over the eastern Pacific from Alaska to Hawaii.

After a major overhaul at Mare Island Shipyard during 1936, *Wright* became the flagship for Patrol Wing 1, then in late 1939, transferred its flag to Patrol Wing 2 and moved to Pearl Harbor, where it assisted efforts to establish aviation bases on Midway, Canton, Johnston, and Wake Islands. When the Japanese attacked Pearl Harbor on December 7, 1941, *Wright* was returning to Hawaii after having delivered personnel and supplies to the bases at Wake and Midway Islands. In the weeks right after the attack, the ship was used to transport Marines and equipment to Midway and bring civilians back to Pearl Harbor. From early 1942 until late 1944, *Wright* saw wide service in the South Pacific, where it acted in the dual roles of seaplane tender to patrol units and transport for Marine aviation personnel and supplies to various island bases. In October 1944 the ship was re-designated AG-79 as a headquarters ship, afterward operating out of New Guinea, Australia, and the Philippines until the war's end. *Wright* was decommissioned in 1946 and sold for scrap in 1948.

Patoka AO-9 (AV-6)—1924

TECHNICAL SPECIFICATIONS

Type: Fleet oiler refitted as airship tender.
Builder: Newport News Shipbuilding and Dry Dock Co., Newport News, Virginia.
Total built: 1 (USN)
Machinery: Two 2,600-shp vertical triple expansion steam engines and a geared, two-shaft drive.

Displacement: 16,800 tons standard.
Dimensions: Length 417 ft. 10 in. overall; beam 60 ft.; draft 26 ft. 2 in. (loaded)
Defensive armament: Two 5-in./51-cal. guns in open mounts.
Performance: Top speed 11 knots; range (not reported).
Aircraft: One airship moored aft.
Crew complement: 168

Though retaining a fleet oiler designation, *Patoka* became the most important support vessel in the Navy's rigid airship program. The ship was commissioned in October 1919 and spent several years as an oiler before entering the Norfolk Navy Shipyard in early 1924 to be fitted with a large (141 ft. above the waterline) mooring mast on its aft end together with repair and storage facilities for airship operations. From mid–1924 to early 1933, *Patoka* served off the Atlantic seaboard and in the Gulf of Mexico and Caribbean in support of all rigid airship operations at sea. It completed the first mooring trials with the airship *Shenandoah* in mid–1924 and after that airship's loss, became a base ship for *Los Angeles* (1925–1932) and ultimately, *Akron* (1932–1933). Following the loss of *Akron* in April 1933, the ship was removed from active service and placed in reserve later the same year.

Patoka was re-commissioned as AV-6 in November 1939 and assigned to Patrol Wing 5 at San Diego, but after less than a year of service, was reassigned to the Naval Transportation Service at Norfolk and reverted to the designation AO-9. Through most of World War II, the ship operated out of Norfolk as a tanker and cargo carrier between ports in the Caribbean and South America. It was decommissioned for the last time in 1946 and sold for scrap in 1948.

The *Patoka* shown in 1924 with ZR-1 *Shenandoah* moored aft. It served as a base ship for all of the Navy's large rigid airships from 1924 until 1933.

Jason AV-2—1930

TECHNICAL SPECIFICATIONS

Type: Coal collier refitted as airship tender.
Builder: Maryland Steel Co., Sparrows Point, Maryland
Total built: 1 (USN)
Machinery: Vertical triple expansion steam engine (shp unknown) and a single-shaft drive.
Displacement: 19,250 tons standard.
Dimensions: Length 536 ft. overall; beam 65 ft.; draft 27 ft. 8 in. (loaded)
Defensive armament: Four 4-in./50-cal. guns in open mounts.
Performance: Top speed 14 knots; range (not reported).
Aircraft: Up to 8 floatplanes embarked.
Crew complement: 82

1930, presumably to reflect that it was no longer classified a coal collier. After being detached from the Asiatic Fleet in mid–1932, the ship returned to the West Coast and was decommissioned at the Navy Yard in Bremerton, Washington later the same year. It was stricken and sold in 1936.

Langley AV-3—1937 see Langley CV-1 under AIRCRAFT CARRIERS

Childs Class AVD-1 through -14—1939

TECHNICAL SPECIFICATIONS

Type: Destroyer refitted as small seaplane tender.
Builder: Various U.S. shipyards: lead ship built by New York Shipbuilding Corp., Camden, New Jersey.
Total built: 14 (USN)
Machinery: Two 13,325-shp steam turbines with four boilers and a geared, two-shaft drive.
Displacement: 1,215 tons standard.
Dimensions: Length 314 ft. 4 in. overall; beam 31 ft. 8 in.; draft 9 ft. 10 in. (loaded)
Defensive armament: Two 4-in./50-cal. guns in open mounts fore and aft and four .50-cal. machine guns amidships (later replaced by eight 20-mm AA guns).
Performance: Top speed 25 knots; range 5,600 mi.
Aircraft: None embarked.
Crew complement: 137

The *Jason* AV-2 seen coaling at Pearl Harbor in early 1932. Note the float-equipped Martin T4Ms carried amidships between the coal derricks. The ship was detached from aviation service later the same year.

USS *Jason* AC-12 served as a fleet coal collier from 1913 until 1925, when it was transferred to aviation duties with the Asiatic Fleet based at Cavite in the Philippine Islands. The ship was not extensively modified, its deck space and holds being used primarily to transport aircraft, personnel, and aviation supplies to various locations in the Far East. *Jason* was re-designated AV-2 in early

In order to keep pace with its rapidly expanding force of patrol aircraft (i.e., 209 Consolidated PBYs procured between 1936 and 1938), the

The *Childs*, name ship of the class, is seen after wartime refit with revised bridge and antiaircraft gun mounts forward of funnels. Forward boilers had been removed to accommodate storage tanks for aviation fuel.

Navy initiated an emergency program during 1938 to convert a number of older World War I–era *Clemson* class four-stack destroyers into small seaplane tenders, commencing in mid–1938 with the USS *Childs* at the Philadelphia Navy Yard. Conversion entailed removing the two forward boilers and stacks and using the added space to extend the bridge superstructure as quarters for aviation personnel, storage tanks for aviation fuel, and space for aircraft spare parts. All torpedo tubes and the two amidships 4-in./50-cal. guns were removed and four .50-cal. machine guns added in their place. (Note, during World War II, 20-mm AA gun mounts were retrofitted and some of these ships replaced their 4-in. guns with 3-in. dual-purpose types.)

Initially, the converted ships were classified as AVPs, but this changed to AVD (aviation tender, destroyer) in late 1940, indicating their dual status as escorts. In all, 14 destroyers had been converted by the end of 1940: *Childs* AVD-1 (ex–DD-241, ex–AVP-14), *Williamson* AVD-2 (ex–DD-244, ex–AVP-15), *George E. Badger* AVD-3 (ex–DD-196, ex–AVP-16), *Clemson* AVD-4 (ex–DD-186, ex–AVP-17), *Goldsborough* AVD-5 (ex–DD-188, ex–AVP-18), *Hulbert* AVD-6 (ex–DD-342, ex–AVP-19), *William B. Preston* AVD-7 (ex–DD-344, ex–AVP-20), *Belknap* AVD-8 (ex–DD-251), *Osmond Ingram* AVD-9 (ex–DD-255), *Ballard* AVD-10 (ex–DD-267), *Thornton* AVD-11 (ex–DD-270), *Gillis* AVD-12 (ex–DD-260), *Greene* AVD-13 (ex–DD-266), and *McFarland* AVD-14 (ex–DD-237). From 1941 through the middle of World War II, most AVDs were deployed in the Pacific Theater, establishing and supporting advance aviation bases as needed. But as more of the newer *Barnegat* class tenders began reaching service during 1942 and 1943, many of the AVDs were relegated to other duties such as convoy escort, ASW patrol, and plane guard and support for escort carriers. Some were converted as high-speed transports (APD) to be used in amphibious operations. Virtually all were decommissioned and sold for scrap after 1945.

Curtiss Class AV-4 and -5—1940

TECHNICAL SPECIFICATIONS

Type: Heavy seaplane tender.
Builder: New York Shipbuilding Corp., Camden, New Jersey.
Total built: 2 (USN)
Machinery: Two 6,000-shp steam turbines with four boilers and a geared, two-shaft drive.
Displacement: 8,671 tons standard.
Dimensions: Length 527 ft. 4 in. overall; beam 69 ft. 3 in.; draft 21ft. 11 in. (loaded)
Defensive armament: Four 5-in./38-cal. dual-purpose guns in turrets and 20-mm AA guns in four quadruple mounts.
Performance: Top speed 20 knots; range 12,000 mi. (est.).
Aircraft: Several flying boats embarked on rear working deck.
Crew complement: 1,195.

The *Curtiss* class is noteworthy in having been the first type of Navy vessel to be built from the keel up as a seaplane tender. Both ships of the class, AV-4 and -5, were laid down in mid–1939 and launched in mid–1940. They had been conceived to function as base ships for long-range patrol seaplanes oper-

ating in forward areas, with onboard facilities to provide maintenance, repair, and logistical support for the aircraft, as well as command and control over the aviation personnel attached to them. The general design emphasized good open-ocean seakeeping, featuring a high-freeboard forward and a low superstructure, with the aft one-third of the deck being left clear as a large seaplane working platform. The superstructure area abutting the platform housed extensive shops that performed aircraft maintenance and repair. AV-4 was commissioned USS *Curtiss* on April 20, 1940, followed by AV-5 USS *Albemarle* on December 20.

Curtiss operated out of NOB Norfolk until the spring of 1941, completing a fit out and shakedown that included installation of CXAM-1, then sailed to Pearl Harbor for permanent duty assignment. During the Japanese attack on December 7, the ship sustained damage from an enemy aircraft crashing into it and a bomb hit that necessitated repairs at San Diego, after which it operated out of Pearl Harbor until mid–1942, when it took station in the Solomon Islands. From mid–1943 to early 1945, *Curtiss* was used to support the invasion campaigns at Tarawa, Kwajalein, Eniwetok, Saipan, and Guam, then in May 1945, after an overhaul, served as a command ship at Okinawa where it sustained damage from a Kamikaze. Following repairs and refit, the ship remained in service during the post-war era, supporting seaplane operations until being decommissioned in September 1957. *Albemarle,* also fitted with radar, was assigned to the Atlantic after commissioning and based at NOB Norfolk at the time hostilities commenced. During World War II the ship provided tender services to seaplane operations across the length and breath of the Atlantic, including deployments from Iceland, the British Isles, Cuba, the Panama Canal Zone, and Brazil. After 1945, it continued in post-war service as a seaplane tender until being decommissioned in October 1960.

Barnegat Class AVP-10, -11, -12, -20 and -21—1941

TECHNICAL SPECIFICATIONS

Type: Small seaplane tender.
Builder: Various U.S. shipyards; lead ship built by Puget Sound Navy Yard, Bremerton, Washington.
Total built: 5 by the end of 1941; 30 from 1942 to 1945 (USN)
Machinery: Two 3,000-shp diesel-electric engines and a two-shaft drive.
Displacement: 2,411 tons standard.
Dimensions: Length 311 ft. 8 in. overall; beam 41 ft. 1 in.; draft 13 ft. 6 in. (loaded)
Defensive armament: Two 5-in./38-cal. dual-purpose guns in turrets and four 50-cal. machine guns (40-mm and 20-mm AA guns added later).
Performance: Top speed 18.5 knots; range 6,900 mi.
Aircraft: 1 floatplane embarked.
Crew complement: 367.

Planned in the late 1930s as a successor to the *Lapwings,* the AVP-10 Class appeared as the Navy's first purpose-built small seaplane tender. In addition to possessing better repair, supply, and handling facilities for aircraft, these shallow-draft ships were designed to operate from the small bays and inlets of forward combat areas and also be able to use their armament, speed, and maneuverability in the role of escorts for larger tenders and other auxiliaries. The first two ships completed, USS *Barnegat* AV-10 and USS *Biscayne* AVP-11, were both laid down in late 1939 and commissioned the same day, on July 3, 1941. Following them into service before the end of 1941 were *Humbolt* AVP-21 (October 7), *Matagorda* AVP-22 (December 16), and *Casco* AVP-12 (December 27). Hull numbers 14 through 20 were skipped when they were temporarily allocated to the *Childs* class in 1940.

Thirty more *Barnegat* class tenders were placed in commission between 1942 and 1946, with six examples in various stages of construction being cancelled prior to acceptance. They saw extensive service in every theater of combat during World War II, a majority in the Pacific. Four were subsequently completed as PT Boat tenders (AGP) prior to commissioning and one as a catapult training ship. Only six of the *Barnegat* class were retained in post-war service as seaplane tenders, though several more were reactivated during the Korean conflict, the very last example being retired in 1966. In 1948 and 1949, 14 mothballed *Barnegats* were transferred to the Coast Guard where some served until the early 1970s. Two, following conversions, became Navy oceanographic survey ships (AGS) and remained active until the late 1960s.

Ironically, four Coast guard ships transferred to the Republic of Vietnam Navy in 1971 were seized by the North Vietnamese in 1975.

Tangier Class AV-8 and -9—1941

TECHNICAL SPECIFICATIONS

Type: Heavy seaplane tender.
Builder: Various U.S. shipyards; lead ship built by Moore Drydock Co., Oakland, California.
Total built: 2 by the end 1941; 5 from 1942 to 1945 (USN)
Machinery: One 8,500-shp steam turbine with two boilers and a geared, single-shaft drive.
Displacement: 11,760 tons standard.
Dimensions: Length 492 ft. 1 in. overall; beam 69 ft. 6 in.; draft 23 ft. 9 in. (loaded)
Defensive armament: One 5-in./38-cal. and three 3-in./50-cal. dual-purpose guns in open mounts and eight 40-mm AA guns.
Performance: Top speed 18.5 knots; range (not reported).
Aircraft: One flying boat and several floatplanes embarked on rear working deck.
Crew complement: 1,075.

By the middle of 1940 it had become clear that the addition of two *Curtiss* class heavy seaplane tenders to the fleet later in the year would not be adequate to support the growing numbers of new patrol aircraft (i.e., PBYs, PB2Ys, and PBMs) expected to enter service from 1942 onwards. As a stopgap measure, the Navy acquired two incomplete C3-type merchant vessels in mid–1940 with plans to convert them into a heavy tender configuration. Changes to the basic merchant layout included provision for a large seaplane working deck aft of the bridge superstructure and a large hoisting crane at the stern. Cargo holds would be remade into personnel quarters, storage areas for fuel, lubricants, and spares, and repair facilities for aircraft. The name ship of the class, USS *Tangier* AV-8, was actually the second to be commissioned on August 25, 1941, having been preceded by USS *Pocomoke* AV-9 on July 18. A third example

The *Tangier*, commissioned in August 1941, as seen in San Francisco Bay in September 1942. Its C3 merchant vessel origins are evident from this photograph. Seven of the class were in service by the end of 1945.

of the class (later became USS *Chandeleur* AV-10) was acquired in mid–1941 but not completed until late 1942. After the U.S. entered World War II, seven more C3 conversions were ordered, four of which reached service in 1944 (i.e., AV-14 through AV-17), the other three being cancelled prior to completion.

Tangier, assigned to Patrol Wing 2 at Pearl Harbor after completing sea trials, was present at the time of the Japanese attack on December 7 and participated in the rescue of survivors from the capsized ex-battleship *Utah*. It remained in the Pacific for the duration of the war, taking part in the Battle of the Coral Sea in May 1942 and thereafter providing tender services in the Solomon campaign, the invasion of the Philippines, and later still, the occupation of Japan. The ship was decommissioned and placed in reserve in 1947 and finally sold for scrap in 1961. Sistership *Pocomoke* was initially attached to Patrol Wing 7 out of NOB Norfolk but transferred to the Pacific Theater in late 1942. The ship was used mainly to transport military personnel, supplies, and ammunition to various combat commands and saw only intermittent service as a seaplane tender. It was decommissioned in 1946 and sold for scrap in 1961.

Note on AV-7 Class Heavy Seaplane Tenders. Hull number AV-7 had been reserved for an improved *Curtiss* class vessel which was not laid down until late 1942, ultimately entering service in June 1944 as the USS *Currituk*, and three more ships of this class reached service before the end of 1945: *Norton Sound* AV-11, *Pine Island* AV-12, and *Salisbury Sound* AV-13.

SEAPLANE-EQUIPPED WARSHIPS

Battleships

The Battle Fleet after World War I. Following the disarmament of Germany, the U.S. Navy possessed the world's second largest fleet of battleships (Great Britain was first), numbering fifteen "pre-dreadnought" types (BB-12 through -22 and -25 through -29), six "dreadnaught" types (BB-30 through -35), and six "super dreadnaught" types (BB-36 through -41), with a further thirteen super dreadnaughts still under construction. Under the restrictions imposed by the Washington Navy Treaty of 1922, all of the Navy's pre-dreadnaughts were soon decommissioned and scrapped and seven of the eight incomplete super dreadnaughts (BB-47, and BB-49 through -54) were cancelled before they could be commissioned. Then in 1931, to conform with the requirements set forth in the newer London Naval Treaty of 1930, the fleet was downsized by three dreadnaughts, *Florida* (BB-30) being decommissioned and scrapped and *Utah* (BB-31) and *Wyoming* (BB-32) both demilitarized and turned into gunnery training ships AG-16 and -17, respectively. No new battleship construction was authorized until 1937, following adoption of the Second London Naval Treaty in 1936, which placed limits on displacement and gun size but not numbers. The first two examples, both ordered in mid–1937, entered service with the fleet during 1941 as *North Carolina* (BB-55) and *Washington* (BB-56). The Navy placed orders for eight more new battleships between 1938 and 1940 (BB-57 through -64), but none would reach service before the end of 1941.

As a consequence of the Japanese attack on Pearl Harbor on December 7, 1941, the centerpiece of fleet tactical doctrine, the battle line, ceased to exist as an effective fighting force. Of the eight battleships present, *Oklahoma* (BB-37) and *Arizona* (BB-39) were total losses; *California* (BB-44) and *West Virginia* (B-48), both sunk, did not rejoin the fleet until mid–1944; *Nevada* (BB-36), heavily damaged and grounded, returned to service in late 1942; *Pennsylvania* (BB-38), damaged in drydock, resumed operations in mid–1942; and *Maryland* (BB-46) and *Tennessee* (BB-42), both escaping with slight damage, returned to service during early 1942.

Catapult Development. Although several types of cata-

Super-dreadnought *Pennsylvania* (BB-38) seen in the mid–1920s carrying two UO-1s on Type-A stern catapult, before the Type-P catapult was fitted to the no. 3 main turret.

The *New Mexico* (BB-40) seen in the late 1930s with one O3U-3 on the turret catapult and second on the stern catapult. The ship was still en route to the West Coast when the Japanese attacked Pearl Harbor.

pults had been tried aboard Navy warships prior to World War I, the first truly practical turntable catapult, the Type A Mark I, powered by compressed air, did not appear until 1920. Successful shipboard launch tests using a Vought VE-7H (see page 104) were carried out in 1922 with a single Type A fitted to the USS *Maryland,* and similar catapult installations followed on *Nevada, Oklahoma, Pennsylvania, Arizona, New Mexico* (BB-40), *Mississippi* (BB-41), *Idaho* (BB-42), *Tennessee, California, Colorado* (BB-45), and *West Virginia*. All of the ships mentioned featured a four-turret super-dreadnaught main armament layout which permitted a catapult and hoisting crane to be sited aft of the number four turret near the stern. The Type P Mark III catapult, driven by an 8-inch powder charge that could propel a 6,000-lb. floatplane to 60 mph within 60 feet, was introduced in 1923 as a fixed mounting on top of a battleship's main turret, the first installation being tested aboard *Mississippi*

in 1924. Type Ps were thereafter fitted as a second catapult aboard all eleven super dreadnaughts and became the single catapult on older dreadnaughts such as *Florida, Utah, Wyoming, Arkansas* (BB-33), *New York* (BB-34), and *Texas* (BB-35). Starting in the late 1920s, the Type P Mark VI (or P-6) lightweight, powder-charged turntable catapult, capable of launching 6,350-lb. aircraft to a flying speed of 64 mph, began superceding Type As and became standard on all battleships. When battleship construction resumed in 1937, all of the new ships (BB-55 and up) appeared with two Type P-6 catapults installed aft near the stern and none mounted to turrets.

Aircraft Utilization. Aircraft became integral to fleet battleship tactics during the 1920s. Navy experiments conducted in early 1919 with aircraft functioning as spotters for the big guns demonstrated a 200 percent average increase in accuracy for hits on targets beyond 18,000 yards. As an interim measure

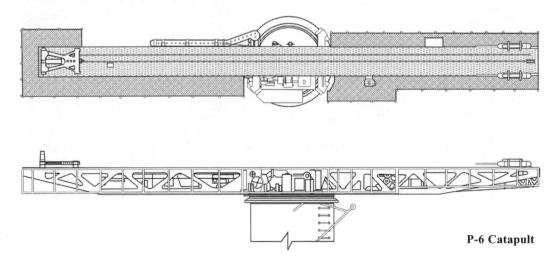

P-6 Catapult

War surplus Nieuport 28 on platform atop *Arizona*'s (BB-39) no. 3 turret. After launching from the platform, aircraft would land in the water and inflate flotation bags. Sopwith 1½ Strutter is being hoisted aboard Oklahoma (BB-37) in 1920 or 1921. Strutters were the first "turret fighters" equipped with radios.

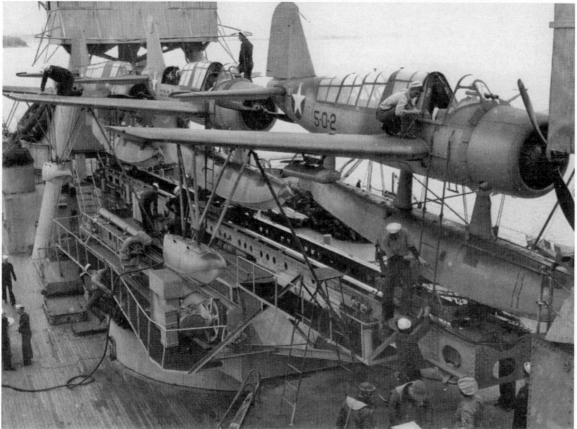

Floatplanes, like this O2U-1 seen on the *Tennessee*'s (BB-43) aft catapult in the late 1920s, became an essential ingredient of battleship combat operations after World War I. The lineup of OS2Us on *New York's* (BB-34) catapult in 1942. The tactical role of floatplanes as gun spotters diminished after fast carrier task forces assumed primacy over the traditional battle line.

from 1919 to 1922, most battleships received a complement of several war-surplus landplane fighters (e.g., Sopwith Camels, R.A.F. S.E.5as, Hanriot Scouts, Sopwith 1½ Strutters, and Nieuport 28s), which were launched from wooden "flying-off" platforms built onto the turrets and recovered in the water via flotation bags. Then, starting in 1922, concurrent with catapult development, NAF-built Vought VE-7Hs, stressed for catapulting, became the first standard floatplane type to be deployed aboard battleships. After efforts during 1923 and 1924 to develop a larger type of armed floatplane for battleship operations met with little success, (see Martin MO and Naval Aircraft Factory NO/Martin M2O on pages 109–111), the Vought UO (see page 108), which was essentially an improved VE-7H, became the next type of aircraft to be adopted for standard shipboard use. The idea of basing fighters aboard battleships to protect the fleet against potential air attack was implemented between 1925 and 1927 when float-equipped variants of the Curtiss TS (see page 61) and Vought FU (see page 108) were assigned to several battleships, but the scheme was dropped in favor of carrier-borne fighters after *Lexington* and *Saratoga* became fully operational within the fleet after 1928.

During 1927 and 1928, Vought O2Us, the Navy's first real purpose-built ship-based floatplane (see page 115), displaced UOs aboard most battleships, and within a similar timeframe, some ships increased their seaplane complement to include one Loening OL amphibian (see page 112) that could serve either as a spotter or a ship-to-shore utility transport. Further improvements upon the basic design of the O2U resulted in the introduction of the Vought O3U (see page 116) in 1931 as the fleet's standard battleship floatplane. As new hangar-equipped heavy cruisers entered service during the early 1930s, BuAer began the trend of issuing distinct requirements between floatplanes, those intended for cruiser duty being classified as scout-

observation (SO) and those for battleships as observation-scout (OS). With the aim of replacing O3Us and procuring additional floatplanes for the new battleships planned (i.e., BB-55 and -56), BuAer issued a new OS requirement in 1936, however, official trials between competing prototypes (see Vought OS2U, Naval Aircraft Factory OSN, and Stearman OSS, pages 132–134) became protracted to the extent that folding-wing Curtiss SOCs (see page 129) were assigned to all battleships from 1938 until they were replaced by Vought OS2Us in 1940 and 1941. OS2Us went on to equip all new battleships commissioned between 1942 and 1944 (i.e., BB-57 through -64), many serving right up through the end of the war in 1945.

Unit Organization. Initially, aircraft assigned to battleships were simply classified as "Ship Air Units, Battle Fleet," but starting in 1926, were reorganized into squadrons under the designator VO (heavier-than-air observation), with at least one squadron of twelve to thirteen floatplanes apiece being allocated to each of the four battleship divisions existing at that time. The suffix "B" following the squadron number (e.g., VO-1B) indicated assignment to the Battle Fleet and "S" to the Scouting Fleet (e.g., VO-5S). The VO squadron numbers between battleship divisions were not sequential inasmuch as they were interspersed with squadrons assigned to cruiser divisions and shore bases. During the late 1920s the fleet began differentiating between battleship and cruiser units, the former retaining the VO designator and the latter becoming VS and later still, VCS.

Cruisers

Cruiser Procurement after World War I. At the time of the Armistice, the U.S. Navy's active cruiser inventory included nine outdated ships classified as armored cruisers (ACR, later CA), all completed in the 1890s, and thirteen equally obsolete

The *Pensacola* (CA-24), the first Treaty Cruiser commissioned in 1929, is seen in the early 1930s with an O3U-1 sited on its port catapult. Floatplane scouts allowed cruisers to remain near the main body of the fleet.

This late 1930s photograph depicts two SOC-1 embarked aboard the catapults of light cruiser *Omaha* (CL-4). The *Omaha* class began carrying floatplanes in mid–1920s before being fitted with catapults.

protected and peace cruisers (C, later CL) that had been placed in commission between 1895 and 1905. Wartime experience had largely reshaped the role of cruisers from one of distant operations (e.g., solitary scouting and commerce raiding) to active defense of the fleet against surface and air attack. New ships had been ordered during 1917 and 1918, ten high-speed scout cruisers (CS-4 through -13), but were still in the early stages of construction. With the adoption of the Washington Naval Treaty of 1922, and the consequent limits placed on battleship tonnage, the protective function of cruisers became more vital. And perhaps most significant, the Treaty itself defined "cruisers" as ships limited to a maximum displacement of 10,000 tons standard, mounting guns no greater than 8 inches. The London Naval Treaty of 1930 took the definition a step further by classifying cruisers with 8-inch guns as "heavy" and those with 6.1-inch or less as "light," with the United States being allowed the tonnage to build 18 heavy cruisers (CA) and approximately 15 light cruisers (CL).

Treaty provisions, combined with the general need to modernize the fleet, resulted in an across-the-board replacement of the Navy's entire cruiser force during the period between the world wars. All nine of the old armored cruisers were either decommissioned or converted to non-combat duties; six of the smaller peace cruisers were retained in the post-war fleet as light cruisers (CL-16 through -21) but all had been stricken from active service by end of 1931. The ten *Omaha* class scout cruisers under construction, re-designated as light cruisers (CL-4 through -13), all entered service in 1923 and 1924. Con-

struction of what were termed "Treaty Cruisers" commenced in 1926 and continued through 1939. Eighteen ships in five classes reached commission as heavy cruisers: two *Pensacola* class in 1929 and 1930 (originally CL-24 and CL-25, changed to CA-24 and -25 in 1931); six *Northampton* class in 1930 and 1931 (CA-26 through -31); two *Portland* class in 1932 and 1933 (CA-33 and -35); seven *New Orleans* class between 1934 and 1937 (CA-32, -34, -36 through -39, and -44); and one *Wichita* class in 1939 (CA-45). These were augmented by nine additional ships, built in two classes, placed in service as light cruisers: seven *Brooklyn* class in 1937 and 1938 (CL-40 through -48); and two *St. Louis* class in 1939 (CL-49 and -50). The USS *Atlanta* (CL-51), commissioned in late 1941, was the first of a series of eleven light cruisers specialized for antiaircraft which had been designed with no provision for seaplanes. Three light cruisers, *Raleigh* (CL-7), *Honolulu* (CL-48), and *Helena* (CL-50), sustained varying degrees of bomb damage at Pearl Harbor during the Japanese attack on December 7, 1941, but all were repaired and returned to service by mid–1942.

Catapult and Hangar Development. Cruisers began carrying floatplanes as early as 1924, but installation of catapults on the ten *Omaha* class light cruisers did not commence until 1927, when *Memphis* (CL-13) received two Type A Mark III turntable catapults mounted to the main deck aft of the funnels. Type P-6 lightweight, powder-charged turntable catapults, initially fitted to the *Pensacola* class heavy cruisers during construction, became the standard type for all cruisers that followed it, and from 1932, P-6s were also retrofitted to the *Omahas*. On

By the late 1920s, floatplanes had been fully integrated into cruiser operations. This O2U-1 was being lowered onto one of the catapults aboard the *Cincinnati* (CL-6) in 1928 or 1929.

the *Pensacola, Portland*, and *Northampton* classes, the catapults were mounted on tall pylons between the funnels to permit launching of aircraft in heavy seas, and a similar configuration appeared on the *New Orleans* class aft of both funnels. Starting with the *Brooklyn* class light cruisers and the heavy cruiser *Wichita*, the catapults were sited aft near the stern. The *Northamptons* were the first cruiser class to feature a pair of seaplane hangars incorporated into the superstructure surrounding the number two funnel. To fit within it, the wings of the aircraft needed to fold to a width of no more than 14 feet 6 inches. The *Brooklyn* class and the *Wichita* relocated the hangar all the way aft as a single hold between the two catapults into which the aircraft could be lowered by a stern-mounted crane, and an identical arrangement appeared on all *Baltimore* class heavy cruisers (15 ships) and *Cleveland* class light cruisers (30 ships) commissioned during World War II.

Aircraft Utilization. As much as with battleships, aircraft became a built-in component of cruiser operations during the 1920s. In their scouting and screening role, use of floatplanes equipped with radios permitted cruisers to canvass huge areas of ocean without distancing themselves from the fleet.

Vought UOs, the same type of floatplane used on battleships, were first assigned to the *Omaha* class light cruisers in 1924 before catapults had been fitted, then in 1927, as these ships received Type A catapults, the UOs were succeeded in service by the newer Vought O2Us. A new requirement issued by BuAer in 1929 for a "light observation floatplane" resulted in the delivery 39 Berliner-Joyce OJ-2s in 1933 for service aboard the *Omahas*. Meanwhile, as the new *Pensacola* and *Northampton* class heavy cruisers began entering service between 1929 and 1931, they were all assigned Vought O2Us or O3Us, typically three aircraft per ship.

Efforts to find a folding-wing aircraft that could be accommodated in the hangars of the *Northamptons* and succeeding heavy cruiser classes began in 1931 when BuAer issued a requirement for a single-engine amphibian; however, all three of the prototypes subsequently evaluated in 1932 and 1933 (see Great Lakes SG, Loening S2L, and Sikorsky SS, pages 126–128) were deemed unsatisfactory. A new requirement issued in 1933 ended with selection of the folding-wing Curtiss SOC in 1935 (see page 129) as the fleet's standard cruiser floatplane, the type being thereafter assigned to all heavy and light cruisers in service, including those without hangars. In 1937, parallel to the effort that produced the monoplane Vought OS2U for battleships, BuAer issued a requirement for a float-equipped monoplane to replace SOC biplanes aboard cruisers. The Curtiss SO3C (see page 136) was ultimately selected for production in 1940, but none began reaching service until the spring of 1942. Ironically, operational short-comings of the SO3C subsequently caused it to be withdrawn from shipboard service, as a result of which, the older biplane SOCs remained aboard most cruisers right up through the end of World War II.

Unit Organization. In 1926, like aircraft attached to battleships, floatplanes serving aboard cruisers were organized into observation squadrons, with the aircraft and personnel of one squadron of fourteen to fifteen aircraft typically allocated between two cruiser divisions. These units switched from VO to the designator VS (heavier-than-air, scouting) in 1929, also using the suffix "B" to indicate Battle Fleet and "S" Scouting Fleet, and changed again to VCS (cruiser scouting) in 1937 to differentiate them from the expanding number of VS squadrons of the Carrier Air Groups. By 1939 the VCS force had grown to eight squadrons serving aboard 36 light and heavy cruisers.

Note on CLV/CF Flying Deck Cruiser. From the late 1920s right up to 1940, naval officials, in particular those of BuShips, studied the feasibility of a hybrid warship that would combine the frontal aspect of a six-inch gun light cruiser with a carrier-type flight deck having an island structure on the starboard side. The ships was envisaged as operating along the sea lanes as a lone hunter, similar on some respects to the commerce-raiding cruisers of the pre–World War era. BuShips developed several imaginative concepts, emerging finally with a 650-foot-long vessel of 10,000 tons displacement that combined the three-turret forward armament of a *Brooklyn* class light cruiser with a 350-foot flight deck and hangar space that housed up to 24 aircraft. Its original CLV (light cruiser-carrier) hull designation was later changed to CF to avoid confusion with the anticipated CVL (light carrier) hull classification. Although the concept

Right, top: **An SOC-1 undergoing maintenance in a seaplane hangar aboard the** *Savannah* **(CL-42), one of seven** *Brooklyn* **class light treaty cruisers entering service in 1937 and 1938.** *Right, bottom:* **Off Iceland during 1941, the** *Tuscaloosa* **(CA-37) is seen hoisting aboard an SOC-1. The seaplane hangar is visible just below the other SOC-1 resting on the starboard catapult.**

CLV-CF Flying Deck Cruiser Concept

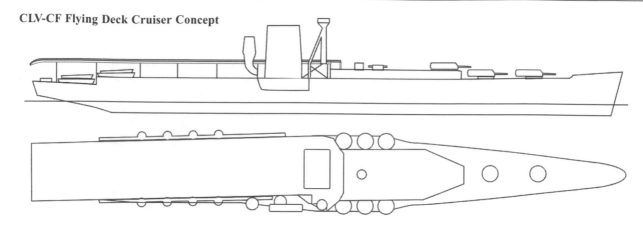

received serious consideration, it remained on hold due to budgetary restraints imposed by the Depression. The Navy Board, amid plans for a huge fleet expansion in 1940, officially cancelled the project after concluding the hybrid design possessed inherent limitations that would render it unsuitable as either a cruiser or an aircraft carrier.

Other Warships

Submarines. Influenced by earlier German and British experiments with submarine-carried aircraft, the Navy acquired two German-made Caspar U-1 submarine scouts in 1922 for evaluations at NAS Anacostia. Following trials with the U-1s, BuAer issued a specific requirement later that year for a very small (18-ft. wingspan by 18 ft. 2 in. length) twin-float biplane that could be dismantled and stowed in an eight-foot-diameter watertight tube mounted on a submarine's afterdeck. Contracts were subsequently issued in 1923 for 12 essentially identical

aircraft, six wooden-framed variants to be built by Cox-Klemin as the XS-1 plus six with metal frames by Martin as the MS-1 (see both, page 110). While the aircraft were being delivered to the Navy, the submarine S-1 (SS-105) was set aside to be fitted with the stowage tube. Operational tests with S-1 and one of the Martin MS-1s commenced in late 1923 on the Thames River near the submarine base at New London, Connecticut and continued off and on until mid–1926, at which point the program was deemed impractical because of the excessive time required (four hours) to assemble and launch the aircraft.

After four years of inactivity, BuAer opted to revive the submarine-scout project with the idea of using a small, boat-hulled monoplane that could be un-stowed and rigged for flight at a much faster rate than a biplane, and with this concept in mind, awarded Loening a development contract in 1930 to build a single prototype as the XSL-1 (see page 120). Testing of the prototype in 1931, while showing that the aircraft could be stowed and unstowed in a matter of minutes, revealed that it

An MS-1 submarine scout seen during trials with S-1 (SS-105) in the mid–1920s. The concept ultimately was deemed impractical due to the time required to assemble and disassemble the aircraft.

was seriously underpowered, and further attempts in 1933 with the re-engined XSL-2 produced only slight improvements in performance. The project was cancelled in late 1933 when the prototype was irreparably damaged during experiments with a submarine.

Destroyers. The Navy originally tested the feasibility of operating a floatplane from a destroyer during the fall of 1923 with a twin-float Curtiss TS-1 fighter carried aboard a *Clemson* class four-stack destroyer, the USS *Charles Ausburn* (DD-294). While underway, the aircraft rested in a cradle forward of the bridge superstructure, then for air operations, was lowered into and retrieved from the water with a small crane installed near the cradle. The forward stowage arrangement was found to seriously restrict visibility from the bridge, plus efforts to handle the aircraft on the narrow deck space available were hazardous at best, thus the after several months, experiments were dis-

continued. This same ship, incidentally, served as a guard ship stationed in the Atlantic for the Army's 1924 around-the-world flight attempt.

As international tensions arose in the late 1930s, the concept was revived to address increasing concerns over protecting merchant convoys from submarine or merchant raider attacks. For convoys typically operating without cruiser or carrier protection, floatplane scouts were seen as a significant means of expanding a destroyer's radius of patrol. New experiments commenced in 1940 when another four-stack destroyer, the USS *Noa* (DD-343), was reconfigured to carry a Curtiss SOC. To avoid the forward visibility problems experienced earlier, the aircraft's nesting cradle was located rearward, just forward of the after deckhouse, and a boom used to launch and recover the aircraft in the water. Although the SOC and associated aircraft equipment were removed from *Noa* after two

Tests were conducted in late 1923 with this TS-1 aboard the destroyer *Noa* (DD-294). The stowage arrangement was found to place severe restrictions on visibility from the bridge.

months of experiments, test results were sufficiently promising that the Navy ordered Type A Mark IV compressed air catapults to be installed aft of the funnels (in place of torpedo tubes) on six *Fletcher* class destroyers then under construction (DD-476 through -481), with the plan of equipping each ship with one Vought OS2U. All six went into service during 1942 and 1943 with aircraft embarked but discontinued aviation operations later in the war as greater numbers of escort carriers arrived to undertake the ASW function.

Gunboats. Though not actually designed to accommodate floatplanes, Curtiss SOCs were nonetheless assigned to gunboats USS *Erie* (PG-50) and *Charleston* (PG-51) soon after their commissioning in mid–1936. Gunboats had been conceived as a loophole in the Washington Naval Treaty allowing a patrol vessel to carry 6-inch guns as long as it did not exceed 2,000 tons displacement or a top speed of 20 knots. Their chief role was protecting U.S. interests abroad by "showing the flag" in foreign waters, with a secondary capability of convoy escort.

One aircraft could be carried in a cradle located aft of the single funnel on the port side and launched and retrieved via a hoisting boom. Both ships operated from the East Coast until late 1940, when *Charleston* was detached to the Pacific for patrol duty between Seattle and the Aleutian Islands and *Erie* stationed off Central America to guard the western approaches to the Panama Canal. In June 1942, while escorting a convoy between Guantanamo Bay, Cuba and Trinidad, *Erie* was sunk after being torpedoed by a German U-Boat. *Charleston* continued operations in Alaskan waters during the war but ceased air operations in 1943. The ship was decommissioned in 1946.

Coast Guard Cutters. Aircraft operating from the Coast Guard's larger cutters and ice breakers at various times between 1937 and 1945 included Grumman JF/J2F amphibians (see page 205) and a float-equipped Waco J2W (see page 221). Thought was given to the idea of installing catapults aboard the three *Wind* class icebreakers built between 1942 and 1944 but never carried out.

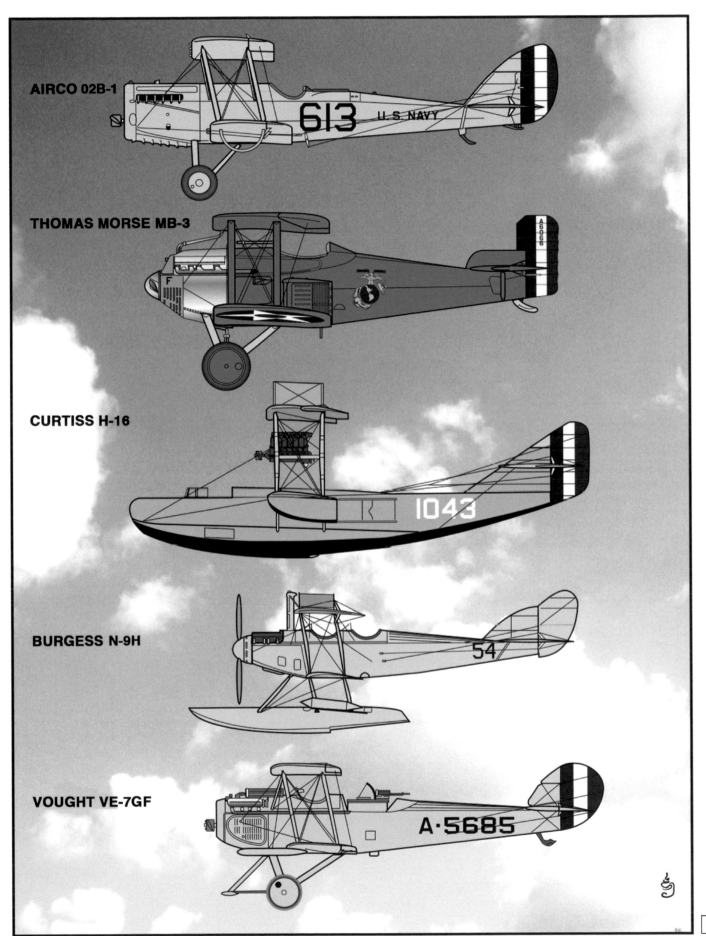

AIRCO 02B-1

THOMAS MORSE MB-3

CURTISS H-16

BURGESS N-9H

VOUGHT VE-7GF

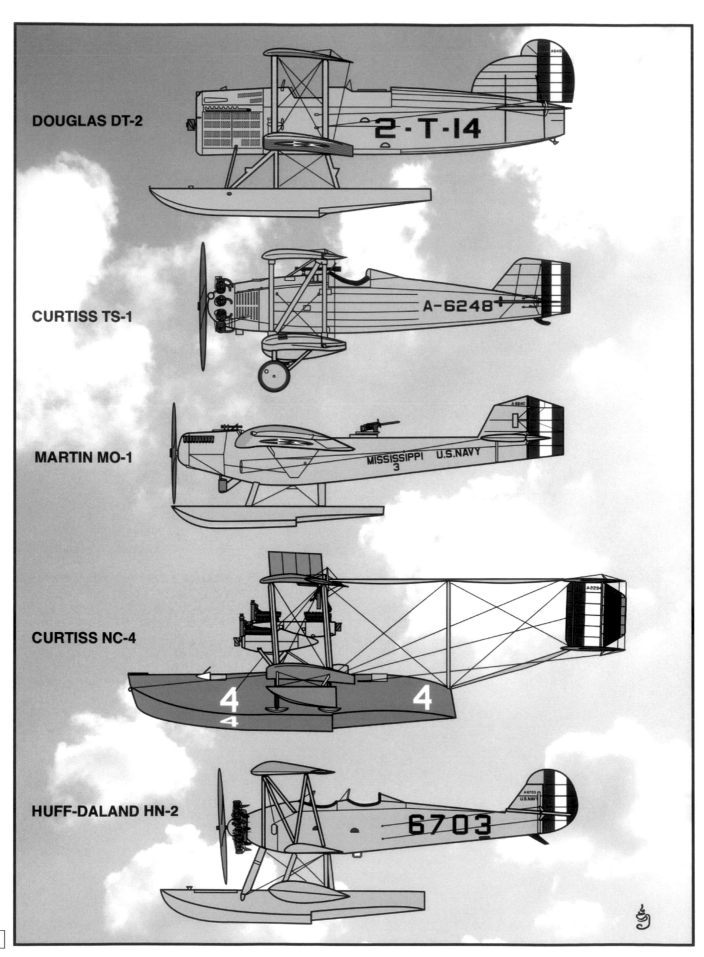

DOUGLAS DT-2

CURTISS TS-1

MARTIN MO-1

CURTISS NC-4

HUFF-DALAND HN-2

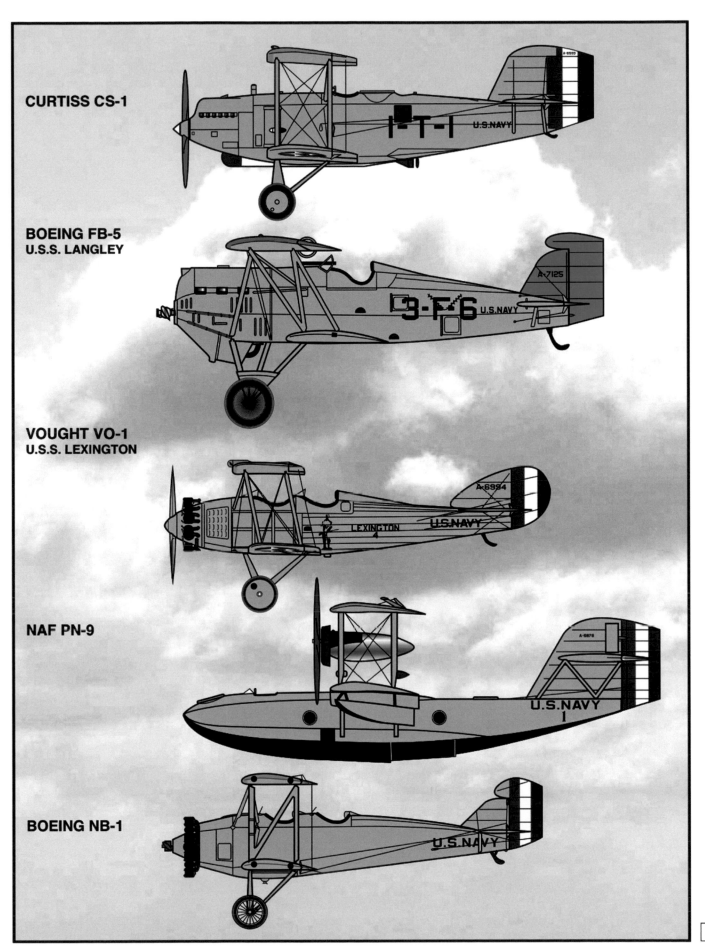

CURTISS CS-1

BOEING FB-5
U.S.S. LANGLEY

VOUGHT VO-1
U.S.S. LEXINGTON

NAF PN-9

BOEING NB-1

C-3

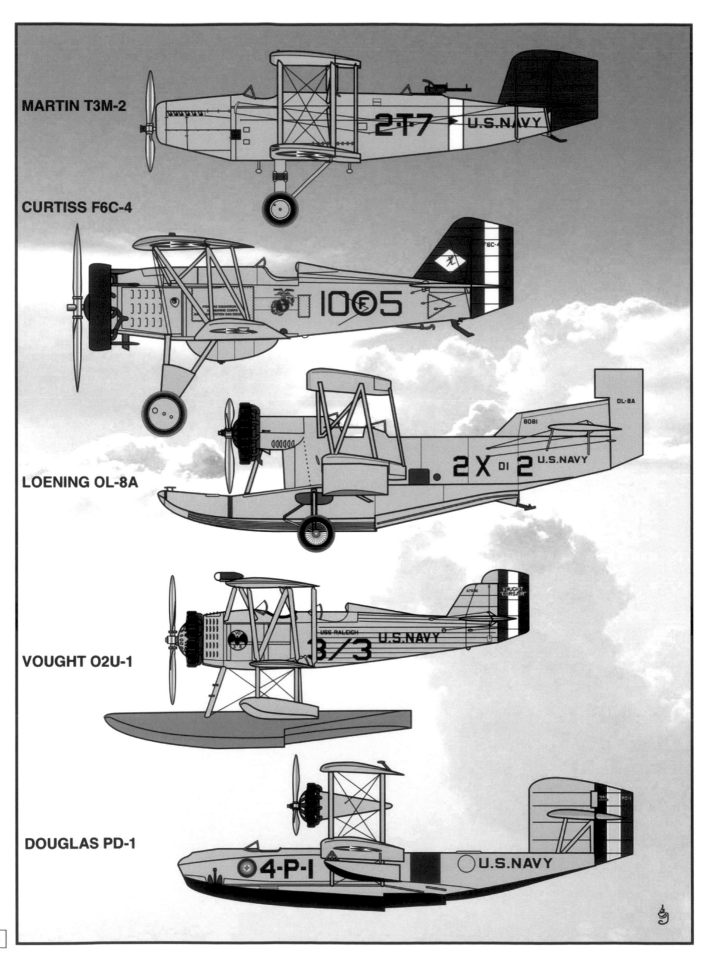

MARTIN T3M-2

CURTISS F6C-4

LOENING OL-8A

VOUGHT O2U-1

DOUGLAS PD-1

C-4

MARTIN T4M-1

BOEING F4B-2

CONSOLIDATED P2Y-2

GENERAL AVIATION PJ-1

CONSOLIDATED NY-2

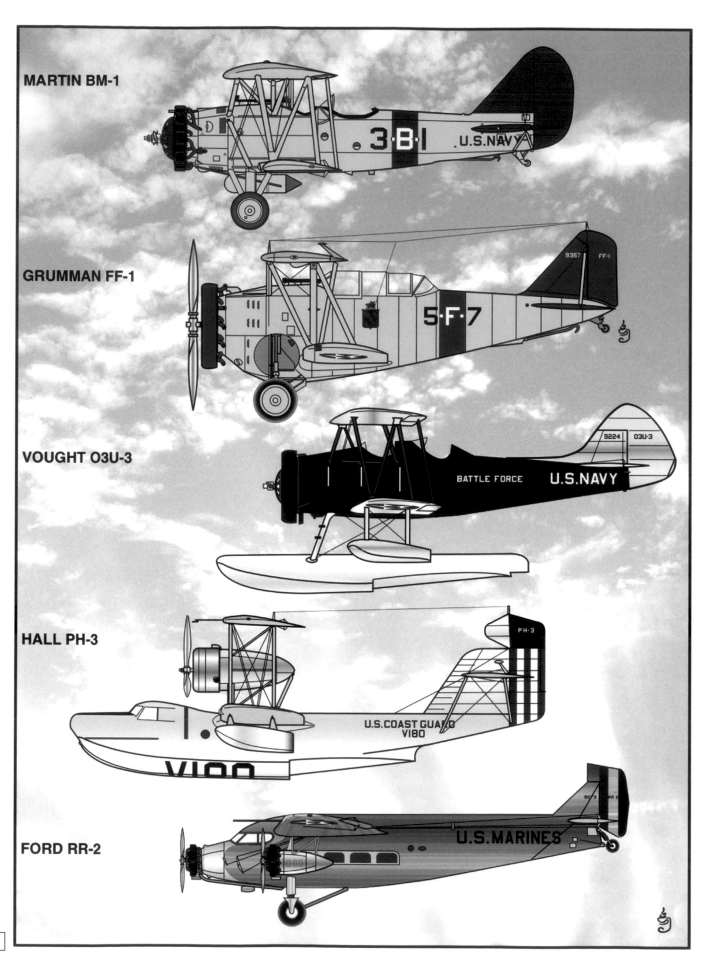

MARTIN BM-1

GRUMMAN FF-1

VOUGHT O3U-3

HALL PH-3

FORD RR-2

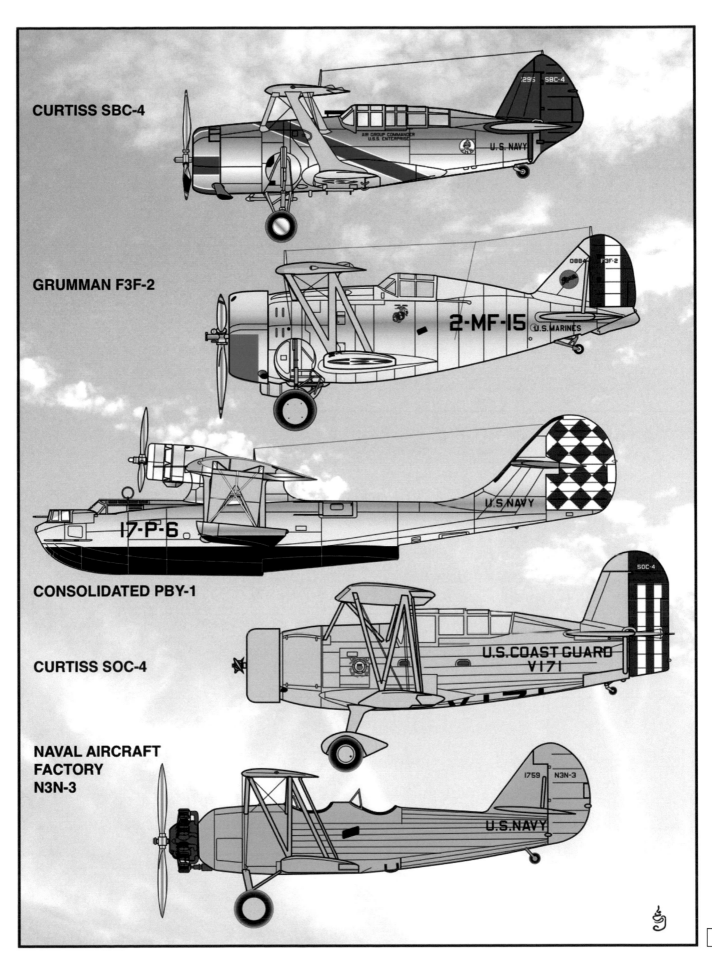

CURTISS SBC-4

GRUMMAN F3F-2

CONSOLIDATED PBY-1

CURTISS SOC-4

NAVAL AIRCRAFT
FACTORY
N3N-3

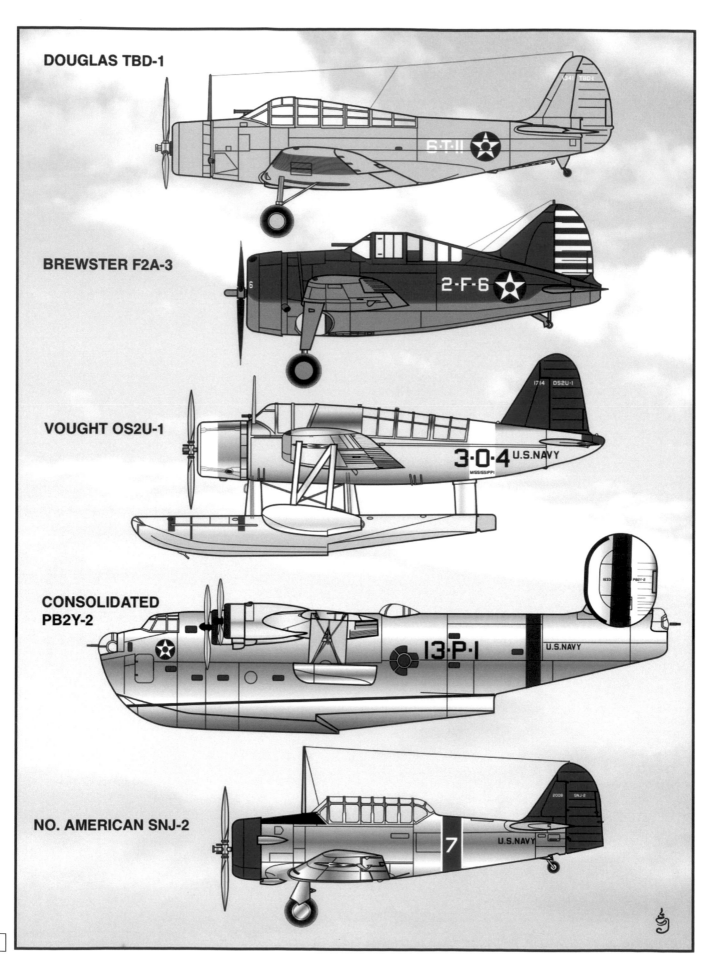

DOUGLAS TBD-1

BREWSTER F2A-3

VOUGHT OS2U-1

CONSOLIDATED PB2Y-2

NO. AMERICAN SNJ-2

Appendix 1: Foreign Aircraft and Airships

Procurement Note. During World War I, due to the limited capabilities of the American aircraft industry, the Navy Department had been obliged to procure sizable numbers of aircraft and airships from its European Allies in order to equip the Navy and Marine aviation units serving overseas. But soon after the war ended, the U.S. government shifted to a general policy of requiring the military services to procure new aircraft from American companies. Occasional exceptions to this policy, as seen below, were permitted for practical reasons. Fifty foreign-built "turret fighters," used as a temporary expedient on battleships from 1919 to 1922, were obtained from war surplus U.S. Army stocks. Another 20 foreign types, sometimes in batches of two or three, were procured between 1920 and 1930 purely for testing and evaluation of structural methods. Several other foreign aircraft were also purchased between 1927 and 1934 for the use of military air attachés in overseas embassies.

Sopwith F.1 Camel (1918)

The Navy Department acquired six Army surplus, British-made Sopwith F.1 Camel fighters in late 1918 to conduct the first experiments launching aircraft from wooden "flying-off" platforms constructed on the main turrets of a battleship, typically the No. 2 (forward) and No. 4 (aft). Dubbed "turret fighters," these aircraft were intended to provide fleet air defense or function as over-the-horizon gun spotters. For water landings, the aircraft was fitted with two under-wing flotation bags and a hydro-vane, a device installed in front of the landing gear axle that was designed to forestall a nose-over as the air-

craft contacted the water. A Camel made the first successful launch from the No. 2 turret of U.S.S. *Texas* (BB-35) in March 1919. General specifications: type, single-seat fighter; one 130-hp Clerget 9B rotary engine; length, 18 ft. 9 in.; span, 26 ft. 11 in.; gross weight, 1,455 lbs.; armament, two fixed Vickers .303-cal. machine guns; max. speed, 115 mph; ceiling, 21,000 ft.; range, 290 mi.

Royal Aircraft Factory S.E.5a (1918)

A standard Royal Flying Corps fighter during the last two years of World War I, the British government transferred 38 SE.5as to the Army Air Service in 1918. Following the Armistice, several surplus examples acquired by the Navy Department were fitted-out as "turret fighters" with flotation bags and hydro-vanes to operate from the flying off platforms on battleships. Records indicate that at least one S.E.5a served aboard *New Mexico* (BB-40) in mid–1919. General specifications: type, single-seat fighter; one 200-hp Hispano-Suiza 8b inline engine; length, 20 ft. 11 in.; span, 26 ft. 8 in.; gross weight, 2,058 lbs.; armament, one fixed .303-cal Vickers machine gun and one fixed .303-cal. Lewis machine

A surplus F.1 Camel at the Naval Aircraft Factory in 1919 being fitted with hydro-vane and flotation bags.

gun on a Foster mount; max. speed 123 mph; ceiling 17,000 ft.; range, 300 mi.

British Admiralty SSZ-23 Airship (1918)

Although the Navy took delivery of six British non-rigid airships during 1918, only one, SSZ-23 (Submarine Scout Zero–type airship No. 23), was reported to have been operated in the U.S. after the war. This airship was deflated and shipped to NAS Cape May, New Jersey in early 1919, where it was erected and flown as

a trainer until April. It was declared unfit and stricken in 1920. General specifications: type, three-place patrol airship; one 75-hp Rolls-Royce Hawk inline engine; length, 142 ft.; diameter, 32 ft.; envelope volume, 70,000 cu. ft.; max. speed, 50 mph. (Note, a second British non-rigid airship operated by the Navy in 1918, the twin-engine North Sea class NS-14, was received at NAS Hampton Roads in 1919, however, there is no record of it having ever been flown.)

Hanriot HD.2C (1919)

Originally manufactured by Hanriot in France during World War I in both wheeled (HD.1) and twin-float (HD.2) fighter versions, 10 Army surplus HD.2s transferred to the Navy Department were delivered to the Naval Aircraft Factory in 1919 to be configured as "turret fighters, which entailed installation of wheeled landing gear, flotation bags, and hydro-vanes. Following these modifications, one HD.2 was embarked aboard each battleship in the Pacific Battle Fleet equipped with turret "flying-off" platforms: *New York* (BB-34), *Texas* (BB-25), *Nevada* (BB-36), *Oklahoma* (BB-37), *Pennsylvania* (BB-38), *Arizona* (BB-39), *New Mexico* (BB-40), *Idaho* (BB-42), *Tennessee* (BB-43), and *California* (BB-44). Due to the understandably high attrition rate of the water recovery operations, the HD.2s served less than a year. General Specifications: type, single-seat fighter; one 130-hp Clerget 9B rotary engine; length, 23 ft.; span, 27 ft. 11 in.; gross weight, 1,540 lbs.; armament, two fixed Vickers .303-cal. machine guns; max. speed, 113 mph; ceiling, 15,750 ft.; range, 186 mi.

Nieuport 28 (1919)

Twelve French-built, Army surplus Nieuport 28 fighters were reassigned to the Navy Department in mid–

Top: **Several S.E.5as were transferred to the Navy from Army surplus stocks and fitted-out as "turret fighters."** *Bottom:* **The airship SSZ-37 was in Royal Navy service and was identical to the six Submarine Scout types transferred to the U.S. Navy in 1918.**

Top: **One of 10 HD-2Cs transferred from Army surplus stocks in 1919. All were equipped with hydro-vanes and flotation bags as battleship "turret fighters."** *Bottom:* **Twelve Army surplus Nieuport 28C.1s were transferred to the Navy in 1919 to replace the HD-2Cs as "turret fighters." The planes were withdrawn in 1922.**

1919 to serve as replacement "turret fighters" for the Hanriot HD.2s. After being fitted with flotation bags and hydro-vanes, they began entering service aboard battleships in the Pacific Battle Fleet during 1920. At this juncture of operations, the platform-equipped battleships typically carried one Nieuport for fighter protection and one Sopwith Strutter (see below) as the gun spotter. All had been damaged beyond repair or withdrawn by the end of 1922. General Specifications: type, single-seat fighter; one 160-hp Gnome 9N rotary engine; length, 24 ft. 4 in.; span, 26 ft. 3 in.; gross weight, 1,635 lbs.; armament, two fixed Vickers .303-cal. machine guns; max. speed, 122 mph; ceiling, 17,390 ft.; range, 180 mi.

Sopwith 1½ Strutter (1919)

The British-designed Sopwith 1½ Strutter was one of the most widely used Allied observation two-seaters during the last years of World War I. The 21 examples acquired in 1919 from surplus Army stocks probably comprised the final batch of replacement "turret fighters" and after being retrofitted with flotation bags and hydro-vanes, became the first shipboard types equipped with two-way radios. By 1920, the usual aircraft complement aboard the turret platform-equipped battleships consisted of one radio-equipped Strutter for gun spotting and one Nieuport

One of the 21 Strutters acquired in 1919 to operate from battleships. It was the first type of spotter to be equipped with a radio.

28 for air defense. With the advent of turntable catapults, all turret fighters were phased-out in favor of recoverable floatplanes during 1922. General specifications: type, two-seat observation; one 130-hp Clerget 9B rotary engine; length, 25 ft. 3 in.; span, 33 ft. 6 in.; gross weight, 2,150 lbs.; armament, one fixed Vickers .303-cal. machine gun and one flexible Lewis .303-cal. machine gun in the rear cockpit; max. speed, 100 mph; ceiling, 15,500 ft.; range, 300 mi.

SCDA O-1 Airship (1919)

Ordered by the Navy Department from the Italian firm Stabilimento Consruzioni Dirigibili de Aerostati (SCDA) in January 1919, O-1 was the only type of semi-rigid airship to ever serve with the Navy. It was a typical Italian design of that era, having a rigid metal keel that ran the length of the gas envelope and an open con-

trol car suspended by cables. After making its first flight in Italy in March 1919, O-1 was deflated and shipped initially to Akron, Ohio to be studied by Goodyear, then arrived at NAS Cape May in June. The airship was erected during the summer of 1919 and its first official Navy flight took place in September. O-1 remained in operation until stricken in late 1921 or early 1922. General specifications: type, three-place patrol airship; two 125-hp Colombo inline engines; length, 177 ft. 10 in.; diameter, 35 ft. 5 in.; envelope volume 127,000 cu. ft.; max. speed, 57 mph.

Parnall Panther (1920)

The two-seat Panther, when ordered by the British Admiralty in 1917, was among the very first aircraft to be designed specifically for carrier operations and did subsequently enter service in 1919 aboard HMS *Argus*. However, the two examples purchased by the Navy Department in 1920 received flotation bags and hydro-vanes for duty aboard battleships equipped with "flying-off" platforms. Although the Panthers were delivered and given Navy serial numbers, there is no record of their having actually been assigned to battleships. In any case, their arrival was probably eclipsed by catapult developments. General Specifications: type, two-seat observation; one 230-hp Bentley BR2 rotary engine; length, 24 ft. 11 in.; span, 29 ft. 6 in.; gross weight, 2,595 lbs., armament, one flexible Lewis .303-cal. machine gun in the rear cockpit; max. speed 109 mph; ceiling, 14,500 ft.; range, 480 mi.

The Italian-made airship O-1 as seen in late 1919. It was the only type of "semi-rigid" airship to be operated by the Navy.

A very rare photograph of a Panther with flotation gear and hydro-vanes installed. Two were tested in 1920 but apparently never deployed aboard battleships.

Blackburn Mk.II Swift (BST-1) (1921)

The Swift, flown in 1919, originated from a Royal Navy requirement for a carrier-based torpedo plane. Two examples purchased by the Navy Department were received for testing and evaluation in 1921. The type received the provisional designation BST-1 (Blackburn Swift Torpedo), but no production was ordered. The Dart, an improved version of the Swift, was ultimately built in quantity for the Royal Navy's Fleet Air Arm. General specifications: type, single-seat torpedo plane; one 450-hp Napier Lion IB inline engine; length, 35 ft. 6 in.; span, 45 ft. 6 in.; gross weight,

6,300 lbs.; armament, one 18-in. aerial torpedo on centerline; max. speed, 106 mph; ceiling, 15,000 ft.; range, 350 mi.

Dornier CsII Delphin (1921)

Developed in Germany as a passenger-carrying civil flying boat, the single CsII purchased by the Navy Department in 1921 featured a one-foot extension to the cabin below the engine. The aircraft had been acquired primarily to study its all-metal construction methods, and after delivery, was turned over to NAF for extensive flight testing and structural analyses. The test program

One of two Swifts acquired in 1921 for torpedo plane tests, seen here after Navy markings had been applied.

This Delphin was turned over to the Naval Aircraft Factory in 1921 for structural tests.

apparently ended in 1922. General specifications: type, eight-place flying boat transport; one 185-hp BMW IIIa inline engine; length, 38 ft. 9 in.; span, 56 ft. 9 in.; gross weight, 4,850 lbs.; max. speed, 93 mph; ceiling, 13,100 ft.; range, 236 mi.

Fokker D.VII (1921)

The U.S. Army obtained 142 German Fokker D.VII fighters after the Armistice with the intention of using them as advanced trainers. When the D.VII first appeared over the Western Front in mid–1918, it was arguably the most advanced operational fighter in the world. Innovative features included a steel tube fuselage structure and cantilevered wings that dispensed with necessity of drag-inducing rigging wires. Six ex–Army D.VIIs were transferred to the Marines in 1921 and thereafter used as trainers at MCAS Quantico until 1924. General specifications: type, single-seat fighter; one 180-hp Mercedes IIIa inline engine; length, 23 ft. 8 in.; span, 34 ft. 10 in.; gross weight, 2,576 lbs.; armament (removed); max. speed, 116 mph; ceiling, 19,600 ft,; range, 400 mi.

One of six ex–Army Fokker D.VIIs transferred to the Marines at MCAS Quantico in 1921 to be used as trainers.

Marine Fokker C.1 seen while serving at MCAS Quantico. Two were used as trainers from 1921 to 1924.

Fokker C.I (1921)

Too late to see combat, the C.I appeared at the close of World War I as a slightly enlarged, two-seat reconnaissance version of the D.VII fighter. In 1921, after the Fokker company had moved its operations to Holland, the Navy Department purchased two C.Is and allocated them to the Marines as trainers at MCAS Quantico. They remained in service until 1924. General Specifications: type, two-seat observation; one 185-hp BMW IIIa inline engine; length, 23 ft. 9 in.; span, 34 ft. 10 in.; gross weight, 2,767 lbs.; armament (removed); max. speed, 109 mph; ceiling, 13,125 ft.; range, 320 mi.

Junkers-Larsen JL-6 (1921)

The New York–based Junkers-Larsen Aircraft Corp. was formed in 1920 to assemble license-built copies of the highly innovative Junkers F.13 transport for the purpose of marketing them to the Army, Navy, and Post Office. Flown in Germany for the first time in 1919, the F.13 was the world's first all-metal airplane. Three American-made examples, listed as the JL-6, were delivered to the Navy in 1921 to be evaluated at NAS Anacostia in both wheeled and twin-float versions. No naval designations were apparently applied. Larsen tried to interest the military services in a 400-hp Liberty powered variant, but no orders resulted. General specifications: type, five-place transport; one 185-hp BMW IIIa inline engine; length, 31 ft. 6 in; span, 48 ft. 7 in.; gross weight, 3,466 lbs.; max. speed, 101 mph; ceiling, 16,600 ft.; range (not reported).

A float-equipped JL-6 evaluated at NAS Anacostia during the summer of 1921. They were license-built Junkers F.13s.

A single Viking amphibian was evaluated at NAS Anacostia during 1921 for potential shipboard use.

Vickers Viking IV (1921)

Developed too late for World War I, the Viking was the forerunner of the type of boat-hulled amphibians like the Supermarine Seagull and Walrus that would later see wide service aboard British warships. The Navy Department procured one Viking IV for evaluation purposes in 1921. The idea of using boat-hulled amphibians on Navy warships, specifically new Treaty Cruisers with seaplane hangars, was revived and tested again during the early 1930s with the Great Lakes XSG-1, Loening XS2L-2, and Sikorsky XSS-1 but ultimately rejected in favor of new floatplanes like the Curtis SOC-1. General specifications: type, four-place amphibian; one 450-hp Napier Lion inline engine; length, 34 ft. 2 in.; span, 50 ft.; gross weight, 5,790 lbs.; max. speed, 113 mph; ceiling (not reported); range, 925 mi.

Macchi M.16 (1922)

The Italian-built M.16 was one of several very small floatplane designs to be tested for the submarine scout role. Originally flown in 1919 as a wheeled sportplane, three float-equipped versions were delivered to the Navy for trials in 1922. Since their airframes could not be readily disassembled for submarine stowage, the M.16s were evidently intended for training. General specifications: type, single-seat floatplane; one 30-hp Anzani radial engine; length 14 ft. 6 in.; span, 19 ft. 8 in.; gross weight, 572 lbs.; max. speed, 83 mph; ceiling (not reported); range, 200 mi.

Three of these very small M.16 floatplanes were purchased in 1922 to be used for submarine scout training operations.

The U.1 could be disassembled for submarine stowage. It was used in 1922 for operational training.

Heinkel-Caspar U.1 (1922)

Another diminutive submarine scout tested by the Navy in 1922, the U.1, unlike the Macchi M.16, had been specifically designed to break-down and fit into the a stowage tube carried on a submarine deck. Designed by Ernst Heinkel and built by the Caspar-Werke firm in Germany, the all-wood U.1 featured a cantilever wing design that permitted rapid disassembly. Two examples ordered for the Navy by BuAer arrived for flight trials in 1922 but appear not to have been used in actual exercises with submarine

S-1 that took place between 1923 and 1926. General specifications: type, single-seat floatplane; one 55-hp Siemens radial engine; length, 20 ft. 4 in.; span, 23 ft. 7 in.; gross weight, 1,124 lbs.; max speed, 93 mph; ceiling and range (not reported).

Handley Page Type S (HPS) (1923)

The Type S (also known as the H.P. model 21) was built by British aircraft manufacturer Handley Page to a specification issued by the Navy Department in 1921 calling for a monoplane scout

The two HPS-1 prototypes were built to U.S. Navy specifications but cancelled before delivery to the United States.

convertible to wheels or floats, with three prototypes subsequently being ordered under the provisional designation HPS-1 (Handley Page Scout). In addition to its monoplane layout, the HPS-1 included a fully cantilevered wing equipped with retractable leading-edge slats and full-span trailing-edge flaps that were expected to significantly reduce takeoff and landing speeds. However, flight-testing of the first prototype in England during the fall of 1923 revealed unacceptable handling characteristics. The second prototype, featuring added wing dihedral, exhibited better flight characteristics when tested in early 1924 but was damaged beyond repair when the landing gear collapsed during load trials. Soon afterward, the Navy cancelled the contract for the third prototype. General specifications: type, single-seat scout; one 230-hp Bentley BR2 rotary engine; length, 21 ft. 6 in.; span, 29 ft. 3 in.; gross weight, 2,030 lbs.; max. speed 146 mph; ceiling, 21,000 ft.; range, 330 mi.

Fokker FT-1 (1923)

The FT-1 was derived from the T.III torpedo bomber built by Fokker after the company relocated to Holland in 1919. It appears to have been a low-wing, float-equipped variation of Fokker's Liberty-powered F.IV monoplane design, two examples of which had been sold to the Army in 1921 as the T-2. In 1923 the Navy acquired three T.IIIs under the designation FT-1 (Fokker Torpedo) and operated them out of NAS Hampton Roads for several years. General specifications: type, three-place torpedo plane; one 400-hp liberty 12 inline engine; length, 51 ft.; span, 65 ft.; gross weight, 7,300 lbs.; max. speed, 104 mph; ceiling and range (not reported).

Dornier (Wright) WP-1 (1923)

The Dornier D.1 Falke, built in Switzerland and flown for the first time in 1922, emerged as an innovative monoplane fighter design featuring an all-metal, aluminum-clad structure. One D.1 air-

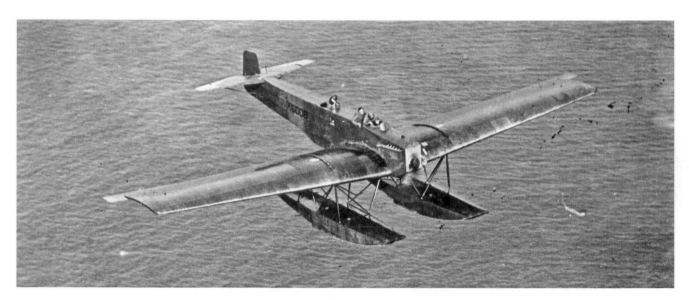

Top: **An FT-1 in flight near NAS Hampton Roads. Three operated from 1923 to 1927 as shore-based torpedo planes.** *Bottom:* **The sole WP-1 is seen at NAS Anacostia in 1923 while being evaluated as a potential carrier fighter.**

frame was shipped to Wright Aeronautical Corp. in 1923 to be fitted with a 320-hp Wright E-3 engine and entered in the Navy carrier fighter competition later the same year. After completing the engine installation, Wright delivered the aircraft to NAS Anacostia where it was assigned the naval designation WP-1 (Wright Pursuit). Although the WP-1 prototype exhibited above-average performance during flight trials, naval officials remained skeptical about the handling characteristics of monoplanes, and further development was discontinued. General specifications: type, single-seat fighter; one 320-hp Wright H-3 inline engine; length, 24 ft. 4 in.; span, 32 ft. 10 in.; gross weight, 2,674 lbs.; max. speed, 162 mph; ceiling (not reported); range, 217 mi.

De Havilland DH.60 Moth (1927)

Introduced in 1925, the DH.60 Moth became one of the most popular club and training aircraft in Britain. The Navy bought a single example in 1927, designated XDH-60, for the use of the Naval Air Attaché at the American Embassy in London. General specifications: type, two-seat trainer; one 60-hp Cirrus inline engine; length 24 ft. 11 in.; span, 30 ft.; gross weight, 1,649 lbs.; max. speed, 102 mph; ceiling, 14,500 ft.; range, 320 mi.

OFM Ro.1 (1928)

Produced in Italy by Officine Ferroviarie Meridionali (OFM), the Ro.1 was a license-built copy of the Dutch-designed Fokker C.V two-seat military observation and light attack aircraft, which had been flown for the first time in 1924. Italian-made Ro.1s began entering service with the Aviation Corps of the *Regio Esercito* (Italian Army) in 1927. The Navy purchased one Ro.1 in 1928 for the use of the Naval Air Attaché in Rome. General specifications: type, two-seat observation and light attack; on 450-hp Bristol Jupiter VI radial engine; length, 31 ft. 2 in.; span, 50 ft. 2 in.; gross weight, 4,909 lbs.; max. speed, 132 mph; ceiling, 19,360 ft.; range, 6721 mi.

Bristol Bulldog IIa (1929)

The Bristol Bulldog served as a frontline fighter with the Royal Air Force and several foreign nations from 1929 until the mid–1930s. BuAer purchased one Bulldog IIa, the main production version, for evaluation purposes in late 1929, but after it was destroyed on its first flight, a second aircraft was acquired in April 1930 to replace it. Reputed to be highly maneuverable, the Bulldog delivered performance comparable to the Navy's contemporaneous Boeing F4B-1 and was similar in structure. General specifications: type, single-seat fighter; one 440-hp Bristol Jupiter II radial engine; length, 25 ft. 2 in.; span, 33 ft. 10 in.; gross weight, 3,490 lbs.; armament, two Vickers .303-cal. machine guns and 80 lbs. of bombs on external racks; max. speed, 174 mph; ceiling, 27,000 ft.; range, 275 mi.

Top: The American-registered DH.60, identical to the XDH-60 flown by Naval Air Attaché in London between 1927 and 1934. *Middle:* Formation of OFM (IMAM) Ro.1s in *Regia Aeronautica* service seen over the Alps during the early 1930s. *Bottom:* The second Bulldog was tested at NAS Anacostia in 1930 after the first had been destroyed the previous year.

American-registered DH.80 of the same type used as that by the Naval Air Attaché in London from 1934 to 1939.

De Havilland DH.80 Puss Moth (1934)

A fabric-covered monoplane first flown in 1929, the DH.80 Puss Moth gained popularity in Britain as a civilian sportplane, selling over 250 examples by the time production ceased in late 1933. The Navy purchased one DH.80 in 1934 to replace the DH.60 (see above) being used by the Naval Air Attaché in London. The aircraft was listed on the inventory as the XDH-80 until late 1939, at which time it was impressed into service by the Royal Air Force. General specifications: type, three-place civil sportplane; one 120-hp Gypsy III inline engine; length, 25 ft.; span, 36 ft. 9 in.; gross weight, 2,050 lbs.; max. speed, 128 mph; ceiling, 17,500 ft.; range, 300 mi.

Caudron C.635 Simoun (1938)

An elegant French design, the first Caudron C.500 Simoun flew in 1934 as a four-seat civil touring and sport plane. A series of improvements and an engine upgrade resulted in the introduction of the model C.635 during the late 1930s, with one being acquired by the Navy for the use of the Naval Air Attaché in Paris in either 1938 or 1939. Though not documented in any ref-

An example of C-635 preserved at the Musee de l'Air in Paris. A similar aircraft was flown by the Naval Air Attaché in Paris in 1938 and 1939.

erence, this aircraft was thought to have been impounded by the German Nazi government following the U.S. declaration of war December 1941. General specifications: type, four-place civil sportplane; one 220-hp Renault 6Q-09 *Bengali* inline engine; length, 29 ft. 10 in.; span, 34 ft. 2 in.; gross weight, 3,040 lbs.; max. speed, 190 mph; ceiling, 20,000 ft.; range, 930 mi.

Messerschmitt Bf.108b Taifun

A direct predecessor of the Bf.109 fighter, the Bayerische Flugzeugwerke introduced the Willi Messerschmitt–designed Bf.108 Taifun (Typhoon) as the M-37 four-seat sportplane in 1934. The most numerous variant, the Bf.108b, appeared in 1935 with an uprated Argus As 10C engine and small aerodynamic improvements. A single Bf.108b was purchased by U.S. government in the spring of 1939 for the use of the Military Air Attachés in the American embassy in Berlin. Though flown by both Army and Navy Air Attachés, the aircraft was entered on the Army inventory as the XC-44. Historical records indicate that the Bf.108b had been grounded by embassy officials a month before being seized by the

A civil-registered Bf.108b of the type used by the Naval Air Attaché in Berlin from 1939 to 1941. The swastika was required by German law.

German government in December 1941. General specifications: type, four-place civil sportplane; one 240-hp Argus As 10C inline engine; length, 27 ft. 2 in.; span, 34 ft. 5 in.; gross weight, 2,976 lbs.; max. speed, 190 mph; ceiling, 20,300 ft.; range, 620 mi.

Appendix 2: Racing and Experimental Aircraft

Historical Note. Official Navy Department policy toward air racing and record-setting underwent several variations during the 1920s. From 1921 to 1926, the Navy was directly involved to the extent of procuring specialized racing aircraft and using Naval Aviators to fly them, actively competing in the Pulitzer Trophy, Curtiss Marine Trophy, and Schneider Maritime Cup races held during that time. Then in 1926, the Secretary of the Navy, Curtis Wilbur, informed Admiral Moffett of the Naval Bureau of Aeronautics (BuAer) that the Navy Department was opposed to "direct involvement" in air racing. But the application of this supposed ban after 1926 was far from uniform. From 1927 to 1930, the Naval Aircraft Factory, under BuAer's direction, collaborated with the Mercury Flying Corp. in the construction and development of the Mercury floatplane racer, with the understanding that the aircraft would be flown by a Marine pilot (i.e., Lt. Alfred J. Williams, who functioned as an advisor to Moffett); however, in 1930 the Navy Department intervened to prevent further Navy involvement in the project, and the completed racer never flew. Likewise, in an apparent departure from official policy, float-equipped Navy Curtiss F6C-3s flown by Marine pilots competed in and won the Curtiss Marine Trophy Race in 1928 and 1930, and a modified F6C-3 with wheels was flown to fourth place by a Navy pilot in the 1929 National Air Race at Cleveland. Another collaborative effort, this time between BuAer and the Curtiss factory in 1930, resulted in development of the highly modified XF6C-6 monoplane racer. This aircraft, flown by Marine pilot Capt. Arthur Page, crashed at the National Air Races in 1930, after which Navy involvement in racing ceased altogether.

Curtiss 18-T (1918)

Originally ordered as a two-seat fighter, the two 18-T triplanes delivered in mid–1918 were subsequently used to capture aviation records and for racing. In August 1918, one Navy 18-T set a new world's speed record of 163 mph for an aircraft carrying a military load, then in September 1919, the other 18-T, fitted with longer wings, established a world altitude record of 34,610 feet. Both aircraft, fitted with short wings and floats, competed in the Curtiss Marine Trophy Race in 1922, though neither finished. General specifications: type, two-seat racer; one 400-hp Kirkham-Curtiss V12 inline engine; length, 23 ft. 4 in.; span, 31 ft. 10 in., gross weight, 3,050 lbs.; max speed, 160 mph; ceiling, 23,000 ft., range (not reported.)

A Curtiss 18-T with short wings and floats. Both 18Ts competed in the Curtiss Marine Trophy Race in 1922.

The CR-1 in mid–1921 with Lamblin-type radiators fitted. This aircraft established a new world speed record of 197.8 mph.

Curtiss CR (1921)

Curtiss received a Navy contract in June 1921 to design and built two aircraft as official Navy entries in the upcoming Pulitzer Trophy race scheduled later the same year. Designated CR-1 and -2 (Curtiss Racer), the design was characterized by an aerodynamically clean molded plywood fuselage and thin-section, fabric-covered wooden wings, and could be converted to wheels or floats depending on the racing format. The CRs were not entered in any 1921 races but a factory test pilot flew one to set a new world's absolute speed of 197.8 mph later in the year. As Navy contestants, CR-1 and -2, rigged with wheels, placed third and fourth in the 1922 Pulitzer Trophy race, and rigged with floats and wing surface radiators and re-designated CR-3 and -4, won first and second places in the 1923 Schneider Maritime Cup race. CR-4 set a closed course speed record of 188 mph in 1924. General specifications (CR-3): type, single-seat floatplane racer; 405-hp Curtiss CD-12 inline engine; length, 25 ft.; span 22 ft. 8 in.; gross weight, 2,746 lbs.; max speed, 177 mph; ceiling, 19,200 ft.; range, 522 mi.

Wright NW (1922)

Wright Aeronautical Corp. received a contract in 1922 to build two racing aircraft according to plans and specifications issued by

The NW-1 as seen in October 1922 with sesquiplane wing incorporated into the landing gear struts. It was forced to ditch in a lake during the Pulitzer race.

BuAer. The first design, known as the Navy-Wright racer or NW-1, featured an unusual mid-wing layout with a small sesquiplane wing mounted on the landing gear legs. NW-1 made its first flight in October 1922 only a few days before being entered in the Pulitzer Trophy race. During the race, NW-1 reached a top speed of 186 mph but irreparably damaged when the pilot was forced to ditch in a lake due to engine overheating. The second prototype, designated NW-2, appeared in 1923 as conventional biplane mounted on twin floats to compete in the Schneider Maritime Cup race. In flight trials prior to the race, NW-2 crash-landed and sank after suffering an in-flight propeller failure. General specifications (NW-1): type, single-seat racer; one 525-hp Wright T-2 inline engine; length, 24 ft.; span, 30 ft. 6 in.; gross weight, 3,000 lbs.; max. speed, 186 mph; ceiling (not reported); range, 300 mi.

The float-equipped NW-2 in 1923 with biplane layout and wing-skin radiators. It did not compete.

The BR-1 in 1922 with Lamblin-type radiators; the BR-2 had wing-skin type radiators. Both were built to compete in the Pulitzer race.

Bee Line (Booth) BR (1922)

Designed by Harry T. Booth and constructed by Aerial Engineering Corp., two aircraft listed as Bee Line BR-1 and -2 (Booth Racer) were built for the Navy in 1922 to compete in the Pulitzer Trophy race. Both aircraft were low-wing monoplanes rigged with wheels, BR-1 having pod-type Lamblin radiators and BR-2, wing skin types. No flight or race records on these aircraft appear to exist. General specifications: type, single-seat racer; one 390-hp Wright H-3 inline engine; length 21 ft. 5 in.; span, 28 ft. 1 in.; gross weight, 2,056 lbs., max speed, 188 mph.

Naval Aircraft Factory TR (1922)

Intended to compete in a forthcoming Curtiss Marine Trophy race, a float-equipped NAF-built TS-3 fighter underwent modifications at NAF in 1922 that included installation of a 180-hp Wright-Hispano engine and streamlining improvements. After being tested as the TR-3, the aircraft entered the race but made a forced landing before finishing. The same aircraft, rebuilt in 1923, emerged as the TR-3A with a larger Wright engine, revised cowling, and flush wing radiators. After recurring engine problems prevented the TR-3A from entering the 1923 Schneider Maritime Cup, further development was abandoned. General specifications: type, single-seat racer (TR-3A); one 275-hp Wright E-4 inline engine; length, 21 ft. 6 in.; span,

Modified from a TS-2, the TR-3A was designed to enter the 1923 Schneider Cup Race in England but did not compete.

25 ft.; gross weight, 2,129 lbs.; max. speed, 159 mph; ceiling 20,700 ft.; range (not reported).

Wright F2W (1923)

Very similar in design and construction to the Curtiss CRs, Wright Aeronautical Corp. built two biplane racers for the Navy

The float-equipped F2W-2 appeared in 1924 with new wings and a Wright T-2 engine but crashed before it could compete.

in 1923 under the fighter designation F2W-1 to compete in the 1923 Pulitzer Trophy race. F2W-1 A6743 took third place at a speed of 230 mph but A6744 crash-landed before finishing. A6744, rigged with floats as F2W-2, was destroyed in a 1924 crash before it could compete in any race. General specifications: type, single-seat racer; one 780-hp Wright *Tornado* inline engine; length 21 ft. 4 in.; span, 22 ft. 6 in.; gross weight, 2,858 lbs.; max. speed, 240 mph.

Curtiss R2C and R3C (1923)

Developed from the earlier CRs, two R2C-1s were built for the Navy by Curtiss to compete in national air races scheduled during 1923. They differed from the CRs in having boosted engines, better streamlining, and upper wings mounted directly to the fuselage. R2C-1 A6692 took first place in the 1923 Pulitzer race with a speed of 243.7 mph, while A6691 took second at 241.8 mph. A6692 became the R2C-2 when converted to floats in 1924

Top: **The R2C-2 A-6692 is seen rigged with floats in 1924. As a wheeled R2C-1 the previous year, this aircraft won the Pulitzer race with a speed of 243.7 mph.** *Bottom:* **This float-equipped R3C-2 competed in but did not finish the 1925 Schneider Cup Race. Lieutenant J. H. Doolittle won the race in an Army R3C-2.**

but was never raced, and A6691 was sold to the Army the same year. A6692 crashed in 1926 while being used to train pilots for a forthcoming Schneider Maritime Cup race. Three R3Cs (A6978, A6979, and A7054) appeared in 1925 and 1926 with more powerful engines and different airfoil sections. A6978, as an R3C-1 rigged with wheels, won the 1925 Pulitzer race at a speed of 249 mph. A6978 and A6979, as R3C-2s with floats, competed in the 1925 Schneider race but did not finish. In 1926, A7045 as an R3C-2, placed second in the Schneider race and A6979, as the R3C-4 with different engine, did not finish. General specifications (R3C-2): type, single-seat floatplane racer; one 565-hp Curtiss V1400 inline engine; length, 22 ft.; span 22 ft.; gross weight, 2,738 lbs.; max. speed, 245 mph; ceiling, 21,200 ft.; range, 290 mi.

Longren Fibre Sport Plane (1924)

Originally flown in 1921 as the Longren AK or "Fibre Sport Plane," BuAer reportedly acquired three of these aircraft in 1924 solely to study the construction methods used. The fuselage was molded from a wood fiber laminate and the folding wings, made of wood, featured a truss system that dispensed with rigging wires. No test results were reported. According to one source, designer A. K. Longren filed for bankruptcy in 1924. General specifications: type, two-seat sportplane; one 60-hp Lawrance L-4 radial engine; length, 19 ft. 7 in.; span, 27 ft. 11 in.; gross weight, 1,195 lbs.; max speed, 87 mph; ceiling, 9,050 ft.; range (not reported).

Naval Aircraft Factory NM (1924)

Built and designed by the Naval Aircraft Factory, the NM-1 (Navy-Metal) appeared in 1924 as a flying testbed for metal structural techniques. If successful, BuAer contemplated producing the design as a Marine armed observation type that would replace the older O2Bs. Fuselage construction used the Dornier method of beaded aluminum skins riveted to stamped metal bulkheads; metal-framed wings and tail group were skinned from smooth duraluminum sheets. Development was discontinued in 1925 after testing revealed serious structural fatigue in the fuselage. General specifications: type, two-seat experimental; one 325-hp

Packard 1A-1237 inline engine; length, 31 ft.; span, 42 ft.; gross weight, 4,190 lbs.; max. speed 108 mph; ceiling 16,900 ft.; range (not reported).

Naval Aircraft Factory Mercury Racer (1928)

Aimed at winning the Schneider Maritime Cup race, the Mercury Racer represented a joint venture between BuAer and Mercury Flying Corp. No bureau number was ever assigned to it. The design emerged as a mid-wing monoplane with a molded, semi-monocoque wooden fuselage. Power was derived from two 500-hp Packard engines arranged in series that occupied nearly half the length of the fuselage. Taxi tests carried out during 1929 revealed serious engine gearing and overheating problems that delayed flight-testing. Interestingly, the project was apparently enjoined by the Navy Department in 1930 before the aircraft could be made ready to fly. General specifications (none available).

Top: **The Bureau of Aeronautics acquired three Fibre Sport Planes in 1924 to study the construction methods used.** *Bottom:* **Pictured in 1924, the NM-1 was built to test various aluminum structural methods. Development discontinued in 1925.**

Top: **The Mercury Racer as seen in 1929. Its two 500-hp Packard engines were arranged in series. It was never flown.** *Bottom:* **Known as the Page Racer, the highly modified XF6C-6 ended all Navy racing when it crashed in 1930, killing Marine pilot Captain Arthur Page.**

Curtiss F6C Page Racer (1930)

Popularly known as the "Page Racer," the XF6C-6 was destined to be last of the Navy racers. It was the brainchild of Marine racing pilot Capt. Arthur Page, who in the spring of 1930 had flown a modified F6C-3 to victory in the Curtiss Marine Trophy race. With the objective of winning the Thompson Trophy race scheduled in September, Page persuaded BuAer officials to authorize an extensive series of modifications to be performed on an F6C-3 at the Curtiss factory. Changes to the basic airframe included replacing the biplane layout with a parasol-mounted monoplane wing, plus installation of a boosted Curtiss V1570 *Conqueror* engine and P-6E–type cantilevered landing gear. The resulting XF6C-3 was expected to reach speeds up to 250 mph. Page was leading the race in the 17th lap when the aircraft inexplicably wandered out of the circuit and crashed into the ground. Page later died from injuries. An investigation of the crash revealed that he had lost consciousness after being overcome with carbon monoxide fumes. General specifications: type, single-seat racer; one 750-hp Curtiss *Conqueror* inline engine; length, 22 ft. 10 in.; span, 31 ft. 10 in; gross weight (not reported); performance details (not reported).

Appendix 3: Naval Aircraft, Airship, Ship, and Aviation Unit Designations, Nomenclature, and Abbreviations

Aircraft

From 1917 to 1922, aircraft were procured and identified under the manufacturer's name and model number as with the Curtiss H-16 and MF and Aeromarine 39-B. In March 1922, the recently formed Naval Bureau of Aeronautics (BuAer) adopted a standardized designation system utilizing a combination of letters and numbers to identify naval aircraft. Initially, the system was sequenced in order of manufacturer, model, type, and production version, e.g., M2O-1 translated to M = Martin, 2 = second Model, O = observation type, and 1 = first version. Then in 1923 the designation order was revised in order of type, model, manufacturer, and production version, e.g., F4B-4 translated to F = fighter type, 4 = fourth version, B = Boeing, and -4 = fourth production version, and with minor variations, this system would remain in effect until 1962. Foreign aircraft (see Appendix 1) sometimes retained their foreign designations as with the Bristol Bulldog IIa and OFM Ro.1 while others received non-standard designations as with the Handley Page HPS-1 and De Havilland XDH80. An "X" prefix ahead of the type designation generally denoted experimental prototype status but was occasionally applied to off-the-shelf civil aircraft acquired for utility or transportation purposes. A letter suffix sometimes added to the production model number indicated special equipment or a modification, e.g., the Grumman J2F-2A identified a Marine version to which machine guns and bomb racks had been added. The following alphabetical codes under the 1922 system apply to aircraft appearing in this book:

Type Designations

		Example	Dates Used
B =	Bomber	BG-1	1929–1940
BF =	Bomber-Fighter	BFC-1	1934–1937
F =	Fighter	F3F-2	1925–1962
G =	Transport, Single-Engine	GB-1	1939–1946
H =	Air Ambulance	XHL-1	1929–1931
J =	Transport	JR-2	1929–1931
J =	Utility	J2F-2	1931–1962
JR =	Utility Transport	JRS-1	1935–1946
LN =	Glider Trainer	LNS-1	1941–1946
M =	Marine Expeditionary	EM-1	1922–1923
N =	Trainer (Primary after 1939)	N3N-3	1922–1962

O =	Observation	O3U-3	1922–1935
OS =	Observation-Scout (BB)	OS2U-1	1935–1946
P =	Patrol	P2Y-1	1922–1962
PB =	Patrol-Bomber	PBY-1	1935–1946
PBT =	Patrol-Bomber-Torpedo	XPBTH-1	1934–1937
R =	Racer	R3C-2	1922–1926
R =	Transport	R2D-1	1931–1962
S =	Scout	SU-1	1922–1935
SB =	Scout–Bomber	SBC-3	1935–1946
SN =	Advanced Trainer	SNJ-2	1939–1962
SO =	Scout–Observation (CA, CL)	SOC-3	1934–1946
T =	Torpedo Plane	T4M-1	1922–1935
T =	Transport	TA-1	1926–1930
TB =	Torpedo-Bomber	TBD-1	1935–1946

Manufacturer Designations

		Dates Used
A =	Aeromarine Plane & Motor Co.	1922
A =	Atlantic Aircraft Corp. (Fokker)	1926–1931
A =	Brewster Aeronautical Corp.	1935–1945
A =	General Aviation Manufacturing Corp. (Fokker)	1931–1932
B =	Beech Aircraft Co.	1937–1962
B =	Boeing Airplane Co.	1923–1946
C =	Curtiss Aeroplane & Motor Co.	1922–1929
C =	Curtiss-Wright Aeronautical Corp.	1929–1946
D =	Douglas Aircraft Corp.	1922–1962
E =	Bellanca Aircraft Corp.	1931–1937
E =	G. Elias and Brother, Inc.	1922–1924
F =	Grumman Aircraft Engineering Corp.	1931–1962
G =	Eberhart Aeroplane & Motor Co.	1927–1928
G =	Great Lakes Aircraft Corp.	1929–1936
H =	Hall Aluminum Aircraft Corp.	1928–1940
H =	Howard Aircraft Co.	1941–1946
H =	Huff-Daland Airplane Co.	1922–1925
H =	Stearman-Hammond Co.	1937–1938
J =	Berliner-Joyce Co.	1929–1935
J =	General Aviation Manufacturing Corp. (Fokker)	1932–1933
J =	North American Aviation, Inc.	1937–1962
K =	Fairchild Airplane & Engine Corp.	1936–1946
K =	Keystone Aircraft Corp.	1929–1931
K =	Kinner Airplane & Motor Co.	1936
L =	Bell Aircraft Corp.	1941–1942

Manufacturer Designations		Dates Used
L =	Loening Aeronautical Engineering Co.	1923–1928
L =	Loening Aeronautical Div., Keystone Aircraft Corp.	1929–1933
M =	Glenn L. Martin Co.	1922–1962
N =	Naval Aircraft Factory	1922–1946
O =	Lockheed Aircraft Corp.	1931–1942
O =	Viking Flying Boat Co. (Stearman-Varney)	1931–1936
P =	Pitcairn-Cierva Autogyro Co.	1931–1936
P =	Mid-Continent Div. of Spartan Aircraft Co.	1940–1942
Q =	Fairchild Aircraft Manufacturing Co.	1928
Q =	Stinson Aircraft Corp.	1934–1935
R =	Stout Metal Airplane Div. of Ford Motor Co.	1928–1930
R =	Ryan Aeronautical Co.	1941
S =	Schweizer Aircraft Corp.	1941–1942
S =	Sikorsky Manufacturing Co.	1927–1929
S =	Sikorsky Aviation Div. of United Aircraft, Inc.	1929–1962
S =	Stearman Aircraft Div. of Boeing Airplane Co.	1935–1945
S =	Stout Metal Airplane Co.	1922
T =	Standard Aircraft Corp.	1930–1934
T =	Northrop Corp.	1933–1937
U =	Chance Vought Corp.	1922–1929
U =	Chance Vought Div. of United Aircraft, Inc.	1929–1962
V =	Vultee Aircraft, Inc.	1940–1945
W =	Waco Aircraft Co.	1934–1939
W =	Wright Aeronautical Corp.	1922–1926
Y =	Consolidated Aircraft Corp. (later Convair)	1925–1962
Z =	Pennsylvania Aircraft Syndicate Ltd.	1934

Airships

Rigid Airships (Dirigibles). The five large rigid airships operated by the Navy from 1921 to 1935 all used alpha-numeric designations common to naval ships rather than aircraft. The letter "Z" denoted lighter-than-air and "R" indicated rigid, as with *Shenandoah* (ZR-1), the unnamed R.38 (ZR-2), and *Los Angeles* (ZR-3), and "S" for scout was added to *Akron* (ZRS-4) and *Macon* (ZRS-5). A one-of-a-kind designation was applied to the smaller ZMC-2, which translated as Z = lighter-than-air, MC = metal-clad, and -2 = second series.

Non-Rigid Airships (Blimps). From 1917 until 1941, non-rigid airships used a simple alpha-numeric that identified them by class (B through O), followed by the envelope number of the class, as follows:

Class and Number	Number Accepted	Dates Served
A (not used)	-	-
B-1 through -20	17 (+3 rebuilt)	1917–1924
C-1 through -10	10	1918–1922
D-1 through -6	5 (D-1 destroyed before delivery)	1920–1921
E-1	1	1918–1924
F-1	1	1919–1923
G-1 (ZNG)	1 (7 accepted after 1941)	1935–1959
H-1	1	1922
J-1 and -2	1 (J-2 cancelled)	1922–1924
J-3 and -4	2 (used Army TC-type envelopes)	1925–1940
K-1	1	1931–1940

K-2 through -5 (ZPK)	4 (128 accepted after 1941)	1941–1959
L-1 through -3 (ZNL)	3 (19 accepted after 1941)	1938–1946
O-1 (see Appendix 1)	1 (Italian-made, semi-rigid)	1919–1921
TC-13 and -14	2 (transferred from Army)	1938–1945

In 1941, with the exception of TC-13 and -14, BuAer adopted a new alpha-numeric system that added Z (lighter-than-air) and N (trainer) or P (patrol) to the existing class codes, as shown above in parentheses.

Aviation-Related Ships

In 1919 the Navy Department adopted a standardized alpha-numeric designation system for all commissioned ships consisting of a two or three-letter hull type followed by the hull number. Aviation-related ships covered in this book may be identified as follows:

Hull Type	Description	Dates Used
AC =	Coal Collier assigned to aviation	1925–1930
AM =	Minesweeper assigned to aviation	1919–1936
AO =	Fleet Oiler assigned to aviation	1924–1935
AV =	Heavy Seaplane Tender	1925–1960
AVD =	Small Seaplane Tender, Destroyer	1940–1945
AVG =	Auxiliary Aircraft Carrier (later ACV and CVE)	1941–1942
AVP =	Small Seaplane Tender	1936–1966
AZ =	Airship Tender	1921–1925
BB =	Battleship	1919–1991
CA =	Armored Cruiser; Heavy Cruiser after 1931	1919–1975
CL =	Light Cruiser	1920–1962
CLV =	Flying Deck Cruiser (not built)	-
CM =	Minelayer assigned to aviation	1919–1931
CV =	Fleet Aircraft Carrier	1922–1952
DD =	Destroyer assigned to aviation	1920–1921
DD =	Destroyer equipped with floatplane	1923–1944
PG =	Gunboat equipped with floatplane	1936–1943
SS =	Submarine	1923–1975
WPG =	Coast Guard Cutter equipped with amphibian	1937–1945

Aviation Unit Organization and Designations

Squadrons formed the basic organizational component for both Navy and Marine Corps aviation units from World War I throughout the interwar period and afterward. A standard alpha-numeric classification system for Navy squadrons was adopted in 1922, and a similar system was applied to Marine Corps units in 1924. Using a scheme analogous to aircraft and airships, squadrons were identified by two letters denoting the aviation class and type of mission followed by a squadron number. The prefix "V" indicated heavier-than-air class (aircraft) and "Z," lighter-than-air (airships).

Prefix	Mission	Dates Used
VA	Training Squadron	1922
VB	Bombing Squadron	1922–1946

Prefix	Mission	Dates Used
VF	Fighting Squadron	1922–present
VG	Fleet or Utility Squadron	1922
VJ	Utility Squadron	1923–1962
VO	Observation Squadron	1922–1945
VN	Training Squadron	1923–1947
VNL	Glider Training Squadron	1941–1943
VP	Patrol Squadron	1922–present
VS	Scouting Squadron	1922–1947
VMSB	Marine Scout–Bomber Squadron	1941–1947
VCS	Cruiser-Scouting Squadron	1936–1949
VT	Torpedo Squadron	1922–1946
VMTB	Marine Torpedo-Bomber Squadron	1941–1947
VX	Experimental Squadron	1927–present
ZJ	Blimp Utility Squadron	1941–1961
ZN	Blimp Training Squadron	1941–1961
ZP	Blimp Patrol Squadron	1941–1961

From 1926, a suffix letter or letters and numbers were added to the squadron number to indicate assignment and/or location. For squadrons assigned to ships, the fleet, and the Marines, the practice was discontinued in 1937. The "M" for Marine Corps assignment after that time became part of the prefix as with VMB-1, VMF-1, etc.

Suffix	Assignment/Location	Dates Used
B	Battle Fleet (e.g., VF-6B)	1926–1937
D + number	Naval District (e.g., VJ-5D11)	1926–1942
F	Fleet (e.g., VP-10F)	1926–1937
M	Marine Corps (e.g., VO-7M)	1926–1937
R	Reserve Squadron (e.g., VS-12R)	1928–1942
S	Scouting Fleet (e.g., VS-10S)	1926–1937

During 1926 and 1927, Navy squadrons assigned to the fleet were organized into carrier air groups, battleship divisions, and cruiser divisions. Carrier air groups (CVGs) were simply identified by ship name (e.g., *Lexington* Air Group or CVG) but after 1942 by carrier hull number (e.g., CVG-9, etc.). In 1937 carrier air groups were further assigned to one of two carrier divisions and patrol squadrons organized into five patrol wings. Marine squadrons were generally grouped by coast location (e.g., First Aviation Group, San Diego 1925-1926; East Coast Expeditionary Force, Quantico, 1927-1934; and Fleet Marine Force [FMF], Air-

craft Two, San Diego 1935-1941). Starting in 1941, Marine Squadrons were further organized into Marine Air Wings (e.g., 1st MAW) and Marine Air Groups (e.g., MAG-21). Until 1942, Coast Guard aircraft were individually assigned by air station (e.g., CGAS Elizabeth City, New Jersey) or by Naval District (e.g., 7th Naval District, Miami, Florida). After 1942, newly organized Coast Guard squadrons were identified by the suffix "CG" (e.g., VP-6CG).

Naval Aviation Abbreviations

ACTG	Advanced Carrier Training Group
BuAer	Naval Bureau of Aeronautics
BuNo	Aircraft or Airship Bureau Number
BuShips	Naval Bureau of Ships
BuWeps	Naval Bureau of Weapons
BAD	Marine Corps Base Air Detachment
BatFor	Battle Force Aircraft Pool
CGAS	Coast Guard Air Station
CVG	Carrier Air Group
FAPU	Fleet Air Photographic Unit
FMF	Fleet Marine Force
LANT	Atlantic Fleet
LSO	Landing Signals Officer
LTA	Lighter-Than-Air
MAG	Marine Air Group
MAW	Marine Air Wing
MCAS	Marine Corps Air Station
NA	Naval Academy, Annapolis, Maryland
NAD	Naval Air Detachment
NACA	National Advisory Committee for Aeronautics
NAF	Naval Aircraft Factory, Philadelphia, Pennsylvania
NAP	Naval Aviation Pilot, Enlisted
NAAS	Naval Auxiliary Air Station
NAS	Naval Air Station
NOB	Naval Operating Base
NPG	Naval Proving Ground, Dahlgren, Virginia
NRAB	Naval Reserve Air Base
NTS	Naval Torpedo Station, Newport, Rhode Island
PAC	Pacific Fleet
SS	Service Squadron
TTS	Transitional Training Squadron
TTU	Transitional Training Unit

Appendix 4: Status of Naval Aviation, December 1941

U.S. Navy Aircraft and Airships

Manufacturer/Designation	Inventory	Assigned to Combat Units
Attack Aircraft:		
Douglas BD-1	1	0
Great Lakes BG-1	22	0
Northrop BT-1 and -2	39	0
Brewster XSBA-1/NAF SBN-1	22	7
Curtiss SBC-3 and–4	174	39
Douglas SBD-1, -2, and -3	242	191
Vought SBU-1 and -2	86	0
Vought SB2U-1, -2, and -3	94	63
Martin T4M-1/Great Lakes TG-1 and -2	7	0
Douglas TBD-1	101	75
Grumman XTBF-1	1	0
Totals	789	375

(Note, acceptance of Brewster XSB2A-1, Curtiss XSB2C-1, and Vought XTBU-1 prototypes pending)

Manufacturer/Designation	Inventory	Assigned to Combat Units
Fighter Aircraft:		
Brewster F2A-1, -2, and -3	144	28
Boeing F4B-3 and -4	34	0
Grumman FF-2	7	0
Grumman F2F-1	23	0
Grumman F3F-1, -2, and -3	117	0
Grumman F4F-3, -4, -5, and -6	185	146
Grumman XF5F-1	1	0
Bell XFL-1	1	0
Vought XF4U-1	1	0
Totals	511	174

Manufacturer/Designation	Inventory	Assigned to Combat Units
Observation/Scout Aircraft:		
Vought O3U-1, -2, and -6	74	0
NAF XOSN-1	1	0
Vought OS2U-1, -2, and -3	536	79
Grumman SF-1	11	0
Vought SU-1, -2, -3, and -4	67	1
Curtiss SOC-1, -2, and -3/NAF SON-1	251	120
Curtisss XSO3C-1	1	0
Vought XSO2U-1	1	0
Totals	942	199

Manufacturer/Designation	Inventory	Assigned to Combat Units
Patrol Aircraft:		
Martin P3M-2	3	0
Consolidated P2Y-2 and -3	41	0
Sikorsky XPBS-1	1	1
Consolidated PBY-1, -2, -3, -4, -5, and -5A	405	248
Consolidated PB2Y-1, -2, and -3	7	4
Martin PBM-1 and -2	22	13
Lockheed PBO-1	18	14
Totals	497	279

Manufacturer/Designation	Inventory	Assigned to Combat Units
Trainer, Transport, and Utility Aircraft:		
Beech GB-1 and -2	27	0
Howard GH-1	6	0
Fairchild GK-1 and JK-1	4	0
Bellanca JE-1	1	0
Waco XJW-1	1	0
Grumman JF-1 and -3	15	0
Grumman J2F-1, -2, -3, -4, and -5	150	19
Lockheed JO-1and -3	2	0
Beech JRB-1 and -2	25	0
Grumman JRF-1, -2, -3, -4, and -5	34	0
North American NJ-1	39	0
NAF N3N-1, -2, and -3	943	0
NAF XN5N-1	1	0
Spartan NP-1	76	0
Ryan NR-1	99	0
Stearman NS-1, N2S-1, -2, and -3	617	0
Consolidated N2Y-1	1	1
Douglas RD-3	2	0
Douglas R2D-1	2	0
Douglas R3D-1 and -2	2	0
Douglas R4D-2	2	0
Lockheed XR2O-1 and R3O-2	2	0
Lockheed XR4O-1	1	0
Lockheed R5O-1, -2, and -3	5	0
Curtiss SNC-1	148	0
North American SNJ-1, -2, and -3	358	14
Vultee SNV-1	171	0
Totals	2,730	34

Manufacturer/Designation	Inventory	Assigned to Combat Units
Non-Rigid Airships (Blimps):		
Goodyear ZNG-type	1	0
Goodyear ZNL-type	3	0
Goodyear ZPK-type	4	4
Goodyear TC-type	2	2
Totals	10	6
Total Navy Aircraft and Airships	5,479	1,061

U.S. Marine Corps Aircraft

Manufacturer/Designation	Inventory	Assigned to Combat Units
Attack Aircraft:		
Curtiss SBC-4	19	12
Douglas SBD-1 and -2	51	46
Douglas SB2U-3	53	49
Totals	122	107
Fighter Aircraft:		
Brewster F2A-2 and -3	14	14
Grumman F3F-2	17	15
Grumman F4F-3	57	50
Totals	88	79
Observation and Scout Aircraft:		
Vought OS2U-3	2	2
Trainer, Transport, and Utility Aircraft:		
Grumman JF-1	1	0
Grumman J2F-1, -2A, and -4	17	13
Lockheed JO-2	4	2
Beech JRB-2	1	0
Grumman JRF-1A	1	1
Sikorsky JRS-1	1	1
Douglas R2D-1	1	1
Douglas R3D-2	3	3
North American SNJ-2 and -3	13	13
Totals	42	39
Total Marine Aircraft	254	227

U.S. Coast Guard Aircraft

Manufacturer/Designation	Inventory	Assigned to Combat Units
All Aircraft Types:		
Grumman JF-2	5	0
Grumman J4F-1	8	0
Grumman JRF-1, -2, and -3	10	0
Fairchild J2K-1 and -2	2	0
Hall PH-2 and -3	12	0
Consolidated PBY-5	1	0
NAF N3N-3	4	0
Consolidate N4Y-1	1	0
Douglas RD-4	7	0
Stinson R3Q-1	1	0
Lockheed R3O-1	1	0
Lockheed R5O-1	1	0
Curtiss SOC-4	3	0
Total Coast Guard Aircraft	56	0
Combined Total All Naval Services	5,789	1,288

Glossary of Naval and Aeronautical Terms

*Where a term and an abbreviation are used together, the abbreviation
will be expressed in parentheses following the term.*

AERODYNAMIC FORCE—A term pertaining to the motion of the air as it acts upon a body (i.e., an aircraft) which is in motion against it.

AERODYNAMIC LIFT—The upward force, perpendicular to the direction of travel, produced by the camber of a wing moving through the air.

AFTERBODY—The section of a flying boat or amphibian hull aft of the step.

AILERONS—Moveable control surfaces on the trailing edge of each wing, which, working in opposition, control the rotational motion of aircraft about its longitudinal axis.

AIRFOIL—The shape of a wing or flying surface as seen in cross-section, sometimes referred to as an airfoil section. Airfoils are designed to produce lift, or in the case of propellers, thrust.

AIRSPEED—The measurement of an aircraft's velocity.

ALCALD—A trademark used by Alcoa Aluminum Company for a high-strength sheet of aluminum consisting of an aluminum alloy core having one or both surfaces metallurgically bonded with a pure aluminum that is electrochemically resistant to corrosion.

ALTITUDE—The height of an aircraft above the ground or water, usually measured in feet.

AMIDSHIPS—The section of a ship or flying boat halfway between the bow and stern.

AMPHIBIAN—As used in this book, an amphibian refers to an aircraft having a boat-type hull or a pontoon forming a permanent part of the fuselage and equipped with retractable landing gear that permits land operations.

ANGLE-OF-ATTACK (AOA)—The angle formed by the chord of an airfoil and the direction of the aircraft into the relative wind.

ANGLE OF INCIDENCE—The angle between the chord line of a wing or horizontal stabilizer and the aircraft's longitudinal axis.

ANTISUBMARINE WARFARE (ASW)—A branch of warfare using ships or aircraft to detect, track, and/or destroy hostile submarines.

ARMAMENT—Refers to any type of weapon carried by a ship or an aircraft, including large rifled guns, machine guns and cannons, bombs, torpedoes, depth charges, and mines.

ARRESTING GEAR—Equipment designed to decelerate and stop the forward motion of an aircraft landing aboard an aircraft carrier. The system originally included a series of elevated traverse and longitudinal wires (pendants), the former to engage the aircraft's tailhook and the latter to guide it in a straight direction; however, the longitudinal wires were deleted in 1926.

ASPECT RATIO—The ratio between the span and the chord width of an aircraft's wing. A high aspect ratio wing is typically long and narrow, while a low aspect ratio wing is short and wide. Aspect ratio is usually expressed as the square of the wingspan divided by total wing area, for example a Consolidated PBY, with a wingspan of 104 feet and wing area of 1,514 square feet, has an aspect ratio of 7.1 $[(104)^2 \div 1, 514]$.

ATHWARTSHIPS—The side-to-side direction, across the beam of a ship.

AUXILIARY SHIP—A naval ship designed to support warships and naval shore operations by providing logistical replenishment, repair, transport, and/or command and control.

BALANCED CONTROL SURFACE—A moveable control surface, such as an aileron or elevator, which incorporates a weight forward of the hinge point to reduce control forces on the stick or yoke.

BARRIER—A traverse system of vertical and horizontal cables, located amidships, raised to stop an aircraft that has missed the arresting wires of an aircraft carrier.

BEAM—The width of a ship at its widest point.

BIPLANE—An aircraft having two wings, an upper and lower. Some early aircraft also featured a biplane horizontal stabilizer and elevator.

BLIMP—An airship with no internal framework using hydrostatic pressure upon its outer envelope to maintain its aerodynamic shape. The term is thought to have been originated by the Royal Naval Aviation Service during World War I as a contraction of B-class airship and "limp."

BOW—The most forward point or nose of a boat hull or float.

CABANE STRUT—Struts used on a biplane, triplane, or parasol monoplane to attach the wings to the fuselage or hull.

CALIBRE—The inside diameter of the bore of a gun barrel and the projectile fired from it, measured in inches (or fractions thereof) or millimeters.

CAMBER—The curvature of the upper and lower surfaces of an airfoil.

CANTILEVERED—An aircraft wing or flying surface wholly supported by its internal structure without need for external bracing.

CATAPULT—A shipboard system for launching aircraft from a ship using air pressure, gunpowder, flywheels, or hydraulics as a propellant.

CEILING—The maximum height above sea level, normally measured in feet, attainable by aircraft under standard atmospheric conditions.

CENTER OF GRAVITY (CG)—The lateral and longitudinal point at which an aircraft balances.

CENTER OF PRESSURE—The aerodynamic point of a wing where

the pitching moment (i.e., tendency to pitch nose up or nose down) is constant with the angle-of-attack.

CHORD—The distance between the leading and trailing edges of a wing. In the case of a tapered or elliptical wing, the distance is expressed as the mean aerodynamic chord. The term is also used in reference to tail surfaces, control surfaces, and flaps.

CONSTANT-SPEED PROPELLER—An electrically or hydraulically controlled propeller equipped with a governor that automatically changes pitch to maintain a constant RPM in response to changes in power settings.

CONTROL STICK—A moveable lever mounted in the cockpit directly in front of the pilot that controls the aircraft's elevators (fore and aft) and ailerons (side to side). Variously known as the joystick or simply the stick.

CONTROL YOKE—A wheel or partial wheel mounted on a shaft or column in the cockpit directly in front of the pilot that controls the aircraft's elevators (pushed and pulled) and ailerons (rotated side to side).

CONVENTIONAL LANDING GEAR—A configuration having the two main landing wheels located in front of the CG and a tailwheel or skid at the rear. Popularly known today as a "taildragger."

COWL FLAP—A moveable flap, usually located at the rear of a engine cowling, that regulates the flow of air through the cowling.

COWLING—A removable fairing around an aircraft engine that improves streamlining and cooling.

DECK—The top section of a flying boat or amphibian hull.

DEPTH CHARGE—An underwater ASW weapon using an acoustic, hydrostatic (pressure), or magnetic fuse to trigger detonation.

DIHEDRAL—An upward angle of the wings or horizontal flying surfaces in relation to the horizontal cross-section of the aircraft.

DORSAL—A location on the upper section of a hull as in a dorsal turret or dorsal fin.

DRAG—The resistance caused by the motion of an aircraft through the air. There are generally two forms of drag: (1) parasite drag caused by the friction of the outer surfaces of aircraft; and (2) induced drag generated by the lift of the wing and other flying surfaces.

DRAG RING—A cambered ring encircling the cylinders of a radial engine for the purpose of improving streamlining and cooling. Also known as a cowl or speed ring.

DRAG WIRE—A rigging wire in an aircraft's structure designed to resist forward and backward aerodynamic loads.

DURAL—Originally a trade name, now used generically, for any wrought aluminum containing alloys of copper, magnesium, and manganese. Also known under the Alcoa trade name "Duraluminum."

ELEVATOR—A moveable surface at the rear of a horizontal stabilizer controlling the pitch (nose up or nose down) of an aircraft around its lateral axis.

EMPENNAGE—The tail group of an aircraft, including the vertical stabilizer and rudder, horizontal stabilizer and elevator, and any supporting structures.

EMPTY WEIGHT—The weight of an aircraft less crew, passengers, cargo, baggage, armament (if military), and usable fuel.

FAIRING—A non-structural component added to the outside of an aircraft to reduce drag.

FIN—See, vertical stabilizer.

FIREWALL—A fire-resistant bulkhead between the engine compartment and the fuselage/hull or nacelles.

FLAG RANK—The naval rank of rear admiral or above, which corresponds to the rank of major general in the Army or Marine Corps.

FLAGSHIP—A naval ship within a fleet, typically a warship, identified as the headquarters of the commanding admiral and from which he "flies his flag."

FLAP—A hinged surface on the trailing edge of the wing which changes the camber in order to increase lift and drag. The lowering of flaps has the effect of lowering stall speeds, decreasing angle-of-attack, and causing the aircraft to fly more slowly. The most common types of flap systems are:

1. SPLIT—A flap consisting of a plate hinged from the bottom surface of the wing.
2. PLAIN—A flap consisting of a hinged section of the entire trailing edge of the wing.
3. SLOTTED—A flap in the shape of an airfoil which, when lowered, is positioned to form a slot between the wing and the leading edge of the flap.
4. FOWLER TYPE—A slotted flap, named for engineer Harland D. Fowler, that moves both rearward and downward on a track, thereby increasing camber and effective wing area.

FLOATPLANE—An aircraft having one or more detachable floats for its primary buoyancy, as differentiated from a boat-hulled flying boat or amphibian.

FLYING BOAT—An aircraft having a boat-type hull that possesses no type of landing gear, retractable or detachable, for land operations. Some flying boats may be equipped with built-in wheels used only for beaching.

FLYING WIRE—A collective term for all of an aircraft's rigging wires: drag wires, landing wires, and lift wires. Early flying boats were highly dependent on flying wires to support and distribute normal aerodynamic loads.

FORMER—A structural or non-structural internal member of a fuselage or boat-hull that forms its outside shape in cross-section.

FRAME CONSTRUCTION—A type of fuselage or hull construction where most of the structural, hydrodynamic, and aerodynamic loads are supported by an internal framework. In early aircraft such frameworks were usually constructed of wood; later methods use welded steel tubing or riveted aluminum extrusions.

FRISE AILERON—A type of aileron, named after engineer Leslie G. Frise, having a beveled leading edge and mounted forward of its inset hinges. When raised, its nose produces drag and decreases adverse yaw, thus requiring less or no rudder input during a banked turn.

FUSELAGE—The main body of an aircraft housing the cockpit, passenger cabin and/or cargo space and to which the wings and tailplane are attached. In the case of a flying boat or amphibian, the fuselage and hull are normally integrated as one structure.

GAP—The vertical distance between the upper and lower wings of a biplane or triplane.

GROSS WEIGHT—The design weight of an aircraft when fully loaded with fuel, crew, passengers, cargo, and armaments (if military). The term is sometimes expressed as normal gross, the weight at which the aircraft remains within its airframe operating limitations, and maximum takeoff, which contemplates that the aircraft will reach normal gross following a predictable fuel burn-off.

HORIZONTAL STABILIZER—The fixed portion of the horizontal tailplane to which the elevator is attached.

HORSEPOWER (hp)—A measure of the motive energy required to raise 550 lbs. to a height of one foot in one second.

INLINE ENGINE—A type of reciprocating piston engine in which an even (4-6-8-12) number of cylinders are arranged either in a straight line or in a V-type configuration directly above (or below) the crankcase. Most early inline aircraft engines were water-cooled via a radiator system, though air-cooled types began to appear during the 1930s.

INTERPLANE STRUT—One or more pairs of vertical (or nearly vertical) biplane or triplane struts, located outside of the cabanes, which transmit aerodynamic loads between wing panels and maintain angles of incidence. Some interplane struts, known as "N" struts, feature an additional drag strut between them.

ISLAND—A superstructure, typically located on the starboard side, amidships, of an aircraft carrier, which houses the bridge, navigation, and flight operations decks.

KNOT—As a measurement of speed, about 1.15 mph, and of distance (i.e., a nautical mile), about 1.15 statute miles or 6,076 feet.

LANDING WIRE—A rigging wire in a wing or tail structure designed to resist negative (downward) aerodynamic loads.

LEADING EDGE—The forward most part of an aircraft's wing or flying surfaces.

LENGTH OVERALL (LOA)—The maximum length of a vessel from two points on the hull measured perpendicular to the waterline.

LIFT WIRE—A rigging wire in a wing or tail structure designed to resist positive aerodynamic (upward) loads.

LOAD FACTOR (G)—A measurement of the force acting upon an aircraft due to acceleration or gravity, usually expressed in units of G times one.

LONGERON—A main longitudinal structural member in a fuselage or hull.

MARITIME PATROL—An over-water military mission that can include long-range reconnaissance, convoy escort, aerial attack, mine-laying, and ASW.

MONOCOQUE—A type of fuselage or hull design in which most of the structural and aerodynamic loads are carried by the outer skin rather than internal bracing.

MONOPLANE—An aircraft having one set of wing surfaces, mounted in various configurations as low-wing, mid-wing, shoulder-wing, high-wing, or parasol-wing.

NACELLE—A streamlined structure used to house engines, landing gear, weapons, or in some instances, a cockpit or cabin

NATIONAL ADVISORY COMMITTEE FOR AERONAUTICS (NACA)—A U.S. government agency established in 1915 to carry out and make available various forms of aeronautical research. Aerodynamic forms tested and developed by the agency, such as airfoils and cowlings, are known by NACA number or type.

NAVAL ATTACHÉ FOR AIR—A naval officer attached to a U.S. Embassy staff who acts as a representative to the host nation and also observes and gather intelligence data relative to the host nation's military capabilities.

PAYLOAD—The proportion of an aircraft's useful load over and above fuel and required crew.

PITCH—The nose up and down motion of an aircraft about its lateral axis.

PLANFORM—The general arrangement of an aircraft as seen directly from above or below.

PLANING SURFACE—The bottom portion of a flying boat's or amphibian's hull or float which is in contact with the water.

PORT—The left side of a boat or aircraft or, facing forward, the direction to the left of it.

POWER-TO-WEIGHT RATIO—For the aircraft, the rated horsepower or thrust divided by the gross weight; for the powerplant only, the rated horsepower or thrust divided by the weight of the engine and accessories.

PROPELLER PITCH—The angle of a propeller blade in relation to its rotational arc; also, the measurement of the forward distance advanced by a propeller blade in one full arc of rotation.

PUSHER—An engine mounted with its propeller facing aft.

PYLON—A streamlined structural member supporting a wing, tailplane, or engine.

RADAR (Radio Detection and Ranging)—An electronic system that uses electromagnetic waves to identify the range, altitude, direction, and speed of moving or stationary objects such as aircraft, ships, weather features, or terrain.

RADIAL ENGINE—A type of reciprocating piston engine in which the cylinders are arranged around the crankcase like the spokes on a wheel. An odd number (5-7-9) of pistons are connected to the crankshaft via a master-and-articulating-rod assembly.

RAMPING—A process by which an amphibian or flying boat equipped with beaching gear uses its own power to taxi from the water onto the shore.

ROLL—The rotational motion of an aircraft about its longitudinal axis.

ROTARY ENGINE—An early type of reciprocating engine in which the cylinders were arranged around the crankcase similar to a radial, but where the crankshaft was fixed and the entire crankcase, to which the propeller was mounted, rotated around it.

RUDDER—A moveable surface at the rear of a vertical stabilizer controlling the yaw (nose left or nose right) of an aircraft about its vertical axis.

SEAPLANE—A generic term for any aircraft capable of taking off from and landing on the water.

SEMI-CANTILEVERED—An aircraft wing or flying surface supported partly by internal structure and partly by external bracing.

SEMI-MONOCOCQUE—A type of fuselage, hull, or nacelle construction where the outside skin is supported by internal formers and stringers that share the structural, hydrodynamic, and aerodynamic loads. It is the most common method used in the fabrication of fuselages and hulls from aluminum.

SESQUIPLANE—A biplane configuration in which the lower wing possesses much less area than the upper wing.

SLAT—A moveable surface on the leading edge of a wing which increases both camber and airflow. Slats can be manual or designed to automatically extend at higher angles-of-attack.

SLOT—A spanwise gap in the leading edge of a wing which increases airflow over the upper surface at higher angles-of-attack.

SPAR—The main structural member of an aircraft wing or flying surface running perpendicular to or across its longitudinal axis. Spars are typically designed to resist any structural or aerodynamic loads, i.e., lift, landing, drag, and torsion.

SPOILER—A moveable plate on the upper surface of a wing for the purpose of causing drag or, when used differentially, to induce roll.

SPONSONS—Buoyant extensions to the sides of a boat hull's forebody. Large airfoil-shaped sponsons, located near the center-of-gravity, have been used in lieu of stabilizing floats under the wings. One-piece stabilizing floats on small amphibians are sometimes referred to as sponsons.

SPRAY RAILS—Metal flanges attached to the chine of a boat-hull or float forebody that are designed to reduce the water spray thrown into a propeller.

STABILIZING FLOATS—Small floats located under the outboard wing panels of a flying boat or amphibian to prevent the wingtips from contacting the water. Also commonly referred to as tip or wing floats.

STAGGER—The relative fore and aft relationship between the leading edges of the upper and lower wings of a biplane or triplane. If the leading edge of the upper wing is forward of that of the lower wing, the aircraft is said to have "positive" stagger. The reverse is true for "negative" stagger.

STALL—An event that causes the wing to lose lift to the extent that it will no longer support the weigh of the aircraft. A stall is caused by an increase in angle-of-attack and resulting loss of airspeed. An "accelerated " stall occurs when the aircraft reaches critical angle-of-attack while accelerating in excess of one-G.

STARBOARD—The right side of a boat or aircraft or, facing forward, the direction to the right of it.

STEP—A transverse gap between the fore-and afterbodies of a boat-hull or float near or just behind the center-of-gravity. In principle, the step allows the hydrodynamic lift generated by the forebody to lift the afterbody clear of the water once sufficient forward speed is attained.

STERN—The most rearward point of a ship or flying boat hull.

STRAKE—A longitudinal member on the outside of a boat-hull or float which adds structural rigidity and directional stability. Sometimes known as a keelson.

STRINGER—A longitudinal member on the inside of a fuselage, boat-hull, or float which adds structural rigidity to the skin. Stingers are also sometimes used for the same purpose in the spanwise construction of wings and flying surfaces.

SUPERSTRUCTURE—Any structure of a ship built above the main deck.

SWEEPBACK—The rearward angle between the quarter chord line (i.e., the distance between the leading and trailing edges) of an aircraft's wing and its longitudinal centerline.

TAILPLANE—See, empennage, above.

TAPER—The angle of a wing or tail surface from root to tip as measured from its leading and/or training edge.

THRUST—An aerodynamic force propelling an aircraft through the air. Thrust may be produced by a propeller or by the expelled gases of a jet or rocket engine. In principle, thrust must exceed drag (aerodynamic and hydrodynamic) in order for an aircraft to achieve flight, and in a level, cruising attitude, thrust and drag are equal.

TORPEDO—A self-propelled explosive weapon launched into the water by a ship, submarine or aircraft.

TORQUE—The rotational force imparted by a turning propeller which causes an aircraft to rotate in the opposite direction, thereby inducing roll and yaw.

TRACTOR—An engine mounted with its propeller facing forward.

TRAILING EDGE—The rear most part of an aircraft's wing or flying surfaces.

TRICYCLE LANDING GEAR—A configuration having the two main landing wheels located aft of the CG and a nosewheel mounted to the front.

TRIM TAB—A small, adjustable or fixed control surface located on or within the trailing edge of a rudder, elevator, or aileron. Adjustable trim tabs, controlled from the cockpit, are used to reduce the aerodynamic forces imposed on flight controls; fixed trim tabs are adjusted on the ground to enable the aircraft to maintain trim in level flight.

TRIPLANE—An aircraft having three wings, an upper, middle, and lower.

TURRET—An enclosed gun mounting on a ship or aircraft that may be simultaneously traversed and elevated.

USEFUL LOAD—The added weight of an aircraft's fuel, crew, passengers, baggage, cargo, and armaments (if military). Armament (i.e., weapons load) may be considered separately.

UTILITY AMPHIBIAN—A type of single and multi-engine amphibian used by all Naval Aviation branches U.S. military branches from 1923 for ship-to shore transportation, search and rescue, and, occasionally, coastal maritime patrol.

VARIABLE PITCH PROPELLER—A hydraulically or mechanically controlled two-position propeller that can be varied from high RPM for takeoff and climb to low RPM for level flight and cruise.

VERTICAL STABILZER—The fixed portion of the vertical tailplane to which the rudder is attached.

WASH-OUT—A feature of wing design in which a slight amount of 'twist' (as seen from the side) reduces angle of incidence from root to tip. For reasons of stability, an amount of washout is normally incorporated to insure that the wing stalls at the root (which has a higher angle-of-attack) before reaching the tip. Wash-in, rarely ever seen, is the opposite of wash-out.

WEAPONS OR BOMB BAY—A fully enclosed compartment in the belly of an aircraft for stowage of weapons such as bombs, torpedoes, or depth charges. In flying boats, the enclosure may be located in the bottom of wing nacelles or within the hull to be launched over the side via a track system.

WEAPONS RACK—An external rack fitted under the wing or belly of an aircraft for the purpose of carrying bombs, mines, depth charges, or torpedoes.

WING LOADING—The wing area of an aircraft divided by its gross weight, usually expressed in pounds per square foot.

WING RIB—A chordwise member of a wing structure that forms its airfoil shape and transmits aerodynamic loads from the skin to the spars. Wing ribs may be fabricated from wood, aluminum, or composite material.

YAW—The side-to-side motion of an aircraft about its vertical axis.

Bibliography

Books and Periodicals

Allward, Maurice. *An Illustrated History of Seaplanes and Flying Boats.* New York: Dorset, 1981.

Althoff, William F. *Sky Ships: A History of the Airship in the United States Navy.* New York: Orion, 1990.

Andrade, Ernest. "The Ship That Never Was: The Flying-Deck Cruiser." *The Journal of Military History,* Vol. 32, No. 3, December 1968.

Bowers, Peter M. *Curtiss Aircraft 1907–1946.* Annapolis, MD: Naval Institute, 1987.

_____. *Forgotten Fighters and Experimental Aircraft U.S. Navy 1918–1941,* Vol. 1. New York: Arco, 1971.

_____. "Scout Bomber." *Wings,* Vol. 15, No. 2, April 1985.

Breihan, John R. *Martin Aircraft 1909–1960.* Santa Ana, CA: Narkiewicz/Thompson, 1995.

Chesneau, Roger. *Aircraft Carriers of the World, 1914 to the Present.* Annapolis, MD: Naval Institute, 1984.

Dean, Jack. "Dive Bomber." *Wings,* Vol. 15 No. 2, April 1985.

Doll, Thomas E., Berkley R. Jackson, and William A. Riley. *Navy Air Colors: United States Navy, Marine, and Coast Guard Aircraft Camouflage and Markings, 1911–1945,* Vol. 1. Carrollton, TX: Squadron-Signal, 1983.

Francillon, Rene J. *Grumman Aircraft Since 1929.* Annapolis, MD: Naval Institute, 1989.

_____. *McDonnell Douglas Aircraft Since 1920.* Annapolis, MD: Naval Institute, 1990.

Friedman, Norman. *U.S. Aircraft Carriers: An Illustrated Design History.* Annapolis, MD: Naval Institute, 1983.

_____. *U.S. Cruisers: An Illustrated Design History.* Annapolis, MD: Naval Institute, 1984.

_____. *U.S. Naval Weapons.* Annapolis, MD: Naval Institute, 1985.

Green, William. *War Planes of the Second World War: Fighters,* Vol. 4. Garden City, NY: Hanover House, 1961.

Grossnick, Roy A. *United States Naval Aviation 1910–1995.* Naval Aviation History Branch, U.S. Government Printing Office, Washington, DC, 1996. Available at www.history.navy.mil.

_____, ed. *Kite Balloons to Airships: The Navy's Lighter-Than-Air Experience.* Naval Air Systems Command, U.S. Government Printing Office, Washington, DC, 1987.

Gunston, Bill. *American Warplanes.* New York: Crescent, 1986.

Hone, Thomas C., and Trent Hone. *Battle Line: The United States Navy, 1919–1939.* Annapolis, MD: Naval Institute, 2006.

Hone, Trent. "Building a Doctrine: U.S. Naval Tactics and Battle Plans in the Interwar Period." *The Journal of Military History,* Vol. 67, No. 4, October 2003.

Johnson, E. R. *American Attack Aircraft Since 1926.* Jefferson, NC: McFarland, 2008.

_____. *American Flying Boats and Amphibious Aircraft: An Illustrated History.* Jefferson, NC: McFarland, 2009.

_____. "Northrop Attack Aircraft 1933–1937." *Skyways Journal of the Airplane,* No. 81, January 2007.

_____. "One Wing or Two? U.S. Navy and Marine Corps Fighters, 1930–1940." *Skyways Journal of the Airplane,* No. 85, January 2008.

_____. "Strike Force in the Making: U.S. Naval Carrier-Based Attack Aircraft Developments from 1926 to 1940." *Skyways Journal of the Airplane,* No. 73, January 2005.

Jones, Lloyd S. *U.S. Fighters, 1925 to 1980s.* Fallbrook, CA: Aero, 1975.

Kuehn, John T. "The Influence of Naval Arms Limitation on U.S. Naval Innovation During the Interwar Period, 1921–1937." Abstract of dissertation, Kansas State University, Manhattan, 2007. Available at http://krex.k-state.edu/dspace/ bitstream/2097/259/1/JohnKuehn2007. pdf.

Larkins, William T. *Battleship and Cruiser Aircraft of the United States Navy.* Atglen, PA: Schiffer, 1990.

_____. *U.S. Navy Aircraft, 1921–1941.* Concord, CA: Aviation History, 1961.

_____. *USMC Aircraft, 1914–1959.* Concord, CA: Aviation History, 1959.

Lawson, Robert L., ed. *The History of U.S. Naval Airpower.* New York: Crown, 1985.

Love, Robert W. *History of the U.S. Navy, Vol. I, 1775–1941.* Harrisburg, PA: Stackpole, 1992.

Margiotta, Franklin D., ed. "History of Airpower." In *Brassey's Encyclopedia of Military History and Biography.* Washington, DC: Brassey's, 1994.

"Marine Corps Aircraft, 1913–1965." Marine Corps Historical Reference Pamphlet, Historical Branch, U.S. Marine Corps, Washington, DC, revised 1967.

Matt, Paul R., and Bruce Robertson. *United States Navy and Marine Corps Fighters, 1918–1962.* Los Angeles, CA: Aero, 1962.

Mersky, Peter B. *U.S. Marine Corps Aviation 1912 to the Present.* Baltimore, MD: Nautical and Aviation, 1983.

Morrison, Samuel Eliot. *The Two-Ocean War.* Boston: Little, Brown, 1963.

Percy, Arthur. *U.S. Coast Guard Aircraft Since 1916.* Annapolis, MD: Naval Institute, 1991.

Preston, Anthony, and Louis S. Casey. *Sea Power: A Modern Illustrated Military History.* New York: Exeter, 1979.

Sheina, Robert L. *A History of Coast Guard Aviation.* U.S. Coast Guard Historian's Office, Washington, DC, 1986. Available at http://www. uscg.mil/history/articles/CGAviation.pdf.

Sherrod, Robert. *History of Marine Corps Aviation in World War II.* Washington, DC: Combat Forces, 1952.

Shock, James R. *U.S. Navy Airships, 1915–1962.* Edgewater, FL: Atlantis, 1992.

Smith, Hershel. *A History of Aircraft Piston Engines.* Manhattan, KS: Sunflower University Press, 1986.

Smith, Peter C. *The History of Dive Bombing.* Annapolis, MD: Nautical and Aviation, 1981.

Swanborough, Gordon, and Peter M. Bowers. *United States Navy Aircraft Since 1911,* 2d ed. Annapolis, MD: Naval Institute, 1976.

Taylor, Michael J. H. *Warplanes of the World 1918–1939.* New York: Charles Scribner's Sons, 1981.

Terzibaschitsch, Stefan. *Aircraft Carriers of the U.S. Navy,* 2d revised ed. Annapolis, MD: Naval Institute, 1989.

_____. *Cruisers of the United States Navy.* Annapolis, MD: Naval Institute, 1988.

Thetford, Owen. *British Naval Aircraft Since 1912*. London: Putnam, 1962.

Trimble, William F. *Wings for the Navy: A History of the Naval Aircraft Factory, 1917–1956*. Annapolis, MD: Naval Institute, 1996.

Ventry, Lord, and Eugene Kolesnik, eds. *Jane's Pocket Book of Airships*. New York: Macmillan, 1977.

Wagner, Ray. *American Combat Planes*, 3d ed. Garden City, NY: Doubleday, 1982.

Wildenberg, Thomas. "Midway: Sheer Luck or Better Doctrine?" Navy Department Library, Naval Historical Center, Washington, DC, 2004. Available at http://www.history.navy.mil/library/online/sheerluck_midway.htm.

Websites

"Air Units of the Imperial Japanese Navy." Global Security Military, http://www.globalsecurity.org/military/world/japan/ijn-air.htm/.

"The Battle of the Coral Sea 7–8 May 1942." Battles of the Pacific War, http://www.microworks.net/pacific/battles/coral_sea.htm.

"The Battle of Midway 4–6 June 1942." Battles of the Pacific War, http://www.microworks.net/pacific/battles/midway.htm.

"Curtiss Aeroplane and Motor Co." Virtual Aircraft Museum, http://www.aviastar.org/manufacturers/0647.html.

"Dictionary of American Naval Aviation Squadrons, Vol. 2." Naval Aviation History Office, http://history.navy.mil.branches/dictvol2.htm.

"The Early Carrier Raids: February and March 1942." Battles of the Pacific War, http://www.microworks.net/pacific/battles/early_carrier_raids.htm.

"Early Years: 1912–1941." History of Marine Corps Aviation, http://www.acepilots.com/usmc/hist1.html.

"The Early Years (1915–1938) and the Growth Years (1939–1956)," Coast Guard Aviation History, http://uscgaviationhistory.aoptero.org/.

Eckland, K.O., ed. "Aircraft A–Z." Aerofiles, http://www.aerofiles.com/aircraft.html.

Flavell, Aird. "Flying Boats of the World, A Complete Reference." World Flying Boat, http://www.msacomputer.com/FlyingBoats-old/.

"Grumman Aircraft." KensAviation.com, http://www.shanaberger.com/grumman.htm.

"Japanese Aircraft Carriers." Imperial Japanese Navy Page, http://www.combinedfleet.com/cv.htm.

"Martin Aircraft." Glenn L. Martin Maryland Aviation Museum, http://www.marylandaviationmuseum.org/history/index.html.

McKillop, Jack, and Craig Swan. "Brown-Shoe Navy." U.S. Naval Aviation Historical, http://www.microworks.net/pacific/aviation/index.htm.

"Midway: The Battle and the Diversions." Encyclopedia of the Naval Battles of World War 2, http://users.swing.be/navbat/bataille/146.html.

"Naval Aviation Chronology Files." Naval Aviation History Office, http://www.history.navy.mil/branches/org4-5.htm.

"Naval Aviation 1911–1986, A Pictorial Study." U.S. Navy History Branch, http://www.history.navy.mil/download/pict-m4.pdf.

"Operations to Relieve Wake Island December 1941." Battles of the Pacific War, http://www.microworks.net/pacific/battles/relief_of_wake.htm.

Pike, John, ed. "1921 Naval Conference, 1927 Geneva Naval Conference, 1930 London Naval Conference, 1932 Geneva Peace Conference, and 1935 London Naval Conference." Global Security Military, http://www.globalsecurity.org/org/military/system.htm.

"Records of the Bureau of Aeronautics 1911–1972." National Archives, http://www.archives.gov/research/guide-fed-records/groups/072.html.

"S-38, S-43, and S/VS-44." Sikorsky Historical Archives, http://www.sikorskyarchives.com/.

"Scouting Airplanes." NavSource Naval History, http://navsource3.org/archives/01/57k.htm.

"Ships or Aircraft Sunk or Survived at Pearl Harbor." Official Site of the Attack on Pearl Harbor, http://www.pearlharbor.org/ships-and-aircraft.asp.

"U.S. Navy Aircraft Carriers, Battleships, Cruisers, Destroyers, and Seaplane Tenders." Dictionary of Naval Fighting Ships Online, http://www.hazegray.org/navhist.

"U.S. Navy Aircraft 1922–1962 Designation System." Navy History and Hertitage Command, http://www.history.navy.mil/photos/ac-usn22/ac-usn22.htm.

"Vought Heritage." Vought Aircraft Industries Retiree Club, http://www.voughtaircraft.com/heritage/years/html/03-16.html.

Index

331

United States Naval
Aviation, 1919–1941